DATE DUE FOR RETURN

2 2 MAY 1997		
2 9 OCT 1998		- 1 FEB 2006
2 1 MAY 1999		
- 1 JUN 1999		
4 MAY 2001		1 2 JAN 2007
1 JUN 2001		
6 FEB 2002		

All communications with regard to the
Society should be addressed to
THE SECRETARY
English Place-Name Society
The University
Reading

ENGLISH PLACE-NAME SOCIETY.   VOLUME XIX

GENERAL EDITORS

ALLEN MAWER *and* F. M. STENTON

27885
18.10.44

THE PLACE-NAMES OF
CAMBRIDGESHIRE
AND
THE ISLE OF ELY

CAMBRIDGE
UNIVERSITY PRESS
LONDON: BENTLEY HOUSE
NEW YORK, TORONTO, BOMBAY
CALCUTTA, MADRAS: MACMILLAN

ENGLISH PLACE-NAME SOCIETY. VOLUME XIX

THE PLACE-NAMES OF CAMBRIDGESHIRE

AND

THE ISLE OF ELY

By

P. H. REANEY
late Leverhulme Research Fellow

CAMBRIDGE

AT THE UNIVERSITY PRESS

1943

The publication of this volume
has been facilitated by a grant
from the British Academy

To the memory of

WALTER W. SKEAT

who, in his *Place-names of Cambridgeshire* (1901),
laid the foundations of modern Place-name study

PREFACE

IT is now a little over forty years since the late Professor Skeat, in his *Place-names of Cambridgeshire*, laid down the fundamental principles on which this study must be based—the collection of early forms and their interpretation in accordance with the laws of phonetics and the history of the language. He realised that the chief handicap of the solitary scholar was a lack of comparative material and with the modesty of the true pioneer he claimed neither finality nor infallibility for his results. Of those who have since pursued, elaborated and improved his methods, not the least was his own pupil, the late Sir Allen Mawer, founder of the English Place-name Society, with its ideal of completeness by means of co-operative study. His profound admiration for the work of Skeat, more than once expressed in print, was repeated in his last letter to me when he suggested the dedication of this volume to Skeat.

The present work deals with over 2000 names, apart from field-names, compared with about 190 explained by Skeat. Fuller forms for such names as Cambridge, Grantchester, Ely and Soham, serve only to confirm his insight and the essential correctness of his methods. Whilst some of his views cannot now be maintained, a new interpretation offered here is due, as a rule, to the discovery of fresh material. Intensive study of his little book, inevitable in the preparation of its successor, leaves one with an enhanced appreciation of the debt due to its author.

Most of the material on which this volume is based had been collected before the outbreak of the present war. This was particularly fortunate, firstly because so many of the early forms are taken from manuscripts now inaccessible, and secondly because, as an evacuated schoolmaster, my time was fully occupied and I was completely cut off from my papers and books and from all access to libraries. After some twelve months, thanks to the award of a Leverhulme Research Fellowship, I was able to devote a whole year to this work, which must otherwise have been postponed indefinitely. For this award I wish to thank the Trustees of the late Lord Leverhulme and their Secretary, Dr L. Haden Guest, for his interest and offers of help. The difficulties due to war conditions were, on the whole, successfully overcome. The earlier muniments of King's College, Cambridge, which would probably have provided useful material for the parish of Isleham, had been removed to a place of safety. Apart from this, the chief handicap has been a lack of opportunity to check forms and references from manuscripts no longer accessible in the British Museum and the Public Record Office, but in no instance has reliance had to be placed on a solitary and unchecked form, so abundant is the material available. Fortunately, too, the resources of the Cambridge University Library continued to be available and the task of checking and verifying forms and references, though not so thorough and complete as I should have liked, has been satisfactorily accomplished, thanks to the unselfish help of various friends in Cambridge.

Here, as in the more recent volumes of the Survey, a full treatment of the field-names of the county has been attempted. For this, the aid of the schools was enlisted and thanks are due to Mr H. M. Morris, the Director of Education for Cambridgeshire, and to those teachers and children who collected and supplied material, often of value and interest, and occasionally remarkably complete and well arranged. Unfortunately, the response was not so general as it has been for some counties and no help at all was received from the Isle of Ely (v. also *infra* 310).

Surprisingly few local documents relating to Cambridgeshire have been printed and whatever merit this book may possess is chiefly due to the material collected from the vast stores of manuscripts preserved at Ely and Cambridge. As one would expect, the College archives have been particularly useful sources and a deep debt is owed not only for permission to consult them, but also to the custodians who were indefatigable in their efforts to help, often at a most inconvenient time. At Corpus, Queens', St John's and Trinity, so numerous are Cambridgeshire documents that nothing but haphazard selection would have been possible had it not been for the previous work of their custodians on their arrangement. For access to their muniments thanks are due to the Masters and Fellows of the following Cambridge Colleges and for facilities and other help to those named in brackets: Christ's (the Bursar and Mr S. G. Campbell), Clare (Mr W. J. Harrison, the Bursar, for facilities, and the Librarian for the use of the Library), Corpus Christi (the Estates Bursar, Mr T. R. B. Sanders, whose information and arrangements saved much time), Downing (the Dean, Mr W. L. Cuttle), Gonville and Caius (the Bursar, Mr E. P. Weller), Jesus (the late Master, Mr A. Gray, who personally produced the documents and gave me the benefit of his unique knowledge of their contents, and Mr F. Brittain), King's (Mr J. Saltmarsh

and Mr R. B. Braithwaite), Magdalene (the Bursar, Mr J. Pope),
Pembroke (the Master, Sir Montagu Butler, who personally produced
the documents and whose courtesy and constant attentions greatly
facilitated the search), Peterhouse (the Bursar, Sir Hubert Sams),
Queens' (the Rev. J. F. Williams, for placing at my disposal his wide
knowledge of the muniments, and the President, who in person
superintended the arrangements), St Catharine's (the President,
Dr W. H. S. Jones, who generously offered the use of his own room
for the work), St John's (the Senior Bursar, Sir Henry Howard, and
Mr H. Gatty, the Librarian, who placed freely at my disposal his
extensive knowledge of the muniments and their contents, saved much
time by offering the loan of his transcript of the Cartulary of St John's
Hospital, and the use of his card index of the charters and deeds, and
provided accommodation in the Library), and Trinity (the Senior
Bursar, Mr T. C. Nicholas, who spared no effort to be of assistance;
he allowed me the use of an index to the muniments and arranged for
the transfer to the Library of rentals, court rolls, etc.; the Sub-
Librarian, Mr C. B. Hurry, for facilities for working on these documents and for help in tracing and checking material from manuscripts
in the Library). Thanks are also due to the officials of the Cambridge
University Library for their invariable courtesy and ready help over
a long period, especially to Mr F. J. Norton for his constant interest
and help of various kinds, to Mr H. R. Mallett of the Map Room,
an enthusiastic and omniscient guide to his treasures, for whom no
request was too trivial, no effort too great, and to Mr H. L. Pink, of
Anderson, who has throughout been a tower of strength. Quite apart
from facilitating the fullest use of the manuscripts in the Library, he
lent me his transcript of the Trinity Hall deeds, acted as guide to the
Peterhouse muniments and arranged for the transfer of many of the
documents to the University Library, and was a never-failing source
of information and help.

Thanks are also due to the Bishop of Ely for permission to consult
the valuable collection of court rolls, plea-rolls, bishops' registers, etc.
preserved in the Ely Diocesan Registry (and to Mr G. H. Ellis, the
custodian, for his constant courtesy in providing facilities), and to the
Dean and Chapter of Ely for access to the extensive collection of
charters, rolls and other documents in their muniment room. For
guidance and facilities I was much indebted to the late Canon G. W.
Evans, then Keeper of the Muniments, and the Rev. Seiriol J. A.
Evans, who lent me their joint transcript of Book III of the *Liber*

Eliensis and helped in other ways. The latter also lent me his card-index and partial transcript of some 800 charters, and thus facilitated a rapid elimination of those not referring to Cambridgeshire. Thanks are also due to the late Canon J. M. Creed and Canon J. S. Boys-Smith, successively in charge of the muniments after the death of Canon Evans, and to the Chairman of the River Great Ouse Catchment Board for access to their muniments, to the Clerk, Mr E. T. L. Baker, and to Mr C. W. Lacey, District Engineer, for facilities at Cambridge and the Fen Office, Ely, respectively.

To the late Dr W. M. Palmer my debt is very great. From the first, he freely placed at my disposal his unique knowledge of the history and topography of Cambridgeshire, his own documents and manuscript collections, his library, and frequently his home. Apart from his familiarity with Cambridgeshire manuscripts in public collections, he had a genius for discovering those in private ownership and regularly supplied me with his own transcripts or made the documents themselves available. He was no arm-chair historian; a good field-botanist and archaeologist, he was able to throw light on many of the innumerable problems arising in place-name etymology. Owing to his sudden death, the volume lacked the benefit of his acute and penetrating criticism.

To some extent, Dr Palmer's place has been taken by his friend, Mr J. H. Bullock who, with the same generosity, has greatly helped the final preparation of the manuscript and the correction of proofs by his gifts and loans of books, and by undertaking that most thankless of all tasks, the checking of another's references and the tracing of those lost. The treatment of Cambridge street-names owes much to his criticism. Others whom I desire to thank are Col. G. Archer (Ely street-names), Dr Helen M. Cam (for valuable historical notes, particularly on Cambridge and the Cambridgeshire hundreds), Professor H. M. Chadwick, Dr H. C. Darby (for his general interest, help and useful discussions and criticisms, particularly relating to the fens), Major Gordon Fowler (for much valuable help on fenland archaeology and topography, particularly decayed rivers and their courses, and for the loan of his transcript of the Stretham parish papers), Sir Cyril Fox, Mr T. C. Lethbridge and Miss M. O'Reilly (for valuable criticisms and suggestions on archaeological problems), Dr H. Godwin (for help in matters of botany), Mr A. T. Hill (Upwell), Dr L. W. H. Payling (forms from Lincolnshire documents), Sir John Russell (help with matters relating to soils, etc.), Professor E. J.

Salisbury (help in matters of botany), Col. L. Tebbutt (guidance in the arrangement of documents in the Fen Office, Ely), Mr T. F. Teversham (material from the Huddleston MSS relating to Sawston), Miss Dorothy Whitelock (forms from the *Libellus Eliensis* from rotographs loaned by Professor Bruce Dickins), and Mr G. M. G. Woodgate for valuable help with Wisbech Hundred. In addition to making available much useful material in the Wisbech Museum and from his own large manuscript collections, his wide knowledge of the history and topography of the district has been constantly placed at my disposal under most pleasant conditions.

For help at the proof stage, I am indebted to Professor Bruce Dickins, Professor J. Tait and Mr J. E. B. Gover, who also supplied field-name material from unpublished Feet of Fines and from the Tithe Awards.

Finally, it is with great pleasure that I express my thanks to the General Editors, the late Sir Allen Mawer and Professor F. M. Stenton. The later stages of the preparation of the volume for press under war conditions threw a particularly heavy burden on Sir Allen. Both he and I were working under evacuation conditions, at a considerable distance apart, and everything had to be done by correspondence. But in spite of his other exacting duties, his courtesy and consideration never failed, and I am happy to pay tribute to the pleasant relations which have always existed between us. Almost the whole book was in type before his sudden death and the remainder lacked only his final criticism. Much of the smoothness with which the long process of revision of manuscript and correction of proofs has been carried out is due to the unfailing care and attention of Miss A. M. Armstrong who has once again placed me deeply in her debt by the cheerful and competent way in which she meets every difficulty. A word of praise is due, too, to the Cambridge University Press for the way in which they have overcome the difficulty of war-time production. The proofs contained very few printer's errors, and I know that Sir Allen Mawer was well satisfied with the rate of progress.

P. H. REANEY

February, 1943

CONTENTS

MAPS

INTRODUCTION

THE district which may conveniently be described as the Cambridge Region offered a natural line of approach towards the southern Midlands to Germanic invaders entering England from the east. The general direction of its main natural features guided movement towards the south-west through a tract of country which had been opened out to intensive settlement before the close of the Roman period. The diversities of soil and contour within the greater part of this region invited an early occupation, and the numerous ancient roads by which the region was intersected permitted easy communication between different bands of colonists. On general grounds, it would certainly be expected that the place-names and archaeological discoveries of the district should yield evidence illustrating the first phase of the Germanic infiltration into southern Britain.

On the archaeological side, the expectation is fully borne out by facts which have become the common property of all historians. It has recently been observed that "in no other region of England is there such a significant concentration of grave-goods for which a really early date can be taken as reasonably certain."[1] The number of sites from which such objects have been recovered is remarkable. Within Cambridgeshire alone, discoveries which clearly indicate an early phase of Anglo-Saxon culture have been made at Little Wilbraham, Haslingfield, Barrington, Trumpington, Soham, Girton and Cambridge itself. The archaic strain in this culture is equally apparent in pottery and in objects of metal-work, and the articles which reflect it are of many different types. Cumulatively, they point to an Anglo-Saxon occupation of Cambridgeshire which was well established before the end of the fifth century.

On the surface, the evidence from place-names is less satisfactory. The names which as a class are most suggestive of early settlement are those which end in the element -*ingas*, and originally denoted not places, but groups of people. Names of this type occur in considerable and sometimes large numbers everywhere within the coastal angle of south-eastern Britain—in East Anglia, Essex, Kent and Sussex. Among the inland counties adjacent to Cambridgeshire, Hertfordshire, Huntingdonshire and Northamptonshire each contain more

---

[1] J. N. L. Myres in *Oxford History of England*, I, 386.

than one example. The fact that no instance occurs in Cambridgeshire itself gives the impression of a definite clash between the archaeological and the place-name evidence for the date at which the county came into English occupation.

But the prevalence of names in *-ingas* is not the only place-name test of early settlement. The occurrence of rare or ancient words and personal names and of primitive forms of compound is at least as significant. When regarded from this standpoint the place-names of Cambridgeshire give, as a whole, an impression of high antiquity. So far as is known, the curious element *dung*, which is compounded in Wilsmere Down near Barrington, does not occur again in England. It is clearly a cognate of the Scandinavian *dyngja*, 'woman's apartment,' but it is never found in Anglo-Saxon literature, and it can safely be regarded as a fragment of primitive Anglian speech which never came to general currency in England. It is a noteworthy circumstance that this archaic word should appear in the name of a site in the neighbourhood of one of the most important burial-grounds in the eastern Midlands. Elsewhere in Cambridgeshire, there are indications of early settlement in the first elements of Yen Hall (*infra* 113), Mepal (*infra* 237) and Malton (*infra* 79), in the river-name *Must* (*infra* 8) and in the locative form from which the name March (*infra* 253) has descended. The Isle of Ely received its name at a time when the rare element *gē* was still in living use, and throughout the adjacent fenland there are scattered names which to all appearance represent an early vocabulary preserved by the isolation of the local inhabitants. In the names Swaffham and Saxon (Street), a tribal name in its stem-form is united with a terminal in a manner which to say the least is unusual in compounds formed in historic times. In several cases, a name which at first sight gives no hint of age, is carried back to a remote period by further investigation. The name Haslingfield, for example, which in its modern form suggests nothing more significant than 'field of hazels,' is recorded in a series of forms which imply that its first element is a group-name formed from the personal name *Hæsela*, cognate with the German *Hasilo*, and never recorded in independent use. On a review of the whole evidence, it is in fact abundantly clear that the place-names of Cambridgeshire, as a series, fully agree with the indications of an early settlement provided by the archaeological materials discovered within the county.

The Celtic element in the place-names of the county is slight. The river-name Grante is the base of Grantchester and of *Grantacaestir*, the original name of Cambridge. Nene is a river-name; Kennett was originally the name of a stream. Chatteris is a hybrid containing the Celtic *cēt*, 'wood' and the English *rīc*, 'stream,' and was once the name of the Ouse. Apart from these, the only traces of Celtic survival occur in the hybrids Chettisham, where the first element may be identical with that of Chatteris, and Crossfield in Fulbourn which contains the element *cors* discussed in PN W (7, 50), *s.nn*. Gauze Brook and Corston. In general, it can be said that the place-names of the county give no support to the theory of a British survival in the Fenland which has sometimes been based on the legend of devils, chattering in the British language, who haunted St Guthlac at Crowland.

Though not to be compared with that of Lincolnshire, and distinctly slighter than that of Northamptonshire, the Scandinavian element in Cambridgeshire is stronger than that in Bedfordshire or Huntingdon-shire and much stronger than that in Essex or Hertfordshire. Only six parish-names—Bourn, Caxton, Conington, Croxton, Toft and Carlton—contain Scandinavian elements, and of these only Toft and Bourn are of pure Scandinavian origin. In Conington and Carlton there has probably been a re-naming by Scandinavians of an original English *cyning-tūn* and *ceorla-tūn*. Caxton and Croxton are hybrids in which the first element is a Scandinavian personal name, but whether we have here the original names of these villages or whether the name of a Scandinavian lord has replaced that of his English predecessor[1], cannot be determined. It is noteworthy, however, that all six are situated on the clay which was probably once well wooded and not particularly attractive to early settlers.

Little evidence is provided by the modern map to remove the impression that Scandinavian influence was but slight. Denny, 'island of the Danes,' is certainly indicative of Scandinavian settlement, but also implies that Danes were in a minority in the district. It is only from a close examination of the unidentified field-names abundantly recorded in medieval sources that a clear impression can be obtained. Here, Anglo-Scandinavian personal names frequently occur together with elements unknown in the major names.

On or near the Huntingdonshire border lie the parishes of Conington, Croxton, Caxton, Bourn and Toft. In Papworth Hundred we have Conington, *le Croke* (1287) in Swavesey, *Bradewonge* (1260) in Box-worth, and *Gangsted* (1311) in Graveley, containing four Scandinavian

[1] Cf. PN Nt xviii–xix.

elements found only in field-names (*infra* 334, 348, 345). In Longstow Hundred, in addition to Caxton, Croxton and Toft, we have *Hosmundeshou* (13th) in Bourn, perhaps the tumulus (*v.* **haugr**) in which was buried a Scandinavian named *Ásmundr*, whilst Little Gransden, in which Gransden Brook was earlier *Holebecke* (*infra* 6), contains two examples of *lundr*, 'wood,' *Langelund* and *Litlelund* (1251). The adjoining hundred of Wetherley contains no evidence of Scandinavian influence in its major names, but across Barrington and Orwell (where was *Mildred becke* 1586), ran *Lunway* (*infra* 27), whilst across Barton (with *Longtoftes* 1463), Coton and Grantchester ran *Clintway* (*infra* 21). In the latter parish were also *Clint* and *Clintefeld*, whilst Clint Hill and Clint Field still survive in Coton. ON *bekkr* is found in Hoback in Wimpole (*infra* 82) and in *le Becke* (1504) in Comberton, whilst in Haslingfield we find *le Bondemadwe* (1259) containing ON **bóndi**, 'free peasant,' *le Mersgate* (1318) and *Holegate* (1224), where the second element is **gata**, 'road' (*infra* 326), *Holegate* being a hybrid in which Scandinavian *gata* has replaced *weg* in the common Holloway (*infra* 24). To the south, in Armingford Hundred, *Lunway*, containing **lundr**, 'wood,' as noted above, passed through Whaddon where we have another Hoback (*infra* 68), whilst in Melbourn we find a further example of *Holegate* (1228) with a field-name *Clippeshull* (1228) containing the Scandinavian personal name *Klyppr*. In Meldreth *Tounhoues* (1319), *Tweynowes* (1526) was the name of two barrows (*v.* **haugr**), whilst in *Houedane* (1319), as in Howden (PN ERY 250–1), ON *hofuð* has replaced OE *héafod*.

Passing east to Thriplow Hundred, we have *Carlecroft* (1308) (cf. Carlton *infra* 116) and *Litlebek* (1317) in Foxton, *Toft* (1397) and *Crookdoole* (1451) in Harston, ON **haugr** in *Nynehoues* (1319) in Newton and *Evereshow* (1219) in Shelford, whilst in Thriplow itself we find an interchange between English and Scandinavian elements in *Kirkefeld* (1251) and *Cherchefeld* (1419). In Whittlesford Hundred *Toftes* occurs in Whittlesford parish (1290) and in Duxford (1315) where we also have *Conegeshou*, *Konewesho* (1316), 'king's burial-mound,' *Houndysthofte* (1483) in Ickleton, and *le Lounde* (1328) in Sawston from **lundr**. In Chilford Hundred *Northgate* has been noted in Horseheath and Camps (*infra* 105), *Brunilde Cruch* (1279) from ON *Brynhildr* in Castle Camps, and in Flendish Hundred, *Krocwere* (1277) in Horningsea. In Staine Hundred we have *le Wro* (t. Ric 2) from ON *vrá*, 'corner,' in Bottisham, and here and in Little Wilbraham *Camgate* (*infra* 21) was a name of part of the Icknield Way.

Bordering on Suffolk, in Radfield Hundred, lies Carlton. In Balsham part of Wool Street was known as *Horninggate* as well as *Horningstrete* (*infra* 32). A similar interchange takes place in *Burstalleweye* (1250) and *Burtallegate* (sic) (1319) in West Wratting, where we also find the same element gata in *Rughegate* (1234), *Denegate* (1250) and *Crossegate* (1319). In Dullingham we have *le Tofte* (1334). In Cheveley Hundred, in Ashley, we find a Scandinavian second element in *Briddesbuske* (1314) and an Anglo-Scandinavian personal name in *Clippescroft* (1280, *infra* 198). In Staploe Hundred, Landwade frequently appears in Scandinavian form as *Langwath* (*infra* 194–5). We have Anglo-Scandinavian personal names in *Thokesdich* (1290), from Old Danish *Toki*, in Isleham, and in Clipsall in Soham (*infra* 198) where also we find three examples of ON *strengr*, 'watercourse,' *Sheldesstreng* (1251), *Strenges* (1393), *le Westrengs* (1393). ON bekkr occurs in Beck Close in Isleham (*infra* 368), in *la Bek* (1342) in Wicken and in *Lytlebek* (1314), *Litlebec(h)* (1387), *Esterbek* (1236), *Osterbec* (1387) (cf. ON *austr*, 'east') in Chippenham where we also find ON haugr in *Tremhowe* (13th).

In the centre of the county, in Cambridge itself we have five examples of vangr, 'meadow,' *Brytheswong*, *Hulkwong*, *Longhauedenwong*, *Pesewong* and *Stonywong* (1432) and one of brinke, *Loderesbrynke* (1380), an element found also in *Wayourbrynke* (1447) in Cottenham in Chesterton Hundred. In Northstow Hundred we have *Clinthauedene* (c. 1250) in Madingley, *Toftes* (1323) in Oakington and *Crocdol* (1251) in Long Stanton, and in Staine Hundred, *Dencheburgwong* (1319) and *Saltbrinkke* (1349) in Swaffham Prior.

In the Isle of Ely there is no parish name containing a Scandinavian element, but there is more evidence of Scandinavian influence on the present-day map, particularly in the north near the Lincolnshire border. Especially noteworthy is the frequency of *gate* from gata. The early forms of Outwell (*infra* 276) possibly show an interchange between OE wudu and ON viðr. Other names are fully dealt with later. To these may here be added some unidentified field-names. In Thorney, Dowsdale, Singlesole, *Toft* (c. 1151); in Whittlesey, Briggate, Claygate, Scaldgate, Flag Fen, Flegcroft, *Gangestede* (1053, *infra* 345), *Longwong* (13th); in Doddington, Coneywood; in Tydd, Broad Gate, Church Lane (with forms *Kirk*-), Eaugate Field, Fengate Field, Grangehill, Kirkgate, Newgate Lane, *Crossegate* (1438), *Seagate* (1579), *Skeppersgate* (1588); in Parson Drove, Gate End Bridge; in Leverington, Bone's Gote, Plain Field (a remarkable hybrid *infra*

272), *Northgate* (1375), *Chapelgate* (1478), (*viam voc.*) *le Kirkgate* (1486), *Southgate* (1570), *Kyrkstrete* (1393), *Kyrkefelde* (1462), *Kyrkelonde* (1519), *Childerhambrynk* (1449); in Newton, Church Croft (with forms *Kirk-*), Fenland Gate, Fitton; in Wisbech, North and South Brink, *Kyrkestede* (1251), *Kirkegote* (1320), *Westlathe* (1368), *Castellathe* (1386), containing ON hlaða, 'barn,' *the Nether gate* (1358), (*communem viam voc.*) *Northgate* (1529), *Medowgatelane* (1587); in Upwell, *Gunnildeslake* (1251), *Pylekok* (*infra* 356), *Appellathe* (1320), *Gongested lake* (*infra* 345); in Littleport, *Ewerestring* (1320), *Snareslodebrynke*; in Ely, *Quaueneybrynk* (1449); in Downham, *Lodesbrinck* (1415); in Witcham, *le Northgate* (1343); in Sutton, *Bradegate* (13th), *Heȝbrenk* (1356), *le Toft* (1357); in Chatteris, *Toft* (1240), *Herberdhouedlond* (13th) (from ON hǫfuð), *le Bondesmade* (1326) from ON bóndi.

In addition there are numerous examples of *holm* and *bigging*, common loan-words of no value as an indication of Scandinavian settlement. It is clearly significant that in Cambridgeshire we have no name ending in -*by* or -*thorp*, and the number of names of Scandinavian origin which have survived is comparatively small. There is distinct evidence, well distributed throughout the county, that the Scandinavian settlers left their mark on the vocabulary and local nomenclature of the county, but the general impression is that of the naming of minor places in a more or less settled time and the gradual replacement of English terms by similar or corresponding Scandinavian ones, some of which became common even in districts where the settlement was not strong. There is no evidence here, as there is in many parts of the Danelaw proper, for the systematic division of the land among Viking settlers and a radical change in place-nomenclature.

Anglo-Norman influence is not strong. Belsars Hill in Willingham, showing a corruption of the common Belsize, and Spinney in Wicken are near the southern borders of the Isle of Ely. The other examples, Dowgate and Portsand, the transferred Marmont and the hybrid Guyhirn, are all in the north of the Isle. Chiefly in the same district are found a few field-names of French origin, including *garitefeld*, *Frauncmauntel* (*infra* 356), several examples of *marais*, 'marsh,' as in *Mareysbanc* and *Maresdrove*, *bois*, 'wood,' in *le Southboys*, and parallels to the Cheshire Malpas in *Malipassdyche*, probably the Car Dyke, and *Maumpasse* (*infra* 34, 356), and to the Wiltshire Devizes, 'boundary,' in *Devyse* in Wisbech. Norman-French influence on pronunciation, much weaker than in Essex, is to be seen in the variation between initial *c* and *g* in the spellings of such names as Croydon, Gamlingay, Grantchester and Girton, and this, coupled with the inevitable difficulties of the Frenchman in pronouncing a succession of liquids, is the real reason why Cambridge is now Cambridge and not *Grambridge*. Grantchester, too, is by no means a normal development. The OE *Grantesæte* should have given a modern *Grantset*, but the Norman confused the second element *-sete* with his pronunciation of *-cestre*, as in the modern Exeter, Towcester, Wroxeter, etc., and the scribe spelled the name accordingly *Grantceter*, *Grantcester*, and this was finally given its modern form *Grantchester*, but at one time popular etymology went a stage farther and Grantchester only just escaped the fate of being called *Grandchester*. The frequent loss of final *th* in early forms of such names as Aldreth, Clayhithe, Meldreth and Shepreth which has finally prevailed in Horseway, Odsey, Ruddery, Swavesey and Willey, is also due to French influence.

As in Huntingdonshire and Hertfordshire, feudal names of the type Hatley St George and Swaffham Bulbeck are neither numerous nor distinctive. They are much fewer and later than in the neighbouring county of Essex, where some of the additions date from a period little later than the Conquest. They were, however, at one time more numerous than they are to-day. So, too, manorial names are less frequent, later and of much less interest than in Essex. Here we have no series of names such as those left on the modern map of Essex by the Gernons and the Bourchiers, nor have we examples of the effect of popular etymology and local pronunciation on difficult foreign names. But we do find evidence of the use of the French definite article to denote manorial possession as in *le Chenez* for Cheyney Lodge, etc. (*infra* 64), a use first noted in Essex. Manorial names are not uncommon in early sources, but many Cambridgeshire manors have disappeared with their names. The manorial *bury* is much less frequent than in neighbouring counties. It is now never found compounded with a personal name, and usually survives simply as The Bury or in conjunction with a parish name as in Melbourn Bury. The compound *Berrystead* which survives occasionally was formerly more common.

The elements found in Cambridgeshire place-names make valuable contributions to our knowledge of the English vocabulary. Hitherto unrecorded elements are **dung* (Wilsmere Down, *infra* 71), **daf* (*Dallode* and various field-names), **graft* (field-names), **grunt* (Grunty Fen), **must* (Must and Muscat), **cwafen* (Quaney and Quaveney), *snote (Snoots, Snout), *til (Tillage), *tydd (Tydd), *crætt (Crackwell, Cratendon), *wīp (Wype), *wride (Wryde), the compound Prickwillow and the mysterious bagatt (Bagott). Others have been previously noted only in counties not yet included in this survey, *bele (Beald, Bield), *cear (Chear Fen, Chainbridge, Old Chair Drain and field-names), *hæfer (Harrimere), *sceldu (Shelford, Shell and Sheldwey). The forms for Creek and Crouch Moor suggest that creek is native and not a Scandinavian loan-word. The first element of Stuntney may be the adjective stunt in its original sense of 'steep'; Utton's Drove, Widden's Hill and numerous field-names derive from OE wiht, 'bend,' which must have developed a specialised meaning in the fens. Common elements like fyrhðe, stede and stow, besides less usual terms such as cradge and crease, are also used in the fenlands in senses not previously recorded. Other elements rarely noted hitherto are *anger, 'grassland' (Anglesey), scydd 'shed' (Shudy Camps) and *crēowel, 'fork' (Crow Hill). The plant-name wrætt, 'cross-wort,' found previously only in Hertfordshire, has been noted in Wrat Field, Wratting and Wratworth, and occurs also in Norfolk and Suffolk. *byde, 'hollow,' first noted in Northamptonshire, and later in Essex, Hertfordshire and Middlesex, is the base of Bedwellhay in Ely and gives us a new derivative *bydel in Bedham. cangle, 'enclosure,' first discussed in Place-names of Essex (434–5), is found in two field-names near the borders of that county, whilst other field-names contain the element mealo, 'gravel,' hitherto known only from Northamptonshire.

As the topography would lead one to expect, there is a marked difference between the nomenclature of Cambridgeshire proper and that of the Isle of Ely. In the former an abundance of medieval material reveals evidence of innumerable roads and tracks whilst in the latter, lost and decayed rivers and water-courses meet us at every turn. Roads and rivers alike had each their different names for particular stretches and in consequence identification is frequently fraught with difficulties. Sidelights are thrown on social history when we find Akeman Street known as Ferdmaneweye, 'the soldiers' road,' and Cowstreet, Ashwell Street as Dedmanyswey, Street Way as Dedcherlway and Icknield Way as Thevestrete and Retherewey, 'cattle-road.' Place-name evidence seems to leave little doubt of the continuance of the Roman road from Red Cross to Grantchester as Grantestrete and on to Bourn as Bourn Way. Elements relating to barrows, earthworks, etc., can often be associated with some of the numerous existing archaeological remains of the county. *ceaster* in *Grantacaestir*, the original name of Cambridge, and in Chesterton, refers to the original earthwork on the site of Cambridge Castle. Alboro, Arbury, Burrough Green, Burrow Moor, Burwell, Vandlebury and Harborough (*v.* Index) all contain an element referring to existing earthworks or fortifications. That at Granham Manor Camp was formerly known as *Aldewerk*, whilst Crow Hill in Steeple Morden, deriving from OE *crog*, *croh*, 'vessel, crock,' may well owe its name to the pottery found in the neighbouring Roman cemetery. In the neighbourhood of the well-known Anglo-Saxon cemetery of Little Wilbraham, Street Way was once known as *Dedcherlway* and hard by was a field called *Dedcherlfeld*. *haugr* and *hlāw* may mean either 'hill' or 'barrow,' but the existence of tumuli is decisively in favour of 'barrow' in Copley Hill, Five Barrow Field, Limlow Hill, Thriplow and Wormwood Hill. Unidentified field-names often suggest the former existence of barrows or earthworks which cannot now be identified. It would be of interest to know whether aerial photography could reveal any trace of the earthwork *Maidenbury* (*infra* 314) which apparently once existed near Whaddon.

The place-names of the Isle of Ely are distinctive and surprisingly numerous. Many of them identify points on the courses of decayed rivers or the sites of drained meres. Oldeamere in Whittlesey was named from a lake no longer existing on the course of the Nene, then called *Oldea*, 'the old river.' The two Bradneys give us another old name of the Nene in Benwick and March, 'the broad river.' Wryde, now a name covering a wide area in Thorney, was originally that of a stream. The extensive Byall Fen took its name from a spot 'by the river' (*Byee*), the meaning was forgotten, the name became that of the river, then of the fen, and was finally corrupted to *Byall*. Similarly the district in March called Creek with Creekgall Fen was originally the name of a stream, whilst Crouch Moor in Littleport was once a mere on a stream of the same name. Rummer's Field in Wisbech was at one time a 'rough mere.'

Of interest for the life of the fens are such names as Manea, 'well-watered land held in common,' where the vill of Littleport actually had a right of intercommon, Nymandole, a *dole* shared by nine men, Halfpenny Field, recalling the rent payable towards the cost of protecting the land from floods, Broken Wash, commemorating a burst dyke, and Wentworth, 'winter enclosure' and Summer Lesure, 'summer pastures,' reminders of the hard fenland winter.

The various types of fen, their products and the fenland industries of sedge and turf cutting are commemorated in numerous examples of Blockmoor Fen, Flag Fen, Fodder Fen, Frith Fen, *Lesh Fen*, *Lugfen*, Mow Fen, Reed Fen, Sedge Fen and Turf Fen (*v.* Index). The great draining schemes of the seventeenth century were shared by those who *adventured* their capital and by those who *undertook* the actual work, and the lands granted to them in return still bear such names as Adventurers' Lands, The Undertakers, etc., whilst the drains they constructed were named after the engineers or Commissioners of Sewers. The abortive reclamation scheme of Charles I is commemorated by Charlemont.

The special topographical conditions in the fenland naturally produced a vocabulary peculiar to this district. Many of the terms now used, such as *gole, gote, clote, galle*, have hitherto been noted only occasionally in counties such as Huntingdonshire, Northamptonshire or the East Riding of Yorkshire, where fenland occurs. Such elements as *drāf, drift, (ge)lād, (ge)delf*, are much more frequent than in any county so far treated. *ēa, ēg, dīc, fenn, lacu, mere, pōl* and *wēr* are naturally particularly common. *barre, *cear, clūse, crease, dolver, *graft, lockspit, snote*, are rare or unknown elsewhere. Other elements, frequent elsewhere, are particularly common in the fens, but are clearly used in a special sense. *hyll* and *hōh* are used of very slight rises in the surface, whilst *holt* and *fyrhð(e)* cannot be used in their usual meaning 'wood.' See also Gores, cote, slæd, stede, stōw, wiht. Particularly noteworthy is the variety of words used of 'lets and hindrances to the passage of the waters' including *cradge, dam, gravel, stamp, turningtree* and *wende*.

The value of place-names as evidence for the former existence of woodland is well illustrated in this county. Place-names provide clear evidence of the existence of woodland on the boulder clay along the Essex and Suffolk borders. In the parishes from Castle Camps east to Woodditton there are some thirteen examples of lēah (four of them parish names), six of (ge)hæg, two each of ryding and stocking and one of holt. Woodditton itself is called *Silvatica* as early as 1086. Other examples have been noted in unidentified field-names. On the western clayland Croydon Wilds and Hatley Wilds with Wild Barns in Wimpole and Wile(s) in Arrington (*infra* 54, 56, 82, 359) all contain OE *weald*, which formerly formed part of the name of Dry Drayton (*Walddraitton*) and is found also in the same district in *Waldis de Brunne*, i.e. Bourn, *Woldeslande* and *Grenewold* (Elsworth), *Kake-*

stunesweald and *Berstunesweald* (Caxton), *le Welde* (Eltisley), *Burne-weld* (Caldecote) and *Schortwalde* (Eversden). Here we have evidence for the use of *weald* for a stretch of high forest land on the clay from Croydon to Dry Drayton, extending across the border into Huntingdonshire, where we have Weald, Weald Farm and Weald House in Eynesbury Hardwicke. Hatley Wilds is near Hayley Wood, and this element *lēah* occurs also in East Hatley, Papley in Eltisley, Swansley Wood in Caxton, Little Childerley and field-names in Hardwick, Gamlingay and Toft. Other woodland terms found in this area are *Stocking* in Gamlingay, Hardwick, Little Gransden, Eversden and Little Childerley, (*ge*)*hæg*, 'woodland enclosure' in Dry Drayton, Papworth, Little Gransden, Hardwick and Gamlingay (2), and *hyrst*, 'wooded hill' in Little Gransden. In spite of a twelfth-century reference to a grant of meadow in Caxton[1], where at the same time Swansley Wood is described as a *nemus*, there can be little doubt that this clayland was once well wooded and that *weald* here means 'high forest land.' In Duxford *le Welde* may mean simply 'high land,' although woodland terms are found among Duxford and Ickleton field-names.

In the Isle of Ely a similar stretch of high clay land from Haddenham (cf. Woolden Lane *infra* 232), through Sutton (cf. Waller Fen *infra* 240), Wentworth (Waddelows Hill *ib.*), Wilburton, Witcham, Mepal and Downham to Ely was named *Wold* (*infra* 246)—a name which survived until the eighteenth century as *Witchford Wold*. There is other evidence of its wooded nature in the occurrence of such woodland terms as (*ge*)*hæg* in Haddenham, Sutton, Wilburton, Witchford and Ely, *stocking* in Sutton, and *lēah* in Sutton and Witchford. As, however, we have a several fishery in Over called *Heye* (1279 RH), it may be that some, at least, of these names containing (*ge*)*hæg* do not refer to woodland. But woodland terms are more common in the Isle of Ely than one would have suspected. We find *hyrst* in Boleness in Wisbech and Shrewsness in Upwell and in field-names in Doddington, Tydd, March, Stretham and thrice in Whittlesey, *holt* in Apes Hall in Littleport, Singlesole in Thorney and Throckenholt in Parson Drove, *stocking* in Doddington and *lēah* in Bradley and two field-names in Whittlesey.

The historical geography of the fenlands provides a series of problems at present insoluble. Recent research, however, has shown that the fens were not always the inhospitable waste of uninhabited

---

[1] *Cott Faust* A. IV, f. 75.

swamp they were once thought to be[1]. Aerial photography and excavation have revealed the existence in Romano-British times of many sites of native villages and groups of associated Celtic fields, particularly in the silt areas and certain islands. Towards the end of the third century, conditions seem to have deteriorated, possibly through a slight subsidence in the whole fenland basin or through a breach in the natural silt defences the sea had built against itself round the southern shores of the Wash. By the fifth century, it seems clear, the general abandonment of the district was inevitable[2]. The Anglo-Saxon invaders made their way up the rivers to higher and drier ground or confined themselves to the islands and more attractive districts around the margin of the fens.

What routes did these invaders follow? Undoubtedly they travelled by water, but the courses of the rivers were certainly not those of to-day. Quite apart from the changes brought about by seventeenth-century (and earlier) drainage works, streams became choked and decayed or changed their courses or split into several channels. Many of these decayed rivers can still be traced on the ground, and the 'roddons' are known to have been active streams in Romano-British times. Changes of this kind were slow and the difficulty is to know where a river flowed at a particular date. Nene, Ouse and Granta, with the Little Ouse and the Wissey formerly entered the sea at Wisbech, not at Lynn as now, this change in the outfall taking place probably by the fourteenth century[3]. Originally the Nene from Peterborough followed in general the course of the stream now variously known as Muscat, Cat's Water, Shire Drain and Old South Eau, whilst the Ouse flowed north from Earith to Benwick and along what the Ordnance map calls 'Old course of the Nene' through March to Outwell. In the thirteenth century Nene and Ouse united at Benwick and flowed (through more than one branch) to Wisbech. The present course of Ouse from Earith along the Old West River to the Cam and Thetford is comparatively late and certainly did not exist in the fifth century[4]. The charter of Wulfhere king of Mercia to Peterborough abbey[5], though an obvious forgery, may contain a fragment of genuine topography in its reference to the *magistram aquam quae ducit ad Elme et ad Wisebeche*. This can safely be identified with the river Nene.

---

[1] H. C. Darby, *Medieval Fenland*, 3–6; J. N. L. Myres, *op. cit.* 384–5.
[2] C. W. Phillips in *The Cambridge Region*, 92–3.
[3] H. C. Darby, *op. cit.* 94–6.
[4] *Infra* 12, 13 and Darby, *loc. cit.* 94–100, CAPr xxxiii, 119–123.
[5] BCS 22.

It flowed *usque ad Trokenholt*, i.e. Throckenholt, on what is now called the Shire Drain. Further, the *pulchra aqua Bradanea nomine*, near *Gretecros*, is clearly the original Ouse, now represented by 'Old Course of the Nene' on which lie Bradney Farm in March and Bradney House in Benwick[1].

The problems of the archaeology of Cambridgeshire have been complicated rather than solved by recent discoveries. The establishment of certain definite facts still leaves many questions unanswered. The Car Dyke has been shown to be a Roman work, made, probably to provide water transport between Cam and Ouse at a time when there was no natural watercourse all the way from Little Thetford to Earith, that is, before the existence of the Old West River as we know it to-day[2]. The present course of this river from Hermitage Sluice, Earith, to Lockspit Hall was thus originally part of the Car Dyke. The cutting of this made it necessary to build a dam or sluice at its mouth to divert enough water into it from the Cam to make it navigable and this sluice or its ruins probably proved a serious obstacle to river traffic from the sea towards Cambridge. With this reduction in the flow of water, the Cam from Waterbeach to Upware probably became useless for navigation. It seems likely that by the seventh century the Car Dyke had been silted up and the Cam forced its way again along its old course from Waterbeach towards Ely, but in the fifth and sixth centuries, the only navigable route from the sea to Cambridge and beyond was from Wisbech, up the Ouse, through March and Benwick to Earith and along the Car Dyke to the Cam.

We are probably on safe ground if we assume that the Anglo-Saxon invaders entered the Fenlands by the Wash near Wisbech. Some of them sailed up the original Nene along what is now the Lincolnshire border to Peterborough; others up the old Ouse, through March and Benwick to Earith, some continuing up the Ouse to Huntingdon, others along the Car Dyke and the Cam to Cambridge. Another group probably sailed from Wisbech up the Welney into Norfolk, and others up the Lark and the Little Ouse into Suffolk. Thus there were two distinct routes, one leading to the early settlements of the Cam valley, the other to those equally early along the Little Ouse and the Lark. This may well account for the differences which have been noted between the Anglo-Saxon settlers of the Lark and Little Ouse areas and those of the Cambridge district.

---

[1] *Infra* 254, 247.   [2] AntJn vii, 141, CAPr xxxiii, 118 ff., xxxv, 90 ff.

The Isle of Ely was sparsely settled[1]. On their way up the rivers, the invaders passed mere after mere. Apart from those better known at Whittlesey, Willingham, Soham and Stretham, the names of many, now drained and fertile, are still preserved, especially near Wisbech and Elm. Names indicative of settlement appear only on the islands or near the former coast, and few give any impression of great age. Wisbech, the valley of the Wisse, and Elm, if this is to be associated with *Ilwan*, preserve the names of tribes probably among the first wave of immigrants. Ely, containing the archaic *gē* found also in Surrey, Essex and Kent, is certainly a name of high antiquity. Hinton in Haddenham is an *-ingatūn* compound, but names in *-ham* are not common and some certainly contain *hamm*. Of the nine compounds of *tūn*, five are formed with a descriptive element, one (Wilburton) contains a woman's name, whilst the remaining three, Doddington, Leverington and Wimblington, are not necessarily indicative of early settlement. A close study of these fenland names confirms the general impression that the earliest invaders, on the whole, found the district uninviting and pushed on up the rivers to more attractive country in Northamptonshire and Huntingdonshire and the upper Cam valley.

Finally, reference should be made to the opinion of the late Mr Arthur Gray[2] that "the evidence of place-names alone is sufficient to establish the conclusion that Cambridgeshire was settled by two races." It was an essential part of this theory that the *-hams* of Cambridgeshire were of East Anglian, and the *-tons* of Mercian origin. In view of the details brought together in this volume, this distinction can no longer be maintained. It was based on the parish-names which occur on the modern map, but for historical purposes the lost *Sigereston* in Stetchworth is as significant as the surviving *Harlton*. Moreover, the modern spelling conceals a *tūn* in Funthams in Whittlesey (*infra* 260) and Bassenhally in the same parish (*infra* 259), and the *ham* in Swillingham was originally *hyrne*. It is a further weakness of the theory that it ignores the distinction between *hām* and *hamm*. Witcham and West Wickham are certainly derived from *hamm*, as, probably, are also Braham, Needham, Barham, the Newnhams and the Coldhams. In Gray's 'Mercian' hundreds seven *hams* have now been found, one of which is undoubtedly from *hamm*, whilst *Dukenham* in Litlington

---

[1] It may be noted that the hundreds of the Isle of Ely are from two to four times the size of those of the uplands. The settlement of some, at least, of the islands is clearly proved by Bede's statement that the Isle of Ely contained about six hundred families (*Hist. Eccl.* iv, 19).

[2] *The Dual Origin of the Town of Cambridge*, 8–9, 29–30.

(13th *Jesus*) and *Totesham* in Arrington (1271 *CartMisc*) look like early names containing a personal name compounded with *hām*. Similarly in his East Anglian hundreds, there occur three lost *tūns*—*Sigereston* in Stetchworth, *Middeltone* in West Wratting and *Beston* in Great Wilbraham, whilst in the Isle of Ely there are seven *tūns* of which account has not been taken.

Historical arguments have been drawn from the "remarkable group of villages in the clay uplands of Cambridgeshire towards Essex whose names include the element 'west'— Weston Colville, West Wickham, Westley Waterless. There are no corresponding 'east' villages near by."[1] *Weston* may simply be the *tūn* west of the lost *Middeltone* in West Wratting which itself implies the existence of at least two others. In West Wickham the attribute has not been noted earlier than 1266. Westley may well be '(place) west of the *lēah*'; it is just on the western edge of the clay. West Wratting is so called because it is west of the neighbouring Great and Little Wratting in Suffolk.

The material on which this volume is based includes but few original Anglo-Saxon documents. Domesday Book for this county is supplemented by the parallel *Inquisitio Comitatus Cantabrigiensis* and the *Inquisitio Eliensis*. For the twelfth century we have not only the Pipe Rolls as usual, but many original charters, notably the extensive collection preserved in the muniment room of the Dean and Chapter of Ely. From this time onwards there is an abundance of material, but curiously few Cambridgeshire records have been printed, and without access to the various collections of manuscripts this volume could never have been written. The frequency of italicised references will show the debt owed to unprinted material. Without its aid many of the most interesting articles would have been reduced to the mere record of an isolated form or two, useless for the purposes of etymology, and, in the light of our present knowledge, definitely misleading[2].

The only published cartulary of a Cambridgeshire house is that of Barnwell which has proved useful, as also have those of Ramsey, Wardon and Colchester from neighbouring counties. Much valuable material has been obtained from the unpublished Red Book of Thorney, from the cartularies of St John's Hospital, Cambridge, and

[1] J. N. L. Myres, *op. cit.*, 391.
[2] E.g. the articles on Beald, Bedham, Brangehill, Crackwell, Harrimere, Shell, Widden's Hill, Wilsmere Down and Wormwood contain only two printed references earlier than the nineteenth century.

Chatteris, and from the magnificent series of cartularies relating to the estates of Ely. For the thirteenth century we have a particularly early Subsidy Roll. Assize Rolls have proved useful, but these and the Feet of Fines for Cambridgeshire do not provide such large numbers of forms for minor names as do those of Essex. Innumerable charters of the thirteenth century and the later Middle Ages are preserved in Ely, Cambridge and London. Many of those at Ely have been copied into one or other of the Ely cartularies which, on the whole, where the original charters cannot be traced, can be looked upon as trustworthy. At Ely, in the muniment rooms of both the Bishop and the Dean and Chapter, and in various College muniment rooms in Cambridge, especially at St John's, Trinity and Corpus Christi, as well as at the British Museum and the Public Record Office, the very large number of court rolls, rentals, surveys and terriers has proved invaluable. Particularly useful are the Cole manuscripts in the British Museum. Although many of the documents copied by Cole have now disappeared, a comparison of his transcript with certain originals which do survive leaves one with a marked feeling of confidence in his care and painstaking accuracy. For the Isle of Ely, the records of the Commissions of Sewers, now in various depositories, are invaluable. Many useful documents are preserved in the Wisbech Museum, but most useful is the vast series of documents preserved in the Fen Office at Ely and the offices of the River Great Ouse Catchment Board at Cambridge. In view of the mass of this material, a judicious selection of certain portions is all that can at present be attempted.

NOTES ON THE DIALECT OF CAMBRIDGESHIRE
AS ILLUSTRATED IN ITS PLACE-NAMES

OE *a*+nasal usually occurs as *a* in ME, but *o* and *u* are also found. This characteristic West Midland development (cf. PN Wo xxvii, PN Wa xxv) has also been noted in Bedfordshire forms (PN BedsHu xxiv) and is found in Essex in Ongar and Stondon Massey (PN Ess 71–2, 81) and in frequent forms with *o*, *ou* for Pant and compounds of -*land* (ib. 9, 200, 388, etc.). In Cambridgeshire it survives in *Sounds* and is evidenced in the forms of Cambridge (*Grontabricc* c. 745, *Contebrig* 1237), Camps (*Comp(e)s* 1298–1633), Granta (*Gronte, -a* c. 745, 13th), Landbeach (*Londbech(e)* 1235–1522), Landwade (*Lonwatha* 1176–85), Long Stanton (*Lungestanton* 1285), Long Stowe (*Lungestowe* 1268), Pampisford (*Pupiswrth* 1215, *Pompeswrthe* 1281). Occasional examples of *hom* from OE hamm are insufficient to enable us to distinguish clearly between hām and hamm.

OE æ usually occurs as *a* in ME which survives. Forms with *e* are occasionally found for *Ash(ley)*, *Ashwell Street*, *Badlingham*, *Balsham*, *Grantchester* and *Wratting*, and more frequently for *Haslingfield*. *Ness* has only *e*, *Freckney* only *a*. For *Wrat Fd*, *Wratworth* and *Wratting*, *o* is common. This is found also in late forms for *Swaffham*.

OE æ, whatever its source, occurs as *a* and *e* in ME, of which *a* is earlier and general. **In ModEng we have [i·]** represented by *ea*, *ee*, in *Breach* (2), *Deal*, *Meadlands*, *Reach* (2), *Streetly*, *Street Way*, *Wheatmath* and *Wool Street*. **When shortened, the vowel usually appears as *a* in ModEng** as in *Haddenham* and *Manages* and also in *Swaffham*, *Wadloes* and *Whaddon* where we have no *e*-forms, but is shortened to *e* in *Meadow*, *Stretham* and *Treading*. In *Manea* (where we have also forms with *o*) and *Swavesey*, *a* has become a diphthong [ei]. For *Horseheath* we have only one form with *a*, whilst for *Ely*, *Reach*, *Upend*, sǣ (*s.n. Roman Bank*) and sǣte (*s.n. Grantchester*) we find only *e*-forms. For *Soham* we have *æ*, *e*, *i*, beside the more common early *a*, with *o* from 1294. brǣdu, hǣð, lǣs, mǣd, slǣp and strǣt have frequent forms in *a* in ME. lǣs appears in ModEng as *Lazier* and *Lesure* and often as *Leys*, probably through confusion with *ley* from lēah.

OE *e* (æ) before nasals usually occurs as *e* in ME, but *a* is **found in ME** forms for *Brook End*, *Denny* and *Wendy* and *s.vv.*

denu, ende, fenn (*infra* 320, 322, 324). This East Saxon peculiarity is common in Essex and Herts and has been noted in Beds, but no trace of it has been found in Hunts (cf. PN Ess xxxv, PN Herts xxiv, PN BedsHu xxiii). Examples come chiefly from the Hertfordshire border, four of -*dane* occurring in Steeple Morden and one in Meldreth. This *a* does not seem to be found in the Isle of Ely and survives only in *The Dane* in Croxton and *Dane Bottom* in Woodditton.

OE *ē* (Angl *ǣ*), when shortened, appears occasionally in ME as *a* in early forms *s.nn. Granham's* (where it survives), *Green Hills, Greenways* and in certain field-names.

OE *ĕa* usually appears as ME *e* and *a*. It survives as *a* in *Saxton* and as *e* in *Chesterton* and *Cheveley*.

OE *ēa* usually gives ME forms in *e* which survives in *Mepal* and *Shepreth*. For the latter, as for *Hinton* and *Shippea*, we find also early forms in *i*. For **bēan** we find only *e* for *Banstead('s)* and *Bendyshe*, only *a* for *Ballond* and *Bancroft*, *a* and *e* for *Bannolds*, and *e, ei, ey* for *Benwick*. **ēast** invariably gives ME *e*, with ModEng *east* except in *Estover*.

OE *eald* (Angl *ald*) occurs in ME as *ald, old*, with only occasional *eld*, but these are well distributed, e.g. *s.nn. Allstreet, The Gores, Offal End, Offals Wood* and *Old Halves*. For *Elford* we have forms in *e* only. In ModEng we have usually **al(d)** or **old** as in *Alboro, Oldeamere, Old Halves*, with a shortened vowel in *Offal*. **eld** survives only in a field-name *Elbrows*.

OE *weald* (Angl *wald*) has ME *ea, e, a* and *o*. Except for occasional forms near Ely, those in *e(a)* are from the Hunts border and survive with *i* in *Croydon* and *Hatley Wilds, Wild Barns* and *Wile(s)*. **wold** is earlier and more common in the Isle of Ely. It survives in *Woolden* and long persisted in *Wold*. We have a shortened vowel from **wald** in *Waddelows* and *Waller*, whilst **weld** is the source of such late forms as *Weeles* in Doddington and Sutton.

OE *ĕo* usually becomes *e*, but we have also early *i* and *u* in *Silverley*.

OE *ēo* usually becomes *e* in ME, but we have also *i, ie* and occasionally *u* in *Barnwell, Girton, Leverington, Stourbridge* and *Thetford*.

OE *īe* (Angl *ē*) usually gives ME *e*, with variant *i* and occasional *u* in *Chiswick, Needham, Shingay* and *Steeple Morden*. For *Fleam Dyke* and *Flendish* we sometimes find AN *a* for *e*.

OE *wielle* usually appears in ME as *welle*. For *Upwell* we have forms with *i*. In certain forms for *Snailwell* and *Outwell* we find

ME *walle* from Angl *wælle* (cf. PN BedsHu xxiv, PN Wo xxvii, PN Wa xxvi), as also in a number of field-names, chiefly near the Suffolk border: *Blakkewalle* (1517) (Haslingfield), *Chaldewalle* (1335) (Burrough Green), *Dernewalle* (14th) (Stetchworth), *Hartewall* (t. Hy 6) (Bottisham), *Tonewalle* (1338), *Wyde-* (1308), *Wodewalle* (1353) (Weston Colville) and *Wytewalle* (1280) (Ashley).

OE *ī(o)w* in the *New*-names shows the same tendency to shift the stress in the diphthong from *io* to *ió* which has been noted in Worcestershire (PN Wo xxviii). This survives in *No Ditch* and is evidenced in *Newnham* and *Newton* in such forms as *Nouham*, *Nuneham*, *Nowetuna*, *Nuenton*.

OE *u* and late ME *u* from OE *ō* appear occasionally in ME as *e* or *i* before point consonants (cf. PN BedsHu xxv, 254, PN Wo xxviii, PN W xx) in such forms as *Metlowe*, *Dedyngton* and *Dynnington* (*infra* 60, 82, 251–2). This survives in *Mettle* Hill.

OE *ȳ* occurs in ME as *e, i* and much less frequently as *u*. *e* seems to be rather more common than *i*. Of these, *e* survives in *Bedham*, *Bedwellhay*, *Kennett*, and *Meldreth*, *i* in *Brinkley*, *Guilden Morden*, *Hill Row*, *Histon*, *Kirtling*, *Nill Well*, *Thriplow*, *Tydd* and *Wimblington*. In *Shudy* Camps, with a preponderance of *u*-forms, *u* survives, but there is evidence that locally *i* persisted in the pronunciation *Cittie*. **bridge, bury, pit, ridge** and **rush,** all with earlier *i, e, u,* now have the standard spelling. **hyrne** has only *i* and *e*, with modern *i*, whilst **hyrst** has usually *i*, with occasional *e*, which, however, survives in *Boleness* and *Shrewsness*. **fyrhþe** has occasional *e* but usually *i* which survives in *Frith* and *Thrift*.

OE *ȳ* usually occurs as *i* or *e*, less frequently as *u*. In *Stetchworth* we have ModEng *e*. Forms in *i* are most common for *Litlington* and *Littleport*, in *e* for *Aldreth* and *Swavesey*, whilst for *Ruddery* we find only *e*-forms. Elsewhere in *hyð*, we have modern [ai] from *ī*, though, earlier, *ē* is almost equally frequent.

OE *ceald, cald* has ME forms in *chald, cald, caud, cad* and *cold*, and occasionally *celd*. *Ch* survives only in *Chardle*. We have initial *c* [k] in *Caldecote*, *Carvers*, *Caudle*, *Caudlehole*, *Cawdle*, *Coldham(s)* and *Cowdell*.

OE *ceaster* has *c* in *Castre-*, *Cestre-*, but usually *ch* in *Chesterton*.

OE *circe*, ME *chirche* has been Scandinavianised in *Kirkgate* (*Bridge*) in Tydd St Giles and sporadically in *Church Croft* (Newton), *Church Field* (Whittlesey) and *Church Lane* (*Bridge*) (Tydd). Other examples are found in field-names: *Kyrke acre* in Fulbourn (*infra*

145), *Kirkgate*, *Kirkegote*, *Kyrkefeld* and *Kyrkelonde* in Leverington (*infra* 326, 327, 371), *Church Field* in Upwell (*infra* 371) and *Kyrkested* (*infra* 345). In Thriplow to-day we have a *Church St* near which, in the thirteenth century was *Kirkefeld*. Similarly **OE bece** has been replaced by Scand **bekkr** in *Birdbeck*, *Hoback* (2), in certain forms for *Waterbeach* and *Wisbech* and in field-names in Chippenham and Foxton. In *Landwade*, the second element varies between **OE wæd** and **ON vað**, and a similar interchange has taken place between **OE weg** and **ON gata** (cf. *supra* xx–xxii, *infra* 21, 32, 326–7).

Prefixed *r* from the dative sing.-fem. of the definite article (ME *atter*) survives in *Ree*, *Rhee*, *Ryecroft* and *Ryland*.

An inorganic *r* is occasionally **inserted in the spelling as a sign of a long vowel** (cf. PN Ess xxxvii) as in *Barston*, *Chardle*, *Starlock*, *Starnea* and *Long Swarth*.

Metathesis of *r* occurs occasionally in the later developments of OE **brycg** *s.nn.* Barton *Bridge* and *Cambridge*, and survives in *Birch* from **brǣc**. (Cf. PN Nth xxxii, PN Wa xxvi, PN W xxi, PN Nt xxiii.)

An **inorganic initial *s*** is sometimes **prefixed** to words beginning with *c* [k] or *p* (cf. PN Sx 190 *s.n.* Poles Pitch, PN Ess 180 *s.n.* Scaldhurst, PN Mx 25 *s.n.* Scrattage). This survives in the dialectal *splash* from **plæsc** and is found in forms for *Cradge* Bank and The *Washes*. Cf. also *Pralleswere* 1221 *ElyA*, *Preileswere* c. 1270 *Thorney*, *Prawlesweere* 1604 *Dugd*, *Sprallesware* 1586 *Ct*, *Spral(l)eswere* 1606 *Depositions*.

Loss of final ð or þ in such elements as **sēað**, **hȳð**, **rið**, etc. (cf. PN Ess 212, *s.n.* Creeksea and IPN 109) is frequent in early forms for *Aldreth*, *Clayhithe*, *Meldreth* and *Shepreth* and persists in *Horseway*, *Odsey*, *Ruddery*, *Swavesey* and *Willey*.

v is found for *th* in forms for *Clayhithe* and survives in *Hive* Rd and Witcham *Hive*, side by side with Witcham *Hythe*. This *v* probably arose from the inflected form with voiced spirant.

The northern tendency to **over-aspiration of OE hw** is evidenced in forms beginning with *Qu-*, *Qw-*, and occasionally *Phw-* for The *Washes*, *Whaddon*, *Whitwell*, *Whitehill*, *Whiting's* Grove, *Whitwell*, West *Wickham*, *Wimpole* and certain field-names. Cf. PN NRY xxxii–iii, 30 (*s.n.* Whenby), PN ERY xxxi, PN Wa xxvi and, for *Ph-*, cf. Falsgrave (PN NRY 107). The falling together of OE *hw* and *cw* is shown in the neighbouring county of Lincoln in Whaplode, earlier *Quaplode*. Cf. also (from the Wisbech court rolls) *le quelewrith* (1317), *quelwrygte* (1318), 'wheelwright'.

OE [χ] in *healh* and *holh* sometimes becomes *f* or *v*. This survives in *Old Halves* and *Swarm Haugh* and in field-names as *Hoof* and *Hove* (*infra* 332). Cf. also *s.n. Capload infra* 240.

Confusion between *burn* and *burgh* is found in forms for *Free School Lane*, *Bassingbourn* and *Fulbourn*.

Initial [j] is developed before OE *ēa* in *Yen Hall* (cf. PN Sx xxix, PN D xxxiii).

Anglian *-us-* for the genitival *-es-* appears in certain forms for *Croxton, Duxford, Hauxton* and *Kingston* (cf. PN Wo xxix, PN Wa xxvii). This *-es-* often also occurs as *-is-* which has survived in Bottisham and Eltisley.

The inflexional *an* of the weak adjective is retained in *Blakeney, Bradney, Deepney, Newnham* (3), *Nornea* and *Sun Doles* and is found in ME forms of such names as *Newton* (2).

The usual present participle form is the Midland *-ende* as in *Hangendewud* (1235), *-brade, -brede, -dole* (1319), *le Rennendeforw* (1300, 1356). We have the **Southern *-inde*** in *Hangindeclay* (13th) and the **Northern *-and*** in *þe furlong lyand* south (t. Ric 2). **Later we have *-ing*** as in *Rennyngforgh* (1383), *le Hangyngfurlong* (1467).

NOTE. Place-names formed with a prefixed prepositional phrase, so marked a characteristic of Devonshire names (cf. PN D xxxvii), are more numerous than in any county so far treated except Devonshire. Most of these have not survived (cf. *infra* 355). In major names bī(g) is preserved in *Beesons* and *Byall*, binnan in *Bin Brook* and *Binnimoor*, and bufan in *Burton*. The preposition has disappeared in *Nornea* and in the neighbouring lost *Sutheneya, Sun Doles* and *Estenhale* (*infra* 43). *v.* also *infra* 112, 130, 239, 244.

BIBLIOGRAPHY AND ABBREVIATIONS

Abbr	*Placitorum Abbreviatio*, 1811.
AC	*Ancient Charters*, ed. J. H. Round (Pipe Roll Soc. 10), 1888.
AD	*Catalogue of Ancient Deeds* (PRO) (1890 and in progress).
AD	Ancient Deeds (PRO).
Add	Additional Manuscripts (BM).
AddCh	Additional Charters (BM).
AddR	Additional Rolls (BM).
AdvL	Schedule of Adventurers' Lands (Fen Office, Ely).
AdvProc	Minutes of the Proceedings of the Adventurers (*penes* River Great Ouse Catchment Board, Cambridge).
AFr	Anglo-French.
AN	Anglo-Norman.
AnctC	C. C. Babington, *Ancient Cambridgeshire* (CAS 20), 1853.
ANG	F. Liebermann, *Ungedruckte anglo-normannische Geschichtsquellen*, 1879.
Annals	C. H. Cooper, *Annals of Cambridge*, 5 vols., 1842–1908.
AntJn	*Antiquaries' Journal*.
AOMB	Augmentation Office Miscellaneous Books (PRO).
ASC	*Anglo-Saxon Chronicle*.
ASCh	A. J. Robertson, *Anglo-Saxon Charters*, 1939.
Ass	*The Assizes held at Cambridge*, A.D. 1260 (Assize Roll 82), ed. W. M. Palmer, 1930.
	Assize Roll 103, ed. W. M. Palmer (EA (NS) VI), Extracts CAPr ix, 209–26.
	The Earliest Northamptonshire Assize Rolls 1202–3, ed. D. M. Stenton (Nth. Rec. Soc. 5), 1930.
Ass	Assize Rolls for Cambridgeshire, nos. 80, 83–6, 90, 93–5, 97–102, 104–8 (PRO).
	Assize Rolls for Divers Counties, nos. 1177, 1181, 1188 (PRO).
ASWills	*Anglo-Saxon Wills*, ed. D. Whitelock, 1930.
Atkinson	T. D. Atkinson, *Cambridge Described and Illustrated*, 1897.
Atkyns	R. Atkyns, *Notes on the Fens of Cambridgeshire*, 1604 (Harl 5011).
Badeslade	T. Badeslade, *History...of the Navigation of the Port of King's Lyn, and of Cambridge*, 1725.
BadesladeA	Map of the Fens (CUL MS Plans 598; Lynam 21).
Baker	*Map of the County of Cambridgeshire and the Isle of Ely.* Surveyed by R. G. Baker, 1816–20.
Banco	*Index of Placita de Banco* (PRO Lists and Indexes, no. 32), 1909.
Barnwell	*Liber Memorandorum Ecclesie de Bernewelle*, ed. J. W. Clark, 1907.
BCS	W. de G. Birch, *Cartularium Saxonicum*, 3 vols., 1885–93.
Bede	*Historia Ecclesiastica*, ed. C. Plummer, in *Venerabilis Baedae Opera Historica*, 2 vols., 1896.
BedL	S. Wells, *History of the...Bedford Level*, 2 vols., 1830.
Beds	Bedfordshire.
Bentham	J. Bentham, *The History and Antiquities of the Conventual and Cathedral Church of Ely*, 2nd ed. 2 vols., 1812.
Berks	Berkshire.
Bk	Buckinghamshire.
BLAcct	Accounts of the Bedford Level Corporation (Fen Office, Ely).
Blaeu	G. and J. Blaeu, *Theatrum Orbis Terrarum...Pars Quarta*, 1645.

Blomefield	F. Blomefield, *Collectanea Cantabrigiensia*, 1750.
BM	*Index to the Charters and Rolls in the Department of Manuscripts, British Museum*, Vol. I, *Index Locorum*, 1900; Vol. II, *Religious Houses and other Corporations and Index Locorum for Acquisitions from 1882 to 1900*, 1912.
BMFacs	*Facsimiles of Royal and other Charters in the British Museum*, 1903.
Bodl	*Calendar of Charters and Rolls preserved in the Bodleian Library*, ed. W. H. Turner and H. O. Coxe, 1878.
Bodl	Charters and Manuscripts (unpublished) in the Bodleian Library.
Borough	W. M. Palmer, *A History of the Parish of Borough Green* (CAS 54), 1939.
Bott	E. Hailstone, *History of Bottisham*, 2 vols. (CAS 14, 16), 1873–8.
Bowen	E. Bowen, *Map of Cambridgeshire*, 1763.
BrC	Cartulary of the Braybrooke family (BM, Sloane MS 186). *v.* EHR 46, 442–3.
BT	J. Bosworth, *An Anglo-Saxon Dictionary*, ed. T. N. Toller, 1898.
BTSupplt	do. *Supplement* by T. N. Toller, 1921.
BuryDoc	*Feudal Documents from the Abbey of Bury St Edmunds*, ed. D. C. Douglas, 1932.
Bushell	W. D. Bushell, *Hobson's Conduit*, 1938.
C	Cambridgeshire.
Cai	*Admissions to Gonville and Caius College*, ed. J. Venn, 1887.
Cai	Caius MS 489.
CaiCh	Charters *penes* Gonville and Caius College, Cambridge.
Caius	J. Caius, *Historia Cantabrigiensis Academicae*, 1574.
Camden	W. Camden, *Britannia*, 1586; *Britain*, tr. Philemon Holland, 1610; ed. E. Gibson (2 vols.), 1772; ed. R. Gough (3 vols.), 1789.
CAPr	*Proceedings of the Cambridge Antiquarian Society*. (In progress.)
CartAntiq	*The Cartae Antiquae Rolls* 1–10, ed. L. Landon (Pipe Roll Soc. (NS) 17), 1939.
Carter	Edmund Carter, *The History of the County of Cambridge*, 1819.
CartMisc	*Cartæ Miscellaneæ* (PRO).
CAS	*Cambridge Antiquarian Society Publications, Octavo Series*. (In progress.)
Castle	W. M. Palmer, *Cambridge Castle*, 1928.
CathAngl	*Catholicon Anglicum* (EETS 75), 1881.
CBD	*Cambridge Borough Documents*, vol. I, ed. W. M. Palmer, 1931.
CCC	Documents *penes* Corpus Christi College, Cambridge.
CCh	*The Charters of the Borough of Cambridge*, ed. F. W. Maitland and M. Bateson, 1901.
CGild	*Cambridge Gild Records*, ed. M. Bateson (CAS 39), 1903.
Ch	*Calendar of Charter Rolls* (PRO), 6 vols., 1903–27.
Ch	Cheshire.
ChancDec	Chancery Decrees (copies *penes* Mr Charles Greenwood).
ChancP	*Calendars of the Proceedings in Chancery, in the reign of Queen Elizabeth*, 3 vols., 1827–32. *Index of Chancery Proceedings* (Series ii) (PRO Lists and Indexes, nos. 7, 24, 30).
Chateriz	*Cartularium de Chateriz* (15th) (Cott Jul A i).
ChR	*Rotuli Chartarum*, 1837.
Christ's	Documents *penes* Christ's College, Cambridge.
ChronRams	*Chronicon Abbatiae Rameseiensis*, ed. W. D. Macray (Rolls Series), 1886.
CHuAS	*Transactions of the Cambridgeshire and Huntingdonshire Archaeological Society*. (In progress.)
Cl	*Calendar of Close Rolls* (PRO). (In progress.)
Clare	Documents *penes* Clare College, Cambridge.

Clerkenwell	Registrum S. Mariae de Clerkenwell (Cott Faust B ii).
ClR	*Rotuli Litterarum Clausarum*, 2 vols., 1833–44.
Cluny	G. F. Duckett, *Charters and Records of Cluni*, 2 vols., 1888.
Co	Cornwall.
Coins	*Catalogue of English Coins in the British Museum, Anglo-Saxon Series*, 2 vols., 1887–93; *The Norman Kings*, 2 vols., 1916; *Anglosachsiska Mynt*, ed. B. E. Hildebrand, 1881; G. C. Brooke, *English Coins*, 1932.
Colch	*Cartularium Monasterii Sancti Johannis Baptiste de Colecestria*, 2 vols. (Roxburghe Club), 1897.
ColchA	Leger Book of St John's Abbey, Colchester (*penes* Colchester Corporation).
Cole	Cole MSS (BM).
Conybeare	E. Conybeare, *Highways and Byways in Cambridge and Ely*, 1897.
Cott	Cottonian Manuscripts (BM).
CPlans	J. W. Clark and A. Gray, *Old Plans of Cambridge*, 1574–1798, 2 vols., 1921.
CR	Pipe Roll, Chancellor's copy.
Crawford	*The Crawford Collection of Early Charters and Documents*, ed. A. S. Napier and W. H. Stevenson, 1895.
CRent	Cambridge Rentals (CUL Add MS 2611).
Crispin	J. A. Robinson, *Gilbert Crispin, Abbot of Westminster*, 1911.
Crowland	F. M. Page, *The Estates of Crowland Abbey*, 1934.
Ct	*Court Rolls of the Abbey of Ramsey and of the Honor of Clare*, ed. W. O. Ault, 1928. *The Court Baron*, ed. F. W. Maitland and W. P. Baildon (Seld Soc. 4), 1890.
Ct	Court Rolls in PRO, BM, CUL, Ely Diocesan Registry, Dean and Chapter Library, Ely Cathedral, Wisbech Museum, Clare College, Gonville and Caius College, Trinity College, Cambridge and private hands.
CTerr	Terrarium terrarum in campis de Cantebrigia (CUL Add MS 2601).
CtWards	Court of Wards (PRO).
Cu	Cumberland.
CUL	Cambridge University Library.
Cur	*Curia Regis Rolls* (PRO). (In progress.)
CurR	*Rotuli Curiae Regis*, 2 vols., 1835.
CWills	*Abstracts from the Wills…of Printers, Binders, and Stationers of Cambridge*, 1504–1699, ed. G. J. Gray and W. M. Palmer (Bibliographical Soc.), 1915.
CWool	Cambridgeshire Wool Tax Returns, 1345 (Caius MS 498).
D	Devon.
Dan	Danish.
Danelaw	*Documents illustrative of the Social and Economic History of the Danelaw*, ed. F. M. Stenton, 1920.
DB	Domesday Book.
Db	Derbyshire.
Deeds	Miscellaneous Deeds in CUL, at Trinity Hall (transcribed by H. L. Pink), and in private hands.
Denny	Denny Rental (CUL Add MS 2601).
DEPN	E. Ekwall, *The Oxford Dictionary of English Place-Names*, 2nd ed., 1940.
Depositions	Exchequer; Depositions by Commission (PRO).
DKR	*Reports by the Deputy Keeper of the Public Records*, vols. 38, 39, 41.
Do	Dorset.

Dodson	W. Dodson, *The Designe for the perfect Draining of the Great Level of the Fens called Bedford Level*, 1665.
Downing	Documents *penes* Downing College, Cambridge.
Draining	As to the Draining of the Fens (Ely Diocesan Registry, A 8).
Drayton	M. Drayton, *Poly-Olbion*, 1612.
Du	Durham.
Du	Dutch.
Dual Origin	A. Gray, *The Dual Origin of the Town of Cambridge* (CAS, 4to Publication, NS 1), 1908.
Dugd	W. Dugdale, *Monasticon Anglicanum*, 6 vols. in 8, 1817–30.
Dugd	Papers about draining of Fens...by Sir William Dugdale (BM Harl 5011).
DugdD	Diary of Sir Wm. Dugdale (BM Lansdowne MS 722).
Dunster	*The Honour of Dunster*, ed. H. C. Maxwell Lyte (So. Rec. Soc. 33), 1917–18.
EA	*The East Anglian*, 4 vols. (OS), 13 vols. (NS), 1858–1910.
EAS	*Transactions of the Essex Archaeological Society* (OS), 5 vols. (NS). (In progress.)
ECP	*Early Chancery Proceedings* (PRO Lists and Indexes, nos. 12, 16, 20, 29, 38, 48, 50, 51, 54, 55), 1901–33.
EDD	*The English Dialect Dictionary*, 6 vols., 1898–1905.
EETS	Early English Text Society. (In progress.)
EFris	East Frisian.
Eg	Egerton Manuscripts (BM).
EgCh	Egerton Charters (BM).
EHN	O. S. Anderson, *English Hundred-names*, 3 vols., 1934–9.
EHR	English Historical Review. (In progress.)
Elem	Cartulary of the Elemosinarius of Ely Priory (14th) (Dean and Chapter Library, Ely).
Elien	Ely Episcopal Registers (Ely Diocesan Registry).
Elstobb	W. Elstobb, *Map of Sutton and Mepall Levells* (CUL).
Ely	*Ely Episcopal Records*, ed. A. Gibbons, 1891.
Ely	Register of Ely Cathedral (Cott Claud C xi).
ElyA	*Vetus Liber Archidiaconi Eliensis*, ed. C. L. Feltoe and E. H. Minns (CAS 48), 1917.
ElyA	Liber de inquisitionibus maneriorum episcopatus Elyensis (Cott Tib B ii).
ElyB	Ely Register—Liber B (15th) (Ely Diocesan Registry).
ElyC	Chartulary of Ely Cathedral (13th) (Add 41612).
ElyCh	Cartae Antiquae *penes* the Dean and Chapter of Ely Cathedral.
ElyCouch	The old Coucher Book of Ely, ff. 1–206 (1251), ff. 209–43 (c. 1330) (Liber R, Ely Diocesan Registry).
ElyD	Ely Cartulary (13th) (Cott Tib A vi).
ElyE	*Registrum Ecclesiae Eliensis* (13th) (Cott Vesp A vi).
ElyF	Ely Cartulary (15th) (Eg 3047).
ElyG	Registrum Cartarum Ecclesiae Eliensis (13th) (Cott Nero C iii).
ElyM	Cartulary of the Church and Convent of Ely (14th) (Ely Diocesan Registry, MS M).
ElyVis	*Episcopal Visitation Returns for Cambridgeshire*, 1638–65, ed. W. M. Palmer, 1930.
EME	Early Middle English.
EModE	Early Modern English.
EnclA	Enclosure Awards.
EPN	*The Chief Elements used in English Place-names* (EPNS), 1924.
EPNS	English Place-name Society. (In progress.)
ER	*Essex Review*. (In progress.)
Ess	Essex.

ESt	*Englische Studien.* (In progress.)
ExcheqDecrees	Transcript of Exchequer Decrees *penes* the Clerk to the March Urban District Council.
Extent	Extents in BM, PRO and Dean and Chapter Library, Ely.
Eyns	*Eynsham Cartulary*, ed. H. E. Salter, 2 vols. (Oxford Historical Soc. 49, 51), 1907–8.
FA	*Feudal Aids* (PRO), 6 vols., 1899–1920.
Farrer	Wm. Farrer, *Feudal Cambridgeshire*, 1920.
Fees	*The Book of Fees* (PRO), 3 vols., 1920–31.
Feilitzen	Olof von Feilitzen, *The Pre-Conquest Personal Names of Domesday Book*, 1937.
Felix	*Vita Sancti Guthlaci by Felix* (ed. W. de G. Birch, *Memorials of Saint Guthlac of Croyland*), 1881.
Fen	W. M. Palmer, *The Fen Office Documents* (CAS 38), 1939.
FenL	Letter Book of the Fen Office, 1672–3 (CUL Add MS 3598).
Fenland	*Fenland Notes and Queries*, 7 vols., 1889–1909.
FenS	Bargains and Sales, Mortgages, Assignments, Leases etc. (Fen Office, Ely).
FF	*Pedes Finium* (Cambridgeshire), ed. W. Rye (CAS 26), 1891.
	Feet of Fines (Pipe Roll Soc. 17, 20, 23, 24), 1894–1908.
FF	Feet of Fines (PRO).
FFEss	*Feet of Fines for Essex*, 2 vols., 1899–1928.
Fine	*Calendar of Fine Rolls* (PRO). (In progress.)
FineR	*Excerpta e rotulis finium*, 2 vols., 1835–6.
Fleet	*A Terrier of Fleet, Lincolnshire*, ed. N. Neilson, 1920.
Flem	Flemish.
For	Pleas of the Forest (PRO).
FörstemannPN	E. Förstemann, *Altdeutsches Namenbuch, Personennamen*, 2nd ed., 1901.
Fox	C. Fox, *The Archaeology of the Cambridge Region*, 1923.
Fr	French.
France	*Calendar of Documents preserved in France*, ed. J. H. Round (PRO), 1899.
FW	Florence of Worcester, *Chronicon ex Chronicis*, 2 vols., 1848–9.
G	C. and J. Greenwood, *Map of Cambridgeshire*, 1832.
Gaimar	Geffrei Gaimar, *Lestorie des Engles* (Rolls Ser.), 2 vols., 1888–9.
Gale	*Historiae Britannicae, Saxonicae, Anglo-Danicae, Scriptores xv*, ed. T. Gale, 1691.
Gardner	R. Gardner, *History, Gazetteer and Directory of Cambridgeshire*, 1851.
Gaunt	*John of Gaunt's Register*, ed. S. Armitage Smith (Camden Soc. 3rd series, 20, 21), 1911.
Ger	German.
Gervase	*The Historical Works of Gervase of Canterbury* (Rolls Series), 2 vols., 1879–80.
GervT	*Des Gervasius von Tilbury Otia Imperialia*, ed. F. Liebrecht, 1856.
GestH	*Gesta Herwardi. v.* Gaimar, *u.s.*
Gl	Gloucestershire.
Goodman	A. W. Goodman, *History of St Botolph's, Cambridge*, 1922.
Goth	Gothic.
Gröhler	H. Gröhler, *Über Ursprung und Bedeutung der französischen Namen*, 2 Parts, 1913, 1933.
Gross	E. J. Gross, *Chronicle of the Estates of Gonville and Caius College.*
Guthlac	*The Anglo-Saxon Version of the Life of St Guthlac*, ed. C. W. Goodwin, 1848.
	Das angelsächsische Prosa-Leben des heiligen Guthlac, ed. P. Gonser (Anglistische Forschungen 27), 1909.

H	W. Harrison, *Description of England* in Holinshed's *Chronicles* (vol. 1), 1577, 1586.
Ha	Hampshire.
Harding	F. Harding, *Map of Middle Level* etc. (CUL; Lynam 37).
Hardwicke	Hardwicke Papers (BM), vol. DCCCLXXXVI, Wimpole Records (1649), Add 36234.
HardwickeA	Hardwicke Papers (BM), vol. DCCCLXXX, Estate and Business Papers, 1610–1759, Add 36228.
Harl	Harleian MSS (BM).
HarlCh	Harleian Charters (BM).
Hayward	W. Hayward, *General Plotte and discription of the Fennes*, 1604.
He	Herefordshire.
Herts	Hertfordshire.
HH	*Henrici Archidiaconi Huntendunensis Historia Anglorum* (Rolls Series), 1879.
Higden	*Polychronicon Ranulphi Higden* (with the English translation of John Trevisa), 9 vols. (Rolls Series), 1865–86.
HMC	Historical Manuscripts Commission. (In progress.)
HMCVar	*HMC Reports on Manuscripts in Various Collections*, 8 vols., 1901–23.
Hollar	W. Hollar, *The Mappe of Norfolke, Suffolke, Cambridgeshire... Exactly Described*, 1644.
Holthausen	F. Holthausen, *Altenglisches etymologisches Wörterbuch*, 1934.
Hondius	*A General Plott and description of the Fennes...H. Hondii*, 1632.
Horns	W. K. Clay, *A History of the Parish of Horningsey* (CAS 7), 1865.
Hosp	Registrum chartarum fratrum sancte domus hospitalis Jerusalem de terris in Chipenham, Asheley et Silverley (15th) (Cott Nero C IX).
Hu	Huntingdonshire.
Huddleston	Documents *penes* Commander Huddleston.
Hughes	T. McKenny Hughes and Mary C. Hughes, *Cambridgeshire*, 1909.
ICC	*Inquisitio Comitatus Cantabrigiensis...Subjicitur Inquisitio Eliensis*, ed. N. E. S. A. Hamilton, 1876.
Icel	Icelandic.
Imb	W. Dugdale, *The History of Imbanking*, 2nd ed., 1772.
InqEl	*Inquisitio Eliensis*, v. ICC.
Ipm	*Calendar of Inquisitions post mortem* (PRO). (In progress.)
IpmR	*Inquisitiones post mortem*, 4 vols., 1806–28.
IPN	*Introduction to the Survey of English Place-names* (EPNS), 1923.
Jespersen	O. Jespersen, *A Modern English Grammar*, 1909.
Jesus	Documents *penes* Jesus College, Cambridge.
Jordan	R. Jordan, *Handbuch der mittelenglischen Grammatik*, I. Teil, 1925.
K	Kent.
Karlström	S. Karlström, *Old English Compound Place-names in -ing*, 1927.
KCD	J. M. Kemble, *Codex Diplomaticus Aevi Saxonici*, 6 vols., 1839–48.
Kendale	W. Farrer and J. F. Curwen, *Records relating to the Barony of Kendale* (Cumberland and Westmorland Arch. Soc. Record Series, Vols. IV, V, VI), 1923, 1924, 1926.
Kip	W. Kip, *Map of Cambridgeshire*, 1607.
Kitchin	T. Kitchin, *Map of Cambridgeshire*, 1747.
Kluge	F. Kluge, *Etymologisches Wörterbuch der deutschen Sprache* (11th ed.), 1934.
KPN	J. K. Wallenberg, *Kentish Place-names*, 1931.
L	D. and S. Lysons, *Cambridgeshire* (Magna Britannia, vol. II), 1808.
L	Lincolnshire.
La	Lancashire.
Landb	W. K. Clay, *A History of the Parish of Landbeach* (CAS 6), 1861.

Landwade   W. M. Palmer, *Landwade and the Cotton Family* (CAPr xxxviii), 1939.
Lat   Latin.
Layer   W. M. Palmer, *John Layer...a seventeenth century local historian* (CAS 53), 1935.
Layer   MS 92 (Ely Diocesan Registry).
Lea   C. Saxton, *Shires of England and Wales*, corrected by...P. Lea, 1690.
Lease   Particulars of Leases, etc. in PRO. (typed catalogue).
Lei   Leicestershire.
Leland   Leland, *Itinerary*, ed. L. T. Smith, 5 vols., 1906–10.
Lewes   *The Chartulary of the Priory of St Pancras of Lewes*, ed. L. F. Salzman (Sx Rec. Soc. 38, 40), 2 vols., 1932–4.
    Cambridgeshire Portion, ed. J. H. Bullock and W. M. Palmer (CAS), 1938; Norfolk Portion, ed. J. H. Bullock (Nf Rec. Soc. 12), 1939.
Lewes   Lewes Cartulary (1444) (Cott Vesp F xv).
LGer   Low German.
LibEl   *Liber Eliensis* (Anglia Christiana Society), 1848.
LibEl   (*a*) Liber Eliensis (Ely Cathedral Library).
    (*b*) Cott Vesp A xix.
Libellus   Trinity College, Cambridge, MS O. 2.41 (James 1145).
Lindkvist   H. Lindkvist, *Middle-English Place-names of Scandinavian Origin*, 1911.
Londin   *Registrum Radulphi de Baldock, etc.*, 1911 ff.
Lot   S. Wells, *The Lot Book of the Bedford Level Corporation*, 1841.
LP   *Letters and Papers, Foreign and Domestic, Henry VIII*, 21 vols., 1864–1932.
LRMB   Land Revenue Miscellaneous Books, vol. 257 (PRO).
LVD   *Liber Vitae Ecclesiae Dunelmensis* (Facsimile, Surtees Soc., 136), 1923.
Lynam   E. Lynam, *Maps of the Fenland* (VCH Hunts iii).
M   P. Morant, *History of Essex*, 2 vols., 1768.
Madox   T. Madox, *Formulare Anglicanum*, 1702.
Magdalene   Documents *penes* Magdalene College, Cambridge.
Manea   T. Neale, *The Ruinous State of the parish of Manea*, 1748.
Map   Unpublished maps and plans (originals and photostats) (CUL).
MDu   Middle Dutch.
ME   Middle English.
MedLat   Medieval Latin.
Meldreth   W. M. Palmer, *Meldreth Parish Records*, 1896.
Memorials   C. H. Cooper, *Memorials of Cambridge*, 3 vols., 1860–6.
Merton   J. M. Gray, *The School of Pythagoras (Merton Hall), Cambridge* (CAS, 4to Publ. NS 4), 1932.
MFlem   Middle Flemish.
MHG   Middle High German.
Middendorff   H. Middendorff, *Altenglisches Flurnamenbuch*, 1902.
Milton   W. K. Clay, *A History of the Parish of Milton* (CAS 11), 1869.
MinAcct   Ministers' Accounts (PRO).
Misc   *Calendar of Inquisitions Miscellaneous.* (In progress.)
MLG   Middle Low German.
MLR   *Modern Language Review.* (In progress.)
ModEng   Modern English.
ModIcel   Modern Icelandic.
ModWFlem   Modern West Flemish.
Moll   H. Moll, *A Set of 50 New and Correct Maps of England*, 1724.
Mont   Montgomeryshire.

Moore	Sir Jonas Moore, *Maps of the Great Level* (1654–1706), *v.* Lynam 8, 9, 14.
Moulton	H. R. Moulton, *Palaeography, Genealogy and Topography*, 1930.
MP	*Matthaei Parisiensis Chronica Majora* (Rolls Ser.), 7 vols., 1872–83.
Mx	Middlesex
N	J. Norden, *An Historical Description of Essex*, 1594 (Camden Soc.), 1840.
Nb	Northumberland.
NCPNW	B. G. Charles, *Non-Celtic Place-names in Wales*, 1938.
n.d.	Undated.
NED	New English Dictionary.
Nf	Norfolk.
NI	*Nonarum Inquisitiones*, 1807.
Nichols	John Nichols, *Bibliotheca topographica Britannica*, 8 vols. in 7, 1780–90; *Miscellaneous antiquities*, 2 vols., 1791–1800.
NLC	*Newington Longeville Charters*, ed. H. E. Salter (Oxfordshire Rec. Soc. 3), 1921.
Norw	Norwegian.
NS	New Series.
Nt	Nottinghamshire.
Nth	Northamptonshire.
NthCh	*Facsimiles of Early Charters from Northamptonshire Collections*, ed. F. M. Stenton (Nth. Rec. Soc. 4), 1930.
O	Oxfordshire.
ODan	Old Danish.
OE	Old English.
OE Bede	*The Old English Version of Bede's Ecclesiastical History* (EETS 95–6, 110–11), 1890–8.
OFr	Old French.
OGer	Old Germanic.
Ogilby	J. Ogilby, *Itinerarium Angliae*, 1675.
OHG	Old High German.
OI	Old Irish.
Old 6″	1st edition of 6″ Ordnance Survey Maps of Cambridgeshire (1887).
OLG	Old Low German.
ON	Old Norse.
Ord	*Orderici Vitalis Historiæ Ecclesiasticæ Libri Tredecim*, ed. A. le Prevost, 5 vols., 1838–55.
OS	Original Series.
O.S.	Ordnance Survey.
OScand	Old Scandinavian.
OSwed	Old Swedish.
P	*Pipe Rolls* (Record Commission), 3 vols., 1833–44. (Pipe Roll Society.) (In progress.)
	Great Roll of the Pipe for 26 Henry 3, ed. Cannon, 1918.
(p)	Personal name.
Pap	*Calendar of Papal Registers* (PRO). (In progress.)
Paston	*The Paston Letters*, ed. J. Gairdner, 3 vols., 1872–5.
Pat	*Calendar of Patent Rolls* (PRO). (In progress.)
PC	*Acts of the Privy Council* (NS), vols. 1–32 (in progress), 1890–1907; *Acts of the Privy Council*, 3 vols., 1921–7.
PCC	Wills proved in the Prerogative Court of Canterbury (British Record Soc.). (In progress.)
Pembroke	Documents *penes* Pembroke College, Cambridge.
Percy	*The Percy Chartulary* (Surtees Soc. 117), 1911.
Peterb	Register of Peterborough Abbey (c. 1253) (Eg 2733).
Peterhouse	Documents *penes* Peterhouse, Cambridge.
Plea	Plea Rolls (Ely Diocesan Registry).

PMLA	*Publications of the Modern Language Association of America.* (In progress.)
PN BedsHu	*The Place-names of Bedfordshire and Huntingdonshire* (EPNS), 1926.
PN Berks	W. W. Skeat, *The Place-names of Berkshire*, 1911.
PN Bk	*The Place-names of Buckinghamshire* (EPNS), 1924.
PN C	W. W. Skeat, *The Place-names of Cambridgeshire*, 2nd ed., 1911.
PN D	*The Place-names of Devon*, 2 vols. (EPNS), 1931–2.
PN Db	B. Walker, *The Place-names of Derbyshire*, 1914.
PN Do	A. Fägersten, *The Place-names of Dorset*, 1933.
PN ERY	*The Place-names of the East Riding of Yorkshire* (EPNS), 1937.
PN Ess	*The Place-names of Essex* (EPNS), 1935.
PN Gl	W. St Clair Baddeley, *Place-names of Gloucestershire*, 1913.
PN Herts	*The Place-names of Hertfordshire* (EPNS), 1938.
PN in *-ing*	E. Ekwall, *English Place-names in -ing*, 1923.
PN K	J. K. Wallenberg, *The Place-names of Kent*, 1934.
PN La	E. Ekwall, *The Place-names of Lancashire*, 1922.
PN Mx	*The Place-names of Middlesex* (EPNS), 1942.
PN NbDu	A. Mawer, *The Place-names of Northumberland and Durham*, 1920.
PN NRY	*The Place-names of the North Riding of Yorkshire* (EPNS), 1928.
PN Nt	*The Place-names of Nottinghamshire* (EPNS), 1940.
PN Nth	*The Place-names of Northamptonshire* (EPNS), 1933.
PN Sf	W. W. Skeat, *The Place-names of Suffolk*, 1913.
PN Sr	*The Place-names of Surrey* (EPNS), 1934.
PN SWY	A. Goodall, *Place-names of South-West Yorkshire*, 1914.
PN Sx	*The Place-names of Sussex*, 2 vols. (EPNS), 1929–30.
PN *vis	R. E. Zachrisson, *English Place-Names and River-Names containing the Primitive Germanic Roots *vis, *vask*, 1926.
PN W	*The Place-names of Wiltshire* (EPNS), 1939.
PN Wa	*The Place-names of Warwickshire* (EPNS), 1936.
PN Wo	*The Place-names of Worcestershire* (EPNS), 1927.
PN WRY	F. W. Moorman, *The Place-names of the West Riding of Yorkshire*, 1910.
Poll	*A copy of the Poll for Knights of the Shire*, 1780 (Institute of Historical Research).
PR	*Cambridgeshire Parish Registers*, ed. W. P. W. Phillimore, etc., 8 vols., 1907–27.
PR	*Register of Orwell*, ed. R. W. Whiston, 2 vols., 1912, 1927.
PRO	Public Record Office.
PromptParv	*Promptorium Parvulorum sive Clericorum*, ed. A. Way (Camden Soc.), 3 vols., 1843–65.
Queens'	Documents *penes* Queens' College, Cambridge.
QW	*Placita de Quo Warranto*, 1818.
R	Rutland.
Rad	A. Gray, *The Priory of Saint Radegund, Cambridge* (CAS 31), 1898.
Rams	*Cartularium Monasterii de Rameseia* (c. 1350) (Rolls Series), 3 vols., 1884–93.
RBE	*Red Book of the Exchequer* (Rolls Series), 3 vols., 1896.
Redin	M. Redin, *Studies on Uncompounded Personal Names in Old English*, 1919.
RegAntiquiss	*The Registrum Antiquissimum of the Cathedral Church of Lincoln* (Linc. Rec. Soc. 27–9, 32, 34), 1931–40.
RegRoff	*Registrum Roffense*, ed. J. Thorpe, 1769.
Rental	Rentals in BM, PRO, CUL, Ely Diocesan Registry, Trinity College, Cambridge.
RES	*Review of English Studies.* (In progress.)
RG	*The Chronicle of Robert of Gloucester* (Rolls Series), 2 vols., 1887.
RH	*Rotuli Hundredorum*, 2 vols., 1812–18.

RHistS	*Transactions of the Royal Historical Society.* (In progress.)
RN	E. Ekwall, *English River-names*, 1928.
RotDom	*Rotuli de Dominabus* (Pipe Roll Soc. 35), 1913.
Rutland	*Manuscripts of the Duke of Rutland* (HMC), 1905.
s.a.	*sub anno.*
Sa	Shropshire.
Sacr	*Sacrist Rolls of Ely*, ed. F. R. Chapman, 2 vols., 1907.
Saints	*Die Heiligen Englands*, ed. F. Liebermann, 1889.
Saxton	C. Saxton, *Atlas of England and Wales*, 1576.
Scand	Scandinavian.
School	Information supplied by the local school.
SD	*Symeonis Monachi Opera Omnia* (Rolls Series), 2 vols., 1882–5.
Searle	W. G. Searle, *Onomasticon Anglo-Saxonicum*, 1897.
Seld	Selden Society Publications. (In progress.)
Sewers	Chanc. Misc. 7/8 (PRO).
SewersA	Orders of Sewers, 1687–1716 (Fen Office, Ely). Copies of Proceedings of different Courts of Sewers relating to the Bedford Level, 1362–1641 (ib.).
SewersB	*Add* 6164–5.
SewersC	*Add* 35171 (17th–18th).
SewersD	Papers relating to the Commission of Sewers, 1528–1653 (*Add* 33466–7).
Sf	Suffolk.
s.n.	*sub nomine.*
SN	Sutton Nicholls, *Map of Cambridgeshire*, 1695.
So	Somerset.
So. Rec. Soc.	Somerset Record Society.
SP	State Papers Domestic (PRO).
Speed	*The Theatre of the Empire of Great Britaine*, 1610.
Spinney	Extracts from a register of Spinney Priory (17th) (CUL, Add MS 3824).
SR	Lay Subsidies printed in EA vi, x–xiii, CGild and CAPr ix.
SR	Lay Subsidy Rolls (PRO).
St	Staffordshire.
StCatharine's	Documents *penes* St Catharine's College, Cambridge.
Stewart	D. J. Stewart, *Architectural History of Ely Cathedral*, 1868.
StJ	*Admissions to the College of St John the Evangelist*, 4 vols. (1882–1931).
StJohn's	Documents *penes* St John's College, Cambridge.
StJohn'sH	Cartulary of the Hospital of St John the Evangelist, *penes* St John's College, Cambridge (c. 1250, with 13th–15th cent. additions).
StNeot	Cartulary of St Neot's Priory (13th) (Cott Faust A iv).
StNP	*Studia Neophilologica.* (In progress.)
Stretham	Stretham Parish Papers (unpublished) *penes* Vicar of Stretham. Transcript *penes* Major Gordon Fowler.
Studies[2]	E. Ekwall, *Studies in English Place-names*, 1936.
Survey	Unpublished Surveys in BM, CUL and in private hands.
s.v.	*sub voce.*
Sw	Swedish.
Sx	Sussex.
TA	Tithe Award.
Tanner	T. Tanner, *Notitia Monastica*, 1744.
Tax	*Taxatio Ecclesiastica*, 1802.
Templars	*Records of the Templars in England in the Twelfth Century*, ed. B. A. Lees, 1935.
Tengstrand	E. Tengstrand, *A Contribution to the Study of Genitival Composition in Old English Place-names*, 1940.
Terr	Manuscript Terriers in various collections.

TextRoff	*Textus Roffensis*, ed. T. Hearne, 1720.
Thorney	Red Book of Thorney (c. 1320) (CUL Add MS 3020).
Thorpe	B. Thorpe, *Diplomatarium Anglicum Ævi Saxonici*, 1865.
Torp	Alf Torp, *Nynorsk Etymologisk Ordbok*, 1919.
Township	F. W. Maitland, *Township and Borough*, 1898.
TRE	Tempore Regis Edwardi.
Trevisa	*v.* Higden.
Trinity	Documents *penes* Trinity College, Cambridge.
TRW	Tempore Regis Willelmi.
Val	*The Valuation of Norwich*, ed. W. E. Lunt, 1926.
VCH	*A History of Cambridgeshire and the Isle of Ely* (Victoria History of the Counties of England), vol. 1, ed. L. F. Salzman, 1938.
VE	*Valor Ecclesiasticus*, 6 vols., 1810–34.
Venn	J. A. Venn, *The Foundations of Agricultural Economics*, 1933.
W	Wiltshire.
Wa	Warwickshire.
Walden	Registrum de Walden (1387) (Harl 3697).
Walde-Pokorny	A. Walde, *Vergleichendes Wörterbuch*, ed. J. Pokorny, 3 vols., 1930–2.
Walker	Plan of the Middle Level (CUL; Lynam 34).
Waltham	Registrum Monasterii S. Crucis de Waltham (13th) (Cott Tib C. ix).
WalthamB	Waltham Cartulary (13th) (Harl 391).
Wardon	*Cartulary of the Abbey of Old Wardon* (13th), ed. G. H. Fowler (Beds. Hist. Rec. Soc. 13), 1930.
Waterb	W. K. Clay, *A History of the Parish of Waterbeach* (CAS 4), 1859.
WC	R. Willis and J. W. Clark, *The Architectural History of the University of Cambridge*, 4 vols., 1886.
We	Westmorland.
Wells	S. Wells, *Map of the Bedford Level*, 1829.
Whitby	*Cartularium Abbathiae de Whiteby* (15th), (Surtees Soc. 69, 72), 2 vols., 1879–81.
Widnall	S. P. Widnall, *History of Grantchester*, 1875.
Will	Unpublished Will.
Winton	*Wykeham's Register* (Hants. Rec. Soc.), 2 vols., 1896–9.
Wisb	Unpublished deeds, etc. in the Wisbech Museum.
Wisbech Map	Map of bounds of Wisbech Hundred, 1597, revised 1657, containing extracts from early documents (Wisbech Museum).
Witcham	Map of part of Cambridgeshire (CUL; Lynam 72).
WMP	William of Malmesbury, *De Gestis Pontificum Anglorum* (Rolls Series), 1870.
WMP	Notes and transcripts from documents *penes* the late Dr W. M. Palmer.
WMR	William of Malmesbury, *De Gestis Regum Anglorum* (Rolls Series), 2 vols., 1887–9.
Wo	Worcestershire.
Works	*Public Works in Mediaeval Law*, ed. C. T. Flower (Seld. Soc. 32, 40), 1915, 1923.
Wren	Bishop Wren's MS (1642) (Ely Diocesan Registry).
Wright	*Vocabularies*, ed. T. Wright, 2 vols., 1857, 1873.
WRY	West Riding of Yorkshire.
Wymond	*Cartularium de Willemundesley* (13th) (Add 43792).
Y	Yorkshire.
YBk	Year Books (Rolls Series), 5 vols., 1863–79; (Seld. Soc.), 1903–. (In progress.)
YCh	*Early Yorkshire Charters*, 6 vols.: Vols. 1–3 ed. W. Farrer; Vols. 4–6 ed. C. T. Clay, 1914–39.

PHONETIC SYMBOLS USED IN TRANSCRIPTION
OF PRONUNCIATIONS OF PLACE-NAMES

p	pay	ʃ	shone	tʃ	church	ei	flay
b	bay	ʒ	azure	dʒ	judge	ɛ	Fr.jamais
t	tea	θ	thin	ɑ·	father	ɛ·	there
d	day	ð	then	au	cow	i	pit
k	key	j	you	a	Ger.mann	i·	feel
g	go	χ	loch	ai	fly	ou	low
ʍ	when	h	his	æ	cab	u	good
w	win	m	man	ɔ	pot	u·	rule
f	foe	n	no	ɔ·	saw	ʌ	much
v	vote	ŋ	sing	oi	oil	ə	ever
s	say	r	run	e	red	ə·	bird
z	zone	l	land				

Examples:

Eltisley [elzli], Sawston [sɔ·sən],
Soham [soum].

NOTES

(1) The names are arranged topographically according to the Hundreds. Within each Hundred the parishes are dealt with in alphabetical order, and within each parish the names of primary historical or etymological interest are arranged similarly, but in a large number of parishes these are followed by one, or two, or three further groups of names. These groups, so far as they are represented, always appear in the following order: (i) minor names of topographical origin found largely in the second name of persons mentioned in the Subsidy Rolls and similar local documents; (ii) names embodying some family name of Middle English or Early Modern English origin; (iii) minor names of obvious origin, or minor names for which we have only very late forms, about whose history it is unwise to speculate. All three types are represented under Fulbourn (*infra* 144–5).

Street- and road-names are given in a note immediately following the interpretation of the parish name, e.g. the street-names of Over are given in a note at the end of the article on Over itself (*infra* 169). The list of street-names in Cambridge is, however, given at the end of all the names in the Borough (*infra* 44–50).

(2) Where a place-name is found only on the 6-inch O.S. map, this is indicated by putting 6″ after it in brackets, e.g. Cloderton (6″).

(3) Place-names no longer current are marked as (lost). This does not necessarily mean that the site to which the name was once applied is unknown. We are dealing primarily with names, and the names are lost. These names are printed in italics when referred to elsewhere in the volume.

(4) Place-names marked '(local)' are not recorded on modern maps but are still current locally.

(5) The local pronunciation of the place-name is given, wherever it is of interest, in phonetic script within square brackets, e.g. Duxford [dʌksə] (*infra* 92).

(6) In explaining the various place- and field-names, summary reference is made to the detailed account of such elements as are found in *The Chief Elements in English Place-names* by printing those elements in Clarendon type, e.g. Caldecote, *v.* **cald, cot(e)**. Clarendon type is also used for reference to those same elements and other additional ones recorded and explained *infra* 311 ff.

(7) In the case of all forms for which reference has been made to unprinted authorities, that fact is indicated by printing the reference to the authority in italic instead of ordinary type, e.g. '1246 *ElyM*' denotes a form derived from a MS authority in contrast to '1636 BedL' which denotes one taken from a printed text.

(8) Where two dates are given, e.g. '974 (14th),' the first is the date at which the document purports to have been composed, the second is that of the copy which has come down to us.

(9) Where a letter in an early place-name form is placed within brackets, forms with and without that letter are found, e.g. *Chyp(p)e-ham* means that forms *Chypeham* and *Chyppeham* are alike found.

(10) All OE words are quoted in the West Saxon form unless otherwise stated.

ADDENDA ET CORRIGENDA

For addenda with appended initials we are indebted to

A.C.W.	Mr A. C. Wood.
E.J.D.	Miss E. Jeffries Davis.
J.B.J.	The Rev. J. B. Johnston.
W.H.	Dr Wilfrid Hooper.

VOL. II

THE PLACE-NAMES OF BUCKINGHAMSHIRE

p. 13, *s.n.* EAKLEY LANES. Add '*Ikeleg*' 1219 Cur.'

p. 31, *s.n.* GT BRICKHILL. Add '*Moche Brikell* 1505 PCC.'

p. 54, *s.n.* EDGCOTT. Add '*Achecott* 1509 PCC.'

p. 109, *s.n.* DODDERSHALL. Add '*Doðesberge* 1204 P.'

p. 122, *s.n.* LONG CRENDON. Add '*Creindon* 1204 P.'

p. 168, *s.n.* THE LYDE. Add '*la Lide* 1212 Cur (p).'

p. 169, *s.n.* SHIMMELL'S FM. Add 'lands called *Shenoldis* 1486 Ipm' (A.C.W.).

p. 184, *s.n.* MOSELEY. Add '*Museley* 1266 Cl.'

p. 205, *s.n.* THE RYE. Add '*Robert atte Reye* 1327 Banco.'

p. 215, *s.n.* BOVENEY. Add '*Boffenay* 1508 PCC.'

p. 219, *s.n.* CHALFONT ST GILES. Add '*saincte Gyles Chaffyn* 1557 PCC.'

p. 233, *s.n.* LENT. Add 'Clemency *atte Leute* (sic) 1328 Banco.'

p. 235. Under DATCHET add 'SUMPTER MEAD (field) is *Sundermede* 1352 Misc.'

p. 244, *s.n.* WYRARDISBURY. Add '*Wradysbury* 1544 PPC.'

VOL. III

THE PLACE-NAMES OF BEDFORDSHIRE AND HUNTINGDONSHIRE

p. 39, *s.n.* HINWICK. Add '*Hanewich* 1204 P.'

p. 62, *s.n.* RENHOLD. Add '*Ro(h)enhal*' 1214 Cur.'

p. 71, *s.n.* MEDBURY. Mr Bannard suggests that the interpretation of this example of *maiden-bury* may be another example of the 'Maiden Castle' type of name, that is 'castle which has never been taken.'

p. 83, *s.n.* BROGBOROUGH. Add '*Brokeneberwe* 1263 Cl.' This form makes it almost certain that the correct etymology is 'broken hill.'

p. 123, under EVERSHOLT. Cf. RADS END. Cf. *Radesho* 1214 Cur.'

p. 144, *s.n.* BIRCHMORE. Add '*Bichemore* 1212 Cur.'

p. 150, *s.n.* WORTHY END. Add '*Wrthinge* 1212 Cur.'

p. 174, *s.n.* APSLEY END. Add '*Aspele* 1219 Cur.'

p. 192, *s.n.* OGERSTON. Add '*Ogierestan* 1202 P (p).'

p. 228, *s.n.* WOOLVEY. The further forms cited under Fenton Lode *infra* 209 suggest that the first element is OE *Wulfgiefu* (f.) rather than *wulf*.

p. 245, *s.n.* WORNDITCH. Add '*Werndich* 1363 Ipm.'

p. 254, l. 4 from bottom. For 'Dinton' read 'Denton.'

VOL. IV

THE PLACE-NAMES OF WORCESTERSHIRE

p. 139, *s.n.* OFFERTON FM. Add '*Okerinton* 1220 Cur.'

p. 159, l. 7. For '*Cestraneslede*' read '*Cestaneslede*.'

VOL. V

The Place-names of the North Riding of Yorkshire

p. 236, l. 10. Delete 'Westley Waterless (C).'

VOL. VI

The Place-names of Sussex (Part I)

p. 61, *s.n.* Northbrook. Add '*Nurburc, Norbroc* 1214 Cur.'
p. 65, *s.n.* Norton. Add '1219 Cur.'
p. 67, *s.n.* Halnaker. Add '*Halfnaked* 1264 Cl.'
p. 94, *s.n.* Crimsham. Add '*Cramesham* 1219 Cur.'
p. 139, *s.n.* Ilsham. Add '*Hiselham* 1214 Cur.'
p. 145, *s.n.* Bilsham. Add '*Bille(s)ham* 1220 Cur.'
p. 156, *s.n.* Rackham. Add '*Recham* 1201 P (p).'
p. 161, *s.n.* Storrington. Add '*Starrington* 1552 PCC.'
p. 190, *s.n.* Poles Pitch. Add '*Spolspiche* 1362 Ipm.'
p. 190, *s.n.* Pondtail Fm. Add '*Pundlond* 1362 Ipm.'
p. 192, *s.n.* Hookland Fm. Add '*Houkland* 1362 Ipm.'
p. 207, *s.n.* Summersdeane Fm. Add '*Somerden* 1362 Ipm.'
p. 227, *s.n.* Hawksbourne. Add '*Alkeburn*' 1269 Cl.'
p. 234, *s.n.* Chowles. Add '*Chosesland* 1362 Ipm.'
p. 247, *s.n.* Brambleden. Add '*Brembolden* 1362 Ipm.'

VOL. VII

The Place-names of Sussex (Part II)

p. 312. After Balsdean, add 'The Bostle is *Baldeshill*' 1210 Cur, *Baldesheld*' 1212 ib. It is close by Balsdean and doubtless takes its name from the same man, hence "*Beald*'s hylde or slope."'
p. 324, *s.n.* Piddinghoe. Add '*Pudenhok, Pudinhok* 1219 Cur.'
p. 330, *s.n.* Cripps's Corner. Add 'cf. *land called Cryppes* 1506 *Ipm*' (A.C.W.).
p. 334, *s.n.* Busses Fm. Add '*Busses* 1506 *Ipm*' (A.C.W.).
p. 334, *s.n.* Harwood's Fm. Add '*Herwerdes in Estgrensted* 1506 *Ipm*' (A.C.W.).
p. 334, *s.n.* Boyleys Fm. Add '*Boylyas* 1506 *Ipm*' (A.C.W.).
p. 390, *s.n.* Alchin. Add '*Alcheshorne* 1363 Ipm.'
p. 419, *s.n.* Exceat. Add '*Execotes* 1220 Cur.'
p. 461, *s.n.* Brooksmarle. Add '*Broxemel, Broximel* 1214 Cur.'
p. 464, *s.n.* Broadhurst. Add '*Bredeherst* 1215 Cur.'
p. 529, *s.n.* Broomhill. Add '*Primhill* 1202 P, *Prunhill* 1202 CR, *Prumhull* 1203, 1204 P, *Primhull* 1205 ib.'

VOL. VIII

The Place-names of Devon (Part I)

p. 134, *s.n.* Limscott. Add '*Luuinecot* 1199 P.'
p. 135, *s.n.* Newland. Add '*Niweland* 1214 Cur.'
p. 140, *s.n.* Vaglefield. Add '*Fagelefeld*' 1266 Cl.'
p. 192, *s.n.* Brimpts. Add '*Birmstestowe, Brimestow* 1199 P.'
p. 235, *s.n.* Tythecott. Add '*Todecote* 1363 Ipm.'
p. 262, *s.n.* Lyneham. Add '*Linham* 1205 P (p).'
p. 284, *s.n.* Bowcombe. Add '*Bocumb*' 1219–20 Cur (p).'
p. 289, *s.n.* Bagton. Add '*Baggeton* 1204 P.'

VOL. IX

THE PLACE-NAMES OF DEVON (Part II)

p. 345, *s.n.* HOLDRIDGE. Add '*Elderig*', *Ellerig* 1219–20 Cur.'

p. 347, under SOUTH MOLTON. Add '*Pattisham's* WOOD (6″). Cf. *Pattesham in the parish of South Molton* 1504 *Ipm*' (A.C.W.).

p. 359, *s.n.* STOWFORD DOWN. Add '*Staff*' 1199 P.'

p. 363, *s.n.* CHAWLEIGH. Add '*Chaflege* 1201 P.'

p. 364, *s.n.* THORNE. Add '*Spina* 1214 Cur.'

p. 374, *s.n.* COLLACOTT. Add '*Colecote* 1199 P (p).'

p. 385. Under BISHOP'S NYMPTON add '*PARKHOUSE* (6″) is *Parke House* 1504 *Ipm*' (A.C.W.).

p. 407, *s.n.* HOOKWAY. Add '*Hocweie* 1205 P (p).'

p. 415, *s.n.* POUGHILL. Add '*Powhill* 1602 PCC.'

p. 425, *s.n.* SHAPLEY. Add '*Sapeleia* 1201 P.'

p. 435, *s.n.* BOYLAND. Add '*Boiland*' 1204 P (p).'

p. 448, *s.n.* ADDISCOTT. Add '*Ailrichescote* 1205 P.'

p. 464, *s.n.* BLACKMOOR. Add '*Blakemor* 1201 P.'

p. 473, *s.n.* NEWTON ABBOT. Add '*Nieweton*' *abbatis* 1201 P.'

p. 527, *s.n.* DEWDON. Add '*Daudon*' 1199 P (p).'

p. 532, *s.n.* DODDISCOMBE. Add '*Doddescumbe* 1214 Cur.'

p. 540, *s.n.* VENLAKE'S COTTAGE. Add 'cf. *Fenlake...within Honeysham* 1492 *Ipm*' (A.C.W.).

p. 609, *s.n.* GODFORD CROSS. Add '*Godeford* 1202 P.'

p. 614, *s.n.* DUNKESWELL. Add '*Dunxwell* 1605 PCC.'

VOL. X

THE PLACE-NAMES OF NORTHAMPTONSHIRE

p. 35, *s.n.* GREATWORTH. Add '*Grantewurth* 1219 Cur.'

p. 53, *s.n.* ASTWICK. Add '*Estweit* 1214 Cur.'

p. 101, *s.n.* DENSHANGER. Add '*Dennes(h)angr*' 1214 Cur.'

p. 132, *s.n.* GT BILLING. Add '*Gratebelling* 1494 PCC.'

p. 135, *s.n.* SPRATTON. Add '*Spretton*' 1205 P.'

p. 165, *s.n.* GEDDINGTON. Add '*Gayngton* 1328 Banco.'

p. 170, *s.n.* OAKLEY. Add '*Akle by Gayngton* 1328 Banco.'

p. 220, *s.n.* THRAPSTON. Add '*Tharpston* 1363 Ipm.'

p. 267, *s.v.* lundr. Add '*parcum suum apud Stoks* (i.e. Stoke Albany) *scilicet Lund*' 1201 P.'

p. 301, *s.n.* KINGSTHORPE. For '135' read '133.'

VOL. XI

THE PLACE-NAMES OF SURREY

p. 22, *s.n.* LAMBETH. Add '*Lamveie* 1219 Cur.'

p. 24, *s.n.* LEVEHURST. Add '*Leferst, Leftherste* 1219 Cur.'

p. 27, *s.n.* PUTNEY. Add '*Puttenhight* 1419 PCC.'

p. 35, *s.n.* TOOTING. Add '*Towtinbeke* 1547 PCC.'

p. 78, *s.n.* ASHURST. Add '*Essehurst* 1201 P (p).'

p. 124, *s.n.* RUNNYMEDE. Add '*Runingemede, Runnemede* 1219 Cur.'

p. 124, *s.n.* ST ANN'S HEATH. This is probably identical with the half hide of land in *Sudinton* (Cur 1214), later *Sintdon, Sundon,* and if so, perhaps derives from (*be*) *suðan dune,* '(to the) south of the hill.'

p. 140, *s.n.* PERYER'S COTTAGE. Cf. 'virgate called Pureys...once of John *Puryer* in Bokeham' (1548 *Survey*).

p. 156, *s.n.* BROOKWOOD. Add '*Brocwude* 1201 P.'

p. 198, *s.n.* LYDLING. Add '*Lydling, Ledlinges* 1219 Cur.'

p. 206, *s.n.* STOATLEY. Add '*Stotel*' 1201 P (p).'

p. 289, *s.n.* WICKLAND. Add '*Wiklond* 1375 Misc.'

p. 295, l. 9 from bottom. DOVERS GREEN is in Reigate and not in Horley parish (W.H.).

p. 296, *s.n.* NORWOOD. Add '*Narrwood* 1616 PCC.'

p. 306, *s.n.* HOOLEY LANE. Dr Hooper suggests that as Hooley Lane lies in a hollow valley the etymology of this name is probably the same as that of Hooley in Coulsdon (PN Sr 45), viz. 'hollow-clearing.'

p. 306, *s.n.* REDHILL. For '1844' read '1841' (W.H.).

p. 307, *s.n.* TRUMPETS HILL. Probably to be associated with the family of Robert *Trumpers* (1577 *Ct*). Cf. 'land called *Trumpers* (1598 ib.)' (W.H.).

p. 330, *s.n.* PUTTENDEN. Add '*Pudinden*' 1203, 1204 P.'

p. 334, *s.n.* STOCKHURST FM. Add 'Symone *de la Stoket* 1271 Cl.'

p. 410, l. 13. Friday St in Rendlesham is identical with that in Eyke and similarly that in Farnham is identical with the one in Saxmundham.

p. 410, l. 19. Add '*Fryday Hawes* in Compton (Sr) 13 and 33 Eliz, *v.* Boston, *Hist. of Compton* 12, 23' (W.H.).

VOL. XII

THE PLACE-NAMES OF ESSEX

p. 87, *s.n.* BECONTREE HUNDRED. Add '*Bergentrie* 1205 P.'

p. 202, *s.n.* HAMPTON BARNS. Add '*Hamptombernis* (sic) 1486 *Ipm*' (A.C.W.).

p. 212, *s.n.* CREEKSEA. Add '*Crixith al. Crixsey* 1611 PCC.'

p. 233, *s.n.* GREAT and LITTLE BADDOW. Add '*Moche Badowe* 1547 PCC, *Lytill Bado* 1500 ib.'

p. 256, *s.n.* GT LEIGHS. Add '*Myche Lyes* 1579 PCC.'

p. 268, *s.n.* CUTON HALL. Add '*Kenytonhalle* (sic) 1370 Misc.'

p. 269, *s.n.* STOCK. Add '*Harforde Stocke* 1580 PCC.'

p. 274, *s.n.* SPARROWHAWK FM. Add '*Sparhauekesbeia* 1214 Cur.'

p. 289, n. 6. Add '*Termyns* 1353 Misc.'

p. 348, *s.n.* ST OSYTHS. Add '*Toozy* 1532 PCC.'

p. 379, *s.n.* COLNE ENGAINE. Add '*Colne in gaine* 1585 PCC.'

p. 452, *s.n.* RAYNE. Add '*Petiterenes* 1265 Cl.'

p. 480, *s.n.* NEWARKS. Add '*Neuwerk in Godythestre* 1349 Misc.'

p. 493, *s.n.* LEADEN RODING. Add '*Ledene Roinges* 1219 Cur.'

p. 504, *s.n.* GT BARDFIELD. Add '*Moche Berdefeld* 1549 PCC.'

p. 528, *s.n.* PLEDGDON. Add '*Plecheden* 1214 Cur.'

p. 553, *s.n.* UGLEY. Add '*Ouglye* 1609 PCC.'

p. 560, *s.n.* horsc. For 'Horse' read 'Horsefrith, Horsepit.'

VOL. XIII

THE PLACE-NAMES OF WARWICKSHIRE

p. xlvi, l. 11. The barrow is in the field and still clearly visible (W.H.).

p. xlvii, l. 21. *Frydaysmede* is in Reigate—not in Betchworth. It is near Reigate town (W.H.).

p. 44, *s.n.* KINGSHURST. Add '*Kyngeshurst* 1495 *Ipm*' (A.C.W.).

p. 53, *s.n.* GROVE END. Mr P. B. Chatwin notes that Grove End is in Sutton Coldfield. The district is called *Bumble End* in Jefferies' map of Warwickshire (1740). The origin of this name is unknown.

p. 55, *s.n.* BARSTON. Add '*Burgestanestowe* 1213 Cur.'

p. 56, *s.n.* RYTON END. Add '*Rividon* 1213 Cur.'

p. 93, *s.n.* SHUSTOKE. Add '*Schystocke* 1549 PCC.'
p. 107, *s.n.* COSFORD. Add '*Casseford* 1214 Cur.'
p. 130, *s.n.* GRANDBOROUGH. Add '*Gremborowe* 1557 PCC.'
p. 197, *s.n.* SHELFIELD. Add '*Selfhill*' 1202 P (p).'
p. 298, *s.n.* BARTON ON HEATH. Add '*Barton on the Yethe* 1551 PCC.'

VOL. XIV

THE PLACE-NAMES OF THE EAST RIDING OF YORKSHIRE AND YORK

p. 100, l. 1. For '*Bofa*' read '*Bōfa*.' Cf. ON Bófi and ModGer *bube*, 'boy.'
p. 252, *s.n.* YARMSHAW. Add '*Yarmes Howe* 1486 Ipm.'

VOL. XV

THE PLACE-NAMES OF HERTFORDSHIRE

p. 16, *s.n.* LYE WOOD. Add '*Leg*' 1220 Cur.'
p. 98, *s.n.* PARKBURY. Add '*le Parc* 1220 Cur.'
p. 100, *s.n.* WATEREND. Add '*Tiebrigg*' 1204 P.'
p. 133, *s.n.* GT MUNDEN. Add '*Mych Munden* 1498 PCC.'
p. 138, *s.n.* BEDWELL. Add '*Bedewell*' 1203 P.'
p. 157, *s.n.* COTTERED. Add '*Codréé* 1202 P.'
p. 174, *s.n.* WARDINGTON BOTTOM. A further example of the stream-name *Lorteburne* is found in *ripam voc. Lurtebourne* (1320 *Ass*) in the Tower Ward of the City of London.
p. 192, *s.n.* GILSTON. Add '*Kedeleston* 1199 P.'
p. 215, *s.n.* BENGEO. Add '*Bedingeho* 1220 Cur.'
p. 230, *s.n.* ST MARGARETS. Add '*pontem de Tiwle* 1214 Cur.'
p. 232, *s.n.* QUEEN HOO. Add '*Quenhag*' 1204 P (p).'
p. 236, *s.v.* brycg. Add '*The(a)le*.'

VOL. XVI

THE PLACE-NAMES OF WILTSHIRE

p. 17, *s.n.* SALISBURY PLAIN. Add '*plein of Salesbury* c. 1300 RG' (J.B.J.).
p. 18, *s.n.* SALISBURY. Add '*Newe Sarum* 1565 PCC.'
p. 73, *s.n.* SEAGRY. The Rev. J. B. Johnston (*Place-names of England and Wales*, *s.n.*) first suggested this etymology for Seagry.
p. 79, *s.n.* GRITTLETON. Add '*Credlinton* 1202 P.'
p. 100, *s.n.* KINGTON ST MICHAEL. Add '*Myghelles Kyngton* 1517 PCC.'
p. 102, *s.n.* LACOCK. This difficult name seems to repeat itself in *Lacoc, Lakoc* in Sutton at Hone and Eynsford (1211–12 Cur).
p. 127, *s.n.* HILPERTON. Add '*Helpringeton* 1205 P.'
p. 175, *s.n.* EAST KNOYLE. Add '*Eastnoile* 1603 PCC.'
p. 224. MAWARDEN COURT should be transferred from the parish of Stratford Tony to the parish of Stratford-sub-Castle (pp. 371–2) (*ex inf.* Rev. W. P. Stubbs).
p. 240, *s.n.* MARKET LAVINGTON. Add '*Stupullavyngton* 1407 PCC.'
p. 243, *s.n.* DEVIZES. Add '*The Devise* 1519 PCC.'
p. 274, *s.n.* CHADDINGTON. Add '*Chedinton* 1202 P (p), *-don* 1203 ib.'
p. 285, *s.n.* BAYDON. None of the forms for this name is really early, and the Rev. J. B. Johnston may be right in suggesting that the first element is the personal name *Bæga*. Cf. the 1249 *Ass* form.
p. 300, *s.n.* FLEXBURGH. Add '*Fleixbir*' 1205 P.'
p. 301, *s.n.* ELCOT MILL. Add '*Elcotes mulle* 1377 Misc.'
p. 321, *s.n.* FRITH WOOD. Add '*La Frith* 1362 Ipm.'
p. 344, *s.n.* COLDRIDGE WOOD. Further reference to *Colungahrycg* would seem to be found in *Colingrugg*' (1264, 1271 Cl).

p. 354, *s.n.* BAGSHOT. Add '*Bekesgate* 1362 Ipm.'

p. 385, *s.n.* ROCHE COURT. Mr H. B. Trevor Cox informs us that the house is now known as Roche Old Court and not as Roche Court as recorded on the 6″ O.S. map ed. 1923–4. It is interesting to note that on the O.S. map of 1807 Old Roche Court is entered as Easton Farm, presumably as representing East Winterslow.

VOL. XVII

THE PLACE-NAMES OF NOTTINGHAMSHIRE

p. 16, l. 15. Miss Whitelock (MLR XXXVII, 83) notes that the *Cokwatergang* referred to here must be associated with the term *cockwater* (sense 2) in NED, 'used of a stream of water brought in a trough through a long pole in order to wash out the sand of the tin ore...in the coffer of a stamping-mill.' The Notts. reference carries the term back from 1753 to 1395.

pp. 22–3, *s.n.* TRENT BRIDGE. Add '*Haygbeche* 1270 Cl.'

p. 28, *s.n.* CLAYWORTH. Add '*Clawude* 1200–5 P, showing confusion of wurðe and wude.'

p. 119, *s.n.* BULWELL WOOD HALL. Add 'cf. *Bullwellwood* 1540 LP' (A.C.W.).

p. 130, *s.n.* THE BARRACKS. Mr H. M. Leman notes for us that the oak whose name lies behind The Barracks is called *ye barred hoc* in the Duke of Rutland's map of Sherwood Forest, and that in the Forest Book it is said to have 'divided the Kings Hay of Linby from the common wood of the same town called *Wyghaw*' (*v.* Wighay, PN Nt 123). This explains the use of the term *barre* as applied to the oak—doubtless there was some boundary bar here.

p. 132, l. 14. For '114' read '140.'

p. 241, *s.n.* SAXONDALE. Add '*Seindal* 1201 P.'

p. 248, *s.n.* RUDDINGTON. Add '*Rutinton*' 1203 P.'

p. 267, *s.v.* stocc. Add 'Stockwell.'

p. 272, l. 9 from bottom. For '*Basa*' read '*Bassa*.'

p. 344. Add 'STOCKWELL GATE, 125.'

VOL. XVIII

THE PLACE-NAMES OF MIDDLESEX

p. xxv. Add 'Smith   H. Llewellyn Smith, *The History of East London*, 1939.'

p. 1, *s.n.* BRENT. A cross-reference to the early form *Breguntford* for Brentford (PN Mx 31) should be added (J.B.J.).

p. 7, l. 7 from bottom. For '*nautgallus*' read '*nantgallus*.'

p. 34, *s.n.* STICKLETON. Cf. Stickle Down (PN Sr 119) (J.B.J.).

p. 47, *s.n.* CATTLIN'S LANE. Mr F. H. Mansford notes that Cattlin's Lane takes its name from Catherine Fm in Eastcote rather than from Catherine's End Fm in Ruislip.

p. 48, *s.n.* POORS FIELD. Mr F. H. Mansford notes for us that this field is dedicated to the use of the poor. It may be that this fact is recorded in the medieval form *Puersfeld*, but the spelling would in that case be rather a surprising one.

p. 49, *s.n.* UXBRIDGE. Add '*Wuxe(s)brig*' 1220 Cur.'

p. 50, *s.n.* BROCKLEY HILL. Mr C. N. Bromehead of the Geological Survey notes for us that the Claygate Beds, consisting of alternations of sand and loam, occur at two points only along the line of Watling Street between London and St Albans, namely Brockley Hill and Elstree. Brockley Hill is thus the first hill out of London on which badgers would have been found. Similarly, the unidentified *Brockehole* in Hampstead (p. 196) may well be accounted for by the occurrence over a limited area of the Claygate Beds and overlying Bagshot Sand, suitable for badgers, in a region mainly clay.

p. 62, *s.n.* CHALKHILL HO (in Kingsbury). Mr C. N. Bromehead of the Geological Survey notes for us a possible solution of the 'chalk' problem in relation to this and other similar names. At various, but somewhat irregular levels in the London Clay, there are layers of large calcareous nodules. Mr Bromehead has himself noted this form of limestone as abundant in parts of Kingsbury and writes: 'It seems not impossible that individual farms where the nodules were abundant erected small kilns and so obtained for a while their own supply of lime, or even ground the rock and applied it raw to the land.' Mr S. W. Hester, also of the Geological Survey, has a map dated 1750 of the Demesne Lands of the Manor of Ruislip; the name 'Marl-pit Field' (*v.* PN Mx 210) which occurs in the midst of a tract of London Clay may be similarly accounted for.

p. 84, *s.n.* CHURCH ST. Add '(now REDCHURCH ST)' and after CHURCH ROW add '(now ST MATTHEW'S ROW)' (E.J.D.).

p. 89, *s.n.* STRAND ON THE GREEN. Add '*la Strond* 1269 Cl.'

p. 97, *s.n.* ALLEN ST. Add '(now DALLINGTON ST)' (E.J.D.).

p. 98, *s.n.* ROSOMAN ST. Add '(now PLACE)' (E.J.D.).

p. 137, under Poplar street-names. Add 'PRIORY ST in Bromley St Leonard takes its name from the priory of Stratford atte Bowe where Chaucer's Prioresse was brought up' (Smith 101).

p. 156, under Stepney street-names. Add 'GRACE'S ALLEY preserves the name of the Cistercian abbey of Eastminster or New Abbey, founded by Edward III "in honour of God and our Lady of Grace" under the title of the Abbey of St Mary of Graces' (Smith 133).

p. 156, *s.n.* OLD and NEW GRAVEL LANE. Here were the pits from which gravel was dug for ballast for ships in the Thames (Smith 206).

p. 157, under Stepney street-names. Add 'KING JOHN ST preserves the name of the house traditionally known as 'King John's Palace,' finally destroyed in 1859' (Smith 262).

p. 157, under Stepney street-names. Add 'PHILPOT ST is so called in commemoration of the family of John *Philpot*, Mayor of London in 1378. He was probably a member of the family of that name which held the subordinate manor of Mile End in the 15th century' (Smith 280).

p. 159, *s.n.* NEWINGTON GREEN. Transfer this to p. 127 under Islington, and add '*v.* Highbury *supra* 125.'

VOL. XIX

THE PLACE-NAMES OF CAMBRIDGESHIRE AND THE ISLE OF ELY

p. 3, *s.n.* CAT'S WATER. Mr G. M. G. Woodgate points out that Cat's Water, like Old South Eau and Shire Drain, was probably once the name of the whole stream as far as Tydd St Giles where Cats Lane (*infra* 284, cf. *Cat Lane* 1779 *Deed*) runs from near the church to the Shire Drain and then along the bank of the stream to Tritton Bridge. The name may well have arisen in this neighbourhood from the *Cat* family of 1285. Later it was extended to the whole river to the west, where Northamptonshire references by name are not earlier than the 16th century. Major Fowler notes that this was the original course of the Nene.

p. 11, *s.n.* OLD WEST RIVER. In the Stretham parish papers (17th-century copies), there is reference to both *Est He* (13th) and *Westee* (1298). Major Fowler suggests that here we have a reference to the time before the formation of the present Old West River. From the watershed near Twenty Pence Ferry, one stream flowed *east* to the Granta (hence *Estee*) and another *west* to the Ouse at Earith (hence *Westee*). Later, the Ouse changed its course at Earith and flowed east to the Granta, forcing its way up the *Westee*, through the low watershed and down the *Estee* to Little Thetford (cf. CAPr XXXIII, 117–24).

p. 11, *s.n.* OLD WEST RIVER. Major Fowler suggests that *Cotingelade* was a name for the Car Dyke.

p. 14, *s.n.* PLANTWATER DRAIN. Mr G. M. G. Woodgate calls attention to the description of the stream at Landwade (*infra* 194) 'full of watercress,' and suggests a similar origin for the name of the Plantwater, choked and decayed probably by phragmites, cladium, or similar plants (cf. H. Godwin in *The Cambridge Region* 45–7).

p. 22, *s.n.* DEADMAN'S WAY. Mr T. C. Lethbridge notes that an Anglo-Saxon cemetery is known to have existed near the Barton-Grantchester boundary, about where INN is marked on the 1″ O.S., south of the Grantchester-Coton road.

p. 29, *s.n.* RIDGEWAYS, and p. 314, *s.v.* burh. Mr T. C. Lethbridge suggests that *Maidenbury* may have some connection with the Bury (Melbourn Bury *infra* 59) beside the course of Ashwell Street at Melbourn, and that Bury Lane (*infra* 60) represents the approximate course of an ancient trackway.

p. 31, *s.n.* WOOL STREET. Mr T. C. Lethbridge is of the opinion (and Sir Cyril Fox agrees) that whilst it is by no means certain that Wool Street is a military earth-work, it is rather more likely to be this than a Roman military road. Hence *Wlmerys-dych* does probably refer to this 'ditch' which in medieval times was regarded as a 'street.' Mr Lethbridge finds it difficult to believe that wolves were numerous in this district in Anglo-Saxon times and suggests that *Wulfmǣr* was the constructor of the dyke (cf. Offa's Dyke), in which case *Wulf(a)* in *Wluestrete* would be a short form of *Wulfmǣr*. Of the three field-names noted, *Woluesden* may well contain a personal name, whilst the other two are much too late for any certainty.

p. 39, *s.n.* CASTLE END. Dr Helen M. Cam notes that *Shire Hill* is historically an older name than *Shirehouse*. The castle site was probably the place where the shire-moot met before the Norman Conquest as the LibEl reference suggests. For county elections it certainly met there either in the Castle yard or in the Shirehouse, down to the end of the 18th century. The Assizes were naturally held in the same place, and after a temporary removal into the town, the Shirehouse has now returned to its original site on Castle Hill.

p. 42, *s.n.* THE KING'S DITCH. Dr Helen M. Cam points out that archaeological evidence strongly suggests that the ditch is older than the Norman Conquest and that *King's* commemorates the improvements of King John and King Henry III (*v.* CAPr xxxv, 49–53). There were other ditches in the town called *King's Ditch* (cf. Rad 125, 127).

p. 46, *s.n.* LENSFIELD RD. The road takes its name from John *Lens*, serjeant-at-law and an original lay fellow of Downing College (1800–25) who owned a field on the south side of Deepway.

p. 78, *s.n.* CANTELUPE FM. Mr J. H. Bullock informs us that the farm derives its name from Viscount *Cantelupe*, son of Earl de la Warr, who owned the village about the beginning of the last century.

p. 105, *s.n.* NOSTERFIELD END. Sir Cyril Fox suggests that this name may provide an indication of a Roman road linking up the Bartlow-Linton settlement area with the Stour valley (and it may account for the great medieval house at Castle Camps, out in the wilds, now destroyed). The road *may* have continued down the valley westward to Cambridge. On the other hand, it may (as suggested *infra* 106) have followed the line of the Roman finds north-westwards. Even if it did, a branch through Street Fm to Bartlow may be envisaged.

p. 136, *s.n.* REACH. Sir Cyril Fox suggests that *Reach* is here used of a straight stretch of water. The Devil's Dyke was probably aligned by the early Dark Age builders on Reach Lode, an artificial cut probably of Roman origin (cf. CAPr xxxv, 93), which looks exactly like a 'stripe.' The hamlet grew out of the traffic up the Reach, hence its position.

p. 138, *s.n.* MUTLOW HILL. Professor Tait notes that the meeting of the three hundreds of Staine, Radfield and Flendish at one common meeting-place would suggest the grouping of hundreds by threes such as we find in the ship-sokes of Kineton, Knightlow and Hemlingford (PN Wa xix), in each of which three hundreds were grouped together for the purpose of supplying a ship to the king for purposes of national defence. Cf. further EHN, Vol. I, xix.

p. 181, *s.n.* MOOR BARNS FM. Dr Helen M. Cam calls attention to the interesting origin of the alternative name *Shire Manor*. 'The manor of *Burlewas*, otherwise called *Shire Manor*, of annual value of £10...the profit thereof to be yearly received and taken towards payment of the fees or wages of the Knights chosen for parliament within the county of Cambridge' (*Statutes of the Realm* III, 924–5 (1542–3), 34 and 35 H. VIII, c. 24). In 1449 the residents of the Isle of Ely compounded for their contributions to the wages of the Knights of the Shire by a lump sum of £200. At some date between 1449 and 1542 *Burlewas Manor* was purchased and its income applied as above, representing one-third of the average expenses of the county M.P.'s. The arrangement is probably unique.

p. 205, *s.n.* CRADGE BANK. An earlier reference is found in 1756 to building 'a small *Cradge* Bank on the north side of the New Bedford River' (H. C. Darby, *Draining of the Fens*, 186).

p. 216, l. 6 from bottom. The note on EGREMONT ST should have been included at the top of p. 215, after the note on Downham St.

p. 221, *s.n.* SPRINGHEAD HO. Col. Archer agrees with Stewart (194) in suggesting that *Blithinghale lane* is an old name for Springhead Lane which originally led down to the only waterway connecting Ely with the Main River. This is what Major Fowler has called Ely Lode (CAPr xxxiv, 25) along which St Withburga's body was carried, after being landed at Turbutsey, and taken by land to Ely. The only possible route was up Springhead Lane. Cf. *viam de Blythinghale* 13th *ElyF*, *Blithynghalelane* 1418 Pat, *Blyþinghalefen* 1277 *Ely*. Possibly 'flat, alluvial land or nook by the bend of the *Bliþing*,' 'the pleasant or quiet, slow-moving one,' from OE *blīðe*. Cf. Blyth (Sf, Nb, Nt), and RN 38–9, 284–5. *v.* healh.

p. 226, *s.n.* CHAIN FM. The change from *chair* to *chain* is probably due to the substitution of an intelligible term for one obsolete and no longer understood. *Littleport Chair* was often used of a specific point dividing Prickwillow Water (the Lark) from Welney Water (Old Croft River). It was about 100 yds. downstream from Littleport Bridge in a big bend of the river opposite Littleport Dock. At or near this was a 17th-century ferry which may have been worked by a chain. Major Fowler notes another possible explanation. Old watermen still living say that where a new toll area began, a chain was placed across the river to prevent them from slipping through at night without paying the toll. Up to 35 years ago there were such river toll chains across the mouth of the river Lark at Branch Bridge, and across the Main River at a spot a few yards south of Littleport Bridge.

p. 229, *s.n.* WILLOW ROW FMS. Mr G. M. G. Woodgate points out that willows were sometimes planted along roadways liable to flooding to mark the track when the floods were out. Willow Row is quite a common name in the fens. He suggests a similar explanation for *Stokewey infra* 25.

p. 274, *s.n.* HASSOCKHILL DROVE is *Hascott Drove* 1713 *Will*. Mr G. M. G. Woodgate calls attention to the frequent references to 'reed ground' in this neighbourhood in the Tithe Reckoning of Leverington (1582).

p. 277, *s.n.* BYTHORN. This name has in error been placed in Parson Drove parish. It should appear under Tydd St Giles parish, and the article be transferred to p. 285.

p. 280, *s.n.* THORNEY. Professor Bruce Dickins notes the comment of Ordericus Vitalis on this name (*Hist. Ecclesiastica*, ed. Le Prevost, IV, 280): *Torneia quippe spinarum insula nuncupatur Anglice, quia diversarum saltus arborum copiosis aquarum gurgitibus circumfluitur undique.*

p. 282, *s.n.* ARCHER'S DROVE, etc. Professor Bruce Dickins notes that Archer's Drove, Green Drove, Harley's Drove and Scolding Drove are recorded in a Court Roll of 1748 (R. Hyett Warner, *History of Thorney Abbey*, 250–2).

p. 285, *s.n.* FURLONG FIELD. Mr G. M. G. Woodgate notes that the sluice would be that at the outfall of the Brass Load, the southern boundary of the field, where it flowed into the sea on the other side of the Roman Bank.

pp. 289–90, *s.n.* SHREWSNESS GREEN. Mr A. T. Hill notes that the change from *Shrewsnest* to *Shrewsness* was helped by the existence of a very obvious *ness* at the ancient junction here of the Ouse and the Nene. Owing to the Old Croft River, this still exists in miniature but formerly it was an outstanding landmark lying between the two rivers, a guide to navigators sailing either to Ely or to Peterborough. Cf. the forms *Shrewysnestpoint* and *Shrewes necke* (1632 Hondius).

p. 293, *s.n.* INLAY'S FM. Professor Tait calls attention to an illuminating example of the use of this word in the Terrier of Fleet, ed. Neilson. In the Introduction, p. lxiii, we have 'The inlikes were the division of the arable in which lay the inter-mixed strips of the tenants.' Miss Neilson also quotes from Ely MSS Ministers' Accounts Wisbech Barton 8 Ed 2 for its use for a tenement let at a rent. It is once spelt *inlye* there.

p. 295, *s.n.* GADDS LANE. Mr G. M. G. Woodgate adds *Geggys Lane* 1417 *Will*, *Gadds or Gedge Lane* 1767 *Deed.* Cf. *Geggis-*, *Geggysdyke* 1452–3 *Will*.

p. 343, *s.v.* slæd. Major Fowler notes that *slade* is also used by the fenmen of the raised and meandering banks of shell marl of a decayed stream after the peat has been washed away from each side (cf. CAPr XXXIII, 110).

DISTRIBUTION MAP. Dullingham should be added to the ingahām names.

CAMBRIDGESHIRE

Grantabricscir(e) c. 1050 ASC (C), c. 1100 ib. (D) *s.a.* 1010–1, *Grantabrycg(e)-* 12th ib. (E) *s.a.* 1010–1, *Grantabrigescira* 1125–35 (1334) YCh

Grauntebreggeschire c. 1045 (14th) ASWills, *-brugge ssire* c. 1330 RG

Granterbrigge syra 1086 ICC, *-sire* 1086 InqEl

Grentebr̃scire 1086 DB, *Grentebrugescira* 1130 P, 1186–94 ib., *-briggescira* 1186–7 ib., *Grenteberg' comitat'* 1279 RH

Cantebrig(g)esira, -e, -y-, -scyra, -scira, -schire c. 1120 HarlCh *et freq* to 15th Trevisa

Chantebrugescire 1167 P, *Cauntebrigeschira* 1230 ib., *Kantebrigesire* 14th HH

Græntebr'scr' 1179 P

Cambrugge schire c. 1400 RG, *Cambrigges(c)hire* 15th Trevisa, 1464 Paston, *Cawmbriggeshire* t. Hy 8 CAPr xxxiii, *Cambridgeshire* 1594 Camden

Cf. Cambridge *infra* 36.

RIVER-NAMES

BECK BROOK (Old West River) is *le Broke* 1483 CRent, *Grytton brooke* 1493 *Rental. v.* Girton *infra* 176 and **bekkr**.

BIN BROOK (6″) (Cam) is *le Binnebrok* c. 1260 *StJohn's*, (ditch called) *Benbrook* 1687 CBD, *Wyttewellebroke* 1349 *StJohn's, Cotenbrook* 1437 *StCatharine's, Whitwel(l)broke* 1497, 1510 ib. For the etymology *v.* **Binbrook Lane** *infra* 44. "Bynbrooke begynnethe at a spring in Whytewell (*infra* 73) and y^{er} is called o^{r} Ladyes well of Whytewell, and so comethe by Coton" (1477 CAPr ix, 74).

The upper waters of the Bin Brook were called *Whitwellbroke*. After flowing through Barton and Coton, the stream becomes the boundary between Coton and Grantchester. A tributary from the Barton boundary which passes Wheat Cases is called *The Brook* (School) and skirts a field in Coton called *Farthing Brook*. This is, no doubt, to be identified with *Fartunebroc* 13th *StJohn's* in Grantchester, which must itself be identical with *Fartwell(e)brok* c. 1250 *StJohn'sH*, 1347 *StJohn's* (in Grantchester), *Fartwelbro(o)k(e)* 1447 *Queens'*, 1510 *StCatharine's* (in Coton), and *For(e)wel(le)brook* 1457 *StJohn's*, *Fertwellbroke* 1459 ib. (in Barton). In Coton, too, we have *Fartwelhed* 1510 *StCatharine's*. The relation between the two names is not entirely clear. The first was presumably 'the brook by a lost *Fartun*,' either OE *fearr-tūn*, 'bull-farm' or *fearh-tūn*, 'pig-farm.' Side by side with *Fartunebroc* there may well have existed a form *Fartunewellebroc*, contracted to *Fartwellebroc*. If *For(e)welle-* is to be relied on, we may have association with OE *fōr*, 'pig,' as possibly in Fairfield (PN Wo 275, PN ERY xlix), *Forfelde* 817 BCS 360. Hence possibly 'stream by the pig-farm.'

BOURN BROOK (Cam) is *Brun(n)ebro(o)k(e)* 1220 *FF*, 1297, 1365 *StCatharine's*, 1302–1542 *Queens'*, *Brunnebroc* c. 1250 *StJohn'sH*, 1289 *Trinity*, *Brounebroke* 1272 *Ass*, *Bronnebroke* 1313 *Queens'*, *(le) Burnebroke* 1480 *Trinity*, 1504 *Queens'*, 1510 *StCatharine's*, *Bourne brooke* 1577 AD v. This is the stream from which Bourn *infra* 155 took its name.

BOURNE, R. (Granta) is *the Burne* 1577 H, *v.* burna, Cam *infra*, Granta *infra* 6 and PN Ess 4. From this were named Bourn Bridge *infra* 100 and Bourne (PN Ess 507). It is also called *Withitheburne* in the bounds of Linton in 1279 (RH), 'withy stream,' *v.* wiþig, and *the Babren* in 1586 (H), a back-formation from Babraham *infra* 100, *Babrenham* 1586 H.

CALLOW BROOK (Beck Brook) is *Colnhellbrok* c. 1250 *StJohn'sH*, *-hilbroc* 13th *CCC*, 1303 *Cole* iv, *Golnhellbroc* 13th *StJohn's*, *Colhil-broke* c. 1300 *StJohn'sH*, 1483 *CRent*, 1493 *Rental*, *Cohilbroke* 1483 *CRent*. Possibly 'the brook by *Cola*'s hill,' *v.* hyll and cf. Colham (PN Mx 41), *Colanhomm* 831 BCS 400, *Coleham* 1086 DB, *Colnham* 1211 RBE. *Colhilbroke* may well have become [kɔləbruk], with later popular etymologising to Callow Brook.

CAM, R.
  (i) *(in) riveram Cantebr'* 1279 RH
  (ii) *(ripam vocatam) Cante* 1340–9 *ElyF*, 1341 *ElyCh*, 1372 WC i, *Cant'* 1383 Works, *Canta...qui hodie Saxonico vocabulo Rheius (quod riuum designat) dicitur* 1574 Caius (all Cambridge)

(iii) *Chamus* 1571 Giles Fletcher (Skeat 32), *alij Grantam, Camum alij nuncupant* 1586, 1594 Camden, *Camus* 1637 Milton, *Lycidas*

(iv) *Cam* 1610 Speed (Guilden Morden, Stretham), 1622 Drayton xxi, 1645 Blaeu (Shingay, Burwell), 1690 Lea (Cambridge to Ditton), 1724 Moll (Shingay), *Cham al. Grant* 1702 WC i

There has been, and still is, considerable variation in the names given to the various branches of the Cam or Granta. The main stream (*a*) rises near Ashwell (Herts) and is joined at Hauxton by (*b*) a stream rising near Elsenham (Ess) which is itself joined near Shelford by (*c*) a tributary from Castle Camps. (*a*) is called *Cam* by Fox, *the Rhee* by Hughes, *R. Cam or Rhee* on the modern 1″ map, whilst it is *Rhee* in Ashwell and *Cam or Rhee* from Guilden Morden to Hauxton on the 6″ map. In early sources this is *Rhee* 1272–1586, *Granta* 1576, *Cam* 1610–1724 and *Barrington water* 1586 H. (*b*) is now *Essex Cam* (Fox), *Granta* (Hughes), *Cam or Granta* (1″ map), *Cam* (Chesterford) (6″ map) and *Cam or Granta* (6″ map) from Ickleton to Sawston. From 1690 to 1830 this is referred to as *Granta*. (*c*) is usually called the *River Bourne* (1″ map), but is also *Granta* in Babraham (1″ map) and from Bartlow to Babraham (6″ map). (*d*) The combined stream is now generally known as *Cam or Granta* in Grantchester and Cambridge and as *Cam* from Cambridge to its junction with the Old West River near Thetford. It is *Cam* at Burwell in 1645 and Ditton in 1690, but *Granta* at Swaffham in 1279 and 1669 and at Ely as late as 1654. Here it is also called *Stuntnye Ryuer* (1611 *AddCh*) and near Barraway, *the olde River* (1609 ib.), possibly with reference to a change of course. *Cante* is a back-formation from *Cantebrigge* and *Cam* from *Cambrigge*, whilst *Camus* is an erudite Latinisation of *Cam*. *v.* Cambridge, Granta, Rhee *infra* 36, 6, 14, Bourne *supra* 2 and PN Ess 4–5.

This is also *ripariam de Heneya* (1260 *Ass*) near *Henney* in Cambridge, *aqua de Haukeston* (1285 *Ass*) in Hauxton, *Chesterton water* (1389 Cl, Pat) from Chesterton to *Estenhale* (*v.* Stourbridge Common *infra* 43), *Cleyhith Water al. voc. Bechewere Water* (1546 *MinAcct*) (*v.* Clayhithe and Waterbeach *infra* 145, 184) and *Ditton river* (1260 Ass) in Fen Ditton.

CAT'S WATER is *Cattesdrit* (sic) 1251 *ElyCouch*, 1277 Ely, *Cattesdich* 15th ib., *Cat(te)swater* 1315 Thorney, 1394 Ct, 1574 SP, *Cattewater* 1636 Fenland vi, *Bull-dike or Cat-water* 1657 DugdD, *Pepper Lake or Catwater* 1771 BedL. It is the name of the stream forming the boundary between Cambridgeshire and Northamptonshire from Peterborough until by the Lincolnshire border the river turns east and becomes the Old South Eau *infra* 10. It was also known as the Muscat *infra* 7 or *Must*. For *Pepper Lake* cf. Old Pepper Lake (Nth). The earlier forms above confirm the suggestion in PN Nth 2 that this was the dyke of a former owner named *Catt*. *v.* Addenda viii.

CHENEY WATER (Cam) is *Cheyneys broke* 1675 *Eg*, *v.* Cheyney Lodge *infra* 64.

CHERRY HINTON BROOK (6″) (Cam) is *le Broke* 1511 *Rental*, *v.* Cherry Hinton *infra* 141.

CRANBROOK DRAIN is *Cranebrook(e)* (*by the Westwater*) 1659 *BLAcct*, *Crainbrook* a. 1700 ib. This forms the boundary between Sutton Fen and Earith Fen. It is possible that Crane's Fen in Willingham (*infra* 175) is pseudo-manorial and was originally *Cranefen*. In that case the fen on the south side of the Ouse and the stream flowing into it from the north were both named from the cranes or herons which frequented them.

DARCEY LODE is *Darsey, Darsye Lo(a)de* 1437 BedL, 1528 Imb, 1618 *AddCh, Darcey Load* 1529 BedL, *Dazzie, Daz(z)y lo(o)de* 1589 *SewersD*, 1636 BedL, 1665 Dodson, *Derseyloade* 1612 *SewersD, Darcy Ea* 1616 BedL, *Darsey Eye* 1617 *SewersD, Darselode* 1629 ib., *Dazey load* 1674 Fen. This seems to be identical with *Darfordes ee* 1563 *SewersD* (in Little Downham, near Manea) and *Darford Ee al. Chaferfenne diche* 1574 *SewersC* (in March). *Chaufer Fen* 1529 BedL, *Chaf(f)er Fen* 1636–7 ib. was near Manea Watering and Wellney Water and was probably the fen between Wateringhill Fm and Welney, near Zig Zag or Dazzle Lode which runs across the Bedford Wash. There was also a *Derfordeshe* (1251 *ElyCouch*) in March which is almost certainly to be associated with Dartford Road *infra* 253. Probably from OE *dēores-ēa*, 'wild-animal's stream,' though Darsey may be a shortening of *Dēorfordes-ēa*, 'stream of the wild-animal ford,' *v.* dēor, ford, ēa. Cf. also Derey Lode *infra* 370.

Identical with Darcey Lode is *Cockes Load* which "beginneth at Huney Corner and endureth unto Maney Field End…to Many Loads End" (1436 BedL), *Cox Lode* 1829 Wells. The upper reaches of Darcey Lode are marked on Jonas Moore's map as *Cox Load* and *Twisle load* (*v.* twisla, 'fork'). At Field Road, in West Field in Maney (?Maney Field End), Darcey Lode turns north and continues as the boundary between Upwell and Manea. Somewhere south of Stonea Fen was *Dollode* (c. 1630 *Map*) which flowed north-east to the Frith in Doddington, east of Great Parke and alongside Block Fen. *Dawe Load* (1529 BedL) ran to Maney Field End and to the Mable at Maney Watering. The exact location and course of this particular stream cannot at present be determined.

At Field Road, Darcey Lode is joined by a stream coming from the south from near Downham Hythe, past Oxlode and crossing the Bedford Wash to Purls Bridge. Abutting on *Cokloode* and Downham Hythe was *Oxwillow lode* (1563 *SewersD*). It seems clear that there has been some interchange or confusion or extension of names here. *Cox Lode* and *Dallode* are recorded earlier than Darcey Lode, Oxlode or *Oxwillow Lode*. Oxlode in Downham (*infra* 225) may possibly be a corruption of *Coxlode* or *Oxwillow lode*.

Cox Lode is earlier *K-*, *Cox(e)lode* 1251 *ElyCouch*, 1277 *Ely*, 1617 Imb, *C-*, *Kok(k)eslode* 1251 *ElyCouch*, 1379–91 *Wren*, *Cokkyslode* 1510 *MinAcct*. 'Cock's or *Cocc*'s watercourse,' *v.* (ge)lād.

Dallode is *Dau(e)-*, *Daw(e)lode* 1251 *ElyCouch*, 1277 *Ely*, 1443, 1510 *MinAcct*, 1529 BedL, *Dollode* c. 1630 *Map*, *Dallode* 1664 *CCC*. There was another stream of the same name in Stretham, *Dau(e)-*, *Daw(e)lode* 1221 *ElyA*, 1251 *ElyCouch*, 1277 *Ely*, 1302 *MinAcct*, 1346, 1549 *Ct*, *Dallode* 1636 BedL. The twofold occurrence of *Daue-* compounded with *-lode* and certain field-names suggests that it is some significant term. Cf. *Dauelond* 13th *AD* iii[1], 1314–19 *Queens'*, 1356–73 *Trinity*, (*le*) *Daw(e)lond* 1337, 1395 *Queens'*, 1373, 1389 *Trinity*, 1465 *Pembroke*, *Daflond* 1312, 14th *Queens'*, *Dallandfeyld* 1477 *Trinity* (Haslingfield), *Dauelond* c. 1250 ib., *Daw(e)lond* c. 1279 *StCatharine's* (Barrington), 1473 *Christ's* (Orwell), *-land* t. Hy 8 *Rental* (Hinxton), *Dallond* 1387 *Wren* (Downham). **daf* may be related to Eng *dabble*, Du *dabbelen*, var. of *dabben*, 'to trample with the feet in mud,' Norw *dave*, 'a pool,' Icel *dafla*, 'to splash,' OSwed *dævin*, 'wet.' In composition with land the meaning might be 'wet' and so 'muddy land.' With (ge)lād the meaning is doubtful; it might be 'muddy watercourse' or one so shallow that one might dabble or splash about in it.

Here, too, may belong *Dar Load* 1575 *Survey* (Over), *Darloade al. Great Swalney* 1618 *Depositions*. Cf. *Sualewenheþe* 1251 *ElyCouch*, 1277 *Ely*, *Swalney Fen* 1575 *Survey*. 'Landing-place (*v.* hȳð) on the *Swalewe*' which must have been used here as a name for the Ouse. Cf. Swale

---

[1] Printed *Danelond*.

(PN NRY 6), *Swalwan* c. 1000 OE Bede, Swallow (L), DB *Sualun*, Swale (K), *Suuealuue* 812 BCS 341 and Swalecliffe (K), *æt Swalewan-clife* 949 ib. 874, which Ekwall derives from the root *suel-*, 'to move, turn, plash' in OE *swillan*, 'to wash,' hence 'winding river,' or it might, as suggested by Wallenberg, be from the root of OE *swellan*, 'to swell,' hence 'the swelling one,' 'river liable to flood,' *v.* RN 383-5, KPN 125, 281.

DELPH, R. is *the Delph or Thirty Feet* 1821 BedL, an artificial drain between the Bedford Rivers for the better draining of water off the Washlands. An earlier reference may be *the Delph* 1617 SewersD, which was for the receipt of water and flowed into the Ouse near Littleport. *v.* (ge)delf.

EASTERN BROOK (6″) (Bourn Brook) in Eltisley flows to the east end of the village from Caxton and is probably to be associated with *Estenddene* 1500 *Pembroke*, *Easton Field* c. 1840 *TA*. The stream was named from this, and its modern form is due partly to lack of stress and partly to popular etymology. *v.* ēast, denu.

GRANSDEN BROOK (6″) (Little Gransden) is probably to be identified with *Holebe(c)k(e)* c. 1185 *StNeot*, 1260 Ass. *v.* holh, bekkr and cf. Hoback Fm *infra* 68.

GRANTA, R.
  Gronte fluminis c. 745 (9th) Felix, *Gronta* 13th ib.
  Grantan stream c. 1000 OE Bede, *(fram) Grante ea* 10th (c. 1050) Guthlac, *Grantee, Granthe* 1279 RH[1], *Grant(e)* 1285 *Ass*[2], 1291 *ElyF*, 1292 Pat, 1596, 1619 Imb, 1611 *AddCh*[3], 1617 *SewersD*[4], 1669 *Ct*[1], *Granta* 1690 Lea[5], 1695 SN[6], 1724 Moll[5]
  Grentam 12th HH
  Graunt(e) 1608-9 *AddCh*[3], 1654 Moore[7]

Probably 'fen river' or 'muddy river.' For a full discussion of the etymology *v.* RN 183-4 and for the alternative *Cam v. supra* 2. See also PN Ess 4-5, Bourne *supra* 2, Rhee, Cambridge and Grant-chester *infra* 14, 36, 75. In Great and Little Abington this is *ripa de Abiton* 1260 Ass, and in Sawston, where it forms the boundary between Sawston and Stapleford, it is *the Old River called Stapleford River, the Stapleford River* 1802 *EnclA*.

---

[1] Swaffham. [2] Cambridge. [3] Ely.
[4] *Joins Owse neare Harramore Hasse.*
[5] Ickleton. [6] Whittlesford. [7] Waterbeach to Ely.

HOBSON'S BROOK (Cam) is *Hobson's watercourse* 1625 *Trinity*, *Hobson's stream* 1851 ib. Its construction is generally attributed to Thomas *Hobson*, the Cambridge carrier (cf. Hobson St *infra* 46), but *v.* Atkinson 68–9.

HOFFER BROOK (6″) (Cam) is *Hoppeforthebroc* 1308 *Trinity*[1], *Hoppefordebroke* 1323 ib.[1], *Horforthbroke* 1540 *Ct*[1], *Hoffer Brook* 1757 *Terr*[2]. Cf. *Apewell(e)broke* c. 1285 *Trinity*[3], *-brook* 1612 *HardwickeA*. *v.* Hoffer Bridge *infra* 85. Locally this is *Hoffer's or Offa's Brook*[4] (School).

HOME DOLE BROOK (6″) (Gransden Brook) is named from *the Home Dole* 1813 *EnclA*, in Little Gransden. *v.* **dāl**.

KENNETT, R. (Lark) is *Kenet* 1249 Cl. Identical with Kennet (Berks) and Kent (We, La). For a discussion of the etymology, *v.* RN 225–8. The name, which is of Celtic origin, has been associated with the Celtic stem *kun-*, 'dog' and with Welsh *cwn*, 'top, summit.' No certainty is possible. Cf. Kennett *infra* 193 and Kentford (Sf), *Cheneteforde* t. Wm 1 (1318) Ch.

LADY NUNN'S OLD EAU is *Priors Ea* 1455 *Wisb*, *Lady Nunns Ee* c. 1600 (1724) *BadesladeA*, *The shire draine* 1632 Hondius, *Lady Nunns Eay* 1706 Moore. This is the name of the Old South Eau (*infra* 10) from Grange Hill to Cloughs Cross, forming the boundary between Sutton St Edmund (L) and Tydd St Giles. *Priors* probably from the Prior of Ely. The monastery had land in Tydd. Cf. Shire Drain *infra* 15. *Lady Nunn* was the wife of Sir Edmund *Noon* who had land in Tydd in 1361 (Cl) and was a commissioner of sewers for the drainage of Elm in 1391. His family gave name to Noon's Manor in Tilney (Nf). *v.* Blomefield, *Hist. Norfolk* (1808), ix, 74.

LARK, R. (Ouse) is probably a back-formation from Lackford (Sf), *v.* RN 236–7. It is called *Pryckewillowewayter* 1549 *Ct* in Littleport, from Prickwillow *infra* 222 and *Mildenhall river or the dead mile* 1604 *Atkyns*, *Mildenhall streame* 1611 *AddCh*, *Millnoll River* 1636 BedL in Ely, Soham and Isleham, from Mildenhall (Sf). For *dead mile*, *v.* Mile End *infra* 222.

LONG BROOK (6″) (Bourn Brook) is so named c. 1825 (O.S.).

MILL RIVER (6″) (Litlington). Cf. *le Melfeld* 14th *Wymond*. *v.* **myln**.

MUSCAT is an alternative for the Cat's Water *supra* 3, not marked on

---

[1] Foxton.   [2] Harston.   [3] Barrington.
[4] The form used in 1929 in CAPr xxx, 112.

the O.S. maps, but found in the map in Hughes's *Cambridgeshire* (1909) and described there (47) as "*the Muscat or Catwater*, north of Peterborough, known also as the South Ea, or Shire Drain." It is

(*to, fra*) *Must* c. 1200 ASC (E), *s.a.* 963, *Must* c. 1151–1314
 Thorney, c. 1225 *ElyCh*, 1251 *ElyCouch*, 1277 *Ely*, *Musc* t. Hy 2
 (1314) Ch, *le Moust* 1328 *Ct*
Musthea 1350, 1597 *Wisbech Map*
Muscote water 1574 *SewersC*, *Mustcote drayne* 1617 *SewersD*,
 Muscot(t) water 1636 *BedL*, 1706 *Moore*, *Muscat R. or Cat's
 Water* 1829 *Wells*
The Murst 1712 *Fenland* iv

As suggested by Ekwall (RN 297, *s.n.* Must), this is probably to be derived from the root *meu- underlying Eng *mud*, Du *modder*, ON *mykr*, etc. It is probably Germanic in origin, meaning 'a muddy stream or ditch.' On the modern map, the name Cat's Water is also given to the stream from the Nene near Peterborough to the Cambridgeshire boundary near Northey. On the Wisbech Map, which is by no means easy of interpretation, *Musthea* is also a stream flowing south of Thorney Bar, Wryde and Knarr. This is possibly the South Must referred to in *Suthmust(es)muthe* 1244 *Rams*, *Southmost'mothe* 1281 *AddCh*, and is probably another name for Cnut's Dyke and King's Dike *infra* 207, 208, just north of which is Must Fm *infra* 261. The dike in this neighbourhood is *Musdike* 1540 *MinAcct*, -*dyke* 1616 *BedL*, *Mustedike* 1617 *AddCh*. The reference in *Eldemust* 1241 *ElyM*, *Thorney*, *Eldemuster* 1241 (1348) *Pat* in the bounds of Thorney and Whittlesey is probably to the Cat's Water between Cambridgeshire and Northamptonshire.

Muscat was originally the name of a cottage by the Must (possibly somewhere near Cat's Water Fm) in Thorney, *Muscote* 1436 *BedL*, 1438 *Imb*, 1469 *Pat*, *Mustcote house* 1617 *SewersD*. Cf. also *Muskett Willowe Rowe* 1540 *MinAcct* (*v.* Willow Hall *infra* 283) and *Musket Hill* c. 1840 *TA* (in Whittlesey). The name was later transferred to the river, *v.* cot(e).

NENE, R.
 Forms from Cambridgeshire documents are:
 (i) (*to*) *Nen* 972 (1121) BCS 1281, c. 1300 *Bodl*[1], *Nene* 1244 *Rams*,
  1330 *Cole* xliii, 1438 *Imb*, 1579 *Depositions*[2], *Neene* 1617
  AddCh

___

[1] Between Thorney and Eye (Nth). [2] Whittlesey.

Nien 1170 LibEl

Neine flu: c. 1600 (1724) *BadesladeA*, *Neeyne* 1617 *SewersD*,
   Neyne, Neine 1621 ib.

Nean(e) 1609 *AddCh*[1], 1617 *SewersD*, (*Old*) 1690 Lea[2]

Nyne 1621 *SewersD*

(ii) *ripa de Wysebeche* c. 1191 *Thorney*, 1285 *Ass*, *the river of Wise*
   1340 *Imb*, *W(e)yse* 1438 ib., *waters of Wysebech* 1358 Pat,
   river of Wisebech 1411 Pat, *the greate river (Ryuer) of Wisbech*
   1436 BedL, 1617 *SewersD*[3], *Wisbeche Ryver* 1615 *AddCh*

(iii) *aqua de Marcheford* 1285 *Ass*, *March stream(e)* 1596 Imb, 1636
   Fenland vi, *river of March called the river of Nyne (or Nene)*
   1600 *AddCh*

(iv) *Bradenhee* 1314 *Ct*[4], *Bradney* 1336 *Rental*[4], *Bradene(e) al. voc.*
   Marche(h)e(e) 1401–28 *Ct*[5]

(v) *the great Eae* 1529 *Dugd*[5], *the Ee* 1542 *Ct*, *River or Eye called*
   Wisbeche Eye 1579 *Depositions*

(vi) *water called Wyseham* 1579 *Depositions*[6]

See further PN BedsHu 9, PN Nth 3 and, for a full discussion of
the etymology, RN 299–300. The meaning is quite uncertain. From
Guyhirn (below Wisbech) the Nene was called Wisbech Great River,
as opposed to the Little River, now the Wisbech Canal *infra* 17. It
was also called *Old Ee* (*v.* Oldeamere *infra* 262), Starnea Dyke and
Plantwater *infra* 15, 14. For *Bradenhee*, *v.* Bradney *infra* 254 and
for *Wyseham*, *v.* Wysemouth *s.n.* Ouse *infra* 12.

THE NEW RIVER (local) is so named in 1634 (Bushell). It was cut in
1610 (*Cole* xli, f. 182 d).

OLD CROFT RIVER (Nene) [ould kraˑft] is *the River of Croft* 1606
Depositions[7], 1609 *AddCh*[8], *the Old Craft River* 1830 BedL[9]. Cf. Croft
Hills *infra* 226. This is the river from which Outwell and Upwell
infra 276, 288 and Welney (Nf) were named:

   aqua (ripa) de Welle 1250–69 RN 447, 1327 *Ct*[9], *ripa de Litleport,*
   de Upwell 1285 *Ass*, *magnam ripam* t. Hy 3 *Ct*[9]

[1] Near Shrewsness.   [2] A continuation of Whittlesey Dyke to March.
[3] From Stangrownd Staffe unto Wisbech high bridge.
[4] Elm.   [5] March.
[6] Whittlesey.   [7] Littleport.
[8] Joined the Graunte near Harrymeare.
[9] Upwell.

Wellenhe 1251 *ElyCouch*[1], 1277 *Ely*[2], 13th *ElyG*[3], *Wellen(ee)* 1259 *ElyM*[3], 1489 *Ct*[3], *Uellenhe* 1277 *Ely*[4], *Welhenhee* 1316 *Ct*[2], *Welnehee* 1391 *Wren*[4]

Holdewellenee 1251 *ElyCouch*[5], 1277 *Ely*[6], *Oldewellenhe(e)* 1251 *ElyCouch*[2], c. 1270 *Thorney*[5], 1334 *Ct*[7], *Eldewellenhe* 1251 *Ely-Couch*[5], 1277 *Ely*[3]

Welnewater 1476 *Ct*[5], (streame) 1610 *SewersD*[2], *Welneywa(y)ter* 1477[5], 1549 *Ct*[2], *Wel(l)n(e)y (Water)* 1529 *BedL*[8], 1606 *Depositions*[2], 1608–9 *AddCh*[2], (ee) 1563 *SewersD*, (river) 1617 ib.[9], 1674 Fen, *Wellnie ryuer* 1589 ib.[2]

'River, stream,' *v.* **wielle**. By the side of this there was also an extended form *Wiellan-ēa* which became Welney, *v.* **ēa**. *Oldewellenhe* implies that the river had changed its course already in the 13th century, *v.* **eald**. At Littleport we also have *the river Little, Littel* 1313, 1314 Pat. This looks like an early back-formation. *v.* also Wisbech Canal *infra* 17.

OLD SOUTH EAU [sauði]

Suthea 13th *Thorney*, *Southea qd nuncupat' le Oldehea* 1340 *Wisbech Map*, *Southhea* 1387 ib., *Sowthea al. Highfen dyke* 1619 *SewersD* *Southee* 1411 *Ct*, *South Ee but anciently Old Ee* 1438 Imb, *le Southhe* 1331 *Ct*, *South Eye* 1579 *Depositions*

Old Southea 1706 Moore, *Old Southeau* 1829 Wells

'The southern river,' *v.* **ēa**. Why *south* is not clear, unless because it forms the south boundary of Lincolnshire. *Old* to distinguish this from the New South Eau *infra* 210. This is the name of the Muscat or Cat's Water *supra* 7, after it turns towards the east near Crowland, though it is occasionally used of the part forming the western boundary of Whittlesey and Thorney. Cf. South Eau Fm in Crowland (L). On the modern map the part from Cloughs Cross to Grange Hill is called Lady Nunn's Old Eau *supra* 7. Where it serves as a boundary between Tydd St Giles and Tydd St Mary (L), it is called the Shire Drain *infra* 15. Here we have Eaudike Bank and Old Eau Field in Tydd St Mary (L), the latter preserving an old alternative name used for the whole, whether the boundary between Huntingdonshire and Cambridgeshire or between Cambridgeshire and Lincolnshire:

[1] Downham, Doddington, Littleport and Upwell.   [2] Littleport. Upwell.   [4] Downham.   [5] Wisbech.   [6] Elm. Elm and Upwell.   [8] Maney.   [9] Near Crouchmore.

Old(e)hee t. Hy 3 *Cole* xliv, 1281 *AddCh*, *Oldhea* 1273 *Wisbech Map*, *Oldee* 1281 *AddCh*, *le Southhea et le Ouldhea idem sunt* 1350 *Wisbech Map*, Old Ee 1570 Imb

From *Nomaneslond* (near Singlesole Fm) in Thorney it is also called *Tidhe* (1277 *Ely*) from the two Tydds, whilst at one time, from Thorney to Throckenholt it was

S(ch)epelak(e) c. 1151, c. 1191 *Thorney*, 1597 *Wisbech Map*, *S(c)epelac* c. 1151, c. 1191, 1314 *Thorney*, *Goldedike or Shepye lake* 1579 *Depositions*

a name which survives in the near-by Shepeau Stow (L) and is probably 'sheep-stream,' OE *scēap-ēa*, to which *lacu* was later added. It is also *aqua de Euerdwic* 13th *StNeot* and *Thorneylake al. Trokenall* 1533 *SewersC* in Parson Drove, v. Throckenholt *infra* 278 and Cloughs Cross, Gold Dike, Shire Drain and Shoffendike *infra* 277, 280, 15, 286. *Oldee* was the old course of the river Nene. For *eau*, v. eā. v. Addenda viii.

OLD WEST RIVER (Cam) is *ripa de Hadenham*, *ripa de Aldereth* 1285 *Ass*, from Haddenham to Aldreth *infra* 231, 232. In Stretham it is clearly referred to as *Estee* 1302 *MinAcct*, *Estae*, *Esteewater* 1356 *Add*, *Estwater* 1589 *Sewers*, because it contained the *east waters* of the Ouse. *Old West* has been transferred to this from (*Old*) West Water *infra* 17, the name for the Ouse when it flowed north from Earith Bridge to Benwick. It is *Lorton delfe* 1632 Hondius, *Looden delfe* ib., 1662 Blaeu. It seems possible that an earlier name was *Cotingelade* 1170 LibEl, c. 1300 GestH, *Cot(t)yng(es)lo(o)de* t. Ed. 3, 1562 *Christ's*, c. 1350 *Cole* xliv. This is certainly not the present-day Cottenham Lode which is modern, but it may be *Cotenhamlode* (1291 *ElyF*). For its history v. CAPr xxxiii, 123–4. The name denotes 'watercourse of the people of *Cotta*,' v. (ge)lād and Cottenham *infra* 149. v. Addenda viii.

OUSE, R.

Forms from Cambridgeshire documents are:

(*into, andlang*) *Use* 1012 (12th) Proc. Soc. Antiq. (NS) iii, 49, 1170 LibEl, 1260 Ass[1], 1279 RH[2], 1438 Imb[3], 1575 *Survey*[1]

Huse 1244 Rams[4], 13th *StJohn's*[1], *Housse* 14th CCC[1]

Ouse 1331 Rams[4], 1349 *Walden*[1], 1576 Saxton[5], 1617 *SewersD*[6],

---

[1] Over.   [2] Swavesey.   [3] Wisbech.   [4] Benwick.
[5] Ely.   [6] Near Crouchmore and Southery Ferry.

Ousa, Wisa, Ysa vel Usa t. Eliz *Draining, Owse* 1608 *AddCh*[1], 1609[2], 1611 ib.[3] *the great, Riuer of Owse* 1609 ib.[4], *Owze* 1618 ib.[1], *ye river Owes* 1643 EA vii, *Old River of Ouze* 1652 BedL, *Old Owse* 1654 *BLAcct, Newe Ouze* 1671 *FenS, Old Ouse* 1690 Lea[5] *Benewykewater(e)* 1461 *MinAcct* (Swavesey), *le hygh Ee* 1473 CCC, *le Streem* 1477 ib. (Over)

This difficult river-name has been previously discussed by Ekwall (RN 313–17), Zachrisson (PN *vis* 13–21) and Smith (PN ERY 9–10). Ekwall identifies *Wusan* (ASC *s.a.* 905) with the Wissey (or, if this really refers to the Ouse, he dismisses it as a scribal error) and derives the river-name *Ūse*, dat. *Ūsan*, from which was formed a shorter *Ūs*, dat. *Ūse*, from a Brit **udso*, 'water,' later **utso, *usso*, with a lengthening of the vowel. With this Smith agrees. To the forms given above, however, must be added those for *Wysemouth*:

Wyshamm(o)uth(e) 1244 Rams[6], 1320 *Elien*[7], 1341 *ElyCh*[7]
Wysem(o)uth(e), -i- c. 1250 *ElyM*, 1298 *Ass*[8] *et freq* to 1529 *Dugd*[9], 1603 *Survey*[10]
Wyshe(e)m(o)uth(e) 1314 *Ct*[10], *Wysea mouth* 1436 *Dugd*
Wysammo(u)(u)th 1341 *ElyF*[7], 1423 *Ct*[11], 1497 *MinAcct*[6]
New Wysemouth 1389 *ElyCouch*[12]

Ekwall cites this name as evidence that the Wissey (Nf) once flowed to Wisbech and suggests that it was the name of the place where the Wissey "joined the main river (Welney?)" (RN 466). The name occurs, as he remarks, in the bounds of Wisbech *Heyefen*[13], but the other points in these bounds show that this extensive fen stretched from Upwell as far as Whittlesey and Thorney. *Wysemouth* is also mentioned in the bounds of Whittlesey and on the boundary between Cambridgeshire and Huntingdonshire. In the latter, it was in Ben-

---

[1] Cottenham.   [2] Well Creek to Salters Load and Littleport.
[3] Turbutsey; joins the Granta at *Harrymeare*.
[4] Near *Harrimeere*.   [5] Whelpmore in Littleport.
[6] Benwick, on bounds of Cambridgeshire and Huntingdonshire.
[7] Doddington.   [8] In March, near Bradney.
[9] Near Whittlesey Dike and Copalder.   [10] Whittlesey bounds.
[11] Whittlesey.   [12] In bounds of Ranson Moor.
[13] The same points occur in the bounds of Wisbech Heyefen in the same order but with variant spellings in *ElyM* f. 390 (c. 1250), *Thorney* f. 193 b (c. 1270), and *ElyF* f. 228 (1341). Cf. 'le Wride, le Knor, Orchierdsted, Stodpath, le Wype, Dedhee, Nimers, Westfencote, Wysemouthe, Swerdesdelf, Gretecros, Hydene, Quedale, Marcheford, le Krike, le Heyerout, Echingee, Þarmeres, Staningmeres, Prallewere, Oldewellenhee, Millestede, Shrewedehirst' (c. 1250 *ElyM*, f. 390). In a survey of Whittlesey of 1603 (CUL, *AddMS* 3826, f. 4), the bounds of Whittlesey begin Le Knar, le Knarstoke, and then continue as above to Great Cross.

wick[1] and this, with its position in the Whittlesey bounds and its association with *Swerdesdelf* (Cnut's Dyke *infra* 207), Whittlesey Dike (*infra* 208) and Bradney in March (*infra* 254), place *Wysemouth* near Benwick and Copalder and south of White Fen, and make it impossible to associate the name with Wisbech and the Wissey. It must refer to the 'mouth of the Ouse' where it joined the Nene in Benwick. The Wissey cannot possibly have flowed so far west and then back to Wisbech[2].

We must, therefore, agree with Zachrisson that Ouse and Wissey are etymologically identical. The nom. was *Wise* and the dat. *Wusan* (from earlier *Wisan*), later *Usan*[3], from which a new analogical nom. *Use* was formed. The original nom. *Wise* is found only in compounds such as Wissey and Wisbech. The dat. *Usan* and the analogical nom. *Use* had a wider currency, as river-names are more often used in the oblique cases than in the nominative. Zachrisson derives the name from the root **vis*, 'to be wet,' but does not account for the difference between *Wise* (Ouse) and *Wisse* (Wissey). Ekwall (RN 465–7) suggests that the latter may be from a side-form **Wisjon-* or, better, from some analogical transformation. He compares the rare OE *wisse*, 'a meadow,' but is probably nearer the truth in associating with this the tribal name *Wisse* which must be located in or near East Anglia and has already been associated by Birch with Wisbech: *in provincia Wissa* c. 745 (9th) Felix, *on þære mægðe Wissa* 10th (c. 1050) Guthlac. Both Ouse and Wissey may well be OE *Wissa ēa*, 'the river of the Wisse.' As a tribe, occupying a *provincia*, they may well have dwelt along the valley of the Ouse, as well as along that of the Wissey, both of which must once have flowed to Wisbech[4]. *Wise* is probably Germanic, from the root **vis*, related to OE *wāse*, 'mud,' ON *veisa*, 'a pool,' Ger *Wiese* 'a meadow,' and probably meant 'water, river.' *v.* also Ouse Fen

[1] *ibi cadit Nene in Huse* 1244 Rams i, 210; *ad villam de Benewyk ubi aquae de Ouse et Nene concurrunt adinvicem* 1331 ib. iii, 146. Cf. also *ladam versus Wysemouthe apud le Wyp* 1286 Ct (Whittlesey), *v.* Wype Doles *infra* 263, *piscar' in Benewyke vocat' Wysammouth* 1497 MinAcct and *water called Wyseham* (near WhittleseyDike) 1579 *Depositions*.

[2] Ekwall (RN 466), commenting on the lack of references in the 13th century to the Ouse north of Benwick, suggests that the Ouse either did not touch Wisbech or else that it divided into several channels and lost the name Ouse in the fen district. The latter is the true explanation. The combined Nene-Ouse split into various channels, each with different names, some of which still survive on the map, *v.* for example Starnea Dyke and Plantwater *infra* 15, 14.

[3] Zachrisson gives some evidence for the early loss of initial *W-*. Some further support is, perhaps, provided by Outwell *infra* 288.

[4] For the changes in the courses of these rivers, *v.* Darby, *Medieval Fenland*, 94–8 and Figs. 14, 15.

and Wisbech *infra* 170, 292. The river-name occurs also in *Ousemor(e)* 1399 *MinAcct*, *-diche* 1408 ib. (both in Chatteris) and in *Hisdelf* t. Hy 3 *Ct* (Swavesey). *v.* also Bluntishmere Drove *infra* 169.

LITTLE OUSE, R. (Great Ouse) is *Owsa parua* 1576 Saxton, *Brandon Water or Ouse parva* c. 1600 (1724) *BadesladeA*. *v.* Ouse *supra* 11. *Brandon Water* from Brandon (Sf).

PLANTWATER DRAIN. Cf. *Plant(e)croft(e)* 1320 *Elien*, 1341 *ElyCh*, *ElyF*, *-feld(e)* 1477–80 *Ct*[1], 1540 *MinAcct*[2], *Idenhea Plant(e)* 1436 BedL, 1617 *SewersD*, *Plant's were* 1438 Imb, *Plantes* 1597 *Wisbech Map*, *Plant(e) water* ib., 1605 Imb, 1808 L, *Plantinwater* 1636 BedL. In 1618 we learn that the "principal river called *Great Cross* or *Plantwater*" was "a branch of or rather the body of Neane and Ouze united" (BedL ii, 83). In 1605 it "cometh out of Nene at Great crosse to the said Hobb's house" (Imb 381), whilst on the Wisbech Map of 1597 it is continued towards Wisbech by the *Idenhea*. This is the "sewer called *Idenhea*, in bredth 32 foote" which was one of the bounds of Heyefen between Wisbech and Thorney (c. 1270 *Thorney* f. 193b, 1436, 1529 BedL ii, 12). It is clear that Plantwater and *Idenhee* were one and the same stream, the two names, as with other streams in the fens, being used indifferently of the whole and various parts. Earlier forms are *Idenhe(e)* 1251 *ElyCouch*, 1277 *Ely*, 1341 *ElyF*, *Hydenee* 1251 *ElyCouch*, 1277 *Ely*, *Idenhea(deepe*, *-croftes)* 1597 *Wisbech Map*. This is possibly a formation parallel with Welney from **wielle** (*v. supra* 10), based on an unexplained river-name *Ide* (cf. Ide, PN D 497, RN 208). With Plantwater, cf. *Plantelode* 1406 *ElyF* (in Lakenheath, Sf) and *Sedgefenn plante* 1403 *SewersA* (in Sutton). This must be OE *plante*, 'a plant, shoot.' The root meaning is 'spreading,' 'a spreading sucker or shoot,' and the word may have been used of some particular spreading plant, then of a place covered by them. Cf. Wype Doles *infra* 263. *v.* Addenda lix.

QUY WATER is so named in 1604 (*Atkyns*). *v.* Quy *infra* 133.

RHEE (Granta) is *Hauxton Ree* 1405 *Ct*, (*le*, *the*) *Re(e)* 1354 EA xii[3], 1407 *StJohn's*[4], 1452 *Hardwicke*[5], 1480 *Cole* xl[6], *the North Ree* 1400 *Huddleston*[7], *le Ee* 1447 WC i[3], *the Ee* 1472 *Rad*[3], *the Comon Ree* 1512 *Hardwicke*[5], *the Raye* 1549 Gray, *Town of Cambridge* 95[3], *the hye*,

---

[1] In Upwell. [2] In Thorney. [3] Cambridge.
[4] Steeple Morden. [5] Wimpole. [6] Trumpington.
[7] Sawston.

Heighe Ree 1569 *Ct*[1], *Granta* 1576 Saxton[2], *the Rea called y*[e] *North Rea* 1580 *Survey*[3], *the Rhee* 1586 H, *Babraham Ree* 1612 *Queens'*, (*reuer called*) *Baburham ree* 17th ib., *ye old Rey* 1624 *Christ's*[4]. By this lived Humphrey and Thomas *Attere* de Clopton (1272 *Ass*) and William *atte Ree* de Grantesete (1285 ib.). OE *æt þære ēa*, ME *at ther ee, atte ree*, 'by the river,' *v.* æt, ēa. Cf. PN Herts 4. From this were named West Rea *infra* 358, *Re(e)strate* 1283–1319 *Bodl*[5], *le Rehil* 1328 *Queens'*[6], *le Reefurlonge* 1466 *Peterhouse*[7], *Reeshotte* 1484 *St John's*[8], *Refelde* 15th *Queens'*[6]. This is also *Wittlesforde Ryver* 1580 *Survey*, "*the Barrington water*, as Leland calleth it, but some other *the Rhee*" (1586 H 102), and *Orwell ryuer* 1600 *Depositions*. *v.* Cam and Granta *supra* 2, 6.

RUNNING DITCH (6″) flows into the North Ditch, a tributary of the Cam or Rhee and is to be identified with a lost *Marditch*. Cf. *Mardyh-furlong* (sic) 1274 Cl (in Abington Pigotts). The stream forms the boundary between Abington Pigotts and Steeple Morden. *v.* (ge)mǣre and cf. Mare Dyke (PN Ess 9).

THE SHIRE DRAIN is that part of the Old South Eau *supra* 10 which forms the boundary between Tydd St Giles and Tydd St Mary (L). It is (*The*) *Shire Drayne* 1578 Fenland v, *the Shere dreine* 1618 *AddCh*, *Clows Cross or Shire Drayne* 1618 BedL, *Sheer Draine* 1695 SN and owes its name to the fact that it serves as the boundary between the shires of Cambridge and Lincoln. In the 17th and 18th centuries, the name was sometimes used of the whole river from Thorney to Wisbech (e.g. 1724 Moll). Evidence of its older name survives near its banks in Eaudike Bank and Field, Eauleet Field *infra* 285 and in Old Eau Field in Tydd St Mary (L). Shire Field *infra* 274 on Lady Nunn's Old Eau (*supra* 7) is a reminder that here too the stream was once called Shire Drain. Cf. *the Upper Shyer goat* 1621 *AddCh* (in Tydd). *v.* also Cloughs Cross *infra* 277.

STARNEA DYKE (*TA*)
> *Upstancote* 1199 *ElyCouch*, *-lake* 1437 *SewersC*, *Upstanycote* 1494–1532 *Ct*, *Upstane(e)* 1236 Ch, 1346 *ElyCh*, *ElyF*
> *Upstauen(e)(cote, -tuisel, -dik)* 1251 *ElyCouch*, 1277 *Ely*, 1356 *Extent*, 1411 Pat, 1411–22 *Ct*, *Upstavinlake* 1438 Imb, *Hup-*

---

[1] Meldreth. [2] Shingay. [3] Sawston.
[4] Whaddon. [5] Chesterton. [6] Pampisford.
[7] Wimpole. [8] Trumpington.

stauene(kote) 1316 *MinAcct*, 1332–46 *Ct, Staven Ea, Eaye, Ee al. Olde Ee* 1579 *Depositions*

Sterne Ee al. Olde Ee 1574 *SewersC*, (*or South Lake*) 1637 BedL, 1829 Wells, *Sterne Eau* 1655 *BLAcct, Starnea Dyke* c. 1840 *TA*

This is the name of a lost stream which flowed through Whittlesey, March, Wisbech and Elm. In 1528 (*SewersC*), *Up Staven Ee* was "an ould dreane...beginninge at Eldernall to a willow at Reedsend." In 1579 (*Depositions*), *Staven Ee* was said to be the boundary between Whittlesey and Wisbech and flowed between *Middfenntree* and *Orchardsteade. Easend* was near West Fen Close and Eldernell (*infra* 258, 259). In 1605 it flowed through Hobb's dike (*infra* 297) into March river and "was wont to run to Tower House and so to Wisbech" (Imb). In 1655, part of the stream was filled up (*BLAcct*). It is marked on Wells's map of 1829 from Eastree Fen (*infra* 259) to Plantwater Drain (*supra* 14) and on a tithe map as the boundary between March and Whittlesey. The *Hoolde Ee* is also mentioned in Elm (1498 *Ct*), near Begdale (*the old ea* 1615 *AddCh*) and near Coldham (*the Old Eaes end* 1600 ib.). In 1575 (*SewersC*), *Olde Ee* begins at *Doddington Barres* and flows past the *Assrowes* and *Fenalder* betwixt *Normore* and the *Frith* and so to *Stetches* (*infra* 265). In 1617, *the ould Ea* is described as a branch of the River of Neene (*AddCh*). This is the stream from which Oldeamere (*infra* 262) is named. Its exact course cannot now be determined. The topography of the whole of this district is difficult. Streams had their courses changed, or decayed; their names varied in different parts and the construction of artificial drains added a further complication. But it seems clear that this was one of several branches of the Nene and, so far as we can interpret the Wisbech map, it seems probable that we should identify it with *Dedhee*, a decayed river passing West Fen Close, which turned towards the east near Knarr Cross, circling round the north of Westry and Norwood to Hobbs House and on through Elm, between Begdale and Coldham. This is (*le*) *Ded(e)he(e)* c. 1250 *ElyM*, 1277 *Ely* (both in Whittlesey), 1251 *ElyCouch*, c. 1270 *Thorney* (in the bounds of Heyefen, near Wype), 1341 *ElyF* (Wisbech). OE *dēad*, 'dead' and *ēa*, 'river.' Hence 'the decayed river.' Cf. *þa deaden lace* 11th Crawford (in Creedy, D), Dautha (We), OScand *dauðā*, 'dead river,' *Dawtha ye ded(e)* 1170–84, and other examples in RN 116.

The derivation of *Upstancote* is not easy. The addition of *ee* from *ēa*, 'river,' is clearly late and it would seem that we have to deal with an original name *Staven*, to which later there was added a prefix *Up-*

(*v.* **uppe**) and suffixes, **cote,** 'cottage,' **twisla,** 'fork,' **lacu,** 'stream' and **dīc,** 'ditch or dike.' *Staven* is probably from OE *æt þǣm stæfum,* ME *atte staven,* 'at the stumps,' *v.* **æt, stæf** and cf. Coton and Wicken *infra* 74, 203. It is just possible that we may have to start with OE *æt þǣm stæfne,* from OE *stæfn,* 'stem, stump,' but from this one would have expected *stam* or *stem.* For this type we may compare Stoven (Sf), *Stoune, Stouone* 1086 DB, *Stovene* 1201, from OE *stofn,* 'stem, tree-stump' (DEPN).

THORNEY RIVER (Nene) is *Thorney leame* 1574 *SP, Thorney water* 1617 *AddCh, v.* **leam.**

VICAR'S BROOK (6″) (Cam) is *Vicaryes Broke* 1480 *Cole* xli, *the Vicar's Brook* 1610 Bushell.

WELL CREEK (Ouse) is *Well Creek(e)* 1609 *AddCh,* 1672 *FenL. v.* Upwell and Outwell *infra* 288, 276 and Old Croft River *supra* 9.

THE WEST WATER (6″) (Nene) is (*ye*) *Westwater* 1589, 1621 *SewersD, the West Watter* 1618 *AddCh, the Old West Water*[1] 1750 *Elstobb,* "all along from Earith Bridge unto Benwicke" (1617 *SewersD*). This is the name given to the west branch of the Ouse. *Old* because decayed, the waters being turned along the Old West River *supra* 11 to the Cam.

GREAT and **LITTLE WILBRAHAM RIVERS** are so named in 1806 (*Map*). *v.* Wilbraham *infra* 137.

WISBECH CANAL is an 18th century straightening of the ancient course of the *Wellestream* between Outwell and Wisbech. It is *Wellestream* 1077 (1444) *Lewes*[2], *Wellestrem* 13th *ElyG*[3], 1285 Pat[4], c. 1350 *Thorney*[5], 1358 Pat[6], 1401 *Ct*[7], *Well Ee* 1340 Imb[8], *le Streme* 1503 *Ct*[7], *river of Elme* 1380 Imb[9], (*called Elme Ee*) 1438, 1580 ib., *ye litle river of Wisbeach al. Elm Eae* 1600 *AddCh, Well Ryver* 1609 *AddCh*[10]. *v.* Old Croft River *supra* 9 and **ēa.** It flows through Elm. *Little* in contrast to Wisbech Great River, the Nene below Guyhirn (*supra* 9). This is perhaps to be identified with *Welles(c)holl* 1380, 1438 *Sewers,*

---

[1] A continuation of Cranbrook Drain in Sutton.
[2] Walton (Nf).   [3] Upwell.
[4] Wisbech, Elm and Outwell.   [5] Flowed into the sea at Wisbech.
[6] Wisbech.   [7] Elm.
[8] Upwell or Outwell.
[9] At Friday Bridge. This points to a change of course. There is no bridge here now.   [10] Outwell.

1445 *Ct, the Sholle of Outwell* 1528 Imb, *Outwell Sholle* 1558 ib., which is mentioned in connexion with Elm, Needham and Friday Bridge. *s(c)holl* is 'shoal, shallow,' and may well have been given as a name to this stream after the main waters had been turned along Well Creek. *v.* Outwell and The Shoals *infra* 276, 175.

ROAD-NAMES

AKEMAN STREET is the name given on modern maps to the Roman road from Ermine Street at Arrington, through Cambridge to Ely and Denver (Nf), *v.* Fox 165–6. This name, which belongs properly only to a Roman road leading to *Acemannes-ceastre* or Bath (cf. PN BedsHu 1–2, PN Mx 10), has here been applied under late antiquarian influence to a Roman road which has nothing to do with Bath (cf. similar early and late application of the names Watling Street, Ermine Street, Icknield Street to roads to which the name does not properly belong, as noted in PN BedsHu 3–4, PN Wo 2, PN NRY 1).

South-west of Cambridge it passes through Orwell and forms the boundary between Little Eversden and Harlton. Here it seems to have been called *Coustratewey(e)* c. 1300 *WMP*[1], 1315–32 *Queens'*[1,2], *le Cowstreteweye* 1457 *Peterhouse*[3], *Cowstreet* 1600 *Depositions*[3]. In Eversden it seems also to have been named *Ferdmaneweye* (13th *Queens'*), i.e. 'soldiers' way,' from OE *fyrdman*. In Haslingfield it is *Stanewey* 1334 *Trinity*, cf. Via Devana *infra* 30 and Stanway (PN Ess 398) as applied to the Roman road from Colchester to London. It is probably to be identified with *le Portweye* c. 1250 *StJohn'sH*, frequently mentioned in Grantchester documents and with *Portweye* 1335 *Queens'*, similarly associated with Harlton. Cf. Portway *infra* 28. It may also be *Potteresweye* 1298 *Christ's et freq* in Harlton. In Barton and Haslingfield it is *Cambriggewey* 1480 AD iv, while in Cambridge itself it is *Granteseteweye* c. 1270 *StJohn's*, i.e. Grantchester-way. In Haslingfield and Harlton it is also referred to as *Heydo(w)n(e)wey(e)* 1312 *Queens'*, 1365 *St Catharine's*, *Heydonhillwey* 1506 ib. Cf. Hay Hill *infra* 77 and *v.* also *Clintway infra* 21.

North-east of Cambridge, in Chesterton and Impington, where the road forms the boundary between the two parishes, it is *Gretmereweye* c. 1260 *StJohn'sH*, *-weie* 13th *StJohn's* (cf. Mareway *infra* 27), *Bechestrete* c. 1250 *Cole* iv, 1493 *Rental*, *Bechestrate* 1303 *Bodl*, (le) *Becheweie* c. 1260 *StJohn's*, 1277 *Bodl*, c. 1480 *CTerr, via de Landbech'*,

---

[1] Little Eversden. [2] Harlton. [3] Orwell.

Landbecheweye 1335 *Bodl* because leading to Landbeach *infra* 179, and *Cretweye* 1228 Merton, *Gretweye* c. 1282 *CCC*, 'great' as distinct from *Smalewey* ib. Walker (CAPr xiv, 154) notes that a lane called *the Mere Way* continues the line of the Roman road to a point where it turns at right-angles into Landbeach village (*Mere Way* 1887 O.S.). In the neighbourhood of Stretham (*infra* 237) it was once called stræt and apparently also in Landbeach, where we have *le Stratefelde* 1374 *CCC*. In Ely, as in Haslingfield, it is *Stanweye* 1319 *ElyF*.

ALFORDWAY (lost) is *Alfordesweye* 14th *Ct* (Grantchester), *Alfurdes-weye* 1497 *StCatharine's* (Barton), *Alfordwey* 1521 AD iii (ib.). This is probably an alternative name for Bourn Way *infra* 20 in Grant-chester and Barton, and is named from a lost *Aldford*, 'the old ford' where the supposed Roman road from Red Cross crossed the Cam in Grantchester. *v.* eald, ford. To it probably led *Alforthpath* 1480 *Trinity*, from Haslingfield. The earthworks marked on the 6″ map near the probable site of the ford are perhaps to be associated with *Aldewerewelle* (sic) 1203 FF, *Aldewerkedic* 1225 *Lewes*, *Audrake Fenne* 1480 *Cole* xli (in Trumpington). 'The old fortification,' *v.* weorc and cf. Granham Manor Camp *infra* 88.

ALLSTREET (lost) is *Ealdestrate* c. 1260 *StJohn'sH*[1], *Aldestrate* 13th *Waltham*[2], 1328 *Queens'*[3], *-strete* 1279 RH[3], *le Oldestrete(wey)* 15th *Queens'*[4], *Allstreet shott* 1570 ib.[4] This must be the road from Stump Cross, at the junction of the boundaries of Great Chesterford (Ess) and Hinxton, to Worsted Lodge on the Via Devana, forming the boundary between Hinxton and Great Chesterford, Hinxton and Great Abington, Pampisford and Great Abington, as far as Bourn Bridge; then for a little it runs through Little Abington, finally becoming the boundary between Babraham and Little Abington. On the 6″ map it is called Icknield Way [Roman Road], a description with which Fox (166–7) agrees. 'The old Roman road,' *v.* eald, stræt. *v.* also Icknield Way *infra* 24.

ASHWELL STREET is *Eswelle strat(e)* t. Hy 2 (1508) Pat, c. 1300 *EgCh*, *Aswellestrate* 1274 Cl, with other references from documents relating to Steeple Morden, Litlington, Melbourn and Meldreth. Cf. also *Aswellewey* 13th *CaiCh*. In 1383 (ib.) the road in Steeple Morden is referred to simply as *le Strat*. This is a 'Hillside' Way. From Ashwell (Herts) to Ermine Street it is a straight road of Roman character.

---

[1] Babraham.   [2] Abington.   [3] Little Abington.   [4] Pampisford.

From Ermine Street to Melbourn its sinuous course, coinciding with parish boundaries, suggests pre-Roman origin (Fox 147–8). For its later course *v.* Street Way *infra* 30.

On a pre-enclosure map of Melbourn, this road, near Grinnel Hill, is *Deadman's Hill Road*, and thence to Heydon Ditch, *Potters Way*, cf. *Potteresweye* 1319 *Extent*, *Potters Way* 1650 *WMP*, *Pedlersway* (sic) 1650 ib. Cf. Potters Way *infra* 29. An alternative name is *Dedmanyswey* 1513 *Christ's* (Kneesworth), *Deadmanwaie* 1615 *WMP* (Melbourn). Cf. *Deadman's Way infra* 22. Cf. also *Maidenberiweye s.n.* Ridgeways *infra* 29. Where it crossed the low-lying land between Fulbourn Lodge and Shardlowe's Well, Ashwell Street was probably named *Eystrate* 1309 *Queens'*, *Eystret(e)wey(e)* 1385 ib., 1435 *MinAcct*, t. Hy 7 *Rental*, 1506 *StCatharine's* from *Eia* 13th *StJohn's*, *Eye* 1283 *Queens'*, 1494 *Rental*, *v.* ēg.

BABRAHAM ROAD (6″) branches off from the Via Devana near Fleam Dyke, on the boundary of Babraham near Copley Hill, and runs through Fulbourn. It is *Baberhamwey* 1210 *FF*, *Badberham Weye* 1279 *RH*, *Babraham weye* 1573 *Queens'*. *v.* Babraham *infra* 100.

BOURN WAY (*TA*[1]) is probably the name of the Red Cross-Grantchester road (cf. Wool Street *infra* 31) in its course from Grantchester to Caxton through Bourn. It is *Brun(n)eweie* c. 1250 *Clerkenwell*, *-wey(e)strate* 1296 *StCatharine's*, *-strete* 1347, 1397 *StJohn's*, *Brunstrate* 1457 ib., *Burneweystret(e)* 1475 *StCatharine's*, *Burneway* 1510 ib. in documents relating to Grantchester, Barton, Coton, Eversden and Caldecote. The evidence as to its history is conflicting, but "it formed, doubtless, a link in the chain of communications from Camulodunum to the Ermine Street, largely native in origin, used by the Romans in the years immediately following the Claudian conquest" (*v.* Fox 169–70). Hence probably the variation between **weg** and **strǣt**. *v.* Bourn *infra* 155.

BROADWAYS. We have many examples of 'broad way' as opposed to the narrow ways enumerated *s.n.* Smallways *infra* 29. The earliest example noted is *Bradeweye* (1219) in Cambridge. Others have been noted in Ashley, Barrington, Boxworth, Comberton, Foxton, Grantchester, Haslingfield, Litlington, Long Stanton, Melbourn, Meldreth, Orwell, Little Wilbraham. Some of the *ways* are doubtless to be identified with other roads dealt with under their individual names.

---

[1] Caldecote.

THE CAMBRIDGE-ST NEOTS ROAD, corresponding generally to a ridge-way from Eltisley to Madingley Hill (*v.* Fox 154), is *Rugweie* c. 1250 *StJohn'sH*[1], *Regweie* 13th *StJohn's*[1], *Rigweye* 1309 *CCC*[2]. *v.* Ridge-ways *infra* 29. It is also *via de Sanctho Neotho* 13th *StJohn's*[3], *Seynt Neteweye* 1336 ib.[3], *Seynt Nedweye* 1342 ib.[3], *Sendnedwey* 1396 *CCC*[3], *Saynt Nideway* 1510 *StCatharine's*[4], *St Noots way* 1607 *Terr*[4]; *Cante-brugestrate* c. 1150 *StNeot*, *Cambrig(g)ewey* 1497 *StCatharine's*[5], *Madingelestret* 1205 *FF*[5], -*strate* c. 1285 *StCatharine's*[6]; *Coteweie* c. 1250 *StJohn'sH*[3], *le Cotenweye* 1293 *StJohn's*[3]; *Crokestoneweye* 1335 *Pembroke*. Cf. also *Stratfurlong* 1384 ib.[7]

CAMGATE WAY (lost) is *Camegate* c. 1235 Bott, *Camgateweye* 1476 *CCC* (in Little Wilbraham), *Kantwey* t. Hy 6 *Rental* (in Bottisham). In Little Wilbraham we also have *Kambesfeld* 1234 Bott, *Cambelfeld* (sic) c. 1235 ib., *Cambusfeld* 1379 *Rental*, *Cambeffeld* 1408 *Ct*, *Came-dene* 1247 *FF*, *Camdenefeld* 1363 *Cole* xviii, *Cambedene* c. 1406 Bott, *Cammdene* 1481 *CCC*, *Camberwe* 1352 *Ct*, *le Compysfeld* 1471 *Ct*, *Combeffelde* 1482 *CCC*, *Combysfelde* 1483 ib., *Comesfelde* 1516 ib., *Combesfeilde* 1667 ib. This is probably a name for the Icknield Way. Its course here is not altogether certain. The present road runs through Little Wilbraham, close to and parallel to the boundary of Bottisham, passing through Six Mile Bottom and climbing Bungalow Hill, about a mile from the higher Cambridge Hill in Burrough Green. It seems possible that *Camberwe* was once the name of Cambridge Hill, and *Camdene* of Six Mile Bottom. The first element in all these names was probably **camb**, 'crest, ridge.' DEPN notes the presence of this element in Cam Fell (Y), Cambo (PN NbDu 38), Cams Head, Cam, Cold Cam, Cambs Ho (PN NRY 194, 196, 258), Combridge (St), Combs (Db) and Combs (PN Sf 121). For *gate*, *v.* **gata**.

CLINTWAY (lost) is *le Clintewaye* 1272 *StJohn's*, *Clynthweye* 1353 ib., *Clyntway* 1510 *StCatharine's*. References to this road are found in documents relating to Grantchester, Barton and Coton. In the latter parish there are still fields named Clint Hill and Clint Field (*Clintfeud* 1235 *FF*) north-west of Barton Fm. In Grantchester too we have *Clint* c. 1250 *StJohn'sH*, *le Clintefeld* 1272 *StJohn's*, *le Clentfeld* 1353 ib. As the name occurs in the three parishes and on both sides of the road, this was probably an alternative name for Akeman Street *supra* 18. There can be no doubt that the first element is the Scandinavian

---

[1] Bourn.   [2] Madingley.   [3] Cambridge.   [4] Coton.
[5] Barton.   [6] Comberton.   [7] Eltisley.

loan-word *clint*, 'hill' (cf. Dan *klint*, OSw *klinter*, 'hill'), though its exact topographical reference is difficult to determine. The same element is found also in Madingley in *Clinthaueden(e)* c. 1250 *StJohn'sH*, 13th *StJohn's*, *Clenthauedon'* 1483 *CRent*. In this case the name presumably has reference to Madingley Hill itself.

DEADMAN'S WAY (lost) was part of a route from the forest land in the west of the county by way of Hardwick to the Cam at Grantchester, possibly a continuation of Hardwick Way *infra* 24. *v.* Fox 154, 169 and AnctC 49. It may have been named from a place in Grantchester, *Dedeman* 13th *StJohn's*, *Dedmanneslond* 14th *Ct*. Cf. *Deadman's Hill Road*, part of Ashwell Street in Melbourn (*supra* 20) and *Dedcherlway*, the name of the Street Way in Little Wilbraham *infra* 30. *v.* Addenda lix.

DOWNS TRACK (not named on map) in Ashley is *Dunewey* c. 1280–7 *Hosp*, *Doneweye* c. 1280 ib., *Downewey* c. 1290 ib. This runs across The Downs *infra* 364 and contrasts with *Deneweie infra* 26.

ELY WAY (6″) is *El(e)ywey(e)* 1378–1417 *Peterhouse*, 1488 *CaiCh*. This name survives in Haddenham. The road continues south as Sand Way (*infra* 29) to Aldreth Causeway and then as a driftway through Willingham, over Belsar's Hill, and as Cuckoo Lane forms the boundary between Westwick and Cottenham. Here it was *Elyweye* 1483 *CRent*, 1493 *Denny* (Cottenham), *Ely Way* 1656 *Terr* (Westwick). It continues through Histon and Impington to Cambridge. Cf. *Hystonway* t. Hy 3 Merton (Chesterton), *Cambrigwey* 1475 *StJohn's* (Impington). "This driftway was from Norman times onwards for 600 years the chief land route into Ely from the south" (cf. Fox 137, 141, 155) and may be prehistoric. Several references to *(H)elyweye* in Long Stanton (1319–90 *Pembroke*) suggest that there was a branch from Willingham, through Long Stanton, perhaps along Hatton's Road to the Via Devana and crossing this, through Dry Drayton to the Cambridge-St Neots road.

ERMINE STREET

(*to, æfter*) *Earninga stræte* 1012 (12th) Proc. Soc. Antiq. (NS) iii, 49[1]
Herningestrate c. 1150 *St Neot*[2], *-strete* 15th *CaiCh*[2]
Erningstret(e) a. 1152 *St Neot*[3], 12th HH, 13th RG, *Ernyng strate* c. 1300 Layer[3]
Aringestrate c. 1205 Wardon[4]

[1] Papworth. [2] Caxton.
[3] Wendy. [4] Arrington.

Arnygestrate t. Hy 3 HMC Rutland iv[1], *Arnyngstrete* 1285 *Ass*[2],
   1333 *Christ's*[3]
Arm'strate 1279 RH[4]
Armingstreet 1281 *Cole* xxxvi[5], *Armyngstret(e)* 1513 *Christ's*[3],
   Armin Street way 1695 SN
le Arnewey 14th *Wymond*[6]
Ermingest strete c. 1440 RG 172, *Ermingstrete* ib., -*streat* 1586,
   1594 Camden
Aryngtonwey 1513 *Christ's*[7], *Arnyngfordstreate, -ing-* 1567 *Ct*[8]

This name has been discussed in PN BedsHu 2–4, PN Herts 6.
The road is Roman and was so called because it passed through the
land of the *Earningas* who gave name also to Arrington, Armingford
Hundred and *Earningaford*, now Arrington Bridge (*infra* 69, 50, 70)
on its course from Royston to Papworth. It was probably also known
as *Potterestrate* c. 1260 *StJohn'sH*[1], *Potteresweye* t. Ed 1 *Christ's*[7],
le Potterstrate 1408 *Pembroke*[5], *Pottersway* 1669 *Christ's*[9]. Cf.
Potters Way *infra* 29.

FIELDEN WAY. We have one example in Ashley of the Fielden Ways
traversing feld or open country discussed in PN Wa 8–9, 15: *Fidene-
weye, (le) Feldewey* c. 1280 *Hosp*. Cf. also *Fylden streate* 1612 *Terr*
(in Ickleton). *filden* is an adjectival derivative of feld, 'open country.'

GRANSTRETE (lost)

   Grantestrate c. 1250 *StJohn'sH*[10], 13th *StJohn's*[10,11], 14th AD ii[10,12],
      1494, t. Ed 4 *Rental*[10,12]
   Grauntestrete 1396 *Queens'*[10]
   Granstrete 1399–1485 *Queens'*[10], 1509 *Ct*[10], -*waye* 1573 *Queens'*[10,13]
   Grandestrete 1417 *Queens'*[10]

These references are to a road in Fulbourn, near Copley Hill and
Shardelows Hyll, probably the hill on which is Hill Plantation between
Wool Street and Old Shardelowes *infra* 144. The name is often coupled
with *Horningstrate*, so that we have to deal with two different roads
in the same neighbourhood and there can be little doubt that *Grantestrate* was the name of the Roman road from Red Cross to Grantchester on the existence of which some doubt has been thrown. It

[1] Papworth.	[2] Stow Hundred.	[3] Kneesworth.
[4] Shingay.	[5] Caxton.	[6] Litlington.
[7] Whaddon.	[8] Bassingbourn.	[9] Bourn.
[10] Fulbourn.	[11] Coupled with *Horningstrate*.	
[12] Near Copley Hill.	[13] Near *Shardelows Hyll*.	

crossed the Granta at *Alford* and continued as *Alfordway* (*supra* 19) and Bourn Way (*supra* 20) to Bourn. 'The strǣt leading to the Granta' (*supra* 6). Cf. also Wool Street *infra* 31 and *v.* Fox 169–70.

GREENWAYS are numerous: *le Grenewey* 1474 *Pembroke* in Linton is the track marked on the 1″ map from Little Linton to Catley. Other examples are *le greneweye called Madyngleweye* 1432 *StJohn's* (Cambridge), *Graneweie* c. 1250 *StJohn'sH* (Caldecote), *-weye* c. 1250 *Trinity* (Barrington), 1395 *CartMisc* (Knapwell). Some twenty other examples have been noted, the earliest being *le Greneweye* 1232 *FF* in Swavesey.

HARDWICK WAY is *Herdewi(c)keweie* t. John Township, c. 1250 *StJohn'sH* (Cambridge), *Hardwicke waie* 1562 AD v (Barton). *v.* Hardwick *infra* 162. It is indicated on the 1836 O.S. map as a track branching from the Arrington Bridge-Cambridge road near Deadman's Hill in Barton and making for Hardwick (Fox 172).

HOLLOWAYS. We have several examples of this name for a road through a valley or hollow: *Holeweye* 1235 Ch (Soham), *Holwey* 1328 *Queens'* (Pampisford). The name was given to parts of the Icknield Way and *Portway infra* 25, 28. *v.* also Whole Way *infra* 31.

ICKNIELD WAY

Ichenild 12th HH, (*viam que dicitur*) *Ikenild(a)* t. Hy 2 (1508) Pat[1], c. 1250 *StJohn'sH* [2]

Hikenuldestrate c. 1225 *ElyF* [3], *Hykenildeweye* c. 1235 ib.[3], *Hikenilddisweye* 1279 RH[4]

Hykenhilte 1274 Cl[1], *Ikenilteweye* 1319 *Extent* [3]

Ykenildes Weye 1279 RH[5], *Ykenilde stret* c. 1330 RG, *Ykeneldes stret* c. 1400 ib., *le Ikenel(e)swey*, *Ikenelsey* 1474 *Rental* [6]

Icknell street 1610 *Cole* xix[7]

This prehistoric track crossed Cambridgeshire from Royston to Kentford. *v.* Fox 143–7, PN BedsHu xl, 4–5, PN Herts 6. The etymology of the name is obscure.

In Duxford it is *Wyt-*, *Witlisfordestrate* 1278, 1316 *CaiCh*, in Pampisford *Briggewey* 15th *Queens'*, *Witesfordbridgway* 1612 ib. and in Whittlesford *Breggecroswey* 1449 *Pembroke*, because leading to

---

[1] Steeple Morden.   [2] Fowlmere.   [3] Melbourn.
[4] Chippenham.   [5] Fulbourn.   [6] Newmarket.
[7] Royston (Herts).

Whittlesford Bridge. In Duxford it was also (*le*) *Dichweie* c. 1235–1316 *CaiCh* and in Whittlesford *Fossoway* (sic) 1449, 1504 *Pembroke*. *Fosseway* is presumably another rendering of *Dichweie*, with reference to the 'ditch' by the road, and reminiscent of the more famous Fosse Way. Cf. PN Wo 3, PN Wa 7, PN W 15, PN Nt 11. It is also named *Roystonwey(e)* 1385 *Peterhouse* (Melbourn), 1504 *Pembroke* (Whittlesford), 1483 *Rental* (Ickleton). Here it is also *Westway al. Roystonway* 1624 *Ct.* This is *Redgway formerly Westway* 1650 *WMP* (Melbourn), earlier *Rigweie* 1228 *FF.* In Melbourn the road to Royston is also called *Ferthyngplotwey* 1476 *St John's* and in Fowlmere, *Royston waie al. Shouldbrode waie* 1593 *Christ's.*

In Whittlesford and Duxford, where the way forms the boundary between the two parishes, it is *Thenestrate* (sic), *Yeuestrate* 1290 Barnwell[1], *Thefstrete* 1313 *CaiCh*[2], *Ewestrate* 1328 ib.[2], *Euestret(e)(wey)* 1449–1504 *Pembroke*[1], *Eustretewey al. voc. Londonwey* 1495 ib.[1], *Esttretwey* 1504 ib.[1], i.e. 'thieves' street' from OE *þeof.* Ermine Street is similarly called *Thevestrat* in Therfield (PN Herts 161). Loss of *Th-* in *Euestrete* is due to mis-division of *Thevestrete* as if for *the Euestrete*; cf. *The Edeway* for þēodweg (PN BedsHu 122, PN Herts 6). This way is also called *Londonwey* 1449 *Pembroke* in Whittlesford and 15th *Queens'* in Pampisford, and *London Way* 18th *Map* in Melbourn.

Where the road crosses Heydon Ditch it divides (*v.* Fox *loc. cit.*), one track forming the county boundary, passing south of Chrishall Grange, across the saddle of Pepperton Hill in Duxford, where it was probably *Rigweye* 1228 *FF*, and following the valley by Ickleton Granges to Ickleton and Stump Cross. Here it was probably *Holwey(e)* 1455 *Rental* and possibly also *Delwey* 1431 *Ct*, *Dealewaye* 1591 ib., *v.* dell. This route may also be identical with *Porteweye* 1455 *Rental.* In Duxford we have *Stocwey* c. 1280 *CaiCh* and in Ickleton *Stokeweye* 1455 *Rental, Stokkewye, Stokkenewey* 1483 ib. This must refer to a road through both parishes, perhaps to this particular route. OE *stoccen*, 'made of stocks,' possibly a road marked by stocks or made passable in the valley by the laying of tree-trunks. *v.* Addenda lx. There was a possible track branching off at Ickleton Granges to Ring Hill and the Essex Cam Valley. This was *Stretehallweye, Waldenweye* 1483 *Rental*, leading to Strethall and Saffron Walden (Ess), *v.* Fox 145, n. 2. The second branch crossed Thriplow Heath and joined the modern Royston-Whittlesford road south of Thriplow, forming the boundary between that parish and Duxford (ib. 145). It is

---

[1] Whittlesford. [2] Duxford.

probably *le Portweye* 1420 *St John's* (Thriplow), *Threploweweye* 1313
CaiCh, *Tryplouweye* 1328 ib. (Duxford). As this became, possibly, the
main route, it may also be *Romweye* 1387 *Walden* (Duxford) from OE
rūm, 'wide.' Cf. Romford (PN Ess 117). From Stump Cross to Wor-
stead Lodge, the road was Romanised. Here it was *Portestrete* c. 1210
HMC vi[1], *Portewey* 1232 FF[2], *Habitoneportweie* 1254 *St John's*[2],
i.e. Abington way. *v.* also *Allstreet supra* 19. Further east Fleam Dyke
was crossed near Mutlow Hill, and here the road forms the boundary
between West Wratting and Great Wilbraham. Here it was *the
Meereway* 1784 *CCC*, 'boundary way,' cf. Mareway *infra* 27. In
BCS 1305 in the bounds of Wratting it is called *stræt* pure and simple.
Continuing east, along the ridge to near New Wadloo Fm it was
probably *Regweye* c. 1250 *ElyM*, *Rugwey* 13th *CCC*, *Riggeweye* 1319
Extent (all in Wratting). Farther east, the course of the way is uncertain, but the occurrence of three distinct road-names running through
the parishes from here to the Suffolk boundary suggests the existence
of three more or less parallel routes, the exact course of which the
material is insufficient to trace (cf. Fox, p. 143, par. 3):

(i) *S(c)held(e)wey(e)*, -*weie* c. 1240–1449 *Clare*[3], 13th *Lewes*[4],
1337 *Clare*[5], 1341 *WMP*[6], *Shelwey(e)* 1472 *Clare*[3], 1483 *CRent*[6].
This is perhaps a compound of OE **sceldu*, 'shallowness,' if this ran
through lower ground, a contrast with *Riggeweye supra*.

(ii) *Retherewey* c. 1250 *ElyM*[3], *Retheresweye*, *Reyerisweye* c. 1250
Add[7], *Reþeresweye* c. 1270 *ElyM*[8], *Rytherweisende* 13th *CCC*[6],
(*viam regalem vocat'*) *Rechirwey* (sic) 1428 *Clare*[3]. 'Cattle road,'
v. hrȳðer and cf. *Coustrate supra* 18.

(iii) (*le*) *Hol(e)wey(e)*, -*wei* c. 1212 *Wardon*[3], 1323 *St John's*[4],
1330–1 *Ct*[9], 1337 *Clare*[5], 1491 *Pembroke*[10]. Cf. Whole Way *infra* 31.
With this, cf. *Deneweie* c. 1280 *Hosp*[11], *v.* denu. Here, too, may belong
Herweye c. 1300 ib.[11], 'army road,' *v.* here and also *Camgate Way
supra* 21.
Through these same parishes ran a trackway, Linton-Balsham-
Stetchworth, which was "probably part of a route to the north-east
from the Essex Cam Valley settlements at Chesterford and Saffron
Walden, duplicating the Icknield Way" (Fox 153). This seems to

---

[1] 'gate of *Wolvestrete* to *Portestrete*' near Coppelowe. [2] Babraham.
[3] Dullingham. [4] Weston Colville. [5] Burrough Green.
[6] West Wratting. [7] Exning (Sf). [8] Stetchworth.
[9] Woodditton. [10] Linton. [11] Ashley.

have been called Port Way, *Port(e)wey(e)* c. 1250 *ElyCh*[1], 1321–9 *St John's*[2], (-*done*) 1328–1401 *Ct*[3], *Westun'portweye* c. 1250 *ElyM*[1], *Porteweie* c. 1280 *Hosp*[4], *Portweyden'* 1240 *FF*[5]. In Balsham, Charterhouse Plantation was earlier *Portfield* Plantation, and an adjoining field was *Port Way Field* (1806 *Map*). *v.* Portways *infra* 28.

IRETON'S WAY is *Iretons Way* 1654 Moore. It was constructed by General Ireton during the Civil War to convey troops from Chatteris to Ely.

LONG ROAD (6″) is *Longwey* 1480 *CTerr*. This road runs south from Madingley in a straight line to Comberton. It may once have continued south through Barrington where we have *Longeweye* (13th *Chateriz*).

LUNWAY (lost) is *Lond(e)wey*, -*weie* t. Ed 1, 1334, 1359, 1449 *Christ's*, c. 1250, 1392 *Trinity*, *Lundwey(e)* c. 1250, 1512 ib., *Lowndwey* 1522 ib., *Lunway* 1593 *Christ's*, 1613 *HardwickeA*. The first reference is to the road in Whaddon, near Malton in Orwell, the rest are equally divided between Orwell and Barrington. They probably relate to a track running through these parishes, possibly towards the *weald* discussed *s.n.* Croydon Wilds *infra* 54. 'Wood, or possibly forest way,' deriving from the Scandinavian *lundr*, 'wood, forest.'

THE MAREWAY is *Mareweie* 1199 *FF*[6], *Meerwaye* 1600 *Depositions*, the *Mareway* 1836 *EnclA*[7]. 'Boundary way,' *v.* (ge)mære, weg. With very slight exceptions, it forms a parish boundary for over 10 miles from Ermine Street to Red Cross (Fox 151). The track, starting at Combe Grove Fm on Ermine Street, still survives as far as Thorn Hill; thence its alignment is marked by parish boundaries to Chapel Hill in Haslingfield (Fox 150). It is a true ridgeway and is *Regweye* c. 1300 *Trinity*[8], the *Rige way* 1593 *Christ's*[7], (*the*) *Ridgeway* 1612 *HardwickeA*[8]. It is also *Whytehill way* 1601 *Trinity*, as leading to Chapel Hill *infra* 78. *v.* also Fox 122, 150. Fox (151) suggests the possibility that a branch of this way, still locally called *Fordway*, led from near Money Hill (*infra* 79) to Harston Ford. This is perhaps the road referred to in *le Fordweyes* 1304 *StCatharine's*, 1317 *Ct* (in Barrington).

MEREWAYS, 'boundary roads,' *v.* (ge)mære, weg. The term *Mare Way*, sometimes used as an alternative name for an ancient road (cf. Akeman

---

[1] West Wratting.   [2] Weston Colville.   [3] Woodditton.
[4] Ashley.   [5] Cheveley.   [6] Wimpole.
[7] Orwell.   [8] Barrington.

Street and *s.n.* Icknield Way *supra* 18, 26), is not necessarily an indication of pre-Saxon antiquity. In the charters it is used of an occupation road on the edge of the ploughland, suggesting that the arable land had extended to the limits of the parish. Cf. Fox 152. We have references to Mereways in Foxton (*Marewye* 13th *Chateriz, the Mareweye* 1315 *Trinity, the Mereweye* 1336 ib.), Great Chishall (*Marwey* 1387 *Walden*), Bourn (*le meare way int' Caxton et Bourne* 1561 *Christ's*), Stapleford (*the Mereway* 1812 *EnclA*, between Stapleford and Great Shelford), Little Gransden (*the Meerway* 1813 *EnclA*, between Great and Little Gransden), Over (*Mareway* 1826 *CCC*), Comberton and Lolworth (*Mereway* c. 1840 *TA*). Cf. Stanton Mere Way *infra* 29.

OLD SUFFOLK ROAD (6″) is *Suffolk Road* c. 1825 O.S. It runs along the boundary between Ashley and Dalham in Suffolk.

PORT WAY (6″) seems to have been the name of an ancient trackway, possibly Roman, but more probably earlier, linking the Cam valley with Ermine Street by way of Hardwick (Fox 171–2, AnctC 21–2). It was probably a continuation of Whitwell Way, branching from Long Road a little south of that way. On the O.S. map the track ends near Hardwick Wood, pointing to Bourn Grange and Caxton. It is *Portweie* 1205 FF[1], c. 1250 *StJohn'sH*[2,3], *le Portweye* c. 1279 *StCatharine's*[4], 1480 *CTerr*[1]. *v.* AnctC 21–2.

PORTWAY (not on map). "An ancient road, doubtless pre-Roman, probably ran from Ermine Street at Royston through Melbourn and Harston to Trumpington. The existing main road (to Cambridge) which passes the Roman camp at Melbourn was there known as *the Portway*" (Fox 172) and in the parish was *Portway Close* c. 1840 *TA*. Earlier references are *Portwey(e)* 1373 *Trinity* (Barrington), (*versus Cantebrege*) c. 1300–15 ib. (Foxton), 1365–1433 *Ct* (Harston), *Portway* 18th *Map* (Melbourn). Near Grinnell Hill this was *Holloway* ib. Cf. Whole Way *infra* 31.

PORTWAYS. Portway is a very common road-name in Cambridgeshire, indicating a road which led to some town or **port**, here usually Cambridge itself. In addition to the examples of the name treated above, the name was also given to some part or other of Akeman Street, Icknield Way (*supra* 18, 24), Roman Way, Street Way and Via Devana (*infra* 29, 30). The road from Saffron Walden to Cambridge is

---

[1] Madingley.   [2] Toft.   [3] Bourn.   [4] Comberton.

referred to in *Porweie* 1219 *FF*, *Portweye* 13th *Jesus* (Great Shelford) and *Portwey* 1542 *WMP* (Sawston), and others leading to Cambridge in *Portwye* 1494 (Fulbourn) and *Portewey* 1476 *CaiCh* (Teversham), where there was also *Portweyefeld* 1346 ib.

POTTERS WAY. Parts of Akeman Street, Ashwell Street, Ermine Street *supra* 18, 19, 22, and Via Devana *infra* 30 were named Potters Way or Potter Street. Cf. also *Pottereswaye* 1230 *StNeot* which was, perhaps, a continuation of the Mareway westward into Gamlingay (*v.* Fox 151) and *Potteres weie* 13th *Waltham* in Shudy Camps.

RIDGEWAYS. We have reference to Ridgeways in Boxworth, Comberton, Grantchester, Harston, Kneesworth, Newton, Trumpington and Whaddon.

A ridgeway probably ran through Whaddon and Kneesworth on high ground in Kneesworth (*Maidenberell'* 1493 *Christ's*, i.e. Maidenburyhill) in the angle between Ermine Street and Ashwell Street and this latter is perhaps to be identified with *Maidenberiweye* (1513 ib.) leading to an otherwise unknown earthwork called *Maidenbury* on *Maidenburyhill*, wherever that was. *v.* Addenda lix.

Ridgeway was also used as a name for parts of Icknield Way, Mareway and the Cambridge-St Neots Road *supra* 25, 26, 27, 21.

ROMAN WAY forms the county boundary between Graveley and Offord Darcy (Hu) and must once have been named *Portway*. Cf. *Porteweyedole* 1398 *Ct* in Graveley and Portways *supra* 28.

SAND WAY (6") is *Sandweye* 1302 *MinAcct*, -*waye* 1518 *Peterhouse*. This is the name of part of Ely Way *supra* 22 in Haddenham.

SMALLWAYS are common. They are narrow (OE smæl) ways in contrast to the Broadways spoken of *supra* 20. One of the earliest examples is *Smalewey* (1210) in Fulbourn. Others are found in Little Abington, Ashley, Chesterton, Dullingham, Eversden, Haddenham, Linton, Litlington, Long Stanton, Melbourn, Swaffham Bulbeck and Prior, Trumpington, Weston Colville, West Wickham. This last is *Smaleweye al. Dygweye* 1408 *Queens'*, doubtless so named for *Dichweye* in reference to Fleam Dyke.

STANTON MERE WAY (6") in Long Stanton All Saints. Cf. *Marefurlang* 1228 *FF*, *Stantonmere* c. 1345 *Cole* xliv, *Stanton meare furlong* 1575 *Rental*. *v.* Mereways *supra* 27. The furlong was on the Willingham boundary.

STREET WAY is *Strateway* 1234 Bott, *Stretewey* t. Ric 2, t. Hy 6 *Rental*, 1459, 1470 *St John's*, 1467 *Ct*, 1483 *CCC*, *le Streytwey* 1451 *AddCh*, *Streetwayroad* 1784 *CCC*. The above references are to this road in Little Wilbraham and Bottisham. By it lies the well-known Anglo-Saxon cemetery of Little Wilbraham (Fox 260–2). Here the road is *Dedcherlway* c. 1274 Bott, cf. *le Dedcherlfeld of Little Wilburham* 1337 AD iv. The road is also called *Chalpitwey* (sic) 1391 *CartMisc* from Street Way Hill Chalk Pit. In Dullingham it is *Stanstrete* 13th ib. and *Hixningewey* c. 1250 *ElyM*, *Exnyngeweye* 13th *ElyF*, *Ixningpath* 1315 *Clare*, leading to Exning (Sf), and in Bottisham, *Portwey* c. 1450 Bott (cf. Portways *supra* 28) and *Newmarketway* 1391 *CartMisc*, leading to Newmarket. Fox treats this as a continuation of Ashwell Street (*supra* 19), though possibly mainly of local importance. It is a 'summer' or 'hillside' way, and "the name 'Street Way' may correctly record its type, that of a pre-Roman Way in places straightened and metalled by the Romans" (Fox 149–50). Cf. *Stretebrede* 1234 Bott, *le Stretedene* 1481 *CCC*, both in Little Wilbraham.

In Chippenham (cf. Fox 149) this is *Dychideweye* 13th *Hosp*, *le Dichweye* 1387 *Walden*, *Grenedichewey* 14th *Hosp*. Near this was *le Grenediche* 13th ib., noted also in Bottisham (1392 *Ct*). Here the road was named from some prominent 'ditch' on one side or both, similar to that which gave name to Fosse Way (PN Wa 7). Cf. also *Dechweye* 1352 *Ct* in Little Wilbraham. For similar names cf. also *s.n.* Icknield Way *supra* 25 and Wool Street *infra* 31.

VIA DEVANA is a modern name and is first recorded c. 1825 (O.S.). It was the name invented by Dr Mason, Woodwardian Professor of Geology 1734–62, for the Roman road which he conceived to run from Colchester through Haverhill (Sf) to Cambridge and Godmanchester (Hu), leading ultimately to Chester (*Deva*), v. CAPr xiv, 161 and Fox 168–70. The road to which he applied this name is mentioned in the bounds of Wratting, *andlang stræte* (974 BCS 1305). On the Gog-Magog Hills, near the place where it markedly changes direction, it was known as *Horningstrete* (possibly containing a word *horning* denoting a bend), near Vandlebury as *Wendelbiristrete*, and from Wormwood Hill, along the boundary of Little Abington, through Linton, past Worsted Lodge and through Horseheath, as Worsted Street or Wool Street, v. *infra* 31. In West Wickham it gave name to Streetly End *infra* 112.

From Cambridge to Huntingdon it is *Stanstræte* 1012 (12th) Proc.

Soc. Antiq. (NS) iii, 49 (near Fen Stanton, Hu), *Stonwey* 1467 *St John's* (Dry Drayton), cf. also *Staniewayes* (-*waies*) *end* 1582 *Magdalene*, *Stanwaye ende* 1617 *EgCh* (Long Stanton). It is also *Huntedon(e)stret(e)* 1251 Ch, 1348 *Pembroke*[1], *Hunteduneweie* c. 1260 *St John's H*[2], *Huntigdonestrate* 1317 *Bodl*[2], *Huntyngtonwey(e)* 1337 ib.[2], 1432 *Ct*[3], *Huntington way(e)* 1617 *EgCh*[1] and *Cambridge waye* 1595 ib. In Madingley and near Howhill Fm in Girton[4] it was *Potterestrate* c. 1250 *St John's H*, cf. Potters Way *supra* 29. In Oakington it is *Porteweye* 1391 Crowland and in Boxworth *Portheweie* c. 1260 *St John's H*, *v.* Portways *supra* 28.

WHOLE WAY (6″) is *Holeweye* c. 1252 *Trinity*[5], *le Holeweye* 1349 *Queens'*[5,6], *Hollewey* 1482 *Trinity*[6], *the hollowway* 1593 *Christ's*[7], *Hollewey* 1482 *Trinity*[6], *Holeway* 1612 *HardwickeA*[5]. This road, climbing steeply from Barrington, crosses the line of the Mare Way at right angles on Chapel Hill and leads to Harlton. On the Barrington side it passes through a distinct hollow formed by the slopes of Cracknow Hill and Wilsmere Down towards the road on each side. It also passes through a hollow on the Harlton side, though this is perhaps less marked. Aptly named 'the road through the hollow,' *v.* holh, weg.

WOODWAYS are frequent from *Wdeweia* c. 1250 *St John's H*. They have been noted in Barrington, Bottisham, Burwell, Comberton, Duxford, Eversden, Fordham, Foxton, Long Stanton, Melbourn, Meldreth, Pampisford, Stow cum Quy, the two Swaffhams, Tadlow, Teversham and Thriplow.

WOOL STREET

    Wluestret(e) 1207[8], 1210[9] FF, 1279 RH[8,10,11], -*strate* ib.[10], *Wholny-strete weye* 1317 *Queens'*[12]

    Woluestrate 1334 *ElyC*[9], 1363 *Clare*[11], -*weye* ib.[11]

    Wolvrestrate 14th *Cole* xxii[12]

    (*le*) *Wul(le)stre(e)te* 1363 *Clare*[11], 1496, t. Hy 7 *Rental*[9], -*weye* 1430, 1443 *Clare*[11], 1523 *Pembroke*[10]

    Wolmerystrete 1479 *Cole* xxii[12]

    Wolf(f)e-, *Wulfe-*, *Wuluestrete* 1494–6 *Rental*[9], *Woolffe streteway* 1573 *Queens'*[9]

---

[1] Long Stanton.   [2] Chesterton.   [3] Girton.
[4] Cf. *Howe opposite Poterestrate* 13th *St John's*.
[5] Barrington.   [6] Harlton.   [7] Orwell.   [8] Horseheath.
[9] Fulbourn.   [10] Linton.   [11] Little Abington.   [12] West Wickham.

Wolstret(t) 1510 *StCatharine's*[1], *-way* 1522 *Pembroke*[2], *Woolstreet-way* 1801 *EnclA*[3]

Olde roade waye, Olderoodswaye 1573 *Queens'*[1]

the old Roman road 1806[1], 1812 *EnclA*[4]

the Hills Road 1812 *EnclA*[4]

Worsted Street 1834 G

This is the name of the Via Devana (*supra* 30) as it passes along the boundary of or through Little Abington, Fulbourn, Linton, Horseheath and West Wickham. Apart from the forms *Wolvrestrate* and *Wolmerystrete*, neither original, and both belonging to West Wickham, this seems to be clearly 'wolves' street' or, possibly, '*Wulf(a)*'s street.' In West Wickham we have also a reference to *Wlmerysdych* (1337 *Cole* xxii). It is probably safer to take these as local names, '*Wulfmær*'s ditch and street.' In Fulbourn we also have *le Wolfheng'* t. Ed 4 *Rental, Woluesden'* 1510 *StCatharine's* and *Woolffenne* 1573 *Queens'*. These are late but they suggest that in this district wolves were once numerous. Cf. also *le Stretefurlong* 1398 *Peterhouse* (Cherry Hinton), *Wolstretfeeld* 1458 *Clare* (Little Abington) and *Wolstrettweyffelde* 1522 *Pembroke* (Linton). The road is also called Worsted Street, a corruption of Wool Street. The process of corruption as illustrated under Worsted Lodge *infra* 115 was probably [wulstri·t], [wu·stri·t], [wu·ste], [wustid].

In the neighbourhood of Vandlebury (*infra* 88) the road was called *Wendelbiristrete* c. 1225 *ElyM, viam de Wendelbir'* c. 1235 ib. Where the road, hitherto aligned directly on Cambridge, makes a marked change of direction, it was known in several documents relating to Fulbourn and one each to Great Shelford and Stapleford as *Horningestrate* c. 1250 *StJohn'sH*, (*le*) *Hornyngstrete* 1387 *AOMB*, 1494 *Rental, Hornyngstretewaye* 1573 *Queens', Horinckestrate* c. 1250 *StJohn'sH, Horn(y)strete* c. 1285, 1398 *Queens', Hornynggyswey, -is-* 1489 *Pembroke, Horningseywey* 1654 ib., *Hornseyway* 1700 ib. This must be from a lost OE *horning*, 'bend,' hence 'road with a bend in it,' cf. DEPN *s.n.* Horning (Nf), 'dwellers by the bend' in the Bure. In Linton the road is also *Ston(e)strett* 1522, 1523 *Pembroke*. In Balsham and West Wratting, near Oxcroft *infra* 122, it is *Oxecroftstrate* n.d. *WMP* (from an old Rental), and in Fulbourn, near Copley Hill *infra* 100, it is *Coppelweweye* 1360 *StJohn's. Horninggate* 1277 *Ely* in Balsham shows a substitution of ON *gata* (cf. *infra* 326) for OE

---

[1] Fulbourn.   [2] Linton.   [3] Balsham.   [4] Stapleford.

stræt. In Fulbourn we find *Grendychewey* 1496 *Rental* side by side with *le Grenedich* 1378 *Queens'*, *Granedyche* 1496 *Rental*. It may refer to this road, cf. *s.n.* Street Way *supra* 30. *v.* also *Alfordway*, Bourn Way and *Granstrete supra* 19, 20, 23. *v.* Addenda lix.

NAMES OF DYKES

BRAN or HEYDON DITCH is *Branedich* 1279 RH, *Brankediche* 1319 *Extent*, 1387 *Walden*, *Brangdyche* 1492 *St John's*, 1593 *Christ's*, *Brentditch* 1610 Camden, *Brangdich* 1637 *Terr*, *the Brane al. Braneditch* 1650 *WMP*, *Brand Ditch* 1821 Baker. Cf. Brand Ditch Field in Heydon, *Brundishfield* 1610 *Cole* v and *Brankedichfeld* 1387 *Walden* in Great Chishall.

BRENT DITCH is *Brundych* 1380 *Queens'*, *Roman Ditch* 1821 Baker. Cf. also *Brunkedichstrete* 1328 *Queens'*, *Brandychewey* 17th ib., *Brankedichfeld* 1359 *Clare*, *Brangdichefelde* 1536 *MinAcct* and *v.* Brent Ditch End *infra* 112. No satisfactory explanation of either of these names can be offered. The early forms forbid our associating them with the word *brant*, *brent*, meaning 'steep.'

CAR DYKE *al.* THE OLD TILLAGE (6″) is *Tillinge* 1235 *FF*, *Tyllinge* 1279 RH, *Tillyng* 1430 Crowland, *Tillage, Landbeach Tilling* 1861 Landb, *the Old Tillage* or *Twilade* 1863 AnctC. The Car Dyke was a broad and deep artificial cut, banked on either side, of Roman origin, and forming part of a canal system from Cambridge to Lincoln. Its course through Cambridgeshire was probably from the Cam near Waterbeach, through Cottenham to the Old West River, along this and the county boundary to Benwick, beyond which it is called Whittlesey Dike, King's Dike (or *Swerdesdelf*), King's Delph and Cnut's Dyke *infra*, 208, 260, 207, to Peterborough. *v.* Fox 179–80, CAPr xxxiii, 118–21, xxxv, 90–3. For the modern name, *v.* PN Nth 5. The above forms refer to the section in Waterbeach and Cottenham. The same name seems to have extended into Chatteris where we have *Tillinge* c. 1160 (1348) Pat and *Tyllinge(s)were* 1240, 1253 Rams, 'the fishing weir in *Tylling*,' *v.* wēr. This is probably a singular name in ing based on OE *till*, 'fixed point, station,' OHG, MHG *zil*, Ger *Ziel*, 'limit, point aimed at.' The OE adj. *til*, 'serviceable, good,' is from the same root, cf. also the OE verb *getillan*, 'to reach, extend,' which is used of the extent of Watling Street and of the Kingdom of Deira. *v.* NED *s.n.* till, v.². The dyke, which is for some distance a parish boundary, must have been a landmark of importance and was probably named from its length, 'the stretcher.' As excavation has shown that by the 7th century the Car Dyke at Waterbeach was impassable to water-traffic, it can scarcely be 'the serviceable, useful one.' Cf. *Malipassedych* in Waterbeach (1432 *Cole* xxxvi, f. 145 d) which Cole suggests is the Car Dyke, a French name identical with Malpas (Ch), 'ditch of difficult passage.'

THE DEVIL'S DYKE

- (i)   *dicum* (dat. pl.)[1] c. 925 ASC (Ā) *s.a.* 905, *le Dych*(*e*) 1336, 1450 *Ct*
- (ii)   *fossam de Reche* 12th LibEl, *Recheresdich* 1335 *Ct*, *Reach*(*e*) *dytch, ditch* 1591–1601 *Ct, Rech-dike al. Deuilsdike* 1594 Camden
- (iii)   *magnum fossatum* 13th *ElyCh et freq* to 1491 *Queens',* (*de Steuechwrth*) c. 1270 *ElyM,* (*apud Reche*) 1294 *Ct*
  le Micheldyche 1315 *Queens', le Mycheldych* 1350 *Ct*
- (iv)   *fossam Sancti Edmundi* 1354 Hyde, 14th Higden, 1574 Caius, *Seynt Edmond his diche, the dyche of Seynte Edmunde* 14th Trevisa, *martyred Edmonds Ditch* 1612 Drayton
- (v)   *Dæmonis fossam* 1574 Caius, (*The*) *Devil's ditch* 1604 *Atkyns,* 1695 SN, 1789 Camden

Like the Fleam Dyke, this was once called simply 'ditch' or 'great ditch,' *v.* dīc. Alternatively, it was named from Reach and Stetchworth *infra* 136, 119. *St Edmund's* as forming the boundary of the Liberty of St Edmund. According to tradition, the dyke was made by Canute "who was a most devout adorer of St Edmund the martyr; and, to make amends for his father Swane's horrid cruelty to the religious of St Edmundsbury, granted them vast privileges, as far as this very ditch," 1772 Camden (i, 390–1). This massive earthwork, the largest of the Cambridgeshire dikes, like others of the same name, is so called "quod dæmonis arte potius quam humana opera factum vulgus putat" (Caius 56). Another (and improbable) explanation is given by Camden, "The *Devils ditch* was probably so called by corruption from one Davilier[2], who held the manor of Broome in Suffolk, by the service of being conductor of the footmen of Norfolk and Suffolk, who were bound to serve the King in his Welsh wars, and their rendezvous was always to be at this ditch" (1789, ii, 141). In the seventeenth century it was "the Ditch that cuts New Market Plaine"

---

[1] With reference to The Devil's Dyke and Fleam Dyke.
[2] Cole (*Add* 5807, f. 138) gives the name as *Deveil.*

(1612 Drayton) and in the eighteenth was also "commonly called *Seven-mile-dike*, because it lies seven miles from Newmarket" (1772 Camden), more probably because seven and a half miles long.

FLEAM DYKE

(i) *dicum* (dat. pl.) c. 925 ASC (Ā) *s.a.* 905[1], *on þa...dic* 974 BCS 1305[2]

(ii) *Flemesdich* c. 1260 Bodl[3], *Flemsdike* 1594 Camden, *Fleames-dike* 1719 Nichols iii

Flemdich 1279 RH[3], 1346 Ipm[4], 1366 Works, *Flemdych(e)* 1415, 1443 CaiCh[5], (*banke*) 1573 Queens'[5], *Fleam Dyke or Balsham Ditch* c. 1825 O.S.

Flemigdich' 1279 RH[5]

Flendish t. Ed 3 *Cole* xxxvi

(iii) *magnum fosse* 13th *Jesus*[2], (*a*) *Magno Fossato* 1279 RH[5], *in magno fossato de magna Wylburgham* 1298 Ass[4]

le Micheldiche 1360 Queens'[5], *le Mechildiche* 1399 ib.[5], *Mekyl-dyche* t. Hy 7 Rental[5], *Mykyldyche* c. 1500 WMP

(iv) *fossatum de Balsham* 1285 Ass

Balsham ditch 1632 WMP, 1801 EnclA (Balsham), 1812 ib.[2]

This was at first called simply 'the ditch,' *v.* dīc, later sometimes 'the great ditch' (cf. The Devil's Dyke *supra* 34), Balsham Ditch from one of the parishes through which it runs, and High Ditch in Fen Ditton (*infra* 142). For further forms and the etymology *v.* Flendish Hundred *infra* 140, which owes its name to the dyke forming part of its northern boundary.

MISCELLANEOUS NAMES

GOG MAGOG HILLS is *amoenissima montana de Balsham* 12th HH, *Gogmagoghil(l)s* 1576 Saxton, 1586 Camden, 1591 *Terr*, *Hogmagogge Hill* 1667 Township, *Hogmagog al. Gogmagog Hills* 1709 *Cole* ix. There seems to be little doubt that, as T. C. Lethbridge has suggested (*The Times*, 12 June 1936), these hills owe their present name to the figure of Gogmagog cut in the downland turf, either inside Vandlebury Camp or on the hillside near it. Camden attributes the name to the scholars of the University (*studiosi vocant*), whilst Layer (110), c. 1635, attributes to them the actual cutting of "a high and

---

[1] *v. supra* 34 n. 1.   [2] West Wratting.   [3] Teversham.
[4] Great Wilbraham.   [5] Fulbourn.

mighty portraiture of a giant...within the said trench" which he had
seen himself. Apparently the figure was renewed from time to time,
for he concludes "but is now of late discontinued." William Cole,
the antiquary, also records that when he was a boy, about 1724, he
was taken with his brother and sisters by his father and mother to
see the figure of a giant carved in the turf. There is now no trace of
it either on the ground or from the air.

Cambridge

CAMBRIDGE[1]

(i) *Grantacaestir* c. 730 Bede, *Grantacester* c. 1000 OE Bede,
Grantaceaster 1170 LibEl
Granteceaster c. 1050 Guthlac, *Grantecestre* 12th HH, *Grante-
cester* 1170 LibEl

(ii) *grontabricc* c. 745 (9th) Felix, *Grontebrugae* 12th Ord
(*to*) *Grantanbrycge* c. 925 ASC (Ā) *s.a.* 921, c. 1000 ib. (B)
s.a. 875, c. 1100 ib. (D), c. 1150 ib. (E), -*bricge* c. 970 ASCh
(*to*) *Grantebrycge* c. 890 ASC (Ā) *s.a.* 875, c. 970 (12th) *LibEl*,
(*to*) *Grántebricge* c. 1050 ASC (C) *s.a.* 876, 1170 LibEl, -*brygge*
ib., -*brig(g)e* 1086 InqEl and so, with variant forms -*brecge*,
-*breg(ge)*, -*brug(g)ge*, -*brucge* to 1285 *Ass*, *Grantebrice* 1086
InqEl, *Græntebrigge* 1186 P
Grantabricge c. 1050 ASC (C) *s.a.* 1010, c. 1100 ib. (D), -*brycge*
c. 1200 ib. (E), *Grauntebryge* 1272 *Ass*
Grentebrige 1086 DB, *Grenteburga* 1086 ICC, *Grentebrigge*
1187 P
Cantebrigie, -*a* 1086 InqEl, *Cantebrigge* 1185 P with variants
-*briche*, -*brigia*, -*brig(g)(e)* -*brug(g)e*, -*brugia*, -*e*, -*breg(g)e*,
-*bregia* to *Cantebrigge* 1540 *Ct*, *Cantibridge* 1639 CHuAS iv,
with occasional initial *K-* as in *Kantebrig* 1196 FF
Cantabrigia, -*e* 1107 YCh *et freq* to 1605 CCh
Canteburge 1191 France, 1201 CCh, -*berg'* 1201 P, *Kanteberge*
1212 ANG
Crantebr' 1219 *FF*
Cauntebrig' 1230 P, with variant forms -*brig(g)e*, -*brigia*,
-*breg(g)e* to *Cauntebrugge* 1351 Pat, *Kauntebrigg* 1232 FF,
-*bregge* 1302 Ipm

[1] Coin forms include *Grant* 979–1100, *Grante*, *Granti* 1016–66.

Cantrebrigg 1322 Pat, *Cantelbrigg* 1390 FF, *Canterbrigge* 1454 Annals

Caumbrig(g)e 1348 Works (p), with variant -*brygge*, -*brege* to 1458 Paston, *Cawmbregge* 1406 Cl, *Kawmbrege* 1449 Paston

Cambrugge 1378 Cl, -*bregge* 1412 Pat, with variants -*brig(g)e*, -*bryg(g)e*, -*brydge*, -*bredge* to 1552 Pat, *Camberage* 1473 Paston, *Camebrygge* 1478 ib.

Caunbrigg(e) 1386 Cl (p), 1396 Pat, *Caundebrugg* 1405 ib., *Cawnbrygg* 1461 Paston

(iii) *Kair-Grant, id est, Granteceastria, quæ modo dicitur Cantebrigia (Grantebrigia)* 12th HH

Caergrant, id est, Cantebrugge 15th Higden, *Caergraunte, Cambrige, Caergrant þat is Cantebrigge* 15th Trevisa

The further forms now collected serve only to confirm Skeat's etymology. Originally 'the Roman fort on the Granta,' later 'the bridge over the Granta,' *v.* Granta *supra* 6, ceaster, brycg. *Caergrant* is a Welsh version of *Grantaceaster*, Brit *caer*, 'fort,' cf. Colchester (PN Ess 369). The normal development of *Grantaceaster* would be to *Gran(t)chester* (the modern village of this name has a different origin, *v. infra* 75). The site of a Norman castle and the centre of Norman administration in the county, the town was subject to strong Norman influence which affected the development of the name. Initial *Gr-* became *Cr-* and the *r* was lost through distant dissimilation in the combination *r--n--r* in *Crantebrigge*. Cf. IPN 114. The only serious criticism of Skeat's etymology, as originally put forward, was the absence of such forms as *Crantebr'* and the invariable initial *Gr-* in Grantchester[1]. The former, though still illustrated only by a solitary

---

[1] This was one of the points made by the late Master of Jesus in his *Dual Origin* (p. 31). The Gloucestershire Cam and Cambridge are certainly not identical in origin with the Cam of Cambridge (*v.* DEPN and RN 65), and Ethelwerd's *Cantbricge* equally certainly has no reference to Cambridge. Neither can a Cambridgeshire river *Cante* contain *ee*, 'water,' or be identical with Kennet. Gray's argument that *Cantebrig* is a name distinct from *Grantebrycge* and "was the name of a bridge which spanned a stream called Cante" cannot be maintained. "I think there is good reason for believing that the name Cantebrig was applied at a very early date to the quarter near the Cante Brig, or to the whole of over-bridge Cambridge", (ib. p. 32), i.e. to the district beyond the Great Bridge, round the Castle. This involves a distinct, geographical difficulty. According to this theory, *Grantebrycge*, the bridge over the Granta at the Great Bridge (*magnum pontem* 1419 *Magdalene*) is to be associated with *Grantacaestir*, the site of the castle. Between these ran the 'watercourse called Cambridge' (*v.* also CAPr ix, 61 *seq.*), earlier *Cantebrig*, 'the bridge over the *Cante*,' the name of a small artificial watercourse between the Great Bridge (*Grantebrigge*) and the Castle, and from this was named Cambridge, beyond the Granta. This watercourse was (*communem*) *cursum aque voc. Cambrigge*, -*brygge*

example, is now supported by *Cantrebrigg* and *Cantelbrigg* and by certain forms for Grantchester showing a similar development, *Crantesete*, *Crauncestre*, *Cantesete* and *Gantesete* and by *Graudene* for Croydon, *Cret(t)on* and *Crytton* for Girton, *Crethowe* for *Grethowe* (*infra* 177) and *Crendon for Grendon* (*infra* 87) and also *Camelinga*, etc. for Gamlingay *infra* 160. From *Cantebrigge* the development is normal, a simplification of the consonant-group *ntbr* to *nbr*, assimilation to *mbr*, a nasalising and a lengthening of the vowel. For -*burge* from -*bruge*, *v.* Introd. xxxvi.

THE WARDS. In DB there were ten wards, numbered one to ten. In the 14th and 15th centuries there were seven: WARD BEYOND THE BRIDGE (*Warda ultra Pontem* 1312 *SR*), BRIDGE WARD (*Bruggewarde* 1086 InqEl, *Warda citra Pontem* 1312 *SR*), HIGH WARD (*Hey(e)warde* ib., (*Ballivo*) *Alti Wardi* 1510 CBD. Cf. King's Parade *infra* 46), MARKET WARD (*Warda de foro* 1312 *SR*, (*Ballivo*) *Wardi Mercati* 1510 CBD), TRUMPINGTON or PREACHERS' WARD (*Trumpton' warde* 1298 *Ass*, *Warda Predicatorum* 1491 CBD. Cf. St Andrew's St *infra* 48), MILNE WARD (*Melnewarde* 1298 *Ass*, *Warda de Melnestrate* 1312 *SR*, *Melneward et Neunham* 1327 SR, *Mellewarde cum Newenham* 1336

1455–91 *Magdalene, the common watercorse callyd Cambridge* 1556, 1603 ib. Earlier it was *vetus fossatum, fossatum* (*domini*) *Regis* t. Ed 3 (1477), CAPr ix, 65, 1419–56 *Magdalene, Old Cantebrig* 1574 Caius, and was clearly, both from its description *fossatum* and from its shape, artificial. It is identical with *fossatum Cant'* (1279 RH) and was probably a ditch made in connexion with the old fortifications near the castle-site (cf. WC ii, 356). In the perambulation of the castle bounds c. 1278, the jurors went *per vetus fossatum* (CAPr ix, 66). Gray translates this 'through' the old ditch, but it is much more likely that the jurors went 'along' the old ditch near the castle, here the boundary between the castle precincts in Chesterton and the town of Cambridge. Hence, probably the name 'watercourse called Cambrigge.' "Cambridge Castle was built on ground taken from the Saxon town.... The ground taken from the borough was added to the King's Manor of Chesterton which adjoins. Thus the castle, although topographically in the borough, was legally in the county, outside the borough, in Chesterton" (CAPr xxvi, 69).

Stress has been laid on the passage "Paid for the quay where the stone lay near the bank of the Caunt (*juxta ripam Cant̄*)" (CAPr xxvi, 83). On p. 84, Dr Palmer gives a photograph of the relevant portion of the MS with the note "This plate was made because a word in the 5th line was read as *Cam̄* in 1896. But by the application of a weak solution of galls, the correct reading is shown to be *Cant̄* for Caunt." To the present writer, however, it seems clear that the mark of abbreviation is longer than that used to indicate the omission of an *n*. It stretches from the *a*, over the *u*, to the *t* and indicates '*ripam Caunt(ebrigge)*,' a common form of river-name. *Cant* or *Caunt*, with a similar mark of abbreviation, is commonly found for Cambridge, e.g. it is printed *Cant'* or *Caunt'* six times between 1260 and 1272 in the Close Rolls (pp. 60, 72, 76, 366, 536) with reference to the prison, the town and the county. Further, we may note that our earliest examples of *Cante* refer to the river between King's College and Trinity College, and can have no reference to the 'watercourse called Cambridge.'

SR. Cf. Queens' Lane *infra* 48) and BARNWELL WARD (*Bernewellewarde* 1336 *SR*, *v.* Barnwell *infra*).

BARNWELL

> *Beornewelle* 1060 (c. 1350) Thorpe
> *Bernewell(e)* 1060 (c. 1350) Thorpe *et freq* to 1470 *CRent*, (*juxta Cantebregiam*) 1330 *Cole* viii, *Bernwell(e)* 1204 Cur *et freq* to 1437 FF, (*Yates*) 1458 Ely, *Bernevell* 1272 Pat, *Ber(e)well* 1213 Rad, 1322 Pat (p)
> *Burnewell* 1235 Cl, 1495 Pat, *Borenewell* 1272 *Ass*, *Bornewell* 1298 ib.
> *Barnewell(e)* 1268 *Ass et freq* to 1594 AD vi, *Banewell* 1553 Pat

This, like Barnwell (PN Nth 178–9), is probably 'warriors' spring,' from OE *beorn* and wielle. '*Beorna*'s spring' is also possible, but the personal name is not well evidenced. As with the Northamptonshire place there was here too a tradition (Barnwell 41) that the name meant 'childrens' spring' from OE *bearn*, but the forms are against this. For other early examples of ME *ar* from OE *eor* cf. Hardwick *infra* 162. For *Yates*, *v. infra* 42.

BUTT GREEN (6″) is so named in 1849 (*Corporation Accts*). Cf. *the towne buttes* 1595 WC iii, 576. This was where the townspeople practised archery. The University butts were on *Butt Close*, now part of Clare and King's College grounds beyond the river (ib. i, 249).

CASTLE END is *ye Castle End* t. Ed 3 (1477) CAPr ix, *le Castelend* 1483 *CRent*, *v.* ende. CASTLE HILL is *le Castelhillys* ib., (*Montes vocatos*) *les Castell hylls* 1515 CBD, *Castle Hill* 1514 *StJohn's*. *Castle* Hill, from the artificial mound of the Norman castle. The plural in the early forms probably refers to the artificial works to the north-west which must once have been clearly visible. Cf. *Castell Hill* and *le Shirhill* c. 1550 Castle 33, the latter possibly owing its name to *the Shirehouse* 1660 ib. 34, the site of the lawcourts. *v.* Addenda lix.

In the last quarter of the 10th century, a great moot was held at Cambridge *subtus Thernigefeld prope Maidenburge* (12th LibEl). Cf. *Themaydenbury* 1453 Queens'. This must have reference to the fortifications on the Castle Hill, from OE *mægdena-burh*, 'the maidens' fort,' i.e. one which has not been captured, cf. Medbury (PN BedsHu 71), Maidenburgh St (PN Ess 371) and *Mayd(en)bury supra* 29. Castle End was called *the Borough* late in the 19th century and the dwellers there were nicknamed *The Borough Boys* (Atkinson 9).

Thernigefeld is OE *þyrning-feld*, 'open country by the place where thorn-bushes grow,' *v.* **feld** and cf. Thurning (PN Nth 221). In 1295 (Barnwell) we have reference to *parochia Omnium Sanctorum iuxta Barbekan* (or *ad Castrum*), with reference to a barbican between the present Castle St and Shelly Row (CAPr xxvi, 74, 79). It was near the walls of *Grantecester* in a place called *Ærmeswerch id est opus miseri* (12th LibEl), *v.l. Ermenswurche, Ermenswithe*. This is *Armeswerk* 1278 Barnwell. It was apparently on the bank of the river beneath the castle. The Ely chronicler's etymology from OE *earm*, 'poor, wretched' is doubtful. As to the real meaning, the variant forms in LibEl suggest that speculation is probably idle.

In the perambulation of the castle bounds c. 1278 (Barnwell) we also have a reference to *Aswykston*, cf. *Asewyston* 1260 Ass, *As(s)h-wyk(e)ston(e)* 1477 CAPr ix, c. 1480 *CTerr*. This was "by yᵉ hie crosse at yᵉ Castle end, south weste of yᵉ stone crosse," i.e. opposite the point where the Huntingdon Road is joined by Pleasant Row (anciently *Hare Hill*) where once "stood yᵉʳon a lyttle stomped crosse" (CAPr ix, 64–5). Cf. (*le*) *St(o)upendecr(o)uche* 1270 Cl, c. 1282 *CCC, le Stupyndecruche* c. 1270 *Cole* xxxi, *Stowpyngcruche* 14th *CCC*, i.e. 'stooping cross.' With such few and late forms it is dangerous to speculate on the meaning of *Aswykston*. It looks rather like a compound of **tūn** with some such personal name as *Æscwīg*, but the forms are difficult. The gallows (*le Galewes* 1340 *CCC*) used to stand amongst the trees at the base of the castle mound.

CHRIST'S PIECE (6″) is *Christ Coll. Peice* 1688 CPlans. This, with Parker St, was formerly *Clayangles* (Township 107). Cf. *Clayhangre* t. John ib., *Clayhang(e)les* t. Ed 1 *CCC*, 1312 AD ii, 1369 Rad, *Cleyanglys* t. Ric 2 *Rental*, c. 1450 Bott, *Clayhanghils* 1591 *Terr, Clay angles* or *Croft land* n.d. Rad 133. The second element, in spite of the initial *h*, is probably *anger, ' grass-land.'

COE FEN (6″) is *Koofen* 1491 Peterhouse, *Co(o)fen(ne)* 1501–61 CBD, *Cowfenne* 1591 *Terr, Choe fenn* 1688 CPlans, *Coe otherwise Cow Fen Leys* 1811 *CCC*. The first element is probably ME *co(o), ko(o)*, 'jackdaw' as in *coo-byrde*, 'monedula' in the Promptorium.

COLDHAM'S COMMON is *Coldham* 1310 Barnwell, *Coldhoom* 1397 *Cole* viii, *Coldhames* 1539 *MinAcct, Neathercoldhams* 1591 *Terr, Coldham's Common* 1877 Atkinson. 'Cold ham(m).'

EMPTY COMMON (6″) is *le Impeye* 1432 *MinAcct, Empty Common* 1877 Atkinson. 'Sapling enclosure' from ME *impe* and (ge)hæg. Cf.

Empty Field *infra* 365, Empty (PN Nth 210), Emply (PN Sr 226) and Imphy (PN Ess 244, 583).

FORDFIELD[1] (6″) is *Fordefeld* c. 1220 Rad, 1248 *FF*, *Fordefel* 1290 Barnwell, *le Forthefeld* 1334, 1376 *CCC*, *le Fortfeld* 1495 *Cole* xli, *Fourde Felde* 1553 Pat, *v.* ford, feld. So called from the ford by which the London road entered Cambridge.

Before the enclosure of the open fields at the beginning of the 19th century, the fields on the eastern side of the town were known collectively as Barnwell Field (*campis de Bernewelle* 1295 Barnwell) and those on the west as Cambridge Field (*campis Cantebrigie* ib.). Each was apparently cultivated on the usual three-field system, Barnwell Field being divided into Bradmore Field[2], Middle Field[3] and Ford Field (including the outlying Stourbridge Field), and Cambridge Field into Grithow Field[4], Middle Field[5] and Carme Field[6] (with which was reckoned Little Field[7]). *v.* Dual Origin 2–4 and Township 55.

GRAVEL HILL FM (6″). Cf. *le grauelpit* c. 1480 *CTerr*, *Gravel Hill* (*formerly St Giles rectory farm*) 1903 *Trinity*. The hill was once called *Grethowe*, cf. Howhill Fm *infra* 177. Near the farm is Trinity Conduit Head, *Branderusche* t. Hy 3 Rad, *Bradrusshe* 14th Bushell, *Bradrush* 1338 *StJohn's*. If the first form is reliable, this is 'burnt rushes,' *v.* brende; otherwise we have rysc used collectively, 'broad place covered with rushes.'

THE HITHES. Along the river, between the two bridges, were the principal hithes, named either from one-time owners or from the commodities landed there. Numerous narrow lanes led from the old Mill St (cf. Queens' Lane *infra* 48) and the High St (cf. King's Parade *infra* 46) down to the quays. *Cholleshethe* 1275 Bott, -*hithe*

[1] Preserved as the name of a house.

[2] *Brademere(feld)* 1248 *FF*, c. 1290 *CCC*, *Bradmorfeilde* 1591 *Terr*. 'Broad mere' as opposed to *Litlemere* t. Hy 3 Merton, *Lyttlemor'* 1279 RH. *v.* mere, mōr. The name survives in Bradmore St.

[3] *Middilfeld* 1296 Barnwell.

[4] *Grethofeld* 13th *StJohn's*, *Grythowefelde* 1453 ib. 'Gravel hill field,' *v.* Howhill Fm *infra* 177.

[5] *Middelfeld* 1248 *FF*.

[6] *le Carm(e)feld* 1312 AD ii, 1320 *CCC*, 1325 *Jesus*, 1346 AD i, 1358 *StJohn's*, *le Cramfeld* 1326 ElyC, *Carmesfeld* 1395 *StJohn's*, *Carnefeld*, *Caromfeld* 1405 ib. Cf. also *Karmeweye* 1293 ib., *Carme(s)dole* 1298 *Ass*, 1320 *CCC*. So called from the house of the Carmelites which stood at Newnham till 1290 (CPlans 54–5), ME, OFr *Carme*, 'a Carmelite,' first recorded c. 1380 (NED). *v.* dāl.

[7] *Litelfelde* c. 1480 *CTerr*. With this went (*le*) *Port(e)feld* 1299 *CCC*, 1320 *StJohn's*, *v.* port, 'town,' cf. Portmeadow in Oxford.

in Water Lane 1366 Rad, *Chollislane* 1296 Barnwell, *Cholleslane al. Whitefrere lane* 1445 Annals i (cf. Absalom *Cholle* a. 1275 Bott). For the white friars or Carmelites, cf. King's Lane *infra* 46; *Strawlane sive Salthithelane* 1455 CCh, *Strawylane* 1279 RH; *Blancwyneshithe* t. Hy 3 Rad; *Flexhethe* t. Ed 1 ib., *Flaxhythe* 1316 ib.; *Keverelleshythe* t. Ed 1 ib.; *le Cornheth* 1341 Pat, *venellam ad portas de Kyngeshall que uocat' Cornehithe* 1483 CRent (Kingshall Lane ran by King's Hall, now merged in Trinity College); *Damenic(h)oleshethe* 1279 RH, *-hithe* 1296 Barnwell. *v.* hȳð.

THE KING'S DITCH was deepened and improved by King John in 1215 and by Henry III in 1267. It marked the limit of 'the urban nucleus' on the south-east, east and north-east sides and was intended as an efficient protection against the freebooters of the Isle of Ely (*insulares*). For its course *v.* Atkinson 61 and Barnwell xxviii *seq.* It is *le Gynggesdich, le Kyngesdyche* c. 1280 CAS xliv, 12, 13, *ripa domini regis* 1291 St John's, *Fossa Regis* 1341 Pat. *King's* because it belonged to the seignory of the Crown and was not controlled by the townsmen (CPlans xxii). Two gates were constructed where the High St and Preachers' St crossed the ditch (Barnwell 122–3): Trumpington Gate (*portas de Trumpiton', Trumpitongate* 1279 RH) and Barnwell Gate (*janua de Burnewell* 1235 Cl, *portam de Bernewell* 1279 RH, *Bern(e)-wellgate* 1347 CBD, (*Yates*) 1458 Ely). *v.* Addenda lix.

MERTON HALL FM (6″). Cf. *curie Scolarium de Mertone* 1286 Barnwell, *terram de Merton'* 1322 Bodl, *Mertonhall* 1374 Merton, *terra clericorum de Mertona* c. 1480 CTerr, *Marton Hawle* 15th Merton, *Schola de Merton* t. Hy 8 Leland, *aedibus quae nomine Anaxagorae appellantur* 1568 Caius, *Domus Pythagorae* 1574 CPlans, *Pythagoras's Farm* t. Chas 1 Merton. So called from the lands here given by Walter de *Merton* to the Scholars of Merton College, Oxford, in 1270. The change to the "House of Anaxagoras" arose from what Professor Maitland has called "the oldest of all the inter-university sports," "the lying match" regarding the relative antiquity of the rival universities. In 1464 John Harrison claimed Anaxagoras as an alumnus of Cambridge and declared he was buried there. The change to the "House of Pythagoras" was due to the substitution of a more familiar name, *v.* further Merton 37–9.

MIDSUMMER COMMON is *Grenecroft* c. 1160 Rad, *Grynecroft* 1348 St John's, *Midsomergreen* 1501 CBD, *Greencrofte now called Midsomer*

Greene 1591 *Terr, Midsummer Common* 1877 Atkinson. *v.* **croft.**
Midsomer from the fair held at that time.

NEWNHAM

Ni(e)weham 1194–5 P, *Nyweham* 1272 *Ass*
Neu(e)ham, Newe- 1195 FF *et freq* to 1285 *Ass*
Newenham 1202 FF *et freq* to 1561 CBD, (*extra Cauntebr'*) 1272
    Ass, (*Elde-*) 1371 *CCC*, c. 1480 *CTerr*
Neuwenham 1267 Misc, 1279 RH, (*Hameletes*) 1312 *St John's*,
    Neunham 1272 *Ass*, 1299 *Hosp, Nuneham* 1260 Pat
Nywenham, -i- 1272 *Ass*, 1286 FF, 13th *St John's*
Nouham 13th *St John's*
'New hām,' or possibly 'hamm,' *v.* nīwe and Introd. xxxv.

STOURBRIDGE COMMON (6″)

Stiebrig' 1199 CurR
Steresbreg(g)(e) 1199 P *et freq* to c. 1480 *CTerr* with variant *Steris-*,
    -brig(g)(e), -brugg(e), -bregge, Sterresbrigge 1323 Sacr
Sturesbrig 13th *St John's*
Sterebrug(g) 1257 Cl, 1444 Pat, *-brigg(e)* 1328 Banco, 1419 Pat,
    (*green*) 1501 CBD, *-brege* 1482 Rad, *Sterbrighe* t. Ric 2 *CCC*,
    Sterbrigge 1455 *MinAcct, -field* 1501 CBD
Styres-, Stiresbridge 1450 Rad, *Stir(e)brigge* 1501 CBD, 1519 CCh,
    Stribyche Faire 1540 *MinAcct, Stirbitch Fair* 1764 *Cole* xx
Sturbrig(g)(e) 1535 VE, 1596 *Cole* xxxvii, *-bridge* 1553 Pat, *Stour-*
    bridge 1763 Bowen, (*al. Stirbridge*) 1817 CAPr xxviii

This name occurs again in Birdbrook (Ess), *Steresbreg'* 1293 *Ct*.
The first element is probably OE *stēor*, 'steer, ox,' hence 'steer's
bridge,' *v.* **brycg.** Cf. Stafford (PN Sx 208), *Stereford* 1327. The
modern spelling is due to a popular association of the name with that
of *the little river Sture* 1789 Camden[1], from which it was supposed to
take its name. Really *Sture* is an antiquarian back-formation from
the bridge-name.

An earlier name of the common was *Estenhal(e)* 1210 FF, t. Ed 1
Rad, 1383 Works, 1389 Pat. The second element is **healh,** which may
have reference to the projection of the parish of Cambridge between
Chesterton and Fen Ditton or to the flat, alluvial land in the bend of

---

[1] Blomefield had earlier rejected this etymology, "STERES-BRIGGE or STURBRIGE
does not take its Name from the Bridge over the River of that Name, but from the
Toll or Custom that was paid at it, for all *Steres* and young cattle that passed here"
(1751 Blomefield 171).

the Cam here. The latter is perhaps more probable and the whole name was originally *be ēastan hēale*, '(common) to the east of the healh.'

CRUSOE BRIDGE (6″) takes name from *Robinson Crusoe Island*, earlier *Swannesneste in Co(e)fen* 1501, 1587 CBD. JESUS GREEN is *Jesus Greene* 16th Dual Origin 22. SHEEP'S GREEN (6″) is *Shipp's Grene* 1636 CAPr xiv, *Sheeps Green* 1688 CPlans.

CAMBRIDGE STREET-NAMES

BENE'T ST is *vicus S. Benedicti* 1574 Caius, *St Bene't St* 1798 CPlans. Named from St Bene't's Church. BINBROOK LANE (now closed) perhaps continued Fisher's Lane along Binbrook which runs into the Cam at the end of Fisher's Lane (CBD i, 83, 134). Cf. *Binnebrok* t. John Township, c. 1270 *StJohn's*, c. 1282 *CCC*, *-broc* 1279 RH, *Bynnebroc* 1288 *StJohn's*, *Vynnebrok* 1313 *Cole* xii, *Bynbrok(feld)* 1329 *StJohn's*, *Benbrooke lane* 1561 CBD, '(land) enclosed by the brook,' *v.* bi(o)nnan, 'within,' brōc. From this the name was transferred to the stream, the Bin Brook *supra* 1. Cf. *Binnebroc* c. 1230 *Trinity* (Harston). BRIDGE ST is *Briggestrate* 1254 Cl, *-strete* 1381 Ass, *Bruggestrete* 1290 *StJohn's*, *Brechstrete* 1370 ib., *v.* brycg, strǣt. CHESTERTON LANE is *Chestretuneslan'* 1298 *Ass*, *Chesterton Lane* 1798 CPlans, leading to Chesterton. CHRIST'S LANE is so called in 1798 (CPlans), from Christ's College. Earlier it was *Hintuneweie* t. John Township, c. 1250 *StJohn'sH*, *lane leading to Hintone*, *Hinton wey*, *lane* t. Ed 2 Rad because leading to Cherry Hinton, *Rokis-*, *Rokeslane* t. Ed 1–2, 1368 ib., *Hangmanneslane* 1371, 1372 ib. *Rokes-lane* was said to mean 'rogues' lane,' an impossible derivation. It is more probably derived from some former land-owner here. It was later *St Nicholas's Lane* (from St Nicholas Hostel), *Emmanuel Back Lane* and *George St* (CAS xlvii, 15). COLDHAMS LANE is *Coldhamlane* 1386 *CCC*. *v.* Coldham's Common *supra* 40. CORN EXCHANGE ST is *le Feireyerdlane* 1495 *Cole* xli, *Slaughterhouse lane* 1596 CAS xlvii, 1798 CPlans. So called from the Hog and Horse Fair held on Hog (now St Andrew's) Hill on the site of the old Corn Exchange (CBD i, 136). DOLPHIN PASSAGE (from an inn), now ALL SAINTS' PASSAGE, is on the site of the Jewry, *vico Judeorum* (*qui descendit a via usque ad cimiterium Omnium Sanctorum*) t. Ed 1 Rad. All Saints' Church was *Omnium Sanctorum in Judaismo* 1428 FA, i.e. in the Jewry. The lane was also called *Pilateslane* t. Ed 1 Rad, *Pylateslane* 1450 ib., probably from Michael *Pilatt*, mayor of Cambridge in 1292 (*Cole* xii, 155). DOWNING ST was formerly Burbolt Lane, Dowdivers Lane, Langrith Lane, Hoghill Lane and Pembroke St (CAS xlvii, 16–17). Burbolt Lane is *Bird-bolt Lane* 1798 CPlans and was so named from an inn called *the Byrdbolte* 1547 *CCC*, *the Burbolt* 1577 CAS xlvii, which stood at the northern corner of St Andrew's St and Downing St. Cf. *Brydbolt or burdebolt* c. 1440 NED "a kind of blunt-headed arrow used for shooting birds." For the other names *v.* Pembroke St *infra* 47. Downing College Grounds are on the site of the former *Swinecroft*, *-y-* 1279 RH *et freq* to 1455 *MinAcct*, *Swinescroft* 1289 Rad, *Swenescroft* 1384 Pat, *le Sweyn Croft* 1450

St John's, Swynescroft al. Seynt Thomas Leys 1521 *CCC, (lees)* 1546 *MinAcct.*
v. **croft, læs.** This was near St Thomas's Hostel (CAS xliv, 51). DRUMMER ST
was formerly *Hinton Lane or the way to Barnwell Fields* (CAS xlvii). *v. supra* 41.
It takes its name from *Drusemere* c. 1248 Rad, *Drosemer* 1333 ib. The first
element is probably OE *drosn*, 'dregs, sediment, dirt.' Hence 'muddy pool,'
v. **mere.** Two ancient watercourses met here, v. Plan in Atkinson 408. For
the first element cf. Drascombe (PN D 432). EMMANUEL ST is *vico Fratrum
minorum* 1303 *Cole* xii, *Coulane* 1348 *CCC, Cowlane* 1490 CAS xlvii, *Blak
Fryers Lane* 1544 Annals i, *Emmanuel lane* 1634 ib., *Preachers' Lane or Black-
friars Lane* CAS xlvii, 15, from the *Priory of Fryers prechers commonly called
the blackfryers* 1583 Atkinson, on the site of which was built Emmanuel
College. In 1240 the Sheriff of Cambridgeshire was ordered to permit the
Friars Preachers of Cambridge to enclose the lane (*vicus*) which lay on the
south part next their church for the enlargement of their cemetery (Cl). Cf.
Regent St *infra* 48. FISHER'S LANE is *Fyssheris lane* 1473 Rad, *Ree or Fyshers
Lane* 1483 CBD, *le Ree lane* 1491 ib. Cf. Rhee *supra* 14. "So called from the
Rhea a ditch or stream which falls in the Ben brook (Bin Brook *supra* 1) now
called Fisher lane" (1604 CBD i, 134). FREE SCHOOL LANE is *Lorteburn(e)-
strate* 13th *St John's, -lane* 1279 RH, 1285 *St John's,* 1296 Barnwell, *Lorte-
burulan', Lorteborustrate* 1279 RH, *Lort(e)buroulane* 1297 *St John's, -boure-*
1318 *CCC, -b(o)urgh-* 1353 Pat, 1455 *MinAcct, -brogh-* 1455 ib., *Lortebur-
strate, -birn-, Lordesburstrate* 13th *St John's, Lourteboroulane* 1319 *Cole* xii,
-burgh- 1353 CGild, *Lurt(e)borowelane* 1319 *Cole* xii, *-burgh-* 1335 Cl, 1348,
1376 Pat, 1455 *Ct, Latbury Lane* 1347 *Cole* xxxvi, *Loteborou lane* 1353 CGild,
Luttburne Lane 1574 CPlans, *Lothburgh Lane* 1612 CAPr xxviii, *Free School
Lane* 1756 *Trinity.* 'Muddy stream,' ME *lort* and burna. Cf. PN Sr 4, PN
Herts 174, PN W 425, RN 259 and *Lurteborne* 1420 Cl (in Bristol). For inter-
change of *-burn* and *-burgh* cf. PN NbDu 270 and *infra* 53. GARRET HOSTEL
LANE. Cf. *Garit hostell* 1448 AD iv, *Garet hostell(e)* 1455 CCh, 1512 CBD,
Garrad Hostel 1503 CAPr xlix, *Gareth hostyll* 1519 ib., *pons Gererdi...a diui
Gererdi hospitio* 1574 Caius, *Garret(t) Hostle Green, Bridge* 1610 *Cole* xii,
(Hostel Lane) 1798 CPlans, *Gerrard hostle bridge* 18th CBD. "So called from
a watch tower, look out place or high window in the original building" (WC
ii, 404). This is a more likely explanation than that of Dr Caius, from a
hypothetical St Gerard. The hostel was incorporated in the foundation of
Trinity College. GONVILLE PLACE was *King's Lane in Middlefield* 1575
CAS xlvii, 16, *Gravel Pit Rd* 1806 ib. GREEN ST is so named in 1688
(CPlans). It was made in 1614 on the estate of Oliver *Green*, annalist of Gonville
and Caius College (ib. 146). GUILDHALL ST was formerly Butchery Row. Cf.
in Carnificio 1279 RH, *Bucheria* 1296 Barnwell, *Bocheria* 1335 *CCC, Bocher-
rowe* 1424 ib., *le Boucheryrowe* 1467 ib., *Butchery rowe* 1723 *St John's.*
HENNEY LANE (lost) is *Henneyestrete* 1329 *CCC, parvam venellam de Henneye*
1362 *Cole* iv. It ran from the river to High St, bounding Trinity Hall on the
north and passing through the present site of Gonville and Caius College.
It is named from *Heneye* c. 1227 Chateriz, 1342 *ElyF,* 1350 *ElyC, Henhaye*
1272 *Cole* xii, *Heneneye* 1340 *ElyF.* 'Island or low-lying land frequented by
wild-fowl,' v. **henn, ēg.** This was described in 1544 as "a filthy and neglected
piece of ground" (WC i, 212). The same piece of land seems to be called
Henabbay 1448 AD iv, *Henabbey* 1455 Pat. HILLS RD is so named in 1858

(*Map*) as leading to the Gog Magog Hills. *v.* St Andrew's St *infra* 48.
HOBSON ST is *Walleslane* 1382 *StJohn's*, 1574 CPlans, *Waleslane* 1425 *St-
John's, Walls Lane* 1688 CPlans. *v.* King St *infra*. *Hobson* from Thomas
Hobson, the Cambridge carrier (d. 1630). Cf. Hobson's Brook *supra* 7.
HUNTINGDON RD is *Huntingdonewey* c. 1282 CCC leading to Huntingdon.
The present road cuts through the old castle grounds, Castle St being partly
on the line of the castle moat. The old road ran round the castle by Shelly
Row. *v.* CAPr xxvi, 74, Castle 32. JESUS LANE is *venella Sancte Radegundis*
1296 Barnwell, *Radegundeslane* 1359 Rad, *Radegund(e)strete* 1328 *Jesus*, 1375
CCC, *Nunneslane* 1435 Rad, 1477 CCC, *Jesus Lane* 1501 CBD. So called
from the nuns of *St Rhadegund*. The site of the nunnery, on which now stands
Jesus College, was earlier *Eldestede* 1246–9 Rad, *Nuns' croft called Eldested-
croft* 1345 ib., *Nunnescroft* 1450 ib. *v.* eald, stede. KING'S LANE is *Kinges
Lane* 1591 *Terr*. Earlier, it is *Segrim(m)eslane* 1279 RH, 13th CCC, *-y-* 1347
Cole iii, *Plotislane* 1295 Barnwell, 1356 CCC, *Segrimeslane que nunc vocatur
Plotteslane* 1346 *Cole* xii, *Noteslane olim Ploteslane* 1397 CCC, *Ploteslane seu
Carmelitarum* 1574 Caius, *Plott and Nuts Lane* 1574 CPlans. *Carmelitarum*
from the House of the Carmelites who removed in 1292 to a site between the
river and the old Mill St (*v.* Queens' Lane *infra* 48), now part of Queens'
College. *Segrimes* from some unknown inhabitant bearing the Anglo-
Scandinavian name *Segrim*. See also *s.n.* Pembroke St *infra* 47. KING'S
PARADE, with Trinity St and St John's St, was *Magna strata* c. 1250 *StJohn'sH*,
(*in*) *alto vico* 1309 CCC, *Alta Strata* 1491 CBD, *via de heistrate* t. Ed 1 Rad,
Heyestrete 1366 Cl, *Highstrete* 1448 Pat, *Highe streate or highe warde streate*
1592 *StJohn's. v.* hēah, 'chief,' strēt. Now named from King's College.
This is also *highway of Hennel* 1362 Bott 286. *v. Henney Lane supra* 45.
KING ST is so named **in** 1798 (CPlans). Earlier it is *Felterestrete* 1199–1216
Rad (*bis*), where lived Ralf fitz Ralf *Filtarius* and where was 'land formerly
of William *Filtarius*' (ib.). Cf. also 'house of Ralf *le Feuterier*' ib. From
English *felter*, 'felt-maker' (from 1605 NED *s.v.*). Cf. Felter Lane (PN ERY
286). This was also *Walis lane* 1296 Barnwell, *a lane to Walesbrigge* 1363
StJohn's, Walyslane 1372, 1408 Rad, *Waleslane* 1377 CCC, (*brigge*) 1456 Rad,
1483 CBD, *Walleslane* 1450, 1462 Rad, 1501 CBD, 1528 CCC, *Wallyslane
brigge* 1472 Rad, *Walls lane* 1561 CBD, *Wall's-end-lane* 1634 CAS xlvii. Cf.
also Hobson St *supra* which ran by the King's Ditch, the boundary of
Cambridge. There was never any town wall here and the reference is to the
walls of the friary of St Francis, now Sidney Sussex College (Memorials iii,
380). LADY MARGARET RD is part of the old Barton Rd which began at
Ashwyke Stone (*supra* 40) near the Castle, crossed the University Rifle Range
and joined the present Barton Rd at Barton Cross (Dual Origin 20, CPlans
59). It is *Bertoneweye* 1299 Rad, 1320 *StJohn's, Grythowwey* c. 1480 *CTerr*.
Cf. Howhill Fm *infra* 177. The Barton Rd from Newnham by Caius Cricket
Ground is *Eldenewenhamweye* 1371 CCC. LENSFIELD RD is *Deepway* 1667
Township. "When the watercourse, known as the New River, was formed,
and a 'cut' was made for the conduit-head along the Deepway..., the lane
obtained the name of *Conduit Road*" (CAS xlvii, 16). *v.* Addenda lix. LITTLE
ST MARY'S LANE is *vici* (gen.) *S. Mariae minoris in suburbio* 1574 Caius,
Little St Mary's Lane 1798 CPlans. MAIDS' CAUSEWAY is *Barnwell
cawsey* 1574 CPlans, *the Maids' Causey* 1634 Bushell. Said to be so called

from almshouses founded in 1647 for two widows and four maids (CPlans 148). MARKET HILL. Cf. (in) foro (Cantebrigie) t. Hy 3 CCC, le Marketstede 1353 ib., le Marketplace 1356 ib., Market hill 1520 StJohn's, v. stede. The meaning of hill here and in Peas Hill, has given rise to much discussion, e.g. "In Cambridge, only the Castle Hill is a hill in the usual sense of the word; elsewhere a hill means an open space amongst the houses such as would be called, in other towns, a place or square" (Bushell 2). The truth is that both Market Hill and Peas Hill were formerly at a much higher level above the river than they are to-day and were "once veritable eminences above the marsh" (Gray, Town of Cambridge 8). "For four centuries and longer Cambridge has been steadily raising the level of the grounds on the western side of the river....It was going on in 1475, when the town covenanted with Queens' College to be allowed to deposit rubbish in the space between the College grove and the road leading to Newnham." And it was still going on at the end of the 19th century, v. Dual Origin 19. MARKET ST is Cordewanaria 1322 StJohn's, Cordewanerrowe 1348 CCC, Cordweiner Row 1561 CBD, Shoo-maker lane 1574 CPlans, Shoemaker Row 1798 ib. The cordwainers were workers in Cordovan leather (cf. NED). MILL LANE is so named in 1798 (CPlans). It led to the King's Mill. NORTHAMPTON ST is so named in 1837 (CAPr xv). Earlier it was Merton Hall Lane 1357 Rad, 1465 Merton, Mertone-lane 1431 ElyCh (v. Merton Hall Fm supra 42) and Bell Lane 1742 Merton, so called from the Bell Inn. PARK ST olim Garlic Fair Lane (Rad 50) was named from the garlicke fayre closse 1578 Rad. Cf. Feyregates 1450 ib., Garlic Fair Gate 1803 ib. The Garlic Fair, granted to the nuns of St Rhadegund by Henry VI, was held in Jesus Lane (Rad 51). PEAS HILL. Cf. Pesemarket 1485 CCC, le Peasemarket Hyll 1570 ib. For Hyll, v. Market Hill supra. PEM-BROKE ST (Pembroke Lane 1798 CPlans), with Downing St supra 44, was anciently Langrith lane or Dowdiver lane (CAPr xxii, 56). The first is Land-grytheslane 1279 RH, Lankrichlane 1455 Ct, Langer lane 1539 CAS xlvii, 37, Langrith lane 1591 Terr. Maitland explained this as a compound of OE land and griÐ, 'peace, truce, protection.' "Is not this the limit of the ordinary land-peace? Within the ditch the stricter burhgriÐ reigns" (Township 101). Such a street-name is somewhat doubtful and land here may be a corruption of lang (cf. Landwade infra 194). The King's Ditch, here running along a depression in the centre of the Intermediate Terrace gravels, may well have followed in part the course of a natural stream, 'the long stream' (v. lang, riÐ) into which flowed the Lorteburne (v. Free School Lane supra 45). The second is Deudeneris lane 1296 Barnwell, Deus Deners lane t. Ed 2 Rad, Deudeuerslane 1455 Ct, Dowdewerslane 1473 CBD, Dowdiuerslane 1574 CPlans. Probably so called from the family of William Duzedeners (t. Ed 2 Rad), i.e. twelve pennies. If so, there must have been a stage in the history of the name when n was misread as u and later interpreted as standing for v. It was also called Plot and Nuts Lane (CAS xliv, 44), also an early name of King's Lane supra 46. It is Plotislane siue Motelane in 1574 (Caius). The Mote may be a piece of etymologising on Dr Caius' part, seeing that the lane was by the King's Ditch. Other references may be to either of these two lanes, Plotteslawe (sic) 1285 Ass, Ploteslane 1314–47 Cole xii, iii, Plotelane 1329 ib., xii, Pluteslane al. Nuttelane 1448 Pat. PETTY CURY is parva Cokeria 1330 CCC, le Petitecurye 1344 CGild, le Peticurie 1362 CCC, le Pety Cury

1364 *St John's*, *le Petycure* 1377 Fine, *le Petykeuri* 1451 Rad, *le Pedicury* 1483 *CRent*, *Petycurye Strete* 1552 Pat. "It is not improbable that part of the Market Hill was anciently called the Cury or Cooks' Row and that the street which is at a right angle with the Market Hill was called the *Petty* Cury to distinguish it from the other or greater Cury" (CAPr i, 63). OFr *curie*, 'kitchen,' cf. Curry (PN Ess 210). PLEASANT ROW is *Pleasance Row* 1883 AnctC and was anciently *Hare hill* 1477 CAPr ix. POUND HILL. Cf. *Pound Green* 1798 CPlans. QUEENS' LANE is so named ib. This, with Trinity Hall Lane, preserves part of the course of the old Mill Street which ran from the King's Mill and the Bishop's Mill at the south end of the town continuing north to a point near the site of the existing sun-dial in Trinity Great Court, where it joined a cross-street to High St. Cf. *Milnestrate* 1258 Barnwell, *in Vico Molendinorum* 1279 RH, *Melnestrete* 1285 FF, *Millestrete* 1318 CCC, *Mulnestret* 1344 Pat, *viam S(ancti) Iohannis, seu milstreat, seu viam molendinarium* 1574 Caius. *v.* myln. REGENT ST is *Preachers Streetway al. Hadstock Way* 1667 Township. *v.* St Andrew's St *infra*. ST ANDREW'S HILL is *le Feyreyerd* 1436 CCC, *Fayreyarde al. Pouchecrofte* 1553 Pat. Cf. Corn Exchange St and Market Hill *supra* 44, 47. ST ANDREW'S ST is so named in 1688 and 1798 (CPlans) from the church of St Andrew the Great. The main street from Magdalene College through the town is now called successively Magdalene St, Bridge St, Sidney St, St Andrew's St, Regent St and Hills Rd. This portion was earlier *Hadestocweye* 1288 *Jesus*, *Hodestokeweye* 1298 *Ass* because leading ultimately to Hadstock (Ess), (*a*) *vico Fratrum Predicatorum* 1349 *Cole* xii, *fryer prechers streate* 1539 CAS xlvii, *le Prechourstrete* 1361 *St John's*, *le Precherche Strete* 1450 Rad, *Preachers strete* 1546 *MinAcct*, (*Streate or Conduite Streate*) 1585 CCC from the Dominican Priory of the Friars Preachers which preceded Emmanuel College. Cf. Emmanuel St *supra* 45. For *Conduite*, *v.* Sidney St *infra* 49. ST BOTOLPH'S LANE is *Pen(n)yfarthing* 1561 CBD, (*lane*) 1574 Caius, CPlans, 1793 CCC, *Botolph Lane* 1798 CPlans. This was on the south of St Botolph's Hospice, "aedes quae ob paupertatem quae in eis sunt, peny farthing lane appellatur" (1574 Caius 120). The old name was clearly one of reproach and probably Dr Caius was right in his conjecture. Cf. Pennyfarthing St in Salisbury (PN W 21). ST JOHN'S ST is *St John's Lane* 1798 CPlans. SENATE HOUSE PASSAGE. The Schools, the centre of the life of the University, existed before any colleges had been founded. The buildings from the first occupied a small part of the present site of the Senate House. *School St* ran from the old Mill St (now Trinity Hall Lane), between the buildings of King's College and Gonville and Caius College, towards High St (King's Parade) as far as the Gate of Honour, corresponding to the western part of the present Senate House Passage. The eastern part was not made until about 1720. Opposite to the Gate of Honour at right angles to School St, ran *North School St*, at the end of which, near King's College Chapel, was the Grammar School or *Le Glommery* Hall. From here to High St, almost opposite St Mary's Passage, ran *East School St* or *St Mary's Lane* or *Glomery Lane* (*v.* Atkinson 270 seq.). SCHOOL ST (lost) is *vico scolarum* 1347 CCC, *le Scolelane* 1406 ib., *Schoolstrete* 1441 ib. GLOMERY LANE (lost) is *venella Glomerie* 1288 CCC, *vieo Glomere, Glomerielane* 1296 Barnwell, *Glomer lane seu vicus Glomer* 1574 Caius. This led to *Le Glomery Halle* or the *Gramerscole* (CAS xlix, 44), over which presided the *Magister Glomeriae* or the *Master in Gramer* (ib. 49, 51). As suggested by Skeat, this is ME *glomarye* or *glamarye*, a corruption of *gramarie* from AFr *glomerie, MedLat *glomeria*, 'grammar' (*v.* NED *s.v. glomery* and CAS xlix, 57). Across the site there also ran *Universitie Street* 1574 CPlans or *Regent Walke* 1647 *CCC*, made by Archbishop Parker in 1574 and leading to the Regent House. SHELLY ROW is so named in 1798 (CPlans). SIDNEY ST is so named in 1838 (CAPr xv) from Sidney Sussex College. Earlier it was *via del cundyt* 1293 *St John's*, *venellam que tendit v'sus le Cundyt* 1315 *Cole* ix, *Cundytstrete* 1366 *St John's*, *Condit-strete* 1366 Rad, *Conduit Strete* 1446 CAS xlix, *Condightstreet* 1530 *CCC*. Cf. *le Cunduith* 1296 Barnwell, *le Cundit* 1315 *Cole* xii, *le Conduyt* 1368 *St John's*. The earliest example of this word in NED is dated 1340. Probably so called from a pump in the wall of the Grey Friars. Their conduit was not made until 1327 (CPlans 109). *v.* also St Andrew's St *supra* 48. SILVER ST is *Smale-briggestrate* 1427 *St John's*, *-strete* 1441 *CCC*, *Sylver Street* 1615 Goodman. So called originally from *Smalebrigges* 1407 Pat, two bridges over the loop of the Cam. *Small* as contrasted with the Great Bridge over the Cam near Magdalene College. The origin of the many *Silver* streets alike in town and country has never been satisfactorily explained. Even in towns they can hardly always be places where silversmiths worked. TENNIS COURT RD is so named from a *tenyse court* mentioned in the Pembroke College Accounts of 1564 (CPlans 45). THOMPSON'S LANE is *Harstonys Lane* 1483 CBD, *Harle-ston(e) Lane* 1491–1524 ib., *Tompson's Lane* 1734 *St John's*, *Thompson's Lane* 1749 CBD. *Harstonys* from Henry de *Herlestone* (1279 RH) who may have come from Harston *infra* 84. *Thompson's* from the family of *Thompson* which lived here from 1520 to c. 1750 (Memorials iii, 270). TRINITY LANE is so named in 1798 (CPlans). Earlier it was *Findsiluerlane* 1296 Barnwell, 1574 CPlans, and *Seynt Micheleslane* 1322 *CCC*, *Michael lane* 1561 CBD, the latter from St Michael's Church and *Michael House*, the elder of the two colleges from which sprang Trinity College. TRUMPINGTON STREET is *Trumpi(n)tonestrate* c. 1200, 1295 *Peterhouse*, leading to Trumpington *infra* 91. WEST RD was earlier *Freshlakeweye* 1325 *Jesus*, *Frosshlakeweye* c. 1480 *CTerr*. Cf. *Froskelade* (*ad introitum ville de Neweham*) 1275 RH. 'The road to or by the frogs' stream,' *v.* lacu and cf. Freshwell (PN Ess 502). WHEELER ST is *Short Butcher Row* 1798 CPlans. Now named from one *Wheeler*, a basket-maker who lived here in the first half of the 19th century (Atkinson 71).

Vendors of different commodities congregated in different parts of the market: *le Chesmarketh* 1415 *CCC*, *foro bladi* t. Hy 3 ib. (i.e. the Cornmarket), *Lethermarket* 1362 *St John's*, *le Maltmarket* 1389 *CCC*, *Milkmarket* 1360 ib., *the Otemarket* 1431 Rad; workers and dealers lived in particular streets: *reugio* (*sic*) *apotechariorum* 1286 *CCC* (*apotecarie* is first recorded in NED in 1366), *Braderers Lane* 1561 CBD (ME *broderer* or *broiderer*, 'worker in embroidery'), *Brasyer Rowe* 1589 CCh (workers in brass), *the Botry rowe* 1501 CBD, *the Boterrowe* 1515 ib., *Comberyslane* 1319 *CCC*, *Kombereslane* 1349 ib., *Com(b)erelane* 1415 ib. (wool-combers, first recorded in NED in 1686), *Cooke Rowe* 1561 CBD, *Culteller'* 1297 *CCC*, *le Cotelerie* 1305 ib., *Cutelererowe* 1320 *St John's*, *Cultellerawe* 1341 ib., *le Cotiler Rowe* 1362 ib., *the Duddrye* 1561 CBD, *le Duddery* 1589 CCh ('place where woollen cloth or articles of clothing are sold,' cf. *dud*, *duddery* (NED)), *le Lorineres-rowe* 1299 *CCC* (i.e. where the makers of metal harness fittings lived),

Potteresrowe 1249 Rad, *Potterslane* 1341 *St John's*, *le Pulterirowe* 1388 *CCC*, *le Pultrye* 1412 ib., *Pewtry rowe* 1589 CCh, *Sherrers Row* 1512 CBD, *Sheerers lane* 1574 CPlans (shearers of woollen cloth), *Shethers lane* 1508 *CCC*, *Sheders lane*, "vicus qui olim artificum nomen refert qui vaginas conficiunt" 1574 Caius (sheath-makers), *le Smeremongger Rowe* 1330 *CCC* (sellers of grease, lard, tallow, etc., OE *smeoru*, 'fat'), *vicus fabrorum* 13th *St John'sH*, *Smitherowe*, -y- 1271–2 *CCC* (later *Wellelane* 1465 ib., *Well Lane* or *Pump Lane* leading to the market cross (1689 *St John's*) from a common pump in the middle of the street), *Soper lane al. Gouldsmiths Rowe* 1589 CCh.

Other unidentified street-names are *Ace(s)lane* 1310 Barnwell, 1312 AD ii; *Alwineslane* 1260 Ass, *Aylwyneslane* 1445 *CCC*; *Aungerys lane* 1311 Rad (Sampson *Aunger* 1451 ib.); *Byrchyn lane* 1561 CBD; *Bischoppesweye* 1298 *Ass*; *Crepers lane* 1574 Caius; *Daleweye* c. 1480 *CTerr*; *the eldernwey* t. Ric 2 *Rental*, v. ellern, 'alder'; *le Endelesweye* c. 1270 *St John's*, so called "because yt nether haeth beginnyng nor endynge" (Township 123), cf. Endless St in Salisbury (PN W 20). There was also an Endless Way in Ely; *Gattunrewe seu Gattonis vicus* 1574 Caius; *vicus qui dicitur Holm* c. 1250 *St John'sH*. Named from *Hulme* 1210 FF, *Holm* t. Ed 1 Rad, a marsh near the western boundary of Greencroft, v. holmr; *Hunylane* 1303 *CCC*, probably a muddy lane; *Horseweye* 1312 AD ii; *little lane* 1463 *CCC*; *Longcowelane* 1424 ib.; *le Longelane* 1368 *St John's*; *Londonweye* 1325 *Jesus*; *Newlane* 1574 Caius; *Processyonway* 1483 CCC. Cf. *infra* 349.

I. ARMINGFORD HUNDRED

Herningeford(a), -y- 1086 ICC, 1169–96 P, 1196 *ElyC*
Ærningef' 1086 InqEl
Erningford 1086 DB, 1199, 1200 P, *Ernyngfforde* 1436 *MinAcct*
Ernin(c)gaford 1086 InqEl, *Erningeford* ib., 1159–99 P, 1236 Barnwell, *Ernigeford'* 1172 P
Ermingeforde 1086 InqEl, *Ermingford'* 1200 P
Arningford(e), -y- 1218 *SR*, 1268 *Ass et passim* to 1523 *SR*, *Arnygford* 1285 *Ass*
Eringford 1236 Barnwell, 1242 P, *Heringford* 1284 FA
Arneford 1260 Ass, *Arinford, Aryfford* 1272 *Ass*
Aringford(e) 1261 Cl, 1268–85 *Ass*, 1275 RH, -forth 1327 SR
Armingforth 1327 SR, *Armyngford* 1336 *SR*, 1482 Pat, 1553 EA viii, 1570 SR, -eforth 1428 FA
Harin(g)ford 1435 IpmR, t. Hy 6 *Cole* xxxvii, *Harnyngford* 1456 IpmR

'The ford of the *Earningas*, the people of *Earn(a)*' who gave name also to Ermine Street *supra* 22 and Arrington *infra* 69. The Hundred

is named from *Ærningaford* 970 (18th) BCS 1265, *Ærnengeford* 12th
LibEl, *Earningeford(e)* 970 (12th) *LibEl*, 12th *Libellus*, 1170 LibEl,
Earmingaford 970 BCS 1266, *LibEl*, *Earningaford* 970 ASCh, *Erningeford* c. 1050 (13th) KCD 907, c. 1060 *ElyM*, 12th LibEl. The ford
was probably where Ermine Street crosses the Cam, at the junction
of the boundaries of Arrington, Wimpole, Wendy and Whaddon (the
first two in Wetherley Hundred, the last two in Armingford), now
the site of Arrington Bridge *infra* 70. In 1224 (*FF*) we have a
reference to *campo de Erningeford* in Whaddon, and in 1272 (*Ass*) to
molendinum de Arneford. The fact that Arrington is not in Armingford
Hundred suggests that the name once covered a wider area than the
present hundred. TRE the Abbot of Ely held 2½ hides in Whaddon,
a sokeman of the Abbot 2 hides in Arrington, whilst under Meldreth
mention is made of the *soc of St Edeldrida*. In LibEl (III, 212)
Earmingaford is a vill, but its exact identification is not clear. The
hundred probably met at Mettle Hill in Meldreth *infra* 60 which lies
on the Meldreth-Kneesworth boundary. Cf. also *Mootelowfurlong*
1627 CAS xl, 332 (in Bassingbourn).

Abington Pigotts

ABINGTON PIGOTTS

    Abintona 1086 ICC, *-tone* 1086 DB, *-ton(e)*, *-y-* 1165–6 P, 1268–85
      Ass, (*de Longrond*) 1272 ib. *et freq* to 1352 Pat, *-don* 1339 *Ass*,
      1344 FF, (*by Bassingburn*) 1375 Cl, 1447 Pat
    Abbinton(a) 1167–1200 (*passim*) P, 1200 Cur, *Abbyndon* 1277 FF
    Albintona 1172 P, *Albyngton* 1298 *Ass*
    Abbingeton 1198, 1200 Cur, 1247 FineR, 1272 Cl, *-tun* 1217 Pat,
      Abbynggeton 1320 FF
    Abigetun 1198 FF, *Ab(b)igton* 1236 Barnwell, c. 1236, 1240
      Wymond, *Abyton* 1298 *Ass*, 1374 FF, *Abidon* 1327 *Ct*, *-ton* 1330
      ib.
    Abbengton' 1199 Cur, *Abbington(e)*, *-y-* 1273 Ipm *et freq* to 1428
      FA, (*juxta Royston, juxta villam de Cruce Roesie*) 1334 FF, *-don*
      1335 *Ass*
    Abinget' 1200 Cur, *-ton* 1202, 1218 FF, 1272, 1285 *Ass*, *-tun* 1218
      SR, *Abinggeton(e)*, *-y-* 1256 Barnwell, 1309 Ipm *et freq* to 1330
      ElyCouch
    Abington, *-y-* 1208 Cur *et freq* to 1551 Pat, (*Sancti Michaelis*) 1254
      Val, (*Pigots*) 1635 Cole xxxvii, (*Magna juxta Mordon*) 1387 *Elien*,
      (*juxta Lytlyngton*) 1457 FF, *Abynkton'* 1333 *Ass*

Habington(e), *-y-* 1236 Barnwell, 1268 *Ass*, (*juxta Shengaye*) 1553
  Pat, *-don* 1285 *Ass*, 1503 Ipm, *Habingeton(e)* 1273 Ipm
Abingdon(e), *-y-* 1285 *Ass et freq* to 1486 Pat

'*Abba*'s farm,' *v.* ingtūn. So also Great and Little Abington (*infra*
99) from which this is distinguished by reference to the names of
neighbouring parishes, Bassingbourn, Litlington, Guilden Morden,
Shingay and Royston (PN Herts 161–2). The church is dedicated
to *St Michael*. *Pigotts* from the family of John *Pykot* (1434 Pat) which
held the manor from c. 1427 to 1802 (Ely 151, L 79). The history of
Longrond, presumably a manorial addition, is unknown. In late
sources this is commonly called Abington *in the Clay* from the soil
which is chiefly clay and gault. Cf. *Le Clay* 1274 Cl (in Abington).

BIBLES GROVE[1] and MOYNE'S MANOR HO (site of) (both 6″) are probably to be associated with the families of Richard *le Byboys* (1274 Cl)
and Alexander *le Moyne* (1236 Barnwell).

BOY BRIDGE (6″) is *Boybridge* c. 1840 *TA*. Cf. *Boybregge s.n.* Boyton
(PN Ess 426) and Boy Bridge *infra* 358. Probably so called from its
users. DOWN HALL is *Dounhalle* 1392 *Elien*, *v.* dūn, heall. HOME FM
(6″). Cf. *Home Fd* c. 1840 *TA* and *infra* 353. MANOR FM is *Domus
Manerii vulgo the Manor House* 1635 *Cole* xxxvii. OAK GROVE (6″) is
so named c. 1840 *TA*.

Bassingbourn

BASSINGBOURN

Basingeburna 1086 ICC
Basingborne 1086 DB, *-b(o)urn(e)*, *-y-* 1237 Fees, 1443, 1482 Pat,
  1457 FF, *-burgh* t. Hy 2 Dugd iii, *Bas(s)i(n)gburg* 1125–35,
  1156–8 (1337) YCh, *Barsingburn'* 1185 RotDom
Bassingeb(o)urn(a), *-y-*, *-(e)* 1158 P *et freq* to 1344 Ch, *-ingge-* 1272
  Ass
Bassingburn(e), *-bo(u)rn(e)*, *-y-* 1218 Fees *et freq* to 1553 Pat,
  (*Wessm'*) 1558 Eg, *Bassigburn'* 1268 *Ass*, *Bassengburn* 1359 FF
Bassynburn 1379 Pat, *-borne* 1501 AD vi, *Bassenborne* 1630 Ely

Probably 'stream of the people of *Basa*,' *v.* inga, burna. For *Basa*
cf. OHG *Baso* and Basing (Ha), *æt Basengum* 871 ASC, *ad Basyngum*
945 BCS 803, Basingstoke (Ha), *Embasinga stoc* 990 KCD 673, Basford
(PN Nt 138), DB *Baseford*, Bassingfield (PN Nt 236), DB *Basingfelt*

---

[1] *Bible Grove* c. 1840 *TA*.

and Bassingham (L), DB *Basingeham*. *Wessm'* from St Peter's, *Westminster*, to whom Hy 7 granted lands here (L 89). Confusion of final **burh** and **burna** is fairly common.

BASSINGBOURN HALL (6″). Cf. *Hallewyke* 1436 *MinAcct*, *v.* wīc. BROOK BRIDGE (6″) is *Brok Bredg* 1622 Ely. BURY FM. Cf. *Aldbury* 1436 *MinAcct*, *the Bury* 1557 EA x, *v.* **burh** (manorial). JOHN O' GAUNT'S HO (6″). The market was confirmed by Edward III to John, duke of Brittany and afterwards to John of Gaunt (L 87). NORTH END is *le Northende* 1345 *CWool*. SHADBURY END is *Shedborough* 1518–29 ECP v, *Shedburgh* t. Ed 6 *Cole* xxxvii, *Shudboroughe (end)* c. 1640 *Layer*, *Shadbury End* c. 1825 O.S. Cf. *Shitborowe Streete* 1627 CAS xl. SOUTH END is *le Sowthende* 1567 *Ct*.

Croydon cum Clopton

CROYDON

    Crauedena 1086 ICC, *Crauden(e)* 1199 CurR *et freq* to 1457 FF, -*denn* 1199 CurR, -*dune* 1200 Cur

    Crauuedene 1086 DB, *Craw(e)den(e)* 1203 Cur *et freq* to 1541 *MinAcct*, -*don* 1303 Pat, 1381 Ass, 1559 *Rental*, *Crauendon(e)* 1324 *MinAcct*

    Crou(e)den(e), -*w*- 1195 P (p) *et freq* to 1362 Ipm, -*done* 1316 FA, *Crowedon* 1276 FF, 1514 EA vii

    Graudene 1377 Cl

    Croyden 1577 EA x, *(cum Clopton)* 1645 ib., *Croydon* 1668 *FF*

'Valley frequented by crows,' *v.* crāwe, denu. For *Graudene* cf. Cambridge *supra* 37. The name shows the same irregular development which we find in *Croyland* for Crowland (L).

CLOPTON

    Cloptune 1086 DB, -*tun* 1199 FF, 1218 *SR*, 1254 Val

    Cloptona 1086 ICC, -*ton(e)* 1196 Cur *et freq* to 1524 *MinAcct*, *(cum Esthattele)* 1285 *Ass*, *(cum Hattele)* 1316 FA, *(by Shingay)* 1470 Fenland iv, *Cloppet'* 1218 *SR*

    Clap(e)ton' 1272, 1285 *Ass*, *Clapton (Fm)* c. 1825 O.S.

    Clapham(gate) 1667 Borough, *(Farm)* 1821 Baker

Clapton Fm and the site of St Mary's Chapel (1886 O.S. 6″) are marked near Croydon Hill, the term **clopp(a)* being probably at one time applied to that hill. Hence 'hill-farm,' *v.* tūn, Studies[2] 136–9 and PN ERY xlvi.

CROYDON WILDS is (*in*) *Waldis de Craudenn* 1285 *Ass*, *Croyden Wilde* 1667 Borough, *Croydon Wold* 1760 EA xiii, *the Wyld* c. 1840 *TA*, *v.* **weald**. Cf. Hatley Wilds, Wild Barns and Wile(s) *infra* 56, 82, 359, in *Waldis de Brun(n)e* 13th *St John's*, n.d. *Cole* xxxvi (Bourn), *Woldeslande* t. Hy 1 Rams and *Grenewold* 1322 *Ct* (Elsworth), *Chakestunes-*, *Kakestunesweald* c. 1150 *StNeot*, *Caxtoneswald* c. 1180 ib., and *Berstunesw(e)ald* c. 1150 ib. (Caxton), *le Welde* 1384, 1500 *Pembroke* (Eltisley), *Burneweld* 1464 *Clare* (Caldecote), *Schortwalde* 14th *Queens'* (Eversden), and Dry Drayton *infra* 152, formerly *Walddraitton*. Here we have evidence for the use of *weald* for a stretch of high land on the clay from Croydon to Dry Drayton, extending across the border into Huntingdonshire, where we have Weald in Eynesbury Hardwicke (PN BedsHu 259), cf. *Wold infra* 246. For the phonology cf. Wild Fm (PN Herts 62) and *v.* Introd. xxvi–xxvii, xxxiv.

CHURCH FM (6″) and CROYDON HILL were the homes respectively of Simon de *Ecclesia* (1231 Rams) and Robert *atte Cherche* (1298 *Ass*) and of Stephanus de *la Hull'* (c. 1280 Wardon) and Hugo *atte Hill* (1347 *SR*).

ROUSES WOOD (6″) is *Rousers Wood* 1797 *Downing*, *Rowsey Wood* c. 1825 O.S. Cf. *Rowys* 1430 FF, *the Rowsys* 1445 Cl, *Rouse maner'* 1471 IpmR, *Wakefeld Rowses*, *Wakefeld and Rowsez* 1518–29 ECP. It is to be associated with the family of Simon Ruffus or *Rus* (1198 FF). *v.* Farrer 276.

GILRAGS WOOD (6″) is so named c. 1825 (O.S.). It is *Jilrags Wood* c. 1840 *TA*.

East Hatley and Hatley St George[1]

HATLEY

  Hateleia 1086 ICC, 1176 BM, *Hatelai* 1086 DB, *Hung'hatele* 1218 *SR*, *Est-* 1302 FA
  Atelai 1086 DB, *Attelee* 1198 Cur, *Atteleye* 1250 Fees, *Hungryattele* 1316 BM
  Etelaie 1086 InqEl (p)
  Hatteleia 1164–95 BM, *Esthatteleia* 1199 P, *-le* 1218 *SR*, *Hattel(e)* 1242 Fees *et freq* to 1405 Pat, (*de S'c'o Georgio*) 1279 RH, (*Hongry*) 1375 Ely, (*Hunger-*) 1429 Cl, *Underhatteley al. Hungrihatteley* 1456 Pat

---

[1] Hatley St George is in Longstow Hundred *infra* 163.

Hatle(e) 1272 *Ass*, 1346, 1428 FA, *Hangryhatle* 1426 Cl, *Undir-hatley* 1460 *Elien, Esthatley* 1552 Pat, *St George Hatley al. Ungrye Hatley* 1614 PCC, *Hungry Hatley al. St George Hatley* 1653 Moulton

Hungerhatton (sic) 1285 *Ass*

These two Cambridgeshire parishes must once have formed, with Cockayne Hatley in Bedfordshire, a single area. Earlier and better forms for the Bedfordshire name (PN BedsHu 105) suggest that the first element may have been a personal name **Hætta*, otherwise unknown, perhaps a pet-form of compound names in *Hæð-* or a derivative of OE *hætt*, 'hat.' It is just possible that the strong form **Hætt* is found in Hassall (Ch), *Eteshale* 1086 DB, *Hattesale* 13th BM, but this cannot be regarded as certain. The three Hatleys are close together on a piece of elevated ground which Ekwall (DEPN *s.nn.* Hatley and Hattingley) suggests may have been called **hætte*, from OE *hætt*, 'hat,' and compares Hatt (Ha), *Hatte* 1206 Cur, situated on Hatt Hill, and possibly Hattingley (Ha), *Hattingele* 1204 Cur. In a document relating to Gamlingay, which borders on Cockayne Hatley and Hatley St George, we have reference to *Hattelawa* (1235 *StNeot*), which might well be the actual hill from which the Hatleys took name. This element was certainly in use in Huntingdonshire, cf. *to þam hætte* (956 *Thorney*) in Farcet (Hu). In Little Gransden, too, we have *Brerehat* c. 1185 *StNeot*, whilst in 1302 (Pat) there lived in Shepreth or Foxton a certain Robert de *Hat*. These may be relevant, but cannot be regarded as certain examples, for *-hat* is a form sometimes found for *-hath*, 'heath,' cf. *Caldemowehat* and *Kaldemowehath* (1251 Rams) in Warboys (Hu) and Heath Plantation *infra* 191. Cf. also *Monekyspat* 13th *StJohn's* (Babraham), *Fredunepat* 13th *CaiCh* (Duxford), *Mydylpat* 14th *Wymond* (Litlington) and *Alfowespat* 14th *Queens'* (Haslingfeld), where *-pat* is for *-path*. Complete certainty is impossible. We may have here 'the hill and wood of **Hætta*' or 'the hill called **Hætte*' and 'the wood by **Hætte*,' v. hlāw, lēah. *East*, the most easterly of the three parishes, was also called *Castell*-Hatley from the *Castell* family (t. Hy 7 L 209). *Hungry* Hatley, probably so called because of its poor soil, owes its present attribute to the family of William de *Sancto Georgio* (1236 Barnwell). Cf. Hungry Bentley (Db) and Hungry Hatton (Sa). *Under-*, because Hatley St George is the lowest of the three Hatleys.

East Hatley

HATLEY WILDS is (*in*) *Weldis subtus boscum de Heyle* 1277 *Ely*, 14th *Cai*, *Hatley Wilds* c. 1825 O.S. *v.* **weald** and Croydon Wilds *supra* 54. It is near Hayley Wood *infra* 162.

BUFF WOOD, HOME FM (both 6″) and LONG LANE FM. Cf. *Buffs Wood*, *Home Pightle* and *Long Lane* c. 1840 *TA* and *v.* **home, pightel**.

Kneesworth

KNEESWORTH

> *Kneneswrde* c. 1216 *Lewes*, *Knenisword* 1272 *Ass*, *Knensworth* 1364 *Christ's*
> *Cnesworth*, *Gneswrth* c. 1218 *SR*
> *Kenesw(o)rth* 1235–85 *Ass*, 1425–56 IpmR, 1426 Cl, *Kensworth* 1400 IpmR
> *Kne(e)sw(o)rth(e)* 1236 Barnwell *et freq* to 1457 FF, -*wurth* 1260 Ass, *Kneseworth(e)* 1316 *Ass*, 1316, 1506 Pat, 1317–1454 *Christ's*, 1349 FF, *Knesseworth* 1398, 1500 *Christ's*, 1472 *Peterhouse*
> *Knethewrth*, *Knetswith* 1236 Barnwell
> *Kney(e)sw(o)rth(e)* 1268–72 *Ass*, 1549 Pat, 1554 EA ix
> *Knyneworth* 1272 *Ass*, *Knynesworthe* 1494 *Christ's* (quater)
> *Kynesworth* 1272 *Ass*
> *Knos(e)worth(e)* 1285 *Ass*, 1347 *SR*
> *Nesworth* 1696 Meldreth

The first element in this **worþ**-compound is, as usual, a personal name. The third series of forms suggests that the name has been compressed through loss of the vowel of the first syllable and that we have to do with a personal name in *Cēn-* or possibly in *Cyne-*, such as *Cēnðegn*, *Cēnwine* or similar compounds of *Cyne-*. For the loss of the first vowel cf. the history of Knayton (PN NRY 206), Kniveton (PN Db 152) and Kneeton (PN Nt 226–7) going back to such forms as *Cheniuetun* and containing the personal name *Cēngifu*.

MILL FM (6″). Cf. *Knesworth mill* t. Hy 3 Ipm.

Litlington

LITLINGTON

> *Lit(e)lingetona* 1086 ICC, *Litlingeton(e)* 1183–4 P, 1306 Ipm, *Lit(t)lington(e)*, -*yng-* 1187 P *et freq* to 1468 FF, (*cum Abingeton*)

1285 *Ass, Lytlington(e), -yng-* 1285 *Ass et freq* to 1542 *Ct,* (*juxta Bassyngbourn*) 1465 FF, *Litli(n)gtun(e)* c. 1250 SR, t. Hy 3 Rental, *Litthlington* 1272 *Ass, Lit(t)elington, -yng-* 1285 ib., 1386 Cl, 1441 Pat, *Lytyll-* 1434 ib., *Lyttel-* 1470 FF, *Lytelton* 1436 Pat, *Litteling(e)dene* 13th, 14th *Queens', Litlyngdene* 1324 ib.

Litlintona 1086 ICC, *-ton(a)* 1182–91 P, 1317 Cl, *-tune* 13th *Jesus, Lytlynton, Lit-* 1298 *Ass,* 1317 Cl

Litingtone, Lidtingtone (sic), *Lidlin(g)tone* 1086 DB, *Linglington* 1298 *Ass, Lynglyngton* 1299 QW, *Lythyngton* 1500 AD vi, *Lidlinton* 1626 *Eg, Lidlington* 1630 Ely

Letlingeton(e) c. 1185 *Wymond,* t. Ed 1 BM, *Letlington(e)* 1280 *Ct,* n.d. AD vi, *-yng-* 1366 *CaiCh*

Luttilington' 1263 Cl, *Lutlingeton* 13th AD i, *Lutlington(e), -yng-* 1263 Cl *et freq* to 1403 ib., *Luttel-* 1388 ib.

Lyllington 1570 SR, *Lylyngton* 1610 Speed

'The farm of the people of *Lȳtel(a),' v.* ingatūn and cf. Lillingstone and Littleworth (PN Bk 44, 88) and Lidlington (PN BedsHu 77–8).

CHARDLE DITCH (6″) is *Kadewellebroc, Chaldewellebroc* 13th *Jesus, le Chal(d)well, Cadwelbroke* 14th *Wymond, Chadwell Brooke* 1627 CAS xl. Near here lived Alan de *Caldewell* (1327 SR). 'Cold spring or stream,' *v.* cald, wielle and cf. Chadwell Heath and Chardwell (PN Ess 91, 517) and Cadwell (O), *Cadewelle* 1086 DB, *Kaldewelle* 1205 Cur, *Caudewell* 1206 ib., *Chadewelle* 1216 ClR.

LIMLOW HILL. Cf. *Limlowfeld* 14th *Wymond, Limbloe Hill* 1821 Baker, *Limlow or Limbury Hill* 1853 AnctC. Possibly 'lime-tree hill or barrow,' cf. Limberrow (PN Wo 215) and Limber (L), *Lindbeorhge* c. 1067 ASWills, *Linberga* 1086 DB, *Limbergia* 12th Danelaw. The late *Limbury* suggests the existence of an alternative name actually identical with these. *v.* lind, hlāw, beorh. The barrow here was destroyed in 1888 or 1892 (Fox 194, 329). Elsewhere in the parish we have *Twymelowe* 1339 *Deed.* 'Two barrows,' cf. Twemlow (Ch), *Tuamlawe* 13th BM.

THE BURY or D'OVESDALE MANOR (6″) and HUNTINGFIELD MANOR FM (6″) are *manor of Ovedale otherwise Dowdale* 1408 Cl, *de Ovedales al. Dovedales* 1635 *Cole* xxxvii, *Bury Fm* 1821 Baker, *v.* burh (manorial) and *terra de Huntyngfeld, -fyld* 14th *Wymond, Huntyngfeldes manoir* 1411 Cl, *manor of Lytlington al. Huntyngfeldes* 1547 Pat. Cf. also *molend' Pet' Douedale* 1336 *Ct.* They are to be associated with the families of John *de Uvedale al. de Ovedale* (1304 FF, 1321 Ipm) and Rogerus de *Huntingefeld* (1242 Fees).

HILL FM (6″). Cf. *Hellecroft* 13th AD i. MALTING FM (6″). Cf. *Malting Grove* c. 1840 *TA*.

Melbourn

MELBOURN

> *Meldeburna* 970 BCS 1266, 1267, (18th) ib. 1265, 1086 ICC, InqEl, (*æt*) (*M*)*eldeburnan* c. 975 ASCh, *Meldeburne* c. 1050 (13th) KCD 907 *et freq* to 1434 Pat, -*bo*(*u*)*rn*(*e*) 1232 *ElyC et freq* to 1392 Pat, *Meldb*(*o*)*urn*(*a*) 1139 *ElyD*, 1342 FF, *Melteborne* 1401 *ElyCh*
>
> *Melleburne*, -*borne* 1086 DB, *Melleborn*(*e*) 1419–97 Pat, 1443 AD vi, *Mel*(*e*)*burne*, -*bo*(*u*)*rn*(*e*) 1204 Cur *et freq* to 1570 SR, (*by Royston*) 1383 Pat
>
> *Mildeburn*(*e*) 1170 LibEl, 1252 FF, 1257 Pat, 1272–85 *Ass* (6), 1291 Tax, -*borne* 1434 Pat
>
> *Medelbne* (sic print) 1207 FF, *Middelburn* 1272 *Ass*
>
> *Muldeburn, Muleburn* 1272 *Ass*, *Moldebourne* 1337 ib.
>
> *Metleburne* 1276 Val, -*borne* c. 1330 *ElyCouch*, *Methelburn* 1285 *Ass*
>
> *Med*(*e*)*b*(*o*)*urn*(*e*) 1285 *Ass*, 1296 FF
>
> *Milb*(*o*)*urn*(*e*) 1428–36 Pat, 1739 *HardwickeA*

The names Melbourn and Meldreth *infra* 60 offer a difficult problem. The places are adjacent and it is natural to assume that the first element is the same in each. Ekwall has suggested in relation to Melbourn that the first element is OE *melde*, 'orach,' and that the whole name means 'stream by which orach grows.' The late Dr Palmer, who came from this district and was at the same time a good field-botanist, considered this derivation impossible. Ekwall himself does not suggest this for Meldreth and we may pretty certainly dismiss it as impossible for both names alike, in spite of the fact that there is one 11th-century form *Meldrethe* which Ekwall did not record.

One might suggest OE *mylde*, 'mould, earth,' as found in Rodmell (PN Sx 325–6), PN Nth 268, PN Wa 331, PN ERY 327, PN Nt 288, but the fragments in ASCh and BCS 1267 are documents in good West Saxon and the word *mylde* would not appear there as *melde*. Further, any interpretation of the compound as a whole would be difficult.

A third possibility has been suggested, viz. that we should take the first element in both names alike to be the personal name *Melda*, which is apparently found in *Meldanige* (BCS 810) in Berkshire. The name *Melda* would seem to be an adaptation for purposes of personal nomenclature of OE *melda*, 'interpreter.' The great difficulty is that for Melbourn we have good late 10th- or early 11th-century forms *Meldeburna* and not any form *Meldanburna* such as we should expect. In these circumstances the interpretation of Melbourn must be left open.

With regard to Meldreth it should be noted that there is only one good early form with a *d*. This occurs in a sentence which also mentions Melbourn and it is just possible that the writing of two successive names beginning with *Mel-*, one of which rightly had *d*, influenced the scribe and made him write the other with a *d* also. If this form can thus be ruled out, the remaining evidence is at least not inconsistent with the etymology suggested by Ekwall (DEPN), viz. a compound of OE *myln* and *rīð*, hence 'mill-stream.' For such early and complete loss of *n* cf. the history of Milbrook (PN BedsHu 82), Milford (PN D 75, 208, PN W 382), Milton (PN Nth 233, PN Nt 56), Milcote, Millburn, Milverton (PN Wa 236, 184, 176), Milkhouse (PN W 349). The early intrusive *d* may be due to the influence of the neighbouring Melbourn, and the rise of the form may have been strengthened later by the common tendency in ME to develop *d* between *l* and *r*.

FIVE BARROW FIELD (not on map[1], *v.* Fox 326). Cf. *ffyvuehoues* 1319 *Extent*. 'Five barrows,' *v.* haugr and cf. Five Fools Mead *infra* 360.

MELBOURN BURY[2] and THE MOOR were the homes respectively of Alice de *Byry* (1272 *Ass*) and Hugo *atte Bery* (1344 *WMP*), of Alexander de *Mora* (1257 Pat), Ralph *in la More* (1272 *Ass*) and William *at More* (1307 Layer). *v.* burh (manorial), mōr.

HOP MALLIONS[3] (6"), MUNSEY'S and NOON'S FOLLY FM[4] are probably to be associated with the families of William and Alice *Mario(u)n* (1324 *Extent*, 1347 *SR*), James *Muncey* (c. 1840 *TA*) and Robert *Noon* (1819 Carter). For *Folly*, *v. infra* 353.

---

[1] Marked on map in AnctC.
[2] *Melborne berry* 1650 EA xiii.
[3] *Maryons* t. Eliz *Cole* xxxvii, *Hobmarians* t. Eliz ChancP. Cf. Malyons (PN Ess 483).
[4] *Knowns Folly* c. 1825 O.S., *Noons Folly* c. 1840 *TA*.

BLACK PEAK (6″) is *le Blakpeke* 1505 *St John's*. GOFFERS KNOLL is *Gaffer* 18.. *Map*. GRINNEL HILL (6″). Cf. *Grenelawe* 1228 *FF*, -*lowe* 1267 ib., *Grynlowewaye* 1615 *WMP*, *Greeneloeways* 1650 *WMP*, *Grindle Hill* 18.. *Map*. 'Green hill,' v. grēne, hlāw. HEATH FM. Cf. *le Oldeheth* 1505 *St John's*, *the heath* 1615 *WMP*. HOLLAND HALL. Cf. *Hollyn* (*path*) 1637 *Terr*. v. holegn. HYDE FM is *le Hyde* 1319 *Extent*, *the Hide* 1650 *WMP*. v. hīd.

Meldreth

MELDRETH

> *Melrede* 1086 DB, InqEl, -*a* 1086 ICC, InqEl, 1109–31 *LibEl et freq* to 1423 Pat, *Melredde* t. Hy 8 *Rental*
>
> *Melreð*, -*reðe* 1086 InqEl, -*reth*(*e*) 1260 FF *et freq* to 1550 Pat, -*rith* t. Hy 3 Ipm, 1553 Pat, *Mellereth*(*e*) 1270 *Ass*, *Melereth* 1298 ib., 1359 Ipm, *Mel*(*e*)*r*(*e*)*heth*, *Melereheth* 1298 *Ass*, *Merlreth*(*e*) 1362 Ipm, Cl, *Melreght* 1510 LP
>
> *Meldrethe* 1086 InqEl, *Meldred*(*e*) c. 1150 *LibEl*, 1230 Ch, 1523 Layer, t. Hy 8 *Rental*, 1643 EA vi, *Meldryth* t. Hy 8 *Rental*, *Meldre* 1236 Barnwell
>
> *Melre*(*e*) 1201–7 FF *et freq* to 1289 ElyA, -*rei*(*a*), -*y*- c. 1210 *ElyM*, 1254 Val, 1277–80 *ElyM*, *Melere* 1272 *Ass*
>
> *Milree* 1201 Cur, *Mil*(*le*)*reth*(*e*) 1272 *Ass*, 1510 LP, *Myldrede* 15th *Christ's*, *Mildred* 1675 Ogilby
>
> *Mulri* 1238 Cl
>
> *Malrede* 1266 FF, 1461 Pat, -*reath* 1588 Fenland i

For the history of this name v. Melbourn *supra* 58.

METTLE HILL (6″) is *Motloweyhil* 1319 *Extent*, *Metlow*(*e*)*hill*(*e*) 1439 *Christ's*, 1594–1606 *Ct*, *Metlyehyll*, 1569 ib., *Metlehill* 1578 ib., *Mutly Hill* 1664 *Rental*, *Mettly Hill* 1735 Meldreth. 'Assembly-hill,' v. (ge)mōt, hlāw. For the development of *o* to *e*, cf. Denton (PN Nth 146), DB *Dodintone*. This was probably the meeting-place of Armingford Hundred. For other 'moot-lows' v. Thriplow and Whittlesford Hundreds *infra* 82, 92.

BURY LANE (6″) and CHISWICK END were the homes of Hugh *ate Bery* (1327 SR) and Ada, daughter of John de *Chesewyk* (1260 FF). Cf. *le Beryende* 1399 *Peterhouse*, 1514 *Ct* and *Chesewik* 1273 *WMP*, *Cheswicke More* 1593 *Ct*, *Chiswicke end* 1637 ib. 'Cheese farm,' v. burh (manorial), cīese, wīc. Cf. also *Chesewic* c. 1260 *St John's H*

(Babraham), *Chesewyc(dale)* 1259 *Queens'*, (*le*) *Chisewik* 1319, 1326 *ib.* (Haslingfield).

SHEENE FM (6") is *terram Prioris de Schene* 1476 *St John's*, *Melreth Shene* 1517 *Ct, the Sheene* (*House*) 1624 *Lease, farm called the Sheene* 1650 EA xiii. It was held of the Prior of the Carthusian House of Jesus of Bethlehem at Sheen (PN Sr 65–6) in 1490 (Ipm).

Guilden and Steeple Morden

MORDEN (GUILDEN and STEEPLE)

> (*æt*) *Mórdune* 1015 (11th) ASWills, *Morduna* 1086 ICC, InqEl, -*dune* 1086 ICC, (*alia*) 1086 DB, -*dun* (*Ylberti de Karenci*) 1194 P, (*Nort*-), (*Su*-) 1218 *SR*, (*Gelden'*, *Stepel*-) 1242 Fees, (*Norþ*-) t. Hy 3 *Rental*, (*Gilde*-) 1272 *Ass*
>
> *Mordona* 1086 ICC, -*don(e)* 1198 FF *et freq*, (*Hildeberti*) 1176 P, (*Gildene*) 1204 Cur, (*Suth*-) 1214 *ib.*, (*Coldene*-) 1254 Val, (*Guldene*-) 1272 *Ass*, (*Stupel*-) 1284 Winton, (*Nor*-) 13th *Wymond*, (*Stepil*-) 1328 Ipm, (*Stepul*-) 1345 *CWool*, (*Stiple*) 1347 FF, (*Gildy*) 1495 Ipm, (*Gil*-) 1535 VE, *Mordoun* 1386, 1433 Cl, *Moredon* 1231, 1271 FF, *Morden* 1237 Fees *et freq*, *Moordo(u)n'* c. 1330 *ElyCouch*, 1387 *MinAcct*, 1413 Cl, -*den* 1553 Pat, *Mourden* 1550 Pat
>
> *Mortuna* 1086 InqEl, -*ton* 1237 Cl *et freq* to 1329 Pat
>
> *Marden* 1274 Misc, 1667 *FF*, *Merdone* 1316 FA
>
> *Guldene* 1298 *Ass*, *Guldene and Morden* 1317 Ch, *Geldenmorde al.* *Geldenmordon* 1302 Ipm, *Mord' Peverel* t. Hy 2 (1508) Pat, *Gilden et Mooreden* 1553 Pat
>
> *Ste(e)ple Morda(u)nt(e)* 1585–1677 *EgCh*

'Marsh-hill,' *v.* mōr, dūn. Guilden Morden is *north* of Steeple Morden, formerly called *South* Morden and now named from the church *steeple* which fell in the great storm of 1703. *Ilbert de Carenci* had land in Steeple Morden in 1176 (P) and William *Peverel* in Guilden Morden in 1166 (RBE). *Guilden* is OE *gylden*, 'golden,' often used as an attribute of places in the sense 'rich, productive, splendid.' Cf. Moreton Pinkney (PN Nth 41), Gilmorton (Lei), *Aurea Morton* 1249 EpReg, *Gilden Morton* 1327 SR, and *þa Gildene burh* 1052 ASC, a name applied to the Abbey of Peterborough because of its splendour (PN Nth lii). The combined parishes are large and in DB included land in Litlington and Shingay. Sutton (*infra* 239) was also called *Golden* Sutton and one of the Swaffhams (*infra* 134) *Gildene* Swaffham.

Guilden Morden

NOTE. CHURCH LANE was probably by the home of William *ate Cherch* (1322 *Ct*). COBBS LANE is to be associated with the family of Thomas *Cobbe* (1339 *Ct*). Cf. *Cobbys* 1465 FF.

ODSEY

> *Odeseie* c. 1150, c. 1400 Wardon, *Odesey(e)* 1296 Barnwell, *Odysey* 1518 ECP
> *Odesheia* c. 1190 Wardon, *Oddes(h)eye* 1232 *FF*, 1252 Wardon
> *Odeseth(e)* 1199 Wardon, 1381 *WMP*, *Oddeseth(e)* 1296 Barnwell, 1322 *Ct*

This is the place from which the Hertfordshire Hundred of Odsey took its name (PN Herts 150–1). Odsey lies in a hollow on the Icknield Way and this may be the sēað, 'pit, hole,' referred to. Near by is a gravel pit and an old chalk pit. '*Odda*'s hollow or pit,' cf. Orsett (PN Ess 165) and Roxeth (PN Mx 53–4). For the loss of *th*, v. IPN 111. It is noteworthy that the alternative forms in -*seles* found for the Hundred name do not occur here.

RUDDERY END (not on map)

> *Redrich* 1227 FF, *Redreth(e)* c. 1278 ElyA, (-*feld*) 1383 CaiCh, 1392–
> 1416 St John's, *Reddreth* 1556 Eg, *Retherethfeld* 1438 St John's
> *Redderia*, *Redreya* 13th Barnwell, *Red(d)re(e)* ib., 1274 Cl
> *Ruddery Field* 1800 EnclA

'Cattle stream,' v. hrȳðer, rīþ. A hamlet with a chapel of ease formerly stood on Ashwell Street near the junction of the parishes of Ashwell (Herts) and Guilden and Steeple Morden. "Houses and chapel, all gone" (c. 1635 Layer). "The bare site is now known as Ruddery end" (Layer 103). Just over the border is Ruddery Spring (PN Herts 154). For the loss of *th*, cf. Odsey *supra*.

THE AVENELS (6″) is *Avenell* 1428 FF, *Avenellys* 1465 ib., and is to be associated with the family of William *Avenell* (1301 (1390) Cl).

COLD HARBOUR is in a remote corner of the parish. v. *infra* 357. GREAT GREEN. Cf. *le Southend de le Green voc. Bennetts Greene* 1610 *Cole* xxxvi. HOOK'S MILL (6″) is *Hokesmelne* 1381 *WMP*. Cf. Hook's

Mill Fm *infra* 67. LITTLE GREEN is *the Little Green* 1800 *EnclA*.
NORTHFIELD is in the *south* of the parish, on the county boundary, not
far from its junction with Station Road in Ashwell. This runs to the
north of the parish, passing Northfields (PN Herts 154), from which
this place must be named. ODSEY GRANGE (6″) is "*grangiam de Oddes'*
quam Willemus Peverell eis (Wardon Abbey) dedit" t. Hy 2 (1508)
Pat, *Odesethegrange* 1381 *WMP*, *Odsey Grange* t. Eliz ChancP. SHIRE
BALK (6″). Cf. "pasture called *the Sheare*" 1665 EA xi, *Shire way*
1800 *EnclA*. It runs along the Hertfordshire boundary, cf. PN Herts
250, *s.v.* balke. TOWN FM (6″) is *Town Hall Fm* c. 1825 O.S. *v.* tūn.
TOWN'S END (6″). Cf. *Townsend Close* 1800 *EnclA*. *v.* tūn.

Steeple Morden

GATLEY END

> *Gatewell(e)* c. 1234, c. 1273 *Wymond*, (*viam*) 13th ib., 1268 *Ass*,
> (*-wei, -y*) c. 1280 *CaiCh*, 1392 *StJohn's*, *-ende* 1504–20 *StJohn's*
> *Gathewell* c. 1260 *Wymond*, *Gattewelle* 1280 *Ct*, *Gatwell* 1517
> *StJohn's*, *Gattle End* 1743 *HardwickeA*, (*close*) 1828 *Eg*, *Gatley*
> *End* c. 1840 *TA*
> *Catewell* 1274 *Cl*, *Catewelleweye* 1465 *StJohn's*

In the neighbourhood were also *Catdelowe* 1275 RH and *Gatesden(e)*
c. 1212, 1273 *Wymond*, *-done* c. 1273 ib., *-dune* 13th *CaiCh*. We have
also to take into account Gatleyway Fm in Kelshall (*Catlou way* 1638,
v. PN Herts 160). Gatley End lies along the valley of Cheney Water
(*supra* 4) on which are Upper and Lower Gatley Fms (6″). *Gatewell*
is possibly an early name of this stream. Gatleyway Fm is situated on
a track which runs to the Icknield Way, pointing directly to Gatley
End, from which runs a track, less direct, past Upper Gatley Fm,
through Morden Grange Plantation, to Ashwell station. It seems
probable that, before the construction of the railway, these tracks were
continuous from Gatley to Gatleyway Fm, passing close by a tumulus
near the Icknield Way. This was probably the *Catdelowe* of 1275 and
the *Catlou* of 1638. Any certain etymology is impossible, but most of
our forms point to a first element *gata*, hence 'goats' stream, valley
and hill,' *v.* wielle, denu, dūn, hlāw. The tumulus was apparently
'wild-cat hill' and we may note that there is still in Kelshall a stream
called Cat Ditch. There may have been confusion between distinct
names, *Gatewellwey* and *Catlowwey*. An interchange of *C* and *G* is
not uncommon, cf. Cambridge *supra* 38.

GLITTON (lost) is *Glette* 1205 Cur, (*campo de Est, West*) c. 1273 *Wymond, Glitte* 1205 Cur, (*West*) *Gletton'* 13th, c. 1272 *Wymond*, 1384 *StJohn's, Westgletten* 1274 Cl, *Glytton* (Steeple Morden) 1375 *StJohn's, Glyttonfeld* (next the land of the Hospital of Shingay) 1466 ib., *Est-, Westglytton* 1483 ib., *Glittonfelde* (in a meadow called *Tadlowemeadowe*) 1541 ib., *Est-, Westglatton* 1377 ib., *Glitton on Northbrook* 1592 *Bodl,* (*al. Northbrook*) 1594 ib., *Glitten al. Northbrooke* 1602 ib. The later forms definitely identify the site with North Brook End *infra* 65, but the name seems to have covered a somewhat extensive area reaching to Tadlow and Shingay, and there can be little doubt that the lost *Glitton* in Ashwell (PN Herts 153) is also to be associated with this place (*Glutton* 1313 *StJohn's, Northglytton* 1406 *Ct*). Cf. also *Glette* (near *Herlestonfeld,* i.e. Harston field) c. 1250 *Trinity* and *le Glytton* 1408 *Ct* (Harston). This looks like ME *glette, glitte,* OFr *glette,* 'slime, filth.' The noun is recorded from 1340 in the sense 'slimy matter, sticky or greasy filth,' the verb from 1527 in that 'to ooze, flow slowly.' Cf. also *gletty,* 'viscosus' 1483 CathAngl, 'green and slimy, applied to the appearance of stagnant water' in Northumberland (1893). *v.* NED *s.vv. gleet, gleety.* Here *glette* is perhaps used of some boggy or marshy ground. The relation of the *Glette* forms to the *Gletton* ones is obscure. *Westgletten* (1274 Cl) suggests the possibility of a weak plural form, but a weak plural form for a word of Romance origin is not very likely and the otherwise universal *ton-*ending is against it. Possibly there were a number of *glett-ton* forms, so called from the character of the soil, but a compound of *ton* with a word of Romance origin is again extremely unlikely.

BROOK END FM and SHINGAY GATE FM were the homes respectively of William, son of Robert *Attebrokhende* (1282 *EgCh*) and Ralph *ate Brokhande* (1327 SR) and of Lucas *ad januam de Seneg'* (13th CHuAS i), *v.* brōc, ende. The former is *le Bro(o)k(h)ende* 1383 *CaiCh,* 1442 *StJohn's.* The latter is *Shingay Gate* (1821 Baker) and is on the boundary of the land of the Preceptory of Shingay *infra* 65.

BROWSE WOOD[1] (6″) and CHEYNEY LODGE[2] are to be associated with the families of Hugo and Robert de *Bruey* (1272 *Ass,* Ipm) and John de *Broweye, Bruay* (1280 *Ct*) and William de *Chaeny* (1248 Ch), *Che(y)ney* (1266 Ipm, 1272 *Ass*).

[1] Cf. *Broweys* 1402 *Ct, Browhouse al. Browesse* 1584 EA ix.
[2] *le Chenez* 13th *Wymond, le Cheyneys* 1464 *StJohn's, Chaines* 1620 *EgCh.* For the early use of the genitival form to describe the manor, cf. Ringer's Fm (PN Ess xxxii, 297), Tadlow Tower Fm, Birdlines Manor Fm and Mines Fm *infra,* 67, 74, 121.

Bogs Gap. Cf. *Bogs Close* c. 1840 *TA*. It lies low. Church Fm. Cf. *Chirchelond* 14th *Wymond*, 1392 *StJohn's*, *Cherchende* 1428 ib., *Cherchefeld* 1473 ib. Fleck's Lane Fm (all 6″). Cf. *Fleckes Close* 1675 *Eg*, *Flecks Lane* 1821 *Baker*, *Flacks Lane* c. 1840 *TA*. Heath Barn. Cf. *le heth* 14th *Wymond*. Moco Fm. Cf. *Mocha Field* c. 1840 *TA*. North Brook End [nɑ·bruki·n] is *North Brook end* 1626 *Eg*, *Narbrooke-end* 1675 ib. Cf. *Northbroc* 1256 BM, *Norbroc* c. 1273 *Wymond* (p), *Glitton al. Northbrook* 1594 *Bodl*. v. *Glitton supra* 64. Thrift Fm (6″) is *Thrift* 1834 G. It adjoins The Thrift (6″) in Therfield. v. fyrhðe and Thrift Fm (PN Herts 167).

Shingay

Shingay

> *Sceningeie* 1086 ICC, *S(c)henyng(h)ey(e)* 1276 FF, 1298 *Ass*, (*cum Wendeye*) 1336 *SR*, *Shenengeye* 1260 Ass
> *Scenegeia* 1086 ICC, 1195 P (p), *Schenegeia* 1196 ib., *S(c)hen(e)-gey(e)* 1256 Barnwell *et freq*, (*ad Wendeye*) 1347 *SR*, *Schenge* 1256 Cl, *Shenegheye* 1272 *Ass*, *Schenekey* 1275 RH, *Chenegeye* 1285 *Ass*
> *Scelgei* 1086 DB
> *Senegaia* 1087–93 (n.d.) France, 12th *Ord*, *Senegheia* c. 1156 Wardon, -*eye* 1272 *Ass*, *Senegey(e)* c. 1185 *Wymond*, 1254 Val, 1275–9 RH, 13th *Ely*, *Senege* c. 1300 ElyA
> *Sungheye* c. 1280 *Hosp* (p), *Schonegey* 1285 HMC vi
> *Synghai* 1513 LP
> *Shyngey* t. Hy 8 *Rental*, 1571 AD iii, *Shingay(e)* 1541 *MinAcct*, (*cum Wendye*) 1570 SR, *Chinghay* 1672 EA xi

'The low-lying land of the people of *Scēne*,' v. inga, ēg. OE *Scēne*, *Scīene* is perhaps found in *Scynes weorþ* 947 BCS 820. It is related to OGer *Scōnea* (FörstemannPN 1306) and is derived from OE *sc(ī)ene*, 'beautiful' or is a pet-form for such a name as *Scēnwulf* (LVD) (cf. OGer *Sconolf* loc. cit.) containing this element. Cf. Shinfield (Berks), DB *Selingefelle*, 1167 P *Schiningefeld*, and Shingham (Nf), DB *Scingham*. For the initial consonant v. IPN 103, 113.

Preceptory is *Schenegeye hospitalis* 1256 Barnwell. This name records the Preceptory of the Knights of the Hospital of Jerusalem. The property was confirmed to the Knights by King John in 1199 (ChR).

Tadlow

TADLOW

> *Tadeslaue* 1086 ICC, *-lawe* 1230 FF, 1332 Ch
> *Tadelai* 1086 DB, *-le(weye)* t. Hy 3 Ipm
> *Tadelaw(e)* 1199 P (p) *et freq* to 1307 Ipm, *-lowe* 1218 *SR et freq*
> to 1399 Cl, (*cum Pynnecote*) 1336 *SR*, (*ad Pynkote*) 1347 ib.
> *Tedelawe* 1199 P
> *Tadlaw* 1218 FF, *-low(e)* 1312 ib. *et freq* to 1552 Pat, *-loo* 1539–41
> *MinAcct*
> *Thadelawe* 1218 *SR*, 1291 Tax, 1298 *Ass*, 1341 NI, *Thadlowe* 1461
> Pat
> *Taddelawe* 1242 Fees, 1256 (1332) Ch, 1257 Pat, 1272–98 *Ass* (ter),
> *-loue* 1285 ib., *-lowe* ib. *et freq* to 1388 Cl
> *Tathelawe* 13th *Ely*, 14th *Cai*, *-laue* c. 1330 *ElyCouch*

The second element is hlāw, 'tumulus,' and the first is, therefore, likely to be a personal name rather than OE *tadde, tāde*, 'toad,' which has been suggested as a possibility. No personal name *Tāda* is recorded but Ekwall (DEPN *s.n.*) suggests that it may have existed side by side with *Tāta*. Hence '*Tāda*'s tumulus.' Cf. Tadley (Ha), (*æt*) *Tadanleage, Taddanleage* 909 BCS 625. For *Pincote, v. infra.*

PINCOTE BARN (6″) is *Pincote, -y-* 1176 P, 1260 Ass *et freq* to 1552 Pat, *Pinnecote, -y-* 1236 Barnwell, 1336, 1347 *SR, Pynecot(e), -i-* 1255 FF, *et freq* to 1296 Barnwell, *Pynkote* 1347 *SR, Pyncott* c. 1525 ECP. Names in *Pin-*, such as *Pinton* (PN Wo 334), *Pinham* (PN Sx 171), Pennicott, Uppincott (PN D 416), Pinhoe, Pinn Court and Pinwood (ib. 443–4), Pinn (ib. 593), Pin Hill (ib. 597), Pinhay (ib. 637), Pinley (PN Wa 167, 219), Pin Green (PN Herts 139), Pinden and Penenden (KPN 304) are not easy to interpret. Occasionally, as in Pinhoe, we have an early form which shows clearly that we have to do with the British *pen*, 'hill,' but for the most part we have no such clear evidence. We know that there was an OE personal name *Pin*, found in DB (TRE) in Gloucestershire and also an OE name *Pinna, Pinnae* in ICC, InqEl in Cambridgeshire in 1086. This name might be adduced in explanation of the Cambridgeshire Pincote, but there are other possibilities. There is an OE word *pinn*, 'pin, peg,' which may enter into some of these compounds. We also have surnames such as Ralph *del Pin* of Ely (t. Hy 3 *AddCh*), Symon Abbot *del Pyn* of Soham (1252 FF), John and Matilda *ate Pyne* of Teversham and Stetchworth respectively (1327 SR) and such compounds as *Pinbregge* (1297 *For*) in Good Easter, *Pynaker* (1359 *Ct*) in High Easter, *Pynstowe* (c. 1300 *ColchA*) in Layer de la Haye, all in Essex, which may derive from this *pinn* or (in some cases) from OE *pynd*, as is the case in Pin Green (Herts). No certainty is possible in relation to Pincote. *pynd* is unlikely but OE *Pinn(a)* and *pinn* are both possible, though the sense of *pinn-cote* is quite unknown.

TADLOW TOWER FM is to be associated with the family of John de *Turri*, de *la Tur* who had land in Steeple Morden in 1271 (FF). It is *Tower Fm* 1821 Baker, *Tadlow Tower Fm* c. 1825 O.S. Cf. *Tourishauedlond* 1377 *St John's*, (*le*) *Toures* 1392, 1461 ib., *Abouetowres* 1422 ib. (in Steeple Morden). Cf. *supra* 64 n. 2.

CHURCH FM (6"). Cf. *Church Pightle* c. 1840 *TA* and pightel. HATLEY GATE is on the county boundary where the road enters Cockayne Hatley (PN BedsHu 105). HOME FM (6"). Cf. *Home Pightle* and *Meadow* c. 1840 *TA*. HOOK'S MILL FM is so named ib., cf. *Hokesdole* t. Eliz *Cole* xxxvii and *supra* 62. NEW ENGLAND FM is *New England* 1821 Baker. It is in a remote part of the parish on the county boundary, cf. *infra* 357. TADLOW BRIDGE FM. Cf. *Tadlowebrygge* 1525 *Ct*. TADLOW GATE (6") is on the boundary where the road from Potton to Cambridge enters the county.

Wendy

WENDY

> *Wendeie* 1086 ICC, -*eie*, -*a*, -*ey(e)* 1195 P (p), 1212 Cur *et freq* to 1457 FF, (*Templariorum*) 1256 Barnwell, (*cum Shenegeie*) 1341 NI, *Wendy(e)* 1272, 1298 *Ass*, 1316 FA, 1413, 1450 Pat, *Vendeia* c. 1180 *Hosp*, -*eye* 1347 *SR*, *Wendhey(e)* 1218 *SR*, 1298 FF, *Weyndeye* 1285 *Ass*, *Wending* 1552 Pat
>
> *Wandrie* 1086 DB
>
> *Wandei* 1086 DB, *Wandeye* 1268 *Ass* (p), 1280 Cl
>
> *Wyndey(e)* c. 1237 Wardon (p), 1272 *Ass* (p), 1366 Pat, 1394-5 Cl, 1444 AD iii, *Windie* 1588 Fenland i

Wendy is in a marked bend of the North Ditch near its confluence with the Cam or Rhee and the first element is probably an OE **wende* from OE *windan*, 'to wind.' *Wende* might possibly have been the name of the North Ditch, aptly called 'the winding stream' or it might have been given to the bend. The second element is ēg. Hence 'low-lying land by the winding stream' or 'in the bend.' Cf. Wendon Lofts and Wendens Ambo (PN Ess 544, 542) and DEPN *s.n.* Wendy.

Lordship Spinney and Whitelands Barn (both 6″). Cf. *Lordships Ground, White Lands* c. 1840 *TA*.

Whaddon

Whaddon

Wadune 1086 DB, InqEl, *Wadone* 1086 DB, 1195 P (p), *Wadona* 1086 ICC, 12th *Lewes*, t. Stephen France

Wæddun 1086 InqEl, *Waddun(e)*, *-a* ib., 1186–9 P (p), 1218 *SR*, *Waddon(e)* 1208 Cur *et freq* to 1341 Cl

Phwaddune 1086 InqEl, *Phwaddon* 1223 FF

Quaddon(e) 1199 CurR (p), 1341 NI, 1387 Cl, 1412 FA, *Qwadone* 1268 *Ass*

Hwaddon 1218 Seld 53, 1381 *WMP*

Watdun 1218 *SR*, *-don* 1223 FF, c. 1237 Wardon (p), 1268 *Ass* (p), *Wathdoun* c. 1250 *Trinity* (p), *Whatdon* 1367 FF

Whaddon(e) 1233 FF *et passim*, (*cum Knesworthe*) 1316 FA, (*cum Whidyhale*) 1346 ib., (*cum Whidale*) 1428 ib., *-doun* 1391 Cl

Whoddon 1610 Camden

'Wheat-hill,' *v.* hwǣte, dūn. Cf. Whaddon (PN Bk 74, 101, PN Nth xlv). *Whidyhale* and *Whidale* are Wyddial (PN Herts 188). For *Knesworthe*, *v.* Kneesworth *supra* 56. Cf. *Hwadundale* 13th *St John's* (Madingley), *Waddonedale* c. 1300 *St John's H* (Eltisley). For the initial *Qu-*, *v.* Introd. xxxvi.

Hoback Fm is *Holebec* 1224 *FF*, *Hobeck* 1624 *Christ's*, *Hoback* 1821 Baker. Cf. *Holbekmede* 1513 *Christ's*. This is named from a stream *Ho back* 1635 ib. which must be the unnamed small tributary of the Cam or Rhee flowing not far from the farm. Cf. also Hoback Fm in Wimpole (*infra* 82) and Gransden Brook *supra* 6. The second element in these names is perhaps OE bece, 'stream,' later replaced by Anglo-Scandinavian *beck*. *v.* bece, bekkr.

Green Fm (6″) was the home of Alexander *atte Grene* (1347 *SR*), *v.* grēne.

Christ's College Fm (6″) is self-explanatory. Dyer's Green is *Dyers Green* c. 1825 O.S. North Road Fm (6″) is on Ermine Street which must here have been called the *North Road*. WHADDON GREEN (6″) is *The Green* c. 1840 *TA*.

II. WETHERLEY HUNDRED

Wedrelai 1086 DB, *Wederlai* ib., 1086 InqEl, *-lea* 1166–93 P, *-le* 1168, 1172 ib., 1478 Pat, *Woderle* 1167 P

Wederlai 1086 InqEl, *-le(a)* 1169 P, 1171–5 ib., *Wetherle(e)* 1218 SR *et freq* to 1401 FA, *-ly(e)* 1381 Ass, 1570 SR, *Whetherley* 1478 IpmR, *Weatherly* 1660 EA vi

Werleia 1086 ICC, *Werle* 1185 RotDom, 1236 Barnwell, *Werele* 1268 *Ass*, *Wherley* 1474 *MinAcct*

Werdeslea 1174 ChancR, *Wether(e)sle* 1236 Barnwell, 1268 *Ass*, *Wethesle* 1279 RH, *Wethele* 1327 SR

Wereslea 1199, 1200 P, *-le* 1275 RH, *Weyeresle* 1268 *Ass*

OE *weðra-lēage*, 'clearing for sheep,' from OE *weðer* and **lēah**, with occasional substitution of the gen. sing. *weðres-* for the gen. plur.

The hundred was named from *Wetherle(e)* c. 1252–1373 *Trinity* and *Wetherle Grene* 1322 *StCatharine's*, near the Whole Way in Barrington. In Little Eversden we have *Wetherle(e)feld* 14th *Queens'* and in Harlton, *Wedyrleweye* 1402 ib., *Wethirlewey* 1483 *Trinity*, *Wetherleywey* 1510 *StCatharine's*. The place must have been near the high ground (once woodland) jutting eastwards into the hundred near the junction of the parishes of Orwell, Little Eversden, Harlton and Barrington.

Arrington

ARRINGTON

(at) Earnningtone c. 950 (14th) ASWills, *ærningetune* 1086 InqEl

Erlingetona 1086 ICC, *Herlingtone* 1087–93 (14th) France, *Erington* 1236 Barnwell, *Eryngeton* 1272 *Ass*

Ernincgetune, Erningetone 1086 InqEl, *Erningatone* 1086–7 France, *-etoñ* 1165 P (p)

Erningtune 1086 DB, *-tone* ib., 13th *Ely*, 1276 Val

Arintona 1087–93 (14th) France, *Arthyngton* 1436 *Hardwicke*

Aring(e)ton(e), -yng- c. 1205 Wardon *et freq* to 1553 Pat, *Aringeston* 1261 FF, *Haryngton* 1272 *Ass*, *-ing-* 1275 RH, *Arrington(e)* 1279 ib., 1570 SR

Ermingetun 13th *St John's* (p)
Arning(e)tun 1218 *SR*, -*ton(e)*, -*yng*- 1254 Val *et freq* to 1490 Ipm,
   Arnington(e) 1254 Val, 1256 Barnwell, *Harnyngton* 1345 *CWool*,
   Arninton 1260 Ass
Armyngton(e), -*ing*- 1285, 1298 *Ass*, 1291 Tax, 1299 QW, 1314,
   1360 Cl, 1346 FA

'The farm of *Earn(a)*'s people,' *v.* ingatūn and cf. Ermine Street
and Armingford *supra* 22, 50. Occasionally the vill is referred to as
Arningaford 963 (14th) *ElyM* or *villa de Arnyngestrete* 1298 *Ass*.

WRAGG'S FM is probably to be associated with the family of James
Wragg (c. 1840 *TA*).

ARRINGTON BRIDGE is *pontem de Arnyngton* 1285 *Ass*. Cf. *Arington
Bridge Field* 1727 *Christ's* in Whaddon, adjoining the bridge, and *v.*
Armingford *supra* 50. DECOY POND (both 6″). Cf. Decoy Fm *infra*
273.

Barrington

BARRINGTON
Barentona 1086 ICC, InqEl, *Barenton(e)* 1086 DB *et freq* to t. Hy 8
   Rental, -*tun(e)* c. 1183 Wardon, 13th *Waltham*, 1302 BM,
   Barinton, -*y*- 1236 Barnwell *et freq* to 1385 Pat
Barn(e)ton(a) 1218 *SR et freq* to 1459 Pat, -*tun* 1334 BM, *Branton*
   1260 Ass
Barington(e), -*y*- 1236 Barnwell (p), 1323 FF *et freq* to 1554 CHuAS
   v, *Barryngton* 1493 Ipm, 1548 Pat
Barletona 1130 P (p), *Warenton* 1345 *CWool*, *Barittone* 1401 FA

'The farm of *Bāra*,' *v.* tūn. This personal name is not recorded in
OE but is probably found also in Barrington (So), DB *Barintone*.
Cf. OHG *Baro* and *v.* DEPN *s.nn.*

NOTE. STEAD LANE. Cf. *Berested* 1542 *Trinity*, *Buryholme* 1364 ib., *Burycroft* 1468 ib. Perhaps to be associated with the manor of Bulbecks, *v.* burh
(manorial), stede.

CRACKNOW HILL
Crakewayn 1314, 1315 *Trinity*, *Crakwenhylle* 1517 ib., *Crackway
   hill* 1631 ib.
Cray(e)way(es) 1585, 1599 *Ct*, *Grayway* 1631 *Trinity*
Crackney Hill 1613 *HardwickeA*, *Crackling Hill* 1877 O.S.

It would seem at first sight that this name is identical with Cracka-way (PN D 40), earlier *Crakewey*, but the early forms in *-wayn, -wen* are disturbing for we have no record elsewhere of a weak plural for the word weg, 'way.' Profesor Bruce Dickins makes the ingenious and likely suggestion that the name is really a nickname, ' crack-waggon hill ' from the steepness, *wen* being from OE *wægn*, 'waggon.'

EDIX HILL HOLE (site of an Anglo-Saxon cemetery, not on map. v. Fox 250–1[1]) is *Edok(k)eshel* c. 1250 *Trinity*, *-hil(le)*, *-is-* c. 1285, 1316, 1332 ib., *Hedokkishilpit* 1316 ib., *(le) Edoxhil(l)* 1333 *StCatha-rine's*, 1522 *Trinity*, *-hell* 1425 *StCatharine's*. Professor Bruce Dickins suggests that *Edok* may be a diminutive for *Edward*, cf. *Willok* for *William*.

FOX HOLE DOWN FM (6″)

> *Focshaledene* c. 1240 *Trinity*, *Foxhal(e)dene*, *-doun* c. 1250 ib., *Foxaldoune* 1333, 1337 *Ct, le foxhall downe* 1538 ib.
> *Fox(h)eld(o)une* c. 1250, 1314 *Trinity*, *-dene* c. 1275, 1285 ib., *Foxseldone* c. 1250 ib., *-dene* c. 1252 ib., *Fox(h)ildene* c. 1285 ib., *-doune* 1316 ib., *Foxhellestounne* 1309 *Cole* ii, *Foxeldoune* 1316 *StCatharine's*, 1551 *Ct, Foxweldownhill* 1522 *Trinity*
> *Fox(e)hole (-doune)* 1456 *Ct*, *(Downehead)* 1489 ib., *(Dounehil)* 1579 ib., *Fox Hole Down Farm* c: 1825 O.S.

'Hill or valley by the nook or hill frequented by foxes.' The second element varied between **healh** and **hyll** and the third between **dūn** and **dene**. Later the name was assimilated to the more common **foxhol**.

WILSMERE DOWN FM

> *Wlmareswong* 13th *Chateriz*
> *Wlmaresdung, -dong(e), -is-* 13th, 1336 *Trinity*, 1337 *Ct, Wulmeres-dunc* 13th *Trinity, Wulmarsdunghel* 1324 ib., *Wolmeresdong* 1331 ib.
> *Wolmeredoune* 1317 *Ct, Wolmersdown(e)* 1585, 1599 ib.
> *Wylmeredunghyll* 1461 *Ct*
> *Wil(l)mer(s)down(e) (end)* 1516, 1522 *Trinity*, 1596 *Ct*, *-don(e)* *(Grass)* 1612 *HardwickeA, le Wylmersdownhawk* 1595 *Ct, Wil-mersh down hill* 1630 *HardwickeA, Wilmots Downs* 1821 *Baker, Wilmottsdown Farm* c. 1825 O.S.
> *Wylmedown hawke* 1548 *Ct, Wilmsdon Grass* 1612 *HardwickeA*

---

[1] It lies immediately to the north of the footpath joining spotlevels 67 and 69, nearer the western boundary of the parish and Malton Fm *infra* 79.

The first element is clearly the OE personal name *Wulfmær*. The second is not so obvious. The first form is probably an eccentric one, due perhaps to repetition of the *w* of the first element at the beginning of the second. If it is genuine, then clearly *Wulfmær*, in addition to giving his name to a *dung* or *dong*, gave it to a *wong* or 'field,' *v.* **vangr**. Apart from this form it is clear that the final element was originally *dung* (*dong, dunc*) rather than *doune*. This is doubtless the word *dung* recorded once in OE poetry in the sense 'subterranean chamber, dungeon,' corresponding to ON *dyngja*, 'woman's apartment,' originally used of a room of which the lower part was underground and probably originally so called because the roof was covered with *dung* (Torp *s.nn. dunge, dyngja*). So similarly MHG *tunc* was used of a spinning room, half underground (Kluge *s.n. Dung*). The exact sense of *dung* as a toponymical term in OE it is impossible now to determine. It may have denoted some primitive form of dwelling or it may be that *dung*, like its Old Norse cognate, had developed some such sense as 'heap,' hence 'small hill.' This word was probably rare and archaic even at the time when it was first used in relation to this place and it was soon confused with the more common dūn (*doun*, down). The word probably repeats itself in the names *Foldedong, Folddung* (13th *Trinity*) in this parish. For *hawk* cf. Hawk Mill *infra* 139. *-hel* is for **hyll**.

MILL COTTAGE (6″) was probably the home of Alexander de *Molendino* (1277 *Trinity*) and Thomas *at(t)e Melne, Molne, Milne* (1306 ib., 1327 SR, 1341 NI). *v.* **myln**.

BULBECK MILL (6″) is *Bulbeksmille* 1375 *Trinity* and is to be associated with the family of Richard de *Bolebek* (1251 FF). Cf. *terram Ricardi de Bolebech* 14th *Walden*.

BALK PLANTATION. Cf. *Bauchweye* 1373 *Trinity*, *le Comene bawke* 1525 *Ct* and *v.* **balke**. BARRINGTON HALL (both 6″). Cf. *le Hallecote* 1384 *Trinity*, *Halle land* 1517 ib. WEST GREEN FM (Kelly). Cf. *le Westgrene* 1462 *Ct*.

Barton

BARTON

> *Barton* 1060 (c. 1350) KCD 809 *et freq* to 1558 AD v
> *Bertona* 1086 ICC, (*Rad de Cahāniis, Chahaignis*) 1168–9 P,
> *Berton(e)* 1086 (13th) BrC, 1086 DB *et freq* to 1553 AD v, (*iuxta*

Gran(te)sete) 1285 *Ass,* (*cum Wytewell*) 1316 FA, (*juxta Cantebrigg*)
1326 Pat
Burton 1202, 1219 Cur, 1342 FF, *Bruton* 1399 FA

'Manor-farm,' *v.* beretūn. William de *Cahainges* held a manor here
of the Bishop of Bayeux in 1086 (DB) and Ralph gave Barton church
to Merton Priory (t. Hy 2 Dugd vi, 247). The *Barton* is distinguished
also by noting its proximity to Cambridge, Grantchester and Whitwell.

WHITWELL FM [witol]

Wurteuuella 1086 ICC, *Wateuuelle* 1086 DB
Witeuuella, -e 1086 DB, *Witewell*(*e*), *-y-* 1207 Cur *et freq* to 1345
 CWool, Wythewelle 1401 *Trinity*
Whitewell(*e*), *-y-* 1199 P (p), c. 1285 *StCatharine's et freq* to 1537
 AD v, *Whitwell, -y-* 1475 ib., 1503 AD iii, *Whyttwell* 1503 ib. iv,
 Whittewell 1516 ib. v
Hwitewelle 1203 FF (p), 13th *StJohn's* (p), *Qwytewellefeld* 1395 ib.
Wetewell 1327 SR, 1465, 1479 *StCatharine's, Whetewell*(*e*) 1391
 StJohn's, 1427 Cl, 1514 LP

'Fair, clear spring or stream,' *v.* hwīt, wielle and Bin Brook *supra* 1.

TOWN'S END FM (6″) was the home of Mabilia *ad Capud* (sic) *Ville*
(1279 RH), *v.* tūn.

BIRD'S FM[1] and THE VATCHES[2] (both 6″) are probably to be associated
with the families of John *Birde* (c. 1440 ECP) and Richard de *la Vach*
(1285 *Ass*).

BARTON BRIDGE (6″) is *Bertonbrygge, -bregge* 1375 *Trinity, -bergge* 1386
ib. *v.* brycg and Introd. xxxvi. CLARE COLLEGE FM (6″) is *land of the
college of Clare Hall* 1480 AD iv. LORD'S BRIDGE is *Ld. Oxfords Bridge*
1821 Baker. UNIVERSITY FM was acquired by the *University* of Cambridge in 1680 (L 87).

Comberton

COMBERTON

Cumbertone 1086 DB, *-tuna* 1155 P, 1218 *SR, Cumberton*(*e*) 1176–
 1202 P *et passim, Cumbirton* 1318 Crowland, *Cumbreton*(*a*) 1168–
 90 P

---

[1] Cf. *Berdyswelle* 14th AD iv.
[2] *Vaches* 1514 LP. Cf. The Vache (PN Bk 221).

    Commertona 1086 ICC, 1172 P, *Comerton(e)* 1279 RH, 1284, 1316
      FA, 1404 Cl, *Cumerton'* 1202 CR
    Comberton(e) 1286 QW *et freq*, *Camberton'* 1187 P, *Combreton* 1198
      Fees, 1387 Pat, 1399 Cl, *Comburton* 1374 Cl

'*Cumbra*'s farm,' *v.* tūn, and for the personal name, cf. Comberton
(PN Wo 193–4).

NOTE. SWAYNE'S LANE is probably to be associated with the family of
Walter *Sweyn* (1279 RH). Cf. *Swaynes Leys* c. 1840 *TA*.

THE OFFAL is (*le*) *Aldefeld(e)* (*de Comb-*, *Cumberton(e)*) c. 1250
StJohn'sH, 13th *StJohn's*, *the Offield* 1706 *Terr*, *Comberton Offal*
c. 1825 O.S. 'The old open country,' *v.* feld and cf. Offal End *infra*
78.

CHURCH END and GREEN END were by the homes of Nicholas *ad
Ecclesiam* and Nicholas *ad le Grene* (1279 RH). Cf. *Gre(e)nes* 1585
EA ix, 1625 *FF*, *Green End* c. 1840 *TA*.

BIRDLINES MANOR FM (6″) is *Burdeleysmaner* 1375 Cl, *Le Burdeleys*
1380 FF, *Burdeleyns* 1419 Cl, *manor of Burdlins* 1553 Pat, *Birdelymes*
1510 *StCatharine's*, *Birdlyns* 1706 *Terr*, and is to be associated with
the family of John de *Burdeleys* (1279 RH). Cf. Cheyney Lodge
supra 64 and, for a somewhat similar development cf. Birdlime Fm
(PN W 380), *Burdlins* c. 1840 *TA*, from the family of Lucia *Burgelon*.

HINES'S FM (6″) is *Hines Fm* c. 1840 *TA*. NORTH FIELD FM. Cf.
le Northffelde 1518 *StJohn's*. OLD FM (6″) is so named c. 1840 (*TA*).
WESTFIELD FM is *Westfeld* c. 1250 *StJohn'sH*, *Westfield Fm* c. 1840
TA.

Coton

COTON

    Cotis 1086 ICC (p), 1345 *CWool*, *Cotys* 1428 FA, *Cotes* 1175–81 P
      et freq to 1428 AD iv, (*al. Coton*) 1445 *Elien*, *Kotes* 1198, 1235
      FF, *Kotis* 1271 Ipm, *le Cotes* 1302, 1308 *CCC*
    Kotene (cruke) c. 1254 *StCatharine's*, *le Cotene (weye)* 1293 *StJohn's*,
      Coten(e) 1354 ib., 1404, 1427 Cl, *Coton* 1392 Pat *et freq* to 1578
      Ely, (*al. Cotes*) 1476 Pat, *Cotin*, *-y-* 1446 ib., c. 1470 ECP,
      Cooton 1530 EA vii
    Cotton 1404 Cl *et freq* to 1553 Pat, (*al. Cottes*) 1535 VE

'The cottages,' *v.* cot(e). The earlier forms are from the strong, the later from the weak plural. Cf. Claycoton, Coton and Cotton (PN Nth 66, 67, 147) and Wicken *infra* 203. For *cruke*, *v.* krókr.

NOTE. BROOK RD is *le Brookstrate* 1436 *Clare*.

CATHERINE HALL FM (6″) (locally ST CATHARINE'S FM) belonged to *St Katharine* the Virgin, now St Catharine's College (1476 *Pat*).

Grantchester

GRANTCHESTER

Granteseta, *-sete* 1086 DB, *-set(e)* 1203–8 Cur *et freq* to 1426 FF, (*iuxta Cantebr'*), (*cum Cotes*) 1285 *Ass*, *-sset(e)* t. Ric 1 Cur, c. 1236 NLC, 1242, 1313 FF, 1272 *Ass*, *Grantisset(e)* 1261 Cl, 1319 FF, *Grantecete* 1270 Ipm, 1279 RH, 1284 FA, 1291 Tax, *Grantsete* 1272 *Ass*, 1294, 1329 Pat, *Grantshet* 1237 FF, *Grantese* 1267 Pat, *Grantece* 1268 *Ass*

Grenteseta 1086 ICC, *Grenteshet* 1212 RBE, *Grentesham* 1214 Cur, *Grencestre* 1426 Cl

Gransete 1199 CurR *et freq* to 1393 FF, (*immo Grandesete*) 1285 *Ass*, *Grancete* 1284 FA *et freq* to 1417 AD iv, *Grancett* 1245 FF, *Granzete* 1284 Ipm, *Gransethe* 1299 SR

Grancestr(e) 1208 Cur *et freq* to 1559 *Rental*, *-cester* 1345 *CWool*, 1349 Crowland, 1570 Ely, 1577 AD v, *-cestour* 1456 IpmR

Cantesete 1218 *SR*, *Gantesete* 13th *StNeot*

Grantesheter 1247 *StJohn's*, *Grauntceseth'* 1254 Val, *Graunt(e)set(e)* 1272 FF *et freq* to 1445 *Elien*

Crantesete 1260 Ass (p), *Crauncestre* 1335–7 Cl

Granseste 1272 *Ass*, *Granceste* 1339 FF, 1341 NI, 1372 *SR*, 1378 SR, *Graunceste* 1446 Pat

Granteceste 1272 *Ass*, 1327 SR, 1417 FF, *Girancecest'* 1279 RH

Graunsete (*immo Grauntesete*) 1285 *Ass et freq* to 1428 FA, *Grauncete* 1315 *Ass*, 1448 Pat, *Grauncethe* 1346, 1428 FA, *Grawnceter* 1553 AD v

Magna Cestre 1287 Cl

Grandeset(e) 1299 QW, 1377 Cl, *Graundeceter* 1518 AD v, *Graundcester* 1549 Pat, *Grandcittie* 1563 Ely, *-citty* 1658 PR i

Grauncestre 1322 Pat *et freq* to 1480 AD iv, *-cester* 1485 Ipm, 1544 AD v, *-cesto(u)r* 1549 BM, Pat, 1559 AD v

Granteseter 1327 Crowland, *Grauntcestr'* 1329 Pat, *-cester* 1485
 AD iv, *Grantcester* 1617 *FF*

Granseter 1349 Crowland (p), *Granceter* 1364 Ely, 1576 Saxton,
 Grancettor 1380 Ely, *Grancetre* 1434 Pat, *Gransyter* 1554 CHuAS
 v, *Granciter* 1579 Ely, *Grancytter* 1582 ib.

Grauncet(t)er 1384 Ely, 1431 AD iv, 1501 ECP, *Grauncetor* 1535
 VE, 1553 EA vii

Graunchester t. Jas 1 *Rental*, *Granchester* 1643 EA vi, *Grandchester*
 c. 1655 ChancP

OE *Grante-sǣte*, 'the settlers on the Granta,' *v.* sǣte, Granta and
Cambridge *supra* 6, 36. For the development cf. *Tempsiter* (Sa), DB
Temsete, Temecester 1540 Leland and *Halcetor* (Mont), earlier *Halch-
seten* 1249 Misc (NCPNW 181). For the variation between *G* and *C*,
v. Cambridge *supra* 38. Initial *Grant-* was at one stage taken to stand
for OFr *gra(u)nt, gra(u)nd* and rendered by the Latin *magna*. The use
of *immo* before certain alternative forms emphasises official uncertainty
as to the correct form of the name.

HAGGIS FM, LACIES FM[1] and MERTON HO[2] (both 6″) are to be associated with the families of one *Haggis* (1758 *Trinity*), Henry de *Lacy*
(1285 *Ass*) and Walter de *Merton* who gave an estate here to *Merton*
College, Oxford (L 202).

BRASLEY BRIDGE is *Bras(s)el or Basley Bridge* 1875 Widnall. CARTER'S
WELL is *Tardryswell* 1659 ib., *Tarter's Well* 1877 O.S., said to be a
corruption of *St Etheldreda's (Audrey's) Well* (Widnall 145). FIELD
COTTAGE (all 6″). Cf. *campis de Gra(u)ntesete* 1285 *Ass*, 1288 *StJohn's*,
Grauncetor Feld 1539 *MinAcct, v.* feld.

Harlton

HARLTON [hɔ·ltən]

Herletona 1086 ICC, *-tone* DB, *-ton(e)* 1185 RotDom *et freq* to
 1285 *Ass*, *-tune* 1196 NLC

Harletona 1086 ICC, 1254 Val, *-ton(e)* 1235 FF *et freq* to 1484 Pat,
 -tun 1198 FF

Harlestona 1086 InqEl (p), *-ton(e)* 1276 Val, c. 1330 *ElyCouch*

---

[1] *terr' quond' domini Henrici de Lacy* 1288 *StJohn's*, *fee of John de Lascy* 1340 ib.
[2] *terre colleg' de Merton* 14th *Ct.*

Herlenton(a), *-e* c. 1150 France, 1155–1240 NLC, *Erlenton* c. 1186 ib.

Harltun 1218 *SR*, *Har(e)l(e)ton(e)* 1291 Tax *et freq* to 1549 Pat, *Harilton(e)* 1296 Barnwell, 1334 FF

Harlenton 1268 *Ass*, c. 1350 NLC

Herleston' 1285 *Ass*

Hardleston 1291 Tax, 1341 NI, 1421 Cl

'The farm of *Herela*,' *v.* tūn and cf. Harlington (PN BedsHu 123–4). The forms in *-es-* are probably due to confusion with Harston *infra* 84.

BUTLER'S SPINNEY (6″) is to be associated with the family of Peter *le Bouteillier* (c. 1232 NLC). Cf. *Botelerislandys* 1421 Cl, *Botellers* 1448 FF. On the enclosure map of 1808 *The Spinney* adjoins *Lordship Butlers*.

HAY HILL (local[1]) is *Heidon(e)*, *-y-* c. 1250 *St John's H*, c. 1300 *WMP*, 1334, 1401 *Trinity*, *Heydounhyll* 1440 *Queens'*, *Hey Hill* 1883 AnctC. Cf. *Heydonhillwey s.n.* Akeman Street *supra* 18. MAY POLE FM (6″) is near the junction of the parishes of Barrington, Orwell and Harlton. It is named from the old Orwell maypole which "until 1870 stood in a clump of fir trees on the hill west of the road, the old Akeman Street" (Hughes, *Cambridgeshire* 244).

✕ Haslingfield

HASLINGFIELD [heizliŋfi·ld]

Haslingefeld(e) 1086 DB, *-ing-*, *-feud* 1275–9 RH, 1293 Cl, *-yngfeld(e)* 1332, 1466 Pat, 1503 AD iv, *Haslinkefeud* c. 1250 *Trinity*
Heslingefelda 1086 ICC, *Heselingefeld'* 1190 P, *-ingafeld* 1156–8 (1337) YCh, t. Ric 1 (1308) Ch, *-inghe-* 1157 YCh, t. Ric 1 (1308) Ch, *-ingfelt* 1125–35 (1337) YCh, *-ingfeld(e)*, *-yng* t. Hy 2 Dugd iii *et freq* to t. Hy 8 *Rental*, *-ynge-* 1299 QW, *Hesligfeld* 1218 SR, *Hæselingefeud'* 1236 Fees (p), *Hecelingfeld* 1254 Ipm, *Eslyngfeld* 1488 Ely
Haselingfeld(e), *-yng-* 1140–54 (1366) Ch *et freq* to 1514 AD v, *-fel* 1206 Cur, 1281 Ipm, *-feud* 1272 *Ass*, 1302 Ipm, *-ford(e)* 1272 *Ass*, 1437 Pat, *-flet* 1335 Cl
Haselingefeld(e), *-ynge-* 1190 P *et freq* to 1558 AD v, *-filde* 1565 ib.

[1] Marked on map in AnctC, and as 'Tumulus' near Lord's Bridge Station, on 6″.

Naselingfeude 1212 RBE
Hasselingfeld 1268 *Ass*, *-yng-* 1338 Pat
Haslefeld 1354 *StCatharine's*, *Haselfeld* 1365 FF
Haislingfild 1647 PR i

Ekwall (DEPN) has suggested that this is probably "the open country of the *Hæselingas*," the dwellers at a lost *Haseley*. Such assumption of one lost place to explain another is dangerous and it is more probable that *Hæselingas* is to be interpreted 'people of *Hæsel(a)*,' a personal name corresponding to OGer *Hasili* (a derivative of *Hasu*) (FörstemannPN 787). This is more probable than any association with a lost OE *hæseling*, 'hazel-thicket' (cf. Hazeldean PN Sx 263, Heslington PN ERY 273–4), as persistent medial *e* in the early forms makes it clear that this name goes back to OE *Hæselingafeld* rather than *Hæselingfeld*. For *Naselingfeude* cf. Nelmes (PN Ess 114) and *v.* æt.

AMPTHILL (lost) is *Amtehelle(s)* 1300, 1376 *Trinity*, *the Auntellys* 1337 ib., *Anthell* 1400 ib., *Antehyll* 1402 ib., *Amptehyll* 1456 ib. 'Ant hill,' *v.* OE æmete and hyll. Identical with Ampthill (PN BedsHu 67–8).

CHAPEL HILL is *le Whyghthill* 1522 *Trinity*, *Whitehill* 1631 ib. and owes its present name to a *chapel* newly founded in 1344 (Pat). It is called the *Chapel of the Blessed Virgin Mary Whightehill in Eslyngfeld* in 1488 (*Elien*) and "a place...called *the Lady of Whitehill* where there was a chapell and the Lady Mary's picture in it" t. Jas 1 (CHuAS i, 358). Cf. *the Chapellfeld*, *Chapellwey* 1480 *Trinity* and Chapel Bush *infra*. The soil is chalk.

LINGEY FEN (6″) is (*le*) *Lengey(e)* (*-dik(e)*) 1311 *Queens'*, (*-dyche*) 1452 ib., *Lenegethdich* 1314 ib., *Lengheyedich* 1369 ib., *Nethyrlengeydyche* 1393 *Trinity*, *the Lynge* 1400 *Cole* xl. The forms are too late for any interpretation to be wise.

OFFAL END is *laudefeud* 1273 *Queens'* (p), (*le*) *Aldefeld(e)* 1286, 1360 *Trinity*, 1300 *Queens'*, (*Ende*) 1453 *Trinity*, *Offal End* c. 1825 O.S. Cf. *Eldefeldehyl*, *Laldefeudhel* 14th *Queens'*, *Alfeld Grene* 1481 *Trinity*, *le Hallfeld Grene* 1504 *Queens'*, *Awfield* 1701 DKR xli, *v.* eald, feld, ende and cf. The Offal *supra* 74, Offals Wood *infra* 359 and Ofields (PN Wa 377). *laude-*, *Lalde-* contain the French definite article prefixed.

CANTELUPE FM is *Cantelope Farm* 1821 Baker. *v.* Addenda lix. CHAPEL BUSH (6″), so named c. 1825 (O.S.), was in *Busshemersshe* (1506 *StCatha-*

rine's) which was near *Chapellwey* "where now is only to be seen certain Trees or Bushes which did inclose it (i.e. the chapel)" (c. 1635 *Layer*). Cf. Chapel Hill *supra* 78. FROG END is so named c. 1840 (*TA*). Doubtless a nickname for a marshy spot. Cf. *infra* 357. MONEY HILL is so named c. 1825 (O.S.). There is a tumulus here, doubtless reputed to contain treasure. SPRING HALL FM is *Spring Hall* 1821 Baker. TRINITY COLLEGE FM (6″) is self-explanatory. WILLOW FM (6″) is so named c. 1840 (*TA*). Cf. *le Wyluholm* 1319 *Extent*, *Willough medowe* 1480 *Cole* xl.

Orwell

ORWELL [*olim* ɔrəl]

> *Oreuuella* 1086 ICC, -*uuelle* 1086 DB, -*well(e)* 1173 P (p) *et freq* to
> 1428 FF, (*cum Malketon*) 1285 *Ass*, *Orrewell* 1322 Ipm, 1336 Pat,
> 1518 AD v
> *Or(e)duuelle*, *Ordeuuelle* 1086 DB, *Orduuelle* 1086 InqEl (p)
> *Horwelle* 1086 InqEl (p), *Hor(e)well* 1203 (p), 1260 Ass, 1285 *Ass*
> *Oruuella* 1086–7 (n.d.) France, *Orwell(e)* 1201 Cur *et freq* to 1459
> FF, (*cum Malton*) 1570 SR

Orwell is situated at the foot of a hill which thrusts itself into the valley and was perhaps called ord, i.e. 'point.' Hence 'spring by the ord,' *v.* wielle. "Orwell of a faire springe risinge there" c. 1640 Layer. For early loss of *d* cf. Orleigh (PN D 89).

NOTE. FISHER'S LANE is *Fishers Way* 1836 *EnclA*. Cf. *Fishers Mead* ib. HURDLE DITCH WAY is so named ib.

MALTON FM[1]

> *Maketon(e)* 1200 Cur, 1272 *Ass*
> *Melketon(e)* 1217 Misc, 1279 RH, *Melton* c. 1540 ECP
> *Malketun* 1218 *SR*, -*ton(e)* 1236–56 Barnwell *et freq* to 1507 Pat,
> (*Grene*) 1352 *Trinity*, *Malkton(e)* 1374 Cl, 1428 FA, 1446 FF
> *Mauketon* t. Ed 1 *Christ's*
> *Malton* 1363 Pat *et passim*, *Maulton ffarme* 1593 *Christ's*
> *Maweton al. Malketon* 1444 *Wren*
> *Molton* 1798 PR, -*ten* 1836 *EnclA*

Malling (K, Sx), earlier *Meallingas*, derives from an unrecorded personal name *Mealla*, cognate with OHG *Malo* (*Mello*), *Mallo*-

---

[1] Formerly an independent parish.

baudes, etc. (*v.* PN in *-ing* 37–8, 60, PN Sx 354, KPN 253, PN K 148). From this may well have been formed another personal name *Mealca, by the addition of the suffix *-(i)ca*. Hence '*Mealca*'s farm,' *v.* tūn.

WRATWORTH (lost)

> *Wrat(t)(e)w(o)rth* 1086 (13th) BrC, 1303, 1393 *Hardwicke*, 1499 EA vii, (*water*) 1531 *Hardwicke*
> *Wretewurda* 1086 ICC, *Warateuuorde, Werateuuorde* 1086 DB
> *Wrotteworth* 1380 Cl, *Wrotford Grene* 1515 Ct

'Enclosure where crosswort grows,' OE *wrætt* and worð. Cf. Wratting *infra* 121. The manor was in Orwell, but extended into Wimpole.

FIELD BARN was the home of Felicia *in Campo* (1279 RH). Cf. *Orwell field* 1403 Layer and *v.* feld.

FOX HILL is *Foxhill* 1593 *Christ's*. GREEN FORD BRIDGE (6″). Cf. *Greenbridge Close* 1836 *EnclA*. KING'S BRIDGE (6″) is *The King's Bridge* c. 1825 O.S. OATLANDS (6″). Cf. *Oatland Field* 1836 *EnclA*. ORWELL HILL (6″) is so named in 1596 (*Ct*). SHARP HILL PLANTATION. Cf. *Sharpe hill* 1593 *Christ's*. SPRING WEST FM (6″) is probably an error for *Springwell* ib. THORN HILL is *Thorn(e)hill* (*Deane*) ib., 1600 *Depositions, Thorneldeane* 1678 *Trinity*. TOWN FM (6″). Cf. *Town meade furlong* 1593 *Christ's*, *le Towneland* 1600 *Depositions*, *v.* tūn.

Shepreth

SHEPRETH

> *Esceprid(e)* 1086 DB, *Sceperia, -eie, -éé* 1086 InqEl, *Scepere* 1218 *SR*
> *Sepeia* 1086 ICC, 1208 Cur, *-eie* 1214 ib., *Syepe* 1281 Ipm, *Schepeye* 1291 Tax
> *Sepere(e), -eye, -ethe* 12th *AddCh*, 1218 *SR et freq* to 1299 QW, *Sepreye* 13th *Ely*, c. 1330 *ElyCouch*
> *Shepree* 1214 Cur, 1285 *Ass*, *Schepreye* 1268 ib., *Shepreth(e)* 1272, 1285 *Ass*, 1330, 1396 FF, *-ryth* 1285 *Ass*, *-red* 1389, 1464 Pat, 1666 CAPr xvii, *-redde* 1553 EA vi, *Schepreth* 1327 SR
> *S(c)hepereth(e), -ryth(e), -rith* 1231 FF *et freq* to 1428 FA, (*al. Shepryght*) 1513 LP, *-rede* 13th *Chateriz*, 1401 Pat, t. Hy 8 *Rental*, *S(c)heper(h)ey(e)* 1262 *Chateriz et freq* to 1298 *Ass*, *-he(a)th* 1290 FF, 1339 Layer, *Seperleye* 1265 Pat, *Chepereye* 1266 ib., *-reth* 1412 FA, *Scepereth* 1345 *CWool*
> *S(c)hipereye* 1272 *Ass*, *-reth* 1298 ib., *Shipreth* 1299 QW

'Brook of the sheep' (OE *scēapa-rīð*), perhaps 'brook where sheep were washed,' *v.* scēap, rīþ. For the loss of *th* in the early forms cf. Odsey *supra* 62.

Note. Huckles Lane is to be associated with the family of Adam and Alan *Huckyl* (1279 RH).

Moor End is *lamoresende* 1539 *MinAcct* and was probably the home of William de *la Mora* (c. 1300 Layer). Cf. *Sheprethmore* 1526 *WMP* and *v.* mōr.

Docuraies Manor, Tyrell's Hall and Wimbish Manor (all 6″) are to be associated with the families of Thomas *Docura* (1552 Layer), Edward *Terrell* (1427 ib.) and Thomas *Tyrell* (1446 FF) and John *Wimbish* (1422 Layer), which must have come from Wimbish (Ess). Cf. *Docuras manor* c. 1635 Layer, *Shepreth al. South Tyrell* 1581 *Cole* xxii, *Terrel's manner* c. 1635 Layer, *Wymbichlond* 1520 Trinity, *Wimbish manor* c. 1600 ChancP.

Brimble Hill and Shovels Plantation are so called c. 1825 (O.S.). *brimble* is doubtless from brēmel, 'bramble.' Hall Yards (6″) is *the Hall Yardes* c. 1635 Layer. L Moor (6″) is named from its shape. Rushmoor Plantation (6″). Cf. *Rush Moor* c. 1840 *TA*.

Wimpole

Wimpole [*olim* wimpl]

> Winepola 1086 ICC, *Winepol(e)* 1086 DB *et freq* to 1242 Fees, -*poll'* 1201–7 Cur, *Winnepol* c. 1300 *St John'sH*
>
> Quenpola sive Wimpoll a. 1086 (c. 1280) YCh, *Wenepol* 1279 RH, *Wempole* 1448 Pat
>
> Wimpol 1195 Abbr, *Wympel* 1297 Pat, -*pol(e)* 1346 FA *et freq* to 1553 Pat, -*pool* 1406–8 FF, 1412 FA, -*poll(e)* 1428 FA (p), t. Hy 8 Rental, *Wympyll* or *Wympooll* 1494 Ipm, *Wympill* 1539–40 MinAcct, -*pull* t. Hy 8 *Rental*, *Wymple* 1553 EA vii, *Wylpole* 1549 Pat, *Whympoole* 1553 ib., *Wimple* 1576 Saxton
>
> Wynepol(e) 1230 FF *et freq* to 1428 Pat, -*poll* 1258 FF, 1291 Tax, -*pool* 1396 Cl, *Wynipole* 1346 FA
>
> Wynpol(e) 1298 *Ass et freq* to 1428 FA, -*pool* 1404 AD i, *Wynnepol* 1270 Ipm, *Winpol* 1320 Pat

'*Wina*'s pool,' *v.* pōl. For *Quen*-, *v.* Introd. xxxvi.

HOBACK FM is *Holbeke* (*next the Comon Ree*) 1512 *Hardwicke*. This is named from the *Hobeck Ryddye* 1593 *Christ's*, *Holback Ridye*, *the river Hoeback* 1836 *EnclA*, apparently the small stream flowing near the farm to the Cam. Cf. Hoback Fm *supra* 68 and Gransden Brook *supra* 6. *Ryddye* is OE rīðig, 'small stream.'

COBB'S WOOD FM and FRENCH HO (6″) are to be associated with the families of Geoffrey *Cobbe* (1377 Ely) and Richard and Stephen *le Fraunceys* (1279 RH). Cf. *Cobbes* (*Dole*) 1403 Layer, *Cobbys* (*Manor*) 1465 EA vii, 1490 Ipm and *Fraunceys maner* 1401 Cl.

COOMB GROVE FM. Cf. *Combe Grove Ho* 1675 *WMP*. HORSE COMMON PLANTATION (6″). Cf. *Horse Common* c. 1840 *TA*. LAMP HILL (6″). Cf. *Lamp Hall* ib. THORNBERRY HILL is *Thornbury Hill F.* 1833 G. WILD BARNS (6″). Cf. Croydon Wilds *supra* 54. WIMPOLE HALL is *Wimple Hall* 1695 SN. WIMPOLE PARK (6″) is *parcum de Wynepol* 1302 *Christ's*.

III. THRIPLOW HUNDRED

Trip(*p*)*elaue* 1086 ICC, *Trip*(*p*)(*e*)*lawa*, -(*e*) 1185–95 P *et freq* to 1336 *SR*, -*lowe* 1260 Ass *et freq* to 1570 SR, *Tryp*(*pe*)*low*(*e*) 1272 *Ass*, 14th *Cai*, 1523 *SR*
Trepe(*s*)*lav* 1086 DB, *Trep*(*p*)*eslau*(*ue*) 1086 InqEl, *Trep*(*p*)(*e*)*lawe*, -(*a*) 1168–1200 P, 1218 *SR*, *Treplauue* 1168 P
Trapelawe 1185 RotDom
Thrippelowe 1332 *SR*, *Thryplowe* 1523 ib., *Thriploo* 1553 EA vi
Thurpelawe 1346, 1428 FA, *Thirppelowe* 1428 FA
Typlowe 1474 *MinAcct*, *Thyplowe* 1482 Pat

For further forms and the etymology, *v.* Thriplow *infra* 90. The hundred probably met in the fields of Newton at *Mothlowe* c. 1250 *ElyM*, *Mot*(*e*)*lowe* 1319 *Extent*, 1323 *St John's*, *Mutlowe* 1418 *Ct*, *Short* and *West Mutler Shot* c. 1840 *TA*. In Harston and Thriplow documents we also have reference to *Motlowe*, -*lawe* c. 1200–92 *Trinity*, c. 1280 *Chateriz*, probably referring to the same place. The road leading to the moot-hill was *Motloweweye* c. 1230 *ElyM* (Shelford), *Mot*(*e*)*loweye* 1319 *Extent* (Newton), 1418 *St John's* (Thriplow), *Metloweye* 1319 *Extent*. *v.* (ge)mōt, hlāw and cf. Mettle Hill *supra* 60.

Fowlmere

FOWLMERE

Fuglemære, Fugelesmara 1086 DB, *Fugelm̄a* 1155–7 P, *Fuelmere*
1086 InqEl (p), *Fulgh(e)mer'* 1220 Cur, *Fowelmere* 1322 Ipm
Fulemere 1086 ICC, 1185 RotDom, 1258 Ch, *-a* 1086 InqEl (p),
Fulmere 1086 ib. (p) *et freq* to 1428 FA, (*al. Foulmere*) 1477 Pat,
Folemere 1227 FF, *Fulmar* 1554 CHuAS v
Foulmer(e) 1313 Pat *et passim, Foulemer'* 1447 *Rental,* 1450 Pat,
Fowlemer(e) 1494 Ipm, 1570 SR, 1583 AD vi, *Fowlmore* 1694 EA
x, *Foul(e)mire* 1616 Ely, 1663 CHuAS v, c. 1840 *TA*

'Wild-birds' mere,' *v.* fugol, mere and cf. Fulmer (PN Bk 237–8).
"An actual mere, noted for its wealth of wild fowl, existed here till
more than half a century ago. It is now a worthless patch of land,
full of springs and runlets" (Conybeare, *Highways and Byways in
Cambs. and Ely* 230). Cf. Foulmire Fen *infra* 233.

BURY FM (local), THE GROVE and ROUND MOAT (both 6″) are all so
named c. 1840 (*TA*). *v.* burh (manorial). For the small oval ring-
work here *v.* Fox 137.

Foxton

FOXTON

Foxetune 1086 DB
Foxtona 1086 ICC, *-ton(e)* 1202–1352 FF *et passim,* (*cum Hard-
liston*) 1334 *Ct, -tun* 1218 *SR, Voxtun* c. 1300 Layer, *Foxston*
1396, 1446 FF, 1485 Ipm, *Faxton* 1549 Pat

'Farm where foxes abound,' *v.* fox, tūn. Cf. also *Foxildounis* 1316
Ct and *Foxholys* 1520 *Trinity* (both in Foxton).

MORTIMER'S FM and WILDBORES FM (both 6″) are to be associated
with the families of William de *Mortuo Mari* (1298 *Ass*) and John
Welbore sonne of Phillip *Wellbore* (c. 1640 *Layer*). Cf. *terram Domini
Roberti de Mortuo Mari* c. 1280 *Chateriz, Mortymeres, -ys* 1409, 1464
Trinity and *Wildboars Close* c. 1840 *TA*.

BURY FM (6″) is *Foxton Burye* 1622 *FF.* Cf. *Berry Close* c. 1840 *TA*
and *v.* burh (manorial).

Harston

HARSTON [*olim* haˑsən]

Herlestona 1086 ICC, InqEl, -e DB, -ton(e) 1175 P (p) et freq to
1499 Ipm, -tune c. 1235 Colch, Herli(e)ston(e) 1246 FF, 1262 Cl,
1268 Ass, 1275 RH, 1296 Barnwell, -ys- 1272 Ass
Harlestone, -a 1086 ICC, InqEl et freq to 1480 CTerr, (Typpetote)
1388 Ct, (Tybbetot') 1396 ib., -tun 1218 SR, Harlyston(e), -i-
1272 Ass et freq to 1428 FA, Harleweston 1272 Ass
Herelestona 1086 InqEl, Hereliston 1275 RH
Erlestuna 1086 InqEl
Hard(e)leston(e) 1218 SR et freq to 1495 BM, (immo Herleston',
Harleston') 1285 Ass, Hard(e)liston(e), -ys- 1297 Ipm et freq to
1395 Ct, Hardlaston 1318 Pat
Herdleston(e) 1239 FF, 1285 Ass, 13th Ely
Hadleston c. 1250 ElyCouch, Haldliston 1302 FA
Harlston 1389 Pat, Harston 1390 Ct et freq to 1553 Pat, (Wygorn)
1465–9 Ct, Herston 1464 Pat, Harstone al. Harlestone 1580 PCC,
Harson, Haston 1757 Terr

This is apparently 'the farm of *Herel*,' the strong form of *Herela*
found in Harlton *supra* 76. *v.* tūn. Ekwall (DEPN) suggests that
Heorulfestun 1015 ASWills may belong here and some slight support
may possibly be found in the 1272 form *Harleweston*. If this is so,
the name is '*Heoruwulf*'s farm,' *v.* tūn. This form may, however, belong
to Harleston (Nf, Sf), both DB *Heroluestuna*, cf. also Harlestone
(PN Nth 83), DB *Herolvestune* and Hardmead (PN Bk 36). *Typpetote*
and *Wygorn* from the family of Sir Robert *Typetot* who held a manor
here in 1298 (*Ass*), and whose descendants later became earls of
Worcester, cf. John *Comitis Wygorn' Lord Typtott* (1448 *Ct*). For
immo cf. *s.n.* Grantchester *supra* 76.

NOTE. CHURCH ST was probably the home of Geoffrey *ad ecclesiam* (1283
Trinity). Cf. *le Chercheweye* 1431 *Ct*.

BAGGOT HALL (6″) was the home of John Walsheman *atte Bagatt*
(1447, 1450 Ct), *atte Bagott* (1453, 1465 ib.) and clearly contains a
significant word *bagatt, bagott* which formed part of his surname. Cf.
further *Bagateswell* 1388 *Ct*, *Bagatdole* 1394 ib. which clearly contain
the same significant word. The history of *baggot* here is quite
distinct from that of the personal name *Bagot* found as that of a
family living in Baggaby (earlier *Bagoteby*) in Warter (PN ERY169)

in the 12th century, whatever the history of that personal name may ultimately be. The etymology of this significant word *bagatt, bagott* is entirely obscure.

HOFFER BRIDGE. Cf. *Ap(p)isford(e)* 13th, 1317 *Queens'*[1], 1389–1433[2], 1411 *Ct*[2], *Apesford* 1391 ib.[2], *Apysworthforthe* 1426 ib.[2], *Appeforde* 1424 ib.[2], *Appelesford* 1380 ib.[2], *Tappesforthe* 1364–74 *Queens'*[1], *-forde* 1400 ib.[1], *Tappysforthe* 1410 *Trinity*[1], *-forde* 1443 *Queens'*[1], *Hopforthe* 1428 *Ct*[2], *(le) Hofforth(e) (-dole)* 1432 ib.[2], 1448 ib.[2], *Hofforde (-holte)* 1448 ib.[2], 1541 *Ct*[3], *Happeforthe* 1451 ib.[2], *Uffer Bridge* 1821 Baker[2], *Hoffer Bridge* c. 1825 O.S.[2] The ford and bridge lie where the Hoffer Brook (*supra* 7) crosses the Cambridge-Royston road (here the Harston-Foxton boundary). A little over a quarter of a mile to the north, the parishes of Harston, Haslingfield and Barrington meet on the Cam, which forms the boundary between Foxton and Barrington, and it is difficult to avoid the conclusion that all the forms given above refer to this same ford and bridge. The interpretation of this name, whether we take the correct form of the first element to be *Appes-* or *Appeles-* is not easy and the whole business is made yet more difficult by the existence of places called *Apewellesheved* 1304 *StCatharine's*, *A(p)pewelle* c. 1250–1340 *Trinity*, c. 1280, 1337 *StCatharine's*, 1463 *Ct*, *Hapewell* 1343 ib. which, with one exception (1316 *Ct* in Foxton), are in Barrington on the opposite side of the Cam. If they can in any way be related to the first series of names then we might perhaps take the original form of all to be *Appelewellesford*, 'ford of the apple-tree spring,' with reference to a ford in Hoffer Brook, called at that time *Appelewell*, but this is entirely speculative and perhaps unwise.

HARSTON MILL (6″) was the home of John, son of Adam *Attemelne* (1279 *Ct*).

HARSTON HILL is *Haston Hill* 1757 *Terr*. MOOR BARN (6″). Cf. *la More* 1228 FF, *le Moorhend* 1411 *Ct*, v. mōr. ST MARGARET'S MOUNT (6″) is *Maggots Mount* c. 1825 O.S., *Maggot* being a popular form for *Margaret*.

Hauxton

HAUXTON [*olim* hɔ·sən]

(*æt*) *Hafucestune* c. 975 ASCh, *Hauochestune* c. 1050 (12th) LibEl, *-tun, -tone* 1086 DB, *-tuna, -e* c. 1120 HarlCh

---

[1] Haslingfield.   [2] Harston.   [3] Foxton.

Hauekestune c. 1050 (13th) KCD 907, 1086 InqEl (p), 1170 LibEl, -*ton*(*a*) 1086 ICC, InqEl *et freq* to 1285 *Ass*, *Hauechestune*, -*a* 1086 InqEl, c. 1120 *LibEl*

Haukeston(*e*), -*a* c. 1060, 1229 *ElyM et freq* to 1445 Pat, (*cum capella de Neutona*) 1254 Val, -*stan* 1339 Cl, *Hauchestuna*, -*e* c. 1150 *LibEl*, *Hawk*(*e*)*ston* 1291 Tax, t. Hy 8 *Rental*, *Haukyston*, -*w*- 1314 *Ass*, 1484 Pat, *Haux*(*s*)*ton* 1359, 1383 *Ct*, *Hawxton* 1572 Ely, *Haukestede* 1371 Pat, *Haugeston* 1272 *Ass*

Hauextona 1086 ICC

Hau(*e*)*ston*(*e*) 1272 *Ass*, 1405 *Elien*, 1447–68 *Ct*, *Haw*(*e*)*ston* 1437 IpmR, 1450 *Ct*, 1553 EA vi, *Hawson* 1589 Cai

'*Heafoc*'s tūn.' This personal name is not on record, but cf. the recorded *Sperhauoc*, *Sparhauoc* and the common Scand *Haukr*. *v*. also MLR xiv, 239.

HAUXTON MILL (FM) and MILL BRIDGE (6″). Cf. *molendini aquatici de Haukeston* 1285 *Ass*, *magni pontis de Hauston juxta molendinum aquaticum in Hauston* 1444 *Cole* xxii, *Hawston Mills* 1563 ib. xii, *Hasonmellfield* 1700 *Pembroke*, *Hockstonmill* 1756 *Jesus*. Here lived Matilda de *Molendin'* (1279 RH). WELL HEAD (6″). Cf. *le Welhed* 1484 *Ct* (in Barrington) and *Apewellesheved* 1304, *s.n*. Hoffer Bridge *supra* 85. *v*. wielle, hēafod.

Newton

NEWTON

Neutune c. 1050 (13th) KCD 907, LibEl, -*ton*(*e*), -(*a*) c. 1060 *ElyM et freq* to 1445 Pat, *Newton*(*a*) 1139 *ElyD et passim*, (*cum Hawxston*) 1372 *SR*, *Newetun*(*e*) 1170 LibEl

Nowetuna c. 1120, 1150 *HarlCh*, -*tona* c. 1120 *LibEl*, c. 1130 *ElyD*

Neotuna c. 1150 *ElyCh*, c. 1170 *ElyM*

Newenton 1271 FF

'The new farm,' *v*. nīwe, tūn. For *Nowe*-, cf. No Ditch *infra* 200 and Introd. xxxv.

COCKLE HILL is *Cokereleslowe* c. 1292 *Trinity*, 1319 *Extent*, *Cockerill Hill* 1757 *Terr*, *Cockle Hill* c. 1840 *TA*. The second element is hlāw, the first, probably, a medieval personal name.

CAMPS PARK (6″) is so named c. 1840 (*TA*). FIELD HOUSES (6″) is so named c. 1825 (O.S.). Cf. *in campis de Neuton* 1323 *St John's*. NEW FM (6″). Cf. *New Farm Field* c. 1840 *TA*.

Great and Little Shelford

SHELFORD (GREAT and LITTLE)

Scelford c. 1050 (13th) KCD 907, 1086 InqEl, 1170 LibEl, (*Magna, Parua*) 1218 *SR*, 1221 *ElyA*, 1279 RH, *-fort* c. 1050 (12th) LibEl, *-forda* 1086 ICC, *-forð* 1086 InqEl, *S(c)hel(e)ford(a)* c. 1060 *ElyM et freq* to 1437 Pat, (*Maior*) 13th *Ely*, (*Petyt*) 1335 *Ass*, (*Moch*) 1465 IpmR, *-forth(e)* 1502 ElyA, 1554 CHuAS v

Escelford(e) 1086 DB, *Esceldford, -forð* 1086 InqEl

Sceldford(a) 1086 InqEl, 1109–31 *LibEl*, *-fort* c. 1120 *HarlCh*, *Scheldford* 1109–33 *ElyM*, c. 1130 *ElyD*, 1176, 1190 P, 1354 CGild

Sel(e)ford(e) 1198 Fees *et freq* to 1289 ElyA, *Seld(e)ford* 1201 Cur, 1236 Barnwell, 13th *Jesus*, 1257 Cl, *-fort* 13th *St John's*, *Shelleford* 1279 *Ct*

Seforð 1199 CurR, *Scheford* 1275 RH

Chileford 1272 *Ass*, *Chel(e)ford(e)* ib., 1277 *Ely*, 1316, 1412 FA *et freq* to 1450 SR

Shaldeford 1343 Pat, *Shulford* 1582 AD vi

Ekwall has suggested (DEPN) that the first element is either OE *sceld*, 'shield, protection,' in the sense 'shelter' as in Sheldwich (PN K 293) or an OE *sceldu*, 'shallowness, shallow place.' The first suggestion is not really satisfactory for, even though there is a camp near by (Fox 178), we have no evidence that OE *sceld* was used of any form of physical protection other than a shield. The second alternative is therefore more probable. Hence 'ford through the shallow place,' *v.* **ford** and Shell Fm *infra* 200.

Great Shelford

SHELFORD MILL (6″) was the home of Gilebertus *ad Molend(inum)* (1279 RH). It is *Chelford mill* 1672 EA xi. Cf. *molendino aquatico de Shelford* 13th *ElyG*.

DE FREVILLE FM and GRANHAM'S MANOR FM (both 6″) are to be associated with the families of Richard de *Frivill* (1275 RH), *al.* de *Frevill* (1298 Ipm) and John de *Grendon* (1355 Pat) or de *Crendon* (1359 Ipm). They are *Frevyles* 1481 IpmR, *Grendon* 14th ElyA, *Grandon(e)s* 1397 IpmR, Pat, *Grendons* 1464 ib., *Gryndons* 1502 ElyA, *Grandames* 1535 VE, *Graundehams manor* 1553 Pat, *Grandhams* 1597

St John's, Granhams 1756 *Jesus, Granham's Fm* c. 1825 O.S. For inter-change of *Gr-* and *Cr-* cf. Cambridge *supra* 37 and for the general development cf. Granham (PN W 308), earlier *Grendon* and Introd. xxiii, xxxiv.

CAIUS COLLEGE FM was purchased by the Master and Fellows of Gonville and Caius College, Cambridge, in 1614 (CAS xl). GRAN-HAM(S) (MANOR) CAMP (local[1]) is probably to be identified with *Aldewerk(e)(hale)* 1221 *ElyA*, 1277 *Ely*, 1322 *MinAcct, Aldework'* 14th *Jesus*. 'The old fortification,' *v.* (ge)weorc, Fox 178, AnctC 50–1 and *Oldwark* (PN Nt 222). See also *s.n. Alfordway supra* 19. THE GROVE (6″) is *Legrove* t. Hy 8 *Cole* xxxvii. HERMITAGE (6″). There was a '*Hermitage* at the *Bridge* between *Great & Little Shelford*' (Blomefield 8–9), probably already in existence in 1398. NINE WELLS is *the Nine Wells* 1575 Bushell. STONE HILL. Cf. *Stonehill way* 17th *Jesus*. WHITE HILL. Cf. *the Whitehill water* 1631 Bushell.

Little Shelford

CLUNCH PIT HILL is *Clunchpitt Hill* 1756 *Jesus*. WELL HEAD PLANTA-TION (6″). Cf. *The Well Head* c. 1825 O.S. WESTFIELD (6″) is (*le*) *Westfeld* 1251 *ElyCouch, v.* feld.

Stapleford

STAPLEFORD

(*ad*) *Stapelforda(m)* 956 (12th) BCS 1346, *Stapelford(e)* c. 1060–1229 (14th) *ElyM et freq* to 1345 *CWool, -fordam* 1086 InqEl, *Stapelforð* ib., *Stappelforde* c. 1150 *LibEl, Stapelefford* 1252 Ch, *Stapalford* c. 1150 *HarlCh, Stapilford(e)* 1275 RH *et freq* to 1493 Pat, (*juxta Babraham*) 1496 *Clare, -forthe* 1410 *ElyB*

Staplesford c. 1050 (13th) KCD 907, *-fort* (12th) LibEl, *Stapelisford* 1372 *SR*

Stapleford 1086 ICC, *-forde* 1086 DB, *-fordam* 1086 InqEl, *-ford* 1347 FF, *-forthe* 1625 *FF, Stableford* 1700 *Pembroke*

'Ford marked by a post,' *v.* stapol, ford.

VANDLEBURY

Wendlesbiri 10th (17th) ChronRams
Wyndilbyry t. Stephen LibEl, 1334 *ElyC*

---

[1] Marked as 'Earthworks' on 6″.

Wandlebiria c. 1211 GervT, *Wandlesbury* 1594 Camden, *Wandle-
bury* 1719 Nichols iii
Wendelbiri c. 1225 *ElyM*, *-beri(gate)*, (*portam de*) 13th *ElyCh*, *ElyF*
Vandlebury Camp 1808 L (map)

'*Wændel*'s fort,' *v.* burh and cf. Wensdon Hill (PN BedsHu 114),
Wellingborough (PN Nth 140), Wandsworth (PN Sr 36), Wallington
(PN Herts 168) and Wansley (PN Nt 132). Gervase of Tilbury
associated this name with the Vandals[1]. The present initial *v* is clearly
an antiquarian spelling due to knowledge of Gervase's story.

WORMWOOD HILL

Wyrmelawe c. 1225 *ElyM*, *-lowe* 1394, 1395 *ElyF*, *Wirmelauhe* 13th
ElyCh
(*campo de*) *Wrmelawe*, *-lowe*, *-laue* (*super le S(c)erdfurlong*) 13th
ElyCh, *ElyF*, *Wurmelawe* ib.

The first element here is probably *wyrm*, 'dragon.' There is a
tumulus here (Fox 149) and it is clear that it was called a hlāw in Old
English times. Barrows are often named after the person (supposed
to be) buried in them, but they are equally often associated with
dragons and the like, so the first element here can be taken to be
wyrma, gen. pl. of *wyrm*, and that is the probable explanation. Cf.
Wormcliff (PN W 85). For the possibilities of a personal name
Wyrma, *v.* Worminghall (PN Bk 129–30) and Warmington (PN Nth
215). *The S(c)erdfurlong* contains as its first element OE sceard, 'gap,'
with reference perhaps to the *unico ad instar portalis aditu* of Vandlebury in the note *infra*.

FOXHILL PLANTATION. Cf. *Foxhil* c. 1235 *ElyM*. HEATH FM is *le Heth*
1390 *ElyF*. THE LOAVES (all 6″) *al.* THE TWOPENNY LOAVES are two
barrows (Fox 329). TELEGRAPH CLUMP (6″) stands high, near Vandlebury, and was probably an old signalling station. Cf. Signal Hill
infra 101 and Telegraph Hill (PN Sx 20).

[1] "In Anglia ad terminos episcopatus Eliensis est castrum, Cantabrica nomine,
infra cujus limites e vicino locus est, quem Wandlebiriam dicunt, eo quod illic
Wandeli, partes Britanniae saeva Christianorum peremptione vastantes, castra
metati sunt. Ubi vero ad monticuli apicem fixere tentoria, planities in rotundum
vallatis circumcluditur, unico ad instar portalis aditu patens ad ingressum" (cf.
portam, *-gate supra*) (GervT LIX, pp. 26–7).

Thriplow

Thriplow

> *Tripelan* (sic) c. 1050 (13th) KCD 907, *-lau* c. 1050 (12th) LibEl,
> *-laue* 1086 InqEl, 1170 LibEl, *-lauua* 12th *LibEl*, *-lowe* 1271 FF,
> *-lawe* 1272 *Ass*, 14th *Cai*, *Triplaw(e)*, *-lowe* 1231 FF *et freq* to 1553
> Pat, *Tripelhawe* 1272 *Ass*, *Trypelawe* 1298 ib., *Tryplowe* 1429
> Pat, 1558 AD vi
>
> *Trippelawe, -a* c. 1060 *ElyM*, 1218 *SR et freq* to 1338 Ch, *Trippe-
> lowe, -y-* c. 1169 *Chateriz et freq* to 1412 FA, *-lawe* 1346 ib.,
> *Tripellowe* 1303 AD iii
>
> *Trepeslau, -lai* 1086 DB, *Trepláu* 1086 InqEl, *-lawe* 1218 *SR*, *-lowe*
> 1275 RH, *Trepelaue* 1086 InqEl, *Trepelowe* 1445 AD vi
>
> *Treppeslaú(e), Treppelau* 1086 InqEl, *-lawe* 1206 FF, 1279 RH,
> *Trappelowe* 1275 ib.
>
> *Threppelawe* 1285 *Ass*, *Threploo* 1554 CHuAS v
>
> *Thrippelowe, -y-* 1298 *Ass et freq* to 1409 Cl, *Thryplowe, -i-* 1341,
> 1541 AD v *et freq* to 1576 *Ct*, *-loe* 1571 ElyA, *-lo(o)* 1506–40 AD v,
> vi, *Thirplowe* 1566 Ely

'*Tryppa*'s hill or tumulus,' *v.* hlāw. This personal name is not on
independent record but, as suggested by Ekwall (DEPN), may be a
short form of such a name as *Þrȳþbeorht* or a nickname from the root
of OE *treppan*, 'to tread.' For further forms *v.* the Hundred name
supra 82.

Note. Church St is *Cherchestret* 1364 AD vi.

Heath Fm and Thriplow Green (6") were the homes of John *ate
Heeth* (1332 *SR*) and John Pryme *atte Grene* (1519 AD v). Cf. *le
Hethfeld* 1251 ElyCouch, 1277 Ely, *le Hathfeld* 1445 AD vi, *common
green of le Grenestrete* 1439 AD vi, *le Grenestrate* 1473 StJohn's.
v. hǣð, feld, grēne.

Bacon's Fm and Barrington's Manor Fm (both 6") are probably to
be associated with the families of Thomas *Bacun* (1316 FF) and
Nicholas de *Barenton* (1250 *AddR*), i.e. Barrington *supra* 70. The first
is *Bakuns* 1489 Ipm, *Bacons* 1576 *Ct*.

Great Nine Wells is so named c. 1825 (O.S.). Mill Ho. Cf.
molend. de Triplawe 1298 *MinAcct*. St John's College Fm (all 6")
was bequeathed by Dr Humphrey Gower (d. 1711) to his successors,
the Masters of St John's College, Cambridge.

Trumpington

TRUMPINGTON

Trumpintune c. 1050 (13th) KCD 907, 1170 LibEl, 1086 InqEl, *Trumpintona* 1086 ICC, *-tone* 1086 DB, InqEl, *-yn-* 1203 Cur *et freq* to 1470 CRent, (*in Kantebrigg*) 1366 Pat, *Trunpintune* c. 1050 (12th) LibEl

Trumpitone c. 1060 (14th) ElyM, *Trumpituna* 1086 InqEl, *Trumpiton(e)*, *-y-* 1202 Cur *et freq* to 1434 Pat, *Troumpyton* 1309 Ch

Trompintona, *-e* 1086 ICC, 1086 InqEl, *-ton(e)* 1272 Ass, 1551 Pat, *Tromphintonam* 1107–28 (1329) Ch, *Tronpinton* 1212 RBE

Trumpington(e), *-yng-* 1198 FF *et freq*, *Trumpingtun* 1218 SR, *Trumpyngdon* 1490 Ipm

Trumpetun(e) 1218 SR, 1252 FF, *-tona*, *-e* 1264 Cl *et freq* to 1421 ib., *Trumppeton* 1271 FF, 1304 Ipm, *Trumpton* 1290, 1314 Cl, 1298 Ass, 1362 Pat

Tromp(y)ton, *-i-* 1261 Cl, 1262 AD, 1285, 1298 Ass, 1313 Ipm, *Trompeton(e)* 1272 Ass *et freq* to 1326 FF

Trompington, *-yng-* 1285 Ass, 1489 Pat, 1539–40 MinAcct

'*Trump*'s farm,' *v.* ingtūn. This personal name is found independently in a signature attached to the Thorney foundation charter as found in the Thorney Cartulary (*ex inf.* Dr Schram). In BCS 1297 it is printed from a late Cottonian charter, with the impossible signature *Trumþ*. It is doubtless short for such a name as *Trumbeorht* or, as suggested by Ekwall (DEPN), it may be derived from Goth *trimpan*, Sw *trumpen*, 'surly,' *trumpe*, 'surly person,' cf. Nicholas *Trumpe* (of Great Abington) 1279 RH, and, for the derivative *Trympa*, Trimpley (PN Wo 252).

NOTE. MILL RD is *Millewey* 1480 Cole xl, *Mill Road or Trumpington New Road* 1862 Trinity, *Mill otherwise Long Road* 1923 ib.

KNEIGHTON[1] is *Kneton'* 1225 Lewes, 1374 Jesus; cf .*Kinetuneweisende* 1228 FF, *Neton Pitte* 1480 Cole xl, *Great, Little Kneighton field* 1841 Trinity. OE *cyne*-tūn, 'royal manor.' For initial *kn* cf. the history of Kneesworth *supra* 56.

ANSTEY HALL is so called from the family of Christopher *Anstey*, rector of Brinkley (d. 1751)[2].

CLAY FM, RED CROSS and VICARAGE FM (6″) are so named c. 1825 (O.S.). TRINITY FM belonged to Trinity College, Cambridge.

[1] Peserved in KNEIGHTON BRAE, on or very near to the site of *Kneton'*.
[2] *Ex inf.* Mr J. H. Bullock.

IV. WHITTLESFORD HUNDRED

Witlesforda, -e 1086 ICC, *Wit(t)lesford(e)*, *Wyt-* 1175–99 P *et freq*
to 1428 FA, *Wytlisford* 1279 RH, 1285 *Ass*, *Wythlesford* 1336 ib.
Witelesford, Witelesfeld 1086 DB, *Witelesforda* 1086 InqEl, *Witel-
(le)sford* 1218 *SR*, *Wittelesforde* 1346 FA
Witleford, Wyt- 1175 P, 1272 *Ass*
Wytford 1272 *Ass*, *Wichesford* 1284 FA

For further forms and the etymology, *v.* Whittlesford *infra* 98.
The meeting-place of the hundred cannot be definitely located. It is
clearly to be associated with *Moutlow mor* 1598 *Pembroke, Muttlow
moor* 1794 ib. in Whittlesford and probably with *Mitlowedene* c. 1280,
1339 *CaiCh* in Duxford which was probably on the borders of the
two parishes.

Duxford

DUXFORD [dʌksə]

Dukeswrthe c. 950 (14th) ASWills, *-w(o)rth(e)* 1211 Cur *et freq* to
1370 Pat, *-uurth* 1218 *SR*, *-w(o)rd(e)* 1218, 1222 Fees, 1230 P,
-wurth 1236 FF, *Doukesworth(e)* 1291 Tax, 1308 FF, *Dukisworthe*
1302 FA

Duchesuurda 1086 ICC (p), *-wrđ* c. 1200 CaiCh, *Ducesuuorthe*
1102–3 Crispin, *Ducchuswrd'* 12th *CaiCh*, *Duckeswurthe* 1218
Seld 53, *Dukkesworth* 1467 Pat

Dochesurda 1086 ICC, *Dochesuuorde* 1086 DB, *Dochesuurda, -đe*
1086 InqEl, *Dokesw(o)rth(e)* 1251 Ch *et freq* to 1435 Cl, (*Sancti
Petri, Sancti Johannis*) 1256 Barnwell, *Dokysworth, -is-* 1356
Walden, 1360, 1442 Pat, 1479 FF

Dodesuuorde 1086 DB, *Dodesuurda* 1086 InqEl (p)

Chochesfordam t. Stephen France, *Cokesworth* 1428 FA

Duk(e)worth 1227 FF, 1284 FA (p), *Dokeworth* 1272 *Ass*

Duxkeswrth 1268 *Ass*, *Duxwurth* 1442 Pat, *Doxe Worth* 1570 SR

Dakesworth 1275 RH, *Dekesworth* 1282 FF, *Dikesworthe* 1298 *Ass*,
Dokenworth 1309 FF, *Dokelesworth* 1340 Pat

Dokesford 1397 Pat

Duxforth(e) (*Petre, John*) 1535 VE, 1548–50 Pat, 1564 Ely, *Duxford
Saynt Johnes* 1548 PCC

'*Ducc*'s enclosure,' *v.* worþ. This personal name is not on independent record, but is found in other place-names. Cf. Ducksworth

(PN BedsHu 45), Duxhurst (PN Sr 293), Dukesfield (PN NbDu 66), Duxbury (PN La 129). There were formerly two churches here, dedicated respectively to St *John* and St *Peter*. For interchange of **ford** and **worþ** cf. PN NbDu 268 (§ 4), Cotchford and Ockford (PN Sx 366, 523-4), PN D, vol. 1, xxxv, Ufford (PN Nth 244) and Chafford (PN Ess 120).

CLODERTON (6″) is possibly to be identified with *Kaleuhel* c. 1235 CaiCh, *Caluedune* 1278 ib., *Calewedone* 1303, 1316 ib., *Kalewedene* 1308 ib., *Collodenhyll* 1589 Ct. 'Bare hill,' v. **calu, dūn**.

COLDHAMS (6″) is *Coldham* c. 1285 CaiCh. Cf. *Coldhomcroft* 1338 ib. 'Cold enclosure,' v. **cald, hamm**.

CRACKWELL HOLE (6″) is *Crattewelledene* 1308 CaiCh, 1483 *Rental*, *Cratwellho(o)le* 1589 Ct, 1612 Terr, *Crackly Hole* 1730 ib. Forms are late and no certainty is possible in the interpretation of this name. The closest parallel in the county is provided by the place-name *Cratendune* 1170 LibEl, 13th ElyCh, *-don* 1251 ElyCouch, 1277 Ely, *Cratenton'* 1221 ElyA, *Cratingdon* 1519 Wren, *Cradiden* 1586 Camden. This is rendered *vallis crati* in LibEl. The name survived as *Cratendon Field* in 1812 "about a mile South of the present city, but the exact situation of it is hardly discoverable at this time" (Bentham i, 54). Cf. also *Craten(h)e(e)* 1251 ElyCouch, 1277 Ely, 1302 MinAcct, *Gratene* 1298 ib., a fishery in Haddenham. The Latin rendering of the lost *Cratendon* suggests that at least in the 12th century that name was understood as containing a personal name. If that was correct, then the name was perhaps *Crætta*, another form of *Cretta*, recorded as the name of a King of Lindsey (Redin 90). There is one difficulty about this interpretation, viz. that the personal name is only recorded in the form *Cretta*, with double *t* and presumably short vowel, whereas the forms of *Cratendon* show persistent single *t*. Another possibility is that these names should be associated with a lost OE word corresponding to Dan *krat*, 'brushwood,' Norw *krat*, 'rubbish,' as suggested by Skeat for Cratfield, DB *Cratafelda* (PN Sf 26) and by Ekwall for a lost *Cratley* (PN Nt 65). In that case we might regard *vallis crati* as a bit of folk etymology and interpret Crackwell as 'spring in the brushwood,' *Cratendon* as 'hill overgrown with brushwood' from an adjective *crætten*, and *Craten(h)e(e)* as 'stream whose banks are overgrown with brushwood.' The relation of these names to Creeting (Sf), DB *Cratingas*, 1199 P *Cretinges*, is difficult. Skeat

(PN Sf 72) associates that name with the OE name *Cretta* as noted above, but it is difficult to explain the long vowel on that basis. Ekwall prefers to assume an OE *Crǣta* related to but not identical with *Cretta*.

PEPPERTON HILL is *Piperton* 1436 IpmR, *Pyperton* 1461 Pat. Cf. Pipton (NCPNW 167), both alike probably containing the ME surname *Pipere*.

TEMPLE FM (6″) is *terram (quond')* *Templar'* 1296, 1313 *CaiCh*, *Templelaundes* 1524 *MinAcct*, *Duxworth Temple* t. Hy 8 *Cole* xxxvii, *Temple Duxford* 1631 *FF*. The Knights Templar held a manor in Duxford in 1275 (RH).

SLOW LINE (6″) was perhaps the home of Gilbert *ate Slo* (1302 *CaiCh*), *v.* slāh, 'sloe.'

BARKER'S FM and LACEY'S FM[1] are probably to be associated with the families of Anthony *Barker* (1550 Pat) and Henry de *Lacy* (1279 RH).

COLLEGE FM was purchased by Gonville and Caius College t. Eliz (L 182). DUXFORD GRANGE. Cf. *Grange Fm* c. 1840 *TA*.

Hinxton

HINXTON

> *Hestitona* 1086 ICC, *Hestitone, Histetune, Histetone* 1086 DB, *Haustitona* 1086 InqEl (p)
>
> *Hincstitona* 1086 InqEl (p), *Hengstiton* 1202 FF, *Henxtenton* 1203 Cur, *Hengsteton'* 1208 Cur, *Henxtinton* 1229 Pat, *Hensington* t. Ed 1 Ipm
>
> *Hinx(s)ton(e)* 1218 *SR et freq* to 1548 Pat, *Hincston(e)* 1265 Misc, 1284, 1316 FA, *Hync(k)ston(e)* 1316 FA, 1570 SR, *Hynkeston* 1332 Cl, 1483 Pat, *Hing(e)ston(e)*, *-y-* 1285 *Ass et freq* to 1428 FA, *Hynkyston* 1423 EA vii
>
> *Henxton(e)* 1220 FineR *et freq* to 1327 SR, *Heng(e)ston(e)* 1227– 1303 FF *et freq* to 1384 Cl, *Hengyston, -i-* 1272 ib., 1274 Ipm, *Heinxton* 1229 FineR, *Henkeston* 1298 *Ass*, 1362 Pat, *Henxston'* 1298 *Ass*, *Hengleston* 1310 Ch, *Heingeston* 1334 Pat
>
> OE *Hengesting-tūn*, 'Hengest's farm,' *v.* ingtūn.

Ickleton

ICKLETON

> (*æt*) *Icelingtune* c. 975 ASWills, *Icelingtune gemæra* 1004 (12th) LibEl, *Ik(e)lington(e)*, *-yng-* 1222 FF *et freq* to 1547 Pat, *Ic-*,

---

[1] *Duxworth Lacyez* 1495 *CCC*, *Lacys* 1508 EA vii.

Iklyngton 1272 *Ass et freq* to 1547 *Pat, Ikilington* 1279 RH,
Igelingtone, -inc- 1302 FA, *Iggleton* 1553 EA vi, *Ickelingeton* 1559
Rental

Clintona 1086 ICC, *Inchelintone* 1086 DB, *Ilkenton* 1226 ChR,
Ilkyngton 1335 Cl, *Inclyngtone* 1346 FA

Hichelintone 1086 DB, *Hiklinton* 1253 FF, *Hiclington(e)* 1285 *Ass,*
Hyclington(e), -yng- 13th *Ely,* c. 1330 *ElyCouch, Hyk(e)lington(e)*
1268 *Ass*

Eclinton(ie) t. Hy 2 (1254) *Pat,* 1159–62 AC, *Eclynton* 1371 Cl,
Ekelington 1268 *Ass, Eclington* 1300 Pat, *Eckleton* 1724 Moll

Yc-, Iclinton, -yn- 1188–94 P *et freq* to 1309 Pat, *Ik(e)linton, -yn-*
1195 P *et freq* to 1455 Pat, *Ykelinton'* 1197 P, *Ikilinton* c. 1210 Rad
Ikel(e)ton(e) 1251 Ch, 1272 *Ass,* 1549–53 Pat, *Icliton(e)* 1254 Val,
1279 RH, *Ikiliton'* 1279 RH, *Ikkylton* 1502 Ipm, *Ickleton* 1574
Ely, *Ickledon* 1600 *Cole* xix

The first element is the old name *Icel* found also in Ickleford (PN
Herts 12) and Icklesham (PN Sx 510). Hence '*Icel*'s farm,' *v.*ingtūn.
St Guthlac was 'of the most ancient and noble race called *Iclingas*'
(Guthlac c. 1).

NOTE. ABBEY ST. Cf. *Abbeywey* 1455 *Rental, the Abbey Street* 1861
Trinity, v. Abbey Fm *infra* 96. CHURCH ST. Cf. *Churchelane* 1539 *Ct.*

BROOKHAMPTON (6″)

Brock-; Bro(o)k(ke)hamton(e) (melne) 1338 *Trinity,* (-*croftes, -felde*)
1431 *Ct,* (-*weye*) 1455 *Rental*
Broketon(eweye, -feld) 1455 *Rental*
Brokenton(e) 1455 *Rental, Brokenfeld, -wey* 1490 *Trinity*
(*le*) *Bro(o)kyngton(e), -ing-* 1455, 1483 *Rental,* 1529–91 *Ct*
Bro(c)k(e)hampton(e) (-*strete*) 1483 *Rental,* 1529–48 *Ct,* (-*brydg,*
-*close*) 1612 *Terr*

'*hamtun* by the brook,' *v.* brōc, hāmtūn and cf. Brookhampton (Sa,
Wa, Wo (bis)) and Brockhampton (Do, Gl (bis), Ha, He (bis), O).

COPLOE HILL. Cf. *Cop(pe)low(e)dene* 1431, 1539 *Ct, (iuxta Valancz)*
1455, 1483 *Rental,* (*le*) *Coppelowe (Valey)* 1483 ib., *Coploden* 1591 *Ct.*
'Rounded hill,' *v.* copp, hlāw and Fox 306. Identical with Copley
Hill *infra* 100. For *Valancz, v.* Vallance Fm *infra* 96.

ORNELDENE (lost). Cf. *Ornedene, -hyll* 1455 *Rental, -hill* 1483 ib.,
Wornelbussh 1455 ib., *Wornehill, Wornelledene, Ornel(l)edene* 1483 ib.

The first element is OE *worn*, *weorn*, 'a swarm, band, flock,' used of
a flock of birds and a herd of pigs. To this was added **denu**, **hyll**, and
then to *worn-hyll* was again added **denu**. Hence 'pig-valley and hill'
and then 'valley by pig-hill.'

SPELVERDEN (lost) is *Spelforthdene* 1431 *Ct*, *Spelfurdene* 1455, 1483
Rental, *Furtherspelleford*, (*le*) *Spyl(le)fordene*, *-furthe-* 1483 ib., *Spel-
for(de)dene* 1529, 1539 *Ct*, *Spelverdene* 1552, 1585 ib., *Spylverden* 1612
Terr. 'Speech-ford-valley,' OE *spell* and **ford**, **denu**. This must have
been a place of assembly, but of what assembly we have no knowledge.

NORMAN HALL (6″) and VALLANCE FM are probably to be associated
with the families of Peter and John *Norman* (1327 SR, 1332 *SR*), Giles
and Agnes de *Valence* (1285 *Ass*). The last is *Walauncz* 1431 *Ct*, terr'
Valauntz 1483 *Rental*, *Ikelton Valence* 1547 *Trinity*, *Valauns* 1561 ib.

ABBEY FM. Cf. *le Abbeygate* 1455 *Rental*, *Abbey land* 1769 *Trinity*.
It is named from the Abbey of Calder (Cu) which also gave name to
THE CALDREES (6″). This is *ten. Abbatis de Caldra* 1285 *Ass*, *Caldernys*
1455 *Rental*, *Caldern(e)s* 1483 ib., *Caldreys* 1529 *Ct*, (*Grange*) 1600
Cole xix, *terra de Caldresse* 1549 *Ct*, *Calderuns* 1561 *Trinity*, *Coldres*
1596 *Cole* xxxvii, *Chalders* 1673 ib. It belonged to that Abbey in 1254
(Val).

Sawston

SAWSTON [*olim* sɔˑsən]

> Salsingetune, Selsingetona, Delsingetune 970 (17th) ChronRams,
>   Sauxington c. 1220 Rad (p)
> Salsintona 1086 ICC, t. Ric 1 (1315) Dugd vi
> Salsiton(e) 1086 DB, -tona 1086 InqEl (p), Salsseton 1231 FF (p),
>   Salxton 1237 Cl, Salsetune c. 1280 Hosp, Salesthon' 13th St John's,
>   Salston(e) 1285 Ass, 1312 Ipm (p), 1789 Camden, Salseston[1] 1305
>   Abbr
> Sauton(e) 1196 Cur, 1380 Cl
> Sausinton(e) 1196-9 FF, 1212 RBE, 1236 Cl, Saucinton 1214 Cur
> Sausetun 1201 Cur, -ton 1242 Fees, 1269 FF, Sausseton 1255 ib.
> Saustun 1235 FF, -ton(e) 1272 Ass et freq to 1435 Cl
> Sausiton(e), -y- 1236 Fees et freq to 13th ElyG
> Sasitun c. 1250 SR, Sason Way 1610 EA xiii, Sarson 1715 PR iv
> Sokeston 1275 RH, Saux(s)ton 1285, 1304 Ass

---

[1] Printed *Salfeston*.

Saw(e)ston(e) 1288 *Ass*, 1427, 1433 Cl, 1441 FF, 1451 Rad
Sawson 1587 Ely, t. Jas 1 *Rental*

'Farm of *Salse*' or possibly, in view of the earliest forms, 'of
Salse's people,' *v.* ing(a)tūn. Cf. DEPN *s.n.* OE *Salse corresponds
to OSw *Salsi*, ON *Sǫlsi* and is a short form of names in *Sele-*.

NOTE. CAMBRIDGE RD is *Canntebregweye* 1400 *Huddleston*, leading to Cambridge. HIGH ST is *Hiestrete* 1437 ib. MILL LANE is *Mellelane* 1461 *Huddleston*
and may have been the home of John *Attemelne* (1279 RH) *v.* myln.
SHINGAY LANE is *Shenegeyelane* 1400 *Huddleston*, *Shyngey lane* 1580 *Survey*,
from the Preceptory of Shingay which held the rectory.

BOROUGH GROVE (6″) is *Burghgrove* 1514 *Terr*, *Burrowe Grove* 1580
Survey. Cf. *Burgh Mille*, *Burghwey* 1391 *Huddleston*, *Boroghe* 1400
ib., *Barroway* 1542 *WMP*, *Burrowe Myll* 1580 *Survey*, *Borough Water
Mill*, *Meadow* 1802 *EnclA*. Borough Mill still survives locally.
William de *Burgo* had a tenement in Sawston in 1236 (Cl). He
perhaps came from Peterborough, and his family may have given
name to the grove and mill.

DERNFORD FM and MILL [dænfə]. Cf. (*in*) *Derneforde* 956 (12th) BCS
1346, 1170 LibEl, 1324 *MinAcct*, 1383 Ch, (*hall*) 1570 SR, *Dernf(f)ord*
1373 Pat, 1490 Ipm, (*mill*) 1530 *CtWards*, *-forth* 1466 Pat, *Darn(e)-
ford(e)* 1279 RH, 1350 *Huddleston*, t. Eliz ChancP, (*Mill, Fm*) 1802
EnclA, *Darnyngford Moor* 1392 *Huddleston*, *Danford*, *Danfer* 1618 ib.,
Damford Fen, *Mill* 1802 *EnclA*. 'The hidden ford,' *v.* dierne, ford.
There was already a mill here in 956.

HUCKERIDGE HILL (local). Cf. *Howcrouch(e)feld* 1346 *WMP*, *-hille*
1514 *Terr*, *Huckeridge* (*Hill*) 1703 *Huddleston*. Apparently 'cross by
the hill,' *v.* hōh, crouche. Identical with *Langley Hills* 1763 ib.

DEAL GROVE (6″) is perhaps to be associated with *more de Dale* 1279
RH, *Dalemore*, *Dail(l)more* 1514 *Terr*, (*the*) *Dale* c. 1520 ECP, 1580
Survey, (*wayer*) ib., *Deal* 1606 *Huddleston*, and was probably the home
of William de *Dal* (1197 FF). *dale* probably derives from OE dæl,
'share, part' *infra* 318. For *wayer*, 'pond,' *v.* weyour.

HUNTINGTON'S FM (6″) is to be associated with the family of Ralph de
Huntingdon (1300 FF), *Huntedon* (1308 Ipm) which must have come
from Huntingdon. It is *Huntyngdons al. Somerys* 1502 Ipm, *Hunting-
tons* 1590 CAPr xxxv.

SAWSTON HALL (6″). Cf. *Halle hooke* 1580 *Survey*.

Whittlesford

WHITTLESFORD [*olim* witsə]

> *Witlesforda* 1086 ICC, *-e* InqEl (p), *Witelesforde* 1086 DB, *-a* InqEl (p), *Wittlesford* 1086 InqEl (p), *Wit(t)-*, *Wyt(t)(e)lesford(e)* 1170 LibEl *et freq* to 1492 Pat, *-forth(e)* 1380 FF, 1563–8 Ely, *Wy(t)thlesford* 1249 FF, 13th *Ely*, *Wit(t)-*, *Wyt(t)(e)lisford(e)*, *-ys-* 1268 *Ass et freq* to 1501 Ipm, *Wyttylsford* 1397 Pat, *Wyttilesford* 1423 FF, *Wyttlesworth* 14th *Huddleston*
>
> *Wyt(t)(e)le-*, *Wit(t)leford* 1241 Cl *et freq* to 1341 NI
>
> *Witheford* 1272 *Ass*, *Wyt(f)ford* 1549 Pat
>
> *Wylysfeud* 1272 *Ass*, *Willesford* 1427 Pat
>
> *Whytleford'* 1348 Works, *Whittlesford* 1643 EA vi
>
> *Wetelesford(e)* 1400 IpmR, 1403–7 Cl
>
> *Wittesford* 1490 Ely, *Wyttisford* 1504 ECP
>
> *Wydford* 1549 Pat, *Widford* 1576 Saxton, 1610 Speed, 1763 Bowen
>
> *Witzer* 1722 StJ

'*Wit(t)el*'s ford,' v. ford and cf. also Whittlesey *infra* 258. The same man also gave name to *Witlisoo* in Whittlesford (1504 *Pembroke*), v. hōh.

RYECROFT FM (6″) is *Rey(ʒe)croft(e)* 1449, 1457, 1482 *Pembroke*, *Ray-crofte* 1478 ib., *Ryecrofte* 1598 ib. v. ēg. ME *at ther eye* has become *at the reye*. The place lies by a stream.

RAYNER'S FM (6″) is probably to be associated with the family of James *Rayner* (1769 *Pembroke*). Cf. *Rayner's Grove* c. 1825 O.S.

CHRONICLE HILLS is so named c. 1825 (O.S.). It is probably a corruption of *Crokelhul(feld)* 1398 *Huddleston*. EARLS HOOK (6″). Possibly a corruption of *Hullishook* 1691 *WMP*. FARRIERS GROVE (6″) is *Farrowes* t. Jas 1 *Cole* xxxvii, *Farrow's Grove* 1812 *EnclA*. FRYING PAN (6″). Cf. (*le*) *Fry(e)ingpanne(s)* 1593 *Ct*, 1665 *Trinity* (in Ickleton). LITTLE NINE WELLS (6″) is so named c. 1825 (O.S.). Cf. Great Nine Wells *supra* 90. MIDDLE MOOR (6″) is *Middelmore* 1290 Barnwell, v. mōr. PARSONAGE FM (6″). Cf. *Parsonage Pitt* 1774 *Pembroke*. THE QUAVE (6″). Cf. Quaveney *infra* 220. STANMOOR HALL is *Stonimere* 1290 Barnwell, *Stanmore shott* 1613 EA xii, i.e. stony pool, v. stānig, mere and scēat. WANCHES PEN (6″) is *Wanshatts Penn* 1794 *Pembroke*, *Wanses pen* c. 1825 O.S. WELLS FM is *Welles* 1578 *Huddleston*. Cf. *Wellemoor* 1449 *Pembroke*. WHITTLESFORD BRIDGE (6″) is *pontem de Wytlesford'* 1242 Cl, *Wytlisfordebrige* 1279 RH, *Witlesford brugge* 1388 Cl, *Widford bridge* 1690 Lea. WHITTLESFORD MILL is *molendinum de Wytlesford* 1260 Ass.

V. CHILFORD HUNDRED

Cildeford 1086 DB, *-forde* 1086 InqEl
Childeforda 1086 ICC, *-ford* 1086 InqEl, 1167 P
Chilleford(e) 1179–1200 P *et freq* to 1334 *Ct*
Chilford(e), *-y-* 1179 P *et freq* to 1429 Cl
Chileford' 1185 RotDom, 1218, 1332 *SR*, 1236 Barnwell, 1268–72
  Ass, *Chyleff ord* 1298 *Ass*
Schelford 1196 ElyC, *Shelforde* 1553 Pat
Chilton 1557 Pat

'Young men's ford,' *v.* cild, ford and cf. Childerley *infra* 148. The meeting-place of the hundred was probably at the original site of Chilford Hall *infra* 110.

Great and Little Abington

ABINGTON (GREAT and LITTLE)

Abintone 1086 DB, *Abintona* 1086 ICC, c. 1212 *Waltham*, *-e*, *-y-*
  (*Comitis Alberici, Comitis Conani, comitis, alia*) 1158 P *et freq* to
  1428 FA, *-tune* c. 1212 *Waltham*, *-don* 1285 *Ass*, 1413 IpmR
Habintona 1086 ICC, *-ton(e)* 13th *Waltham*, 1299 QW, *Habington'*
  13th Fees, *-yng-* 1298 *Ass*, *Habiton(e)* c. 1212 *Waltham et freq* to
  1347 *SR*
Abictona 1125–35 (1337) YCh, *Abiton(e)*, *-y-* 1199 Cur *et freq* to
  1484 Pat, (*Magna, Parva*) 1218 *SR*, (*Litle-*) 1336 Ch, *-toun* 1331
  Bodl, *Abeton'* 1244 Cl
Abingtuna 1157 (1337) YCh, t. Ric 1 (1308) Ch, *-ton* 1215 Cur
  et passim, (*Gret, Litill*) 1523 *SR*, *Abyngton(e)* 1291 Tax *et freq* to
  1553 AD i, *-don* 1285 *Ass*, 1426, 1548 Pat
Abbint(h)on 1218–22 Fees, 1263 Ipm, *-don* 1275 RH
Abbiton' 1218 Fees (p), 13th *WalthamB*, 1253 Ch
Abbingeton' 1218 Fees, *Abbington* 1291 Tax

'*Abba*'s farm,' *v.* ingtūn and cf. Abington Pigotts *supra* 51. Great Abington (*comitis Alberici*) from Aubrey de Vere, Earl of Oxford, Little Abington (*comitis Conani*) from Conan, Earl of Richmond.

Great Abington

ABINGTON PARK was the home of William de *Parco* (1331 Ipm). It is *Abington Park* 1801 *Map*.

LAGDEN'S GROVE (6″) is to be associated with the family of *Lagden* of Bourn Bridge (1724 *Cole* xxii).

ABINGTON HALL is so named in 1716 (*Map*). BUSH PARK. Cf. *Peak Bush* ib. THE GROVE is *Abington Grove* 1663 EA xiii. HALL FM (all 6″). Cf. *Hall Low* 1610 ib.

Little Abington

BOURN BRIDGE is *ponte de Abiton' Parva* 1279 RH, *Burnebre(d)ge* 16th Queens', *Burnbridge* 1690 Lea, *Bournbridge* 1724 *Cole* xxii. The stream here is the Bourne or Granta *supra* 2. CLAYPIT PLANTATION (6″). Cf. *Cleypetfelde* 1328 *Clare*. v. clǣg, pytt

Babraham

BABRAHAM [beibrəm]

> *Badburgham* 1086 DB *et freq* to 1488 Pat, -*borueham* 1218 *SR*, -*ber(g)ham* 1270 FF, 1272 *Ass*, 1279 RH, -*borouham* 1279 RH, -*bourgham* 1361–4 Ipm, 1363 Pat, 1403 FF
> *Bathburgeham* 1086 ICC, *Bathbirenham* 1267 Pat, *Batburheham* 1141–7 Colch, *Batburg(e)ham* 1193 *WalthamB*, 1198, 1202 FF, 1202 Cur, *Bat(h)burham* 1268 *Ass*, 13th *Ely*
> *Badburgeham* 1086 InqEl, 1164–74 P, 1191 *Waltham et freq* to 1242 Fees, -*hamm'* c. 1260 *St John's H*, *Badburcham* 1288 Wardon, *Badburnham* 1310 Ipm
> *Badburgh, Badburham* 1086 DB, -*ham* 1203 Cur *et freq* to 1553 Pat, *Badburgéé* 1086 InqEl, *Badbarwham* c. 1300 *St John's H*, *Badburwham* 1380 Cl
> *Baburg(e)ham* 1176 BM *et freq* to 1492 *AD*, *Babburham* 13th *WalthamB*, 1254 Val, 1332 *SR*, *Baberwham* 1357 Pat, *Baburham* 1428 FA, 1464 Pat, 1502 Ipm, *Baberham* 1408 Cl, 1491 Pat, *Baburuham* 1540 Ct, *Babarham* 1565 Ely
> *Babram* 1488 PCC *et freq* to 1663 EA xiii, *Babraham* 1575 Ely

'The hām of a woman named *Beaduburh*.'

NOTE. LOVE LANE is so named in 1802 (*EnclA*). MILL RD is *Mylleway* 15th *Clare*.

COPLEY HILL is *Coppelawe* 1164 BM, 1345 *CWool*, 1347 *SR*, *Coppe-lowe* c. 1210 HMC vi *et freq* to 1494 *Rental*, *Coplaue* 13th *ElyCh*, *ElyF*, *Coplow* (*farm*) 1535 EA xii. 'Rounded tumulus,' v. coppe, hlāw and cf. "the great tumulus Copley Hill" (Fox 148). Identical with Coploe Hill *supra* 95.

MILL HOLE (6″) and REED FM were probably the homes of John de *Molendin'* (1279 RH) and Adam *atte rude* (1322 *Clare*). With the first, cf. *Sutmelnefeld* 14th *Clare*. *v.* myln. The second is *Reade* 1436 IpmR, 1461 Pat, *Reed Barn Fm* c. 1840 *TA*. Forms are late and this may contain OE **rīed, rȳd,* 'cleared land,' discussed *s.n.* Inchreed (PN Sx 378), or it may be identical with Reed (PN Herts 161), with early forms *Ruith* 12th, *Rued* 1254, *Red(e)* 1204. This is derived from OE **rȳ(h)ð,* an unrecorded derivative of rūh, 'rough,' in the sense 'rough land.'

CHALK FM (6″). Cf. *C(h)alche(n)ho* c. 1260 *St John's H*, *-hill* 13th *St John's, v.* cealc, hōh. CHURCH FM (6″). Cf. *(le) Cherchestrate, -strete* 1333, 1347 ib., *Churchefyld* 15th *Clare, Church Street Fm* c. 1840 *TA*. COTT FM is *Cot Fm* c. 1825 O.S. HILL COTTAGES (6″). Cf. *The Hill Houses* ib. MEGGS HILL is *Maggeshel* c. 1260 *St John's H*, 13th *St John's.* PAMPISFORD WITCH (6″) is *Pampeswurth wiche* 1525 *Queens', Pampisford Witch* 1703 *Huddleston, v.* Pampisford *infra* 111 and wīc, 'dairy farm.' POPPY HILL (PLANTATION) (6″), ROWLEY FM, SIGNAL HILL (PLANTATION) (6″) are so named c. 1825 (O.S.). Cf. Telegraph Clump *supra* 89. SLOUGH COTTAGES (6″) are so named ib. Cf. *Slo* c. 1260 *St John's H*, *le Sloo* 1420 *Clare* and *v.* slōh.

Bartlow

BARTLOW

> *Berk(e)lawe* 1232 FF *et freq* to 1485 BM, *-lau* 1352 Pat, *-low(e)* 1260 Ass *et freq* to 1435 FF, *Borklawe* 1272 *Ass*
>
> *Berclawe* 1236 Barnwell *et freq* to 1387 *Walden, -lowe* c. 1330 *Ely Couch, Bercklowe* 1558 AD vi
>
> *Bertelawe* 1448 *Cole* xxii, *Bart(e)lowe* 1559 *Rental*, 1570 SR, 1576 Ely, 1579 EA xiii, (*al. Barclowe*) 1599 Ely, *Barlow* 1724 Moll
>
> *Bark(e)low(e)* 1490 Ipm, 1532 AD ii, *Barcklowe* 1565 Ely

'(At) the mounds of the birch-trees,' OE *(æt) beorca-hlāwum, v.* beorc, hlāw, i.e. the great Bartlow Hills tumuli which dominate the church and village. As Sir Cyril Fox notes, there is no natural hill here. For *-lawe*, cf. *infra* 330 and *Tremelau* (PN Wa 247). Cf. the neighbouring Bartlow End, named from this (PN Ess 507).

THE HALL (6″). Cf. *terram aule Berklow* 1522 *Pembroke, Bartlow Hall* c. 1655 ChancP.

Castle and Shudy Camps

CAMPS (CASTLE and SHUDY)

> *Campes* 1086 ICC *et freq* to 1578 BM, *Campis* t. Ric 1 Cur, *Kampes*
> 1218, 1233 FF, 1285 *Ass*, *Champes* 1268 *Ass*, *Camps* 1331 FF
> *et passim*, *Campus* 1345 C*Wool*, *Campys* 1433 FF
> *Cāpas, Canpas* 1086 DB, *Caunpes* 1428 FA
> *Chaumpes* 1231 FF, *Caumpes, K-* 1218 *SR et freq* to 1428 FA,
> *Kaumpis* 1343 FF, *Cawmpes* 1462–3 Pat
> *Camp(e)* 1260 Ass *et freq* to 1298 *Ass*, *Caump(e)* 1263 Ipm *et freq*
> to 1378 SR
> *Comp(e)s* 1298 *Ass*, 1416 AD iii, 1417 Cl, 1633 *Will*

OE *campas*, 'fields or enclosures,' *v.* camp.

Castle Camps

CASTLE CAMPS

This was formerly called *Great* (*Magna Ca(u)mpes* 1236 Barnwell,
1271, 1314 FF) and also *Earl's* (*Caumpes Comitis* 1218 *SR*) from the
Earl of Oxford, a descendant of Aubrey de Vere who held the manor
in 1086 (DB). *Castlecampes* (1384 FF) and *Campes ad Castrum* (1446
Cole iv) from the *castle* of the de Veres, now completely destroyed. "It
is called castle Campes of yᵉ faire auncient howse and seate of yᵉ
Earles of Oxford" c. 1640 *Layer*.

HOLMSTEAD[1] HALL and OLMSTEAD GREEN are *Halmestede* 1235 FF,
Almystede 1428 FA, *Olm(e)stede* 1260 Ass *et freq* to 1416 AD iii,
-hall(e) ib., 1474 IpmR, *Elm(e)sted(e)* 1272, 1285 *Ass*, *-halle* 1399 FF,
Olnested 1281 *Cole* xxxvi, *Olmisted* 1316 FA, *Holmsted* 1327 SR (p),
Ampsted Greene 1693 *Huddleston*. Formerly partly in Helion Bumpstead, these names have been treated in PN Ess 509 where forms in
Holm- are more numerous. The *H* is inorganic and the modern forms
are from *ulmestede*, a derivative of OE *ulm(treow)*. Here we also have
the more common type from *elm*. 'Place where elms grow,' *v.* elm,
stede. *Halm-, Alm-* are due to French influence. Cf. IPN 112–13
and Elmstead (PN Ess 337).

WILLESEY is *Wilnesle* 1275 RH, *Wylsey Hall* 1553 *Cole* xli, *Wilsie way*
1637 *Terr*, *Willesey Wood* 1821 Baker, c. 1840 *TA*, *Wilseys* c. 1825
O.S. The first form is probably an error for *Wiuelsle*. Just over the

---

[1] Holmsted (6″).

border, in Bartlow End, is Wilsey, the home of Humphrey de *Wyueleshey* (14th *Queens'*) who probably came from here. Cf. PN Ess 507–8. Hence '*Wifel*'s (ge)hæg.'

HILL FM, PARK FM and WESTOE FM (all 6″) were the homes of John *del Hil* (1279 RH), William *o the hil* (1313 *AddCh*), Thomas *ate Hul* (1327 SR), Robert *attehell* (1446 *Cole* iv), Thomas *atte Park* (1345 ib.) and Alicia de *Westho* (1199 CurR). Cf. *the Park* c. 1840 *TA*, *Westho* 1298 *Ass*, *Westo* 1342 FF, *Westhoo by Campes* 1361 Cl, Ipm. 'West ridge,' v. hōh. *West*, as opposed to Northey *infra* 105.

COOPER'S FM, HART'S Ho[1] and PARKIN'S FM (all 6″) are probably to be associated with the families of John *Cooper* (c. 1840 *TA*), John *le Hert* (1360 *Cole* iv) and William *Parkin* (c. 1840 *TA*).

LITTLE BIGGIN COMMON. Cf. *Biggin* c. 1840 *TA* and bigging, 'building.' CAMPS END and GREEN are so named c. 1825 (O.S.). CASTLE FM (6″). Cf. *Castle Field* c. 1840 *TA*. LANGLEY WOOD. Cf. *Langeneyefeld* 1360 *Cole* iv, *Langley Wood* c. 1840 *TA*. The land is not low-lying, so if *Langeneye* is correct, it must stand for earlier *Langenhey*, 'long enclosure' (v. (ge)hæg), rather than *Langeney*, 'long marshy land' (v. ēg). MASCAL'S FM (6″) is *Maskalls* t. Eliz ChancP. WIGMORE POND. Cf. *Wigmore Ley* c. 1840 *TA*. WOOLPACK GROVE (6″) is *Wool Park Grove* ib.

Shudy Camps

SHUDY CAMPS

This was formerly called *Little* and *Wood* Camps: *Parva Campes* 1316 FA, *Woode Campes* 1570 SR.

The element *Shudy* occurs in the following forms:

Sude- 1218 SR, 1236 Barnwell, *Sudi-* 1242 Fees, *Sudes-* 1272 *Ass*, *Sode-* c. 1278 ElyA

S(c)hude- 1256 Barnwell, 1279 RH, *Schudde-* 1298 *Ass*

S(c)hode- 1285 *Ass*, *Shodi-* 1327 Cl, *Shod-* 1361 ib., *Shodo-* 1428 FA

S(c)hudi- 1286 Cl, 1299, 1347 *SR*, 1304 FF, 1345 *CWool*, *Scudi-* 1302 *SR*, *Shudy-* 1331 Pat

Suth(e)- 1260 *Ass*, 1272 *Ass*, *Suþe-* 13th *Ely*, *Sut(e)-* 1268–72 *Ass*, *Souþe-* c. 1330 *ElyCouch*

[1] *Harts* c. 1840 *TA*.

Shuthe- 1260 Ass, *Shuti-* 1331 FF
Shyde- 1285 *Ass*, *Shidi-* 1341 NI
S(c)hite- 1298 *Ass*
Shedi- 1298 FF, *Schede-* 1346 FA
Side- 1298 *Ass*, *Sythe-* 13th *Waltham, Citie Campes al. Shudy-campes* 1547 Pat, *Cytty(e)* 1609, 1640, 1710 *FF, Sittycomps* 1633 *Will*
Shad(e)y Campes 1616, 1715 *Cole* ii

There was apparently a tradition at Ely in the 13th century that *Shudy* preserved the name of the benefactress who bestowed lands here on the monastery: "Northo is a hamlet belonging to Shudecamps and the monks of Ely have it by the gift of Shudda (*de dono Shudde*) formerly lady of Shudecamps from time out of mind" (RH ii, 428). Dr Palmer, however, has shown that the lady's name was really Juliana de Campes (CAS, 4to, N.S. v, 36) and we should therefore abandon this interpretation. The variation in the vowel in the early forms points to OE *y*, though *u* is more common than one would have expected in this district. The element, whatever it was, was early confused with *south*, but late forms such as *Citie* point to the survival of the normal Cambridgeshire *i*. We have probably to do with OE *scydd*, 'shed,' as in Limbo and Gunshot (PN Sx 117–18, 132), Puckshot (PN Sr 206) and *Sheddon* (PN Ess 344). The name may have been given because of mean buildings likely to be common in a parish called *Wood* Camps, or it may be that the place was called *Shed* Camps in jest or derision, in contrast to *Great* or *Earl's* Camps with its 'Castle.'

FRECKNEY POND (local). Cf. *Fragenhou, -ham* 1219 FF, *Frakenho* 1263 Ipm, 1279 RH, c. 1300 *ElyM*, 1418 *Ct, Frakeho* 13th, 1303 *Waltham, Frakners* c. 1840 *TA*. The second element is clearly hōh, 'hill-spur.' The first is probably a personal name. Cf. *Frǣccændun* (KCD 673) in Wootton St Lawrence (Ha) which survives in the name of a field called Frog Down (Grundy, *Saxon Land Charters of Hampshire* 315) and Freckenham (Sf) in DEPN. *Frǣcca* is probably a name which is ultimately of nickname origin from OE *frǣc*, 'greedy, voracious, bold' (cf. Holthausen *s.n.*).

MANAGES (local) is *Manheg(ge)* 1219 *FF*, 13th *Waltham, Manhedg* t. Jas 1 *Cole* xxxvii, *the Manages* 1831 *Trinity, Managers Field* c. 1840 *TA*. 'Common hedge or enclosure,' from OE *gemǣne* and hecg. It is near the parish boundary. Cf. Man Wood (PN Ess 316, 495) and Manhood (PN Sx 79).

NORTHEY WOOD. Cf. *Norro* 13th *Waltham*, *Nort(h)ho(u)* 1260 Ass *et freq* to 1317 FF, *Norhou* 1265 Cl, *Northoo* 1414–18 *Ct*, t. Hy 8 *Rental*, *Northowe* 1541 *MinAcct*, *Northey* c. 1840 *TA*. 'North ridge or spur of land,' *v.* hōh. *North* in distinction from *Westoe supra* 103. Cf. also Nosterfield and Street Fm *infra* 107.

NOSTERFIELD END

> *Nostresfeld(a)* 1086 ICC (p), c. 1300 *AddCh*, 1311 FF, *Nostrefeld(e)*
>   t. John BM *et freq* to 1401 Cl, *-feud* 1235 FF, 1272 Ass, *-feuld* ib.,
>   *Nostrifeld* 1287 FF, *Nostrisfeld* 1347 *SR* (p)
> *Ostre(s)feld'* 1179–81 P, *Osterfeld'* 1236 Cl, *Rostresfeld* 1309 Pat
> *Nosterfeud* 1231 FF, *-feld(e)* 1232 ib. *et freq* to 1360 Ipm, *-fild* 1381
>   FF, *Nostelfeld'* 1233 Cl, *Nosturfeld* 1298 *Ass*, *Nousterfeld* 1359
>   IpmR, *Nostirfeld* 1360 Ipm, *Nostredfelde* 1429 Cl
> *Northfeud, Nostrefeud, Nortstretesond*[1] 1272 *Ass*
> *Nostesfeld* c. 1275 *AddCh*, *Nostefeld* 1327 Pat (p)
> *Nesterfeld vel Nosterfeld* 1436 IpmR
> *Noffeld* 1519 *Cole* iv

This name has been explained by Skeat (PN C 62) as possibly short for *Paternoster Field*, in PN NRY 223, *s.n.* Nosterfield as 'at the sheepfold field,' from OE *æt ðǣm ēowestrefelda*, ME *at then (e)ostrefeld*, *(atte) Nostrefelde*, and by Ekwall (DEPN) from an element *oster*, 'hillock,' postulated by Wallenberg for Osterland (KPN 286) and related perhaps to OE *ōst*, 'a knot, knob,' in the sense 'hillock.' Cf. also Oyster Bridge (PN Ess 506) and Osterley (PN Mx 25).

None of these etymologies satisfactorily fits all the forms given above. The most interesting are *Northfeud*, *Nortstretesond* and *Nostredfelde*. The first two of these suggest the possibility that the first element is really norþ followed by a second element strǣt, while the third one (admittedly a late one) also suggests the possibility of strǣt. The possibility of such elements being present in this name is strengthened by a reference to *Nordhoustret* in Horseheath in 1205 (FF), which in its turn clearly links up with Northey *supra* and possibly with *Northgate* in Horseheath (1279 RH) and *Northgate* in Camps, near Nosterfield (1313 *AddCh*). *gate* may possibly show substitution of Anglo-Scandinavian *gate*, 'road,' for English *strete* in the

---

[1] These might be read *Northsend, Nostresend, Nortstretefond.*

compound *Northoustret*. Just what road is so named it is a little difficult to say. There is no known Roman road to which *strǣt* can refer. From Nosterfield End the road runs west to Shudy Camps Park and then divides, encircling the park to north and south, a diversion clearly due to the enclosing of the park, beyond which it continues the alignment from Nosterfield, past Street Fm, south of and below Northey Wood, to Bartlow, where there are entrenchments, and on to Linton, the site of a Roman villa. Street Fm certainly suggests that we are on the line of this street, but the road here does not actually pass over *North-ho*. From the northern branch of the fork round the park, a road leads north to Horseheath, passing a tumulus, and crossing the higher ground north-west of Northey. This road winds more than one would expect from a Roman road, but footpaths cut off various bends and it looks from the map as if there might once have been a fairly straight road from near Mark's Grave on the Via Devana towards Steeple Bumpstead. On Fox's map of the Roman Age, this route is marked by a series of finds of coins and by the site of a single burial. Cf. also AnctC 34–5. It is difficult to choose between these two possibilities for the line of *Northoustrete*, but it is clear that it must be brought into account in explaining some at least of the forms of Nosterfield, possibly all of them. Our choice lies between taking the original form of the name to have been *Norðhōhe(s) strǣt feld* with very early reduction of this to *Nostresfeld*, *Nostrefeld* and chance archaic survival of the fuller form in the 13th century, or believing that the early forms derive from (*æt ðǣm) ēowestre felda* and that the difficult 13th-century forms are due to contamination by the name of a neighbouring topographical feature. On the whole the former is the more likely process. A word *oster*, 'hillock,' would not suit the site of Nosterfield. *v.* Addenda lix.

BARSEY FM is *terram Willelmi de Berardeshey* t. Ed 2 Cole xxii, *Barcy's* 1748 ib. xxxv, *farm called Barcy* 1783 *Trinity*, *Barsey Fm* c. 1840 *TA*, *Borsey farm* 1851 Gardner, and was the home of William de *Berardesheye* (1268 *Ass*), *Berardesye*, *Bernardesey* (1272 ib.). It is probably local in origin. '*Beornheard*'s enclosure,' *v.* (ge)hæg.

CARTER'S FM and SHARDELOW'S FM (both 6″) are probably to be associated with the families of John and Rebecca *Carter* (c. 1840 *TA*) and Sir John de *Shardelowe* (1350 *Cole* ii). The latter is *Shadows farm* 1851 Gardner.

BURNTHOUSE FM. Cf. *Burnt House Field* c. 1840 *TA*. DUNCEY
PLANTATION. Cf. *Dunsey* ib. HOME FM. Cf. *Home Close and Meadow*
ib. and *infra* 353. LOWER HO FM. Cf. *Lower Fm* ib. OAKS PARK is
Okes 1303 *Waltham, Oaks Park* c. 1840 *TA*. PRIORY FM is *Nostrefeilde
al. Pryors* t. Eliz *Cole* xxxvii, *Priors or Prewers* 1784 *Trinity, Priory Fm*
c. 1840 *TA*. The Prior of Hatfield Broad Oak had land in Nosterfield
(*supra* 105) in 1279 (RH). STREET FM (all 6″). *v.* Nosterfield End
supra 105.

Hildersham

HILDERSHAM

Hildricesham 1086 DB, *Hildrichesham* 1086 ICC *et freq* to 1313
YBk, *Hildrikesham* c. 1185 *Clerkenwell*, 1242 FF, *Hyldrichesham*
1247–9 FF, *Hildricsham* 1260 Ass, *Hildrichissam* 1270 FF, *Hil-
dricheham* 1431 Pat

Heldrikham 1185 RotDom, *Heldrichesham* 13th *Clerkenwell*

Hildresham, -y- 1239 FF *et freq* to 1388 Cl, *-is-* 1239 FF *et freq* to
1346 FA, *Hilteresham* 1267 Pat, *Hilderesham* 1268 *Ass*, *Hylders-
ham, -i-* 1285 ib. *et freq* to 1470 Pat, *Ildresham* 1302 FA

Hildesham 1272 *Ass*, 1316 FA

Eldresham 1392 Pat, *Heldresham* 1428 FA, *Heldersham* 1474 *Cole* vii,
1532 AD ii, 1610 EA xiii

'The hām of *Hildrīc*,' a personal name unrecorded in OE but
common on the Continent. Cf. Förstemann PN 834–5.

ALDER CARR (6″). Cf. *The Alders* 1795 *Map, Alder Car* c. 1840 *TA*.
car(r) is clearly the word *carr* denoting a marsh grown over with
brushwood, a loan-word deriving ultimately from ON *kiarr*. It is
not found elsewhere in Cambridgeshire. It is found in Essex (PN
Ess 583), but even there is very rare except in the compound
Aldercar, the earliest example dating from the 15th century.

HILDERSHAM WOOD (6″) is so named in 1795 (*Map*) and was near the
home of William *atte Wode* (1325 *Ass*).

BURGOYNE'S PLANTATION (6″) is probably to be associated with the
family of John *Burgoyn* (1427 *Layer*).

COOK'S PEN (6″) is *Cooks Pen* c. 1840 *TA*. FURZE HILL is *The
Furs* 1795 *Map, Furs Hill* c. 1840 *TA*. HILDERSHAM HALL (6″) is
Hildrishamhall 1545 *Bodl*. HILDERSHAM MILL (6″) is *molendino de*

Hildrikesham c. 1185 *Clerkenwell*. PENN FM. Cf. *The Pen* 1795 *Map*. ROUND PLANTATION (6″) is so named c. 1840 *TA*. ST MARGARET'S GREEN (6″) is *Margaret's Green* 1573 (1851) *Gardner*, *Margates Green* 1795 *Map*. THE SALLOWS (6″) is so named ib., *v.* sealh.

Horseheath

HORSEHEATH

> *Horseda* 1086 ICC, *Horsede* 1285 *Ass*, 1387 *Walden*, 1413 Pat, 1433 FF, *Hors(e)hed(e)* 1411, 1548 Pat, 1511 EA vii, *-hedd* t. Jas 1 *Rental*, *Horside* 1577 Cai
>
> *Horsei* 1086 DB, *Horseye, -i-* 1195 Abbr *et freq* to 1272 *Ass*, *Horse(e)* 1199 CurR, 1203–6 FF, *Horsheye* 1268 *Ass*
>
> *Horeseia, -ey(e), -eya* t. Hy 2 BM *et freq* to 1378 Pat, *Horeseg* 1200 CurR
>
> *Horesathe* 1198 AC (p), *Hortseth* 1284 FA, 1298 *Ass*, *Horeseth* 1285 ib.
>
> *Horset(e)* 1199 FF *et freq* to 1410 Cl, *Horcet* 1383 Cl
>
> *Oreseie* 1199 CurR, *Orsey* 1350 Pat
>
> *Horseth(e)* 1218 *SR et freq* to 1416 Pat, *(al. Orsett)* 1547 Pat, *Horsheth(e)* 1272 *Ass*, 1283 Pat, 1298 FF, 1426 Cl, *Horseath* 1307 FF, *Horsheath* 1311 FF
>
> *Orset(t)* 1230 Cl, 1490 HMC Var ii

Probably 'horse-heath,' *v.* hǣþ.

LINACRE (lost) is *Linacra* 1086 ICC (p), *-acre* 1203 FF, *Lynaker* 1313 *AddCh*. 'Flax-acre,' *v.* līn, æcer.

CARDINAL'S GREEN and LIMBERHURST FM (6″) are to be associated with the families of Peter *Carbonel* (t. Ed 3 *Walden*) and Walter de *Limberh, Lymbyri(g)* (1268–72 *Ass*) and John de *Lymbery* (1298 *Cole* xxii) which probably came from Limbury (Beds) (PN BedsHu 155). They appear later as *manor of Carbonell* 1433 FF, *Carbonelles* 1490 Ipm, *manor of Lymbury* 1367 Cl, *Lymbery(e)s* 1480 IpmR, 1516 EA vii, *Limberhurst Fm* c. 1840 *TA*. For the development of *Carbonelles* to *Cardinal's*, cf. Cardinal's Fm (PN Ess 429), from the family of William *Carbonell*.

HORSEHEATH PARK is *the Parke of Horset* 1515 *Cole* xxii, *Horseth Parkes* 1553 ib. xli. William Alington had licence to make a park in Horseheath in 1448 (ib. xxxiii).

Linton

LINTON[1]

> (*æt*) *twam Lintunum* 11th (15th) KCD 725, *duo Lintunum*, (*in*)
> *Lintune* 1008 (12th) LibEl, *Lintona* 1008 (14th) *ElyM*, 1086 ICC,
> *Lintone, alia Lintone* 1086 DB, *Linton Magna, Parua* 1218 *SR*
> *et passim*, *Lyntone* (*juxta Waldene*) c. 1250 RegRoff *et passim*,
> *Lytton* 1355 FF, *Lynton the more* 1493 PCC
>
> *Lymton* 1310 Cl
> *Lenton* t. Eliz ChancP

'Flax-farm,' *v.* līn, tūn. *twām*, 'two' (dat. pl.), i.e. Great and Little
(*infra* 111). *Waldene* is Saffron Walden (PN Ess 537).

BARHAM HALL [bærəm]

> *Bercheham* 1086 ICC, DB, *Bercham* a. 1086 (1337) YCh, c. 1210
> Wardon *et freq* to 1339 Pat, *Berkham* 1218 *SR et freq* to 1316 FA,
> *Berkam* 1285 *Ass*, *Bergham al. Berkham* 1609 PCC
> *Ber(e)w(e)ham* 1199 Wardon, 1313 Ipm, 1327 SR, 1332 *Ass*, 1359
> Pembroke, 1380 Cl, *Beru(gh)ham* 1218, 1372 *SR*, 1298 *Ass*, 1311
> FF, 1346 FA, *Bergham* 1277 FF *et freq* to 1435 IpmR, *Berewgham*
> 1406 Pembroke, *Barugham* 1428 FA, *Bargham* 1456 IpmR, 1546
> Pembroke
> *Buruuham* 1199 Wardon, *Boruham* 1272 *Ass*, *Burgham* 1285 FF,
> 1298 *Ass*, 1299 QW
> *Berh(h)om* c. 1205 Wardon, 13th BM, *Berham* 1313 *AddCh*, 1345
> *CWool*
> *Barcham* 1285 *Ass*, *Barkham iuxta Lynton* 1540 *MinAcct*
> *Bar(re)ham(e)* 1539–40 *MinAcct*, 1550 Pembroke, *Bareham al.*
> *Barkham* 1552 Pat

'Enclosure on the hill,' *v.* beorg, hamm and cf. Barham (PN
BedsHu 233) and Barham (Sf), *Bercheham* c. 1050 (13th) KCD 907,
Bercham 1086 DB, *Beorcham* 1144 *ElyM*, *Berucham* 1279 ib.

BORLEY WOOD is *Bor(e)ley(wode)feld(e)*, *Borle(e)* (*-wey*) 1487 *Pembroke*,
(*wood*) 1562 ib., *Borleywoodway* 1531 *WMP*. Forms are late, but as
this is on a hill, we may possibly compare Boreham (PN Herts 74–5)
which Ekwall (Studies[2] 132–3) explains as containing OE **bor* in the
sense 'eminence, elevation.' Hence 'wood or clearing on the hill,'
v. lēah.

---

[1] *Lintune* 970 BCS 1268, identified with this in DEPN, really refers to Linden
End *infra* 234.

CHILFORD HALL with LITTLE CHILFORDS

> *Chilford* 1279 RH, (*campo*) 1298 *Ass*, *Chilfordefeelde* 1600 *WMP*,
> *Chilfords* 1662 *Deed*
> *Chilleford* (vill.) 1298 *Ass*

The above forms refer to the place from which Chilford Hundred (*supra* 99) was named. The modern places of this name, however, are not on the same site. They date from c. 1840. The hundred meeting-place was on the Linton boundary, between Great and Little Linton, at a ford through the Bourne due south of Little Chilfords.[1]

MARK'S GRAVE may be associated with "terra quondam Johannis *Marke* de London iac. in Stonstrett" 1522 *Pembroke*. *Stonstrett* is probably Wool St *supra* 31. Cf. "highway to a place called *Nan Saxby's Grave* where the road from Linton to Balsham crosses at right-angles the Woolstreet road" 1761 *Pembroke*. Both names may refer to burials at cross-roads, but we may note that Mark's Grave is at the junction of the boundaries of four parishes and may contain mearc, 'boundary.'

RIVEY HILL. Cf. *le Wivy* 1279 RH, (*le*) *Ryvyden*(*ffelde*) 1522, 1523 *Pembroke*, (*al. London Lane*), *Reuydenfeelde* 1600 *WMP*, *The Rivey* (*-den*) 1768 *Pembroke*, c. 1825 O.S. RIVEY WOOD (6″) is so named c. 1840 (*TA*). No explanation of this name can be offered in view of the uncertainty of the early forms.

LINTON MILL (6″) was probably the home of John de *Molendin'* (1279 RH). There were two water-mills here in 1271 (Ipm). Note also MILL LADE (6″). The word *lade* denoting a 'channel, watercourse' cannot derive directly from (ge)lād which gives ME *lode*, ModEng *lode*, *load*. NED suggests that it is a new formation from that element as found in Cricklade (PN W 42), Lechlade (PN Gl 99), but the persistent preservation of *a* in those names, as against the regular development to *o* in Evenlode (PN Wo 123), is equally strange.

PAIN'S PASTURE (6″) is probably to be associated with the family of Richard *Payn* (1327 SR).

LITTLE BARHAM[2] (6″) is so named in 1761 (*Pembroke*). CATLEY PARK is *Catteleg* 1279 RH, *Catleye* 1522, 1523 *Pembroke*. 'Wild-cat wood

---

[1] *Ex inf.* the late Dr W. M. Palmer.
[2] THE BEECHES, BURTLE VILLA, GRIP FM and MORTIMER HO (all 6″) are all modern names.

or clearing,' v. catt, lēah. Cow Gallery Wood (6") is *Cow Gallery*
c. 1825 O.S. Greenditch Fm. Cf. *Grenedich(e)* 1463 *Pembroke*.
Heath Fm (6"). Cf. *Fritheath* 1281 *Cole* xxxvi, *the heath* 1531 *WMP*,
v. fyrhþ(e). Lady Grove (6"). Cf. *Ladyland* 1768 *Pembroke*, c. 1840
TA. Little Linton is *Parva Linton* 1218 *SR*. The two Lintons
were distinct already in 1008, v. *supra* 109. Short's Corner (6").
Cf. (*le*) *Short(e)wo(o)d(e)* 1279 RH, 1522–3 *Pembroke*, 1531–8 *WMP*,
(*corner*) 1765, 1768 *Pembroke*. *Shortwood Corner* would seem to have
been simplified to *Short's Corner*.

Pampisford

Pampisford [pa·nzə]

    Pampeswrda 1086 ICC, *-uuorde* 1086 DB, *-worda* 1086 InqEl,
    c. 1170 *ElyM*, *-uuorð(a)* 1086 InqEl, *-wurda* 1171 P, *-wrth(e)* 1199
    CurR *et freq* to 1290 Pat, *-worthe*, *-a* 1134–44 *ElyCh et freq* to
    1532 AD ii, (*al. Pampesforde*) 1489 Ipm, *-wurda* 1169 P, *-wurth(e)*
    1272 *Ass*, 14th *Walden*, *-wrt* 1279 *ElyM*, *-ford* 1603 *FF*, *Pampis-*
    worth(e), *-ys-* 1284 FA *et freq* to 1434 Pat, *-ford* 1608 *FF*, 1663
    EA xiii

    Pampeworda 1086 InqEl, *Pampeworth(e)* 1170 LibEl, 1272 *Ass*,
    1280 FF, 1377 Fine, *-wrde* 1285 *Ass*

    Pamsforth(e) 1535 VE, t. Eliz ChancP, *Pam(m)esworth* 1587–9 *Add*,
    Pamsford 1610 Speed, 1627 *FF*

    Paunsworthe 1539 *MinAcct*, *Paunsforth* 1550 Pat, 1553 EA vi,
    Pan(ne)sworth(e) (*al. Pamsworthe*) 1553 Pat, 1661 Cai, *Pawnsford*
    1603 *Map*, *Pantisford* 1660 CAPr xvii

    Palmeforde 1559 *Rental*, *Palmesfourde* 1588 AD vi, *Parmeforth* 1672
    EA xi

    Panser 18th *Huddleston*

Probably '*Pampe*'s enclosure,' v. worð. This personal name is found
as a surname at Whittlesey in 1335 (Pat) in the names Andrew and
John *Pampe*. It is related to ME *pampe*, 'to pamper,' ON *Pampi*, a
nickname used of a thickset man. Cf. DEPN and Pandon (PN NbDu
155). Here, we may have ON *Pampi* itself. For *-ford* cf. Duxford
supra 92.

Creek's Plantation (6") is to be associated with the family of John
de *Crek* (1305 FF) which may have come from Creake (Nf).

BRENT DITCH END (6″), locally BRANDY GIN, is *Brand Ditchend* 1821
Baker, *v.* Brent Ditch *supra* 33. HAYFIELD PLANTATION (6″). Cf.
Hayfeld 1232 *FF*. 'Open land marked by an enclosure,' *v.* (ge)hæg,
feld and cf. Pampisford Hay *infra* 362. LANGFORD ARCH is *Longe-
forthebrige* 1290 Barnwell, *Langeford* 1309 Pat, *Langefordebrigge* 1449
Pembroke. PAMPISFORD MILL (6″) is *molendinum de Pampesworthe* 1353
Queens'.

West Wickham

WEST WICKHAM[1]

> (*oð*) *wichamme* 974 BCS 1305, *Wicham* 1086 ICC *et freq* to 1318
> Pat, *Wickhum* 1210 FF, *Wikham* 1218 *SR*, (*West*) 1266 Pat *et freq*
> to 1428 FA, (*by Strettelee*) 1328 Banco, *Wykeham* 1218, 1231 FF,
> *Wykham, -c-* 1251 *ElyCouch et freq* to 1426 Cl, (*juxta Balsham*)
> 1366 *Cole* xxii, *Wykam* 1279 RH, *Wickham* 1344 FF, *Wikam*
> *Wolvis* 1470 IpmR
>
> *Wicheham* 1086 DB, *uuichehâm* 1086 InqEl
> *Quicham* 1267 *ElyG*, *Whykham* 1317 Queens'

'Enclosure by the wīc,' *v.* wīcham(m). *Wolvis* from the knight's
fee held in 1373 by William *Wolf* (Cl). For *Quicham*, *v.* Introd. xxxvi.
West probably in relation to Wickhambrook (Sf), earlier *Wickham*.

BURTON END is (*camp. voc.*) *Boueto(u)n* 1232 *FF*, 1340 *Cole* xxii, *-feld*
1340 Queens', *-strete* 1380 *Cole* xxii, *Button* (*End*) 1580 ib. xli, (*Field*)
1812 *EnclA*, *Burton End* c. 1825 O.S. 'Above the *tun* or hamlet,'
v. bufan, tūn. It lies farther up the hill than West Wickham. Cf.
Abouethon 1267 *FF*, *Magna Boueton(e)* 1390 *Peterhouse*, 1505 *St John's*,
Mychboton 1455 *Peterhouse*, *Magna Boton* 1459 ib., *great Bouton* 1637
Terr (in Melbourn).

STREETLY END

> *Stradleia* 1086 InqEl, *Strattleie, Stratleie* ib., *-lege, -legh, -le(e)*,
> *-ley(e)* 1202 FF *et freq* to 1428 FA, (*cum Henhall*) 1570 SR
> *Stretlaie, Stretle* 1086 InqEl *et freq* to 1366 FF, *-lye, -leg(h), -ley*,
> *-lie* 1272 *Ass et freq* to 1630 Ely, *Strethle* 1170 LibEl, *Stredlegh*
> 1275 RH, *-l(e)* 1285 *Ass*, *Stretele(e), -ley(e)* ib. *et freq* to 1434
> Pat, *Strettle* 1316 FA, *Streetley End* 1812 *EnclA*
> *Streleye* 1230 Cl, *Strale* 13th *Ely*

---

[1] *Wichamm* (BCS 1268), identified with West Wickham in DEPN, really refers
to Witcham *infra* 244.

'Wood or clearing by the Roman road' (known popularly as Wool Street) (*supra* 31). *v*, strǣt, lēah.

YEN HALL

(*to, of*) *eanheale* 974 BCS 1305, (*strata de*) *Enhal(e)* c. 1200 *ElyCh et freq* to 1428 FA, (*-weye*) 1298 *Cole* xxii, *Enehale* 1298 *Ass*, 1299 QW, *Enhall(e)* 1316 FA, 1327 *Ct*, 1395 *Cole* xxii, *Eenhale*(*weye*) 1340 *Queens'*, *Enalehall* 1436 *WMP*, *Eynall* 1556 Pat, *Eanallffeild* 1632 *WMP*, *Eynell* 1776 L

(*æt*) *Heanhealan* c. 975 ASWills, *Henhal(e)* 1272–85 *Ass*, 1319 *Extent*, *Heynhall* 1597 *Bodl*

Yenhall 1549, 1576 *Queens'*, *Yenoll* 1629–32 Ely, *Yennald Farm* 1821 Baker, *Yan Hall* 1851 Gardner

Probably, as suggested by Ekwall (DEPN), 'lamb-nook' or 'lamb-valley,' from OE **ēan*, 'lamb.' Cf. OE *geēan*, 'with lamb,' *ēanian*, 'to yean,' and *v*. healh. Cf. also Kings and Knights Enham (Ha), *Eanham* 1008 Laws, and Studies[2] 70–1.

HILL FM, LEYS WOOD (6″) and OVER WOOD were the homes of Seman *ate Helle* (1350 *Ct*), William de *la Lee* (1302 *Cole* xxii) and William de *Sur le boys* (14th *ib*.). The last two are *Layyswode* 1395 *Cole* xxii, *Layes* 1419 *Queens'*, *Leyes* 1495 Ipm and *le Overwode* 1384 *ib*. *v*. hyll, lēah. It is possible that Leys may be manorial rather than local.

CADGE'S WOOD and HARE WOOD are probably to be associated with the families of Richard *Cagghe* (1279 RH) and Thomas de *le Hayr* (1327 *Cole* xxii). Cf. *crofto voc. Walteriscaygges* 1457 *ib*., *three cornered Cadges, Long Cadges meadow, Cadges Wood* 1812 *EnclA* and *Heirs* 1383 *Cole* xxii, *Hare Wood* 1812 *EnclA*.

SKIPPER'S HALL FM. Cf. *Skippers Lane* (*Road*) 1812 *EnclA*. STREETLY HALL is *Stratlehall* 1298 *Ass*, 1388 IpmR, *Stretlehalle* 1325 Cl, *Stretley Hall* 1495 Ipm, 1851 Gardner.

VI. RADFIELD HUNDRED

Radefelle 1086 DB[1]
Radefelde 1086 InqEl, *Radesfeld(a)* 1086 ICC, *Rad(e)feld(e)* 1157 P *et freq* to 1428 FA, *-feud* 1260 Ass, 1272 *Ass*, *-felt* 1381 Ass

---

[1] It was apparently also called *Weslai hund*' (DB fol. 199) from Westley Waterless *infra* 120.

Ridefeld 1166 P, *Redefeld'* 1185 RotDom, c. 1250 SR
Ratefeld 1251 *ElyCouch*, 1277 *Ely*

The hundred was named from *Radefelde* 1335–9 *Clare*, *Radfe(i)ld* 1504, 16th *Pembroke*, *-fyld* ib., *-filld* 17th ib., *Wrat Field* 1815 *Pembroke*, *Rad Field* c. 1840 *TA*. This was 'in campo de Burgh' near the land of Batemans Chantry and north of Widgham, stretching apparently into Dullingham[1]. Probably 'red open country,' *v.* **feld**. Patches of gravel on the chalk make the soil look rather reddish. The hundred probably met at Mutlow Hill (*infra* 138).

Balsham

BALSHAM [*olim* bɔ·lsəm]

> *to bellesham gemære* 974 BCS 1305, *Belesham* c. 1050 (13th) KCD 907, c. 1060 (12th) ib. 932, c. 1050, 1170 LibEl, 1086 DB, ICC, InqEl *et freq* to 1277 *Ely*, *Belessham* 1086 DB, *Belsham* 1221 *ElyA*
>
> *Balesham* c. 1060 (14th) *ElyM*, 1086 InqEl *et freq* to 1284 FF, *Balsham* 1267 Pat *et passim*, *Ballesham* 1279–82 FF, 1376 Cl, *Balseham* 1285 *Ass*, 1434 Pat, *Balisham* 1291 Pap, *Balescham* 1298 ib., *Balsam* 1476 *Pembroke*, 1506 Pat, *Baldesham* 1272 *Ass*, 1571 ElyA, *Balsome* 1623 Blomefield
>
> *Bælesham*, *Bælessam* 1086 InqEl
>
> *Valesham* 14th HH, *Walsham or Balsam* 1510 LP

'*Bælli*'s hām.' For this personal name cf. Balsall (PN Wa 53–4).

FROGS HALL (6″) is perhaps to be associated with the family of Hugh *Frogg* (1356 *Extent*). Alternatively it may be used of a farm on a marshy site, for it is on the site of an old swamp (School). Cf. *infra* 357.

BALSHAM PLACE (6″) is *Balsham ye place* c. 1640 *Layer*. BALSHAM WOOD is *Balsham whode* 1317 *Queens'*. CHARTERHOUSE PLANTATIONS. The manor and advowson of Balsham were part of the endowment of the *Charterhouse*, London, founded in 1611 by Thomas Sutton, a former inhabitant of the parish (L 84). DOTTEREL HALL and GUNNER'S HALL are so named c. 1825 (O.S.). DUNGATE FM is *Dungate* ib. PARSONAGE FM is *Parsonage Farm or Rat Hall* c. 1825 O.S. Cf. *infra* 357.

---

[1] Marked on the tithe map reproduced in W. M. Palmer's *History of Borough Green* (facing p. 124).

PLUMIAN FM. Cf. *allotments to Plumian Professor* 1801 *EnclA*, part of the endowments of the Plumian Professor of Astronomy in Cambridge. STOCKING TOFT (Kelly). Cf. *Sto(c)king(e)* 1251 *ElyCouch*, 1277 *Ely*, (*Pen, Bottom*) 1801 *EnclA*. *v.* stocking. WORSTED LODGE is so named ib. and is *Wool Street Lodge* 1806 *Map*, *Worcester Lodge* 1852 ib., from Wool Street *supra* 31. YOLE FM is *the Yowls* 1801 *EnclA*, *Yole Fm* c. 1825 O.S., *Yould Fm* 1851 Gardner, *Youle Fm* 1852 *Map*. Cf. *Zolefeld* 1395 AD iv (in Newton in the Isle of Ely).

Brinkley

BRINKLEY

Brinchel' t. Hy 2 (1508) *Pat*, *Brinkelai, -y-, -leia, -leie, -lay, -le(e), -leg(h), -ley(e)* 1177–94 France *et freq* to 1551 *Pat*, *Brinkel* 1246–52 FF, 1261 Ch, *Brinckley* 1313–33 FF, *Brynckele* 1342 ib.
Bringkele t. Hy 3 *ElyCh*, t. Ed 1 *Cole* xix, *Bryng(e)le* 1369 Ipm, 1370 Cl, 1398, 1406 *Cole* xviii, *Bryngley* 1409 Borough, *Bringkley* 1523 *SR*
Brun(c)kele 1272 *Ass*, 1291 Tax
Brenkele 1272 *Ass*, *Brenk(e)ley* 1444, 1465 *Elien*, 1516 EA vii
Brinklow 1576 Saxton, 1610 Speed

'*Brynca*'s clearing or wood,' *v.* lēah. Cf. Brinklow (PN Wa 98–9). The early forms are inconsistent with association with the common word *brink* and this would not be apt topographically.

Burrough Green

BURROUGH GREEN

(*at*) *Burg* c. 1045 (14th) ASWills, 1234 FF *et freq* to 1336 ib.
Burch 1086 ICC, DB, *Burc* 1176 P, t. Hy 2 (1508) *Pat*, c. 1205 Wardon, 13th Misc
Borw c. 1278 ElyA, *Borghwe* 1422 PCC, *Borow* 1501 ECP, *Borough* 1529 EA vii, *Borough(e)grene* 1571 Ely
Burgh 1285 *Ass et freq* to 1449 *Pat*, (*cum Westele*) 1372 *SR*, (*by Dullyngham*) 1392 *Pat*, *Bourgh* 1345 *CWool*, *Burrowgh* 1553 Pat, *Burrowe* 1606 Ely, (*Green*) 1640 EA vi
Brough 1360 *Cole* xviii, t. Hy 8 *Rental*

'Fort,' *v.* burh. Remains of this earthwork still exist in Park Wood (Borough 2).

BURDEN GRANGE (lost) is *grangia de Burchesdan'* t. Hy 2 (1508) Pat, *Boruedene* c. 1240 *Clare*, *Burgdene grange* 1337 ib., *Burdon graunge* 1344 Cl, *Burwedene* 1390 ib., *Burghden Grange* 1501 EA vii, *Burden* (*Graunge*) 16th *Pembroke*, 1554 EA viii. 'The denu or valley by burh or Burrough Green.' This was a grange of Wardon Abbey.

THE CHANTRY is *Batemannes Chaunterie* 1445 Pat, *the chantry of Batemans in Borough* 1553 ib., *the Chantree Pinne*[1] 1615 Borough. In 1445 John *Bateman*, parson of Burgh, had licence to found a *chantry* in the chapel of the Conception of Burgh (Pat).

RAVENS' HALL [rænsɔ·l] is *Raven(e)sholt(e)* t. Hy 2 (1508) Pat, 1291 Tax, 1386 Pat, 1389–90 Cl, (*al. Ransholt*) 1716 Borough, *-hout* c. 1210 Wardon, *Ravenshold(e)* 1539–41 *MinAcct*, *Rammsholt* 1279 RH (p), *Ramenshold* t. Hy 8 *Rental*. 'Raven's wood,' *v.* hræfn, holt. A personal name is also possible, cf. *Hrafn* (Feilitzen 292–3).

BUNGALOW FM and HILL. Cf. *Bangalore Barn* c. 1825 O.S., *Bungalow Fm* c. 1840 *TA*. BURROUGH END is so named c. 1840 (*Map*). BUSHEY GROVE (6″). Cf. *Bushy Close* ib. CAMBRIDGE HILL is probably to be identified with *Camberwe supra* 21. FOX HALL (6″). Cf. *Fox Yerthes* 1563 Borough, *Fox-hole or Owls-harbour* c. 1825 O.S. THE GREEN (6″) is *Burgh grene* 1481 *Pembroke*. THE HALL. Cf. *Hall Fm* c. 1840 *TA*. OUT WOOD is so named c. 1825 (O.S.). PADDLE HOLE END (6″) is *Padlow End* 1756 Borough, c. 1840 *TA*, *Padloe End* c. 1825 O.S. PARK WOOD and PARTRIDGE HALL are so named c. 1840 (*TA*). PLUNDER WOOD (6″) is so named c. 1825 (O.S.). SIPSEY BRIDGE is *Sybbysforth* 1481 *Pembroke*, *Sippesford Bridge* 1639 Borough, c. 1840 *TA*, *Sipsey Bridge* c. 1825 O.S. Probably '*Sibbi*'s ford.' SLUGGS GREEN (6″) is *Struggs Greene* 1615 Borough. SPARROWS' GROVE is so named c. 1825 O.S., and may possibly be associated with the family of Richard *Sparrow* (1662 Borough), but cf. *Spruethorn* (sic) c. 1236 *Clare*, *Sparwethorn* 1377 ib. UNDERWOOD HALL. Cf. *Underwood Field, Farm* c. 1840 *Map*. WICK FM (6″). Cf. *Wig(ge)lane* 1618, 1663 Borough, c. 1840 *Map*, *Wick Lane* 1756 Borough, *the Wick Fm* c. 1840 *TA*.

Carlton cum Willingham

CARLTON

Carletunes (gen.) c. 990 ASWills, *-tun(e)* t. Hy 2 Colch, (*cum Willingham*) 1218 SR, *Carletona* 1086 ICC, *-tone* 1086 DB,

---

[1] *le Peend* 1407 Borough. Cf. Pen Hill (PN Sx 220), from OE *pynd*, 'enclosure.'

-ton(e), K- 1202 FF *et freq* to 1551 Pat, (*Parva*) 1275 RH, (*Canvile*) 1559 *Rental*, (*Much*) t. Eliz ChancP

Carlentone 1086 DB, *-tona* t. Wm 1 (1417) Cluny, 1121 AC, *-tuna*, *-e* c. 1160 Colch, *Karlentona* c. 1098 (15th) Lewes

Carlton t. Stephen France *et freq*, *Karlton* 1260 Ass, 1268 *Ass*, *Car(r)eltun* 1257–68 *AD*, *-ton* 1268 *Ass*, 1365 FF

Charleton 1587 Ely, 1645 Blaeu

OScand **karlatún**, 'the tún of the free men or peasants.'

NOTE. BROOK LANE. Cf. *Brook Lane Close* 1799 *EnclA*. ROODHALL LANE is *Rood Hall* (*lane*) ib.

WILLINGHAM

Willingeham c. 1095, 1098 (15th) Lewes, *Willingham*, *-y-*, *-yng-* 1254 Val *et freq* to 1551 Pat, *Willigham* c. 1250 SR, *Wyllyngeham* 1306 Lewes

Wellingeham c. 1095 (15th) Lewes, *Welingeham* t. Stephen France, Cluny, 1249 FF, 13th AD v, *Welyngham* 1397 Lewes, 1417 FF

Wilingeam 1121 AC, *Wilingham*, *-y-*, *-yng-* 1306 FF, 13th AD v *et freq* to 1338 Seld ix

'hām of the people of *Willa*.' *v.* ingahām.

CRICK'S FM is to be associated with the family of John de *Creke* (1298 *Lewes*) which may have come from Creake (Nf). LOPHAM'S HALL and WOOD are *parua Karleton* 1236 Barnwell, *Barbedors* 15th *Lewes*, *Loppehams* 1466 Pat, *Loppams* 1528 EA vii, *Parva Carleton al. Barbydours or Lophams* c. 1530 ECP vi, *Lopham Hall Wood, Lopham's Wood* 1799 *EnclA, Map*. Named successively from the families of Roger *Barbedor* (1298 *Ass*) and John de *Lopham* (1375 *Elien*). The last must have come from Lopham (Nf).

CARLTON GRANGE (6"), GREEN and HALL (6") are so named in 1799 (*EnclA*). CARLTON WOOD is *bosco de Karleton* 1268 *Ass*. CHURCH FM is so named in 1799 (*EnclA*). COCKSEDGE FM. Cf. *Cock's Head land, Farm* ib., *Cockshed* (*Meadow*) 1799 *Map*, c. 1825 O.S. Possibly the plant-name *cock's head*. Cf. Cockhides (PN Ess 132). NORNEY'S FM is *Nawney* 1821 Baker, c. 1825 O.S. RAYNOR'S BRIDGE (all 6"). Cf. *ad pontem Reyn'* c. 1258 *Lewes*. WILLINGHAM GREEN is so named in 1799 (*EnclA*).

Dullingham

DULLINGHAM

> (*at*) *Dullingham* c. 1045 (14th) ASWills, *Dullingham* 1086 DB, -*yng*- 1200–3 Cur, 1271 FF *et passim*
>
> *Dullingeham* 1086 DB, ICC, 1086 InqEl (p), 1170 LibEl, 1200 FF, 1272–98 *Ass*
>
> *Dulingham* 1086 DB, -*yng*- 1208 Cur *et freq* to 1361 Ipm
>
> *Dollin(c)geham* 1086 InqEl (p), -*y*- 1244 FF *et freq* to 1412 FA
>
> *Dulingeham* 1204 Cur, 1210–15 Wardon
>
> *Dolingeham*, -*y*- 1214 Cur, 1270 FF, -*ing*-, -*yng*- 1305 Pat, 1307, 1311 Ipm, 1478 Pat
>
> *Dun(n)ingeham* 1219 Cur, *Donyngham* 1373 Cl
>
> *Dulligham* c. 1220 *AOMB*
>
> *Dillyngham* 1298 *Ass*, *Delyngham* 1510 LP, *Dallingham* 1643 EA vi

'The hām of *Dull(a)*'s people,' *v.* ingahām. This personal name is not on record, but is probably from the stem of OE *dol*,' dull.' Cf. OHG *Dolleo* and, for the derivative *Dylla*, cf. Dillington (PN BedsHu 269–70). See also PN in -*ing* 139.

BEDHAM HILL (6″)

> *Bethlinge* 1314 Clare, -*lyngfeld* 1337 ib.
>
> *Bedlingge* 1315 Clare, -*lynge* 1344 ib., -*hyll* 1428 ib., 1478 *St-Catharine's*, *Bedlengefeld* 1334 Clare
>
> *Bedhynggfeld* 1327 Clare
>
> *Bedlam Hill* c. 1825 O.S.

We possibly have here a compound of *bydel, a diminutive of *byde, 'hollow, depression,' discussed *s.n.* Bidwell (PN Nth 222), and hlinc, 'hill by the hollow,' cf. PN in -*ing* 28–30.

HARLOCK'S MOOR (6″) is *Heylocks* 1674, 1761 Borough and is probably to be associated with the family of John *Heylok* (1395 ib.).

CLAREHALL FM was part of the possessions of Clare College, Cambridge. CROSS GREEN (both 6″) is so named c. 1825 (O.S.). Cf. *Cr(o)uchweye* c. 1250 *ElyM*, (*le*) *Crouch(e)feld(e)* c. 1290–1455 *Clare*. *v.* crouche. DULLINGHAM HO, JACK'S GALLOWS, LOWER HARE PARK, THE MOATS and TODD'S POND (all 6″) are so named c. 1825 (O.S.). DULLINGHAM LEY is *Dullinghamleye* 1444, 1490 *Clare*, *v.* lēah. GRANGE

FM (6″). Cf. *grangie prioris de Tyfford in Dullingham* 1285 *Ass*. WHITE WOOD (6″) is *Whitewood* ib. WIDGHAM GREEN is *Widgham* ib.

Stetchworth

STETCHWORTH

  Steuicheswrðe c. 1050 (13th) KCD 907, *Steuicesuuorde* c. 1050 (12th) LibEl, *Steuecheswode* 1086 InqEl, *Steu(e)chesw(o)rth* 1279 *ElyM et freq* to 1378 FF, *Stechysworth* 1410 *ElyB*

  Steu(e)chw(o)rth(e) c. 1060 (14th) *ElyM et freq* to 1340 *Ass*, *Steueg-worþe* 1268 *Ass*

  Steuecheworð 1086 InqEl, *Steu(e)chew(o)rde*, *-a*, *-w(o)rthe* c. 1060 (12th) KCD 932 *et freq* to 1341 NI, *Stefecheworþe* 13th *Ely*, *Steuekewrth* 1268 *Ass*

  Stuuicesworde 1086 DB

  Sticesuuorde 1086 DB, *Stichew(o)rth*, *-y-* 1268 *Ass* (p), 1388 Pat

  Stiuicesuuorde 1086 DB, InqEl, *-uuorð* ib., *Stiuechesuurda* 1086 ICC, *Stiuic(h)esuuorð*, *-uuorda* 1086 InqEl, *-wrde* c. 1150 *HarlCh*, *-worthe* 1235 FF

  Stew(e)ch(e)wrda, *-w(o)rth(e)* 1216, 1223 *ElyM*, 1375, 1456 AD vi, i

  Stiwechuurth 1218 SR, *Stowecheworthe* 1316 FA

  Stiuechewrda, *-w(u)rth*, *-y-* 1249 *ElyM*, 1260 Ass

  Stekworth 1277 *ElyM*, *Stech(e)worde*, *-worth(e)* 1374 *Elien et freq* to 1567 Ely, *Stecheford* 1510 LP

  Stachworth 1576 Saxton

This is probably *styfic-worþ*, 'stump-enclosure.' Names in *-worþ* usually have a personal name as first element and this, perhaps, is the explanation of the forms with genitival *s*. Apart from this name, there seems to be no evidence for a personal name *Styfic*, as suggested by Skeat. For another example of *worþ* compounded with a descriptive element, cf. Wentworth *infra* 243. *v.* styfic, worþ.

LEY FM (6″) was the home of Walter *Attelegh* c. 1250 (*ElyM*). *v.* lēah.

BASEFIELD WOOD is so named in 1814 (*EnclA*). GREAT and LITTLE CHITLINGS WOOD and COMBERS WOOD (both 6″) are so named c. 1825 (O.S.). KIDNEY PLANTATION (6″) is so named from its shape. LINGAY HILL. Cf. Lingey Fen *supra* 78. MARMER'S WOOD is *Marmons Wood*

1814 *EnclA*, c. 1825 O.S. PICKMORE WOOD is *Pikemere* c. 1330 *ElyF*, *Pickmore Wood* 1814 *EnclA*. STETCHWORTH LEY is so named c. 1825 (O.S.). TWO CAPTAINS (6″) is *The Two Captains* ib. From these barrows are named a neighbouring field TWO HILLS (School) which is to be identified with *tuomhowe* 14th *ElyF*. '(At the) two hills,' or rather 'barrows,' *v.* OE **twām** and **haugr** and *v.* also *s.n.* Beacon Fm *infra* 135.

Westley Waterless

WESTLEY WATERLESS

> (*at*) *Westle* c. 1045 (14th) ASWills, *Westlai* c. 1050 (13th) KCD 907, 1086 ICC, InqEl, *Westley*(*e*) c. 1060 *ElyM et passim*, (*Waterle*) 1389 *Cole* xxxvii, (*Waterleys*) 1483 ib. xviii, (*Waterley*) 1523 *SR*, *Westleg*(*h*) 1242 P, 1298 *Ass*, 1299 QW
>
> *Vueslai* c. 1050 LibEl, *Weslai* 1086 DB, InqEl, *Wesle* 1297 Abbr
>
> *Wvestle* 1086 InqEl, *Westle*(*i*)*a Gun*(*n*)*or*(*r*)*e de Valoin'*, (*Valoignes*) 1196–7 P, *Westle*(*e*) 1220 FF *et freq* to 1441 Pat, (*Waterles*) 1285 *Ass*, 1290 Cl, 1297 Abbr, 1308 *Cole* xviii, (*Waterlees*) 1285 *Ass*, (*cum Burgo*) 1341 NI, (*al. Westerle*) 1428 FA, (*Waterle*(*e*)) 1455, 1485 *Cole* xviii, 1490 Ipm, *Westle Waterle* 1508 PCC, *Westley Waterless* 1599 ib.
>
> *Westele*(*ye*) 1254 Val, 1391 Cl, 1445 Pat, *Westelee Waterlees* 1541 PCC, *Westeley* (*Waterlesse al. Westley Waterleyes*) 1556 Pat, (*Watlesse*) 1559 *Rental*
>
> *Westerle* 1291 Tax

'West lēah.' Westley is *west* of Dullingham Ley and south-west of Stetchworth Ley. The whole district was, however, probably once well wooded and it may have been called simply lēah. *Waterless* is a corruption of *Waterlees*, containing the plural of lēah. Hence 'water clearings.' Dr Palmer points out that there is no lack of water here. *Burgo* is the neighbouring Burrough Green *supra* 115. This must be the manor in Radfield Hundred held in 1185 by Agnes de *Valuines* (RotDom) which Farrer (106) places in Stetchworth. *Gunnora* was the grand-daughter of Agnes.

HUNGRY HILL. Cf. *Hungerhalle* 1426 IpmR, *Hungry Hill* c. 1825 O.S. and *infra* 357. LADIES GROVE is *Lady Grove* c. 1840 *TA*. WESTLEY BOTTOM (6″) is so named in 1812 (*EnclA*). WESTLEY HALL is *aule de Westle* 13th *Jesus*. WESTLEY LODGE FM is so named c. 1840 (*TA*).

Weston Colville

WESTON COLVILLE

(oð) *West tuniga gemæra* 974 BCS 1305
Westona 1086 ICC, *-tune* 1086 InqEl, *-tone* 1086 DB, InqEl, *-ton(e)*
1176 P *et passim*, (*Coluyle*) 1236 Lewes, (*Coleuill'*) 1285 *Ass*,
(*cum Parva Carletone*) 1316 FA, (*juxta Westerattyng*) 1423 FF,
(*Shrubb*) 1641 *Cole* xviii, (*Couell*) 1645 Blaeu
Westkoleville 1324 Ipm, *Westcolvill* 1327 ib.

'West farm,' *v.* tūn. **West**, probably because *west* of Carlton.
Colville from the family of William de *Coleville* (1203 Cur).

NOTE. CLAMP'S LANE. Cf. *Clampiswaye* 1329 *St John's*, *Clampescroft* 1364
ib.

HILL CROFTS was perhaps the home of William *del Hill* in 1236
(Lewes), *v.* hyll.

MINES FM and WHITING'S GROVE (both 6″) are probably to be associated with the families of John *le Moyne*, *Moigne* (1272 *Ass*, 1298
Lewes) and William *Quyting* (1236 ib.). Cf. (*le*) *Moignes* 1361–9 Cl,
1368 Ipm, *Weston Moynes* c. 1530 ECP, *Wytinges croft* c. 1300 *St John's*,
terr' voc' Whyting 1360 ib., *Whytinges* 1364 ib. Cf. *supra* 64 n. 2.
For *Qu-*, *v.* Introd. xxxvi.

CARLTON GREEN is *Karlet* t. Hy 3 AD iii, *Carletonegrene* 1339 *St John's*.
v. Carlton *supra* 116 and grēne. CHILLY HILL is *Chilhowe* 1236 Lewes,
-brede c. 1300 *St John's*, *Chillowe(brede)* 13th, 1331 ib., *Chilly Hill*
c. 1825 O.S. The second element is hōh. FINCHLEY GATE FM (6″).
Cf. *Finchele* 1236 Lewes, *Finchley Gate* c. 1825 O.S., *v.* finc, lēah and
cf. Finchley (PN Mx 92). LARK HALL is *Larks Hall* c. 1825 O.S.
LINNET HALL is *Linnets Hall* ib. WESTON GREEN is so named ib.,
cf. *Neugrene* 1329 *St John's*. This may refer to LITTLE GREEN. WESTON
WOOD'S FM is *boscum de Westuna* 14th *Jesus*.

West Wratting

WEST WRATTING

(æt) *Wreattinge* 974 BCS 1305, (æt) *Wrættincge* c. 975 ASWills
(æt) *Wretting* 974 BCS 1305 *et freq* to 1273 FF, *Wrettinges* 1200
Cur, *Wretinge* c. 1150 LibEl, *Wrettinga* 12th *ElyM*, *Old Wret-*
tingg(e) 1268 *Ass*, 1309 Pat

Wratinge c. 1050 (12th) LibEl, c. 1050 (13th) KCD 907, 1086 InqEl, c. 1150 *LibEl*, 1170 LibEl, c. 1185 Wardon, *Wratinga* 1086 InqEl, *Wratyngg* 1353–9 Pat

Wratting(e) c. 1050, 1229 (14th) *ElyM et freq*, (*cum Oxecroft*) 1218 SR, *Wrattinga* 1086 ICC, *Wrattincge* 1086 InqEl, *Westwratting(e)*, -*yng(e)* 1272 *Ass*, 1284 FF *et freq*, *Wrattenge* 1278 ElyC, *Wrattingg(e)*, -*y*- 1299 QW *et freq* to 1363 Pat, *Westwrattinges* 1315 FF

Waratinge 1086 DB, InqEl, *Waratincg(e)* 1086 InqEl, *Waratige* 1170 LibEl, *Wartinga* 12th *LibEl*, *Wartting* 13th *Jesus*, *Westwarttynge* 1347 *Cole* xxii, *Wrautinge* 1246 *ElyM*

Wrotting(e), -*y*- 1199 *ElyC* (p), 1247 FF *et freq* to 1450 Rad, (*West*-) 13th *ElyCh*, *Wrottyngge* 1329 Misc, 1363 Pat

Wroting(e) 1200 Cur, 1212 RBE, 1257 FF, *Westwrotyng(e)* 1285 *Ass*, 1405 Pat, *West Wratten* 1493 *Pembroke*, 1549 *Add*

Worthing(e) 1272 *Ass*

A singular name in ing based on OE *wrætt*, 'cross-wort,' hence 'place where cross-wort grows,' *v.* PN in -*ing* 14–15 and cf. *Wratworth supra* 80, Wrat Field *infra* 273, Wratten (PN Herts 11), Wretham (Nf), DB *W(e)retham*, and Wretton (Nf), *Wretton* 1198 FF. *West* because *west* of Great and Little Wratting (Sf), DB *Wratinga*, one of which is called *Estwrattyng'* in 1382 (*Ass*). The three parishes must once have formed a whole.

Note. Slough Hill Lane is *the old Slough Road* 1813 *EnclA.* Cf. *le Sclohell* 1402 *Peterhouse*, *Slohyll* 1438 *WMP.*

Conger's Well (6″) is *Cungrauewellehil* c. 1250 *ElyM*, *Congerswell* 1436 *WMP*, *Congreswell* c. 1500 ib., *Conger's Well* c. 1825 O.S. Possibly 'well by the grove in the valley,' *v.* cumb, grāf(a) and cf. Congreve (St), *Comegrave* DB.

Oxcroft Fm (6″) is *Ox(e)croft(e)* 1218 *SR et freq* to 1426 Cl, (*aula*) c. 1250 *ElyM*, (*by Balesham*) 1324 Pat, (*Halle*) 1355 Ipm, *Execroft* 1346 FA, *Os(e)crofthalle* 1371, 1385 Pat, *Oxcroftehall al. Ox(e)wyckhall*, -*wicke*- 1572, 1597 *Bodl*, *Fosters al. Oxcrofthall* ib. *v.* oxa, croft. *Fosters* from the family of John *Foster* (t. Ed 3 *Bodl*).

Wadloo Fms

Ward(e)lou(h)(e)feld c. 1250 *ElyCh*, 1319 *Extent*, -*lauheweyefeld* t. Hy 3 *ElyCh*, -*laweweye*, -*feld* 13th *ElyM*, -*lowe(feld*, -*weye*) c. 1250 *ElyM*, 1309, 1352 *Peterhouse*, -*hul* 1319 *Extent*, -*hill* 1414

Ct, Ward(e)loweye c. 1250 *ElyM*, 13th *Jesus*, 1319 *Extent, Ward-lofeld* 1320 *StJohn's, Wardele(ye)feld* 1432, 1533 *WMP, Warde-hillwye* 1414 *Ct, Wardilhill* 1533 *WMP*

Warloweye c. 1250 *ElyM*, 14th *Jesus, Warlouel, Warlowefeld, Warloueweye* 13th *ElyM*

Wadeloweweye 1319 *Extent, Wadl(e)y* (*-feld*) 1589 *Rental*, (*Hall*) c. 1825 O.S., *Wadloo Field* 1605 *Peterhouse, Wadlow Field, Way* 1632 *WMP*

'Look-out hill,' OE *weard-hlāw*, with occasional addition or substitution of hyll. Cf. Wardlow (Db), *Wardelawe* 1258 FF.

CHALICE'S TREE[1] (6″), RAND'S WOOD[2] and SCARLETT'S FM[3] (6″) are probably to be associated with the families of Stephen de *Eschaliers* (12th *Peterhouse*), John and William *Randes(s)on*' (1347 *SR*) and William *Scarlet* (1441 *WMP*).

BEDFORD GAP is so named c. 1825 (O.S.). THE GROVE (6″) is *le Grove* 1518 *StJohn's*. HALL WOOD is so named in 1813 (*EnclA*). LORDSHIP FM is *the Lordship Farm* 1775 *WMP*. LOWER HEATH PLANTATION, NEWHEATH PLANTATION. Cf. *Hatheweye* 1319 *Extent, the Heath* 1432 *WMP, Littelheath* 1443 ib. PADDOCK PLANTATION. Cf. *the Valley Paddock* 1813 *EnclA*. WAVERS POND (all 6″) is *the Waver Pond* 1813 *EnclA*. WEST WRATTING GRANGE is *Wratting Grange* c. 1825 O.S. WEST WRATTING GREEN (6″). Cf. *le gretegrene, le mychegrene* 1483 *CRent, Wratting Green* c. 1825 O.S. WEST WRATTING VALLEY FM is *Valley house* 1813 *EnclA*. Cf. *Wratting Valley* c. 1825 O.S. WRATTING COMMON is so named ib.

VII. CHEVELEY HUNDRED

Caueleie 1086 ICC, *Cauelai* 1086 DB, InqEl, *Cauele* 1218 *SR*
Chauelai 1086 DB, *Chauelæi* 1086 InqEl, *Chauelai, -e(e), -e(a)* 1166 P *et freq* to 1316 FA
Cheauele 1175 P, *Cheavely* 1641 EA ix
Cheuele(a) 1198 P *et freq* to 1428 FA, *Chevell* 1553 Pat

v. Cheveley *infra* 125.

[1] *Chalers* 1497 *Peterhouse, Charlers* 1563 ib., *Charles* ib., (*al. Chalyers*) 1589 *Rental*, 1632 *WMP, Challures* 1582 *Peterhouse, Challispasture, -hill* 1632 *WMP*.
[2] *Randesbushe* 1483 *CRent, Raunds Wood* 1813 *EnclA, Rans Wood* c. 1825 O.S.
[3] *terram quond' Willelmi Scarlet* 1493 *Denny, Scarlettes* 1563 *Peterhouse*.

Ashley cum Silverley

ASHLEY

> Esselei 1086 ICC, Esselie 1086 DB, Esle(ge) 1272 Ass, 13th Hosp
> As(se)le(e), -leg, -leia, -leie, -lye 1228 FF et freq to 1311 Walden
> Ays(s)le 1260 FF, c. 1280 Hosp, 1285 Ass, 1291 Tax, Aisseleye 1374
>   Pat
> As(s)h(e)le(e), -ley(e), -legh 1260 Ass et freq to 1428 FA, As(s)chele
>   1298 Ass, 1299 QW, (cum Sylverley) 1316 FA, Axele al. Assele
>   1292 IpmR, Has(se)le 1298 Ass, 13th Cole xviii, Haschele 1449 Pat

'Wood of the ash-trees,' v. æsc, lēah.

NOTE. ASHLEY RD is Asselegewey 13th Hosp.

SILVERLEY

> Seuerlai 1086 DB, ICC, -lei 1086 ICC (p), Seuerlaio 1086 InqEl (p)
> Seilverleia 1086 InqEl (p), Selverleia t. Hy 2 BM, -leg' 1199 CurR,
>   1222 FF, (et Ascheleg) 1246 ib., -le(e), -ley(e) 1218 SR et freq to
>   1315 Ass, Selvirle 1279 RH
> Silverleg(h), -le(e), -ley(e), -y- 1195 Abbr et freq to 1553 Pat, (cum
>   Asshele) 1285 Ass, Sylvyrle 1260 FF
> Suluerle(ye) 1285, 1298 Ass, 1299 Hosp, 1389 Cl, -legh 1299 Hosp

The first element is OE seolfor, 'silver,' possibly, as suggested by
Ekwall (DEPN), used elliptically for some plant- or tree-name such
as silver-weed or silver-wort. v. lēah and see further Sylhall Plantation
infra. Cf. Siluergore c. 1260 StJohn'sH (in Fulbourn), Silver Ley
(PN Ess 627), Selverleg' (1222 FF) in Helion Bumpstead (Ess),
Selvercroft (13th WalthamA) in High Ongar (Ess) and Selverland
(1223 FF) in Stambourne (Ess).

GESYNS[1], HOUGHTON FM (both 6″) and RAYNER'S FM (local) are to be
associated with the families of John de Gynes (1295 Layer), H.
Houghton (1815 Map) and William Rayner (ib.). For Gesyns cf. the
history of Guyzance (PN NbDu s.n.). The family came from Guisnes
(Pas de Calais).

ASHLEY GAP is so named c. 1825 (O.S.). ASHLEY HALL (both 6″) is
aulam de Asselege c. 1280 Hosp, cf. Asselehallecroft c. 1300 ib. ASHLEY-
HEATH FM. Cf. le Hethe c. 1280 Hosp. DUKE'S FM (Kelly) belonged
to the Duke of Rutland (1815 Map). SYLHALL PLANTATION (6″). Cf.

---

[1] Gosehams c. 1825 O.S.

Siluerlehallegate c. 1300 *Hosp*, *Sylhall* c. 1825 O.S. Sill Hall Field contains the site of the old *Sill Hall* (School), *v. supra* 124. TRINITY PLANTATION is the property of Trinity College, Cambridge (School).

Cheveley

CHEVELEY [tʃiˑvli]

(*æt*) *Cæafle* c. 1000 ASWills, *Ceaflea* (*villam silvosam*) 1022 (12th) LibEl, *Ceauelai* (*silua*) 1086 InqEl, *Chef(f)le* 1170 LibEl, c. 1280 *Hosp*

Cheaflea 1022 (18th) KCD 734, t. Cnut (14th) *ElyM*, *Chiauel'* 1200 CurR, (*Silva regis de*) *Cheueleie* 1086 ICC, InqEl, *-lea* 1188 P, *Chevele(e)*, *-ley(e)* 1170 LibEl *et freq* to 1539 *MinAcct*, *-legh* 1287 Fine, *-ly* 1340 FF, *Cheule* 1268 *Ass*, *Cheeveley* 1535 VE

Cauelai 1086 DB, *Caueleio* 1086 ICC, *Cauelaio* 1086 InqEl (p), *Cauele* 1218 SR, *Caveley* 1246 Cl

Chauelai (*silua*) 1086 DB, *Chauelai*, *-ly*, *-le*, *-lay*, *-leye*, *-leg* 1160 P *et freq* to 1342 Ipm, *Chafle* 1242 Fees

Cheleia 1086 InqEl (p)

Chaluelega 1167 P, *-lea* 1171–92 ib.

Chivele 1361 Pap, *Chyvele* 1438 Pat

The first element is OE *ceaf*, 'chaff,' possibly in the sense of 'rubbish, fallen twigs,' as suggested by Ekwall (DEPN); the second is lēah, here, clearly, 'wood,' as shown by the references to a *silva* from DB onwards.

BANSTEAD MANOR (6″) is *Benstedys* c. 1484 EA vii, *Benstede manor* 1582 BM, *Bansted(e)s al. Bensted(e)s* 1587 Moulton, (*al. Cheveley*) 1669 ib., *Bansteeds al. Bansteddes* 1613 ib., and is to be associated with the family of John de *Benstede* (1315 FF).

BROAD GREEN is *Broad Greene* 1675 *WMP*. CASTLE PLANTATION (6″). Cf. *Castle Hill* c. 1825 O.S., *Castle Folly* c. 1840 *TA*. There was formerly a castle here, surrounded by a deep ditch, the residence of the lords of the manor (*Layer*). For *Folly*, *v. infra* 353. CHEVELEY BELT is *Belt Plantation* c. 1840 *TA*. CHEVELEY PARK is *the parke of Cheueley* 1528 CtWards. GIPSY'S WALK (6″) is *Gipsey Walk* c. 1840 *TA*. LITTLE GREEN (6″) is so named c. 1825 (O.S.). LONG HOLE FM. Cf. *Long Holes* c. 1840 *TA*. LONG TONGUE (6″) is *Long Tongue Plantation* ib. SHEPHERD'S HO and WARREN HILL (both 6″) are so named c. 1825 (O.S.).

Kirtling

KIRTLING [*olim* kætlidʒ]

> Curtelinga, -e 1086 ICC, Curtling' 1219 Cur, Quetelinge 1086
> InqEl
> Chertelinge 1086 DB, InqEl, 1170 LibEl, Chertelinges 1166 RBE,
> Kert(e)ling(a), -(e), -yng(g)(e) 1167–8 P et freq to 1509 LP,
> Kertlingh 1298 Ass, Kertelenge 1381, 1456 AD i, 1434 Pat,
> Kertlinges, -yng- 1176 P, 1241 FineR
> Chirtlyng 1272 Ass, Kirt(e)ling(g)(e), -yng(e), Kyrt(e)l- 1268 Ass
> et freq to 1489 Pat, Kyrtelynche 1438 IpmR, Kirtlyche t. Hy 6
> Cole xxxvii, Kirtling quæ & Catlidg nominatur 1594 Camden
> Kart(e)lyng(e), C- 1450 SR et freq to 1553 EA viii, Cartlenge, K-
> 1501 Rental, 1553 EA viii, Cartelage 1553 Pat, Kertlidge 1640 EA vi
> Catlidge 1576 Saxton, 1607 Kip
> Cateledge 1616 Cai, Kirtling, Catlige or Catlage 1808 L

This name has generally been explained as derived from OE *Cyrt-lingas*, 'the settlement of *Cyrtla*'s people,' v. ing, PN in -*ing* 82 and DEPN, and cf. Kirklington (PN NRY 220, PN Nt 170) and Kirtling-ton (O), *Kyrtlingtun* c. 1050 (*s.a.* 977) ASC (C). The rarity of forms in -*es*, the numerous spellings in -*inge* and the ultimate development to *Catlidge* suggest that the second element is OE hlinc rather than ingas, and that the original form of the name was *Cyrtlan-hlinc*, '*Cyrtla*'s ridge.' This would suit the site well. For similar development of hlinc through *linge* to *ling* cf. Swarling (PN K 547) and Sydling (PN Do 201).

UPEND is *Upheme* 13th *Hosp*, (*in Hamelet*) 1483 Pat, *Upyeme* 1477 Madox, *Upyng* 1669 Moulton, *Upend* 1612 FF, c. 1825 O.S., *Upping* 1821 Baker. Here lived Geoffrey de *Hupheme* c. 1250 (*Hosp*) and Walter de *Upheme* in 1298 (*Ass*). This would seem to derive direct from OE *upp-hǣme*, 'up-dwellers.' The exact significance of *in Hamelet* is obscure.

PARSONAGE FM was the home of Adam *atte Persones* of *Kertlyng* (1328 Banco).

BANSTEAD'S FM and PRATT'S GREEN FM (6″) are probably to be associated with the families of John de *Benstede* (1298 *Ass*) and John *Prat* (1327 SR). The first is *Bumpsteds* 1563 *Cole* xxii. This is the same family as that mentioned under Banstead Manor *supra* 125.

Hill Fm and Kirtling Green are so named c. 1825 (O.S.). Lucy Wood is *Lowcey Wood* 1821 Baker, *Lucy Wood* c. 1825 O.S. Possibly 'pig-stye enclosure,' *v.* hlōse, (ge)hæg and cf. Luceys Field (PN Ess 643).

Woodditton

Woodditton

> *Dictun(e)* 1022, c. 1050 (12th) LibEl, 1086 InqEl, *Dichton* 1218 FF, *Dicton* 1285 ib., 1298 *Ass*
>
> *Dittune (siluatica)* 1086 InqEl, (*Silvestre*) 1170 LibEl, *Dittona* 1086 ICC, *Ditton(e)*, -*y*- 1169–71 P *et passim*, (*Valoynes*) 1218 *SR*, (*Wode-*) 1227 FF, (*Waleyns*) 1300 *MinAcct*, (*Valoygnes*) 1308 FF, (*Valouns cum parte Novi Mercati*) 1316 FA, (*Valence*) 1318 FF, (*Valoys*) 1327 SR, (*Valoynetz*) 1332 *Ct*, (*Valeys, Valois*) 1346 FA, (*Valeyntz*) 1353 AD ii, (*Valeyns*) 1363 AD i, (*Waleys*) 1366 Pat, (*Waloys*) 1389 Cl, (*Valans*) 1501 *Rental*, (*Valaunce*) 1553 Pat, (*Vallence al. Wooditton*) t. Jas 1 *Rental*
>
> *Ditone* 1086 DB, *Diton Saxtone Valeyns* 1272 *Ass*, *Wodeditton Valeynce* 1319 FF, *Ditton Camoys* 1370 Pat

'tūn by the dīc,' i.e. the Devil's Dyke (*supra* 34). *Valoynes* from the family of Robert de *Valoines* (Farrer 43). For *Saxtone* and *Camoys*, *v.* Saxon Street and Camois Hall *infra* 128. "Called '*Wood*' to make a distinction from yᵉ other Ditton (Fen Ditton *infra* 142) beinge well wooded and in the wood country as wee call it" (c. 1640 *Layer*).

Derisley Fm is *Deresleg*, -*le(e)*, -*ley* 1239 FF *et freq* to 1465 *Ct*, *Dersle(e)* 1302 FA, 1337–1400 *Ct*, 1394 *MinAcct*, (*Valey*) 1501 *Rental*, *Derisle(e)*, -*y*- 1300 *MinAcct*, 1327–43 *Ct*, *Deeresleigh* 1467 *Ct*, *Deersleys Farm* c. 1825 O.S. Probably 'Dēor's wood or clearing,' *v.* lēah and cf. Desborough (PN Nth 111) and Deresbridge (PN Ess 257). If the first element were dēor, 'animal,' we should not expect a genitive singular.

Saxon Street and Saxton Hall

> *Sextuna* 1086 ICC, *Sextone* 1086 DB, -*ton(e)* 1208 Cur (p) *et freq* to 1285 *Ass*
>
> *Saxton(e)* 1236 Barnwell *et freq* to 1484 Pat, (*cum Nouo Mercato*) 1336 *SR*, *Saxston(e)* 1331 *Ct*, 1411 SR, 1412 FA
>
> *Saxon* 1570 SR, *Saxum* 1576 Saxton, 1607 Kip, *Saxham* 1695 SN

Ekwall (DEPN) would interpret this name and Saxton (PN WRY 162), with similar forms, either as 'Saxon farm' or as 'farm by the *seax or hill,' grouping the name in the latter case with Saxham (Sf), DB *Sexham, Saxham*.

The difficulty about the first interpretation is that we should have expected ME forms *Saxeton, Saxeham*, deriving from OE *Seaxatūn* and *Seaxahām* (with gen. pl. *Seaxa*), rather than *Saxton* and *Saxham* going back apparently to OE *Seaxtūn* and *Seaxhām*. These can only be interpreted as 'tūn or hām of the Saxons' if we believe that direct compounds of the stem *Seax-* with tūn and hām could be formed to denote 'Saxon-*tun*' and 'Saxon-*ham*[1].' There is apparently a parallel for such formation in Swaffham (C, Nf) *infra* 133 where we seem to have a similar direct addition of hām to the stem of the tribal name *Swǣfe*. Such a name applied to isolated Saxon settlements in Anglian areas is historically quite a likely one. Cf. further *Sackbridge* (lost) in Bottisham, found in *Saxbriggemore* 1391 *CartMisc, Saxbrugge* 1429 *Ct*, *Sakebridge, Sackbridge* 1655 *Terr*, where we seem to have reference to a Saxons' bridge. The second explanation gets over the formal difficulty, but is not at all satisfactory from the semantic point of view. There are hills here and at Saxton and Saxham, but they are not of that rough or craggy character which one would have expected if there had been an OE *seax* which could be used of a hill.

WELL BELT (6″) was near the home of John *atte Welle* (1405 *Ct*).

CAMOIS HALL is *Ditton(e)* 1236 Barnwell, (*Kamoys*) 1260 *Ass*, (*Cameys*) 1275 RH, (*Camois*) 1290 *Rental*, (*Caumays*) 1300 FF, *Dytton Canons* 1570 SR and is so called from the family of Ralph de *Kameys* (1209 FF). *v.* Woodditton *supra* 127.

CHALKPIT PLANTATION (6″) is so named c. 1825 (O.S.). Cf. *le Chalk-hill, le Chalkpittes* 1501 *Ct*. CHURCH HALL FM. Cf. *Cherchehalle Wode* 1411 *Ct*. COURT BARONS is *Court Barns* c. 1825 O.S. DANE BOTTOM is *Danes Bottom* ib., probably from denu, 'valley,' cf. Introd. xxxiii. DITTON PARK WOOD. Cf. *Ditton parke* 1501 *Rental, Ditton Wood al. Nonnes Wood* t. Jas 1 ib. *Nonnyswode* (1406 *Ct*) was part of the possessions of the nuns of Swaffham Bulbeck (CAPr xxi, 51). HOUGH-TON GREEN (6″) is *Heighton Green* 1821 Baker, *Hoghton Green* c. 1825 O.S. MOORLEY PLANTATION is so named c. 1825 (O.S.). Cf. *la More* 1243 *FF*. PARSONAGE FM (6″). Cf. *Person(n)esfeld* 1335 *Ct*, (*le*) *Person(n)age(s)feld(e)* 1410–1501 ib.

[1] Cf. *Saxmere* 1260 Ass (in Chilford Hundred).

VIII. STAINE HUNDRED

Stane 1086 ICC, InqEl, *Stan(e)* 1185 P *et freq* to 1523 *SR*
Stanes 1086 DB, 1268 *Ass*, *Stanas* 1086 InqEl
Stone 1268, 1272, 1285 *Ass*
Stayne 1553 EA vii, 1592 BM

'Stone' or 'stones,' OE stān or *stānas*. Anderson (EHN i, 100)
notes that Skeat's suggestion that the modern form is due to Scandinavian influence is scarcely possible, for there is no trace in the early
forms of the diphthong we should expect from ON *steinn*. Cf. Staines
(PN Mx 18) where the *ai* is similarly late in appearing, though in that
name there is no trace of any *o*-forms at all. He suggests that it is
probably an inverted spelling due to the falling together of *ā* and *ai*
in early ModE. This name cannot be associated with such names as
Old Steine (PN Sx 292) and Steane (PN Nth 57) where we have early
forms like *Stene(s)* in the 13th century, from OE *stǣne*, 'stony place.'
Cf. also Long Stanton (*infra* 184) which occurs as *Stainton* in 1438.
The meeting-place of the hundred was probably at Mutlow Hill in
Great Wilbraham (*infra* 138).

Bottisham

BOTTISHAM [*olim* bɔtisəm, bɔtsəm]

Bodekesham 1060 (c. 1350) KCD 809, 1077 (17th) ChronRams *et
freq* to 1494 AD i, -*is*-, -*ys*- 1284 FA *et freq* to 1492 AD i, *Bode-
chesham* 1168, 1176 P, *Bothekesham*, -*is*- 1218 *SR*, 1350 FF,
Bodekesam 1227 NLC
Bodichesham 1086 ICC, *Bodichessham* 1086 DB, *Bodikisham* 1357
Pat
Bodischesham 1086 ICC (p), *Bodeske(s)ham* 1172, 1242 P, 1275 FF,
Bodkesham 1236, 1274 Cl, 1371 FF
Boding(e)s(h)am 1155, c. 1186, 1227 NLC, t. Hy 2 (1313) Ch
Bodeg(h)esham 1195 P *et freq* to 1496 AD i
Bodesham c. 1210 Wardon (p) *et freq* to 1527 Bott
Bo(c)kesham 1213 Cur (p), 1291 Tax, 1411 SR, 1412 FA
Bot(h)ekesham, -*is*-, -*ys*- 1218 *SR et freq* to 1468 Pat, *Botkysham*,
-*is*-, -*es*- 1399 FF *et freq* to 1430 Pat
Bodelsham 1272 *Ass*, *Botelesham*, -*ys*- 1384, 1443 Pat

Bot(t)esham 1298 *Ass et freq* to 1605 Imb
Bottisham, -ys- 1434 Pat *et passim, Bottessam* 1512 CAPr xxxi,
Botsom 1558 *Ct, Bosham* 1712 *CCC*

'*Boduc*'s farm,' v. hām, as suggested by Skeat and Ekwall. This
personal name is not on record, but is a derivative of the *Boda* found
in Bodiam (PN Sx 518), Bodenham (He) and Bodham (Nf). In the
12th century confusion with a more common type of name in *-inges-*
such as Horningsea (*infra* 145) seems to have taken place.

NOTE. WILBRAHAM RD is so named in 1801 (*EnclA*).

BOTTISHAM LODE is *ladam de Bodekesham* 1279 RH, *Bodkesham lo(o)de*
1388 *Ct, Botesham Loode* 1390 Ely, v. (ge)lād.

BRADDONS PLANTATION (6″) is *Brodyng(es)* t. Ric 2 *Rental,* c. 1450
Bott, *Bradding, Bradynsfeild* 1615 *Magdalene, the Bradens* 1801 *EnclA*.
Probably an *ing*-derivative of brād, 'the broad place.' Cf. *Bradyng
medow* (Soham) t. Ed 4 *Pembroke,* Weeting (Nf) < OE *wǣt,* 'wet,'
Steeping (L) < OE *stēap,* 'steep,' PN in *-ing* 15, 16, 21 and *infra* 333.

BOTTISHAM HALL was the home of John *atte Halle* (1321 *Ct*).

ALLINGTON HILL[1], BENDYSHE FM[2] and ST IVES WOOD[3] are to be
associated with the families of William *Alyngton* (1410 Cl), Thomas
de *Bendish* (1321 *Ct*), which probably came from Bendysh (PN Ess
513), and William de *Sancto Ivone* (1294 *Cole* xxii) which came from
St Ives (PN BedsHu 221).

BOTTISHAM HEATH FM (6″) is so named c. 1825 (O.S.) and, with
HEATH ROAD (so named 1801 *EnclA*), takes name from *le Heth* 1451
AddCh. HALL FM (6″) and SPRING HALL are so named c. 1825 (O.S.).
TOWN END (Kelly). Cf. *Northtounshende* 1347 *AD, Esttowneshende de
Botesham* 1428 *Ct, Southtowneshende* 1429 *Ct,* v. tūn. TUNBRIDGE
HALL (6″) is *terram prioris de Tonebrig* 1302 *Cole* iv, *Tonebregghall* 1354
MinAcct. Part of the possessions of the Prior of Tonbridge (K). THE
VINEYARDS (6″) is *Vineʒerd* t. Ric 2 *Rental, le Vynneʒerde* 1451 *AddCh,
le Wynneyerde* 1470 *StJohn's,* v. wīngeard. WHITELAND SPRINGS (6″)
is *Withelond* t. Hy 6 *Rental, White Land-hill* 1719 Bott, *Whiteland
Springs* c. 1825 O.S.

[1] *terra Willelmi Alyngton* t. Ric 2 *Rental, Alingtons* c. 1450 Bott.
[2] *Bendissh* t. Ric 2 *Rental, Bennys* 1545 Bott, *Benditch Fm* 1851 Gardner.
[3] Cf. *Sent Yvespath* t. Ric 2 *Rental, Seyntyvescroft* t. Hy 6 ib.

Lode[1]

LODE

> Lada 1154–89 AddCh (p), (de Bodekesham) c. 1251 Cole iv, la Lade
> c. 1260 Bodl, 1279 RH, Ladam 1321 Ct
> (le) Lode 1345 Cole iv, 1462 Pat
> Botesham Lode 1396 Cole iv, 1521 Bott, Bosham Load 1712 CCC
> (le) Lodestrete 1429 Ct, 1539 MinAcct

'Watercourse,' v. (ge)lād. Named from Bottisham Lode.

NOTE. SANDY RD. Cf. Sondipece t. Ric 2 Rental.

ANGLESEY

> Angleshey(e), -heia, -ys-, -is- 12th AD iii et freq to 1553 Pat, (juxta
> Stowe) 1362 Cole iv, Angelsheye 1253 FF
> Anglesie 1213 Cur, -eia, -eie, -eye, -eya 1221 FF et freq to 1539
> MinAcct, -ee 1227 NLC, -ea c. 1278 ElyA, Anglysseye 1444 AD i
> Angylsey 14th Wymond, 1489 AddCh, Angelsey 1451 ib.
> Engles(s)(e)ye 1262 AOMB, 1272 Ass, FF
> Hangleseye 1272 Ass, 1311 Queens'
> Angeseye 1578 Queens'

No certainty is possible with regard to this name. At first sight
Ekwall's interpretation (DEPN) 'isle of the Angle' is attractive, but
the reason for such a name is difficult to find. 'Isle of the Angle' is
unlikely in territory which was essentially Anglian rather than Saxon.
The possibility of some other interpretation is suggested by the
existence near by of a hamlet Angerhale in Bottisham (1279 RH)
and the mention at an earlier date of Angerhale, a place to which the
monks of Ely took their treasures in the troubled days of Hereward
(v. Gesta Herewardi 391). It is further mentioned as Hangerhale 1268
Ass, 1451 AddCh, Angerhale 1348 Ct, 1451 AddCh, Ang(e)rale t. Ric 2
Rental, 1428 Ct. We have also mention of Anglemedwe, -croft t. Hy 6
Rental. Angerhale is clearly a compound of OE *anger, 'grass-land'
(cf. Ongar, PN Ess 71–2) and healh, hence 'grass-land nook'. It may
be that from Angerhale was formed a compound Angerhales-ēg,
'marshland by Angerhale,' and that this developed to Anglehalesey,
Anglesey, v. ēg. For angle from angre, v. IPN 107 and cf. the similar
development of hangra in Barnacle (PN Wa 101), Rishangles (PN Sf
124), Hangleton (PN Sx 168, 289), Nether hangeles 1270 St John's
Horningsea), Fleghangelles infra 324 and s.n. Christ's Piece supra 40.

---

[1] Formerly part of Bottisham.

HOLMES PLANTATION[1] and LODEMOOR DROVE (both 6″) were probably
near the homes of Thomas and Wimer de *Hulmo* (c. 1251, t. Hy 3
Cole iv) and John *atte More* (1308 *Ct*). *v.* holmr, mōr.

BULL'S FM, HARVEY'S DROVEWAY[2] (6″) and HATLEY'S FM (6″) are
probably to be associated with the families of Thomas *le Bole* (1336
Ct), Simon fitz *Heruey* (13th *AOMB*) and Nicholas *Heruy* (1335 *Ct*)
and Thomas *Hatley* (1814 *Lot*).

BLOCK FEN DROVEWAY (6″). Cf. *Blackfen Lake* 1357 *Cole* xxxvi. Cf
Blockmoor Fen *infra* 198. BOTTISHAM POORS' FEN (6″) is *Bottisham
Poor Fen* 1801 *EnclA*. On enclosure, 217 acres of fen land were
allotted to the poor of Bottisham (Bott 15). CRANNEY DROVEWAY is
Cranneys Drove 1775 *Map*. CRANNEY HALL is *Craney(e)*, (*mariscun*
de) 1305, 1337 *Cole* iv. 'Crane or heron marsh,' *v.* cran, ēg. DAM
DROVE (6″). Cf. *le Wrongdam* 1429 *Ct*, *the Dam-root* 1719 Bott, *v.*
wrang, 'crooked.' DOCKING DROVEWAY (6″) is *Dockin(g) droveway* ib.
1825 O.S. Cf. *le dokky halfacre* t. Hy 6 *Rental*. FENHEAD (6″) is so
named in 1719 (Bott). LONG MEADOW is *Langmedwe* 1260 *FF*, *Lange-
mede* t. Hy 3 *Cole* iv, (*de Bodekesham*) 1336 ib. xxii, *Longum Pratum*
1279 RH. Self-explanatory. QUEEN'S FEN is so named in 1801
(*EnclA*). Cf. *Queen's ground* 1719 Bott. WHITE FEN (6″) is so named
in 17th (*AdvL*).

Stow cum Quy

STOW

> *Stoua* 1086 ICC, (*alia*) *Stowe* 1189, c. 1270 Rams, *Stowe* 1236
> Barnwell *et passim*, (*Engayne*) 1218 *SR*, (*West*) 1301 *CaiCh*,
> (*juxta Angleseye*) 1307 FF, (*iuxta Quie*) 1327 *Ass*
> *Stowe et Coye* 1279 RH, *Stowe cum Quey* 1316 FA, *Stowequeye*
> 1372, 1384 Pat, *Stowe Cumquy* 1383 Cl, *Stowequye* 1420 Cl
> *Stoquie, -ye* t. Hy 8, 1559 *Rental*, *Stow sid Quy* 1667 CWills
> *Stokequy(e)* 1462, 1489 Pat, *-qui* 1546 *Rental*

'Place,' *v.* stōw. *Engayne*, from the family of Richard *Engaine*
(1184–9 Rams). Cf. *D'Engayne's Fm infra* 133. *West* in contrast to
Long Stowe *infra* 163.

NOTE. COLLIER'S LANE is perhaps to be associated with the family of
Trignell *Collyer* (c. 1840 *TA*). DUNSLEY CROSS RD is *Dunsey Crossway* 1591
EA xiii, *Dunsicroseway* 1615 *Magdalene*.

[1] Cf. *Holme* 1279 RH.
[2] Cf. *t'r' Thomae Hervey sup' Lodeweye* t. Hy 6 *Rental*.

QUY [kwai]

Choeie 1086 ICC, Coeia 1086 DB, InqEl, Coeie ib., Coy(e) 1275–9
RH, 1284 FA, 1285, 1298 Ass, Coieye 1346 FA (p)

Cuege 1086 InqEl, Cueya, -e 1185 RotDom, 1218 SR, 1242 Fees,
1285 Ass

Queya, -e, -eie 1218 SR et passim, (juxta Wilburgham) 1308 FF,
(juxta Anglesey) 1324 ib., Qweye 1272 Ass, 1291 Cl, Tax, 1345
CWool

Cow(e)ye 1268 Ass, 1270, 1271 FF, Coueye al. Couue 1272 Ipm,
Couye 1298 Ass, 1317 Ipm

Quie, -y- 1327 Ass et freq to 1434 Pat, Qwye 1340 ElyF, 1450 SR,
Qwoye 1285 Ass, Quoy, -i 1605 Imb, 1719 Bott

'Cow-island,' v. cū, ēg. For the development cf. Quickbury (PN
Ess 51).

D'ENGAYNE'S FM (6″) is to be associated with the family of William
Denganye, de Engann' (1279 RH). It is Engaynesmaner 1402 FF. Cf.
also Gaines close 1615 Magdalene, Gains Plantation c. 1840 TA and
Colne Engaine and Gaynes Park (PN Ess 380, 84, 133).

CREAKHILL is Creakhill(s) c. 1840 TA. QUY MILL is Stowquy Water
Myll 1589 StJohn's, Quymill 1636 BedL. SPRING PLANTATION (6″) is
so named c. 1840 (TA). STOW CUM QUY FEN is Qui fenn 1623
Magdalene.

Swaffham Bulbeck and Swaffham Prior

SWAFFHAM (BULBECK and PRIOR) [swɔfəm], olim [sɔfəm]

Suafham c. 1050 (13th) KCD 907, 1086 ICC, DB, InqEl, 1272
Ass, (by Cambridge) 1312 Misc

Suafahm (sic) c. 1060 (12th) LibEl, Suafam 1086 DB, InqEl,
Swafam c. 1300 ElyA

(Altera) Suuafham 1086 InqEl, Swafham c. 1150 LibEl et passim,
(Bolebek, Prioris) 1218 SR, (prioris Elyensis) 1232 ElyC, (alia)
1236 Barnwell, (le Cunte) 1252 FF, (magna) 1253 ib., (Sancti
Cyricii, Sancte Marie, Monialium) 1254 Val, (Long-) 1258 Cl (p),
(Prior) 1261 FF, (Bulebec) 1268 Ass, (Prior de Ely) 1279 RH,
(iuxta Riche, Gildene) 1285 Ass, (iuxta Reche) 1285 FF, (le Counte)
1324 Abbr, (Peche) 1334 Ct, (Comitis) 1451 IpmR

Sæufham 1170 LibEl, Saufham 13th ElyCh, Sawfham 1284 FA
1394 MinAcct, Saffeham Monialium 1487 Elien
Swaffham 1196 FF et passim, (cum Reche) 1298 Ass, (Litle) 1643
Blomefield
Swauesham 1197–8 P, 1199 ElyC, 1285 Ass, Swaveham 1471 Pat
Swapham 1256 Barnwell et freq to 1529 LRMB, (and Bulbech)
1464 Pat, Swefham 1556 Pat
Swof(f)ham 1272 Ass et freq to 1553 EA vii
Sofham 1440 Ct, Soff(e)ham 1442 ib. et freq to 1574 Ely, Sopham
1481 MinAcct, Soffhom, Soughom 1501 Ct, Shoffam 1550 Pat

OE Swāfhām or Swǣfhām, 'the Swabian home,' the first element
being the stem of the tribal name Swǣfe. Cf. Swaffham (Nf), DB
Suafham and v. also Swavesey infra 172 and Introd. xxxiii. For the
formation cf. Saxon Street supra 127. Bulebec from Hugo de Bolebec(h)
1086 ICC, InqEl. It was also called magna[1], le Cunte or Comitis from
the family of Aubrey de Vere, earl of Oxford (d. 1214), who married
Isabel de Bolebec (v. Farrer 128–9), and Monialium from the nuns of
Swaffham Bulbeck Priory founded before the reign of King John
by one of the Bolebecs (Tanner 46) (cf. Nunnysmill, le Nunnys
Weyer 1536–9 MinAcct). For Gildene, cf. Guilden Morden supra
61, and for Reche, v. infra 136. Long because Swaffham Bulbeck lies
along the road, cf. Long Stanton infra 183. Swaffham Prior called
also Little[1], was a manor of the Prior of Ely. There were formerly two
parishes here (united in 1667) and two churches dedicated to St Cyric
and St Mary. Peche from the fee of Hamon Pecche in Swaffham Prior
(1236 Barnwell).

Swaffham Bulbeck

NOTE. FEN LANE is le Fenn lane 1605 Ct. QUARRY LANE. Cf. John atte
Quarrere 1329 Cole iii and le quarre 1549 Ct. SWAFFHAM FIELD RD. Cf.
camp. de Swafham Bolebek 1319 Extent, Swafhamfelde 1457 Ct.

CROW HILL PLANTATION (6″). Near here and possibly identical in
name with Crow Hill was a fen called le Croyell' 1573 Ct, (the) Croyle
1637 BedL et freq to 1775 Map. The topography is uncertain, but we
probably have here OE *crēowel, 'fork,' found in Croughton (PN Nth
51) and Cryfield (PN Wa 181–2). For these we have forms Croyle-,

---

[1] Swaffham Bulbek or Great Swafham, Swaffham Priors or Little-Swaffham 1751
Blomefield.

Crouel-, *Crowell-*. The form *Crow Hill* would then have arisen through popular etymology.

HILL Ho was the home of Roger *atte Hull* (1369 CAPr xxxi).

ASHMAN'S FM (6"), BURGH HALL[1] and SORREL FM[2] (6") are probably to be associated with the families of Benjamin *Ashman* (1722 Lot), Thomas de *Burgh* (of Burrough Green) (1327 SR) and Sarra *Sorel* (1318 CAPr xxxi).

ADVENTURER'S GROUND FM. Cf. *Adventurers Lands* 1775 *Map* and Adventurers' Land *infra* 292. CHALK FM is so named in 1829 (Wells). Cf. *Chalkehul* c. 1210 Wardon. COW BRIDGE is so named in 1775 (*Map*). FOUR MILE STABLE FM. Cf. *Four Mile Stables* 1829 Wells. GUTTER BRIDGE (6") is *Guttars brugge* 1409 Borough. HARE PARK is *Upper Hare Park* c. 1825 O.S. Cf. Lower Hare Park *supra* 118. HIGHBRIDGE FM is *Hyebrigge* 1445 *Ct*. HUNDRED ACRE DROVEWAY (6"). Cf. *Swaffham Common called the Hundred Acres, The Hundred Acre Droveway* 1775 *Map*. KING'S GAP (6") is so named in 1821 (Baker). MITCHELL HALL (6") is *Michelhall, -y-* 1429 *Ct*, t. Hy 8 *Cole* xxxvii. Probably 'great hall,' *v.* micel. NEW ENGLAND is *New England Fm* c. 1825 O.S. It lies on the parish boundary, cf. *infra* 357. NEW MILL (6"). Cf. *Newemelleweye* 1330 *Ct*. SWAFFHAM BULBECK LODE is *ladam de Swafham Bolbek* 1279 RH, *Swaffham lode* 1539 *MinAcct, v.* (ge)lād.

Swaffham Prior

BARSTON BRIDGE and DROVE. Cf. *Baston(e)* 1319 *Extent*, 14th *Queens'*, 1342–1663 *Ct, le Baston* 1563 ib., *Basson* 1600–69 ib., (*ripa de*) *Barsondich* 1610 ib., *Baston Bridge* 1805 *EnclA, Barson Bridge* 1829 Wells. Probably 'lime-tree farm,' from OE *bæst* and tūn. *v.* Bassen-hally *infra* 259.

BEACON FM is *Bacon Fm* c. 1825 O.S. So called from *The Beacons*, two barrows at the "east end of 4-mile race-course" (Fox 327). These barrows are probably to be identified with *Tweynhowes* 1279 RH (on the bounds of Swaffham Prior), *v.* haugr.

---

[1] *Burghall* 1319 *Extent, Burrowhall* 1668 *Ct, now corruptly called Budge-hall* 1808 L.
[2] *terram Sarre Sorel* 1319 *Cole* iii.

REACH

> *Rete, Reche* 1086 InqEl, (*littus*) *Reche* c. 1122 (17th) ChronRams
> *et freq* to 1552 Pat, (*iuxta Swafham*) 1315 *ElyF*, (*Sopham*) 1481
> *MinAcct, la Reche* 1230 *ElyC* (p), *Reeche* 1446 *MinAcct, Reach*(e)
> 1552 Pat, 1564–92 *Ct*, (*East, West*) 1660 ib., *West Retche* 1661 ib.
> (*littus de*) *Rechere* c. 1135 Rams
> *Rache* 1517 EA vii

This name has been discussed *s.n.* Reach (PN BedsHu 125–6), the name of a place which is on rising ground in a shallow valley, the village lying along the road which runs up the valley. The Cambridge-shire Reach lies alongside the end of the Devil's Dyke, and, as Skeat has pointed out, old maps show that it stood at the very edge of the waters of the fenlands, on a rounded projection from the old shore. It was once a busy spot where sea-going ships were loaded and unloaded (cf. Conybeare 194). There is another Reach in Whittlesey (*infra* 264), a stretch of marsh-land near the King's Dyke, with nothing distinctive in the topography. It seems difficult to find a common element in the sites of these places. It has been suggested (*loc. cit.*) that the source of this name was an OE *rǣc*, cognate with ON *rák*, 'stripe, streak,' the source of the English *rake*, 'way, path,' and that the reference in the Bedfordshire place was to the steep narrow road in the valley, whilst that in Cambridgeshire was named from the Devil's Dyke which was used as a *reach* or path. The fact that there was also a *Recheweye* is not an insuperable difficulty, but it seems impossible to apply the term 'road' to Reach in Whittlesey. Ekwall (DEPN) suggests the same OE *rǣc*, cognate with ON *reik*, 'parting of the hair,' Sw *rēk*, 'a stripe,' with a probable meaning 'strip.' This seems, on the whole, the best interpretation, *rǣc* referring in the Bedfordshire name to the strip of rising land, and here and in Whittlesey to the strip of land bordering on the fens or the dyke (note the use of *littus supra*). The hamlet is partly in Burwell and partly in Swaffham Prior, the two parts being known as *West* and *East* Reach respectively. They were separated by the Devil's Dyke. *v.* Addenda lix.

DELVER END and BRIDGE (both 6″) are *Delvesende* 1442 *Ct, Delfend* 1529 *LRMB, Delphend* 1663 *Ct, Delfe Bridge* 1585 ib. *v.* (ge)delf, ende.

REACH LODE is *lada de Reche, Rechelod*(e) 1279 RH, (*al. voc. le Myle*) 1457 *Ct, Reach Loades End* 1618 ib. *v.* (ge)lād and cf. Mile End *infra* 222.

REACH BRIDGE (6″) was probably near the home of Geoffrey *Attebrigge* of *Swafham iuxta Riche* (1285 *Ass*).

BYE'S FM, HUBBERSTEAD'S FM, LORD'S GROUND FM, RAND HALL[1] and DROVE[1] (6″) and SHADWORTH MANOR FM[2] (6″) are probably to be associated with the families of John *Bye* (1665 *Ct*), John Lodge *Hubberstye* (1814 Lot), Adam *le Lord* (1280–3 *Ct*), John *Rande* (1368 CAPr xxxi) and John *Shadworth* (1399 *Cole* xxxvii).

BEACON COURSE (6″). Cf. *the Beacon Course Road* 1805 *EnclA*. BLACK DROVEWAY (6″) is so named c. 1825 (O.S.). BUNBURY FM. Cf. *Bambury('s) Mile* 1821 Baker, 1829 Wells. CHAPEL FM (6″). This is near a Methodist chapel from which it may well be named, but cf. also *terram capelle* 1301 *Ct*, *le Chapellonde* 1474 *Queens'*. CHURCH HILL (6″) is *Churchehill* 1663 *Ct*. Cf. *le Cherchehelfelde* 1338 *Queens'*. DRIEST DROVEWAY (6″). Cf. *ye common called ye Dries* 1669 *Cole* iii, *Driest Droveway* 1805 *EnclA*. FAIR GREEN (6″). Cf. *Horssefeyr' in Reche* (p.n.) 1349 *Ct*, *Rechefeyre* 1424 ib. Self-explanatory. The earliest mention of *horsefair* in NED is dated 1369. THE HALL (6″). Cf. *Hallfeild* 1579 ib., *la Hallande* 1599 ib., *the Hall maner* 1669 ib. HEADLAKE DROVE (6″) is so named in 1805 (*EnclA*). Cf. *le Headlake* 1588 *Ct*, v. lacu. HIGHFEN FM. Cf. *le Heyfen* 1569 *Ct*, *the High Fen* 1637 BedL. LITTLE FEN DROVE (6″) is so named in 1805 (*EnclA*) from *le lyttellfenne* 1564 *Ct*. LOWBRIDGE HOLE and MILL DRAIN (both 6″) are so named c. 1825 (O.S.). The former is *Low Bridge Hale* 1775 *Map*. PARTRIDGE HALL FM (6″) is *Partridge Hall* c. 1825 O.S. RAIL DROVE is so named in 1805 (*EnclA*). RIVER BANK. Cf. *communem ripariam in Reche* 1453 *Ct*. ROUND COURSE and SPLIT DROVE (both 6″) are so named in 1829 (Wells). SEDGE FEN (6″) is *le Segghffen* 1431 *Ct*. SWAFFHAM PRIOR FEN is *Swafham ffen* 1455 *Ct*. WHITEWAY DROVE (6″) is *White Drove* 1805 *EnclA*, *White Droveway* c. 1825 O.S., *Whiteway Drove* 1829 Wells.

Great and Little Wilbraham

WILBRAHAM (GREAT and LITTLE)

(*æt*) *Wilburgeham* c. 975 ASWills, 1086 ICC, InqEl (p) *et freq* to 1428 FA, *Wilburgesham* 1185 P, *Wilburheham* c. 1240 AD v

---

[1] *terr' Rogeri Rant* 1569 *Ct*, *Ran(d) Drove* 1805 *EnclA*, c. 1825 O.S.
[2] *Manor of Shadeworth* 1436 *Ct*, *Shaddeworthes* 1456 ib.

Witborham, Wiborgham 1086 DB, *Wiborgeham, Wiburgeham* 1086
  InqEl (p), *Wi-, Wyburham* 1156 France, 1249 FF, *Wy-, Wiburg-
  ham* 1230, 1242 P, 1368 FF, 1480 *CTerr*
Wilburcham 1150 BM, 1199 CurR, c. 1240 AD v, *Wil-, Wylburgham*
  c. 1169 *Hosp et freq* to 1461 Pat, (*magna, parua*) c. 1250 *Hosp*,
  (*Kinges-*) 1272 Ass, *Wilborham* 1280 Fine, *Wilborugham* 1325 *Ct*,
  Wylborgham 1337 *Ass*, *Wilbourgham* 1363 Ipm
Wil-, Wylburham a. 1169 *ElyM et freq* to 1553 Pat, (*Parua*) 12th
  AD iii, (*Regis*) 1218 *SR*, (*Alia*) 1236 Barnwell, *Wilburuham* 1268
  Ass, *Wilbirham* 1298 ib., *Wilberham, -y-* 1290 Ch, 1325 FF, 1552
  Pat
Winburgeham c. 1180 *ElyF*, *Wyneburgham* 1271 FF
Wolburham, -bor- 1283 FF, *Wulburgham* 1328 Banco
Wilbram, -y- 1360 Ipm *et freq* to 1550 Pat, (*Litle*) 1500 PCC,
  (*Moche*) 1515 *Cole* xxii, (*Myche*) 1548 PCC
Wyl-, Wilbraham t. Hy 8 *Rental*, 1539 *MinAcct*, 1643 EA vi

'The *hām* of a woman named *Wilburg*,' a name found also in Wilburton *infra* 243, *v.* hām. *Regis* and *Kinges-* because the manor of
Great Wilbraham was held by the King (TRE).

Great Wilbraham

Mutlow Hill is *Mutlow Hill* 1812 *EnclA*, *Motlow Hill* c. 1825 O.S.
It is a tumulus on the Fleam Dyke at the junction of the boundaries
of Great Wilbraham (Staine Hundred), West Wratting and Balsham
(Radfield Hundred) and Fulbourn (Flendish Hundred), and is, no
doubt, identical with Mutlow Hill (PN Ess 543). 'Assembly hill,'
v. (ge)mōt, hlāw. Situated as it is at the meeting-point of three
hundreds, this must, presumably, have been the place of assembly of
all three. The sheriff's tourn for Flendish Hundred (*infra* 140) was at
the Fleam Dyke. In Balsham in Radfield Hundred was (*campo voc.*)
Schameles 1251 *ElyCouch*, whilst in Wilbraham in Staine Hundred we
have reference to (*ad*) *Shamele* c. 1320 *Deed*, *Sameles* 14th AD v.
This is OE *sceamol*, 'a bench,' clearly that on which sat the members of
the Hundred court. Cf. *Tendryngshameles* (PN Ess 325) and Shamwell
Hundred (PN K 107), DB *Essamels*, 1226 *Ass Shamele(s)*. *v.* Addenda
lix.

Wilbraham Temple is *Wilburham Magna Templariorum* 1254 Val,
the Temple of Wylburgham 1298 Pat, *Templum de magna Wilburgham*

1340 *Ass*, *le Temple* 1424 *Hosp*. The manor was held by the Knights Templar in 1226 (Pat).

CHURCH END, CROSS ROAD FM, TEMPLE END (FM)[1] (all 6″) and GREAT WILBRAHAM HALL were probably the homes of William *Attecherch* (1333 HMC Rutland iv), John Hancock *atte Crosse* (1476 Bott), Richard *del Temple* (1325 Pat) and John de *Aula* (1327 SR). *v.* cirice, cros.

SHARDELOWES WELL (6″) is so named c. 1825 (O.S.) and is to be associated with the family of Edmund de *Sardelowe* (1279 RH) and John de *Shardelou* (1325 Pat).

APPLETON PLANTATION. Cf. *Appelton*(*clos*) 1424 *Hosp*. 'Orchard,' *v.* æppeltūn. FROG END is so named c. 1825 (O.S.). Used of a marshy spot. It is low-lying. THE GRANGE (6″). Cf. *finem occidentalem grangie* 1428 *Hosp*. HEATH FM (UPPER and LOWER). Cf. *le Heth* 1424 ib.

Little Wilbraham

NOTE. MILL RD is *le Melneweye* 1379 *Rental*. By it lived Walter *Attemulwey* (1272 *Ass*).

HAWK MILL is *molendinum de Halke* 1279 RH, *Halkmylne* 1398 Cl, *Hawkemyll* 1570 CCC. It takes its name from *le Halke de Wilburham* 1245 *AD* which gave name also to *Halkpath* 1339 *CartMisc*, *Halkestrete* 1446 *Rental*, 'mill in the nook or corner,' *v.* halke *infra* 328.

WELLS'S FM (6″) is probably to be associated with the family of Thomas *Welle* of Botekesham who had land in Little Wilbraham in 1470 (*Ct*).

CORPUS CHRISTI FM (6″) represents the manor of Rycots given to Corpus Christi College, Cambridge, in 1571 (CAS i, 98). COVENTRY FM is *Lands of the City of Coventrey*, *Coventrey Land* 1667 CCC. It was given in 1625 by Thomas Wale to the corporation of the city of Coventry in trust for charitable uses (CAS i, 99). SIX MILE BOTTOM is (*the*) *Six Mile Bottom* 1801 *EnclA*, c. 1825 O.S. It is a hamlet in a hollow six miles from Newmarket and was possibly at one time named *Camdene*, *v. Camgate Way supra* 21.

---

[1] Cf. *croft' templar'* 1446 *Rental* and *supra* 138.

IX. FLENDISH HUNDRED

Flamingdice, Flammindic, Flammidinc, Flammiding 1086 DB, *Flam-mincdic, Flammigedic, Flammicgedic, Flammingedich, Flammedige-dig* 1086 InqEl, *Flamencdic* 1086 ICC
Flammedich 1155–7 P, *Flamedich(e)* 1175–9 ib., 1251 *ElyCouch*, 1277 *Ely*, 14th *Cai, Flaundishe* 1553 Pat
Flem(e)dich(e), -y- 1188 P *et freq* to 1523 *SR, Flemesdich* 1218 *SR*, 1284 FA, 1298 *Ass, Flemedic* 1218 *SR, Flemdik(e), -y-* 1268, 1285 *Ass, Flem(i)sdich* 1279 RH, *Flemdisch* 1372 *SR, Flem(e)dys(s)h* 1457 IpmR, 1523 *SR*
Flendiche 1428 FA, 1570 SR, *Flendishe, -y-* t. Hy 6 *Cole* xxxvii, 1560 *Depositions, Flendick* 1570 SR
Flyndiche 1553 Pat, *Flyndysshe* 1557 ib.

The hundred is named from Fleam Dyke *supra* 35, its northern boundary. Skeat's suggestion that the first element was OFr *Flamenc*, 'Fleming,' can scarcely be accepted in the light of the full 11th-century forms, nor is Anderson's explanation (EHN i, 100–1) altogether satisfactory. He takes it to be OE *flēmena-dīc*, 'fugitives' dyke' (OE *flēma, flīema*, 'fugitive'), possibly influenced first by OE *flēming*, 'fugitive,' and later by ME *flḗme* < OE *flēam*, 'flight,' a word found in Flamstead (PN Herts 32). More probably we have to start with OE *flēminga-dīc*, 'dyke of the fugitives[1].' For this type of name cf. Wrekendike (Du), a Roman road, which Ekwall (DEPN) explains as OE *wrǣccna dīc*, 'dyke of the fugitives.' The earth-work is certainly post-Roman and was probably constructed at a time of great danger by the East Anglians in the late pagan or early Christian period to protect their frontier against the Middle Anglians. It runs across the narrow belt of open country between forest and fen, the most easily defensible position on a vulnerable frontier, and was at one time, as excavation has proved, the scene of fierce fighting (*v.* Fox 125, 129–31, 292–4). Some such struggle, ending in the defeat and flight of the East Anglians, may have given rise to the name.

[1] Gray (CAPr xxxi, 86) suggested a derivation from OE *flȳming*, 'fugitive,' but with a different explanation, probably because "ditches were looked upon as refuges for the homeless after the raised banks had ceased to serve as practical lines of defence." The 18th century was also on the right track, cf. "Fleamdike, that is 'Flight-dike,' as it seems from some remarkable flight at this place" (1772 Camden i, 390).

References to the dyke itself by name are rare and late, but one (*Flemigdich'* 1279 RH) shows a trace of the medial *-ing-*. Most of our forms are for the hundred-name on which AN influence is likely to be strong. Further, three of our forms for the dyke itself refer to the holding there of an earl's tourn. The early disappearance of all trace of the medial *-ing-* is, therefore, probably to be compared with that found in such names as Hinckford Hundred in contrast to the fuller form preserved in the parish name of Hedingham, both deriving from the same first element (cf. PN Ess 405, 438–9 and IPN 97). *-dish* is much too late a development to be ascribed to AN influence. The hundred probably met at Mutlow Hill in Great Wilbraham (*supra* 138).

Anderson's suggestion (EHN i, 101) that we have a counterpart of this name in *le Flemdich* (AD v, in Little Waltham, Ess) cannot be upheld. The frequency of this type of name was noted in PN Ess 578 where a connexion with OE *flīema* was suggested. Further examples make this unlikely. A *fleame* was "the water-course or race of a mill-stream, the channel of water from the main stream to the mill, below which the streams unite. It also describes a large trench or main carriage in water, cut in meadows to drain them" (ER xlv, 135). Cf. the reference to the presentation of Peter Cleare at Rochford (Ess) in 1638 for encroaching upon the glebe "by landing up part of a Fleame or Brook Ditch" (ib.). See also PN Mx 3.

Cherry Hinton

CHERRY HINTON

> *Hintone* 1086 DB, *-a* 1086 ICC, *Hinton(e)*, *-y-* 1218 *SR*, 1237 Fees
> et freq, *-tune* 13th Misc, *Brok-*, *Brochintone* 1301–16 *CaiCh*
> *Hingtone* 13th *Jesus*, *Hynkton* 1420 Rad
> *Heyneton* 1269 Pat, *Hyneton* 1299 ib., 1437 FF
> *Henton* 1428 *MinAcct*
> *Cheryhynton* 1576 Saxton, *Cherry Hinton* 1658 PR i

No satisfactory suggestion can be made for the main part of this name. Ekwall (DEPN) doubtfully suggests the possibility of a derivation from *hīgna-tūn*, 'tūn of the monastic community' or *hind-tūn*, 'tūn where hinds (females of the hart) were found.' But the new forms *Hingtone* and *Hynkton* suggest that there has been a wearing down of the first element, and speculation as to its original form is useless.

Cherry "from the abundance of cherry trees formerly growing there" (1789 Camden ii, 141). Cf. Cherry Burton (PN ERY 191) and Cherry Willingham (L). *Broc-* from Cherry Hinton Brook (*supra* 4).

NOTE. COLDHAM'S LANE, *v.* Coldham's Common *supra* 40. DAWS LANE is *Daweslane* 1532 *Peterhouse.* MILLEND RD. Cf. *le Mylhende* 1511 *Rental.*

WORTH'S CAUSEWAY (6″) is *Worts's Causeway* 1812 *EnclA,* (*Worts*) c. 1825 O.S. and was so named from William *Worts* (d. 1709) who left £1500 to "be applied to the making of a calcey or causeway from Emmanuel College to Hogmagog alias Gogmagog Hills" (CAS xlvii, 6–7).

BROOKFIELDS (6″) and CHURCH END were probably the homes of Henry de *Brok'* (1275 RH) and Robert *atte Cherch* (1327 SR).

CHERRY HINTON HALL. Cf. *Hall close* 1549 Pat. MISSLETON HILL. Cf. *Meselles* 1511 *Rental.* NETHER HALL is *Netherherhall* (sic) 1372 Pat. UPHALL FM (6″) is *Uphall* 1382 *MinAcct.* WAR DITCH (6″), locally WAR DITCHES. No specific reference has been found to this circular single-ramparted fortress (cf. Fox 136, 177–8).

Fen Ditton

FEN DITTON

- (*æt*) *Dictunæ* c. 975 ASWills, (*æt*) *Dictune* c. 1000 (11th) ib., c. 1050 (12th) LibEl, *Dictun* 1022 Gale iii
- (*at*) *Dittone* c. 950 (14th) ASWills, *Dittune* c. 1050 (13th) KCD 907, (*non illam Silvestrem*) 1170 LibEl, *Dittona* 1086 ICC, *Ditton(e),* -*y*- 1200 Cur *et passim,* (*Fen*) 1281 Pat, (*Fenny-*) 1285 *Ass,* (*cum Horningeshey*) 1316 FA, *Duton* 1336 Cl

'tūn by the dīc,' i.e. Fleam Dyke (*supra* 35) which here joins the Cam, in contrast to Woodditton *supra* 127. It adjoins Horningsea *infra* 145.

NOTE. HIGH DITCH RD is *High Ditch Lane* c. 1825 O.S., *High Dyke Road* 1829 Wells. Cf. *Heydich* 13th *StJohn's.* The road runs along the course of Fleam Dyke *supra* 35 which must here have been called *High Ditch.*

BIGGIN ABBEY is *le Biginge* c. 1260 Bodl, *Biggin Hall* c. 1553 ECP, *v.* bigging, 'building, dwelling place.' There is no authority for the abbey.

WADLOES FOOTPATH (6″). Cf. *Woteleuuemedwe* 1251 *ElyCouch*, 1277 *Ely*, *Whatelowe* 1316 *MinAcct*, *Wallowe* 1549 *Ct*, *Watloe* 1807 *Map*. Probably 'wheat-hill,' *v*. hwǣte, hlāw. For the variation between forms from hlāw and hlǣw cf. *Watlowedole* 1290 Barnwell, *Watlewdole* 1449 *Pembroke* (Whittlesford), (*le*) *Watlew*(*e*) 1329–1425 *Queens'* (Haslingfield).

DITTON HALL is *Fenditton Hall* 1593 ChancP, *Fenditton al. Dytton Hall* 1634 *Cole* xxxvii. LITTLE DITTON (6″) and GREEN END are so named c. 1825 (O.S.). GREENHOUSE FM is so named in 1829 (Wells). WHITE HILL FM (6″) is *White Hall* c. 1825 O.S.

Fulbourn

FULBOURN

> *Fuulburne* c. 1050 (13th) KCD 907, c. 1050, 1170 (12th) LibEl, 1086 InqEl, *Fuleburna* 1086 ICC, -*burne* 1086 InqEl *et freq* to 1308 Pat, *Fuleberne* 1086 DB, 1202 FF, *Fulburne* c. 1060 (14th) *ElyM*, 1086 InqEl (p), -*burn*(*e*) 1196–8 P *et freq* to 1517 AD ii, (*Omnium Sanctorum, Sancti Vigoris*) 13th *Ely*, *Fulbourn*(*e*) 1291 Ch *et freq* to 1442 AD ii, -*born*(*e*) 1339 Pat *et freq* to 1441 FF, (*Wigors*) 1550 Pat
>
> *Fuelburne* 1086 InqEl (p), *Fugelburn*(*e*) 1170 LibEl, 1190–1 P (p), 1198, 1209 FF, 1214 Cur, *Fulgelburn'* 1190 P (p), 1199 FF, *Fulghburn'* 1220 Cur
>
> *Foleborne*, -*a* 1157 France, t. Ric 1 (1332) Ch, -*burn*(*e*) c. 1190 *AddCh*, 1260 Pat, 1286 FF, *Folbourne* 1328 Ipm, 1439 Pat, -*burne* 1310 Pat, -*berne* 1246 Cl, *Folleburn* 1260 FF
>
> *Full*(*e*)*burn*(*e*) 1219 Cur, c. 1259 SR, 1275 RH, 1291 Tax, -*borne* 1422 FF, *Fulbrun* 1475 ECP
>
> *Foul*(*e*)*bourn*(*e*) 1298 *Ass*, 1323, 1462 Pat, -*borne* 1325 FF, *Foulbourg* 1361 Cl

'Stream frequented by birds,' *v*. fugol, burna. Fulbourn now consists of the united parishes of *All Saints* and *St Vigors*.

NOTE. COLE'S LANE is *Colles Lane* 1435 *MinAcct*, *v*. Cole's Green *infra* 144. DOGGETT'S LANE. Cf. Henry, son of Robert *Doget* (1279 RH), *terra quondam Dokettes* t. Hy 7 *Rental*, *Doggettes* 1503 Peterhouse. IMPETT'S LANE is perhaps to be associated with *Ympey* 1435 *MinAcct*, *Ympies* 1806 *EnclA*. Cf. Empty Common *supra* 40. MILL LANE. Cf. *le Melnewey* 1360 *Queens'*, *Mellewey* 1397 ib., *Millestrete* 1454 ib. TEVERSHAM DROVE WAY is *Theuereshamwaie* 1293 *Queens'*. WRIGHT'S LANE. *v*. Wright's Grove *infra* 144.

BISHOP'S CHARITY FM is *Bysshopes* 1435 *MinAcct*, *Rev. Jeffery Bishop's Charity* 1806 *EnclA*. Geoffrey *Bishop*, Vicar of All Saints, Fulbourn (1458–76), gave for the use of the poor a messuage called *Guild-Hall*, a croft and 63 acres of arable (*Cole* xix, f. 14).

CROSSFIELD (*TA*) is *Chors* c. 1225 *AD*, 14th *AD* iv, (*campo de*) *Cors* 1294, 1324, 1325 *Queens'*, t. Ed 4 *Rental*, *Corys* 1315 *Peterhouse*, *Cors(se)f(f)eld(e)* 1293 *Peterhouse et freq* to 1509 *Ct*, *Corisfeld* 1308 *Peterhouse*, *Crosfeld* 1540 *MinAcct*. The first element here is a British word related to Welsh, Cornish *cors*, 'reeds, bog,' Breton *kors*, 'reeds.' *v.* RN 95 and Gauze Brook, Corston and Corsley (PN W 7, 50, 152). There is much marsh in the parish.

THURLOW HILL (lost) is *Thirllouhil* 1332 *ElyC*, *Thrillowe* 1360 *Queens'*, *Thurlow(e)hill* 1465 *CaiCh*, *Thirlowhill in le Combes* 1494 *Rental*. The first element may be OE *þyrel*, 'pierced,' and the second hlāw, 'hill' or 'barrow.' Cf. Thurland's Drove *infra* 290 and Durlett (PN W 247), or the name may be identical with Thurlow (Sf), *Tritlawa*, *Tridlauua* 1086 DB, *Thrillauue* c. 1095 BuryDocs, which Ekwall (DEPN) derives either from OE *þrȳþ-hlāw*, 'famous tumulus,' or from an OE *þride-hlāw*, 'deliberation-hill.' In view of the complete absence of early forms for Mutlow Hill (*supra* 138) it may be that here we have an earlier or an alternative name for the hundred meeting-place which is only just outside Fulbourn.

FULBOURN FEN and MILL HILL were the homes of John *del Fen de Fuleburne* (1298 *Ass*), Matilda de *Molendino* (1279 RH), William *atte Miln* (1341 NI) and Thomas *ate Melne* (t. Ed 2 *Rental*). The latter is *Mellehelle* 1496 ib., *v.* myln.

BUTCHER'S FM, COLE'S GREEN (both 6″), NEW SHARDELOWES FM, OLD SHARDELOWES and WRIGHT'S GROVE (both 6″) are *Bochercroft* 1388 *AOMB*, *terram Johannis Cole* 1318 *Queens'*, *Schardelowys* 1392 (1455) Pat, *Old Shardelowe* c. 1825 O.S., *Wrights Heath* t. Eliz *Cole* xxxvii, and are probably to be associated with the families of Joseph *Butcher* (1806 *Map*), Robert *Cole* (1279 RH), John de *Schardelowe* (1327 SR) and John *le Writhe* (ib.), Ralph *le Wryte* (1370 *AOMB*) and Robert *Wright* (1433 Pat).

BROAD GREEN is *Brodgren'* 1505 *Ct*, *Bradgreene* t. Eliz *Cole* xxxvii. *Broad*, as opposed to *Lytelgrene* 1435 *MinAcct*. CAUDLE DITCH is so named in 1806 (*Map*). Cf. *Caldewell* 1279 RH[1] and Cawdle Fen

---

[1] In the bounds of Teversham, i.e. Caudle Ditch.

infra 222. CHURCH HO (all 6″). Cf. *Kyrke acre* 1362 *Queens', le Chirche glebe* 1461 Pat. FULBOURN VALLEY FM is *Valley Fm* 1832 G. HAGGIS GAP (6″) is *Haggis's Gap* 1806 *EnclA*. HALL ORCHARD is so named ib. Cf. *Halcot* 1501 *Ct*. HEATH FM is *the Hethe* 1403 Cl. HIGHFIELD (6″). Cf. *Highfeild meadow* t. Eliz *Cole* xxxvii. HIND LODERS. Cf. *Looderes* 1494 *Rental*. OLD MILL HO is *Mill Ho* c. 1825 O.S. PETERHOUSE FM (all 6″) is self-explanatory. QUAKER'S CHARITY is so named in 1806 (*Map*). QUEENS' COLLEGE FM (6″) is *the queenes Collegge londe* 1573 *Queens'*. THE TEMPLE is *le Temple* 1509 *Ct*. WHITEHILL PLANTATION (both 6″). Cf. *le Witehil* 1360 *Queens', qwythel* 1379 ib. For *qwythel*, *v.* Introd. xxxvi.

Horningsea

HORNINGSEA [*olim* hɔ·nsi]

   (*æt*) *Horninges ige* c. 975 ASCh, *Horningesei(e)*, -(*a*) 870, 975, 1071, 1170 (12th) LibEl, 1086 ICC, InqEl, *Hornincgeseie* 1086 InqEl, *Horningesie* 1086 DB, *Horninggeseie* c. 1050 (13th) KCD 907, *Horning(e)sey(e)*, -*yng*- c. 1060 (14th) *ElyM et freq* to 1505 Pat, *Ornyngseye* 1432 FF
   Horniggeseie 870, 946, 975 (12th) LibEl, *Hornigeseiæ* 1086 InqEl, *Hornigesheye* 1279 RH
   Hornungesheia c. 1150 Rad, *Horningesheye*, -*yng*- 1251 *ElyCouch et freq* to 1348 FF
   Horingeseye 1272 *Ass*, *Horinggesheye* 1279 RH
   Hornsey 1719 Bott, 1808 L

'Island or marshy land of *Horning*,' a personal name probably derived from OE *hornung*, 'bastard.' *v.* ēg.

CLAYHITHE

   Cleie 975 (12th) LibEl, *Gleyham* 1228 Pat, *Clehe* 1279 RH, *Claye* t. Eliz ChancP
   Clayheth 1268 *Ass*, *Claethe* 1298 ib., *Claihythe* 1313 *St John's*, *Clayhith(e)* 1333 ib., 1607 Imb, *Clayeth* 1372 Horns, *Claye Hyve* 1580 Ely, *Clay hive* 1618 BedL
   Cleyheth(e) 1279 RH, 1284 FA, 1363 *Ct*, 1381 Ass, -*hothe* 1279 RH, *Cleythe* 1302 *St John's*, *Cleyhygh* 1323 ib., -*hith(e)*, -*y*- 1429, 1450 FF, 1502 Ipm, *Cley Hyve* 1581 Ely

Originally simply 'clay,' later 'landing-place on the clay,' *v.* clæg, hȳð. *Gleyham* is probably from a Latinisation to *Cleiam*, with AN *g* for *c* (cf. IPN 114). For loss of -*th*, cf. Odsey *supra* 62, and for *hive*, *v.* Introd. xxxvi.

EYE HALL FM

> *Eie* 870, 975 (12th) LibEl, *Eye* 1260 FF *et passim*
> *Ey(e)halle* 1356 FF, 1364, 1373 Pat, 1412 FA, (*al. Highall*) 1634 Cole xxxvii, -*hale* 1412 FA
> *Hyehall* 1378 St John's, *Hihall* 1518 Horns, *Highall* 1555 Pat

'Island' or 'well-watered land,' *v.* ēg.

NORTH HILLS is *Northale(feld)* 13th, 1313, 1333 St John's, *Noryhale* 13th ib., *v.* healh. This is in a corner of the parish bounded by Bottisham Lode and the boundary. It is low, but the farm is on a slight rise and this may have given rise to the later corruption.

KING'S FM (6″) is probably to be associated with the family of Rogerus *le Kyng* (1251 *ElyCouch*).

HONEY HILL. Cf. Honey Hill *infra* 166. LOW FEN DROVEWAY (6″). Cf. *Low-Fen* 1649 Badeslade. SNOUTS CORNER. Cf. snote *infra* 344.

Teversham

TEVERSHAM

> *Teuuresham* c. 1050 (12th) LibEl, *Teuresham* c. 1050 (13th) KCD 907, 1086 DB, 1198 Fees, 1205 Cur, 1310 FF
> *Teueresham* c. 1060 (14th) *ElyM et freq* to 1392 Cl, -*is*- 1317 FF, *Teuueresham* 1086 InqEl
> *Teuersham* 1086 DB, ICC *et freq* to 1553 Pat, *Teuersam* 1086 InqEl, 1285 *Ass*, *Tebersham* t. Hy 8 *Rental*
> *Theueresham* 1086 InqEl *et freq* to 1357 Pat, *Theversham* 1249 Ch *et freq* to 1340 FF, *Theuresham* 1277 Ely, *Theuersam* 1285 *Ass*
> *Taversham* 1130 P (p) *et freq* to 1588 Ely, *Taueresham* 1167 P (p)
> *Evresham* 1204 Cur
> *Treusham* 1570 SR

This is a difficult name. Smith (PN NRY 34–5, *s.n.* Terrington), citing the parallels of this name, Tyersall (WRY) and Teversall (PN Nt 135–6), notes that all these places are in Anglian territory, and suggests that they contain an OE *Tĕofer, an *r*-derivative of the name-theme *Tēof* which is found in the Anglian personal name *Tĕoful*, recorded in Bede. Ekwall (DEPN) suggests the possibility that the first element may be an OE *tīefrere* (*tēfrere*), 'painter,' perhaps in the sense of 'one who marks sheep.' The second element is hām.

TEVERSHAM FEN and MANOR FM were the homes of John *Atefen* and Henry de *Manerio* (c. 1260 Bodl).

ALLEN'S FM (6″) is *Allens* (1553 Pat) and is to be associated with the family of John *Aleyn* (1386 ib.).

WILLOWS FM (6″) is *Willowes's lands* 1799, *Willowes's Fm* 1810 (Gross). The estate was devised to Gonville and Caius College in 1503 by Thomas *Willowes* (Gross 86).

X. CHESTERTON HUNDRED

Cestretune, Cestretona 1086 InqEl, *Cestretone* 1086 DB, -*ton*(*e*) 1130 P *et freq* to 1304 Pat, *Cestertun* 1218 *SR*, -*ton*(*e*) 1236, 1296 Barnwell, 1268 *Ass*, 1275 Misc, 1284 FA
Chesterton(*e*) 1346, 1428 FA, 1478 Pat, *Chestirtone* 1401 FA
Cheserton' 14th *Cai*

v. Chesterton *infra.*

Chesterton

CHESTERTON

Cestretone 1086 DB, -*ton*(*a*), -(*e*) 1086 InqEl *et freq* to 1394 Cl, -*tun* 1157 P, 1227 FF, *Cesterton*(*a*), -(*e*) 1172 P *et freq* to 1456 Pat, -*tune* 1199 FF, *Cestreston* 1195 P
Chesterton(*e*) 1206 FF *et freq* to 1552 Pat, (*juxta Cantebregiam*) 1316 Cole xix, *Chestreton* 1272 *Ass et freq* to 1405 Pat, *Chesturton* 1480 CTerr, *Chisterton* 1640 PR i
Castreton 1242 P, 1272 Pat, *Casterton* 1324 FF
Chastreton 1277 Cl, 1323 Pat, 1376 Rad, *Chasterton* 1304–54 FF, 1313 *Ass*, Pat, 1345 CWool, 1357 Crowland, *Chastirton* 1327 ElyC

'Farm by the fortified place,' i.e. the Roman station north of the Cam at Cambridge. *v.* ceaster, tūn, and *Grantacæstir* as the earlier name for Cambridge (*supra* 36).

NOTE. GREEN END RD and WATER ST are probably to be associated with Nicholas *Attegrene* and Alexander *Attewater* (1279 RH). Cf. *Grenend close* 1555 Pat and *Water Lane* c. 1840 *TA*.

ARBURY CAMP is *Herdburw* 13th *CCC*, *Herburg* 13th *St John's*, *Herdburg'* 1282 *Bodl*, *Ertburg'* 1293 ib., *Erthburg'* 1302–38 ib., *Erburgh* 1445 *Queens'*, *Arbrow(medow)* 1475 *St John's*, *Narborough* 1499 *Min-Acct*, *Arborough* 1572 *Terr*, *Arbury* (*Hedges*) a. 1760 EA xiii, *Arbury or Arborough* 1772 Camden, *Harboro Close* c. 1840 *TA*. OE *eorþburh*, 'earthwork,' here probably prehistoric, *v.* Fox 137, 141, 157 and cf. Arbury (PN Nth 13, PN La 98, PN Wa 79–80) and Harborough (PN Wa 289). For *Narborough* from *at then Erburgh*, cf. Nelmes (PN Ess 114).

KING'S HEDGES is *Alborough al. Kinges Headge* 1588 *Terr*, *Kinges Hedges*, *Allbrow* 1656 ib., and is probably to be identified with *terr' Thome Albourgh* 1328 *Bodl*. There is an earthwork here of doubtful age (*v.* Fox 178, AnctC 14–15) near Akeman Street *supra* 18, which is perhaps to be identified with *Thistilburg* 1277 *Bodl*, *Systelburth* (sic) 13th Merton, *Yistilburg* 1310 *Bodl*, *Thistilborw* 1329 ib., *Thistelborgh* 1334 ib. 'burh overgrown with thistles.'

CLOSE FM adjoins The Close in Howe Ho *infra* 178. TRINITY HALL FM (both 6″) is *Trinitie Hall* 1615 *Cole* xli.

Childerley

CHILDERLEY

Cildrelai, *Cilderlai* 1086 DB, *Cilderlaio*, *Cildrelaia* 1086 InqEl, *Childerle(e)*, -*y*-, -*leg(h)*, -*ley* 1208 FF *et freq* to 1448 Pat, (*maior*) c. 1250 *ElyA*, (*Minor*) 1254 Val, (*magna, parva*) c. 1278 ElyA, (*le greindur*) 1394 Cl, (*Litel*-) 1396 FF, (*the More, the Less*) c. 1480 ECP, *Childrele* 1269 Cl, *Childirle(e)*, -*yl*-, -*yr*- 1346, 1428 FA, 1393 Cl, 1432 AD ii, *Childurleye* 1381 Pat
Chirderl' 1267 Cl, *Chyderlee* 1279 RH, -*leie* 1298 *Ass*
Chyldrerley 1272 *Ass*, *Childerley* 1425 FF, *Childersley* 1576 Saxton, 1610 Speed
Chelderle 1439 Cl

'Wood or clearing of the young men,' *v.* **cild**. The exact sense of OE *cild* cannot be determined in such a context. Cf. Chilford *supra* 99 and Hanley Child (PN Wo 50–1).

BLACK PARK and GREAT PARK are so named c. 1840 (*TA*). WEATHER-
FIELD PLANTATION (all 6″). Cf. *Wether Field* ib.

Cottenham

COTTENHAM
> Cotenham 948 (c. 1366) Crowland, p. 981, c. 1050, c. 1071 (12th)
>   LibEl, c. 1050 (13th) KCD 907, c. 1060 (14th) *ElyM*, 1086
>   InqEl *et passim* to 1500 Pat, (*cum Westwyke*) 1316 FA
>
> Cothenham c. 1020 (12th) LibEl, c. 1250 *ElyCouch, Cotheham* 1218
>   SR
>
> Coteham 1086 DB, InqEl *et freq* to 1315 Crowland, *Koteham* 1252
>   FF
>
> Cotham 1086 InqEl (p), *Cottham* 13th Barnwell
>
> Cottenham 1246, 1458 FF, 1549 Pat, *-yn-* t. Hy 8 *Rental*
>
> Cotingham, -y- 1272 *Ass*, 1312 Seld 33 (p), 1349 Pat, 1461 FF,
>   *Cottingham(e)* t. Hy 8 *Rental*, 1562 *Christ's*
>
> Cot(t)nam 1511 CAPr xxxiv, 1668 *FF*

'*Cotta*'s hām.' Cf. Old West River *supra* 11.

NOTE. BROAD LANE is *le Brodelane* t. Ed 3 *Christ's*. HAY LANE was
probably near the home of Alexander de *la Haye* (1252 FF). *v.* (ge)hæg.
TWENTY PENCE RD. Cf. *a place called twenty penn*[c] 1596 ib.

ALBORO CLOSE DROVE (6″). Cf. *Aldebur* 1202 FF, *Audeburg'* 1228 *FF*,
Aldeburgh(feld) 1323 Crowland, *-borowefeld* t. Ed 3 *Christ's, -burghaye*
c. 1350 *Cole* xliv, (*le*) *Alburgh* 1492, 1527 *Christ's, Alborough* 1596 ib.,
Awbrose (*Fen*) 1604 *Atkyns, Alboro Close* c. 1840 *TA*. 'The old fort,'
v. eald, burh. Roman and other remains have been found in the
neighbourhood. Not far away, on Bullocks Haste Common, earthworks are marked on the O.S. map. These Fox (223) describes as an
elaborate system of shallow ditches, probably irrigation works of
Roman date. Either these were mistaken for earthworks, one of which
is referred to in *le Arburgh* 1483 *Christ's* (cf. Arbury *supra* 148), or
there was once a fort here of which all visible trace has been lost.

CHEAR FEN is *Char(e)fen(n)* 1343 *Cole* xlix, 1596 *Christ's,* (*of Cottenham,
Common Fen*) 1604 *Atkyns*, 1772 Imb, *Chaireffen* (*Hill*) 1605 *Depositions*[1], *Charfenn hills* 1706 Moore[1], *Chaff Fen* c. 1825 O.S. The first
part of this name is found in (*ad, de la*) *Char'* 1279 RH, which is given

---

[1] From Stretham documents.

as one of the points on the bounds of *mariscum de Coteham*, which include *pontem de Halderheth* (High Bridge on the Old West River) and *Tyllinge* (Car Dyke *supra* 33). CHEAR LODE (6″) is *Char(e)lo(a)de* t. Ed 3, 1596 *Christ's*. It is a continuation of Beach Ditch which here forms the boundary between Cottenham and Waterbeach. Near it must have lived Robert *atte Char* in 1329 and Richard *at the Chayre* of Waterbeach in 1347 (*Cole* xxxvi). There can be little doubt that the word *chare* is to be identified with an OE **cear*, an unmutated form of OE *cierr*, 'turn,' as suggested for the first element of the name of the Cherwell (RN 75) and found in certain street-names, notably in Newcastle, in the sense 'winding lane, passage.' The *cear* in Chear Fen probably has reference to one of the sharp bends in the Old West River. It may be that we have reference to the same bend in Chear Lode, but no certainty is possible. From denoting a bend in a stream it would seem to have come to be used at times of the stream itself (cf. *s.nn.* Chair Drove, Chain Fm, Chainbridge and Old Chair Drain *infra* 192, 226, 254, 289).

LOCKSPIT HALL DROVE (6″). Cf. *Lockspit Hall* 1883 AnctC. This, with Lock Spit Fm and Hall and Long Lockspits (*infra* 228, 235, 176), is named from the *lockspits or small trenches* dividing fen lands (1637 BedL ii, 270). *v.* NED *s.v.* lockspit, from *lock* sb.[2] or v.[1] and *spit*, 'a turf.' First recorded in 1649–50, cf. *Sutton Lockspittes* 1654 BLAcct, *Lockspits in the Old Hawes* (in Chatteris) 1678 *FenS*.

THE LOTS is *The Lotts* 1604 Atkyns, *Cottenham Lottes* 1636 BedL. This consisted of "about 200 acres wherein every house hath an acre" (*Atkyns*). Cf. *les Fenlotes* (Whittlesey) 1402 Ct, *les lotez* 1423 ib., *lez lotes* (in Elm) 1446 Ct, *Lotts in Gallfenn* (in Haddenham) t. Jas 1 *Cole* xxxvii, *the lot or dole of John Belwood* (Witcham) 1637 BedL, *the Lott Landes of the said Edward Love* (Sutton) 1678 *FenS*. The name derives from the drawing of *lots* for land in the fens. Cf. The Lots and Hobb's Lots *infra* 202, 297.

SETCHEL FEN is *Seghchawfen* 1343 *Cole* xliv, *Sechall*, *Sedghall* 1596 *Christ's*, *Sechell* 1604 Atkyns, *Seechhill* 1636 BedL, *Sech Hill Fens* 1637 ib., *Sech Hills* 1829 Wells. This is apparently OE *secg* and haga, i.e. 'sedge-enclosure,' with later confusion of *hall* and *hill* in the unstressed position. For *haw* > *hall* cf. PN Nth 173–4.

SMITHEY FEN is *Smithyfen* 1343 *Cole* xliv, *Smythyfen* 1464 *Christ's*, *Smytheffen* 1483 ib., *Smetheffen* 1493 ib., *Smethy Fen* 1604 Atkyns.

This is probably 'marsh in smooth low-lying land,' v. smēðe, ēg, fenn.

Top Moor is *Tappingmore, -y-* 1303 Abbr, 1343 *Cole* xliv, *Tappigmor* 1325–6 *MinAcct, Tappyn' moore* 1546 ib., *Tapymore* 1596 *Christ's, Topham More* 1604 *Atkyns.* '*Tæppa*'s marsh,' v. mōr, with connective ing. For the personal name cf. *s.n.* Taplow (PN Bk 231). It is possible that we may have a significant word *tæpping* associated with OE *tæppa, -e,* 'band, ribbon, tape,' in the sense 'strip of land.'

The Undertakers. This is part of the land granted to those who undertook 'effectively to drain and dry the whole level and latitude of the Fens.' *Undertakers* were distinct from *adventurers* who 'adventured' their capital. Cf. Adventurers' Land *infra* 292.

The Green and Willow Fm (both 6″) were the homes of Henry *Attegrene* (1279 RH) and John *in le Wilugwes* (1315 *Cole* xliv). They are *the Grene* 1409 Crowland, *Wylowe* 1604 *Atkyns.*

Ablett's Row (6″), Lamb's Cross[1], Mason's Pastures, Smith's Path and Taylor's Lodge (both 6″) are probably to be associated with the families of Jabez *Ablett* (c. 1840 *TA*), Henry *Lamb* (1279 RH) and Robert *Lomb* (1327 SR), Edward *Mason* (c. 1840 *TA*), Richard *le Smyth* (1341 NI) and William *Taylor* (1780 Poll).

Bullocks Haste Common is *Bullocks Harst* 1596 *Christ's, (Hast)* 1636 BedL. *haste, harst* are dialectal forms of *haslet,* a common dialect term for the lights of an animal, especially a pig. The Causeway is *Calcetu' de Cotenham* 1272 FF, *calcetum* being the Latin term for a causeway. Church End and Hill (all 6″) are so named c. 1840 (*TA*). Church Field is *Churchfeild* 1596 *Christ's.* Cottenham Lode is *Cotenhamlode* 1291 *ElyF,* v. (ge)lād. Cow Pastures (6″) is *ye Cow pasture* 1596 *Christ's.* Dunstal Field (6″) is *Tunstallefeld* 1316 CCC, *Dunstalfelde* 1424 ib., *Donstalle ffylde* 16th *Christ's, Dunstan Field* c. 1825 O.S. 'Farm-steading,' v. tūnsteall. Further or Farm Field (6″). Cf. *fearne feild* 1596 *Christ's, Farm Field* c. 1840 *TA.* Green End is so named ib. The Holme is *Holm* 1483 CRent, v. holmr. Mitchell Hill Common. Cf. *Michell Ley* 1596 *Christ's, Cottenham Fennes voc. Michlaye* 1604 (1727) Hayward, *Michelle(e)* 1604 *Atkyns, fenn voc. Mukle* 1660 Dugd, *Mitchell Hill* c. 1840 *TA.* This was apparently at

---

[1] *Lambes Crosse* 1596 *Christ's.*

first micel-lēah, 'large clearing.' GREAT and LITTLE NORTH FEN are *Northfen* 1343 *Cole* xliv, *Little North fenn* 1596 *Christ's*. OXHOLME (6″) is so named in 1549 (*Ct*). THE PUNT (6″) is *le punt* t. Ed 3 *Christ's*, *le poynte* 1562 ib., *The Punt* c. 1840 *TA*, *Punts* 1870 *Witcham*. Cf. *Puntelode* 1393 *Ct* (in Soham), *Punt mede* 1493 *Rental* (in Oakington). TWO MILL FIELD (6″) is *Two-mill Field* c. 1825 O.S.

Dry Drayton

DRY DRAYTON

> *Draitona* a. 1086 (c. 1280) YCh, 1086 InqEl, *Draitone* 1086 DB *et freq* to 1362 Crowland, -*tun* 1218 *SR*
>
> *Dratona* 1086 InqEl, 1130 P, *Drydraton* 1540 *MinAcct*, c. 1570 ChancP
>
> *Dreituna* t. Stephen (1307) Ch, -*ton(e)* 1199 Cur, 1223 FF, (*Drie*) 1286 Pat, (*Dry*) 1478 Pat
>
> *Waldretton'* 1176 P, *Dratton* 1227 FF, *Drettone* 1346 FA
>
> *Waldraittona* 1176 CR, *Woldrayton* 1324 *MinAcct*
>
> *Driedraiton* 1218 *SR*, 1281 Ipm, *Dreie*- 1227 FF, *Drere*- 1300 Misc, *Dridrayton* 1254 Val, *Dry(e)*- 1272, 1334 *Ass*, *Drigh*-, *Dregh*- 1312 FF, *Drydraytone cum Childerley* 1316 FA, *Dreydrayton* 1405 PCC
>
> *Drayton(a)*, -(*e*) 1231 FF *et freq*, -*tun* 1235 FF

'Farm by the hill,' *v.* dræg, tūn. The road leaving the church on the left rises steeply and *dræg* here probably has the sense 'a stiff hill, a steep slope or ascent where more than ordinary effort is required.' Cf. Fen Drayton *infra* 166 and *v.* DEPN. Dry Drayton is on the western clay area which was once well-wooded and was formerly called *Wald*, cf. Croydon and Hatley Wilds *supra* 54, 56. The reason for the epithet *dry* is not obvious as the parish is well-watered. Cole says "Drye-Drayton, so called not from the *Drynesse* of the *Soile*, but for that it *standeth* in the *Upland* and Champion Countrie, thereby to *distinguish* it from the other *Drayton*, which taketh Appellation from the *Fenne*" (xlviii, f. 156).

EDINBURGH FM is north of Scotland Fm. THE FOLLY (6″) is a small wood, *v. infra* 353. SCOTLAND FM (6″) is so named c. 1825 (O.S.). It lies well away from the village, *v. infra* 357.

Histon

HISTON [*olim* hisən]

Histonona (sic) 1086 InqEl

Histuna, -e 1086 InqEl, -tone 1086 DB, InqEl, -ton(e) 1157–63
  RegAntiquiss *et passim*, Hystun' 1248 Cl, -ton(e) 13th Barnwell
  et freq to 1434 Pat, (*Abbatis, Sancti Andree*) 1291 Tax, (*Sancte
  Ætheldrede*) 13th *Ely*, (*E(y)nsham*) 1539 Eyns, (*Dennye al. Bowyer*)
  c. 1570 ChancP, (*Awdry al. Evensham*) t. Jas 1 *Cole* xxxvii, *Hissen*
  1592 PCC

Heston' 1165 P (p), a. 1169 *ElyM*, 1203 Ass, 1363 Pat

Huston(a) 1188–99 P, 1199 CurR, 1206 Cur, 1224 FF, 1225 *SR*,
  1251 Eyns

The first element in this name is difficult. Ekwall (DEPN), relying
on a form *Hestitona* (1086 ICC), which really refers to Hinxton *supra*
94), interprets the name as *Hȳþsǣta-tūn*, 'the tūn of the dwellers at
the hȳþ or landing-place.' But, with the correct identification of
Hestitona, there is no evidence for the medial -*sǣta*-, and a landing-
place here is doubtful or impossible, for Beach Dyke does not reach
Histon. We may perhaps compare Husborne Crawley (PN BedsHu
118–19) and Hurstbourne (Ha), both of which occur in charters as
Hysseburnan. The first element there may be OE *hysse*, 'a tendril or
vine-shoot,' used of some plant, or, perhaps OE *hyssa*, gen. plural
of *hyse*, 'young man, warrior.' *Hysse-tun*, or *hyssa-tun* would account
for the variation between *i, e* and *u*. The entire absence of any sign of
the *ss*, or of the intermediate vowel is somewhat disturbing, but
as none of the forms is really early, this is not an insuperable difficulty.
There were two parishes with churches dedicated to *St Andrew* and
St Etheldreda. The manor of Histon St Andrew came, about 1391, to
Denny Abbey and on the dissolution was granted to Sir William
Bowyer (c. 1570 ChancP); that of Histon St Etheldreda (or *Audrey*)
belonged to the Abbot of Eynsham.

NOTE. GUN'S LANE. Cf. *Guns Headland* 1746 *Terr*. PARK LANE is *yᵉ Park
Lane* ib. PIG'S LANE. Cf. *Pigs Lanesend* 1749 ib. WATER LANE. Cf. El'
Atewater 1279 RH.

THE CAMPING CLOSE (6″). Cf. *le Campinge close* 1600 *Depositions* (in
Orwell). As a field-name this also occurs in the TA's for Chesterton,
Girton, Soham, Little Thetford, Thriplow and Wentworth. It is from
ME *camping*, 'contending in a camp-ball or camping-ball match,' cf.

NED *s.v. camping* sb. The camping close was clearly the village football ground where was played a game with indefinite numbers on each side, somewhat similar to that which survives in the well-known Shrove Tuesday football match at Ashbourne in Derbyshire. Cf. also *le Campingplace* 1540 *MinAcct* (in Fulbourn).

BOWER'S FM (6″) is to be associated with the family of John *Bowyer* (c. 1640 *Layer*).

ABBEY FM, from the Abbey of Eynsham, cf. *supra* 153. MILL LANE FM. Cf. *Mill Lane* 1746 *Terr*. MOOR DROVE (6″). Cf. *Hystonemore* 1253 *FF*. SWAN POND (6″). Cf. *Swanspond pits* 1746 *Terr*.

Westwick

WESTWICK

> *Westuuiche* 1086 DB, InqEl, *-wich'* 1196 P, 1199 CurR, 1201 P, *-wyche* 1279 RH
>
> *Westuuica, uuestuuic* 1086 InqEl, *Westwic(a)* 1130, 1197 P, 1199–1201 Cur, 1227 FF, *-wik(e)*, *-y-* 1218 *SR et freq* to 1428 FA, *(juxta Hokyngton)* 1493 EA x, *-wyck* 1272 *Ass*
>
> *Westewyke* 1393 Cl, *Wessewyk* 1472 *Pembroke*

'West dairy-farm,' *v.* wīc.

WESTWICK FIELD was the home of Matilda *atte Feld* (1334 *Ct*), *v.* feld.

XI. LONGSTOW HUNDRED

Stouue 1086 ICC, *Stou* 1086 DB, *Stouu(e)* 1086 InqEl, *Stou(e)* 1200 P, 1279 RH
Sto 1161 P, *Stowa* 1185 ib., *Stow(e)* 1199 ib. *et freq* to 1482 Pat *Longstow* 1653 *Rental*

v. stōw, here probably used in the sense of 'meeting-place,' cf. Northstow Hundred *infra* 176. One would suppose that the hundred was named from Long Stowe *infra* 163. At the opposite end of the hundred, however, and apparently just over the border, in the field of Harlton called *Northfeld*, was another *Long(e)stowe* 1349 *Queens'*, 1393 *Trinity*. This was near Bourn Brook. In Harlton too, and near Eversden, was *Stowefurlonge* 1332 *Queens'*. Near by was *S(c)hortestowe* 1349 ib., 1373 *Trinity*, 1506–10 *StCatharine's*.

Bourn

BOURN

Bronna 1086 ICC, 1176 BM, *Bronne* 1236 Barnwell *et freq* to 1445
  Elien

Brona 1086 ICC (p), *Brone* 1086 DB

Brunna 1086 ICC, *Brunna, -e* 1185 P *et freq* to 1445 FF, (*juxta*
  Caxtone) 1283 ib.

Brunam 1086 DB, *Brune* ib. *et freq* to 1361 Ipm, *Bruin(n)e* 1227 FF,
  1408 Pat

Broun(n)e 1285 *Ass et freq* to 1476 AD v

Burn(e) 1441 Pat *et freq* to 1506 EA vii

Boorn 1512 EA vii, *Borne* t. Hy 8 *Rental*, 1536 EA xiii, 1549 Pat,
  1582 EA x

Bourne 1540 *MinAcct*, 1552–3 Pat, 1553 EA viii

Buene 1576 Saxton, 1610 Speed

With this name must be taken Bourne Eau (L), *Brunne* 1327 Ch,
(*le*) *Brunne Hee, Brunhee* 1354, 1383 Works, and Bourne (L), *Brunne*
c. 960 (18th) BCS 1060, *Brune* 1086 DB, which are distinct from other
bourne-names in having invariably early forms in *Brun(n)e, Bronne*
instead of *Burne, Bo(u)rne*. Ekwall (RN 41–4, DEPN) derives all from
OE burna, a metathesised form of an original *brunna*. "There is no
reason to look upon these [forms in *brunne*] as due to Scandinavian
influence." It is to be noted, however, that Bourn is near the Huntingdonshire border, adjoining Caxton and not far from Croxton, each of
which contains a Scand personal name. Lincolnshire is, perhaps, the
most Scandinavianised county in England. Of the very large number
of forms noted for Bassingbourn, Fulbourn and Melbourn, only one,
and that very late (*Fulbrun* 1475 ECP), does not end in -*b(o)urne*. In
the neighbouring counties which have already been treated in full,
Beds, Hu, Nth, Herts, Ess, no forms in *brun(n)e* are found. It is only
in the North and East Ridings of Yorkshire, where Scandinavian
influence is strong, that we have names with only *brunn*, others with
only *burn*, and still others with a mixture of the two. For Bourn Brook
and Bourn Way (*supra* 2, 20) we have no form in *Burn-* before the
middle of the 15th century. It seems clear, therefore, that Bourn (C)
and Bourne (L) both derive from ON brunnr, 'spring, stream,' here
the Bourn Brook.

NOTE. CHURCH ST. Cf. *le Chyrcheweye* 1343 *St John's*.

BOURN WOOD, BROOK FM[1], GREAT BRIDGE and TOWN'S END FM (all 6″) were probably the homes of Robert *atte Wode of Brunne* (1319 Pat), Henry de *Broc* (1279 RH) and Robert *atte Brok* (1319 Pat), John *atte Brygge* (1341 NI) and Albric' *ad Capud Vill'* (1279 RH). v. tūn.

BARANCE'S FM (6″) and GILL'S HILL are probably to be associated with the families of Ann *Barrans* of Hardwick (1639 PR i) and John *Gill* (1700 *Christ's*). The latter is *Gills Hill Fm* c. 1840 *TA*.

ARMS HILLS (local). Cf. *Alms Hill Fm* c. 1840 *TA* and v. Fox 194–5. THE BARRACKS is *Broadway or Barracks Fm* c. 1840 *TA*. It lies on BROAD WAY (6″). Cf. *Broadwayfield* 1668 *Christ's* and Broadways *supra* 20. BROOK END FM (6″). Cf. *le Brookend* 1539 *MinAcct* and Brook Fm *supra*. CAXTON END. Cf. *Caxton End Fm* c. 1840 *TA*. It lies towards Caxton. CHURCH FM (6″) is *The Hall or Church Fm* ib. CROW END FM, EDGEHILL FM (both 6″), Fox FM (Kelly), GRANGE FM and HEADINGS FM (both 6″) are so named ib. HOME FM (6″). Cf. *Home Meadow* ib. MONKFIELD FM is *Monkefeld* 1553 Pat. It formerly belonged to the monks of St Neots. NEW BARNS PLANTATION (6″). Cf. *New Barns Fm* c. 1840 *TA*. NEWZEALAND (6″) lies remote, towards the parish boundary, v. *infra* 357.

Caldecote

CALDECOTE [*olim* kɔ·kət]

> *Caldecote* 1086 DB *et freq* to 1552 Pat, (*juxta Brunne*) 1292 FF, (*by Kyngeston*) 1389 Cl, *Kaldekote* 1198, 1252 FF, *Caltecote* 1428 FA, *Caldycote* 1552 Pat, *Caldecotte* 1582 Ely
> *Caudecot(e)* 1227, 1260 FF, 1272 *St John's*, 1275 RH, *Cauldecot* 1494 Ipm
> *Chaldecotes* 1247 FF
> *Calcot(t)(e)* 1429 Pat *et freq* to 1559 *Rental*
> *Cawket* c. 1570 ChancP, *Cawcote* 1576 Saxton, 1607 Kip, *Cowcote* 1644 Hollar, 1690 Lea

'Cold cottage(s),' v. cald, cot(e). A common term, probably only of reproach, just possibly with some technical significance. Cf. Coldharbour *infra* 357.

MITCHEL'S WOOD and STINNAGE'S WOOD (both 6″) are *Mitchells Wood* and *Stenniges Wood* c. 1840 *TA*, and are probably to be associated

---

[1] Cf. *Brooke Close* 1700 *Christ's*.

with the families of Robert *Michel* (1341 NI) and William *Stinnet* and Robert *Stenet* (1636, 1679 PR iii).

CHRIST'S COLLEGE FM (6″) and CLARE FM (Kelly) are self-explanatory. HIGHFIELD FM. Cf. *High Field Wood* c. 1840 *TA*.

Caxton

CAXTON

> *Caustone* 1086 DB, 1559 *Rental*
> *Kachestona* t. Stephen France, *Ka(c)kestune* c. 1150 *StNeot*, *Kaccestune* c. 1183 Wardon (p), *Kakeston(a)* 1183–94 P, 1206 Cur, *Kaxton* 1195 P *et freq* to 1330 FF, *Kaxston* 1298 Ipm
> *Chachestun* c. 1150 *StNeot*, *Chakeston'* 1186 P, 1303 *Lewes*, *Cakeston(a)* 1187 P *et freq* to 1324 Pat, *Caqueston(a)* 1191 *AD*
> *Caxton(a)*, -(e) c. 1150 *StNeot et freq* to 1488 Pat, *-tun* c. 1250 SR, *Cakston* 1346 FF, *Caxston(e)* 1353 FF, 1401 FA, 1487 Pat
> *Caston* 1380 Cl

As suggested by Ekwall (DEPN), this is probably '*Kakkr*'s farm,' *v.* tūn. This Scand personal name is found in Kaksrud (Norway) and may be from Norw *kakk*, 'nose' or ON *kǫkkr*, 'lump,' Norw *kakk*, 'a knob.' The persistent ME forms in -*es*- make Ekwall's alternative suggestion that this might be from Scand *käx*, a side form of *kax*, 'umbelliferous plants,' the source of English *kex*, unlikely.

SWANSLEY WOOD FM. Cf. (*nemore de*) *Swanesle(hul)* c. 1150, 1180 *StNeot*, 1279 RH, 1345 *CWool*, *Swannesle(hul)* c. 1150, 1180 *StNeot*, c. 1250 *StJohn'sH*, 1324 *MinAcct*, *Swanlehille* 15th *CaiCh*, *Swanneley* 1553 Pat. It is impossible from the early forms to decide whether this is 'the wood of the peasant' (*v.* swān) or that of the swan (OE *swan*). A late form, however, *Swaneholmbroke* 1511 *Cole* iii, with its reference to 'low-lying land by a stream' (*v.* holmr) and the brook which flows past the farm, is in favour of the latter. *v.* lēah.

CAXTON GIBBET and PASTURES are so named c. 1825 (O.S.). MILLHILL SPINNEY (6″). Cf. *Mylnehylfelde* 1487 *Pembroke*, *v.* myln. THE MOATS is so named c. 1825 (O.S.). There are earthworks near by. RED LION FM (6″). Cf. (messuage or inn called) *the Red Lyon* 1535 AD v.

Croxton

CROXTON

> Crochestone 1086 DB, -tune 1086 InqEl (p), Crocestona 1086 ICC
> (p), Crokeston' 1184–6 P, 1285 Ass, 1346 FA, Crokuston 1335
> Pembroke
>
> Crochetone 1086 InqEl (p), Crocton 1257 FF
>
> Croxton(e) 1199 CurR et freq, (near Eltesle) 1301 Pat, (by Cawm-
> bregge) 1406 Cl, Crocstun(e) 1202 FF, 1210 Cur, -ton 1202 FF,
> Croxston(e) 1298 Ass, 1314 Ipm, 1316, 1401 FA
>
> Croston' 1200 Cur
>
> Crokesden 1447 EA vii, 1465 Pat

'Crocc's farm,' v. tūn. Cf. Crocc t. Cnut (Searle). This name is ON
Krókr which is found very early in Croxall (St), Crokeshalle 942 (13th)
BCS 773. Cf. also Croxton (Nf), Crochestune c. 1050 (12th) LibEl.

INGLES SPINNEY and KING'S SPINNEY (both 6″) are probably to be
associated with the families of William Ingree (1689 PR iv) and Richard
Kynge (ib.).

CROXTON PARK is The Park 1826 Map. HILL FM, MANOR FM, SOUTH
LODGE and WHITE HALL (all 6″) are so named c. 1825 (O.S.). MEADOW
FM is The Meadow Fm 1826 Map. WESTBURY FM is Westbery 1346
FF, Westbury de Croxton 1363 ib., v. burh (manorial).

Eltisley

ELTISLEY [olim elzli]

> Hecteslei (sic) 1086 DB, Helteslay 1202 FF, -l(e) 13th Ely, c. 1260
> StJohn'sH, c. 1330 ElyCouch, Helteysleye, Heltisle 1272 Ass
>
> Eltisle(e), -ys- 1218 SR et freq to 1434 Pat, -ley 1500 ib., Eltesle(e),
> -leg, -ley(e) 1227 FF et freq to 1448 Pat
>
> Eltesie t. Hy 3 HMC Rutland iv, Elteseye 1272 Ass
>
> Elesl' 1285 Ass, Ellesley 1548 Pat, Elsley(e) 1553 EA viii, 1576
> Saxton, 1675 Ogilby
>
> Eltesele 1386 Pat, Elstisleye 1480 CTerr

'Wood or clearing of Elti,' the strong form of the weak Elta found
in Elkington (PN Nth 70). v. lēah.

Papley Grove and Hollow. Cf. *Pappele* 1279 RH, 1334, 1385 BM, *Papledene* 1500 *Pembroke*. 'Pappa's wood,' *v.* lēah. The *dene* (*v.* denu) may well be the hollow itself. They are near Papworth *infra* 171 and are probably named from the same man.

Church End (6″) was the home of Marg(aret) *ad Ecc(lesi)am* (1279 RH).

Caxton End lies towards Caxton. Green Fm (6″). Cf. *Green Close* c. 1840 *TA*. Jesus College Fm and Pembroke College Fm (6″) are self-explanatory. Potton End is on the road to Potton (PN BedsHu 106).

Great and Little Eversden

Eversden

> *Euresdone* 1086 DB, 1199 CurR, *Evresdon* 1200–3 Cur, 1317 Ch, 1382 FF, *Eversedon* 1310 ib.
>
> *Eueresdona* 1086 ICC, (*Michel-*) 1272 Ass, *Euerisdone* (*magna*) ib., *Everesdon(e)* 1202 FF *et freq* to 1448 ib., (*Magna, Parva*) 1240 FF, *-dun* 1227 ib., *-doun* 1391, 1401 Cl, *-den(e)* 1254 Val *et freq* to 1340 Ipm, *-ton* 1387 Cl, *-isdon, -y-* 1279 RH, 1282 Ipm, 1475 Pat
>
> *Euersdon(e)* 1086 (13th) BrC, 13th *Ely*, *Eversdon(e)* 1239 FF *et freq* to 1503 AD iv, *-dune* 1239 FF, *-den* 1303 FF, 1553 Pat, *-doun* 1420 Cl, *-ton* 1442 IpmR
>
> *Au(e)resdone* 1086 DB, *æuerdune, Neuueretona* 1086 InqEl
>
> *Euerdon(e)* 1199 P (p), (*maior*) 13th *Ely*, *Everdon'* 1205 Cur, 1229 Cl, 1524 AD v, *-den* 1549 Pat, *Evyrdoun* 1403 Cl
>
> *Heversdun* 1218 SR, *Heverisdon'* 1275–9 RH
>
> *Evesdon* 1239 FF, *Hevesdon* 1271 ib., *Evysdon* 1492 Ipm

'Boar's hill' or that of *Eofor*, *v.* eofor, dūn. For the compound cf. Eversholt (PN BedsHu 123), *Euereswell(e)(felde)* c. 1250 *StJohn'sH*, 1440 *Queens'* (Eversden), *Euereshel* c. 1206 *ElyCh*, c. 1250 *ElyM* (Ely), *Eueresdune* ib. (West Wratting) and *Euereshow* 1219 FF (Great Shelford).

Great Eversden

Note. Church Lane is *le Cherchelane* 1302 *Queens'*.

Church Fm (6″) and Eversden Wood were the homes of John *atte Churche* (1346 Cl) and Everard *atte Wode* (1272 Ass) and Henry *ad Boscum* (1279 RH).

HOLBEIN FM (6″) is probably to be associated with the family of John *Holben* (1811 *EnclA*).

EVERSDEN FM and SING CLOSE are so named c. 1825 (O.S.). REDHOUSE FM (all 6″) is *le Redehous Croft* 1306 *Queens'*.

Little Eversden

NOTE. BUCK'S LANE. Cf. *Buck's Close* 1811 *EnclA*.

MARSH CLOSE (6″). Cf. *le Merssh* 14th *Queens'*. QUARRY FM. Cf. *Eversden Quarry* c. 1825 O.S. RECTORY FM (6″) is *terram rectoris ecclesie de parua Eueresdon'* 1300 *Queens'*.

Gamlingay

GAMLINGAY

> *Gamelinge, Gamelingei* 1086 DB, *Gamelingee, Gmelingéé* 1086 InqEl, *Gamelingeie* ib., *Gamelingei(e)*, *-(a)*, *-ey(e)* 1199 CurR *et freq* to 1432 Pat, *Gamelyngey(e)*, *-eie*, *-ay(e)* 1271 Pat *et freq* to 1477 FF, *Gamelengeia* 1155 P, *Gamblingay(e)* t. Eliz ChancP
> *Gamelingeheia* 1086 InqEl, *-heye* 1277 *Ely*, 14th *Cai*, *Gamilenk-*, *-inkeia* t. Hy 2 BM, *Gamelinghey* 1218 SR, 1364 Pap, *Gamilingeye* 1252 Cl
> *Camelinga* 1086 InqEl, *Camelegeia* 1153 BM, *-eye* 13th *Ely*, 1276 Val
> *Gamel(e)g(e)a*, *-eia*, *-eya*, *-eie*, *-eye*, *-aia*, *-aye*, *-ia*, *-ie*, *-ye* 1119, a. 1185 Colch *et freq* to 1405 Pat
> *Gaminggeia* 1170 LibEl, *Gam(e)neg(h)eia*, *-heye*, *-ay* c. 1210 Fees *et freq* to 1333 *ElyC*
> *Gamelegeheie* 12th Colch, *Gamelekeye* 1218 SR, *Gameligh* 1275 RH, *Gameleye*, *Gamylygaye* 1361 Cl, *Gamylgy* 1364 Pat
> *Gemelegehya* a. 1202 Colch, *Gemelyngeye* 1327 SR
> *Gamegeya* 1218 Fees
> *Gameneygeye* 1285 *Ass*, *Gamennigeye* 1372 Cl (p)

'The low-lying land of the people of *Gamela*,' a personal name to be associated with OE *gamol*, 'old,' probably found also in (*æt*) *Gamelanwyrðe* 946 BCS 813. v. inga, ēg. For the AN *c* for *g* and interchange and loss of *l* and *n*, v. IPN 114, 106.

NOTE. COW LANE and STOCKS LANE are so named c. 1840 (*TA*).

PARK FM (6″) is *Shackledon Grange al. le Park* 1637 *Cole* xxxvii. The earlier name is *Scacresden* 1153 BM, *Shakild'n* 1279 RH, *Shakelden Graunge* 1547 *Pat*, from OE *scēacere*, 'robber' and **denu**. We probably have parallels in *Schakeldene* 1319 *Extent* (West Wratting) and *Saclesdell* c. 1212 *Wymond* (Steeple Morden). For interchange of *r* and *l*, *v*. IPN 106.

DENNIS GREEN[1] (6″) is probably to be associated with the family of Thomas *Dennis* (1672 *Rental*).

THE BUTTS. Cf. *Butt Close* c. 1840 *TA* and *v*. **butte**. DUTTER END. Cf. *Dearetree pasture* 1672 *Rental*. FOXHOLE WOOD. Cf. *Foxalls* t. Eliz ChancP, probably for 'foxholes.' GAMLINGAY CINQUES is *the Sinks* 1672 *Rental*, *Gamlingay Sinks* c. 1825 O.S., *Sinks Common* c. 1840 *TA*. ME *sinke*, LG *sinke*, 'hollow or depression in the ground,' used from 1596 of 'a flat, low-lying area where waters collect, a bog, marsh,' *v*. NED *s.v. sink* sb.[1] GAMLINGAY GREAT HEATH is *Great Heath* 1601 *Cole* xxii. Cf. *le hath in Neutonhide* 1229 *StNeot*. LITTLE HEATH is so named in 1601 (*Cole* xxii). MERTON GRANGE and MANOR FM are *Mertonhalle* 1346 *Elien*, *Mertonage* 1601 *Cole* xxii. This was part of the endowment given to Merton College, Oxford, by its founder, Walter de Merton. WOODBURY is *Wodebury* 1336 FF, *v*. **wudu, burh** and cf. *le Wodefurlong* 1229 *StNeot*, *Hestwode* 1230 ib. WOODBURY HALL (all 6″) is *Woodburrough Hall* 1683 *Cole* ix.

Little Gransden

LITTLE GRANSDEN

> *Grantandene* 973 (14th) *Thorney*, *Grantendene* 1086 InqEl, 12th *LibEl*, c. 1185 *StNeot*, *Grantendene*, *Grantendena* 1086 InqEl, *Grauntenden'* 1228 Cl
>
> *Grentedene* c. 1050 (13th) KCD 907, (12th) LibEl, *-dena* 1086 ICC, *Grentesden* 1230 *ElyCouch*
>
> *Grantedene* 1086 DB, InqEl *et freq* to c. 1278 ElyA, *Gratedene* (sic) 1086 DB
>
> *Grantsedene* 1199 CurR, *Grantesden(e)* 1230 *ElyC et freq* to 1415 Pat, (*Little*) 1294 ib., (*cum Herdwyke*) 1316 FA, *-denne* 1388 Pat, *Grantisden* 1230 *ElyC et freq* to 1391 Pat, *Grauntesdene* 1298 *Ass*, *Grancesden* 1492 Ipm

---

[1] So named c. 1840 (*TA*).

Granden(e) 1236 Barnwell, 1285 *Ass*, 1327 SR, *-don* 1298 *Ass*,
  Graundone 1285 ib.
Grandesden c. 1330 *ElyCouch*, 1387 *MinAcct*, 1396 Pat, 1408
  CTerr (p)
Gran(n)(e)sden 1485 Ipm, 1571 ElyA, *Graun(e)sden* 1486, 1548 Pat,
  Gramysden 1548 ib., *Gramsden* 1645 Blaeu, *Grampdon* 1672 EA xi

'*Granta*'s or *Grante*'s valley,' *v.* denu. *Little* to distinguish this
from the neighbouring Great Gransden (PN BedsHu 258). For the
personal name cf. further Gransmoor (PN ERY 88–9).

HAYLEY WOOD is *Heile* 1164 BM, (*boscus*) *Heyle* 1251 *ElyCouch et freq*
to 1316 BM, *Hayly Wood* 1602 *Cole* xlii. Probably 'hay-clearing' as
in Green Hailey (PN Bk 171), earlier *hegleage* (BCS 603) and Hailey
(PN Herts 212), *v.* hēglēah. A compound of (ge)hæg is also possible,
denoting 'a woodland enclosure.' See Hayley Green (PN Wo 295),
Hailey (PN Sx 305).

HILL FM (6") was the home of Robert *ate Hul* (1327 SR).

FULLER'S HILL FM is probably to be associated with the family of
John *Fuller* (1780 Poll).

GRANSDEN LODGE. Cf. *Lodge Fm* 1690 DKR xli, *Gransden Lodge Fm*
1813 *EnclA*.

Hardwick

HARDWICK

Hardwic c. 1050 (13th) KCD 907, *-uic* c. 1050 (12th) LibEl, 1086
  DB, InqEl, *-wyk* c. 1060 (14th) *ElyM*, *-uuic*, *-wich*, *Hardewic*
  1086 InqEl
Herdwich 1086 InqEl, 1167 CR, 1277 *Ely*, 1279 RH, *-wic* 1167 P
  (p), 1170 LibEl, 1201 Cur, 1254 Val, *-wik*, *-wyk(e)* 1252 FF *et freq*
  to 1436 Pat, *-wick* 1277 *Ely*, *-wykes* 1313 FF
Ordewic(o) 1212 RBE
Herdewyk(e), *-wik(e)* 1251 Ch *et freq* to 1393 FF, *Herthwyk*, *-wik*
  1260 Ass, *Heredewyk* 1376 Pat
Herwich 1277 *Ely*, *Herewyke* 1399 Cl, *Harwicke* 1668 FF

'Sheep-farm,' *v.* heordewīc.

HARDWICK WOOD is *le Hardwykwode* 1496 *Clare*. RED BRICK FM (6")
is *Red Brick House* c. 1840 *TA*. STARVE GOOSE PLANTATION (6"). Cf.
Stir-goose Close c. 1825 O.S. and *infra* 357.

Hatley St George[1]

NOTE. BAR LANE is *Burr Lane* c. 1840 *TA*.

CHURCH FM (6″). Cf. *Church Piece* c. 1840 *TA*. HATLEY PARK. Cf. *Heldepark* 1279 RH, i.e. probably *Eldepark*, 'old park.' *v.* Introd. xxxiv. PARK FM (6″) is *The Park Farm* c. 1840 *TA*.

Kingston

KINGSTON

Chingestone 1086 DB, *Chingestuna, Chinchestune* 1086 InqEl
Kingestona 1086 ICC, -*tuna* 1086 InqEl, -*ton(e)*, -*y*- 1242 Fees
   et freq to 1443 FF, -*tun* 1235 ib., *Kingiston*, -*yng*- 1254 Val, 1275
   RH, 1345 *CWool*, *Kyngtone* 1272 *Ass*, *Kingheston* 1297 Ipm,
   Kingstone cum Caldecote 1316 FA, *Kynguston* 1363 Pat
Kinkestune 1218 *SR*, *Kynkeston'* 1279 RH, *Kyneston* 1291 Tax,
   Kynxston 1553 EA viii, *Kynston* 1630 StJ
Chinston c. 1265 Misc

'The king's farm,' *v.* tūn. This was a royal manor TRE.

NOTE. CRANE'S LANE is so named c. 1825 (O.S.).

ARMSHOLD FM (6″). Cf. *Areneshowe* 1203 FF, *Arniggesho* 13th *Queens'*, *Arneshowe* 1312 *Deed*, *Arnyshowehyl* 15th *Queens'*. These references are from Great Eversden. The farm is just over the border, whilst ARMSHOLD LANE (6″) forms the boundary between Kingston and Great Eversden. 'Hill of *Earn* or *Earning*,' *v.* hōh. This may be that now known as CLAYPIT HILL in Great Eversden.

KINGSTON WOOD (FM) is *bosco de Kingeston* 1298 *Ass*, *Kington Wood* (*Farm*) 1810 *EnclA*. PINCOTE WOOD (6″) is so named c. 1825 (O.S.). Cf. Pincote *supra* 66. QUEEN'S COLLEGE FM (6″) is self-explanatory.

Long Stowe

LONG STOWE

Stou 1086 DB, *Stowea* 1200 Cur, *Stowe* 1204 FF *et passim* to 1428
   FA, (*juxta Brunne*) 1271 FF, (*cum Hattele*) 1279 RH, (*Wid,*
   Wythe) c. 1350 Rams, *Stouwe* 1346 FA
Lungestowe 1268 *Ass*, *Longa Stowe* 1271 FF, *Longstowe* 1272 *Ass*,
   (*juxta Caxton*) 1391 FF, *Langestowe by Brunne* 1316 Pat

---

[1] For the parish name, *v.* East Hatley *supra* 54.

'Place, site,' *v.* stōw. *Wid, Wythe* possibly from *Wido* de Auco or *Guido* de Stowe who held land in Stowe in 1130 and 1189 respectively (Rams ii, 261, iii, 48). "Called soe (i.e. *Long*) in respecte of ye length and to distinguishe from other townes of ye name in this country" (c. 1640 *Layer*).

LONGSTOWE HO is so named in 1604 (Borough).

Toft

TOFT

Toft(e) 1086 InqEl *et passim*, (*juxta Cumberton*) 1314 FF, (*juxta Kingstone*) 1316 FA, (*cum Herdwik*) 1334 *Ct*
Tofth 1086 DB, *Tost(a)* 1086 ICC, InqEl, *Topht* 1279 RH
Toftes 1086 InqEl, 1170 LibEl, 1246, 1314 FF, *Thof(f)tes* 1170 LibEl, 1493 Ipm, *Thoft(e)* 13th *Ely*, 1235 Cl, 1302 FA, *Thofth* t. Hy 3 Ipm

'Small homestead,' *v.* topt.

NOTE. MILLER'S RD is probably to be associated with the family of the Rev. George *Miller* (c. 1840 *TA*). PINFORD WELL LANE was probably the home of William *Atewelle* (1347 *SR*).

WOOD BARN was probably the home of William *ad Boscum* (1279 RH). Cf. *Wood Close* c. 1840 *TA*.

XII. PAPWORTH HUNDRED

Papeword(e) 1086 DB, *Pap(p)ewurðe, -wurde, -word(e), -worth(e)* 1176 P *et freq* to 1401 FA, *Papworth* c. 1250 SR *et passim*
Pāpesword 1086 DB, *Pampeswrda, Pampeuuorda, -e* 1086 InqEl, *Papesw(o)rd'* 1086 (1337) Ipm, 1200 P, *Pampeworth, Pa'ppeworth* 1275 RH

For further forms and the etymology, *v.* Papworth *infra* 171.

Boxworth

BOXWORTH

Bochesuuorde 1086 DB, 1086 (1337) Ipm, *-worth* 1086 (1313) ib., *Bokesw(o)rth(e)* 1199 Cur *et freq* to 1479 FF, *-wurth(e)* 1235 FF, 1251 Ch, 1284 FA, 1299 QW, (*Parva*) 1298 FF, *-word(e)* 13th BM, 1291 Tax

Bukeswurthe 1185 RotDom, *-wrth* 1228 FF
Bokiswurth, -y- 1243 FF, 1290 *Ct, -worth(e)* 1313 Ipm, 1316 FA,
   1421 FF
Bukisworth' 1261 Cl, *Bukkesworthe* 1428 FA, *Buxworth* 1480 Pat
Box(e)w(o)rth 1272 *Ass,* 1332 Pat, 1479 *AddCh*
Boxford 1510 LP

'*Bucc*'s enclosure,' *v.* worþ. For this personal name, which is not
on record, but is probably from OE *bucc,* 'buck,' *v.* MLR xiv, 236,
and cf. Buxhall (Sf), *Bucyshealæ* c. 995 BCS 1289.

Note. Thorofare Lane. Cf. *the Thorofares* c. 1840 *TA.*

Asplen's Mount[1], Bird's Pastures Fm[2], Page's Fm and Samson's
Barn (all 6″) are probably to be associated with the families of William
Aspelun (1279 RH) and William *Aspland, Aspline* (1684, 1690 PR iii),
James *Bird* (1763 ib.), John *Page* (1782 ib.) and Geffrey son of
Sampson or Matilde *Sampson* (c. 1260 *StJohn'sH*).

Browns Leys Grove is so named c. 1840 (*TA*). Honeyhill Wood.
Cf. Honey Hill *infra* 166. Lap Close Spinney. Cf. *Lap Close* c. 1840
TA. L Grove is *Ell Grove* ib., so called from its shape. Overhall
Grove. Cf. *Overhall* 1386 IpmR. View Ponds and Spinney. Cf.
the Views c. 1840 *TA.* White Grove (all 6″) is *White's Grove* ib.

Conington

Conington

   æt Cunningtune c. 975 ASWills, *Cunington, -yng* 1214 Cur (p), 1260
      Ass, 1291 FF, 1348 Works, *Cunnyngton* 1576 Saxton
   (*be*) *Cunigtunes* (*gemæra*) 1012 (12th) Proc. Soc. Antiq. (N.S.) iii,
      49, *Cunigtona* 1254 Val
   Cunitone 1086 DB, *-ton* 1199–1212 Cur, *-tun* 1218 *SR*
   Contone 1086 DB, 1086 (1337) Ipm
   Cuninton 1199, 1202 FF, 1214 Cur, *Kunintun* 1199 FF, *Cunninton'*
      1213 Cur
   Coniton(e), -y- 1200 Cur *et freq* to 1502 Ipm
   Con(n)inton(e), -y- 1242 Fees (p) *et freq* to 1316 FA
   Conigton(e), -y- 1254 Val *et freq* to 1336 *SR*
   Conyngton(e), -i- 1265 Misc *et freq* to 1570 SR, (*iuxta Fennedrayton*)
      1285 *Ass,* (*juxta Ellesworth*) 1374 FF, *Connyngton* 1553 Pat

---

[1] Cf. *Asplin Close* c. 1840 *TA.*   [2] *Birds Pasture* ib.

Like Conington (PN BedsHu 182), this is probably a Scandi-navianising of OE *Cyning-tūn*, 'King or royal farm,' under the influence of ON *konungr*, v. tūn.

Fen Drayton

FEN DRAYTON

> *be Drægtunes gemæra* 1012 (12th) Proc. Soc. Antiq. (N.S.) iii, 49
> *Draitone* 1086 DB, InqEl, *-ton* 1203 Cur, 1281 Ipm
> *Fendreiton', -y-* 1188 P (p) *et freq* to 1279 FF, *Fendret(t)on* 1199, 1231 FF
> *Fendrayton(e)* 1218 FF *et freq*, *Fenny-* 1285, 1334 *Ass, Fandraitun* c. 1250 SR, *Fennedraittone* 1316 FA, *Fyn- al. Fynne- al. Fenne-drayton* 1462, 1468 Pat
> *Fendraton* 1228 Eyns, 1296, 1324 FF, 1402 Cl
> *Fendryton'* 1279 RH, *-driton* 1345 CWool

This name is a compound of *dræg* and tūn, but the significance of the element in this particular case is by no means clear. There is no hill here as in Dry Drayton *supra* 152 up which something has to be drawn, neither is there any reason for portage in cutting off a bend in a stream, and Ekwall himself in his original article on the *dray*-names (*Germanska Namnstudier tillägnade Evald Lidén* 60) found it difficult to explain. *Fen* in contrast to *Dry* Drayton.

NOTE. BROWN'S RD. Cf. William *Browne* (1619 PR). COOTE'S LANE. Cf. Elizabeth *Coote* (1703 ib.). HIGH ST is *le H(e)yestrēte* 1422 St John's.

HONEY HILL (6″) is so named c. 1840 (TA). Cf. *Honehill* 1494 *Rental*, 1510 St Catharine's, *Honyhell* t. Hy 7 *Rental* (in Fulbourn) and *Hunihul* c. 1250 PN Nt 285. This name is found six times in the county and thrice as a field-name, usually in parishes with much marsh. *Honey* probably has reference to the stickiness or muddiness of the soil. Cf. *Hunibuttes* 1228 FF (Stanton), *Honiefelde* 1504 *Pembroke* (Whittles-ford). Honey Hill in Chatteris (*infra* 249) has a different origin.

DAINTREE'S FM and MIDDLETON'S FM (6″) are probably to be associated with the families of Thomas *Daintree* (1637 PR) and William *Middleton* (1749 ib.). For *Daintree* cf. Daintree Fm (PN BedsHu 214). The family must have come from Daventry (PN Nth 18).

ELNEY is *Ellney* c. 1205 (16th) SewersD, v. ēg. FAR FEN is *Fur Fen*

1603 *Christ's*, *Far Fen* c. 1840 *TA*. Low Fen. Cf. *Lowefendyche*
1422 *St John's*. Oxholme (all 6″). Cf. *Oxeholmedyche* ib., *v.* holmr.
St John's College Fm is self-explanatory.

Elsworth

Elsworth

> *Eleswurth(e)* 974 (1334) BCS 1311, 1249 *AddCh*, -*worth* 974 (14th)
> BCS 1310 *et freq* to 1363 Pap, *Elesworð* 1060 (c. 1350) KCD 809,
> *Elesuuorde* 1086 DB, -*wrde* 1198 FF, 1233 AD i, -*wrth(e)* 1327
> Ipm, *Els(e)wyrth* 1272 *Ass*, -*worth* 1337 ib., *Elysw(o)rth* 1286,
> 1290–4 *Ct*
> (*be*) *Elleswyrðe gemæra* 1012 (12th) Proc. Soc. Antiq. (N.S.) iii, 49,
> -*wurth(e)* 1077 (17th) ChronRams, 1218 FF, 1254 Val, -*worth(e)*
> 1130–1253 (c. 1350) Rams *et freq* to 1473 *Ct*, -*wurð(a)* 1176 P,
> 1245 AD i, 1251 Ch, *Ellisworth(e)*, -*y*- 1261 Cl *et freq* to 1454
> AD i
> *Helesworde* c. 1150 *StNeot*, *Hel(l)esworth(e)* 1200 Cur, 1240 Rams,
> 1298 *Ass*, 15th *CaiCh*
> *Elewurde* 1198 FF, *Elleworth* 1285 *Ass*, *Elliworth* 1364 Pap

'*Elli*'s enclosure,' *v.* worð.

Cowdell End (6″) is *Caldewell* 1290 *Ct*, *Cawdleend close* 1640 EA xiii,
v. cald, wielle.

Elsworth Wood (6″) was the home of Matheus *Atewode* (1279 RH).
Cf. *le Wodecroft* 1322 *Ct*.

Brown's Fm (6″) is perhaps to be associated with the family of John
Brown (1290 *Ct*).

Claypit Fm (6″), Common Fm and New Fm (6″). Cf. *Elsworth Clay
Pits*, *Elsworth Common* and *New Barn* c. 1825 O.S. North Meadow
Barn. Cf. *Northmadedole* 1322 *Ct*, *v.* mǣd, dāl. Pitt Dean Fm (6″)
is *Pit Dean Farm* c. 1825 O.S., *Pedoan Farm* 1821 Baker. Cf. *Pitdeane
Feilde* 1672 *Ct* and *v.* denu. Rogues' Lane Fm (6″). Cf. *Rogueslane*
c. 1825 O.S.

Graveley

Graveley

> *Greflea* 974 (1334) BCS 1311, 964, 1077 (17th) ChronRams,
> *Grevelee* 1411 SR

Grauel' 974 (14th) BCS 1310, *Gravele* 974, 1317 (17th) Chron-
Rams, 1078 (c. 1350) Rams *et freq* to 1434 Pat, *Gravelei* 1086 DB,
-leye 1367 Pat
Græflea 1060 (c. 1350) Thorpe, *Groflea* c. 1350 Rams

The second element here is clearly lēah, 'wood, clearing.' The first
is uncertain. Some of the forms look as though the correct form was
OE *græf*, 'pit, trench.' Some of the later forms suggest association
rather with OE **græfe**, **grāf(a)**, 'grove, thicket.' Somewhat similar
difficulties of form are found in the not very distant Raveley (PN
BedsHu 217), early *Ræflea*, later *Rauelai*.

LODGE FM (6″). Cf. *Graveley Lodge* c. 1825 O.S.

Knapwell

KNAPWELL
(*at*) *Cnapwelle* c. 1045 (14th) ASWills, 1045 (17th) ChronRams *et
passim* to 1329 AD ii, *Cnapp(e)well(e)* 1251 Ch, 1286 *Ct*, 1298
Ass, 1302 FA, *Canappewelle* 1286 *Ct*
Cnapanwelle 1077 (17th) ChronRams, *Cnapen(e)welle* c. 1350 Rams
Chenepewelle 1086 DB, *Cnepwell* 1196 FF
Knapwell(e) 1208 FF *et freq*, (*olim Little Wellesworth*) 1746 *Cole*
xviii, *Knap(p)ewell* 1233 FF *et freq* to 1349 Pat
Clapwelle 1284 FA

This may be '*Cnapa*'s spring,' *Cnapa* being on record as the
name of a moneyer; *cnapa* in its original sense 'boy' is also a possibility. Cf. *Chnapecoteweye* 1277 *Bodl* (in Chesterton), *Cnapewell*
(PN Nt 293), *Cnapewelleheved* 1300 Misc (in Marton, Y), Knapton
(PN ERY 136), Knapeney and Knapthorpe (PN Nt 54–5, 184).

KNAPWELL WOOD FM was the home of John *ad boscum* (1311 *Ct*).
Cf. *Cnapwollegraue* 1278 *Ct* and *v.* **græfe**.

COLDHARBOUR FM is in an exposed position, on a hill. Cf. *infra* 357.

Over

OVER
Ouer 1060 (c. 1350) KCD 809, *Ouere* 1086 InqEl, *Over(e)* 1247 FF
et passim, (*by Rampton*) 1357 Ipm

Oura(m) 1086 ICC, 1165 P, *Oure, Ovre* 1086 DB *et freq* to 1337 Pat, (*iuxta Cantebrig'*) 1285 *Ass, ouro, ourt* 1086 InqEl, *Owre* 1576 Saxton

Ofre 1086 InqEl

ouuere 1086 InqEl, *Owver* 1553 Pat

Hovere 1200 Cur

'Bank of the river' (i.e. of the Ouse), *v.* **ofer.**

NOTE. COX END LANE. Cf. *Maggecocks* 1552 *CCC, Madgecokes* 1564 ib., *Coxes* 1575 *Survey, Coxhill* 1587 *Rental, Coxe townsend* 1826 *CCC* and Samson *Cock* (1294 *Ct*). DOLE LANE. Cf. *the Dole Land* 1575 *Survey, v.* **dāl.** FURTHER WAY is *Fotheweye* (sic) 1300 *Ct, le Forthwey* 1540 *MinAcct, Farther Way* 1774 *Terr.* Cf. *le Forthwere* 1307 *Ct.* HIGH ST is *le High Street* 1552 *CCC.* HITHER WAY and LONG LANE are so named in 1774 (*Terr*). MIDDLE WAY is so named in 1826 (*CCC*). MUSTILL'S LANE. Cf. *Mussel* 1826 *CCC* and Jonas *Mustill* (1891 *Trinity*). SKEGG'S LANE. Cf. *Skeggs(fen)* 1575 *Survey,* (*Way*) 1774 *Terr, Skegg Fenn* 1684 Moore. In *Witcham* (1870), *Skeg's Way* runs across *Skeggings.* It may perhaps be associated with the family of John *Skegg* of Godmanchester, freeholder in Over in 1819 (Carter 251).

BLUNTISHMERE DROVE (6"). Cf. *Blunt(e)smere* 1277 Fleet, (*-fen*) 1575 *Survey,* (*Drove*) 1777 *Terr, Blunte Meer* 1637 BedL, *Blunsmare* 1652 *FF, Far Bluntmere* 1826 *CCC, Over Blunt Fen* 1829 Wells. The Ouse here forms the boundary between Over and Bluntisham (PN BedsHu 204) and the first element is the personal name found in Bluntisham itself and the second is probably (ge)**mǣre,** 'boundary.' The Ouse was called *aquam de Erhe* (i.e. Erith) *vel Bluntesdich* 1251 *ElyCouch.* If the 1829 form is reliable, *Blunt* gave name also to the **dīc** and fenn.

GRAVEL BRIDGE and RD (6") are *Gravel way bridge* 1710 *Trinity, the Gravel Road* 1774 *Terr, Gravel Bridge road* 1826 *CCC*; cf. *Golea* (*Golay*) *Field* (*al. Grauelley Brig Field*) 1774 *Terr.* This latter alternative is *Goldey(e)* 1357, 1383 *CCC,* (*-bro(o)ke*) 14th, 1448 ib., *Gooldey-brook* 1477 ib., *Go(o)l(e)yfield* 1575 *Survey. v.* **ēg** and cf. *Goldiford* (PN BedsHu 195) from OE *goldeg* (BCS 909), probably used of marshland covered with some 'golden' flower such as marigold.

LANGDRIDGE FEN and DROVE (6"). Cf. *Langedych* 1307 *Ct, Langdisch* 1357 *CCC, Longedyche* 1489 *Ct, Langridge(fen)* 1575 *Survey,* 1870 *Witcham, Chattox* 1604 *Atkyns,* 1870 *Witcham, Langridge al. Clattockes, Langreche* 1618 *Depositions, Clattockes* 1621 *SewersD, Clattox al. Langrach* 1636 BedL, (*or Langrige*) 1637 ib., *Chaddocks* 1654

BLAcct, Clatter Common 1662 Blaeu, *Landgridges Way* 1774 *Terr,
Over Chattox* 1829 Wells. It is clear that there has been some confusion or corruption. If the earliest forms belong here, this is simply
'long ditch,' *v.* lang, dīc, but the later corruptions would then be
surprising. The second element may be identical with Reach *supra* 136,
with reference to a strip of land near the now drained Willingham
Mere. But we have probably to take into account also *Langereche* 1251
ElyCouch (in Chatteris), *Langrede* 1471 *Rental* (ib.) and *Estlongriche*
1274 HMC vi, *Estlongreche* 1315 *Ct* (in Sutton). These three places
were probably near the course of the Ouse when it flowed north to
the Nene and may contain the element rīc found in Chatteris (*infra*
247), itself an old name of the Ouse.

FEN DROVE and HILL FM (both 6″) were near the homes of William
atte Fen (1294 *Ct*) and William *of the Helle* (1376 *CCC*). The latter
is *the Hill farm* 1851 *Trinity, v.* fenn.

PORTER'S FM (6″), WATTS' FEN FM and WHITE'S BANK (6″) are probably
to be associated with the families of William *Porter* (c. 1517 ECP),
William *Watts* (1787 PR ii) and Hugo *White* (1376 *CCC*).

BARE FEN (6″) is *Barefen(n)* 1575 *Survey, Bar-fen* 1826 *CCC*. BARE
HILL is *Barrhill* 1774 *Terr.* CHAIN DITCH (6″). Cf. *Over Chain* 1870
Witcham and *v.* Chain Fm *infra* 226. CHURCH END (6″) is *Le Church
End* 1552 *CCC*. COLD HARBOUR FM is in a lonely, remote situation,
cf. *infra* 357. HAWCROFTS (6″). Cf. *Hawcroftfen, Holcroft ditch* 1575
Survey, The Holcrofts c. 1825 O.S., *Hawcroft* 1830 *Trinity*[1]. LITTLE
GULL. *v.* gole *infra* 327. LONG HOLMES is *Longeholme* 1473 *Ct, v.*
holmr. LONG HOLME DROVE is *Long Holme Way* 1774 *Terr.*
MAN LODES (all 6″) is *Manload* 1575 *Survey.* OUSE FEN is *Owseffen*
1445 *CCC*, (*le*) *Housefen* 1539 *MinAcct, Ouzefen* 1575 *Survey, Howse
fen* 1604 *Atkyns, Oze Fenn* 1774 *Terr. v.* Ouse *supra* 11. OVERCOTE
FERRY (6″). Cf. *Over Cote, Over Coat* 1575 *Survey, Over Ferry* 1774
Terr and *feryeweye* 14th *CCC, v.* cote. OVER END. Cf. *Overendditch*
1575 *Survey*. ROSE COTTAGE. Cf. *messuage called the Little Rose* 1674
Lease. SANDPIT POND. Cf. *Sandpit(wey)* 1510 *StCatharine's.* TRINITY
COLLEGE FM (all 6″) was in the possession of Trinity College, Cambridge, in 1575 (*Survey*).

---

[1] The identification of all these forms is probable but not certain.

Papworth Everard and St Agnes

PAPWORTH (EVERARD and ST AGNES)

> be Pappawyrðe gemæra 1012 (12th) Proc. Soc. Ant. (N.S.) iii, 49,
> Pappeworda 1086 InqEl, -w(o)rd(a) 1147 BM, 1291 Tax,
> -w(o)rth(e) 1199 CurR et freq to 1553 Pat, (alia) 1236 Barnwell,
> (Everard) 1254 Val, (Petri, Anneis) c. 1260 StJohn'sH, (Agnes)
> 1281 Cl, (Magna) 1285 Ass, (Over-) 1557 Pat, Pappesw(o)rth 1236
> Barnwell, 1285 Ass, 1362 FF, 1372 Gaunt
> Papeuuorde 1086 DB, -worð 1086 InqEl, -wurth(e) 1185 RotDom,
> 1198 Cur, -w(o)rth(e) 1250 Fees et freq to 1416 Pat
> Pampeuuorð, -worda 1086 InqEl, -w(o)rth(e) 1166 RBE, 1299 QW,
> Pampesworth (Anneys) 1275 RH, (Everard) 1276 Val, 13th Ely
> Papw(o)rth(e) 1240 FF et freq, (Pet', Agnetis) 1218 SR, (Anneys)
> 1240 FF, (Peres) 1272 Ass, (Parva) 1281 Ipm, (Olde-) 1285 Ass,
> (Anney) 1298 ib., (Annes) 1539 PCC, (Nether or Little) 1643 Cole
> ix, (Uper) 1664 CHuAS iii
> Papesworth 1272 Ass, Pabworth 1458 Pat

'Pappa's enclosure,' v. worþ and cf. the neighbouring Papley Grove
in Eltisley (supra 159), both probably named from the same man.
Papworth Everard, so called from Evrard de Beche (1155–75 Farrer
97), was also called Parva, Over, Upper and Petri (Peres) from the
dedication of the church. Papworth St Agnes, so called not from a
St Agnes, but from Agnes de Papewurda (1160 P), is also called Magna
and Olde. The series of forms with medial m is due to confusion with
Pampisford supra 111.

Papworth Everard

KISBY'S HUT is Kesby's hut c. 1825 O.S. and is to be associated with
the family of Samuel Kisbey (1769 PR iv).

CROW'S NEST FM is (le) Croweneste(s) 1346, 1404 Pembroke. Cf.
Crownest(e) 1448, 1493 Rental (Knapwell), Crowneast (PN Wo 91)
and Starkesnest 1513 Cole (Waterbeach). FIRTREE FM is Fir Tree Farm
c. 1840 TA. PAPWORTH WOOD (all 6″) is so named c. 1825 (O.S.).

Papworth St Agnes

NOTE. BARNFIELD LANE is so named c. 1825 (O.S.). Cf. Barn Field c. 1840
TA.

NILL WELL. Cf. *Nil Well Field* c. 1840 *TA*. It was by the home of Gilbert de *Knille* (1279 RH) and Richard de *Knoll* (1281 Cl). For cnyll as a mutated derivative of OE cnoll cf. Knell (PN Sx 169), where this name is cited and the Herefordshire parallel Knill (DB *Chenille*) noted.

DUMPTILOW FM (6″). Cf. *Dumptilow* (*Barn*) c. 1825 O.S., c. 1840 *TA*, *Dumphlow* ib. HILL FM is *The Hill Fm* c. 1825 O.S. RIDGEWAY PLANTATION (6″) is so named c. 1825 (O.S.), cf. *Ridgeway Field* c. 1840 *TA* and Ridgeways *supra* 29.

Swavesey

SWAVESEY

Suauesheda 1086 ICC, -*hed'* 1176 P, -*hide* 1203 Cur, *Suauishith* 1290 *Ct*

Suauesham 1086 ICC, *Swavesham* 1237 Fees

Swavesey(*e*) a. 1086 (c. 1280) YCh, 1228 Ch *et passim*, -*eia*, -*eie*, -*ay*(*e*), -*y*(*e*), -*ie*, -*e* 1086 (1337) Ipm *et passim* to 1339 Pat, -*heie* (*Alani de Roham*) 1196–7 P, 1199 FF, -*hey*(*e*) 1230 Ch *et freq* to 14th *Cai*, -*he*(*e*) 1275 RH, 1277 Misc, 1281 Ipm, *Swaviseye* 1261 Ch, 1285 FF, 1313 Ipm, *Swavsey*(*e*) 1297 FF, 1316 FA, *Swayveseye* 1338 Cl, *Swaf*(*e*)*sey*(*e*) 1346 FA, 1404 SR, *Swathesey* 1442 ECP, 1450 Pat

Suauesy(*e*) 1086 DB, -*eye* 1236 Fees, 1268 *Ass*, -*heia* 1199, 1200 P, 1224 Pat, -*hey*(*e*) 1218 *SR*, 1327 Ipm, *Suaviseye* 1265 FF

Swavesche t. Hy 2 France, *Soaveshey* 1254 Val, *Swawesch* 1263 Ch, *Swhavesheth* 1267 Pat

Swaveshith, -*y*- 1212 Cur *et freq* to 1313 *Ass*, -*heth* 1267 Pat, 1285 *Ass*, 1290 *Ct*, *Swaueseth* 1298 *Ass*, 1450 Pat, -*ith* 1333 *ElyC*

Swauseth 1268 *Ass*, *Swaweseth* 1272 ib., *Swausey* 1309 FF

Swasheth 1285 *Ass*, -*ithe* 1304 Pat, -*ethe* 1340 ib., -*ey*(*e*), -*ye* t. Hy 8 Rental *et freq* to 1565 Ely, *Swaisey* 1559 *Rental*, *Swasey* 1606 *FF*, *Swacye* 1613 ib.

'*Swǣf*'s landing-place,' v. hȳð. *Swǣf* is found in *Swǣfesheale* BCS 762 and is a short form of names in *Swǣf*-. Cf. Sacombe (PN Herts 137), DB *Sueuechāp* from *Swǣfa*. It is just possible that we have here 'the Swabian's landing-place,' cf. Swaffham *supra* 134. *Alan de Rohan* held land in Swavesey in 1237 (Fees). For the loss of final *th* cf. Odsey *supra* 62.

NOTE. GIBRALTAR LANE. Cf. *Gibraltar Close* c. 1840 *TA*.

BUCKINGWAY HO (6″). Cf. *Bokkyngweye* 1287 *Rental*. Swavesey
parish is adjacent to Boxworth *supra* 164 and though there is no direct
track from Boxworth to Buckingway Ho, there is a track from Boxworth to the Cambridge-St Neots road and another from that road
past Buckingway Ho, so that there can be little doubt that *Bokkyngweye* is from *Buccingaweg*, 'the track of the people of Boxworth,' or
perhaps simply *Buccingwey*, '*Bucc*'s track.'

UTTON'S DROVE (6″) is *Wiʒtton dyche* 1287 *Rental*. Cf. *Wytton medowe*
ib. The first element is probably a compound of ME *wiʒt* and tūn.
For the meaning of *wiʒt*, v. wiht *infra* 351.

COVELL'S BRIDGE is probably to be associated with the family of Henry
de *Colevill* (1252 FF) and Mary *Covil* (1768 PR ii). Cf. Colville Hall
(PN Ess 495), earlier *Covell*. THORP'S FM (both 6″) is *terram nuper
Thome Thorppe* 1287 *Rental*.

BOXWORTH END. Cf. *Buxworthdole* 1287 *Rental*. It is the end of the
village lying towards Boxworth *supra* 164. BRICKKILN DROVE (6″).
Cf. *Brick Kiln Drain* c. 1840 *TA*. CASTLE HILL. Cf. *Castel Crofte* 1287
Rental, *Castle Close* c. 1840 *TA*. There are some remains of a castle
here, probably the ancient seat of the Zouches. COW FEN (6″) is *Cow-
fenne* 1677 Fen. FRIEZLAND FM lies isolated in the fen, cf. *infra* 357.
HALE WINDMILL (6″). Cf. (*campo de*) (*le*) *Hale* 1287 *Rental*, 1497 *Min
Acct*, *Hale Regewey* 1287 *Rental*, v. healh. LAIRSTALL DROVE (6″). Cf.
Lairstall Close c. 1840 *TA* and *infra* 353. LONG STANTON FIELD FM.
Cf. *campo de Longstanton'* 1287 *Rental*. It lies towards Long Stanton
infra 183. MANOR FM (6″) is so named c. 1825 (O.S.). MARE FEN is
Marefenne 1677 Fen, v. (ge)mǣre. It borders on Over. MIDDLE FEN
(6″) is *the Middle fen* 1571 CHuAS i. MOW FEN is *the Mowe fen* ib.,
Swacye Mowfen 1636 BedL, v. *infra* 179.

Willingham

WILLINGHAM
Uuinlingeham (sic) c. 1050 (13th) KCD 907, *Vuivlingeham* c. 1050
(12th) LibEl, *Wiuelingeham* 1086 ICC, InqEl, 1221 *ElyA*, *Wiue-
lincgaham*, *Wuiuelingeham*, *Wiuelincgeham* 1086 InqEl, *Wyve-
lingeham* 1238, 1244 Cl
Wyuelingham, -*yng*- c. 1060 (14th) *ElyM et freq* to 1575 *Rental*,
Wywelingham 1277 Ely, *Wyveleyngham* 1379 FF, *Wyvelington*
1549 Pat

Wivelingham 1086 DB, InqEl *et freq* to 1638 ElyVis, *Wiflyngham,
-ing-* 1272 *Ass*, 14th *StCatharine's, Wivlingham* 1549 Pat
Wiueligeham 1086 InqEl, *Wyueligham* t. Ed 1 *MinAcct*, 1346 FA,
Wiveligham 14th *Cai*
Wevelingeham 1130 P, *-ing-, -yngham* 1294 Rams *et freq* to 1565
Ely, *Wewelyngham* 1345 *CWool, Welyngham* (*by Overe*) 1416 Pat,
1496 Ipm, 1539 *Rental, Weavlingham* 1588 Fenland i, *Wellingham*
1690 Lea
Wil(l)yngham, -y-, -ing- 1272 *Ass et freq* to 1553 EA ix

'The home of the people of *Wifel*,' *v.* ingahām.

Note. Sneesby's Rd is to be associated with the family of Susannah
Sneesby (1745 CHuAS i).

Belsars Field is (*in campo de*) *Belasis(e)* 1221 *ElyA*, 1251 *ElyCouch*,
1277 *Ely*, 1279 RH, *Belsar(y)esfield* 1575 *Rental, Bels(a)iesfield* ib.,
c. 1840 *TA, Belsyes, Belseys field* 1622 EA xiii, *Bellses(s) Field* 1754
Venn, 1803 CHuAS i, *Belches Field* 1799 ib., *Belchers Field* 1816 ib.
Belsar's Hill is *Belsars Hills* 16th *Cai, Belsair hills* a. 1760 EA xiii.
Belsar's Hill is an earthwork described by Camden (ed. Gibson 410)
as "a rampart nigh Audre, not high, but very large, called Belsar's
Hills, from one Belisar; but what he was I know not." The camp lies
on the edge of the fen, commanding the southern approaches to
Aldreth Causeway, the chief land-route into the Isle of Ely from the
south (*v.* Fox 137, 155). Its ditches are referred to in the phrase
in fossatis de Belasis 1251 *ElyCouch*. The name is the common OFr
bel assis, 'beautiful seat,' found in Bellasis (PN NbDu 16), Bellasize
(PN ERY 245), Belsize (PN Nth 232, PN Mx 112). Cf. also *Belassise*
(Whittlesey) c. 1291 *Thorney* and *Bellasses* (Linton) 1411 *WMP*. The
forms as given above effectively dispose of Camden's *Belisar*.

Hempsalls Fen is *Hemeshale* 1221 *ElyA, Heueneshal(e)* 1251 *Ely-
Couch*, 1277 *Ely*, 1279 RH, 1352 *Layer, Hempshill* 1575 *Rental,
Hempsallfen* 1604 *Atkyns, The Hempsall* c. 1840 *TA*. 'The nook of
Hefin,' a derivative of the recorded *Hefa, v.* healh. Cf. Heveningham
(Sf), DB *Heueniggeham*.

Mere Holes (6″) is *Mere Holes* c. 1840 *TA*. Named from the now
drained Willingham Mere, *mara de Wiuelingeham* 1221 *ElyA, Wyve-
lyngham mere* 1361 FF, *v.* mere.

Queen Holme is *Quenholm* 1221 *ElyA*, 1251 *ElyCouch*, 1277 *Ely*,

Henholm ib., *Queneholme* c. 1465 *ElyB*, *the Quinam Ware* 1569
CHuAS i, *Queenhams* 1638 ElyVis, *the Queenhams or Showells* 1638
CHuAS iv, *Queenholmes, Queensholms* c. 1840 *TA*, *Queenham's* 1870
Witcham. It is impossible to say whether this takes name from some
unknown *queen* or from OE *cwene*, 'woman'; cf. *Quendolf* (1395 EA
iv) in Newton. For *Showells*, *v.* The Shoals *infra.*

LONG and SHORT SHELFORDS with SHELFORD'S FM (all 6″) are
Shelek(es)holes 1251 *ElyCouch*, 1277 *Ely*, *Shelfold(e)* c. 1465 *ElyB*,
t. Hy 8, 1575 *Rental*, 1604 *Atkyns*, (*le*) *Schelf(fh)ol(l)es, Schefolles* 1539
Rental, *Schelfforthe* 1549 *Ct*, *Shelfo(u)ld(e)s* 1575, 1600 *Rental*, 1575
Survey, (*Great, Little*) 1636 BedL, *Shelford* (*corner*) 1575 *Survey*,
(*Long*) c. 1840 *TA*, *Shelford(e)s, Shefelds* 1575 *Rental*. This is probably
a compound of OE *sceolh*, 'oblique, awry' in the sense of 'shelving,
sloping' and so 'shallow,' and **holh**. Hence 'shallow hollow(s).' The
places lie along the Ouse and near Mere Holes, the site of Willingham
Mere. Farther along the Ouse were The Shoals *infra.*

THE SHOALS (6″) is *the Sholds* 1636 BedL, *the Queenhams or Showells*
1638 ElyVis, *Willingham Flat or the Shoals* c. 1825 O.S. 'Shallows,'
v. NED *s.v.* shoal sb.[1] *v.* also Flat Bridge *infra.*

THE STACKS (6″) is (*le*) *Stackes* 1251 *ElyCouch*, 1277 *Ely*, 1316 *MinAcct*.
Cf. *le Stak* 1414 *Wren* (Downham). ME *stak*, the root meaning of
which is 'a pile,' hence 'a heap' and so 'an obstruction,' cf. *Stacke
or heap, agger* c. 1440 NED *s.v.* The Stacks is a low-lying area and no
doubt owes its name to obstructions in some watercourse here.

BOURNEY'S MANOR FM[1] and CRANE'S FEN[2] (both 6″) are probably to
be associated with the families of John de *Brune* (1391 *Layer*) and
Joan *Burne* (1496 Ipm) which probably came from Bourn *supra* 155,
and Robert *Crane* (1307 *Ct*).

BERRY CROFT is so named in 1575 (*Rental*). BLACK PIT DROVE. Cf.
Short Blackpitt ib. CADWIN FIELD. Cf. *Short, Water Cadwin, Cadwyn
field, Cadwing feild* ib. FLAT BRIDGE. Cf. *Willingham* (*Cote called the*)
Flat 1604 *Atkyns*. HAVEN DROVE. Cf. *the Havon* 1622 EA xiii.
HERMITAGE SLUICE BRIDGE is *Great Bridge at Hermitage* 1654 *BLAcct*.
This is near Hermitage *infra* 235. HILLS (all 6″). Cf. *Middlehill* 1636

---

[1] *Bornes* 1495 *Layer*, *Burnes' Manoir* 1496 Ipm, *Bournis, Burnys* 1618 *Depositions*,
Burney's dole 1754 Venn, *Brunes Manner corruptly Bornes Manner* 1776 Cole xlviii.
[2] *Crane Fen* c. 1840 *TA*. See also *s.n.* Cranbrook Drain *supra* 4.

BedL. The Irams is *Ilamcorner* 1575 *Survey*, *Irames* 1621 *SewersD*, *Iram* 1636 BedL, *The Irams* c. 1840 *TA*. Long Lockspits (6″). Cf. *Litt Lokpit* 1793 CHuAS i, *Lockspit* c. 1840 *TA* and Lockspit Hall *supra* 150. Long Swarth Barn. Cf. *yᵉ long swathes* 1575 *Rental*, *Long Swarths* c. 1840 *TA* and *v.* swæð. Lord's Ground is so named ib. Lordship Terrace (all 6″). Cf. *Lordships Close* ib. Middle Fen is *Middelfen* 1251 *ElyCouch*. Milking Hills Corner. Cf. *ye Brinks or Milking Barrs* 1575 *Rental*, *Fen called Milkinghill* 1636 BedL, *Milking Hills* c. 1840 *TA*. Pound Ground (6″), Reed Ground (Fm), Rose Hill (6″) are so named ib. Shoalmill Drain. Cf. *Shoal-mill* c. 1825 O.S. and The Shoals *supra* 175. The Sponge is *the Spong* c. 1840 *TA*, *v. infra* 354. The Washes is *The Wash* ib., *v. infra* 212. Weathersome Common (all 6″) is *Weathersome* ib., (*Common*) 1870 *Witcham*. Cf. *Wetherstuble* 1575 *Rental*. West Fen Fm is *Westfen* 1251 *ElyCouch*. Willingham Lode (6″) is *ladam de Wyuelingham* ib., *Wyuelynglode* 1307 *Ct*, *v.* (ge)lād.

XIII. NORTHSTOW HUNDRED

Nordstouua 1086 ICC, *Nordstou(u)e* 1086 InqEl, *Nordstow(e)*, *-a* 1168–99 P, 1279 RH, *Northsto(u)we* 1170 P *et freq* to 1482 Pat
Nortstou 1086 InqEl, *Nortsto(u)we* 1218 *SR*, 1268 *Ass*, 1279 RH
Norestov 1086 DB, *Norstowe* 1086 InqEl, *Nor(e)stowe* 1185 Rot-Dom, 1268 *Ass*, 1444 *Cole* xii
Orneston 1086 DB, *Norston* 1200 P, *Northston* 1236 Barnwell

'North stōw,' i.e. probably 'north meeting-place.' *North* to distinguish this from Longstow *supra* 154. The hundred is probably named from (half an acre in) *Nortstowe* 13th *StJohn's* in Dry Drayton, a parish which forms a narrow, elongated projection of Chesterton Hundred into Northstow.

Girton

GIRTON

Grittune c. 1060 (c. 1350) Rams, *Gryttune* 1060 (c. 1350) Thorpe, *Grittona*, *-(e)*, *-y-* 1135 Rams *et freq* to 1541 *MinAcct*, (*cum Bertone*) 1428 FA
Gretton(e) 1060 (c. 1350) Thorpe *et freq* to 1382 FF, *Gret(t)ona* 1086 ICC, *Grettona* 1086 InqEl (p), ICC (p), 1123 (c. 1350) Rams, *Grettun(e)* 1086 InqEl (p), 1235 FF

Gretone 1086 DB, *Gretona* 1086 InqEl (p), *Greton(e)* 1195 FF, 1206
Cur, 1260 Ass, 1279 RH
Creton 1195 FF, *Cretton al. Gretton* 1288 Ipm, *Grutton* 1299 QW,
Grotone 1411 SR, *Crytton* 1435 Pat
Girtonhale 1367 Crowland, *Gerton* 1399 FA, 1441 IpmR, *Girton*,
-y- c. 1460 CRent *et freq* to 1540 *MinAcct*, *Gurton* 1639 PR i

'Gravel-farm,' OE grēot and tūn. Cf. Howhill Fm *infra*. For the
metathesis cf. Girtford (PN BedsHu 108) and Girton (PN Nt 204).
For *Cr-*, *v.* Cambridge *supra* 37.

NOTE. CHURCH LANE is *le Chirchlane* 1434 *Ct*.

HOWHILL FM (6″) is so named in 1900 (*Trinity*). The name is
to be associated with *le Howeshil* (1300 Misc), 'the hill to *Howes*,'
surviving in Howe Ho *infra* 178. Cf. *Hoes* 1219 Cur, (*le*) *Ho(o)wes*
ib. *et freq* to 1480 CTerr, *Houwes* 1227 FF, *Hoghes* 1260 Ass, *le
Houis* 13th CCC, *Hoses* 1480 CTerr, *House(s)* 1533 Pat, 1535 VE.
Cf. also *Howescroftesande* t. John Township, *Howseshedge* 1432 Ct,
le Howescroft 1480 CTerr. *Howes* was a hamlet which Gray (Merton
20) located 'in a corner in the north-west end of Grithow Field'
in Cambridge. Cf. *Gretthawe* c. 1225 Rad, (*le*) *Grethowe*(*hil*) 1240
FF, c. 1250 *St John'sH*, *Crethowe* 1293 ib., *Grythowefelde* 1453
St John's, 'gravel ridge,' *v.* grēot, and cf. Girton and Gravel Hill
Fm *supra* 176, 41. For *Crethowe*, *v.* Cambridge *supra* 37. Dr
Helen M. Cam notes that the Enclosure maps for St Giles parish,
Cambridge (1803) and Girton (1814) show the hamlet extending
from Girton Corner to the Cambridge borough boundary, partly in
Impington, partly in Girton. The Huntingdon Rd was *Hows Lane*.
It is always difficult to distinguish between ME *howe* from OE
hōh, dat. *hōge*, and *howe* from ON haugr 'barrow.' The topography
does suggest a possible derivation from hōh, but the invariable
plural form is a difficulty. Lysons (44) records the destruction of
a barrow (probably near Bunker's Hill) in making the present
turnpike road. In Impington, too, we have a field called *le Borow-
feld*, *litill Barowfelde* (1475 *St John's*), whilst Mr T. C. Lethbridge
suggests that there may once have been many barrows here. Whilst
certainty is impossible, *Howes*(*hil*) is probably from haugr, and
Grithow from hōh. Dr Cam suggests that the site may have been
occupied from British times and may have been connected with the
cemetery in the grounds of Girton College.

COLE'S PLANTATION (6″) is probably to be associated with the family of Robert *Cole* (1633 PR iii).

BUNKER'S HILL, *v. infra* 357. CATCH HALL (both 6″) is *Catch Hall farm* 1895 *Trinity*. DUCK END is so named c. 1840 (*TA*).

Impington

IMPINGTON

> *Impintune, -a* c. 1050 (13th) KCD 907, 1086 InqEl, 12th LibEl, *Impinton(e), -y-* 1201 FF *et freq* to 1574 Pat, *Ympintuna* 1134–44 ElyCh, *Impenton* 1246 *ElyM*, *Hinpinton* 1269 Pat
> *Impeton(e)* c. 1060 (14th) *ElyM et freq* to 1365 FF, *-tune* 1170 LibEl
> *Empintuna, -tona* 1086 InqEl, *-inton(e), -y-* 1196 P *et freq* to 1285 *Ass*
> *Empituna* 1086 InqEl, *-iton(e), -y-* 1194–9 P *et freq* to 1298 *Ass*
> *Impitune* 1086 InqEl, *Impiton(e), -y-* c. 1170 *ElyM et freq* to 1482 Pat
> *Epintone* 1086 DB, *Epintonam* c. 1086 LibEl
> *Inpetuna* 12th *LibEl*
> *Empington* 1201 Cur, 13th *ElyF*, 1315 Cl, *Empigton(e)* c. 1250 *ElyCouch*, 1284 FA, 14th *CaiCh*
> *Impingtun* 1237 *ElyM, -ington, -y-* 1271 FF *et freq* to 1539 *MinAcct*
> *Inpyton* 1250, 1405 FF
> *Empeton(e)* 1277 *ElyF*, 1285 *Ass*

Forms with initial *e* and *i* are so evenly balanced that no certainty as to the etymology of this name is possible. If *e* has been raised to *i* before nasal *m*, then we may compare Empingham (R), DB *Epingeham*, c. 1110 RegAntiquiss *Empingeham*, 1210 FF *Impingeham*, 1286 *Ass Impyngham* and *Empenbeorch* 956 (14th) BCS 970 in Wiltshire. 'tūn of *Empa* or *Impa*,' *v.* ingtūn.

HOWE HO is *Howhouse farm* 1895 *Trinity*. It is near the site of *Hows House*, an inn which was demolished *c.* 1879. This stood near the top of a long rise on the Huntingdon Road from Cambridge. At the top there is a slight dip, followed by a slight rise and steeper drop. On the slope of this is Howhill Fm in Girton (*supra* 177, where the etymology is discussed).

Burgoynes Fm (6″) is *terra Johannis Burgone* 1475 *St John's*, *Burgoyns* 1558 EA viii, and is to be associated with the family of John *Burgoyn* (1429 *Ct*).

Landbeach

Landbeach

Bece, Bech 1086 DB, *Beche* 1086 InqEl, *Bech(e)* 1242 Fees *et freq* to 1434 Pat

Land(e)bech(e) 1218 *SR et freq* to 1480 *CTerr*, (by Rampton) 1357 Ipm, -*beach* 1320–9 FF, -*beeche* 1580 AD vi

Lond(e)bech(e) 1235, 1346 Cl, 1383 Pat, 1522 *SR*

Inbeche c. 1250 *ElyA et freq* to c. 1330 *ElyCouch*

Lanbech(e) 1268 *Ass et freq* to 1535 VE

Lang(e)bech(e) 1272–85 *Ass*, 1472 IpmR

Lambech(e) 1284 FA *et freq* to 1547 *Add*

The *Bech(e)* of DB and InqEl is identified by Farrer (190) with Waterbeach and *Utbech* (v. Waterbeach *infra* 184) with Landbeach (ib. 188). Ely, however, had interests in both and in later Ely documents *Inbeche* is clearly distinct from Waterbeach. It must therefore represent Landbeach, whilst *Utbeche* must be Waterbeach. Both were originally called simply *Beche*, OE *bece*, 'stream, valley.' They were later distinguished as *Land* and *Water* Beach from their topographical situation. They were also distinguished as *In-* and *Utbeche*; *Inbeche* probably represents the manorial nucleus of the estate, *Utbeche* its outlying portion. For confusion of *land* and *lang* cf. Landford (PN W 386–7) and Landwade *infra* 194.

Note. Cockfen Lane. Cf. (*clauso voc.*) *Kokfennys* 1520 *CCC*.

Frith Fen (Drove) (6″) is (*le*) *Frithf(f)en*, -*y*- 1326 *MinAcct*, 1350–70 *CCC*, *Fritfen*, -*y*- 1336–47 ib., *le Frefen* 1347 ib. This preserves the name of one of the common types of fen. In 1552 (Pat) we read of *segefennis*, *ffoderfennis* and *frythefennis* in Wicken, Soham and Wisbech. Cf. also, in Lakenheath (Sf), "Fen groundes...of seuerall natures That is to say some mowinge groundes some feedinge groundes some used for digginge the necessary firinge of the Inhabitants there as flaggs hassocks and turffes and a great parte wheron there groweth Reed and sedge" 1621 *SewersD* f. 200. Most of these are represented in the Isle of Ely to-day. Cf. Sedge Fen, Fodder Fen, Mow Fen, Flag Fen, Turf Fen and Reed Fen *infra* (Index).

Frith was a common fenland term, cf. "the Isles of Norney and Thorney have certain low grounds called Fryths on the skirts of the highland belonging to them...on which they gather winter fodder" 1604 *Atkyns*, "one rood of *frethfen*" (in Fen Drayton) 1422 *St John's*. This must be **fyrhð(e)**, 'wood,' which must have been used in the fens in the specialised sense of 'brushwood, undergrowth.' NED *s.v. frith*, sb.[2], gives similar meanings for later dates, "a piece of land grown sparsely with trees or with underwood only" (1538), "brushwood, underwood" (1605). Cf. (in Wicken) *Frithefen* 1232 *FF*, (Swavesey) *le Frethefenne* 1287 *Rental*, (Doddington) *frithfen* 1298 *MinAcct*, (Sutton) *le Frithfen* 1319 *Ct*, (Cottenham) *le Frithfen* 1339 Crowland, (Waterbeach) *Frithfenne* 1437 *Cole* xxxvi. Cf. also *le Frythmor* 1357 *CCC* (in Landbeach).

GOOSE HALL (6″). "Goose-hall, or, as it is in the maps, Goose-house ...was so named from a practice which, since the introduction of railways, has entirely ceased. For previously large numbers of geese were wont to be driven periodically along the highway from the northern part of the Isle of Ely to London, and here, next after Ely, they rested during the night" (1869 Milton 26).

WORT'S FM (6″) is to be associated with the family of William *Worts* (1709 *Cole* ix).

BEACH DITCH is *ladam de Beche* 1235 *FF*, *Bechelode* 1279 RH, *v.* (ge)lād. THE COMMON (6″) is so named in 1614 (Landb). HIGH FEN (6″) is *le High Fen'* 1518 *CCC*.

Lolworth

LOLWORTH [loulə]

> *Lollesw(o)rth(e)* 1034 (17th) ChronRams, 1202 FF *et freq* to 1378 SR, *Lolleswrda* 1086 ICC, -*uurth* 1218 *SR*
>
> *Lolesuuorde* 1086 DB, -*uuorda*, -*uuorð(e)*, -*wrtha*, *losewrða* 1086 InqEl
>
> *Lulleswrðe* 1199 P, *Lulleworth* 1272 *Ass*, 1284 FA, *Luesworth* t. Eliz ChancP
>
> *Lollew(o)rth(e)* 1242 Fees *et freq* to 1553 Pat, -*word(e)* 1279 RH, 1291 Tax, -*wurth(e)* 1259–98 FF
>
> *Lal(le)worth* 1285 *Ass*, 1486 Pat
>
> *Lolworth(e)* 1346 FA *et passim*, -*werth* 1480 CTerr

Lowl(e)worth(e) 1553 Pat, 1576 Saxton, t. Jas 1 *Rental, Loworth*
    1640 EA vi, *Lowlwor* 1688 PR i
Lolor(way) 1617 *EgCh, Lowlow* 1702 PR (Orwell), 1788 ib. ii

'*Loll* or *Lull*'s enclosure,' *v.* worð. Cf. Lowleth (PN Sr 381),
Spitalfields (PN Mx 151) and Lulworth (PN Do 140–1). All these
names alike alternate between forms in *Loll* and *Lull* and between
forms based on strong *Loll* or *Lull* and weak *Lolla, Lulla*.

HALL FM (6″) was the home of Walter de *la Halle* (1279 RH).

Madingley

MADINGLEY [mædɪŋli]

    Mading(e)lei 1086 DB, *Madingele(e)*, *-yng-*, *-ley* 1198 FF *et freq* to
        1480 *CTerr*
    Matingeleia 1086 ICC, *Madineglea, Meddingale* 1086 InqEl, *Medyg-*
        ley 1480 *CTerr*
    Maddingeleá, *-leæ*, *-le* 1086 InqEl, *-le(e)*, *-lea* 1193 P *et freq* to 1298
        Ass, *-leie* ib.
    Madingle, *-leg(a)*, *-ley*, *-le(e)* 1200 Cur *et passim* to 1539 *MinAcct*
    Maddingle(e), *-leye*, *-leia*, *-le(y)gh*, *-yng-* 1203 Ass *et freq* to 1470
        CRent, Magding(e)le 13th *Ely, Maddigl'* 1268 *Ass, Maddynle* 1291
        Tax, 1346 FA, *Maddenlaye* 1565 Ely, *-lie* 1662 ElyVis

'Wood or clearing of the people of *Māda*,' *v.* inga, lēah. *Māda* is
not on record, but is possibly a nickname derived from OE *mād*,
'foolish,' as suggested in DEPN *s.n.* Cf. Madeley (St), *Madanlieg*
975 BCS 1312 and Madeley (Sa), DB *Madelie*.

MOOR BARNS FM is *Morebernes* 1499 *MinAcct, More al. Morebarnes*
1539–41 ib., *Mower Barnes* 1539 ib., *Burley Wash otherwise Moor
Barnes* 1895 *Trinity*. It takes its name from *Maddinglemor* 1309 *CCC*.
Burley Wash is the manor of *Burlewas al. Shire Manor* c. 1630 Landwade, *Burleywash al. Moorbarnes farm* c. 1700 ib., so called from the
family of William *le Burdeleis* (1199 CurR). *v.* Addenda lx.

WRANGLING CORNER is *Wrangelond* 1235 *FF, Wrongelond* 13th *CCC*.
'Twisted land(strip),' *v.* wrang, land.

HOME FM. Cf. *Home Close* c. 1840 *TA.* MADINGLEY HALL and WOOD
(all 6″) are *Maddingley Hall* and *Wood* 1612 CAS xxxviii. MADINGLEY
PARK. Cf. *in magno parco* 1232 *FF, the Park* 1612 CAS xxxviii. PARK
FM and THE VIEW (6″) are so named c. 1840 (*TA*).

Milton

MILTON

(*fram*) *Middeltune* c. 975 ASCh, 975 (12th) LibEl, c. 1060 (14th)
ElyM, -*tun*(*a*) 1086 InqEl, 1253 Pat, -*tona* 1086 InqEl, -*tone* 1086
DB, -*ton*(*e*) 1196 P *et freq* to 1399 Pat, *Middleton*(*e*), -*y*- 1227
Ch, 1274 FF, (*juxta Landbeach*) 1325 ib., *Middilton*(*e*), *Myddel*-,
Myddyl- 1260 FF *et freq* to 1446 ib.

Mideltune c. 1050 (13th) KCD 907, -*ton* 1232 Cl *et freq* to 1364 Pat,
Midilton(*e*) 1261 Cl, 1309 Ipm, 1346 FA, *Mydelton* 1341 NI

Meddelton' 1235 Cl, *Med*(*d*)*ilton* 14th *Cai*, 1516 Milton

Milton 1275 RH *et passim*, *Mylton* 1436 Pat, 1570 SR, *Melton*
t. Hy 8, 1559 *Rental*, 1636 BedL

'The middle farm,' *v.* tūn. *Middle* possibly because situated between
Impington and Fen Ditton.

BAITS BITE LOCK is *Basebytt* 1424 *Cole* vi, *Basbet* 1621 *SewersD*,
Basebitt (*furlong*) 1634 Milton, *Backbyts* 1665 Dodson, *Baitsbite* (*Bank*)
1807 *Map*, *Baits Bite* c. 1825 O.S., *Backsbite* 1829 Wells, 1869 Milton.
The second element may be byht, 'curve, bend'; the first is quite
uncertain. MILTON FEN (6″) is *le Fen* 1424 *Cole* vi.

Oakington

OAKINGTON

Hochinton(*e*) 1086 DB, -*ton*, -*tun* 1086 InqEl, -*tona* 1130 P,
Hocchintuna, -*tona*, *Hokintona* 1086 InqEl, -*ton*(*e*), -*yn*- 1166
RBE *et freq* to 1529 Crowland, *Hockinton* 1268 *Ass*, *Hokenton*(*e*)
1302 FA, 1315 Crowland

Hogintune 1086 InqEl, *Hogynton* 1411 SR, t. Hy 8 *Rental*, -*don*
1502 EA vii, *Hogyngton*, -*ing*- 1415 Cl *et freq* to 1539–41 *MinAcct*,
Hogginton 1576 Saxton, (*otherwise Oakington*) 1854 *Trinity*

Okinton', -*y*- 1176 P, 1272 *Ass*, 1327 Pat, 1499 Ipm, *Ocinton* 1272
Cl, *Oketon* 1285 *Ass*, *Okington*, -*yng*- 1327 Pat, 1364 Cl, 1570 SR,
t. Eliz ChancP, *Okeington* 1595 Ely, *Oggington* 1640 EA vi,
Oak(*e*)*ington* 1660 PR i, 1685 CAPr iii

Hokiton(*e*), -*y*- 1200 Cur *et freq* to 1403 Crowland, (*cum Westwyk*)
1341 NI, -*tun* (*Abbatis* (*de Croyland*), *Comitis*) 1218 SR, *Hoke-
ton*(*e*) 1201 Cur *et freq* to 1357 Crowland

Hokincton' 1207 FF, *Hokington*(*e*), -*y*- 1284 FA, (*iuxta Cantebr'*)
1285 *Ass et freq* to 1549 Pat, *Hockynton'*, *Hokyngdon* 1480 *CTerr*,
Hokkyngton 1490 Ipm

Hogyton(e) 1279 RH *et freq* to 1412 FA, *Hoggiton(e)* 1284 FA, 1382
 FF, *Hog(g)eton* 1357 ib., 1393 Cl, 1412 FA
Rokyngton 1361 Cl

'The farm of *Hoc(c)a*,' *v.* ingtūn. *Croyland* from the manor of the
Abbot of Croyland and *Comitis* from that of the Earl of Huntingdon.

NOTE. COLES LANE is so named in 1833 (*EnclA*); cf. Robert *Cole* (1570
PR iii). MILL RD. Cf. *le Milneweye* 1362 Crowland. WATER LANE is so
named in 1833 (*EnclA*).

PHYPER'S FM (6″) is to be associated with the family of John *Phypers*
(1617 *EgCh*).

MEADOW FM (6″). Cf. *Medewefurlong* 1327 Crowland.

Rampton

RAMPTON

Ramtona 1086 ICC, *-ton(e)* c. 1251 *ElyCouch et freq* to 14th *Cai*,
 Ramtune, -a 1086 InqEl, *Rantone* 1086 DB
Ramptune 1086 InqEl, *Rampton(e)* 1247 FF *et freq*, *Rampeton'* 1299
 QW, *Rempton* 1403 Pat

Probably 'ram-farm,' from OE *ramm* and tūn.

NOTE. CUCKOO LANE is so called in 1829 (Wells). Cf. *Coockowe Brooke*
1654 *BLAcct*.

PAULEY'S DROVE (6″) is probably to be associated with the family of
William *Pawley* (c. 1840 *TA*).

BROOK FIELD, LITTLE FIELD and MILL FIELD (both 6″) are so named
in 1754 (Venn). GIANTS' HILL is *Giant's Hill* 1883 AnctC. Close
behind the hill is an oblong mound called *Giant's Grave* ib. MOW
FEN. Cf. *supra* 179. NEW GROUND COMMON. Cf. *The New Ground*
1754 Venn. RAMPTON BRIDGE is *Rampton Brigge* 1315 *Cole* xliv.
REYNOLDS DROVE and DITCH. Cf. *The Runholds* 1789, 1791 CHuAS i,
Renolds 1793 ib., *the Reynolds* 1796 ib., *Reynold Ditch* 1797 ib.,
Renold's Ditch 1799 ib. SNOUT COMMON (all 6″) is *The Snout* 1754
Venn, *Snout Common* c. 1840 *TA*. *v.* snote and Snoots *infra* 262.

Long Stanton All Saints and St Michael

LONG STANTON (ALL SAINTS and ST MICHAEL)

Stantune 1086 DB, InqEl, *Est Stantun* c. 1250 SR

Stantona 1086 ICC, (*Rollandi de Dinan*) 1168 P, *Stantone* 1086 DB,
   Stanton(e) 1161 P *et passim*, (*magna, alia*) c. 1250 *ElyA*, (*Omnium
   Sanctorum, Sancti Michaelis*) 1254 Val, (*Lunge-, Segraue*) 1285
   Ass, (*Long*) 1281 Ipm, (*by Rampton*) 1357 Ipm, (*al. Covelles*) 1580
   EgCh, *Longstanton All Hallowes* 1553 EA ix
Staunton(e) 1205 RBE *et freq* to 1553 Pat, (*Longa*) 1272 *Ass*,
   (*Lange*) 1337 FF, (*Michaell*) 1595 *EgCh*
Long Stainton 1438 IpmR, 1576 Saxton, 1690 Lea

'Stone farm-enclosure,' *v.* stān, tūn. *Long* from the long, straggling
village, so named in distinction from Fen Stanton (PN BedsHu 267).
Roland de Dinant had land in St Michael which is *east* of All Saints
in 1161 (P). The latter is also called *Magna* because larger than St
Michael, and *Segrave* from Nicholas de *Segrave* (t. Hy 3) and Stephen
de *Segreve* (1279 RH). *All Saints* and *St Michael* from the dedications
of the respective churches. For *Stainton*, cf. Staine *supra* 129.

Long Stanton All Saints

NOTE. CHURCH LANE is so named in 1580 (*EgCh*). MILLS LANE. Cf.
Millway 1617 ib.

GREEN END (6″) was the home of Andrew de *la Grene* (1251 Ch) and
William *super le Grene* (1279 RH).

HATTON HO and HATTON'S RD (both 6″) are to be associated with the
family of Sir Thomas *Hatton* (d. 1658 *Cole* i).

HOME FM (6″). Cf. *Home Close* c. 1840 *TA*. NOON FOLLY FM (6″).
Cf. Noon's Folly Fm *supra* 59.

Long Stanton St Michael

INHOLMS FM is *Inhams* 1595 *EgCh*, *the Inholmes* c. 1840 *TA*, *v.* innam.
MAGDALENE COLLEGE FM is self-explanatory. MOOR BALK (6″). Cf.
Le mor 1319 *Pembroke*, *v.* mōr, balke. NEW CLOSE FM. Cf. *the olde
newe close* 1595 *EgCh*.

Waterbeach

WATERBEACH

Bechia a. 1086 (c. 1280) YCh, *Beche* 1169–70 *ElyM et freq* to 1412 FA
   Vtbech 1086 DB, *Udbec(h)e, Udbecce, Vtbeche* 1086 InqEl
Waterbech(e) 1237 FF *et freq* to 1395 Cl, -*becche* 1326 ib., -*beke*
   t. Eliz ChancP, *Watirbeche* c. 1278 ElyA, 1331 FF, 1376 Pat,

Watre- 1351 ib., *Watterbech* 1281 Ch, *-beach* 1568 RHistS (3) i,
266, *Waterbeach* 1337 FF, (*cum Denny*) 1740 *Cole* viii, *-beyche*
1279 RH

v. Landbeach *supra* 179.

BANNOLDS (6″). Cf. *Ban(e)hale(feld)* 1205 FF, 1348, 1356 *Cole* xxxvi,
Ben(e)halemed 1325 *MinAcct, Banalefield* 1484 *Cole* xxxvi, *Bannold-
field* 1514, 1553 ib., *Baynall* 1559 ib., *Banhold Field* 1569 ib., *Ban-
nowllde* 1621 *SewersD*. 'Nook whcrc bcans grow,' *v.* bēan, healh.
BANNOLD DROVE (6″) is *Banald Drove* c. 1825 O.S.

CHALICE FRUIT (local) is *Charlesfrith* 1542 *Bodl*, 1555 *Pat, Challys
ffrythe, Challes frethe* 1546 *MinAcct, Churles Frythe* 1576 *Cole* xxxvii.
The second element is fyrhŏe, perhaps denoting 'brushwood,' *v.*
supra 179. Forms are too late for any certain suggestion as to the first.
It may be OE ceorl, 'churl.'

CHITTERING is *Chit(t)ering(e)* 1426, 1434 *Cole* xxxvi, 1621 *SewersD,
Chet(t)ering(e), -yng* 1423–1559 *Cole* xxxvi, 1521 Milton, *Chitterings*
1604 *Atkyns*. No explanation of this name can be offered.

DENNY ABBEY
    Deneia (insula), -eya, -e, -aya 1160–71 (14th) YCh, 1176 Templars
      et freq to 1279 RH
    Daneya, -eia, -eye, -eie t. Hy 2 *ElyM*, 1176 Templars *et freq* to
      1313 Cl
    Denney(e), -y(e) 1285 *Ass et freq*

    Probably 'Danes' island,' *v.* ēg and Introd. xix.

ELMNEY HILL (local) is *Elmeneya (insula)* c. 1167, 1169 *ElyM,
Elmenea, -eia, -eye* c. 1169 *Hosp et freq* to 1325 Misc, *-hey* 1326
MinAcct, Ameneya, -eia c. 1176, 1180 *ElyF, Helmenhey* 1325 *MinAcct,
Elmeley* 1341 *Cole* xxxvi, *High, lowe Elmholm* 1542 *Bodl, High, Lowe
Elmone* 1546 *MinAcct, Elmeham* 1555 *Pat, High, Low Elman* 1672
EA xi, *High-elm or Elmere* c. 1825 O.S., *High Elmer* 1870 *Witcham*.
Probably 'elm-grown island,' from *elmen*, adj. 'with elms,' and ēg.

FIDWELL FEN (6″) is *Lugf(f)en* 1373, 1414 *Cole* xxxvi, "later called
Fyde" ib. It is, perhaps, to be associated with the family of John, son
of Geoffrey *Fyde* (1352 Pat), cf. Fidwell Fen in Stretham *infra* 238.
Lugfen from the flags or *lugs* growing there, cf. '*iiii colar' de Lugges,*
1324 *MinAcct* (Harston), *Lugffen* 1636 BedL (Soham).

GARDEN TREE (lost) is *Garentre* 1279 RH, -*were* 1426 *Cole* xxxvi (cf. *Garentre piscaria* 1546 *MinAcct*), *Garden tree* 1604 *Atkyns*, 1679 *FenS*. The second element is **trēow**, 'tree'; the first may well be a personal name *Gāra*, a short form of names in *Gār-* (cf. Garford (PN Berks 38), *æt Garanforda* 940 BCS 761). It is possible, however, that the place-name is related to the obscure *Gartree* of Gartree Wapentake (Lei, L), with early forms *Geretrev*, *Gairtre*, *Cheiretre* and the like (EHN i, 46–7, 53). The origin of that name is obscure, but it would seem to be related to ON *geirr*, 'spear.'

JOIST FEN is *Agist fen, Gyste Fenn* 1507 Waterb, *the giest Fenne* 1546 *MinAcct, Ge(e)yst Fenne* 1558 Pat, *Giste Fenne* 1566 *Cole* xxxvi, *Geist fen* 1604 *Atkyns, Joyce Fenn* 17th *AdvL, Joist Fen(e)* 1618 *SewersA*, 1636 BedL, *Gest fen* 1621 *SewersD*. 'The marsh on which cattle were *agisted*,' from ME *agist*, OFr *agister*, Lat *jacitare, 'to take in live stock to remain and feed at a certain rate,' originally 'to admit cattle for a defined time into a forest.' The Denny Court Rolls record that in 1347 the provosts of the marsh were fined 20s. for not mentioning the total of the cattle in the marsh and for not making *agistment* accordingly, whilst *s.a.* 1559 they contain an order that "no man was to keep any *Geste* Cattle in Midlelode, Bannold and Wyngfold unless great neede require" (*Cole* xxxvi, ff. 136d, 155d). An earlier example of *joist* occurs in 1606 (*Depositions*) in a reference to "joist cattle in Rackefenne" (in Littleport). Cf. *Wicken Joyst fenn* 1708 *FenS*. See further *joist* v. and sb.[2] (EDD) and Justment (PN D 449).

WINFOLD FM is *Wulfholes* 1205 FF, *Wulfholefeld* 1207 FF, *Wolfollfeld*, *Wynfollfeld* 1375 Waterb, *Wynfold(e)(feld)* 1422 *Jesus*, 1546 *MinAcct*, *Woulfoldfelde, Wonefoldefelde* 1422 *Jesus, Wullefulfield* 1484 *Cole* xxxvi, *Weynfold* 1432 ib., *Winfold* 1526 ib., *Wyngfold, -i-* 1559, 1740 ib. Probably 'wolf-hollow,' v. **wulf, holh**.

DENNY GATE (6") was probably the home of Henry *atte Gate* (1329 *Cole* xxxvi), v. **geat**.

ADAMS'S CROSSING and MASON'S DROVE (both 6") are probably to be associated with the families of Thomas *Adams* (1619 *Cole* xxxvi) and Albric' *le Masun* (1279 RH).

BANK FM. Cf. *Waterbeche Banc upon the Eye* 1350 *Cole* xxxvi. For *Eye* cf. *the Ee* 1357 *Cole* xxxvi, v. **ēg**. BROWN'S PLANTATION. Cf. *feod' Broun, prat' voc. Brounes* 1493 *Denny*. THE CAUSEWAY. Cf. *the Dele Causey* 1514 *Cole* xxxvi, *Cleyhithe Causey* 1520 ib. CAUSEWAY END FM (all 6″) is so named in 1740 (ib. viii). CHITTERING HILL (6″) is so named in 1596 (*Christ's*). THE GREEN (6″) is *the Grene* 1427 *Cole* xxxvi, *Beech greene* 1428 Waterb. THE HALL is *le Hall* 1340 *Cole* xxxvi, *Bechehall* 1417 ib. MIDLOAD (6″) is *Middelloyd* (sic) 1346 ib., *Midlelode* 1559 ib., *v.* (ge)lād. NORTH FEN is *the Northffenne* 1331 ib. NORTHFEN DRAIN (6″). Cf. *aqua de Norffen* 1285 *Ass.* NORTHFEN FM is so named c. 1825 (O.S.). WATERBEACH JOIST FEN (both 6″) is *Waterbeach Ioyst Fenn* 1706 Moore, *v.* Joist Fen *supra* 186,

XIV. STAPLOE HUNDRED

Staplehou 1086 DB, ICC, InqEl, *Stapleho(w)(e)* 1260 Ass, 1553 Pat
Staplefo. ... 1086 ICC, *Stapel(e)ford(e)* 1175–1200 P, 1302, 1346 FA
Stapelhowe 1086 InqEl, 1268 *Ass*, *Stapelho* 1168 P *et freq* to 1381 Ass, *Stapelhou* 1175–7 P, 1285 *Ass*, *Stapilho(e)* 1275–9 RH, 1336 SR, 14th *Cai*, 1401 FA, *Stapilhow* 1279 RH, *Stapulho* 1428 FA, 1523 *SR*, *Staploo* 1560 *Depositions*
Stapelawa 1193 P, *Stapellauwe* 1196 *ElyC*

'Spur of land marked by a pillar' and probably, as suggested by Anderson (EHN i, 98–9), used as a meeting-place, *v.* stapol, hōh. *Stapelford* and *Stapelawa* are due to the influence of hundred names like Whittlesford and Thriplow which sometimes immediately precede it (e.g. 1175, 1193 P).

The hundred is named from a place *Stapelhoo* (1298 *Ass*) in Burwell. "A *balk* in Burwell field is called Staploe *balk*" 1808 L 97. The road leading thither is frequently mentioned as *viam de Stapelhoue* 1198 FF[1], *Stapilhamweye* 1451 *Queens'*, *Stapillo wey* 1521 ib., *Staplowey* 16th ib. Cf. Staploe (PN BedsHu 58).

Burwell

BURWELL
Burcwell 1060 (c. 1350) KCD 809, *Burghwell(e)* 1298 *Ass et freq* to t. Hy 8 *Rental*, *Burgewelle* 1346, 1428 FA
Borewell(e) c. 1070 (17th) ChronRams *et passim* to 1384 Pat
Buruuella 1086 DB, *Buruuelle* ib., 1086 ICC, *Burwell(e)* 1227 FF *et passim*
Bureuuelle 1086 DB, InqEl (p), *Burewell(e)* 1170 LibEl *et freq* to 1372 Pat, (*Sci Andree*) 1291 Tax

[1] In Exning (Sf).

Bureswell(e) 1258 FF, *(Sce Mar')* 1291 Tax
Barewell 1285 *Ass*, *Barwell* 1548 Pat, 1648 Cai
Borwell(e) 1304 *MinAcct et freq* to 1421 FF
Bourrewell 1332 *Pembroke*, *Burelle* 14th Rams

'Spring by the fort,' *v.* **wielle, burh.** There is a field near the site of the castle which is still called SPRING CLOSE. The castle was Norman, but probably the Norman castle occupied the site of an earlier earthwork, *v.* CAPr xxxvi, 127. There were formerly two churches here, dedicated respectively to *St Andrew* and *St Mary*.

NOTE. HIGH ST is *Heystrete* 1347 *Queens'*, *le Highstrete* 1452 *Ct*. NORTH ST is *Northstrete* 1351 *Queens'*. PARSONAGE LANE is *le Personslane* t. Hy 8 *Rental*. SCOTRED LANE. Cf. *Scottridge Close* c. 1840 *TA*. TOYSE LANE is to be associated with the family of John *Toyse* (1446 *MinAcct*).

ADVENTURERS' FEN. Cf. "lands in Burwell common part and parcell of the 95,000 acres of *Adventure land* allotted and sett forth by Act of Parliament for setling the draining the Great Levell of the Fenns called Bedford Levell" 1717 *FenS. v.* also Adventurers' Land *infra* 292.

BREACH FM is *(le) Breche* 1232 *FF*, 1357 *Cole* iii, 1419 *Ct*, *le, la Brach(e)* 1294, 1322 *Ct*, 1378 FF, 1398 *MinAcct*, 14th Rams, *le Braach* 1398 *MinAcct*. 'Land newly taken into cultivation,' *v.* **bræc.**

NESS HO is *Nest House* c. 1825 O.S., *The Ness House* c. 1840 *TA*. Cf. *molendinum del Nees* 1267 Rams, *Nesmelne* 1279 RH, *le Nesse* 1307 *MinAcct*, *the Nest* 1691 *SewersA. v.* **næss**, 'projection.'

THE LEYS (6″) is *le Layes* 1439 *Ct*, *le leese feld* 1473 ib. and may have been the home of William de *la lee* in 1388 (FF). If so, there has been confusion between lēah 'clearing' and lǣs 'pasture.'

BAKER'S FEN and DROVE, BUNTING'S PATH[1] and DYSON'S DROVE (all 6″) are probably to be associated with the families of Thomas *Bakere* (1394 Cl), Thomas *Bunting* (1279 RH) and John *Dyson* (c. 1840 *TA*).

THE BROADS is *le Broud* 1398 *MinAcct*, *The Broads* c. 1840 *TA*, *v.* **brode.** BURWELL FEN is *Borewellefen* 1373 *Ct*. BURWELL HO (6″). Cf. *Houslond* 1398 *MinAcct*. BURWELL LODE is *Burwell Loade* 1650 *FenS.* THE CAUSEWAY (6″) is *le Causie* 1604 *Ct*. CROWNALL FM. Cf. *Cromwell* 1307 *Ct*, 1332 *Pembroke*, *Crampwell* 1307 *Ct*, *Crownall*

---

[1] *Buntyngespath* 1460 *Pembroke*.

Close c. 1840 *TA*. 'Crooked spring,' if this sequence of forms is correct. DITCH FM. Cf. *Dichefeld* 1232 *FF*. Near the Devil's Dyke *supra* 34. DRAINER'S DITCH (6″) is *the Drainors ditch* 1678 *FenS*. GOOSE HALL (6″) is so named c. 1840 *TA*. HALLARD'S FEN is *Hallard Fen* ib. It is perhaps to be identified with *Hallode in maresco* 1419 *Ct*. HIGH BRIDGE (6″) is *Haybrige* ib. HIGH TOWN and HIGHTOWN DROVE (6″) are both so named c. 1825 (O.S.). HOWLEM BALK (6″) is *Howland Balk* 1760 *Pembroke*, possibly from hōh and land. HYTHE BRIDGE (6″) is so named c. 1840 (*TA*). KLONDYKE FM (6″) lies away from the village, towards the fen, *v. infra* 357. LARK HALL. Cf. *Larklond* 1398 *MinAcct*, *Larkedene* 1460 *Pembroke*. LITTLE FEN is so named c. 1840 (*TA*). NEWNHAM (6″) is so named in 1446 (*MinAcct*). Cf. Newnham *supra* 43. NEWNHAM DROVE is so named c. 1825 (O.S.). PARSONAGE FM. Cf. *terram persone* 1307 *MinAcct*. PIT'S FM (all 6″). Cf. *Pit Close* c. 1840 *TA*. PRIORY. Cf. *Priory Close* ib. RUNNING GAP (6″) is so named in 1829 (Wells). SOUTHFIELD (Kelly) is *Southfeld* 1232 *FF*. TUNBRIDGE FM (6″). Cf. *Tunbridge Water Close* c. 1840 *TA*. WARBRAHAM FM is *Walbrom* 1398 *MinAcct*, *Walbron* 1504, 1537 *Queens'*. This looks like a derivative of OE brōm, 'broom,' but no certainty is possible.

Chippenham

CHIPPENHAM

Cypeham 1086 ICC, *Cipeham* 1086 InqEl (p), t. Hy 2 (1268) Ch, 1204 FF

Cipenham, -y- t. Wm 1 TextRoff (p), 1170 LibEl, *Cippenham* 1272 Ass, 1327 Pat

Chipeham 1086 DB *et freq* to 1302 FA, *Chippeham* 1235 Pat, 1238 Cl *et freq* to 1285 Ass, *Chyp(p)eham* 1246 FF, 1298 Ass, *Chepeham* 1306 FF

Chipenham 1086 InqEl (p) *et freq* to 1346 FA, FF, *Chippenham, -y-* 1169 Walden *et freq*, *Shipenham* 1285 Ass

Chipham 1226 Pat, 1293 FF

Chepenham 1279 RH, (*cum Budlingham*) 1316 FA *et freq* to 1554 BM, *Chepingham* 1484 IpmR, *Chypnam, -i-* 1540 Fenland vi, 1640 EA vi

'*Cippa*'s hām.' For the personal name cf. Chippenham (PN W 89) and also *campo de Cippenhale* 1272 Ass, in or near Chippenham (C).

BADLINGHAM

> *Bellingeham* 1086 DB, ICC (p), *Belincgesham* 1086 ICC, *Bellincgesham, Billingesham, Bethlingeham* 1086 InqEl (p), *Bedlingham* t. Hy 2 (1268) Ch, *Bedelingham* 13th *Hosp*
>
> *Baddlingham* 1218 *SR*, *Badlingham*, -*y*- 1231 FF *et passim*, *Badelingeham* 1268, 1285 *Ass*, 1302 FA, *Bad(e)lyn(g)ham* 1285 *Ass*, 1400, 1422 FF, *Batlingham* a. 1387 *Walden*
>
> *Bodelingham* 1270 Ch, 1272 *Ass*, *Budlingham* 1316 FA
>
> *Bal(l)ingham* 13th Misc, 14th *Hosp*, *Badyngham* 1272 *Ass*, *Baldingham* 1285 ib.

'The hām of the people of *Bæddel*,' a diminutive of the recorded *Badda*, *v.* ingahām.

GRANGE FM is *grangiam de Chippenham, grangiam monialium de Chykesonde* 13th *Hosp*, *le Brende Grange* 1540 EA vii. The site of the grange was given to the Priory of Chicksands by Rohaise widow of Geoffrey Earl of Essex c. 1155 (Beds. Hist. Rec. Soc. i, 112). *Brende* refers to some unrecorded fire.

LA HOGUE HALL [hɔg hɔ·l] was built by Edward Russell, the commander of the English fleet which defeated the French at La Hogue in 1692 (*Cole* vi, f. 13). It is *La Houge Hall Fm* c. 1840 *TA*, *Hogg Hall* 1851 Gardner.

SOUNDS FM is *Sounde* c. 1135, 1184 *Hosp*, (*le*) *Sund'* 13th ib., *Chalk or Sounds Fm* c. 1825 O.S. Possibly from *sand*, 'sand, sandy soil.' There are sand pits near by. Cf. Sound (Ch), *Sonde* 1274, 1282 DEPN and *v.* Introd. xxxiii.

STANNEL WOOD is so named c. 1825 (O.S.). Cf. *Stahulla* c. 1135 *Hosp*, *Stanhille* 1184 ib., *Stamhell* a. 1387 *Walden*. 'Stone-hill,' *v.* stān, hyll.

WATER HALL and WATERHALL FM (both 6″) are *Water Hall* c. 1825 O.S. and *Water Hall Fm* c. 1840 *TA*. Here lived Matilda *Attewater de Chepenham* (1279 RH).

GIFFORD WOOD (6″) is so named c. 1825 (O.S.) and is probably to be associated with the family of Richard *Giffard* (c. 1238 *Hosp*).

ASH WOOD and LOW PARK CORNER are so named c. 1825 (O.S.). DEER PARK. Cf. *Deer Plantation* c. 1840 *TA*. FOXBURROW PLANTATION. Cf. *Fox(eh)oles* a. 1387 *Walden*, *Fox Burrows* c. 1825 O.S. HEATH

PLANTATION is so named ib. Cf. *Sudhed, Sudhet* t. Hy 2 (1268) Ch, *v.* hǣð. JERUSALEM WOOD (all 6″) is so named c. 1825 (O.S.). Cf. *the Jerusalem Estate* 1751 Blomefield. This was part of the lands *de domo Hospitalis Jerusalem* (1204 FF). PARK FM. Cf. *the Park* c. 1840 *TA*. REDLODGE PLANTATION and ROUNDABOUT PLANTATION (both 6″) are *Red-lodge Pln* and *Round-about* c. 1825 O.S. SCOTLAND (6″) is *Scotland Cottages* c. 1840 *TA* and is perhaps to be associated with (*campo vocat'*) *Scote* 13th *Hosp*, a. 1387 *Walden*.

Fordham

FORDHAM

> (*æt*) *Fordham* c. 972 ASCh, 1086 InqEl *et passim*
> *Fordam* 1086 ICC, 1199, 1200 P, 1284 FA, 1367 Cl, *Fordan* 1495 Paston
> *Fordeham* 1086 DB *et freq* to 1428 FA
> *Forham* 1086 DB, *Fordthham* 1305 FF, *Frodham* 1510 LP

'The hām by the ford.'

NOTE. CARTER ST is *Carter(e)stret(e)* 1397 *Ct*, 1541 *StJohn's* and is to be associated with the family of John *Carter* (1567 *Ct*). KING'S PATH is *Kyngs-path* 1432 CAS xxxviii. Cf. *Kingesdun* t. Ric 1 (1251) Ch. MARKET ST is *le Marketstrete* 1439 *StJohn's*, *-weye* 1448 ib. MILL LANE. Cf. Agatha *ad Molendinum* (1279 RH). MOOR RD is *le Moorstrete, -lane* 1397 *Ct*. WATER LANE is *Waterlane* 1406 *Add*.

BIGGEN COTTAGE[1] (6″) and MOOR FM[2] were the homes of William *atte Byggyngge* (1397 *Ct*) and Richard de *Mora de Fordham* (c. 1258 *Add*), Gilbert de *la More* (1279 FF), Philip *ate More* (1303 Ipm) and Henry *in the Mor* (1327 SR). *v.* bigging, mōr.

BASSINGBOURNE MANOR FM[3] and LORDS BARN (6″) are probably to be associated with the families of Humfrey de *Bassingburne* (1280 FF) which came from Bassingbourn *supra* 52 and John and Henry *le Lord* (1327 SR).

BLOCK FM is *Black Fm* 1829 Wells. *v.* Blockmoor Fen *infra* 198. COLLIN'S HILL (6″) is *Collings Hill* 1702, 1727 *Christ's*, *Collin's Hill* 1761 ib. FORDHAM ABBEY is so named in 1829 (Wells). FORDHAM BRIDGE (6″) is *pontem de Fordham* 1272 *Ass*. FORDHAM MOOR is

---

[1] Cf. *Byggynscroft* 1379 *Spinney*, *Biggin Cottage* 1829 Wells.
[2] *le mor* 1316 Pembroke.
[3] *Bassyngbornes* 1428 FF, *the manr of Bassyngbowrnes* t. Hy 8 *Rental*.

Fordhammoor 1397 *Ct.* HALL YARD WOOD (6″). Cf. *Hall Yard* 1616 *Christ's.* TRINITY HALL (6″) was purchased by Trinity Hall, Cambridge, in 1563 (L 194). UNDERDOWN PLANTATION (6″). Cf. *Under Down* c. 1825 O.S. WEST FEN is *Westfen* 1279 RH.

Isleham

ISLEHAM [izləm]

> (*in*) *Yselham* 895 (12th) BCS 571, 1167–8 P, (*Parua*) 1236 Barnwell, *Iselham* 12th RegRoff *et passim* to 1548 Pat, *Iseleham* 1256 (1332) Ch, *Islam* 1270 *ElyF*, 1381 Pat, *Isleham* 1284 Misc *et passim*, *Iselesham* 13th *Hosp*, *Isselham* 1316 FF, 1330 Pat, 1333 Cl, *Iselam* 1363 FF, t. Hy 8 *Rental*, *Isham* 1396 Pat, *Islem* 1440 ib., *Iseham al. Iselham* 1451 ib.
>
> *Gyselham* 1086 ICC, 1304 *MinAcct*, *Gisleham* 1086 DB, *Giselham* t. Wm 1 RegRoff, TextRoff, c. 1180 *ElyF*, c. 1250 *ElyCh*, *Yiselham* 1326 Pat
>
> *Hislaham* c. 1140 Whitby, *Hyselham*, -i- 1218 *SR et freq* to 1433 Cl, *Hiselam* 1268 *Ass*, *Hisenham* 1312 Whitby, *Heselham* 1432 *MinAcct*
>
> *Isilham* 1284 FA, 1331–9 Pat, 1334 *Ct*, 1376 FF
>
> *Yeselham* (*magna*) 1285 *Ass et freq* to 1416 Cl, *Yesilham* 1316 FF, 1327 SR, 1328 Banco, 1349 BM, (*Litle-*) 1322 *Spinney*, *Eselham* 1377 IpmR, *Yestelham* 1429 Pat

'*Gīsla's hām.*' This is the same personal name which is found in Islington (PN Mx 124).

CHAIR DROVE (6″) is a short straight road leading to the Lark. The first element of this name is found in *Charlake* 1425 *Ct* and *Charelakeload* 1611 *AddCh*. The load, we are told, flowed from *Thorneye fryth* (*v.* Thorney Hill *infra* 221) by *Chare Lake* to *Thirtyware Lake*. This was earlier *þritawere* 1251 *ElyCouch*, *þrittywere*, *þrithiwere* 1277 *Ely*, *Thrittewere* 1303 Sacr, and was in the great stream, i.e. Ouse. Further, the *load called Charelake* passed from the corner of *Thorneyfryth* to a place in *Mildenhallstreame*, i.e. the Lark (cf. *supra* 7), "between the common Mowefenn of the towne of Ely called *the lytle Shield* (Shell Fm *infra* 200) and the commen fenn of the town of Soham called *Mettly fenn*" (*v.* Mettleham *infra* 200). A later hand has added in the margin *Cawldelfen lode* (*v.* Cawdle Fen *infra* 222). The topography is difficult as the courses of both the Ouse and the Lark have changed. It may be that the old course of the Lark was once known as *Chare*. This name (*v.* Chear Fen *supra* 149) would be appropriate to the winding course of the old Lark If that is the case, there is some support for Skeat's suggestion (PN Sf 33–4) that the old name for the sluggish Lark was *lacu*, found as the first element in Lackford (Sf), DB *Lacheforda*, on its banks.

SPOONER'S DROVE (6″) is probably to be associated with the family of William *Spooner* (1780 Poll). Cf. *Spooners Close* c. 1840 *TA*.

BASKEYBAY is *Baskey Bay* 1829 Wells. BLACK DROVE (6″). Cf. *Black Fen Drove* c. 1840 *TA*. CAUDLEHOLE DROVE. Cf. *Cadwell* 1514 *Spinney*, *Caudle Hole* c. 1840 *TA* and Caudle Ditch *supra* 144. COMMON GATE DROVE. Cf. *the Common gate* 1689 Pembroke, *Common Gate Drove* c. 1840 *TA*. *Gate* is here probably ON **gata**, 'road.' CROOKED DITCH (all 6″). Cf. *Crooked Dyke Ground* c. 1840 *TA*. EAST FEN, WEST FEN DROVE (6″) and HALL FM are so named c. 1840 (*TA*). FIELD FM (6″) is so named c. 1825 (O.S.). INHAMS. Cf. *Borlesynnham* 15th *Pembroke*, *Enamgate* 16th *ib.*, *Inhams* c. 1840 *TA* and *v.* innam. ISLEHAM FERRY is so named in 1829 (Wells). ISLEHAM FIELD. Cf. *campis de Giselham* c. 1250 *ElyCh*, *Isleham Feilde* 1689 *Pembroke*, *v.* feld. KNAVES ACRE DROVE (all 6″). Cf. *Knaves Acre* c. 1840 *TA* and *infra* 357. LARK HALL FM is *Larkhouse Fm* ib. LITTLE LONDON (DROVE) (6″). Cf. *infra* 357. PRIORY (6″). Cf. *the pryory londe* 16th *Pembroke* (belonging to Isleham Priory). THE TEMPLE is *Manerium Templi* 1290 RegRoff, *the Temple* c. 1840 *TA*. The Master of the Templars in England had a messuage here in 1279 (RH). THE WASH (6″) is *Wash* c. 1840 *TA*.

Kennett

KENNETT

Kenet 1086 ICC *et freq* to 1488 Pat, (*juxta Kentford*) 1320 FF, (*cum Badelingham*) 1327 SR, *Keneth* 1302 FA, *Keneyt* 1327 Ipm, 1372, 1384 Pat, *Kenett* 1570 SR
Chenet 1086 DB, 1159–62 P (p), *Cheneta* 1086 InqEl
Kentefarye 1279 RH, *Kent cum Kentesford* 1316 FA

Named from the R. Kennett *supra* 7. *Kent(es)ford* is Kentford (Sf), also on the Kennett, sometimes stated to be in Cambridgeshire. For Badlingham *v. supra* 190. *farye* is presumably for *ferye*, 'ferry,' with reference to some small ferry across the Kennett. For such an early use of the word cf. PN BedsHu 294.

THE HALL (6″) is *Kennet Hall* 1669 *WMP*.

Landwade

LANDWADE

> *Langwaðe* 1060 (14th) Thorpe 383[1], *Lang(e)worth* 1235 FF, *-wath* 1246–57 *Add*, 1272, 1285 *Ass*, *-uad(e)*, *-wad(e)* 1252 *AD et freq* to 1476 *Ct*, *-wat* 1257 *Add*
>
> *Landuuade* t. Wm 1 RegRoff, TextRoff (p), *Lantwadam* a. 1194 Landwade, *Landwad(e)* 1236 Barnwell *et freq* to 1475 Pat, *-wath(e)* 1195 FF *et freq* to 1366 Ipm, *-wat(e)* c. 1250 *Add*, 1285 FF, 1341 NI, *-waye* 1279 RH, *-wod(e)* 1426 Cl, 1448 Pat
>
> *parva Lonwatha* 1176–85 Templars
>
> *Lanwad(e)* 1236 Barnwell *et freq* to 1682 Landwade, *-wath(e)* c. 1250 SR, *Lanewade* 1425 Landwade, *Llanwade* 1540 CAPr xxvii, *Laynewarde al. Langwith* 1541 *MinAcct*, *Lanward* 1570 SR, 1644 PR i, *Lanworthe* 1576 Saxton, *Lan(d)ward (al. Lanworth)* 1604 *Atkyns*
>
> *Landewade* 1298 *Ass et freq* to 1419 Cl, *Landewath* 1360 Ipm

This is a difficult name. The second element was probably originally OE *wæd*, 'ford,' with later substitution of the cognate Scand *vað*, the English word ultimately surviving. As a first element, *Lang-* and *Land-* are almost equally early, but the latter is much more frequent than for Lamport (PN Bk 48), DB *Lan(d)port*, Lamport (PN Sx 430), 1054 *Lantport*, and Old Langport (PN K 483–4), DB *Lam-*, *Lantport*, all of which certainly derive from OE *lang-port*. Similar difficulties of interpretation arise in Landford (PN W 386–7), DB *Langeford*, 1242 *Laneford*, 1295 *Landeford*. Here the choice lies between *lang*, 'long' and *lanu*, 'lane.' The latter is impossible for Landwade. The ford here is on the county boundary, where the road crosses the small 'sluggish stream, at present full of watercress[2],' and although there were two water-mills here in the 14th century, the stream can hardly have been wide enough to justify the name 'long ford.' Langford (PN Nt 205–6), with a long series of forms in *Lande-* and a place hard-by called *Landeleie*, is derived from a personal name *Landa*, but forms for Landwade with a medial *e* are late and rare. Ekwall, who gives

---

[1] From an inspeximus. [2] Landwade 2.

only forms in *Land-*, has suggested (DEPN) that the first element is OE *land*, and while admitting that "the exact meaning of the name *land-ford* is not clear," suggests 'chief ford' as a possible explanation. This is not satisfactory for a ford through so small a stream. OE *land* is used however in the sense 'region, district, province' (BT), and the ford may have been so called because the road here crossed from the county of Suffolk to that of Cambridge, perhaps at a time when this was the boundary between East Anglia and Mercia. This part of Suffolk forms a curious projection into Cambridgeshire (by which it is almost surrounded), the historical reason for which is unknown. For a similar use of *land*, cf. Landmoth (PN NRY 206, PN D liii), DB *Landemot*, 'district meeting-place,' and, possibly, *Landelod(e)* 1221 *ElyA*, 1251 *ElyCouch* in Stretham on the southern boundary of the Isle of Ely. When the name was Scandinavianised, it was probably associated with the common Danish place-name *Langevad*. Hence the numerous and early forms in *Lang(e)-*. Cf. Langwith (PN ERY 269), earlier *Lang(e)wath*. The real difficulty in this interpretation is that one would expect a ford with such a name to be on a route of some importance. The present road does not meet this requirement. There was, however, a very ancient trackway from Little Thetford and Old Fordey (*infra* 198) round the south of Soham Mere to Wicken which may have continued round the edge of the high land to Landwade. Cf. also *viam regiam in Al(l)ing(ge)worye* in the bounds of Landwade (1279 RH), *Hillingworth* 1331 *Add*, *Helyngeworth* 1402 ib., and *pontis et calseti de Languade* (1360 *ElyC*).

Snailwell

SNAILWELL

    Sneillewelle c. 1050 (c. 1350) KCD 907, 1170 LibEl, 1387 *Walden*, *-uuelle*, *-a* 1086 InqEl, *Sneiluuelle* c. 1050 (12th) LibEl, *-well(e)* 1242 Fees, 1279 RH, 1354 FF, *Sneilewelle* c. 1060 (14th) *ElyM*, 1302 FA, *-uuelle*, *-a* 1086 ICC, InqEl, 1193 P, *Snail(l)(e)-*, *-ay-*, *-ey-* 1203 Cur *et freq* to 1552 Pat, *Snaylewall'* 1254 Val, *Snalewell* 1576 Saxton

    Snegeluuelle 1086 InqEl, *Sneyelwell* 1304 FF

    Snelleuuelle 1086 DB, InqEl, *Snelewell* 1195 FF, 1272 *Ass*, 1348 Pat, *Snelywell* 1330 FF

    Sneleswell(e) 1176 Percy, 1272 *Ass*, *Sneil(l)es-*, *-ey-*, *-ay-*, *-ai-* 1214 Cur *et freq* to 1436 Pat

    Sneinewell 1268 *Ass*, *Sneyneswell* 1272 Pat

This is probably from OE *snægel-wielle*, 'snail-stream,' used of a sluggish stream, the "little river Snail" which "crawls away into the adjacent fen" (Conybeare 176). This would seem on the whole more likely than Ekwall's "stream frequented by snails" (DEPN). *v.* wielle, and for the last forms *v.* IPN 106.

GRAVELPIT PLANTATION. Cf. *Gravel Pit* c. 1840 *TA.* PHILADELPHIA (both 6″) is in the extreme south of the parish, *v. infra* 357.

Soham

SOHAM [*olim* soum]

(*æt*) *Sægham* c. 1000 (11th) ASWills
Saham 1086 ICC, DB, InqEl *et passim* to 1463 FF, (*juxta mariscum de Ely*) c. 1195 *Pembroke,* (*cum Berewey*) 1218 *SR,* (*prope Ely*) 1285 *Pembroke*
Seham 1170 LibEl *et freq* to 1327 SR (p), *Sigham* 1198 P
Soham 1294 FF, 1353 *MinAcct et passim*
Some 1427 Pat, 1570 Fenland iv, (*Sohome or*) 1510 LP, 1628 Cai, *Soome* 1541 PCC

This is a difficult name. If the Snail, which probably owed its name to its sluggish flow (*v.* Snailwell *supra* 195), always followed its present course along what is now Soham Lode[1], the first element in Soham might well be an OE **sæg*, 'slow-moving stream,' as in Seabrook (PN Bk 97, PN D 455), Sellake (ib. 550) and possibly Seaton (R), *v.* DEPN. But we must note also Saham Toney (Nf), DB *Saham*, 1300 P *Seham*, and Earl and Monk Soham (Sf), DB *Saham*, 13th Misc *Saham ad Stagnum*. So long as there are no forms in *Sæg-, Sag-* for these names, they are best derived from OE *sæ, *sā* in the sense 'lake.' Ekwall derives the Cambridgeshire Soham in the same way, discounting the form *Sægham* (RN 284-5, DEPN). It is our oldest form, however, and is supported by *Sigham.* The first element was thus probably an OE **sæg, *sāg*, as suggested by Skeat, who called attention to Bavarian *saig*, Tyrolese *sege, söga* from the stem **saig-*, 'a depression or swamp.' In early times Soham was invariably associated with Soham Mere, cf. "Saham quae est ad stagnum," "Seham quae est villa juxta stagnum" (LibEl 21, 183), "Seham quae est villa juxta stagnum, quod volentibus ire in Heli quondam periculosum navibus, nunc, facta via per palustre harundi-

[1] This is doubtful, *v.* CAPr xxxiii, 116-17.

netum, transitur pedibus" (WMP 147, 153, 318). The first element may thus have referred to the mere and the meaning be 'swamp, inundated land, lake.' Saham and the two Sohams would then have the same meaning, 'hām by the lake.' Cf. Sealodes *infra* 200.

NOTE. BROOK DAM is *Brook Dam Lane* 18.. *Map.* Now NEW ST. BROOK ST is *Brokstrete* c. 1270 *Pembroke.* CHERRYTREE LANE is named from *The Cherrytree* (inn) c. 1825 O.S. CHURCHGATE ST is *Cherchegatestrete* 1462 *Pembroke.* CLAY ST is *Cleystrete* 1540 ib., *Clay or Meer Street, Bull Lane or Clay Street* 18.. *Map.* Cf. *le Cley* 1397 *Ct, le Cleymere* 1404 ib. The subsoil is clay. CROSS GREEN is *Cross Green or Wallis Hill* 18.. *Map.* Here was the home of Symon *atte Cros* (1374 *Ct*). FOUNTAIN LANE is *Fountain Lane or Lion Lane* 18.. *Map.* Named from the *Fountain Inn.* HALL ST is *le Hallestrete* 1397 *Ct.* Cf. *Hallewey* 1452 *Pembroke.* Here in 1272 lived Thomas *ad Aulam* (*MinAcct*). HIGH ST is *Highstreete* 1601 *Eg.* LONGMERE LANE is *Long-meare lane* 1601 Fenland ii. Cf. *Langemere* 1221 *ElyA, Langmore* 1658 BedL. NORTHFIELD RD is *Northfield Lane or Bancroft Lane* 18.. *Map.* PADDOCK ST is *Paddocke Streete* 1645 *Eg.* PRATT ST is probably so called from the family of Mabilla and Thomas *Prat* (1312 *SR,* 1374 *Ct*). REDLAND or ROSEFIELD LANE runs past both *Redland Field* and *Rose Field* in 18.. *Map.* The second is *Roluesfeld* 1302 *Pembroke, Rosefeild* 1584 *Eg, Roastfield Hill* 1720 *BLAcct.* The first element probably goes back to the Anglo-Norman *Rolf.* SAND ST is *Sandstret* 1404 *Ct.* There is an out-crop of sandy gravel here. SPEED LANE is *Speeds Lane or Cross Lane* 18.. *Map.* STAPLES'S LANE is probably to be associated with the family of Edward *Staples* (1768 *Pembroke*). TANNER'S LANE. Cf. *Tanners* 1343 *MinAcct.* THORN ST is *Thornstrete* 1510 *Pembroke* and was probably the home of Henry de *Spinis* (1312 *SR*). It is bordered by high thorn-bushes. TOWN END is *Soham town's end* 1604 *Atkyns.* VAXEN LANE is a corruption of 'Backs and Ends' (School).

BARCHAM FM

Bercham 1235 Ch, c. 1280 *Pembroke,* 1343 *MinAcct,* 1397 *Ct,*
   Berc(h)gham c. 1280 *Pembroke, Bercheham* 1349 *MinAcct*
Barcham 1272 *Ass,* 1558 Fenland iv
Birch(e)ham 1272 *MinAcct,* t. Eliz *Bodl*

'Birch ham(m),' *v.* bierce.

BARWAY, with BARWAY FEN (6″) and BARRAWAY SIDING (6″)

Bergeia, -eie, -eya 1155 P *et freq* to 1230 ib., *Berheia(m)* 1158–77 ib., c. 1170 *ElyM, Bercheia, -eya* 1170–90 P, *Bericheia* 1174 ib., *Berecheya, -eia* 1181–5 ib., *Bereg(h)eia* 1183–93 ib., *Bergee* 1190 *Pembroke, Burgeye* 1218 FF
Ber(e)wey(e) 1218 *SR et freq* to 1494 *Ct,* (*iuxta Saham*) 1298 *Ass,* (*juxta Middilton*) 1369 *St John's,* (*cum Henneye*) 1470 IpmR,

Ber(e)wy(e) 1251 *ElyCouch*, 1260 Ass, 1277 *Ely*, 1379 Cl, *Berewe* 1279 RH

Barewe 1265 Misc, 1285 Abbr, *Barueye* 1285, 1291 *Pembroke*, 1285, 1320 Pat[1], *Bar(e)wey* 1359 *ElyF*, 1448 *Pembroke*, 1564 *Ct*, *Barwye* 1360 Sacr, *Barway(e)* 1602 Fenland ii, 1611 *AddCh*, (-*ffen*) 1636 BedL

Bar(r)oway(e) t. Hy 8 *Pembroke*, 1544–86 Fenland iv, 1561 *Ct*, *Barraway* 1604 *Atkyns*, *Barrow Fen* c. 1840 *TA*

'Hill-island,' *v.* beorh, ēg. Barway and Barraway are alternative developments. "It is a myerie island...and is environed with fens on each side" (*Atkyns*).

BLAKENEY FEN (6″). Cf. *Brodblakeneye* 1407 *Ct*, *Blakene(hull)* 1420 ib., *Blackneye* 1562, 1585 ib., *Blakeney Fen* c. 1840 *TA*. 'Black low-lying land or island,' from the colour of the peat, *v.* blæc, ēg.

BLOCKMOOR FEN is *Blokmoor* 1397 *Ct*, *Blakemere* 1415 ib., *the Block Fen* 1814 *Pembroke*, *Blackmoor Fen* c. 1825 O.S., *Blockmoor* c. 1840 *TA*. Probably 'black marsh,' but in this name, as in Blockmoor Fen, Block Moors, Block Fen *infra* 241, 230, 250 and Block Fen Droveway *supra* 132, there are difficulties. ME and EME forms in *blok-* may go back to OE *blāc* which is found side by side with the more usual *blæc*, 'black,' used of the dark peat-coloured marsh. They may equally well go back to OE *blāc*, 'pale,' but these are peat fens and black, and when covered with undergrowth, green[2].

CLIPSALL FIELD and CORNER. Cf. *Clippeshal(e)*, -*y*- 1262 *AD et freq* to 1364 *MinAcct*, *Clypsale(fen)*, -*i*- 1324 *StJohn's et freq* to 1397 *Ct*, *Clipsalefelde* 1467 *Pembroke*, *Clippsalls* 1601 *Eg*, *Clipsall feild* 1654 *Pembroke*, (*Corner*) 1687 *BLAcct*. 'Clipp's nook,' *v.* healh. For this Anglo-Scandinavian personal name cf. Clipston(e) (PN BedsHu 122, PN Nth 111, PN Nt 73) and also *Clippeshull'* 1228 *FF* (in Melbourn), *Clippescroft* c. 1280 *Hosp* (in Ashley).

DELPH BRIDGE is *le Delfbregge* 1397 *Ct*, *Delphbridge* 1604 *Atkyns*, *Dull Bridge* 1675 Ogilby. 'The bridge over the *Delf*,' now the Crooked Drain *infra* 209.

OLD FORDEY FM is *Fordey(lake)* 1480, 1526 *StJohn's*, (*Great*) 1541 *Spinney*, *Fordy* 1604 *Atkyns*, *Fordea* 1636 BedL. NEW FORDEY FM (6″) is *Little Fordey* 1541 *Spinney*. 'Low-lying land by the ford,' *v.*

---

[1] Printed *Barneye*.   [2] *Ex inf.* Major Gordon Fowler.

ford, ēg. An old chalk and gravel ford through the Ouse has been discovered by the site of Little Thetford Chapel, with a piled causeway in the peat leading to it from Fordey, *v.* CAPr xxxiii, 112.

HARRIMERE DRAIN. Cf. *Hauering(e)mere, -yng-* 1221 *ElyA*, 1251 *ElyCouch et freq* to 1564 *Ct, maram de Haueringe* 1279 *ElyM, Auering(g)(g)(e)mere* 1251 *ElyCouch,* 1277 *Ely,* 1279 RH, *la mare de Aringe* 1285 *Ass, Herymer* 1531 *Cole* xlvi, *Har(r)ymeare* 1561 *Ct, -mare* 1583 ib., 1617 Fenland v, *-more* 1611 *AddCh, Harramore* 1612 *Eg.* The first element of this name is probably a singular name in *-ing* identical with the second element in Quadring (L), *Quadheuringe, Quedhaueringe* 1086 DB, *Quadringe* 1271 *Ass*[1]. This is from OE **hæfer,* cognate with a lost Ger *haver,* 'higher, raised ground,' Dan *Hevring, v.* ing and PN in *-ing* 85–6. The mere has now disappeared, but several neighbouring names have reference to rising land in the fens. Cf. Barway *supra* 197, Henny Hill (*infra*) and Fordy Hill and Padney Hills. The actual reference may, perhaps, be to the piled causeway mentioned *s.n.* Old Fordey *supra* 198. Hence 'lake by the piece of higher, dry land in the fen.'

THE HASSE, GREAT and LITTLE HASSE FM and DROVE [hæsi]. Cf. *Wolmereshaslond* 1404 *Ct, the Hasse* 1636 BedL, *Hassecroft* 1636 *Eg, Great, Little Hasse Drove* 18.. *Map, The Hasse of Soham* 1829 Wells. Cf. also *Hassecroft* 1251 *ElyCouch,* 1277 *Ely, Hascroft(e)* 1460, 1587 *Ct,* (*dyke*) 1428 Imb (Tydd St Giles), *Hesland* c. 1295 *ElyM, Prykkeshasse* 15th *Ely* (Sutton), *Haselond* 15th Pembroke (Isleham), *Hassedole* 1252 Rams in Upwood (Hu). *hasse* is a difficult word. The only suggestion that can be made is that it is the stem from which the equally difficult OE *hassuc,* 'coarse grass,' is derived. The sense 'coarse grass' would not be inappropriate for places in these fenland parishes.

HENNY HILL and FM

  Haneia 1086 DB, InqEl
  Henney 1086 InqEl, *Heneie(h)am* 1144 *ElyD,* 1144, 1229 *ElyM, Hen(n)ey(e), -eie* 1190 Pembroke *et freq* to 1490 Ipm, (*Hyll*) 1557 Fenland iv, *Hennehill* 1636 BedL
  Enneye 1279 RH

---

[1] Ekwall now (DEPN) prefers to take the second element in this name as a patronymic. The first is OE *cwēad,* 'dirt,' with reference to the fens here.

'Island frequented by wild-fowl,' v. henn, ēg. Described as an island in 1086 (DB, InqEl).

METTLEHAM FM is *Metlehom* c. 1280 *Pembroke, Metleham* ib., 1343–49 *MinAcct, Mettlham* 1397 *Ct, Mettilham* 1397, 1404 ib., *Mittilham* 1397 ib., *Metlam* 1503 *Pembroke,* 1588 Fenland iv, *Meatlam* 17th *AdvL, Great, Little Metland* 1636 BedL. This is not an easy name. It may possibly be from OE *middel,* 'middle' and ham(m). There was a lost *Littleham* in the parish, forms for which are given under Ham Corner *infra* 202. This may have been on the far side of Mettleham from Barcham. Cf. Mitley (PN Nth 68), *Mittelowehul* t. Hy 3, probably from *middel.*

NO DITCH FIELD is *New(e)dich(e)* 1235 Ch, 1467 *Pembroke, -felde* 1349 *MinAcct, Neudich(feld)* 1343–64 ib., *Nowdich(felde)* 1397 *Ct, No(o)-dych(e)fen* 1404 *Ct,* 1541 *Spinney, Nowedych* 1439 *St John's, Noditch-(feld)* t. Eliz *Bodl.* 'New ditch,' v. nīwe, dīc. For the sound-development v. Introd. xxxv.

WET and DRY SEALODES (6″) is *(le) Se(e)lode* 1260 Ass, 1279 RH, 1343, 1486 *MinAcct, Seuelodes* 1277 *Ely, Wet, Dry Sealodes* 18.. *Map.* This is an area of marsh adjoining Soham Mere and was probably originally the name of a watercourse running from the mere to the Ouse, possibly that now called Soham Lode *(infra* 201). The first element is thus probably identical with that of Soham *supra* 196, v. (ge)lād.

SHELL FM. Cf. *Sceldwere* 1221 *ElyA,* 1251 *ElyCouch,* 1277 *Ely, Sheldesstreng, Echelmere* 1251 *ElyCouch,* 1277 *Ely, (le) Sheld(e) (Litil-)* 1425 *Ct, (Grete-)* 1471 ib., *(marisc. voc.) le Hall shelde* 1475 ib., *Great Sheild* 1582 ib., *Shell (Lake)* 1612 *Eg, Ely Greate (Little) Shell* 1632 Hondius, 1690 Lea, *Little Shell or East Eastmore* 1637 BedL, *Moon-shell* 1658 ib., *Shell Barn* c. 1840 *TA.* The farm is on the Ely boundary. In 1632 *Shell* was a stretch of marsh near Burnt Fen on both sides of the Ouse. Greatshell was near Shippea, Littleshell near Weltmore. The name thus covered a large stretch of low-lying land on both sides of the river. It is probably OE *sceldu,* 'shallowness, shallow place' and, if *Echelmere* (in Littleport) is to be relied on, may have been the name of a mere. The second element in *Sceldwere* (in Littleport) is wēr, 'fishing weir,' and in *Sheldesstreng* is ON *strengr,* 'water-course' (cf. Ellingstring, PN NRY 231), and this may be identical with the later *Shell Lake* (v. lacu, 'sluggish stream'). Another example of *sheld* is apparently found in *Grenesheld ad Gretho* in Cambridge (t. John Township). Cf. also Shelford *supra* 87.

SOHAM MERE is *mara de Saham* 1086 ICC, DB, *le Meer* 1391 *MinAcct*, *v.* mere.

SOHAM LODE was probably by the home of Richard de *la Lad'* (1234 Cl), *v.* (ge)lād.

DAY'S FM, HICK'S DROVE, HODGE'S HILL[1], KEY'S CROFT (all 6″), LEONARD'S FM, NEWMAN'S POND[2] (6″) and SLACK'S HILL (6″) are probably to be associated with the families of John *Deye* (1404 *Ct*), Robert *Hicks* (c. 1840 *TA*), John *Hogge* (1353 Pat), Elizabeth *Key* (c. 1840 *TA*), George *Leonard* (ib.), Robert *Neuman* (1370 Pat) and Jeremy *Slack* (1680 *FenS*).

ANGLE COMMON is so named c. 1825 (O.S.). ANGLE FM is *The Angle Farm* ib., from ME *angle*, Fr *angle* in the sense 'outlying spot or corner,' *v.* NED *s.v. angle* sb.[2] They lie on the opposite side of the river, away from the village, cf. The Angle *infra* 287. ASH CLOSES is so named in 1814 (*Pembroke*). ASH TREE FM. Cf. *Forromes ashen tree* 1601 Fenland ii. BANCROFT FIELD is *Bancroft(e)* 1364 *MinAcct*, *Bangcroft* 1502 Fenland ii, *Bancrofft felde* t. Hy 8 *Pembroke*, *Bamcroft* t. Eliz *Bodl.* 'Bean-croft,' *v.* bēan. BARWAY BRIDGE is *Barraway fen bridge* 1672 *FenL*, *v.* Barway *supra* 197. BLACK DROVE (all 6″) is so named c. 1825 (O.S.). THE BRACKS is *Bracks* c. 1840 *TA*. Cf. *Brackelake* 1393 *Ct*. BRACKS DROVE (6″). Cf. *Bracks Drove Pieces* 1814 *Pembroke*. BROAD HILL. Cf. *Broad Hill ground* ib. BROAD HILL DROVE (6″) is so named in 18.. (*Map*). BROAD PIECE is so named in 1814 (*Pembroke*). BURGESS CORNER (6″). Cf. *Burgess Ware* (near Crowthorne *corner*) 1617 *Wisb.* *v.* wēr. BURRY CROFTS FIELD (6″), now simply [ðə kræfts], is *le Burycroft* 1397 *Ct*, *Burrie Croft* 1558 Fenland iv, *v.* burh (manorial). CASTLES FM. Cf. *Castle Ground* 1680 *FenS*, *Castles Farm* c. 1825 O.S. COLLEGE FM (6″) was part of the Barway manor of the Master and Fellows of Pembroke College in 1604 (*Atkyns*). CROW FEN (6″) is *Crowfen* 1570 *Eg*. CROW HALL. Cf. *Crow Hall* (*closes*) 1814 *Pembroke*, c. 1825 O.S. DOWN FIELD (6″) is *Dune* 13th *Pembroke*, *Doun(e)feld(e)* 1302 ib., 1343–9 *MinAcct*, 1393 *Ct*, (*le*) *Down(e)feld(e)* 1393 *St John's*, 1448 *Pembroke*. EAST FEN COMMON (6″) is *Est(e)fen* 1374, 1393 *Ct*. EAST FEN DROVE (6″) is so named in

---

[1] Cf. *Hodges Lane or Bullard's Lane* 18.. Map.
[2] Cf. *Normans Pond Acre* c. 1840 *TA*.

1814 (*Pembroke*). Eau Fen Fm is *Ee fenne* 1526 *St John's*, *Eau Fenn* 1655 *BLAcct* and is named from (*the ryuer called*) *le Ee* 1452 *Ct*, *v.* ēa and cf. Old South Eau *supra* 10. Eye Hill Drove (6″) is so named in 1821 (Baker), *v.* ēg. Eye Hill Fm. Cf. *Eye Hill* c. 1840 *TA*. Fodder Fen is *Foderfen* 1325 *MinAcct*. Cf. Fodder Fen *infra* 203. Fodder Fen Drove (6″) is so named in 1829 (Wells). Foxlow Field is *Floxlewe* (sic) 1235 *Ch*, *Foxlow Felde* c. 1465 *Pembroke*. 'Fox hill,' *v.* hlāw, hlǣw. Frith Fm is *le Fryth* 1397 *Ct*, *v.* fyrhþ(e). Gault Pit. Cf. *Gault Piece* c. 1840 *TA*. Goose Fen is so named in 1840 (*TA*). Cf. *Gosmere* 13th *ElyE*, *Gosemore* 1600 *Ct*. Goose Fen Bridge (all 6″) is *Goose fenn bridge* 1699 *SewersA*. Great Fen is *Great Freffen* 1630 *Eg*. Cf. *Frythfen* 1343 *MinAcct*. Near Frith Fm *supra*. Great Fen Drove (6″) is so named c. 1825 (O.S.). Green Hills is so named in 1814 (*Pembroke*). Cf. *Grenehowe* 1324 *St John's*, *Grane-howe* 1484 ib., *v.* grēne, hōh and cf. Grinnell Hill *supra* 60. Half Acre Fm is *Halfe Acre* c. 1650 *Rental*, (*House*) 1604 *Atkyns*. Ham Corner (6″) is perhaps to be associated with *Litleham* 1349 *MinAcct*, *v.* hamm. Hodson's Fm is *Hodsons* c. 1840 *TA*. The Holt is so named ib. Horse Bridge is *Horsecroft Bridge* 1665 Fenland ii. Horse Crofts (all 6″) is *Horsecrofte* 1343 *MinAcct*. North and South Horse Fen are *Hors(e)croftf(f)en* 1393–7 *Ct*, 1541 *Spinney*, *the Horse-fen* 1814 *Pembroke*. Wet Horse Fen (6″) (near Fordham Moor) is *Fordham horse Fen* 1612 *Eg*, *Wet Horse Fen* 18.. *Map*. Horsefen Drove (6″) is *Horse Drove* 1829 Wells. All these places are named from an extensive fen round Horse Crofts. Hundred Acres is *The Hundred Acres* c. 1825 O.S. Lode End Bridge (6″). Cf. *Lodesende* 1277 *Ely*. Long Dolver Drove is so named in 1814 (*Pembroke*), *v. infra* 352. The Lots (6″) is *fenground called Common Lots* 1658 BedL, *Soham Lotts* 1699 *SewersA*. Cf. The Lots *supra* 150. Mere Side is *ye Mare sid* 1602 Fenland ii, *v.* Soham Mere *supra* 201. Mettleham Drove is *Soham Metlam Drove* 1687 *BLAcct*, *v.* Mettle-ham *supra* 200. Mill Croft is so named c. 1840 (*TA*). Moat Closes (all 6″) is *the Mote Closes* 1814 *Pembroke*. North Field is so named c. 1840 (*TA*). Parish Bush Drove (6″) is *Parysbush* 1604 *Atkyns*. This is on the Isleham boundary. Qua Fen Common [kɑˑfen] is *Caffen*, *Quaffen al. Calffen* 1636 BedL, *Calf Fen* 1637 ib., (*Common*) c. 1825 O.S., *Qua Fen* c. 1840 *TA*, *Qua Common* 18.. *Map*. Redland Field (6″) is so named in 1814 (*Pembroke*). Cf. *Litelredlonde* 1400 *Ct*. Probably 'red-land,' *v.* rēad, land. There is a good deal of red marl here (School). St John's Fm belonged to St John's College,

Cambridge. LONG SANDFORD. Cf. *Sandford Hill* 18.. *Map.* SAYER'S
LAKE DROVE and FIELD (all 6″) are so named ib. Cf. *Say's Lake Field,
Sear's Lake Closes* 1814 Pembroke, *Searls Lake* c. 1840 *TA.* SEDGE
FEN is so named in 1604 (*Atkyns*). Cf. Sedge Fen *infra* 204. SHADE
COMMON is *Shade Common or Towns End Sheate* 18.. Map. Cf. *the
Shade* 1814 Pembroke, *Soham Shade* c. 1825 O.S. SHORT BUTTS (6″)
is so named in 1814 (*Pembroke*). SMALL PATH (6″) is *Smalpath* 1397
Ct. SOHAM CAUSEWAY is *calcetum de Saham* 1322 Sacr, *Soham Causey*
1604 *Atkyns, Soame Calcy* 1636 BedL. SOHAM COTES is *Soham Coates*
1668 *BLAcct.* SOHAM FEN is *Saham Fen* 1425 *Ct, Soame Fennes* 1636
BedL. SOHAM TUNNEL DROVE and DRAIN (6″). Cf. *Soham Tunnell*
1720 *BLAcct, Tunnel Drove Drain* 1829 Wells. STUDFIELD FM is
Stutfelde 1528 Pembroke, *-folde* 1551 ib., *-field* (*Closes*) 18.. *Map.* If
the forms are to be trusted, the first element is OE *stūt*, 'gad-fly.'
TIGER COTTAGES. Cf. *Tiger Inn* 18.. *Map.* TILED HO FM is *Tile
House* c. 1825 O.S. THE WASH. Cf. *Wash Land* c. 1840 *TA* and
The Wash *infra* 212. THE WEATHERALLS (all 6″) is *Weatheralls* ib.

Wicken

WICKEN

> *Wich* 1086 ICC, *Wicha* 1086 DB
> *Wicrena* 1125–35 (1337) YCh, *Wicre(s)* 1156–8, 1160–71 (1337) ib.
> *Wiken, -y-* c. 1200 Deed *et freq* to 1570 SR, *Wykyn(e), -i-* 1337
>   Pembroke *et freq* to 1541 MinAcct, *Wykyng* 1504 St John's, 1540
>   Fenland vi, *Wycken, Wyckham* 1552 Pat
> *Wikes, -y-* 1208 Cur, 1218 SR *et freq* to 1428 FA, *Wykis* 1279 RH,
>   *Wykys* 1327 SR, 1419 Cl
> *Wyk(e)* 1227 FF, 1285 *Ass,* 1299 QW, 1341, 1353 Pat

'Dairy-farm(s),' *v.* wīc, with variation, first between the singular
and plural and secondly between the strong and weak plurals, cf.
Wicken (PN Nth 107–8), Wicken Bonhunt (PN Ess 544), Wyken
(PN Wa 192) and Coton *supra* 74.

NOTE. DOCKING'S LANE and HAWE'S LANE are probably to be associated
with the families of John *Dorking* and James *Hawes* (c. 1840 *TA*).

FODDER FEN (DROVE) (6″). Cf. (*treys acres de*) *fodder fen* 1345 *Cart
Misc, the fother fenn* 1541 Spinney, *Fodder Fen* c. 1840 *TA.* A fen
from which fodder was obtained. Cf. Frith Fen *supra* 179 and *fenfoder*
1356 *Extent* (Stretham and Wisbech), 'tithes of grain, hay, thacke

and *ffoder'* 1540 *MinAcct* (Waterbeach), *Fodderfen* 1326 ib. (Waterbeach), *le fodderfen* 1431 *Peterhouse* (Haddenham), *fodderfen* 1406 *ElyF* (Lakenheath, Sf). In Lincolnshire we have the term *thacfother*, of doubtful significance, but probably a payment for licence to cut rushes or for the relaxation of thatching services (Croyland 93).

SEDGE FEN DROVE (6″). Cf. *Segfrythfen* 1345 *CartMisc*, *Seggefen* 1449 Pat. The name is self-explanatory. Cf. Frith Fen *supra* 179 and *Segenefenweybrede* 1251 *ElyCouch* (Fen Ditton), *Sechfen* 13th *St John's* (Haddenham), *Seggefen* 1427 *Ct* (March), *le Seggeffen* 1449 *Ct* (Ely).

SPINNEY ABBEY

> (*de*) *Spineto* 1227 FF *et freq*
> *Spinney* 1267, 1301 Pat, 1438 Imb, (*La*) *Spyn(n)ey(e)* 1279 RH
> *et freq* to 1403 EA xiii, *Spine* c. 1290 *Hosp*, 13th *Cole* xviii
> *Speney(e)* 1374 *Ct et freq* to 1511 CAPr xxxiv

"The spinney," OFr *espinei*, "a place where thorn-trees grow." Cf. "the prior and convent of St Mary and St Cross in *the Spinney* of Wykes" (1269 Pat). Often referred to by its Latinised name *Spinetum*, 'thorn-thicket.'

THORN HALL is *Thornhalecroft* t. Hy 3 AD iii, *Thornhall* 1333 Pat, *Thornham al. Thornhall* 1685 Fenland vi. 'Thorn-covered nook,' *v.* þorn, healh.

UPWARE is *Upwere* 1170 LibEl *et freq* to 1419 Cl, *Hupwere* 1268 *Ass*, *Up(pe)were* 1453–4 *Ct*. 'Upper fishing weir,' *v.* wēr.

DIMMOCK'S COTE[1], GRAY'S FM, HOWE'S FM and ST EDMUND'S FEN are probably to be associated with the families of Hugo *Dymmok* (1394 *Ct*) and Mr Willis *Dymocke* of *Dymockes Coate* (1669 Ely), John de *Grey* (1327 *Spinney*), John *How* (c. 1840 *TA*) and Geoffrey de *Sco Edmundo* (1285 *Ass*).

AFTERWAY HOUSES. Cf. *Afterway Close* c. 1840 *TA*. AMERICA FM is some distance from the village, *v. infra* 357. CROOKTREE FM (all 6″) and FEN SIDE are so named c. 1825 (O.S.). FIELD FM. Cf. *Wicken field* 1604 *Atkyns*. GREAT WOOD (6″) is *Greatwood or Wicken Ash* c. 1825 O.S. HIGH FEN FM is so named ib. Cf. *Wicken Highfen* 1612 *Eg*. PADNEY is *Padeneye* 1405 BM, *Padney Field* c. 1840 *TA*. Probably 'frogs' low-lying land,' *v.* ēg and cf. Padnal *infra* 222. TITHE FM (6″)

---

[1] *Dymocks, Dymokes cote* 1604 *Atkyns, Dimock Court* 1687 *BLAcct*.

is so named c. 1825 (O.S.). THE WEIGHTS (6″). Cf. (*wood called*) *Wayte* 1541 *Spinney*. WEST HILL is so named c. 1840 (*TA*). WICKEN DOLVERS (6″). Cf. *Dolver, Church Dolver, Great Dolver* ib. and *infra* 352. WICKEN FEN is *Wickin fenn* 1690 Lea. WICKEN LODE is *Wickin Lode* 1636 BedL.

THE ISLE OF ELY

insula…que a solicolis celebri Ely nuncupatur onomate 970 (18th)
  BCS 1265, *insula ely* 1086 InqEl, *Isle dely* c. 1254 Ct, *þe yle of ely* c. 1330 RG, *Ilde of Ely* 1627 PR i
helig ealond c. 1000 OE Bede, *insula de Hely* 1085–6 (13th) Crispin

v. Ely *infra* 213.

NAMES OF BANKS

CRADGE BANK (6″) is (*the*) *Cradge Bank* 1830 BedL, c. 1840 *TA* (Downham, Upwell and Welney), *Scradge Bank* ib. (Coveney and Sutton). *Cradge* is a word used in Eastern England for "a small bank made to keep out water" (1854 NED). Here it is used of the eastern bank of the New Bedford River. It is probably the same word as *cratch* sb.[1] (NED), ME *crecche*, OFr *creche, cresche*, 'manger, crib,' used also of a wooden grating or hurdle. For the change from *cratch* to *cradge*, cf. *crutchback* (1592 NED) and *crudge bak* (1519 ib.) for *crouchback*. *v.* Introd. xxxvi and Addenda lx.

CREASE BANK (6″), along King's Dike in Whittlesey, is *The Crease* c. 1840 *TA*. Cf. *The Creasse or Broad Drove* (Tydd St Giles) 1788 *Wisb* "every man shall sufficiently repaire and make good his *creasing* or *bancke*" 1638 *Ct* (Wilburton). This is probably identical with the common word *crease* (NED sb.[2]), 'furrow, wrinkle, ridge,' which is occasionally found in the form *creast(e)*, perhaps by confusion with the word *crest* (also spelled *creast*), used of a roof-ridge, a cresting generally. Cf. '*crests*, cradges and ward-dykes' (1854 NED) and 'any wardiche or *crest*' (1438 Imb), 'warddich seu *crestam*' (1437 SewersC). In 1438 (*Sewers*) we have frequent references to *crests* in the fens. These were banks four feet high and eight to twelve feet wide. There was *unam crestam* in Leverington, beginning at *Neuton Gordyk* (Goredike Bank *infra* 206) and continuing past *Bondesgote* (Bone's Gote *infra* 271) as far as *Rechemound* (Richmond Field *infra* 273). This is clearly Turnover Bank in Leverington. Cf. further *creste dicte sewere de Coldham, crestam super Syddyk* ib. The word was also applied to a drove as in *quedam cresta in Uppewell vocata Piysdrove* (Pius Drove *infra* 291). The two words *crease* and *crest* had become completely confused in form and meaning.

CROOKED BANK (6″) is so named in 1829 (Wells) and is probably to be identified with *le Sediche* 1340 *Dugd, le Sedyke* 1450 *Ct.* Cf. Roman Bank *infra*.

ELBOW BANK with ELBOW FIELD (6″) in Parson Drove. Cf. *Elboefeild* 1611 *SewersD, Elloe Bank* 1786 *Wisb, Parson Drove Gate or Elbow Lane* 1746 ib. This bank is a continuation of Elloe Bank *infra* and Shoffendike *infra* 256. *Elbow* is a corruption of *Elloe*, favoured by the topographical use of *elbow*, cf. "y^t one *Elbow* nere Earith bridge... shalbe digged and taken away for ye more comodious fall of ye waters" (1618 *Sewers*).

ELLOE BANK (6″) is *Southea Banck* 1654 Moore, *Elloe Bank or Shoffen-dyke* 1817 *Deed*. This is part of the bank once known as Old South-eau Bank *infra* and is continued in Parson Drove as Elbow Bank *supra*. It serves as a boundary between Cambridgeshire and Elloe Hundred (L).

GOREDIKE BANK (6″), from Elloe Bank, is *Gerdyke* 1395 EA iv, so called because it runs alongside Gorefield *infra* 272.

NORTH BANK is *North Bancke and Draine* 1654 Moore, *North banke of Mooreton's Leame* 1658 *BLAcct*.

OLD SOUTHEAU BANK is *South Ee dike* 1438 Imb, *Southee bancke* 1617 *SewersD, Old South Eau Bank* c. 1825 O.S. It is identical with South Eau Bank in Holbeach (L), *fossatum de Southee* 1313 Fleet and is named from the Old South Eau *supra* 10.

ROMAN BANK

> (*le*) *Se(e)dic(h)(e)*, *-y-* 1221 *ElyA*[1] (p) *et freq* to 1340 Imb[1], *-dik* 1376 *Ct*[1], *-dyk(e)* 1395 EA iv[2], *le Siddich* 1306 *Ct*[3], *Seddyke* 1438 Imb[4], *Tyd Sydeyk* 1438 *Sewers*, (*Tyd*) *Seadike* 1438, 1570 Imb[4] *fossat' mar' de Leueryngton* 1340 *Ct*[1]
>
> *the* (*ould and auncyent*) *Seaban(c)ke* 1617 *Depositions*[1,2], *the great Sea banke of Ouse* 1657 *DugdD*[5], *The Old Country Banck against the sea* 1706 Moore
>
> *the old Roman Bank* 1696 *Wisb*[1], *Roman Bank* 1786 ib.[2]

[1] Leverington.   [2] Newton.   [3] Wisbech.
[4] Tydd St Giles.   [5] Walsoken.

The course of this embankment, as its old name indicates, marks the former coast-line of Cambridgeshire. Through Long Sutton (L) and Tydd St Mary (L), where we now have 'Roman Villa,' it ran through Tydd St Giles, past Tydd Gote and the Four Gotes, through Newton, where there was a 'Chapel of the Sea' (*v.* Chapel Drove *infra* 275), *Segate* and *Semylle* (1395 EA iv) and also Bank Barn, through Leverington (cf. Roman Ho and Sea Field and Horseshoe Lane *infra* 274, 271) to Wisbech St Peter, where part is known as Mount Pleasant Bank. Passing round the inside of Crabb Marsh[1] and Turnpike Marsh, it turns north through Walsoken, West Walton (*Old Roman Bank* 1829 Wells), Walpole St Peter and St Andrew, Terrington St Clement and Clenchwarton (*fossa maris de Klenchworton* c. 1210 Lewes). Here it must once have been called **weall**, from which Walpole and Walton are named. *Roman* is due to antiquarian speculation. Such names are not older than the end of the 17th century and there is no evidence of Roman work. *v.* **sǣ, dīc**. It is possible that some of the forms *Sedich*, etc. refer, not to this bank, but to Sea Dike Bank *infra*. New sea-dikes were erected as new land was reclaimed. Cf. "they have made the sea banckes nearer the Sea than now they are" (1617 *Depositions*). One of the objects of this enquiry was to ascertain "what severall sea banckes or sea ditches have been heretofore made for the defendinge of the landes from the force and Rage of the sea." Cf. also Crooked Bank *supra* 206.

SAND BANK (6″) is so named in 1821 (Baker). Cf. *Newdike al. Sandy dike, Sondy dike al. Sorrelldike* 1570 Imb, *Sorellesdike* 1437 Ct, *Sondike* 1620 *SewersD*. *Sorelles* from the family of Thomas *Sorel* (1301 *Ct*).

SEA DIKE BANK (6″), between Parson Drove and Leverington on the north and Wisbech on the south, is probably referred to in *Seadyke* (*Sand*) 1604 *Dugd*. Cf. Roman Bank *supra* 206.

SOUTH BANK is *South banck of Mortons Leam* 1654 Moore.

NAMES OF DYKES

CNUT'S DYKE

> *Suthende de Kinggesdelfe* 1285 *Ely, Suthenkyngesdelf, Suthenkindelf* 1286 Rams
> *Swords Delfe al. Kenouts Delfe* 1604 (1727) Hayward, *Knuts delph*

[1] Cf. *the sea banke on Crabmershe side* 1620 *SewersD*.

1605 Imb, *Sword dike* 1617 *SewersD*, *Ravenswillow dike al*
Sworde Dike or faltdike 1629 ib., *Swards Delft* 1664 BedL
Canutus or Kings Dyke 1695 SN

This was the name of the southern portion of King's Dike *infra*
In 1617 *Sword dike* is said to run from *Horsey Gate* (Horsey Hill
PN BedsHu 199) to Ramsey and "parteth *Whittlesey Kyngs Delfe*
(*v.* King's Delph *infra* 260) and *Farsett Kings Delfe.*" This must be
Cnut's Dyke or Oakley Dike, the boundary between Farsett (Hu) and
Whittlesey. In 1629 the heading is *Whittlesey Dike*, but the reference
must be to this dike. It ran from *Ravenswillow* (marked on map in L
(1808) near King's Delph Fm in Whittlesey) to *Okye* (Oakley Dike
infra). *Faltdike* is *Dock a Falt* (PN BedsHu 189), a place on the
east of Whittlesey Mere. It is clear there was confusion in the use of
the names of these dikes and King's Dike *infra*. For *Swards Delft*
and *Sword Dike* cf. King's Dike *infra*, *Sword Point* (PN BedsHu
190–1) and Swasedale *infra* 221. *v.* also *s.n. Must supra* 8.

King's Dike

> *Swerdesdelf* c. 1250 *ElyM*, *Suerdesdelf* 1251 *ElyCouch*, c. 1270
> Thorney, 1341 *ElyF*, *Swerdessedelfe* 1597 *Wisbech Map*, *Delf dike*
> *al. Swoordsdelf* 1636 BedL
> *Northende de Kinggesdelfe* 1285 *Ely*, 1294 *ElyC*, *Northenkyngesdelf*
> 1286 Rams
> *Knutus Dyke Kings Dyke* 1690 Lea

This is a continuation of Cnut's Dyke *supra* 207 running east through
Whittlesey, past King's Delph Fm. East of Whittlesey it is known as
Whittlesey Dike *infra*. *Suerdesdelf* (*v.* PN BedsHu 190–1) was on
the bounds of Wisbech *Heyefen*, between *Wysemouth* and *Gretecros*
(*v.* Ouse *supra* 12). *v.* King's Delph *infra* 260.

Oakley Dike (6″) is *Knutus or Okley Dike* 1821 Baker, *Oakley Dyke*
c. 1825 O.S. It is the name of part of what was once called Cnut's
Dyke *supra* 207. *Oakley* is a late corruption of *Okey* 1403 *SewersA*,
Okye 1629 *SewersD*.

Thorney Dike is *the Abbott of Thornye his dike* 1579 *Depositions*,
Cnorre Dyke 1597 *Wisbech Map*, *Thorney dike al. Gore dike* 1772 Imb.

Whittlesey Dike is *Wittlesey ditch* 1436 Dugd, *Whittlesea Dike* 1668
Fenland i.

NAMES OF DRAINS

BEVILL'S LEAM (Whittlesey) is *Bevills Leame* 1636 Fenland. Constructed in 1605 and named from the family of William and Robert *Bevil* (1603 *Survey*) who had land in Whittlesey. *v.* leam.

BUCKWORTH'S DRAIN (6″) (Tydd St Giles) is *Buckworth Drain* 1829 Wells and is so called in 1741 (*Ct*) from Everard *Buckworth*, one of the commissioners of sewers in 1618 (*AddCh*).

COUNTER DRAIN (6″) (Whittlesey) is *Counter* (*Banke*) *Drain*(*e*) 1720 *BLAcct*, 1753 BedL.

CROOKED DRAIN is *Abbotesdelf nunc vero Biscopesdelf vocitatum, Anglice Abbotesdelf, Latine autem Abbatis fossa* 1170 LibEl, *Bysshoppesdellfe* 1403 *SewersA, yᵉ delph* 1618 *Sewers, Crooked Drain* c. 1825 O.S. This is the sewer spanned by Delph Bridge *supra* 198. *v.* (ge)delf. It bounded the land of the Abbot, and later of his successor, the Bishop of Ely.

DIVISION DRAIN (6″) (Sutton) is so named in 1808 (L).

DOWSDALE ARM or PORTSAND DRAIN (6″) runs from Portsand Fm in Thorney to Dowsdale Bank in Croyland (L) on the Lincolnshire side of the Old South Eau. In 1574 (*SP*) we have reference to the *Ryver of Dowsdale* (from Croyland to Wisbech), which must be another name for the Old South Eau *supra* 10. *v.* Dowsdale Plantation, Portsand Drain and Portsand Fm *infra* 280, 210, 281.

FENTON LODE or TWENTY FOOT DRAIN is *Wylleueylode, Wulleueylode* 1238 *ElyCouch, Fentonlode* 1238 ib., *Fenton's Loade* 1656 BedL, *Twenty foot dreyne* 1672 *FenS, Wolvey lode* (which by some is called *Fenton lode*) 1772 Imb. The stream flows through Fenton (PN BedsHu 211), past Wolvey Fm (ib. 228). *v.* (ge)lād.

FORTY FOOT DRAIN or VERMUDEN'S DRAIN is *Vermu*(*y*)*dens Eau* 1654 Moore, 1655 *BLAcct, Adventurers Forty foot Dreyne* 1664 *CCC*. It was made in 1651 by Sir Cornelius *Vermuyden*. *v.* ēa and Adventurers' Land *infra* 292.

HAMMOND'S EAU is *Hamonds Eau* 1652 *AdvProc*, (*Eav*) 1654 Moore, *Hammonds Ea* 1700 *SewersA*. *v.* ēa. It is named from Anthony *Hamond* who was concerned in the proposal "for the drayning of that parte of the great Levell wch lyeth betweene Bedford River and Medland Banke" (*v.* North and South Meadlands *infra* 241) in 1649 (*AdvProc*).

KINDERSLEY'S CUT (from Wisbech to the sea) was so called from Charles *Kinderley* who first suggested the cut in 1721. *v.* VCH Hu iii, 282.

MORETON'S LEAM is a cut made in 1478 by John *Morton*, Bishop of Ely, from the Old Nene near Peterborough to Guyhirn. It is *the New Leame* 1529 BedL, *river of Neane called the New Leame al. Moretons Leame* 1616 ib. *v.* leam and VCH Hu iii, 266.

NEW BEDFORD RIVER or HUNDRED FOOT RIVER (parallel to the Old Bedford River *infra*) was constructed in 1651 and is so named in 1652 (BedL).

NEW CUT (Thorney) is *the Newe Cutt* 1621 *AddCh*.

NEW SOUTH EAU [sauði] is *New Southea* 1654 Moore, *New South Eau* 1747 Kitchin. *v.* ēa.

OLD BEDFORD RIVER is a new channel for the Ouse made in 1631. It is (*the said New River called*) *Bedford River* 1637 BedL, *Old Bedford River* 1654 Moore (in contrast to New Bedford River *supra*). See also Bedford Level *infra* 211 and VCH Hu iii, 271.

PEAKIRK DRAIN (6″) was made in 1631. It is *Peakirke Drain* 1664 BedL and takes its name from Peakirk (PN Nth 241).

POPHAM'S EAU is a cut begun in 1605 by Sir John *Popham*, chief justice of the King's Bench 1603–7, *v.* VCH Hu iii, 270. It is *loade or Ryuer called Popham Ea* 1609 *AddCh*. *v.* ēa, (ge)lād.

PORTSAND DRAIN (6″) is *Postland waters* 1672 FenL, *Porsand water* 1694 Fen, *Porsland al. Portsland waters* 1697 *SewersC*. *v.* Portsand Fm *infra* 281.

SANDY'S or SANDALL'S CUT is *Sandes Cutt* 1655 BLAcct, *Sandy's River* 1664 BedL, *Sandy's or Sandell's Cut* c. 1825 O.S. Sir Miles *Sandys* was one of the Adventurers of 1631 (BedL i, 112–13).

THURLOW'S DRAIN or SIXTEEN FOOT RIVER is *the Sixteene foote draine* 1669 *ChancDec, Thurlow Drain* 1690 *Lea, Thurloes Draine* 1695 SN. Made in 1651 and named after Mr *Thurlow*, one of the Bedford Level Commissioners (BedL i, 200).

WISBECH DRAIN is *le gote de Wysebeche* 1465 *Ct*. Cf. Four Gotes *infra* 285 and gote.

MISCELLANEOUS NAMES

BEDFORD LEVEL is *the Great Level (of the Fens)* 1632 *SP*, 1663 BedL, *Bedford levell* 1661 Fenland i. So called from Francis, Earl of Bedford, who undertook the draining of the fens in 1631. In his *Discourse* of 1642, Vermuyden divided the Great Level into three areas; these are now NORTH, MIDDLE and SOUTH LEVEL (*North, Middle, South Levell* 1652 BedL).

BYALL FEN is a large fen stretching from Chatteris to Little Downham. The name survives in:

BYALL FEN FM (Chatteris). Cf. *Byhe* 1251 *ElyCouch, Bye(f)fen* 1461 *MinAcct*, 1462 *Wren, Bya-, Biafen* 1464–7 ib., *Byalfen* 1605 Imb, *Biall Fen* 1636 BedL.

BYALL FEN DROVE (6″) (Coveney), so named in 1829 (Wells).

COVENEY BYALL FEN (Coveney). Cf. *Bye...Bye Eae cote* 1403 *SewersA, Biall Fen* 1636–7 BedL, *Byefenn...*the said *Biall fen* 1658 *Ct*.

BYALL FEN (Downham), *Byefen* 1381 *Wren, Bie(e)fen* 1386, 1489 ib., *Byaffen* 1482–95 *Ct, Byallfen* 1489 ib., *Bialfenne al. Balstaff Moore* 1632 Hondius, *Byall or Balstaff Fen* 1830 BedL.

BYALL FEN BANK (6″) (Manea). Cf. *Bialffen* 1636 BedL.

BYALL FEN (Welches Dam). Cf. (*piscandi in*) *le Behee* 1315 *Ct*, (*piscaria*) *Bye(e)* 1378–1405 ib., *Wychamee al. Biehee* 15th *ElyM*, (*river*) *Byhey* 1522 *Wren, Biallffen* 1636 BedL.

BYALL FEN (Witcham Gravel) is *Byhe* 1277 *Ely, Byee* 1318 *ElyF, Byall fenne* 1589 *Depositions*.

The fen clearly takes its name from a place *By(h)ee*, 'by the river,' *v.* bī(g), ēa. For the type of name cf. Bin Brook *supra* 1. This river, which flowed through Chatteris, Sutton, Doddington, Witchford, Witcham and Downham, is *le Byee* c. 1300 *SewersD*, *le Behee* 1315 *Ct*, *Byelake* 1379 *Wren*, *Byhey* 1522 ib., *Byeau* 1706 Moore. Its course cannot now be determined exactly, but it seems to correspond to the river called *The fyrthe dick* 1576 Saxton, *The Fyrthe dyke* 1610 Speed, which flowed across the fen from Chatteris to Littleport and probably owed its name to *Duditunefrith* (1221 *ElyA*) which stretched from Wimblington to Chatteris. It may, perhaps, correspond to the *Frith(e)lake* 1329–42 *Ct*, *Frethlake* 1356 ib., *Fritlake* 1449 ib. (in Sutton), and seems also to have been called *the new Chaire* (*v.* Chain Fm in Littleport *infra* 226).

The lost alternative in Downham is *Bal(d)staf(f)(mor(e))* 1251 *ElyCouch*, 1277 *Ely*, 1563 *SewersD*, *Le Bal(l)derstaffe* 1403 *SewersA*, probably from ME *ballede*, probably in the sense 'smooth, bare' and *stæf*, 'staff.' The fen must have been named from some smooth or bare pole used as a landmark.

THE WASH is the name given to the strip of land between the banks raised along the two Bedford Rivers to prevent the floods of the Ouse from spreading over the countryside. This area between the rivers comprises 5600 acres and is variously known as *The Receptacle* 1654 Moore, *the Wash* 1654 *BLAcct*, *the Wash upon Bedford River* 1658 ib., *ye Wash of Byea ffenne al. Byall ffenne* 1676 Pembroke, *the Wash near unto Meapole Bridge* 1715 *FensS*, *the Washlands* 1756 *Act*, *The Hundred Feet Washes* 1812 ib.

THE WASHES (6″) is a name given to various pieces of land on the banks of the Ouse or Old West River liable to floods in Willingham (cf. *Squasselode* 1279 RH, *The Wash* c. 1840 *TA*), Haddenham (*the Wash* 1720 *HardwickeA*), Cottenham and Wilburton. These latter are on the boundary of Stretham where we have *Wasselode* 1251 *ElyCouch*, .1277 *Ely*, *Quasselode versus Theford* 13th *ElyM*, 14th *Elem*, (*drauam voc.*) *Wasschelood* 1549 *Ct*. *Washlode* must, therefore, be an old name of the Old West River (*supra* 11) from Haddenham to Thetford. The first element is OE (ge)wæsc, recorded c. 1440 as '*wasche*, watur or forde, *vadum*' and a. 1548 as *the wasshes*, i.e. The Wash (L). *v.* (ge)lād. For *Quasse-* and for *Squasse-*, *v.* Introd. xxxvi.

THE TWO HUNDREDS OF ELY

(into) *þam twam hundredum* 970 BCS 1267
In Duob' Hvnd' de Ely qui conuenivnt apud Wiceforde 1086 DB
the two hundreds (with)in the isle of Ely 1233 (1328) Ch

To-day, the Isle of Ely contains the hundreds of Ely, Wisbech and North and South Witchford. In DB there are two, *unum* (containing Whittlesey, Doddington with March and Benwick, Chatteris, Little-port, Stuntney, Little Thetford, Stretham, Wilburton, Coveney and Haddenham), *aliud* (comprising Wisbech, Ely, Henny (in Soham), Downham, Witchford, Wentworth, Witcham and Sutton). In InqEl a similar arrangement obtains. In 1298 (*Ass*), 1336 and 1372 (*SR*) there are three hundreds—Ely (containing Ely, Littleport and Down-ham), Wisbech and Witchford. In the charter of privileges granted to Ely by King Edgar (LibEl 169) the two hundreds of the Isle are said to meet at Ely or *Wicheforda* "quae caput centuriatuum insulae dicitur" or "ad *Modich* quae quarta pars est centuriatuum." Cf. *Mudeke* (in Littleport) 1221 *ElyA*.

XV. ELY HUNDRED

Hvnd' de Ely 1086 DB, (*cum Hundred de Wycheford'*) 1450 SR
Hundr(ed) Elyens' 1251 *ElyCouch*, 1277 *Ely*

Ely

ELY

(*in regione quae uocatur*) *Elge* c. 750 Bede, c. 1150 FW, 1170 LibEl, *elgae* 8th Bede

(*æt*) *Elige* c. 900 ASC (Ā) (*s.a.* 673), *in þæm þeodlonde þe is geceged Elige* c. 1000 OE Bede, *in regione Elig* 970 BCS 1266, (*on, into*) *Elig* 970 ib. 1267, *Elyg* 1004 (18th) KCD 711, 1086 DB

(*on*) *Eligabirig* c. 1000 Saints, (*to*) *Eligbyrig* 11th ASC (C) (*s.a.* 1036), (*to*) *Elibyrig* c. 1050 ib. (D) (*s.a.* 1036)

hélige c. 1000 OE Bede, (*æt*) *Helige* 12th ASC (E) (*s.a.* 673), (*æt*) *Helig* 957 (18th) BCS 999, (*into*) *Helig* 11th (12th) KCD 722, (*to*) *Hélig* 11th ASC (D) (*s.a.* 1072)

(*into*) *Ælig* c. 1000 (11th) ASWills, *æl æg* c. 1040 OE Bede
Ylig 11th ASWills

(*in*) *Hely* c. 1050 (13th) KCD 885, 1108 *LibEl et freq* to c. 1400 RG, (*into*, *to*) *Heli* c. 1050 (12th) LibEl, c. 1130 SD, c. 1260 Gervase, (*æt*) *Hele* p. 1066 (12th) KCD 897

(*æt*) *Eli* c. 1100 ASC (F) (*s.a.* 673), 1155–61 P, 1203 Cur, (*in*) *Ely* 956 (12th) BCS 1346, 970 (18th) ib. 1265, 1086 ICC, DB, InqEl *et passim*

Ealye 1591 *Depositions, Elley* 1616 Bentham

OE *æl-gē, ēl-gē*, 'eel-district,' as already suggested by Skeat and Ekwall. Ely is called by Bede a *regio*, rendered in the OE version by *þeod-lond*, 'people-land,' a satisfactory translation of the rare *gē* which is found also in Surrey (PN Sr xi, 1–2), Vange and *Ginges*, now Margaretting, Ingatestone, etc. (PN Ess xxi, 174–5, 258–9) and in Eastry, Lyminge and Sturry (KPN 73, 25–6, 6). This archaic element early fell into disuse and was easily confused with OE *ēg*, 'island,' which happens to be particularly apt topographically. As early as the 8th century etymological speculation had begun with Bede's "Est autem Elge...regio...in similitudinem *insulae* uel paludibus, ut diximus, circumdata uel aquis, unde et a copia *anguillarum* quae in eisdem paludibus capiuntur nomen accepit[1]." This was repeated by the Ely historian and the chroniclers with more fanciful alternatives. The former, after quoting Bede, continues "quae mutato nomine meliorando 'Ely' nuncupatur, modo scilicet digna Dei domus, cui nomen convenit ejus; vel sicut quidam ex duobus verbis Ebraicis disserunt, 'Elge:' quoniam dicitur 'el' Deus, 'ge' terra, quod simul dei terra sonat. Digne enim insula tali signatur onomate[2]...." Rents of eels were a fruitful source of income for the abbots and bishops of Ely.

ELY STREET-NAMES

NOTE. Ely is now divided into three wards, Steeple-high Ward, Fore-hill Ward and Castle-hithe Ward. In 1425 (*Ct*) we have four: *Warde de Stepilrow, Castelheth, Sce Marie, Brodheth*. The fourth is now St Mary's Parish, *Seyntmaryward* 1472 ib. Cf. also *Castelward* 1425 ib., *Hye Rowe ward* 1475 ib. v. High St, Fore Hill and *Castle Hithe infra* 215, 216.

ST MARY'S PARISH

BEDWELL HAY LANE is *Bedwellhayewaye* 1556 *Ct, Bedlehayway* t. Eliz *Rental, Bedleyhay highway* 1676 EA xiii, v. Bedwellhay Fm *infra* 217. CAMBRIDGE RD is *Stanweye* 1319 *ElyF, Thetfordwey* 1425 *Ct*. For *Stanweye* cf. *supra* 19. CHURCH LANE is *le Chirchelane* 1342 Sacr. Near St Mary's Church. COW LANE is *Cowelane* 1553 *Ct*. DEAN'S LANE is so named c. 1840 *TA*. DOWNHAM

[1] *Hist. Eccles.* iv, 19. [2] LibEl, p. 47.

S<small>T</small> is *Dunhamstrete* 13th *ElyM*, *Downhamwey* 1334 *ElyF*, *-lane* 1583 *Ct*. T<small>HE</small>
G<small>ALLERY</small> is *le Galelylane* 1438 *Plea*, *(le) Gal(l)ery* 1481 *Ct*, *(way)* 1649 Stewart.
Commonly said to take its name from a *gallery* which led from the Bishop's
Palace to the west transept of the Cathedral, but the first form suggests that
it was really named from the *Galilee* or porch of the Cathedral (cf. *novam
galileam* c. 1215 Stewart). *Galilee-lane*, with its triple liquids, would easily
be corrupted to *Gallery-lane*, especially as in the reign of Henry VIII the
term *Gallery* was applied to the western boundary of the priory generally
(*v.* Stewart 241–2). This is also called *Pale(y)slane* 1437–40 *Ct*, from the
Bishop's Palace. K<small>ILBY'S</small> C<small>ORNER</small> is *Kilbyes Corner* 1418 *Ely*, so called from
Richard *Kilby* (ib.). M<small>ARY'S</small> S<small>T</small> is *regia via versus le Grene* 1418 *Ely*, *St Mary's
St* c. 1840 *TA* and is named from St Mary's Church. M<small>EPSALE'S</small> C<small>ORNER</small> is
so called from John *Mepsale* (1416 Stewart). M<small>ILL</small> R<small>D</small> is *Mellane* 1432 *ElyCh*,
Milnelane 1450 *Ct*, *v.* m<small>yln</small>. S<small>ILVER</small> S<small>T</small> was in succession (1) *Swaulewelane*
13th *ElyM*, *Swal(e)uyslane* 1280 *Rental*, *-wis-* 1326 Sacr, *Walweslane* 1322
ib., i.e. swallow(s) lane, (2) *Walpol(es)lane* 1331, 1371 *ElyF*, *Walpullane*
1449 *Ct*, from the family of Henry de *Walpol* (13th *ElyF*). From this ran
Lardenereslane, so called from Isabell *Lardener* (1418 *Ely*). S<small>MALE'S</small> C<small>ORNER</small>
is *Smales corner*, where was the *ten. Radulphi Smale* (1418 *Ely*). S<small>MOCKMILL</small>
A<small>LLEY</small> is *Smock Alley* c. 1840 *TA*. A *smockmill* is a windmill with a
revolving top. U<small>PHERD'S</small> L<small>ANE</small>. Cf. *Upherds Ground* ib. W<small>EST</small> F<small>EN</small> R<small>D</small> is
strate de Westfen 1418 *Ely*, *Westfenwey* 1499 *Ct*, *-stret* 1502 ib. We also have
Cattyslane 1280 *Rental*, cf. *Cattesland* c. 1195 *ElyE*, *Catyscrosse* 1453 *ElyB*.

TRINITY PARISH

A<small>NNESDALE</small> is *Auntresdale* 1418 *Ely*, *le Awtersdale* 1475 *Ct*, *Ansdale* c. 1840
TA, *v.* d<small>æl</small>. A stream formerly ran from Cawdle Fen to the river through
Annesdale (Stewart 181). B<small>ACK</small> H<small>ILL</small> is so named c. 1840 *TA*. B<small>RAYES'</small> L<small>ANE</small>
is *Brayeslane* 1561 *Ct*. So called from the manor of *le Brayys* 1349 *ElyF*,
Braystede 1361 *CartMisc*, belonging to the family of Agnes *le Bray* (1300
ElyF). Cf. terram *Agnetis le Bray* ib. *v.* s<small>tede</small>. B<small>ROAD</small> S<small>T</small> is *(del) Brodlane*
1280 *Rental*. B<small>ULL</small> L<small>ANE</small> is so named c. 1840 *TA*. Earlier it was *Lyldeslane*
1280 *Rental*, *Lileslane* 1418 *Ely*, near which were *Lilesholt*, *-place* 1379, 1398
ElyF, all named from the family of John *Lyle* (1450 *Ct*), which must have been
here much earlier. T<small>HE</small> B<small>UTCHERY</small> is *Bocherisrowe* 1382 EA vi, *Bocheria* 1418
Ely. C<small>ROYLE'S</small> L<small>ANE</small> is *Croyleslane* 1418 Pat. D<small>OVEHOUSE</small> Y<small>ARD</small> is *Dufhouszerde*
1418 *Ely*. F<small>ORE</small> H<small>ILL</small> is so named c. 1840 *TA*. G<small>AOL</small> S<small>T</small> (now M<small>ARKET</small> S<small>T</small>) is
Gaol Lane c. 1840 *TA*. So named from the Bishop of Ely's gaol. H<small>IGH</small> S<small>T</small> is
le Hyestrete 1478 *ElyCh*, *Heystrete* 1514 ib. Earlier it was *le Heyrow* 1351 ib.,
le Hyerowe 1361 *CartMisc* and *le Steplerowe* 1280 *Rental*, from a steeple
connected with one of the gates of the priory (Stewart 201). M<small>ARKET</small> P<small>LACE</small>
is *le Marketstede* 1332 *ElyCh*, *Market Place* c. 1840 *TA*, *v.* s<small>tede</small>. N<small>UTHOLT</small>
L<small>ANE</small>. Cf. *Nut Holt* c. 1840 *TA*. This was formerly *Redcrosselane* 1556 *Ct*,
so called from *rubiam crucem* 1418 *Ely*, *le Reed Crosse* 1490 Ely, which stood
at the junction of this street and Egremont St with the Lynn Rd (Stewart
195). Earlier it was *S(c)henteforth-*, *-furthlane* 1280 *Rental*, *Schendelford
(venella)* 13th *Elem*, *S(c)hend(e)ford(lane)* ib., 13th *ElyM*, 1418 Pat, *Shen-*,
Shynfordelane 1418 *Ely*. T<small>HE</small> P<small>OTTERIES</small> is *Pottereslane* 1280 *Rentul*, *-strete*

1411 *Elem*, "ubi domus figuli quondam situata fuit" (Stewart 185). THE QUAY is *Bradehide* c. 1210 *ElyM*, *le Brodhyth* 1390 *ElyCh*, *-hethe* 1402 ib., *-hith* 1418 *Ely*, *Brodhye* 1497 *Ct*. 'Broad landing-place,' *v.* hȳð. Near here were also *Castelhiþe* 1295 *ElyCh*, 'landing-place by the castle,' *comyn stathe versus Castelhythe* 1476 Stewart, *v.* stæþ, 'landing-place,' *Monkeshith* 1418 *Ely*, that of the monks, and *Stokhith* ib., one 'made of timber,' cf. Stockwith (PN Nt 39). WATERSIDE ST. Cf. *the Water side in Ely* 1670 *Bodl*. WINFARTHING LANE. Cf. *Wynferthing* 1418 *Ely*.

Ely College

ELY COLLEGE is *Ely College* 1591 *WMP*. After the surrender of the Monastery of Ely in 1539, Henry VIII founded the church anew and endowed it with the site of the dissolved monastery. This is now extra-parochial, the first reference by name being "The Boke of the erection of the King's *newe College at Elye*" c. 1540. *v.* Bentham 225–7, App. xxxiv.

CHERRY HILL (6″) is *Mount hill* 1610 Speed, *the Mill-hill* 1649 Stewart, *Cherry Hill* 1821 Baker. There was a wind-mill here in 1229 (Bentham ii, 53).

ELY PORTA (6″) is *porta monachorum* c. 1300 *ElyCh*, *novas portas* 1397 Bentham, *portas magnas* 1404 *Ct*, *Ely Porta* 1509 *Wren*, *Elyeporte* 1566 *Ct*, *Walpols Gate House* c. 1840 *TA*. The first reference must be to an earlier gate, for the present great Gate of the Monastery was begun by Prior Bucton (1366–97) and completed by his successor, William *Walpole*. Here were held the manor courts of the Prior and of the Abbey (Bentham i, 222, ii, 50). Also known as *Stonegate* (1438 *Plea*).

Ely St Mary

ELY ST MARY is *parochia Ste Marie de Ely* 1275 *ElyF*, *Ely Seynt Mary infra Insul' Elien'* 1553 EA ix. So called from the dedication of the church.

NOTE. EGREMONT ST is probably to be associated with the family of Thomas *le Akerman* (14th *Elem*). It is *Akermannysstrete* 1280 *Rental*, *Akirmanstret* 1438 *Plea*, *Egreman St* 1868 Stewart. *v.* Addenda lx.

BARTON FM (6″) is *Berton(a)* c. 1120 *HarlCh et freq* to 1432 *Ct*, *Ely Barton* 1436 *Ct*, *Barton ferme* 1591 *Depositions*. *v.* bere-tūn. This was a manor of the Bishop of Ely.

Bedwellhay Fm

Bidewelle 1302 *MinAcct*
Bed(e)wel(l)hay(e), *-hey* 1403 *SewersA et freq* to 1570 *Ct*
Bedelhey 1576 Saxton, *Beadall Haye* 1606 *Depositions*, *Beddlehay*
1615 *Elien*

'Enclosure by the spring in the hollow,' *v.* **byde, wielle, (ge)hæg.**
Cf. Bidwell (PN Nth 222) and Bedlar's Green (PN Ess 35).

Braham Fm

Bramewere 1086 InqEl, 1251 *ElyCouch*, 1277 *Ely*, *-weyre* 1556 *Ct*
Brama t. Hy 2 *ElyCh*, *Brame* c. 1200 *ElyE et freq* to 1541 *MinAcct*,
Breame ib., *Brayme* 1553 PCC
Braham 1199–1281 FF, 1285 *Ass et passim*

Possibly 'bramble **ham(m)**,' *v.* **brame.** Cf. Braham (WRY), DB
Michel-, Litelbram, Braham 1242 Fees, Bramham (WRY), DB *Bram(e)-*
ham, Braham, and for *Breame*, Bream's Fm and Braham Hall (PN
Ess 257, 333). *Bramewere* was a fishery of the monks of Ely, *v.* **wēr.**

Chettisham

Chetesham c. 1170 *ElyM*, c. 1195 *ElyE et freq* to 1475 *Ct*, (*-wode-*
gate) 13th *ElyF*, *Chetisham*, *-ys-* 1240 Rams (p) *et freq* to 1490
Ely, *Chettysham* 1497 *Ct*, *Chetsham* 1579 Ely
Chedesham 1221 *ElyA et freq* to 14th *Cai*, (*bosco*) 1277 *Ely*, *Chedis-*
ham 1292 Sacr
Schetesham 1298 *ElyF*, *Scheteham crouch'* 1349 ib.
Checham bushes 1606 *Depositions*, *Churcham* 1638 ElyVis, 1763
Bowen, (*or Chetisham*) 1808 L

This is not an easy name. The first element looks like a personal
name *Cett*, the strong form of *Cetta*, confused with *Cedd*. The forms
in *Chedes-* are later than those in *Chetes-* and are probably due to
voicing of intervocalic *t*. There was also in the neighbourhood a place
called *Chetesfeld*[1] or *Chedesfeld* (1251 *ElyCouch*, 1277 *Ely*). The first
element might well be taken as British *cēt*, 'wood,' from which
were formed two genitival compounds similar to *Chettisholt* (PN D
604), were it not that a compound *Chetesfeld*, 'open country of the
wood,' seems unlikely. *v.* **feld.**

---

[1] Also 1302 *MinAcct*.

EMERY BARN FM is *Amery(e)barn(e)* 1536 CHuAS v, 1544 *WMP, the Ambry Barnes* c. 1550 ECP, *Almery or Amery Barnes* 1584 CHuAS v. Cf. also *le Awmerye* 1448 *Ct,* (*le*) *Ambryland* 1570 ib. This was part of the endowment of the almonry (OFr *au(l)mosnerie*) of Ely. Cf. Amery Court (PN K 491), Armoury Fm (PN Ess 360–1) and *The Ambry* (PN Mx 166).

ORWELLPIT FM is *Orrell Pytt(s)* 1528 CAPr xxxvi, *Orwell' pitte* 1570 *Ct.* Cf. *Horewell(e)* 1263, 14th *Elem,* 13th *ElyCh,* (*viam de*) *Horeswell(e)* c. 1300 *Elem, Orwel(l)wey(e)* 1494 *Ct,* 1512 *ElyB.* 'Pit(s) by the muddy well,' v. horh, wielle, pytt.

WALWORTH (lost) is *Walewrth* 13th *ElyM, Walew(o)rd(e)* 13th, 1300 *ElyCh,* 13th *ElyF.* 'Farm of the serfs or Britons,' or that where they worked, v. wēala, worð. Two other examples have been noted, (*campo voc.*) *Waleuort* 1251 *ElyCouch* (in Horningsea) and *le Waleworthell* 1339, 1340 *Queens'* (in West Wickham), v. hyll. It is noteworthy that all three became early extinct.

CHURCH FM (6″) was probably the home of Nicholas de *Ecclesia* and William, son of John de *Ecclesia* (1251 *ElyCouch*).

FOX'S DROVE is probably to be associated with the family of Henry *Fox* (1251 *ElyCouch*). Cf. *terra Roberti Fox* c. 1195 *ElyE, ffoxiscroft* 1280 *Rental, tenement Foxes* 1418 Pat, *ffoxeslond* 1425 *ElyB.*

THE BALK is the boundary between Ely St Mary and Downham, *v. infra* 311. BRICK HILL is near disused brickworks and is as usual probably a corruption of *brick-hill* from *brick-kiln,* cf. Brickhill St (PN Wa 43). ELY FIELDS FM. Cf. *campis de Ely* c. 1195 *ElyE, Ely Fields* 1457 Fenland v. FIELD COTTAGE (all 6″). Cf. *campo de Ely versus Dunham* 13th *ElyCh, Field House Fm* 1821 Baker. This was probably part of *Northfeld* 13th *ElyE.* FIELDSIDE is so named c. 1840 (*TA*). It was probably *Middelfeld* 13th *ElyE.* PARADISE FM. Cf. *Paradise close* 1564 *WMP, close of the Prior of Ely called Parradise North* 1630 CAPr xxxvi. The term is probably used here of the garden of a convent, cf. NED *s.v. paradise*[6]. ST JOHN'S FM (6″). Cf. *terram Hospitalis Sancti Johannis de Ely* 1305 *ElyCh.* TEA CLOSE and WEST END (both 6″) are so named c. 1840 (*TA*). WOOD HO is so named in 1695 (SN).

Ely Trinity

ELY TRINITY is *magna parochia de Ely* 1279 *ElyCh*, *Trynetye Parisshe in Ely infra Insul' Elien'* 1553 EA ix. *Magna* because larger than St Mary's in the suburbs. *Trinity* from the dedication of the Cathedral which contains Trinity Church, formerly a chapel of the monastery.

NEWNHAM (6″) is *Newham, Neuenham* c. 1195 *ElyE, Newenham* 1280 *Rental et freq* to 1457 Fenland v, *Newnham* 1283 *ElyF, Newnam* 1450 *Ct.* 'New hām,' or possibly 'hamm' v. nīwe.

TURBUTSEY FM (6″)

  Tidbrithseseye, Tidbrithti insula 974 (12th) LibEl
  Tidbritheseya c. 1120 *ElyM, Tidbriteseia* 1144 *ElyD, Tydbryttesheya*
    1293 Sacr
  Tidbrithteseia c. 1120 *LibEl, Tithbrichteseia* c. 1120 *HarlCh*
  Tidbricheseia c. 1120 *ElyM,* c. 1150 *LibEl, Tithbricheseia* c. 1130
    ElyD, Tythbertseya 1279 *ElyF*
  Tybricteseya 1139 *ElyM, Tybricheseie* 1139 *ElyD, Tibertseia* 1279
    ElyF, Titbridseye 1342 Sacr
  Tirbutsey 1417 *Ely, Tyrbytseye* 1315 *ElyF, Turbutsey* 1417 *Ely,*
    1418 Pat, *Tibirsey* 1418 *Ely,* Pat, *Tirbysey* 1450 *Ct, Tyrbursey*
    1453 ib., *Turbetsey* 1561–71 ib., *Turbesey lake, Turbysey* 1611
    AddCh, Tarbetsey 1684 Moore

'*Tīdbeorht*'s island,' v. ēg. Turbutsey Fm was destroyed to make room for the Ely Beet Sugar Factory in 1925 (CHuAS v, 383).

BABYLON is *tenementa ultra aquam* 1418 *Ely, Babylon* 1618 BedL. An isolated district beyond the river. Cf. *infra* 357. ELY COMMON (both 6″) is so named ib. HIGHFLYER'S FM is *High-flyers Hall* c. 1825 O.S. Cf. *Highflyer Hill* c. 1840 *TA.* LITTLE LONDON is so named c. 1825 (O.S.), v. *infra* 357. NEWBARNS HO is *Newbernys* 1504 *ElyB.* THE VINEYARDS (6″) is *vineam in Hely* 1109–31 *LibEl, le Vyneyerd* 1482 *Ct, le Wenyerde* 1493 ib., *the vyneards* 1684 Moore. v. wīngeard.

Ely Trinity Detached

NOTE. THOROUGHFARE LANE. Cf. *Thoroughfare Piece* c. 1840 *TA.*

NORNEA FM is *North(e)ney(e)* t. Hy 3 *WMP, (Michele, Little)* 1298 *Ass, Northeye* 1279 *ElyM, Nordeney(e)* 1313 *Ct,* 1428 *ElyF,* t. Hy 8 *Rental, Norney* 1576 Saxton, *Northnye* 1611 *AddCh, Nornea* 1684

Moore. OE (*bī*) *norðan ēge*, 'to the north of the marshy land,' *v.* **ēg** and cf. Norney (PN Sr 199). There was also a *Sutheneya* 13th *Elem.*

QUAVENEY HILL [kweini] is *Quaueney*(*e*) t. Hy 3 *WMP*, 1279 *ElyM*, 1298 *Ass*, 1335 Sacr, *-brynge* 1432 *Ct*, *-brynk* 1449 ib., *Ʒeueneye* 1348 *ElyC*[1], *Quaney* 1576 Saxton, *Quavenye brinck* 1611 *AddCh*, *Quayney* 1617 *SewersD*, *Quanea* (*Brink or Lode*) 1636 BedL. The first form for Quaney Field (*infra* 288), viz. *Whaueney*, is reminiscent of some of those for the River Waveney (Nf, Sf) and Wawne (PN ERY 44–5). These names, with Warne (PN D 201), Ekwall (RN 440) derives from an OE *wagen (cf. OE *wagian*, 'to wag') in the sense 'quaking bog.' Here we may have a similar formation, *cwafen, related to an OE *cwafian of parallel formation to *cwacian*, 'to quake,' *v.* NED *s.v.* *quave.* Hence *cwafenēg, 'quaking-bog island.' Here too possibly belong *Quamming*(*e*)*were*, *Quammingeswere* 1086 InqEl, alternative names of a fishery which may have been in this neighbourhood. In this case, the basis may be *cwafening*, an *-ing-* derivative of *cwafen*, with early assimilation of *fn* to *mn* and *mm*. The more common noun is found in Bottisham in *the Quave* 1569 CHuAS i. *v.* **brinke.**

ROSWELL PITS (6″). Cf. *Roueshil* 1221 *ElyA*, (*cum Stanpettes et Cley-pettes*) 1251 *ElyCouch*, 1277 *Ely*, *Roweshill* 13th *ElyE*, (*grauellpittes in*) *Roushyll* 1381 *Wren*, *Rossell* 1548 CHuAS v, *Rossehill* 1604 *Atkyns*, *Rosshall* 1674 Fen, *Roslyn or Roswell Hill* c. 1825 O.S., *Roswell Hill pits* 1830 BedL. The first element is probably a contraction of a personal name, either OE *Hrōþwulf* or Norman *Rolf.* Cf. Rousham (O), DB *Rowesham*, c. 1200 Bodl *Rodolvesham* and Rowsham (PN Bk 89–90).

STUNTNEY

> *Stuntenei* 1086 DB, *-*(*e*)*ie* 1086 InqEl, *-eia*, *-eya*, *-ey*(*e*) 1109 *LibEl* > et freq to 1418 Pat, *Stounteneye* 1323 Sacr, *Stuntney* 1436 *Ct*
> *Stonteneia* 1086 InqEl, *-ey*(*e*) 1285 *Ass et freq* to 1490 Ely
> *Stumteneye* 1283 Pat, *Stumpney* 1541 *MinAcct*
> *Stynteneye* 1298 *Ass*
> *Stantney* 1576 Saxton, 1610 Speed

Both Skeat and Ekwall explain this name as '*Stunta*'s isle,' the personal name deriving from OE *stunt*, 'foolish,' *v.* **ēg.** Cf. Stonesfield (O), *Stuntesfeld* DB, from the strong form *Stunt.* It is perhaps worth

---

Documents relating to Doddington dated at.

noting that in the Cambridgeshire dialect, *stunt* means both 'blunt of manner' and 'steep.' The ultimate history of OE *stunt* is uncertain, but probably the physical sense 'cut off, abrupt, steep' is the earlier one, and possibly we have the adjective here, in which case the meaning would be '(at the) steep island.' Cf. "This Isle…riseth suddenly…" (1604 *Atkyns*).

SWASEDALE FM is on a projecting piece of land near Crooked Drain, once known as *Abbotesdelf* or *Biscopesdelf* (*supra* 209). The drain was apparently also known as *Swerdesdelf(fe)* 1427–53 *Ct*[1], *Sward(e)sdelfe*, *-delphe* 1564–6 ib., *Swarsedelfe* 1565 *Ct*, *Swarsdelph* 1604 *Atkyns*, *Swasdale* 1629 *SewersD*, *Swavesdell* 1636 *BedL*. This would seem to be identical with the old name for Cnut's or King's Dyke *supra* 207–8. In view of the origin of the latter name, deriving from a point of land in the old Whittlesey Mere, one can only suggest that the name of one famous dike was transferred to another.

THORNEY HILL takes name from (*insula de*) *Torneie* c. 1206 *ElyCh*, *Thorneye* 1280 *Rental* (p), *Thornee* 1349 *MinAcct*. 'Island covered with thorn-bushes,' *v*. ēg and cf. Thorney *infra* 280.

HATCH'S FM (6″) is probably to be associated with the family of John *Hatch* (1802 *Lot*). Cf. *Hatches Hill* c. 1840 *TA*.

BRADFORD FM is *Bradfords* c. 1840 *TA*. Cf. *Bradford(es)were* 1369, 1586 *St John's, Bradford(lode)* 1443–1583 *Ct, Bradfurthwer'* 1454 ib. 'Broad ford,' *v*. wēr, (ge)lād. This is, no doubt, the ford which preceded Delph Bridge *supra* 198. CORPORATION FM (6″). Cf. *Corporation Holt* c. 1840 *TA*. THE DUNSTALLS is *Tunstal* 13th *ElyE, Dunstall'* 1411–1576 *Ct, v*. tūnsteall. LONG HOLT (6″) is *long Holt* 1558 *WMP*. MOW SIDES (6″) is *Mow Sides* c. 1840 *TA*. Cf. *Mowe Fenn* 1582 *Ct*, *the commen Mowefenn of the towne of Ely* 1611 *AddCh* and Mow Fen *infra* 227. NEW WORLD FM is in a remote part of the parish. QUAVENEY DROVE and FM (both 6″) are *Quaney Drove* 1829 *Wells, Quanie Farm* 1658 *BedL. v*. Quaveney Hill *supra* 220. RED HO. Cf. *Red House Piece* c. 1840 *TA*. SKIRTS ROW (6″). Cf. *Long, Short Skirts* ib. This is a long row of trees near the edge of the fen, *v*. skirt(s). SPRINGHEAD HO. Cf. *Spring Head* c. 1840 *TA. v*. Addenda lx. STUNTNEY OLD HALL is *aula de Stunteneye* 1348 *ElyM, v*. Stuntney *supra* 220. TURF FEN (all 6″) is *Turfefen* 1564 *Ct*. Cf. Turf Fen *infra* 247.

---

[1] Near by was the *lada de Swerdesderneslake* 1298 *Ass*. Probably this is for *Swerdesderueslake* from *Swerdesdelueslake* with common AN confusion of *r* and *l*.

Intermixed Lands rated to Ely St Mary and Ely Trinity.
No. 1

CAWDLE FEN

> Cald(e)well(e) 13th *ElyE*, *-fen* 1251 *ElyCouch et freq* to 1418 *Ely*,
> Cawdewelffen 1495 *Ct*, Cawdlefen 1591 *Depositions*
> Chaldewelle 13th *Elem*
> Cadewellfen 1417 *Rental*, Cadlefen(n) 1591 *Depositions*

'Cold spring or stream,' *v*. ceald, wielle. Cf. Caudle Ditch *supra* 144.

MILE END. Cf. *Mildenhall river or the dead mile* 1604 *Atkyns*, *Dead miles end* 1661 *BLAcct*, *Mile End* 1829 Wells. *Dead Mile* (still the watermen's name for the Lark *supra* 7 from Prickwillow Bridge to Mile End Corner), probably because particularly sluggish. Cf. *Dedemile* 1244 Rams (Whittlesey), *Dedhee s.n.* Starnea *supra* 16, Reach Lode *supra* 136 and *le Myle* 1371 *ElyF*, *draine called the Mile* 1529 BedL (Sutton).

PADNAL FEN is *Pandenhal(e)* (sic) 1221 *ElyA*, 1251 *ElyCouch*, *Padenhal(e)* ib., (*-fen*) t. Hy 3 *WMP*, 1277 *Ely*, *Padenalefen* 1450 *Ct*, *Padnale* 1432–79 ib., *Padnal(l)* 1561 ib., *Padnoll* 1658 *BLAcct*. As always in *Pad*-names one is presented with the alternative of derivation from the OE personal name *Pad(d)a* or from OE *pada*, 'toad, frog.' In fenland one is naturally inclined to the latter, with what measure of justification it is impossible to say. Hence either 'frog's or *Pada*'s nook,' *v*. healh. For the former we may perhaps compare *Pathewere*, *Padewere* 1086 InqEl, a fishery of the monks of Ely.

PRICKWILLOW is *Pri(c)kewylev* 1251 *ElyCouch*, 1277 *Ely*, *Prikewiluh* 1279 *ElyM*, *Pricwylgh* c. 1320 CAPr iv, *Prikwylwe* 1387 *ElyF*, *Prikwhelwe* 1438 *Plea*, *Prykwylowgh* 1475 *Ct*, *Prykewylow* 1480 ib., *Prickwillowe* 1570 *Eg*. The compound *prick-willow* is not on independent record, but presumably it is used, like the compounds *pricktimber*, *pricktree* and *prickwood*, to denote a tree from which wooden skewers are made. If so, it goes back some 300 years earlier than any of those compounds.

SHIPPEA HILL FM

> Sepeye 1260 *ElyCh*, S(c)hepey(e) t. Hy 3 *WMP et freq* to 1541
> *MinAcct*, Chepeie 1279 *ElyM*, Sheppy 1604 *Atkyns*
> Shypeye 13th *Elem*, 1355 Sacr, Shippy 1582 *Ct*

'Sheep-island,' *v*. scēap, ēg.

KETTLESWORTH[1] (6"), ROLL'S LODE[2], SCOTT'S DROVE[3] (6"), SINDALL-
THORPE HO[4] and SPOONER'S FM are probably to be associated with the
families of John de *Ketene* (1309 *ElyC*) which came from Ketton (R),
Jefferie *Rolls* (1617 *Wisb*), John *Skot* (1417 *Rental*), John *Sendale* (ib.)
and Katerine and Geoffrey *Sponer* (1566 *Ct*).

BLACK WING DROVE is *Blackwing Drove* 18.. *Map*. BLUE BOAR DROVE
is so named c. 1840 (*TA*). BUNKER'S HILL HO (all 6"), *v. infra* 357.
CLAYWAY FM. Cf. *Claywaye* 1611 *AddCh*. ELY HIGH BRIDGE is *le
Heyebregge* 1348 *ElyM*. FOLLY FM, *v. infra* 353. HALL DROVE (6").
Cf. *Hallewere* 1480 *Ct*, *v.* wēr. LOT'S FM. Cf. The Lots *supra* 150.
MIDDLE FEN is *Middelfen* 1251 *ElyCouch*. PHILLIPS' HILL FM is *the
Phillips* 1664 *BedL*. PRICKWILLOW BRIDGE (6") is so named in 1677
(*FenS*). PYPER'S HILL is *Pypers Hill* 1604 *Atkyns*. QUEEN ADELAIDE,
locally ADELAIDE, is so named from a public-house. REDMOOR PLANTA-
TION. Cf. *Redmere* t. Hy 3 *WMP*, *Redmore* 1480 *Ct*. 'Reed-mere,'
v. hrēod, mere and cf. Redmere and Redmoor *infra* 229, 270. WATER-
DEN FEN. Cf. *Waterden* 1221 *ElyA*. WILLOW FM (6"). Cf. *Willowes*
1582 *Ct*.

Intermixed Lands rated to Ely St Mary and Ely Trinity. No. 2

BEALD FM is (*vaccaria in*) *Biela* 1109–31 *LibEl*, *Bela(m)* 1109–1279
ElyM, 1120–50 *HarlCh*, 1130–44 *ElyD*, 1279 *ElyF*, *Bele super Dedhil*
c. 1195 *ElyE*, (*super Longelonde*), (*le middelhoue de*) 13th *Elem*, *le Bele*
1403 *SewersA*. BEALD DROVE (6") is *Belyslanes(ende)* 1280 *Rental*,
viam de Bele 13th *ElyE*, *Belewey* 1512 *ElyB*, *Beald Drove* c. 1825 O.S.
Cf. also *Belilake* 1251 *ElyCouch*, 1277 *Ely*, (*piscaria*) *Belwere* 13th
Hosp, *Beleslond* 1436 *Ct*, *Belehedge* 1582 *Ct*. This is the same word as
Beel 1276 RH (WRY) which Ekwall (*Studies*[2], 159 ff.) finds in such
names as Belaugh and Bylaugh (Nf), Beltoft (L), Belton (Lei), etc.
Though not evidenced as a common noun in OE, it is clearly so used
here. Ekwall suggests that we may have a Germanic cognate in
Beelen in Münster (*Belaun* c. 1030, *Belon* c. 1050, dat. pl. *Belen* 1134,

---

[1] *Ketyneshord* 1452 *Ct*, *Ketyls* 1472 ib., *Ketonshorde* 1495 ib., *Ketyllforth closse*
1514 CAPr xxxvi, *Ket(t)leworth* 1706 Moore, *Kettlesworth Close* c. 1840 *TA*, *v.* ord,
'spit of land.'
[2] Cf. *a loade…in* the use of *Jefferie Rolls* 1617 *Wisb*, *Roll's Load* c. 1825 O.S.,
v. (ge)lād.
[3] Cf. ten. *Joh' Skot* 1417 *Rental*, *Scotts Holt* c. 1840 *TA*.
[4] ten. *John Sendale* 1417 *Rental*, *Sendales* 1564 *Ct*. A very late *thorpe*-formation.

Beele 1188) and Beelen in Gelderland (*Belen* 1103, *Bele* 1188). Its meaning is unknown, but Ekwall suggests a connexion with ON *bil*, Dan *bil*, *bæl*, 'point of time,' literally 'interval, interspace,' with a possible meaning in place-names of 'a glade in a forest' or 'a piece of dry land in fenny country.' The latter is apt here, where we have it associated with *Dedhil* and *Middelhoue*, and in Beild Drove *infra* with *le Knol* and *-houe*. In both we have reference to a *weg*. The road to Beald Fm follows a peculiarly winding course through the fen, clearly keeping to what was once the only passable route. *v.* also Beale Close *infra* 370, Beild Drove and Pymore *infra*.

Little Downham

LITTLE DOWNHAM

> *Duneham* 1086 DB, InqEl, 1267 Pat, *Dunham* 1086 InqEl *et freq* to 1294 Pat, *Dunneham* 1291 Tax
> *Donham* 1086 InqEl, 1275 RH, *Doneham* 1086 InqEl
> *Dounham* 1286 *MinAcct et freq* to 1506 Pat, (*in Insula Elyense*) 1336 ElyC, (*Lytle*) 1357 ElyCh, (*parua*) 1403 Ct, *Douneham* 1327 Pat, *Downeham in the Ile of Ely* 1559 AD v

'hām on a hill,' *v.* dūn, hām. *Little* is a late addition to avoid confusion with Downham Market (Nf).

NOTE. CLAYWAY LANE. Cf. *Clay Way Field* c. 1840 TA and *Claihill* 13th ElyM. RAM'S HORN LANE is so named c. 1840 (*TA*).

DOWNHAM HYTHE is *Dunham hythe* 1251 ElyCouch, *Dounhamhethe* 1405 Ct, *Downeham Hythe* 1549 ib., *v.* hȳð.

MARSHAL DROVE is *Mers(c)hale* 13th, 1391 ElyF, *Merchehale* 13th ElyCh, *Merishale* 13th Elem, *Marshall* (*Fenne*) 1548 CHuAS v. 'Nook in the marsh,' *v.* mersc, healh.

PYMORE is *Be(e)leffen* 1449 Ct, *Belfen al. Pymoor* 1497 ib., *Byemoor* 1786 Lot. Perhaps 'insect-infested marsh,' from OE *pēo*, *pīe*, or possibly 'magpie,' and mōr. Cf. Pymore (PN Do 255). The earlier name is from the neighbouring Beild Drove *infra*.

ADVENTURERS' DROVE (6″) is *Adventurers Dr.* 1829 Wells. Cf. *Adventure Land* 1713 FenS and Adventurers' Land *infra* 292. BEILD DROVE (both 6″) is *Belewey* 1494, 1570 Ct. Cf. *Beild Field* c. 1840 TA. It takes its name from Beald *supra* 223. BISHOP'S PALACE is *The Bishops-*

hall 1660 *Dugd*, formerly a residence of the Bishops of Ely (L 178). BLACK BANK is *Blak Bankes* 1636 BedL. CALIFORNIA lies well away from the village, *v. infra* 357. COFFUE DROVE (6″). Cf. *Corfew Acre* c. 1840 *TA*, perhaps involving a corruption of the first element of *Kalfeycnol* 13th *ElyCh*, *v*. cealf, ēg, cnoll. COPHALL is *Copehall* 1435 *Wren*, *Copthall* 1576 Saxton, possibly 'peaked hall,' cf. Copped Hall (PN Ess 24). DENMARK FM (6″) is in a remote situation. DUNKIRK. Cf. *Dunkirk Drove* c. 1825 O.S. and *infra* 357. FODDER FEN is so named c. 1840 (*TA*), *v*. Fodder Fen *supra* 203. FRITH HEAD. Cf. *le Frith* 1449 *Wren*, *Frith Head Lot* c. 1840 *TA*, *v*. fyrhð(e). GUILD-ACRE FM (6″) was probably part of the land acquired by the gild of St Mary de la Porche and St Leonard, founded in 1475 (Pat). HEAD-FEN FM. Cf. *Head Fen* c. 1840 *TA*. NORTH FEN FM. Cf. *Northfen* 1251 *ElyCouch*. OTTERBUSH FM is *Otrebush* 1403 *SewersA*, *le Otterbush* 1478 *Wren*, (*the*) *Attarbushe* 1617 *SewersD*, *Artle Bush Fm* 1887 Old 6″. Presumably self-explanatory. OXLODE is *Oxload* 1683 *BLAcct*, *Ox Lode* c. 1825 O.S. PARK FM (6″). Cf. *parcum de Dunham* 1221 *ElyA*. THE SLIPE (6″) is *Slipe* c. 1840 *TA*, *v. infra* 354. STRAIGHT FURLONG DROVE (6″) is so named c. 1825 (O.S.). THE WASH is *the Washes* c. 1840 *TA*, *v*. The Wash *supra* 212. WEST FEN is *Westfen* 1251 *ElyCouch*. WEST MOOR FEN is *Westmore* 1414 *Wren*, (*Fennes*) t. Ed 6 CHuAS i.

Littleport

LITTLEPORT

> *Litelport* 1086 DB, InqEl, *Liteport* 1169–86 P, *Lit(t)elport* c. 1250 Ct *et freq*, *Lit(t)leport(e)* 1170 LibEl *et freq*, *Litillport* 1456 Pat, *Lytylport* 1508 ib.
> *Lutelport* c. 1250 Ct, *Lutleport* 1324 Pat, 1331 Rams
> *Lettelport* c. 1250 Ct

'Small town,' *v*. port.

NOTE. COMMON ACRE LANE. Cf. *the Common Acre* 1637 BedL. NEW DITCH WAY. Cf. *Nowedik* 1251 *ElyCouch*, *Newedik* 1277 *Ely*, *le Newditch* 1287 *Wren*. Cf. No Ditch Field *supra* 200.

APES HALL is *Apesholt(e)*, *-is-* 1251 *ElyCouch et freq* to 1606 *Depositions*, *Apeshold*, *Abshold* 1433 *Wren*, *Apshall* 1589 *Depositions*, *Apeshall* 1606 ib., *Aspeholt* 1660 *Dugd*. Probably 'aspen-tree wood,' with early metathesis of *aspe* to *ap(e)s*, *v*. holt.

BURNT FEN is *Brendefen* 1277 *Ely*, 1306, 1334 *ElyCouch*, t. Hy 5 Fleet, *Bryntfen* 1432 *Ct*, *Brenteffen* 1471 ib., *Burnt Fenne* 1606 *Depositions*, *v.* brende, fenn. It has been suggested that it owes its name to the burning of the fen by Hereward.

CAMEL DROVE (6″). Cf. *Camhale* 1251 *ElyCouch*, 15th *ElyM*, -*halle* t. Hy 3 *WMP*, *Camoll loode* 1563 *SewersD*, *Cammalle* c. 1600 *Bades-ladeA*, *Cammell Load* 1617 *SewersD*. It is difficult to suggest any satisfactory etymology for this name. The second element is clearly healh, 'nook, corner.' The first is perhaps *cam*, 'crooked.' If so, the word must, as suggested in NED (*s.v.*), have been loaned from British into popular speech at a much earlier date than any independent record suggests. Cf. Camel Gate in Spalding (L), *Camellgate* 1526 *Terr*.

CHAIN FM (*TA*)[1]. Cf. *le Charre* 1306, 1334 *ElyCouch*, *Lytilport Chaire* 1548 Imb, *ye Chayer* 1591 *Hayward*, *Lyttleport Chayre* 1608 *AddCh*, *the Old Chaine* 1662 *BLAcct*, *Littleport Chayne* 1674 Fen[2], (*Charer*) 1677 ib. It lies at a sharp bend in the Old Croft River (*supra* 9) and the term *chare*, originally applied to the bend, may have come to be used of the river itself as in Chear Lode *supra* 150. It seems to be used of the river in the following passage: "A myle beneath *the Old Chare*, *the new Chaire* w[ch] is a great Navigable River falleth into the said river of Owse and out of the said *New Chare* falleth a great parte of the West Waters under Earyth bridge, descending northward by Sutton, Mepal, Wicham, Coveney and so to Downham hithe by the frythe ditche" (1530 *Draining*, f. 182). Here it seems to be an alternative name for *Byhee* (*v.* Byall Fen *supra* 211). The reason for the change from *chair* to *chain* is obscure. The ferry may have been worked by a chain. See however Chainbridge *infra* 254. For inter-change of *char* and *load* cf. Brangehill *infra* 239. *v.* Addenda lx.

CROFT HILLS is so named c. 1825 (O.S.). Cf. *Littleport Crofts* 1606 *Depositions*, *Lyttleport Craftes* 1672 *FenL*. Hence was named the Old Croft River *supra* 9. Major Gordon Fowler points out that Jonas Moore's map shows that in his day the old flood plain of the course of the Welney north of Littleport was occupied by an almost con-tinuous line of little *crofts* or small holdings, abutting upon the river (CAPr xxxiv, 24).

---

[1] The name survives in Chain Drain in Southery (Nf) from the Ouse, opposite Horse Fen Fm, to Willow Row Drain.

[2] A ferry was maintained here (1660, 1674 Fen).

CROUCH MOOR is *Crech(e)mere*, K- 1221 *ElyA*, 1251 *ElyCouch*, 1268 *EA* vi, (-*lake*) 1621 *SewersD*, *Cro(w)ch(e)mere* (*lo(o)de*) 1563, 1574 *SewersC, D*, *Crichmere* t. Jas 1 *Cole* xxxvii, *Crickmere* c. 1600 *BadesladeA*, *Creakemere*, *Cruchmere(lake)* 1606 *Depositions*. CROUCH MOOR FM is *Crutchmerhall* 1591 *Hayward*. *v*. Creek *infra* 254.

DEEPNEY DROVE (6″). Cf. *Depenhe(e)* 1277 *Ely*, 1298 *Ass*, (*ripam de*) *Depheʒ*, *Depenhey* 1298 *Ass*, *Depenee* 1403 *SewersA*, *Deeping Drove* c. 1825 O.S. '(At the) deep river,' *v*. dēop, ēa.

HALE DROVE (6″). Cf. *Halewere* 1221 *ElyA*, *Halywerelak* 1251 *Ely-Couch*, *Alywerelake* 1277 *Ely*, *Haylewood delff* 1549 *Ct*, *Haleward lake* 1606 *Depositions*, *Hale al. Blackmore Hale* 1611 *ExcheqDecrees*, *The Hale* 1636 *BedL*, *v*. wēr, lacu. The first element may be healh, 'nook, corner,' with reference probably to the land in the bend of the Old Croft River.

HAWKINS'S DROVE (6″). Cf. *Hawkins Bytt* 1436 *BedL*, 1609 *AddCh*, *Hawckinges bitt* 1629 *SewersD*, *Hawkins* 1656 *AdvProc*. The drove runs through the middle of a bend in the course of the Old Ouse. *bytt* is for byht, 'bight, bend,' with reference to the bend. *Hawkins's* from the holding of William *Hawkins* (1658 *Cole* xxxvi), the 'several fen ground of William *Haukins*' (1637 *BedL*). By a curious chance, an earlier name of this fen seems to have been *Hacunfen* 1221 *ElyA*, 1251 *ElyCouch*, *Hakounfen* 1318 *Ct*, deriving from Anglo-Scandinavian *Hacun*.

MOW FEN is *Littleport mowefen voc. mourefen* 1660 *Dugd*, *Mow fenn* 1706 Moore. Cf. "Mow Fens or Lamas Grounds consisting of the Lots or doles of divers persons...out of the mowing grounds" 1637 *BedL* ii, 264 (Wicken), *Draiton Mowffen* 1636 *BedL*, *le Mowe fenne* 1661 *Ct* (Upwell).

SKETCHDOLES FM (6″). We have no early forms for this place-name, but it has its parallel in *le Scach(e)dole* 1494 *Rental*, *Skatchyddole* 1496 ib. in Fulbourn, and we have reference in the same document (1496) to a field with a *skatche on þe est syde*. So also we have *Skacched Akyrr* 1528 *CAPr* xxxvi in Ely and 2 *roods* 20 *poles called a Sketch on the Brickkiln* 1800 *EnclA* in Guilden Morden. The same element seems to be found in fields called *Scachbowe*, *Schachebowe*, *Skac(c)hebowe*, *Skatchebowe*, *Scatchbold* 1332–1786 *CCC*. The history and meaning of this element *skacche* is entirely obscure.

SPAINDELF FM is *Spanidelf* 1251 *ElyCouch*, *Spandelf* t. Hy 3 *WMP*, *Spanisdelf* 1277 *Ely*, *Spaindelf* 14th *Cai*, *Spanydelfe* 1606 *Depositions*,

Spains Delph c. 1840 *TA*. This is probably a compound of OE *spann*, 'a hand's breadth, a span' and (ge)delf, perhaps a derogatory name for a very narrow dike. Cf. further Spon End (PN Wa 167–8). The earliest forms might be read as *Spain-* or *Spani-*, but the form *Spany-* suggests that the second is the correct reading, with later corruption of a name no longer understood.

WELTMORE FM is *Welpingmor* 1251 *ElyCouch*, 1277 *Ely*, *Welpmor* 1306 *ElyCouch*, t. Hy 5 Fleet, *Whelpmore* 1334 *ElyCouch*, 1609 *AddCh*, *Whelpyngmore* 1556 *Ct*. The forms in *W(h)elping-* make derivation from a personal name *Hwelp* more likely than derivation from OE *hwelp*, 'cub,' hence '*Hwelp*'s marsh,' *v.* mōr. Cf. Kirkwhelpington (PN NbDu 129). For the possibility of a native English name *Hwelp* cf. Feilitzen 297 *s.n. Hvelpr* and Tengstrand 367, *s.n. Uuelp*.

WOOD FEN is *Penhenorte* 1251 *ElyCouch*, *Penstr(e)* 1306, 1334 ib., *Pensenort north fenne or Woodfenne*, *Penhenorte al. Penynorth* 1606 *Depositions*, *Penkenort* 1611 *ExcheqDecrees*, *Wood Fen* 1636 BedL. This name must in its earlier form remain an unsolved problem.

BATES'S DROVE[1], BELL'S DROVE[2] (both 6″), BUTCHER'S HILL FM[3], CAVE'S FM, HORN'S DROVE[4] (6″) and MARTIN'S DRAIN are probably to be associated with the families of William *Bates* (c. 1840 *TA*), Alice *Belle* (1327 SR), Edward *Butcher* (1780 Poll), Thomas *Cave* (c. 1840 *TA*), John *Horne* (1654 *BLAcct*) and ..... *Martin* (c. 1320 CAPr iv) and William *Martin* (1802 BedL).

BLACK BANK, BLACK HORSE DROVE, OLD POOL DROVE, POPLAR DROVE and WILLOW ROW DROVE (all 6″) are so named c. 1840 (*TA*). BLACK HORSE FM is *Black Horse* 1821 Baker. BURNT CHIMNEY DROVE and DAIRY HOUSES (both 6″) are so named in 1821 (Baker). BURNT FEN BANK is so named in 1660 (*Dugd*). CROSS DROVE (both 6″) is *the Cross Drove* 1658 *BLAcct*. GRUBB'S FM is *Grub's Fm* c. 1825 O.S. HILL FM (6″) is *Hills Farm* ib. THE HOLMES (6″) is *Hulmo* c. 1320 CAPr iv, *v.* holmr. THE HUNDREDS. Cf. *croft voc. hundreth ac'* 1549 *Ct*, *the Hundred Acres* 1637 BedL. LITTLEPORT BRIDGE. Cf. (*altam viam prope*) *pontem* c. 1320 CAPr iv, *Littleporte brigge* 1606 *Depositions*. LITTLEPORT FIELDS is *Littleport feild* ib., *v.* feld. LOCK SPIT FM (6″). Cf. Lockspit Hall *supra* 150. MARE FEN is *Marffen* 1636 BedL, *the*

---

[1] *Bates Drove* c. 1825 O.S.
[2] Cf. *Bell Croft* 1637 BedL, *Farm House of Mr Philip Bell* 1714 *Cole* xlvii.
[3] *Butchers Hill* 1821 Baker.　　　　[4] *Horns Drove* c. 1825 O.S.

Mare Fen 1637 ib. Probably from (ge)mǣre, as it is near the parish boundary. MIDDLE DROVE (6″) is so named c. 1825 (O.S.). MILDEN-HALL DRAIN (6″) is *Mildenhall Dreyne* 1677 *FenS*, from Mildenhall (Sf). THE PLAINS is *La Plaine* c. 1320 CAPr iv. PORTLEY HILL (local) is *Portlow* ib., v. **port**, **hlāw** and Littleport *supra* 225. RACK FEN is *Rakfen* 1306 *ElyCouch*, t. Hy 5 Fleet, *Rackefenn* 1582 DKR xxxiii, 1584 *Depositions*. SANDHILL.. Cf. *Sandhill poynt* 1629 *SewersD*. SCOTLAND FM (6″) is on the parish boundary, v. *infra* 357. WADLODE FM is *Wadlode* 1610 *SewersD*, *Waddload* 1621 ib. WEST MOOR DROVE (6″) is so named in 1829 (Wells). WEST MOOR FEN (6″). Cf. *Westmor* 1306 *ElyCouch*. WHITE HALL FM is *Whithall* 1629 *SewersD*. WHITE HO FM is *White House* 1821 Baker. WHITE HOUSE DROVE (6″) is so named c. 1825 (O.S.). WILLOW ROW FMS is *Willow Roe End* 1655 *BLAcct*, *Willow Row Fms* 1821 Baker. v. Addenda lx.

Redmere

REDMERE FEN (6″) is (*maram de*) *Red(e)mere* 1251 *ElyCouch*, 1277 *Ely*, 1302 *MinAcct*, *Rodemere* 1298 ib., *Redmore* c. 1825 O.S. 'Reed-mere,' v. **hrēod**, **mere**.

DECOY WOOD (6″). Cf. *Decoy Fen* c. 1825 O.S. REDMERE FM (6″) is *Redmere House* ib.

WITCHFORD HUNDRED

(*in*) *hundredis suis de Wichefort* c. 1128 *Thorney*, (*in*) *hundredis suis* (*Eliensis ecclesia*) *de Wichefordia* t. Hy 2 (1314) Ch, (*hundredo de*) *Wich(e)ford(e)*, *-y-* 1178–89 (17th) ChronRams *et freq* to 1399 *MinAcct*

Wiceford t. Hy 5 Fleet, *Wecheforde* 1418 *MinAcct*

In DB and InqEl, the two hundreds of Ely are said to meet at Witchford (v. *supra* 213). Later the "hundred courte (was) houlden at *Witchforde Stoune*" (1596 *Depositions*). Cf. *Wichfordstone* 1419 *ElyCouch*. In 1657 and 1660 we have reference to the "court kept at *Lowhill* called the Shereffesturn" (*Ct*). Cf. *cur' de Wychamlowe* 1409 ib., *Wychamlowfurlong* 1423 *ElyCh* (apparently in or near Sutton)[1].

---

[1] The tourn was held at Witchfordstone at Michaelmas and at Witchamlowe on the feast of St Peter in Cathedra (1377, 1395, 1429, *ex inf*. Mr E. Miller). In 1377 "Hundreda de Wichford tenta apud Sutton et apud Hadenham" (*Wren* f. 341).

v. hlāw. In Witcham, too, we have *lauehove* 1306 *ElyF*, *Louehoue*
t. Ed 1 *ElyCh* and (*le*) *Loweweye*(*howe*, *-houe*) 13th, 1304–12 *ElyCh*,
Lowway 1693 *Ct*, *v.* hōh, weg. *Louehoue* is presumably identical with
Lowhill and *Loweweye* is the road leading to the meeting-place of the
hundred.

XVI. HUNDRED OF SOUTH WITCHFORD

Coveney

Coveney

> *Coueneia* c. 1060 (12th) KCD 932, 1170 LibEl, (*insulam de*) *Coueneya*
> c. 1160 *Ely*, *-ey*(*e*) 1251 *ElyCouch et freq*, *Couenhe* ib., *Covene*
> 1310 Pat
> *Conye* 1319 Cl

This may be '*Cofa*'s island' or it may be 'island in the bay' as
suggested by Ekwall (DEPN). For *Cofa* cf. Covington (PN BedsHu
238). OE *cofa*, 'cave, den,' is found in place-names in the sense
(among others) 'bay, creek.' *v.* ēg. The topography suggests that
when Coveney was an island it was situated in a deep bay, now
represented by the West Fen.

BLOCK MOORS is *Blockemor* 1326 *MinAcct*, *Blokmoor* 15th *Ely*, *Block
Moors* 1637 BedL, *Blackmores* 1653 *FenS*. Cf. Blockmoor Fen *supra*
198.

WARDY HILL is *Wardey*(*e*) 1251 *ElyCouch*, 1277 *Ely*, 1423–34 *Ct*,
Wardheye 1277 *Ely*, 14th *Cai*, *Werdey* 1481 *Wren*, *Wardie hill* 1589
SewersD, *Waudy Hill* 1821 Baker, *Wardow Hill* c. 1825 O.S. 'Island
from which watch was kept,' *v.* weard, ēg.

BARBER'S DROVE (6″) is probably to be associated with the family of
Elizabeth *Barber* (c. 1650 *SewersA*). Cf. *land in Blockmoor formerly
Barber's* a. 1769 BedL.

ASHWELL MOOR is *Ashwelle* 1375 *Ct*, *Asswelmoor* 1428 ib., *v.* mōr.
COVENEY FEN (6″) is *Coveny Fen* 1636 BedL. FROG'S ABBEY FM (6″)
is *Frogs Abbey* 1829 Wells. Cf. *infra* 357. GREAT DAMS FEN. Cf.
"certain severalls...called *Covenie dames*" 1636 BedL, *the New Dams,
the Town Dam* 1637 ib. HALE FEN is *Fen called Hales* 1636 ib., *Hale
Fen* 1637 ib. HALL FEN is *Hallfen* 1653 *FenS*. JERUSALEM (6″) is on
the parish boundary, *v. infra* 357. NEW DROVE and SHORT CAUSEWAY

are so named c. 1825 (O.S.). OLD FEN (all 6") is *Oldfenn* 1621 *SewersD*.
SEDGE FEN DROVE. Cf. *Seggefen* 1414 *Wren*, *Sedgefenn* 1658 *Ct*.
STRAIGHT DROVE (6") and WAY HEAD are so named in 1829 (Wells).
SWEET HILL DROVE (6") is so named in 1870 (*Witcham*). WAY HEAD
DROVE (6") is *Wayhead Drove* c. 1840 *TA*.

Grunty Fen

GRUNTY FEN

> *Gruntifen(n)*, -y- 1221 *ElyA et freq* to 1558 *Ct*, *Grontefenfelde* 1532
> *Peterhouse*, *Grauntye Fenne* 1618 *SewersA*
> *Gruntyngfen(felde)* 1370–1440 *Peterhouse*, (*furlonge*) 1488 *CaiCh*[1],
> *le Gruntyngmede* 1432 *Peterhouse*[1]
> *Grundefen* 1604 *Atkyns*

We have probably to do with a first element *grunting*, but its history
and meaning are obscure. The Teutonic stem **grunþo* has given rise
to ON *grunnr*, *gruðr*, 'shallow, bottom,' Sw *grund*, and the stem
*grundu-s has given OE *grund*, 'ground.' *grunting* is perhaps allied to
these and may denote a shallow place. It has been suggested that
grunþ goes back to *grumþ* and is related to Norw *grumen*, 'muddy,'
hence 'muddy shallow,' *v. ing.*

GRANGER'S GRUNTY FEN FM (6") is probably to be associated with the
family of John *Granger* (1672 *Bodl*).

GRUNTY FEN DRAIN (6") is *Grunty Fenn Draine* 1654 Moore.

Haddenham

HADDENHAM

> (*on*) *hædan ham* 970 (12th) BCS 1268, *Hadenham* 1086 InqEl *et freq*
> to 1484 Pat, *Hadinham* 1247 FF, 1276 Pat, 1335 *ElyC*, *Hadnam*
> 1496 Ipm, 1565 PCC, *Haddenham on the hill* 1537 *CaiCh*, *Hadna-
> ham* 1576 Ely
> *Hadreham* 1086 DB, *Hæderham*, *Haddreham* 1086 InqEl, *Hadyrs-
> ham* 1487 Pat
> *Hedreham* 1089 BM, *Hederham* 1170 LibEl
> *Hadeham* 1170–1 P (p), 1285 Ass, *Haddeham* 1172 P, *Hadman* 1436
> Pat, *Hadden within the Isle of Eley* 1548 ib.
> *Hadingham* 1247 FF, 1324 Pat

---

[1] In Haddenham.

'*Hǣda*'s homestead,' *v.* hām. Cf. Haddenham (PN Bk 161). For the AN *r* for *n*, *v.* IPN 106–7.

NOTE. BERRY LANE leads to the manor of Lindon (*Lyndonbury* 1356 *Extent*). CHEWELL'S LANE is *Chewellewey* 1383 *Peterhouse*, *Chewelleslane* 1554 ib. Cf. *terram Ricardi de Chewell'* 1221 *ElyA*, *Chewell* 1368 *Misc*, *Chewelles* 1485 *Wren*. COW WAY is *Cowey* 1532 *Peterhouse*, *Cowewaie* 1610 *Terr.* HINTON HEDGES RD. Cf. *Henghtonehegge* 1496 *Peterhouse* and Hinton *infra* 233. LODE WAY is *Loadewaye* 1615 *Ct*, *v.* (ge)lād. MADDINGLEY WAY is *Madyngleeweye* 1461 ib. PERRY WAY is *Perywey* 1488 *CaiCh*. 'Pear-tree road,' *v.* pirige. SMITH'S LANE is probably to be associated with the family of John *Smyth* (1431 *Peterhouse*). Cf. *terr. Johannis Smyth'* 1488 *CaiCh*. STOCKING LANE. Cf. *Stockynge* 1368 *Peterhouse*, *v.* stocking. TINKER'S LANE. Cf. *Tinkers Close* c. 1840 *TA*. WOOLDEN LANE. Cf. *Waldune* 13th *ElyCh*, 'the dūn by *Wold*' *infra* 246.

ALDRETH

Alrehed(a) 1169–72 P, *-heðe*, *-hede* 1170 LibEl, *-hethe* c. 1300
  GestH, *-huða* 1171 P, *Aldreheþe* 1251 *ElyCouch*, *-hethe* 1298 *Ass*
Alderheþe 1251 *ElyCouch*, *-heth(e)* 1279 RH *et freq* to 1345
  CWool, *-hithe* 1298 *MinAcct*, *-heath* 1358 FF, *Ælderheþe* 1277 *Ely*
Halderheth 1279 RH, *Altherhethe* 14th Rams
Aldereth 1302 *MinAcct*, *Ald(e)ryth* 1311, 1315 *ElyF*, *Aldreth* 1499
  Ipm, *Alreth* 1443 *MinAcct*
Audre 1576 Saxton, *Athered hodie Audre* 1586 Camden, *Aldrey*
  1605 Imb

'Landing-place by the alders,' *v.* alor, hyð. For loss of final *-th* cf. Odsey *supra* 62.

ALDRETH CAUSEWAY is *calceta de Alreheda* 1178 (17th) ChronRams, *la chaucee de Alderhethe* 1339 Rams, *Elderyth cawse* 1540 *MinAcct*, *via Etheldredæ quæ vulgo vocatur S. Audreyes causeye* CHuAS i, 8, 51. The building of the causeway is traditionally assigned to William the Conqueror (but cf. H. C. Darby, *Medieval Fenland* 110), and for centuries it was the chief entrance from the Cambridge district. When the name had developed to *Audrey* it was quite naturally associated with *St Audrey* or *St Etheldreda*, the foundress of the monastery at Ely.

UPPER and LOWER DELPHS is *le Delue* 1330 *Ct*, *le Delf* 1343 ib., *ye Delfes* 1563 Fenland v, *the Delphs*, *the Nether delph*, *the Upper delph* 1604 *Atkyns*, *v.* (ge)delf. Alternatively they are known as *Lesdelfes called Delff et Osdelff* 1549 *Ct*, *Delfe et Esdelfe* 1595 *SP*, and the second of these is called *Hisdelfe* 1207 (1344) *Rams*, *Hosedelf* 1221 *ElyA*, *Os(e)delf* 1251 *ElyCouch*, 1277 *Ely*, *Osdel(were)* 1435 *Peterhouse*, *Ouse-delph* 1604 *Atkyns*. The Delphs are on the banks of the Ouse, but the forms suggest that *Osedelf*, etc. refer not to the position by the Ouse but to the *ose* or *ooze* (OE **wāse**) found in them.

FOULMIRE FEN (6″). Cf. *Fulmere(s)(lode)* 1251 *ElyCouch*, 1277 *Ely*, 1298 *Ct*, *ffoul(e)merelode* 1405–51 *Ct*, 15th *Ely*, *Folmere* ib. Either 'foul, muddy mere' (*v.* **fūl**) or identical with Fowlmere *supra* 83 and so 'wild-birds' mere,' *v.* fugol.

HILL ROW

> (*on*) *hylle* 970 (12th) BCS 1268, 1086 InqEl, *Hylle*, *Hille* 1170 LibEl *et freq* to 1298 *Ass*, *Hilrowe* 1638 ElyVis
> *Helle* 1086 DB, InqEl, 1170 LibEl, *Heilla*, *Heille*, *Hælle* 1086 InqEl, *Hulle* 1380 *Peterhouse*

Self-explanatory.

HINTON HALL

> *Henegetun(e)* 973 (12th) *LibEl*, 1170 LibEl, *-ton(e)* 1221 *ElyA et freq* to 1298 *Ass*, *Henegent'* c. 1250 *ElyCouch*, *Hynegeton* 1341 *Elien*, *Henig(h)ton* 1498–9 *Ct*, (*al. Henton*) t. Eliz *Cole* xxxvii
> *Haningetuna*, *Ha(n)ningatuna* 1086 InqEl (p), *Honegetone* c. 1260 Bodl
> *Heneketon(e)* 1281 Cl, 1298 *Ass*, 1302 FA, 1341 *Elien*, *Hynke-*, *Hinketone* 1378–83 *Peterhouse*, *Henkentonfeld* 1455 ib.
> *Hynton*, *-i-* 1304 *ElyF et freq*
> *Hington* 1387, 1507 Pat, *Heng(h)ton(e)* 1485–8 *Wren*, 1541 *MinAcct*, *Hosp*, t. Hy 8 *Rental*
> *Heyngton(e)* 1417, 1508 *Peterhouse*, 1496, 1502 *Ct*, 1510 LP, t. Hy 8 *Terr*, *Heyn(y)ton(e)* 1498 *Ct*, 1517–20 *Peterhouse*
> *Henton* c. 1460 ECP, t. Hy 8 *Rental*, 1506–7 *Ct*

This would seem to derive from an OE *Hēaningatūn*, but the ultimate history of such a name is entirely obscure. No personal name *Hean* is on record. *Hean*, often quoted as the name of the first abbot of Abingdon, is really an oblique case of *Hæha*. OE *hēan*, 'low, abject, mean,' could hardly give rise to a personal name. For the development cf. Danbury and Hanningfield (PN Ess 248, 250–1).

LINDEN END[1]

> (to) *Lindune* c. 975 ASCh, 1086 InqEl, 1086, 1170 (12th) LibEl,
> *Lindone* 1086 DB, *Lindona* 1086 InqEl, -*don(e)* 1221 *ElyA*, 1247,
> 1310 FF, 1251 *ElyCouch*, 1277 *Ely*, (*End*) 1686 *Cole* ix, *Lyndon*
> 1251 *ElyCouch*, *London* (sic) *End* c. 1825 O.S.
> (into) *Lintune* 970 (12th) BCS 1268, *Ætlintune* 970 (12th) LibEl,
> *Lenton Croft* 1686 *Cole* ix

This may be 'flax hill' as suggested by the topography and the
form *Lindun* in an original 10th-century document. v. līn, dūn.
'Lime-tree hill' is also possible, v. lind. Cf. Linwood Wood *infra* 257.

STAPLE LEYS FM (with Staple Leys in Wentworth *infra* 243) is
Stapyllleyes 1431 *Peterhouse* and takes name from *Staple* 1251 *Ely-
Couch*, some forgotten stapol or pillar, which also gave name to
Stapelweye 13th *ElyCh* and *Stapelfeld* 1341 *Ct.* leyes is probably a
late form for læs, 'pasture.' The 'staple' was probably in Wentworth.

THE GREEN and LINDEN END DOLES (both 6″) are *le Grene* 1549 *Ct*
and *Lindon Dowles* 1596 *Cole* xxxvii and were the homes of Robertus
del grene (1221 *ElyA*) and Robert de *la Dale de Lindon* (1285 *Ass*). v.
grēne and Linden End *supra*. *la Dale de Lindon* must derive from
dæl rather than from dāl.

GRANGER'S DROVE (6″), SALMON'S FM and SETCHELL'S FM (6″) are
probably to be associated with the families of Samuel *Granger* (1669
FenS), John *Salmon* (1819 Carter) and Oliver *Setchell* (c. 1840 *TA*).

THE ADVENTURERS (6″). *the Adventurers for y*ᵉ *Fennes* had land here
in 1654 (*Terr*). ADVENTURERS' HEAD DRAIN, LITTLE ADVENTURERS'
DRAIN (both 6″). Cf. *the dreyne from Adventure Grownd in Gall fen*
1654 BLAcct. ADVENTURERS' HEAD DROVE (6″) is so named c. 1825
(O.S.). Cf. Adventurers' Land *infra* 292. ALDRETH FIELD (6″) is so
named in 1604 (*Atkyns*). BEDLAM FM is *Bedlam House* 1821 Baker,
v. *infra* 352. BERRY FEN FM. Cf. *Berry fen* 1604 *Atkyns*. THE BOOT
(6″). Cf. *Mere Boot* (in Willingham) 1870 *Witcham*. THE BRINKS is
so named c. 1840 (*TA*). BUTLERS DROVE (both 6″). Cf. *Butylers* 1514
Peterhouse. CHURCH FEN, EWELL FEN and SMALL FEN (6″) are so
named in 1604 (*Atkyns*). COLLEGE FM. Cf. *College Close* c. 1840 *TA*.

---

[1] BCS 1268 gives us the bounds of Linden End (*into Lintune*). With the exception
of Hill Row *supra* 233 the points given are names of parishes. Ekwall (DEPN)
wrongly identifies *Lintune* with Linton *supra* 109.

DAM BANK DROVE (6″). Cf. *Dambanke* 1636 BedL. FLAT BRIDGE FM
is *Flat-house* c. 1825 O.S. Named from Flat Bridge in Willingham
supra 175. FOULMIRE DROVE, HADDENHAM PASTURES and RED HO (6″)
are so named c. 1825 (O.S.). FROG'S HALL (6″) is *Frog-hall* c. 1725
Cole ii, *v. infra* 357. GALL FEN is *Gallefenne* 1549 *Ct*, *Gaul Fen* 1637
BedL, *v.* galle. THE GULLS (6″). Cf. *Gull Drain* c. 1825 O.S. and
gole. HADDENHAM END FIELD is *Haddenham End Fields* 1663 *Hard-*
wickeA. HADDENHAM ENGINE DRAIN (6″) is so named in 1883 (AnctC).
THE HERMITAGE is *the Heremitage* 1604 *Atkyns*, *the Armitage* c. 1695
Celia Fiennes' *Diary*. The causeway over Haddenham Fen was looked
after by "poor hermits of Haddenham" (1406, 1491 Ely). HIGH
BRIDGE FM is named from *le Heigbrigg* 1370 *Peterhouse*, earlier *pontem*
de Alderhithe 1240 Rams. HILL ROW CAUSEWAY (6″) is *Hyllwey* 1488
CaiCh. HILL ROW DOLES is *Hulledoles* 1396 *Peterhouse*, *Hilledoles*
1417 ib., *v.* dāl. HILL ROW FIELD (6″) is *campis de Hille* 1348 *CaiCh*,
Hullefelde 1383 *Peterhouse*, *Hillrow field* 1668 EA xiii, *v.* Hill Row
supra 233 and feld. HOGHILL DROVE. Cf. *Hoggeshill* 1604 *Atkyns*,
Hoghill Drove c. 1825 O.S. HOLME FM and FEN. Cf. *The Holmes*
1604 *Atkyns*, *Holme Fen* c. 1840 *TA*. *v.* holmr. LAKES DROVE (6″)
is so named in 1690 (*SewersA*). LINDEN END FIELD is *Lyndonfylde*
1436 *Peterhouse*, *Lindon End Field* 1686 *Cole* ix. LOCKSPIT HALL (6″).
Cf. *Adventurers Lockspits* 1733 *Terr* and *v.* The Adventurers *supra* 234
and Lockspit Hall *supra* 150. LONG DROVE (6″) is so named c. 1825
(O.S.). MADDINGLEY FM (6″) is *ten. Maddyngle* 1366 *Ct*, *terram*
Maddynglie 1383 *Peterhouse*, *Madyngleyes* 1432 ib., *Maddingly Farme*
1733 *Terr*. Probably a manorial name from some tenant belonging to
Madingley *supra* 181. MILKINGHILL BRIDGE (6″). Cf. *Milking Hill*
1697 *HardwickeA*, (*Bridge*) 1870 *Witcham*. NORTH FEN (6″) is *North-*
hayfen 1277 Ely, *North Fen* 1604 *Atkyns*. "Fen by *Northey*, the low-
lying land in the north (of the parish)." Cf. *Northey* 1221 *ElyA* and
Northey and North Fen *infra* 261, 262. PINGLE HO. Cf. *le Pyngle*
1549 *Ct*, *the Pingles* "be 2 parcels of meadows...one...called *My*
Lord's Pingle" 1604 *Atkyns* and *infra* 340. SHEPHERD'S HO (6″). Cf.
Shepherds Close c. 1840 *TA*. THE WASHES (6″) is *the Wash* 1720
HardwickeA. Cf. *supra* 212.

Manea

MANEA
    Moneia, -eya, -eye 1177 P (p) *et freq* to 1326 *MinAcct*, *Monea* 1576
    Saxton, 1695 SN

Maneia, -ey(e), -aye, -ye 1178 P (p) *et freq* to 1575 Ely, *Mane* 1570
SR
Mawna 1499 Ipm

"Well-watered land that served as common pasture," from OE
(*ge*)*mǣne* and ēg. Cf. "*Moneyeslode* (i.e. Manea Lode) ubi tota villata
de Lytleport debent communare" (1251 *ElyCouch*) and Maney (PN
Wa 49–50).

NOTE. DAY'S LODE RD is probably a corruption of Darcey Lode *supra* 4,
olim [deizi]. FODDER FEN RD is *Fodder Fen Drove* 1829 Wells. Cf. *supra* 203.
HIGH ST is so named c. 1840 (*TA*).

CHARLE MONT (6″) is *Charlemont* 1638 Imb. "On 23 July 1638 (owing
to the opposition of the fenmen) Charles I declared himself the sole
Adventurer for the reclamation of the Fens....An eminent town was
to be built in the midst of the Level, on the site of the little village of
Manea, to be called *Charlemont*, the design whereof the King drew
himself..." (Fenland v, 365).

CRANMOOR LOTS is *Cranemoore* 1473 *Wren, Cranmore* 1679 *FenS.*
'Crane or heron marsh,' *v*. cran, mōr. For *Lots* cf. The Lots *supra*
150.

BARNES'S DROVE (6″), BOND'S FM[1] and CARROLL'S FM and GROUNDS
are probably to be associated with the families of George *Barnes*,
Sergeant-at-Mace to the Bedford Level Corporation, 1663–7 (Fen 95),
John *Bond* (1819 Carter) and John *Carill* (1649 *AdvProc*). The latter
are *Mr Carrills House* 1661 *BLAcct, grounds called Carrel's Hundred*
1714 *Cole* xlvii, *Carrells Grounds* c. 1840 *TA.*

BEDLAM FM is *Bedlam* 1714 *Cole* xlvii, *v. infra* 352. THE BIGGINS is
High, Low Biggins c. 1840 *TA, v.* bigging. CLAYPITS (6″), COW
COMMON and WEST FIELD are so named c. 1840 (*TA*). THE DAMS is
Manea Dammes 1636 BedL. FIFTY DROVE (6″) is so named in 1829
(Wells). Cf. *the ffifties end* 1688 *SewersA* and Manea Fifties *infra.*
FODDER FEN COMMON is *Fodder Fen* c. 1840 *TA.* Cf. Fodder Fen
supra 203. FODDER FEN HO (6″) is so named in 1829 (Wells). MANEA
FIFTIES is *the Fiftys* c. 1702 Fen. Cf. Fifty Drove *supra.* PURLS
BRIDGE is so named in 1720 (*BLAcct*). WATERINGHILL FM. Cf.
Maney Watering 1529 BedL.

[1] *Bonds* 1748 Manea.

Mepal

MEPAL [mepəl]

Mepahala 12th *LibEl*, *Mepehale* 1362 Pat, 1379–87 *Ct*
Mephal(e) 1199 FF *et freq* to 1428 FA, (*iuxta Sutton*) 1321 *ElyCh*
Mephall 1285 *Ass*, 1579 Ely, 1605 Imb, *Mepalle* 1523 *SR*, 1670
    Hardwicke A, Mepalt 1706 StJ
Mepale 1467 *Wren*, 15th *ElyM*, t. Hy 8 *Rental*
Mepole 1607 Kip, *Mep(p)le* 1636 BedL, 1675 Ogilby, *Meepole* 1685
    CAPr iii, *Meypole, Maple* 1695 SN

This name must be compared with Meopham (KPN 71, 359, PN K
103–4), *Meapaham* 788 BCS 253. Skeat suggested that the first
element of both was the genitive plural of a tribal name *Mēapas*, and
the first form given above, unknown to Skeat, certainly supports this.
Wallenberg (PN K *loc. cit.*), withdrawing his first suggestion that the
first element was topographical, explains *Mēapas* as "the mopers, the
sulkers, the grumblers," from the root **maup-*, cognate with English
mope. Ekwall (Studies[1] 24–5) prefers a personal name *Mēapa* from
the same root. No certainty is possible.

NOTE. GREEN LANE is so named c. 1840 (*TA*). It was possibly the home
of John *Grenelane* who had a tenement in Haddenham in 1411 and 1428 (FA).

COLE'S FM and FORTREY HO[1] (both 6″) are probably to be associated
with the families of William *Cole* (c. 1840 *TA*) and Samuel *Fortrey*
(1662 *AdvProc*).

MEADLANDS FM is *Mead Landes* 1658 *BLAcct*. MEPAL BRIDGE (6″) is
Mepale Bridge 1636 BedL. PINGLE DROVE (6″). Cf. *Pynns Pingle* 1659
BLAcct, *Pennyspingle Bridge* 1662 ib. *v.* pingel. WITCHAM MEAD-
LANDS is *Wychammedwelonde* 1318 *ElyCh*, -*medelond* 1318 *ElyF*. This
was, presumably, once part of Witcham *infra* 244.

Stretham

STRETHAM

(*æt*) *Strǣtham* c. 975 ASCh
Stratham c. 970 *LibEl*, 1086 InqEl *et freq* to 1303 Cl, (*by Ely*)
    1257 Pat
Stradham 1086 DB, InqEl

        [1] *Fortry Hall* 1829 Wells.

Stretham 1170 LibEl *et freq* to 1550 Pat, (*cum Theford*) 1327 SR,
    Stret(t)(e)ham(e) 1378, 1381, 1553 Pat, 1546 *MinAcct*
Straham 1170 LibEl *et freq* to 1302 *MinAcct*
Streham 13th *Elem*, 1298 *Ass*, *Streeum* 1688 PR i
Traham 1272 Ch
Streatham 1565 Ely, *Stritham* 1662 Blaeu

'hām on the strǣt,' i.e. the Roman road known as Akeman Street
supra 18. For *Traham* cf. Trafford in Stretford (PN La 32).

ELFORD CLOSES take name from *Elforde* 1221 *ElyA*, *Eleford*, *Eldeford-*
(*brigge*) 1251 *ElyCouch*. Possibly *Eldeford* reveals the real origin of
the name, viz. 'the old ford,' *v.* eald, ford. This must have been the
ford and bridge where Akeman Street crossed the Ouse.

HOLT FEN (6″) is *Holefen* 1251 *ElyCouch*, 1277 *Ely*, *Holffen* 1549 *Ct*,
Hold Fen 1636 BedL, *Howle Fen* 1674 *BLAcct*, *Whole Fenn* 1692
SewersA, *Holtfen* c. 1840 *TA*. 'Hollow marsh,' *v.* holh, fenn.

LAZIER FEN (6″) is *Lazar fenn* 1605 *Depositions*, *le Leasouwe Fen* 1612
Ct, *the Lazure* 1689 DKR xli. 'Pasture fen,' *v.* lǣs.

STARLOCK HAY FEN is a composite name combining (i) *Stanlake* 1221
ElyA, *Stallock* 1608 *Stretham*, (ii) *Hay* 1221 *ElyA*, (iii) *Hayfen*
1302 *MinAcct*. 'Marsh by the enclosure by the stony stream,' *v.* lacu,
(ge)hæg.

STOW BRIDGE (FM) (6″) is *Stoubrigge* 1417 *Rental*. The meaning is
uncertain. It may be a compound of stōw as used in the fen district
with a significance which is not clear (*infra* 345) or it may be for
Stonbrigge with loss of *n*. For similar loss of *n* cf. *s.n.* Stoford (PN D
41), Sto(w)ford, Stowell and Storridge (PN W 124, 199, 228, 326,
150).

HILL FM (6″) was the home of Richard *Attehil* (1277 *Ely*).

ADVENTURERS LAND, cf. *infra* 292. BEGGAR'S BUSH FIELD is *Begger(s)-*
feild 1606 *Depositions*, *Beggar's Field* 1639 *Stretham*. BERRY GREEN is
so named ib. Cf. *Birilode* 1251 *ElyCouch*, *Berelake* 1302 *MinAcct*.
v. burh (manorial). BROOK FIELD (all 6″) is *Brocfeld* 1221 *ElyA*.
CHEAR FEN, *v. supra* 149. CHITTERING FM is *Chitterings* 1604 *Atkyns*.
Near Chittering *supra* 185. FIDWELL FEN (6″) is *Fedall Fen* 1573
Stretham, *Fydall fen* 1604 *Atkyns*, *Feadallffen* 1606 *Depositions*,

Fidwell Fen 1637 BedL. GRAVEL FM. Cf. *Hole Fen Gravel* 1667
Stretham. MERE MILL DROVE (6″). Cf. *Mere Mill* c. 1825 O.S.
MILL WAY is so named in 1639 (*Stretham*). PARSON'S DROVE. Cf.
Parsons Holt 1636 BedL. THE PINGLE. Cf. *the little Pingle* 1667
Stretham. PLANTATION CLOSES (all 6″). Cf. *Plantation House* ib.
RED HILL FM. Cf. *le Redehil* 1388 *Ct*. SNOOTS COMMON is *the
Snowte* 1606 *Depositions*, *Common called Snout* 1657 *Bodl, v.* snote.
STRETHAM FERRY BRIDGE (6″). Cf. *Stretham Ferry* 1604 *Atkyns*.
STRETHAM MERE is *mare de Straham* 1170 LibEl, *Strethammere*
1356 *Extent, v.* mere.

Sutton

SUTTON

> *Sudtone* 1086 DB, *Suttuna*, *Suttona* 1086 InqEl, *Suttun(e)* 1170
> LibEl, *Sutton(e)* 1246 FF *et passim*, (*in Heyland, iuxta Ely, iuxta
> Hadenham*) 1285 *Ass*, (*infra insulam Eliens'*) 1302 *ElyCh*, (*cum
> Mephale*) 1327 SR, (*in the Ilande*) 1367 FF, (*Golden*) 1599
> ChancP, (*in the Isle*) 1609 *SewersD*

'South farm,' *v.* tūn. In the *south* of the Isle of Ely. For *Golden*
cf. Guilden Morden *supra* 61. *Heyland* is for *eyland*, i.e. 'island.'

NOTE. BROOK RD. Cf. *Brokweyesende* 1399 *Ct*. STIMSON'S LANE. Cf. John
Stimpson c. 1840 *TA*.

THE BEESONS is *Estounesende* 1302 *ElyCh*, *Beestoun* 1348 *ElyCh*, *the
Besons* 1742 BedL. OE *bī ēastan tūne*, 'to the east of the hamlet,'
v. tūn and cf. *Westounesende de Sutton* 1324 *ElyCh, bisuthentun* 13th
ElyM (Stretham), *Attewestounesende de Wynteworthe* 1314 *Ct* and
Bestwall (PN Do 146).

BRANGEHILL DROVE (6″)

> *Berengal(e)* 1285 *Ass*, -*hal* 1315 *Ct* (p), *Bering(e)hal(e)*, -*y*- c. 1295
> *ElyM et freq* to 1391 *Ct*, -*droue* 1318 ib.
> *Ber(e)neiale* 13th *ElyCh*, *Berneiale* 1457–9 *Ct*
> *Berg(e)hale* t. Ed 1 *ElyCh* (p), -*feld* 1438 *Ct*
> *Berinshale* 1309 *Ct* (p), *Beringeslade* 1327 *Ct*
> *Berninghale* 1330 *Ct*, *Bornenghale* ib. (p)
> *Berenialelode* 1337–43 *Ct*, *Berineiale(char) subtus Mepale* 15th *ElyM*
> *Bernegaledoune* 1369 *Ct*, *Bernemalefelde* 1461 ib.
> *Ber(y)alelo(a)de* 1403 *SewersA*

Baringaleffeld 1423 *ElyB*
Brangells 1572 *WMP, Branghill* 1720 *BLAcct*

Possibly 'the nook of the people of *Beorn(a)*,' *v.* inga, healh. It lies low near the New Bedford River and Gault Hole near the boundary of Mepal in a corner of Sutton parish. drāf, dūn, feld and (ge)lād have been added to some of the forms. For *char v.* Chain Fm *supra* 226.

CAPLOAD (lost) is (*piscaria de*) *Quappelode* 1307 *Ct, Cappelode* 1316–1449 ib., *Caplode* 1379, 1474 ib., *Suffen Haffes or Cap Loade* 1617 *SewersD.* 'Eel-pout stream,' from OE **quap*, 'eel-pout' and (ge)lād. Identical with Whaplode (L), *v.* DEPN. For *Suffen Haffes, v.* South Fen and Old Halves *infra* 242, 249.

GAULT BRIDGE (6″) is *Sotton Galt Bridge* 1662 *BLAcct.* GAULT HOLE (6″) is possibly *Gaull extra Whiddon* 1392 *Wren.* SUTTON GAULT is *Sutton Galt* 1637 BedL, *Sutton Golt or Gravell* 1672 *FenS.* Cf. also *Gaule Fen, the Gaultway* 1637 BedL, *the Gault Causeway* 1785 ib., *Gault Close* c. 1840 *TA.* Gault Bridge is over the New Bedford River, Sutton Gault is in the Wash, across which runs The Causeway (*infra* 241), probably *the Gaultway* and *the Gault Causeway supra*, and Gault Hole lies under the Hundred Foot Bank, some little distance from Widden's Hill *infra*, so that the name must once have covered a wider area. All lie low and we probably have ME *galle*, 'marshy ground,' cf. *infra* 325. The final *t* is dialectal. There is clay near, but no gault.

SUN DOLES (*TA*) is *Suþendune* 13th *ElyCh, Sunedune* 13th *ElyM, ElyF, Sonnedone(forlong)* 1302*Ely Ch.* OE *bī sūðan dūne*, 'to the south of the hill,' *v.* dūn, dāl.

WALLER FEN (*TA*) is *Walowffen* 1480 *Ct*, taking name from *Waldelowe* 1320–1 ib. (surviving in Waddelows Hill (*TA*) in Wentworth), i.e. 'fen by *Wold*-hill,' *v. Wold infra* 246. So also in Sutton we have *Waldhethe, -weye, -were* 13th *ElyM,* 1294 *ElyCh,* 1330 *Ct* and *Heghwolde* 1399 ib., *the Weeles* 1610 *SewersD. v.* hȳð, hēah, wēr.

WIDDEN'S HILL (6″)
  Estwidun(e), -done, -y- 13th *ElyCh,* 1327 *ElyF,* 1474 *Ct*
  Widdon(e), -y- 1309 *Ct et freq* to 1475 ib., (*super le Redelond*) 1302
    ElyCh, (*Nort-*) 1303 *Ct,* (*North*)*wytdone(cnol)* 1309 ib., (*-knol*)
    1317 ib., (*West-*) 1474 ib.
  Whiddon 1392 *Wren, The Widdens* c. 1825 O.S.

This is a difficult name and the forms are too late for any satis-factory interpretation. If the form *wytdone* is significant, then it may be that the first element is the common word hwīt, 'white,' or the rare wiht discussed *infra* 351. The name has left further traces in Widen Close in Mepal and Widden Close in Witcham (*infra* 370) which must take their name from the same dūn.

BEDINGHAM'S FM, BLABY'S DROVE[1] (6″), CHAFFEY'S FM, CHARTER'S FM[2] (6″), FEARY'S FM, HAMMOND'S EAU FM[3], ROBINSON'S FM (6″), TUBB'S FM[4] and WATT'S DROVE[5] (6″) are probably to be associated with the families of Richard *Bedyngham* (1461 *Ct*), Sarah *Blaby* (1692 *SewersA*), Rev. William *Chaffey* (c. 1840 *TA*), William *Charter* (1811 *BedL*), Stephen *Feary* (1773 ib.), Anthony *Hamond* (1649 *AdvProc*), John *Robinson* (1768 *BedL*), William *Tubb* (1654 *BLAcct*) and William *Watte* (1369 *Ct*).

AMERICA, so named c. 1825 (O.S.), is in a remote part of the parish, *v. infra* 357. BETWEEN DITCHES DROVE (6″). Cf. *Tween Ditches* 1637 *BedL*, *Between Ditches* 1800 ib. BLOCKMOOR FEN is *Blokemor* 1459 *Ct*, *Blockmoor* c. 1840 *TA*. Cf. Blockmoor Fen *supra* 198. BROADPIECE FM and WEST FEN DROVE (6″) are so named c. 1825 (O.S.). BURYSTEAD FM is *Burystead* c. 1840 *TA*, *v.* burh, stede. There is a rectangular earthwork here. THE CAUSEWAY (6″) is *Sutton Causey* 1637 *BedL*. CHAIN CAUSEWAY (6″) is *the Chain Cause-way* 1828 ib. Cf. Chainbridge *infra* 254. THE GROVE is *Graue apud Sutton* 13th *ElyCh*, *v.* grǣfe. THE GULLET is *Gull in Bedford North Bank neere Tubbes his howse* 1655 *BLAcct*. It is near Tubb's Fm *supra*. *v.* gole. JOLLY BANKER'S (BRIDGE) (6″) is *The Jolly Bankers* c. 1825 O.S., from an inn. THE LAWNS is *Great, Little Lawns* c. 1840 *TA, v. infra* 337. NORTH and SOUTH MEADLANDS (both 6″) are *le North-medelond* 1315 *ElyF*, *le Nort(h)medwelond* 1316 *ElyCh*, *le Suthmedwelond* 1315 *Ct*, *Southmedlond* 1388 ib. MILL HO is *Oueremillehoue* 1324 ib. NORTH FEN is *le Northfen* 1338 ib. LONG and SHORT NORTH FEN DROVE (both 6″) are so named in 1819 and 1767 (*BedL*). NORTH MIDDLEMOOR (6″) is *le Middilmoor* 1379 *Ct*. ROW END FM is *Rows End* c. 1840 *TA*.

---

[1] *Blaby's Drove* 1785 *BedL*.
[2] *Willm Charters Farm* 1750 *Elstobb*.
[3] Cf. *Mr. Hamonds Lands* 1656 *AdvProc*. The name *Hamond* is found here already in 1410 (*Ct*).
[4] *Tubbes (his) howse* 1653 *BLAcct*. The name *Tubbe* is found here already in 1341 (*ElyCh*).
[5] Cf. *terram Willelmi Watte* 1356 *ElyCh*, *Watts's Drove* c. 1825 O.S.

RYMANMOOR DROVE (both 6″) is *Ryman Moor* 1805 BedL, *Rymermoor* (*Drain*) 1821 Baker. SOUTH FEN is *Suthfen*(*muthe*) 1240 Rams, *Suffen-*(*mowthe*) 1473 *Ct*. SUTTON HOLWOODS is *Hollod*(*e*) 1298 *Ct et freq* to 1480 ib., *Holewlodemor, Holewodemor* 1371 Misc, *Hollwoods* 1636 BedL. This is part of Holwoods Fm in Chatteris *infra* 248. SUTTON MEADLANDS is so named in 1672 (*FenS*). SUTTON MILL (6″) is *molendinum de Sutton* 1278 *ElyCh*. SUTTON WEST FEN is *le Westfen* 1325 *Ct*.

Little Thetford

LITTLE THETFORD

    (*æt*) *þiutforda* c. 972 ASCh
    Liteltedford 1086 DB, *Liteltædford* 1144 *ElyD*, *Liteltiedford* 1144 *ElyM*, *Tef*(*f*)*ord* 1198 FF *et freq* to 1285 *Ass*, *Tethford* 1251 *ElyCouch*, 1277 *Ely*, *Tetford* 1394 *Ct*, 1412 FF
    Littleteodford, Litel teodford, Litlet(*h*)*eotford, Litel teoforð* 1086 InqEl
    Thedford' c. 1155 Thorney, *Litletheford* 1229 *ElyM*, *Thef*(*f*)*ord*(*e*) 1233 Cl *et freq* to 1357 *ElyCh*, *Thetford*(*e*) 1251 *ElyCouch et freq*, (*in Insula Elyeñ*) 1365 *ElyCh, parua Theford iuxta Ely* 1298 *Ass*, *Thetfurthe* 1553 EA ix, *Thetforth* 1564 *Ely*, *Fetford* 1586 PCC

Þeodford, which is a compound of *þeod*, 'nation, people' and *ford*, probably denotes a ford which carries a *þeodweg*, i.e. a national road. *Little* to distinguish this from Thetford (Nf).

NOTE. WATSON'S LANE is probably to be associated with the family of *Watson* (1617 *Wisb*).

GOLD'S MERE[1] (6″) is probably to be associated with the family of Richard *Golde* (1285 *Ass*).

CHAPEL HILL is so named in 1829 (Wells). Cf. *Chapelhow* 1411 *Ct*. Here stood the *capelle S Georgii de Thetford* (1489 Ely). HALL FEN (6″) is *Halle Fen* 1394 *Ct*. REED FEN is *Reed Fen* c. 1840 *TA*. THETFORD FIELD (both 6″) is *Thetforde Feildes* 1636 BedL.

Welches Dam

WELCHES DAM is *Welshes Dam* 1651 *AdvProc, Welsh his dam* 1652 ib. and is named from a dam across the Old Bedford River made by Edmund *Welsh*, an under overseer to the Adventurers (*AdvProc*).

    [1] Cf. *Gold mere dyke* 1549 *Ct, Golsmore* 1563 *SewersD, Goldsmere* 1605 *Depositions*.

COOPER'S FM is *Coopers Farm* c. 1840 *TA*. FORTREY'S HALL is *Fortrey Hall* ib. Cf. Fortrey House *supra* 237. HUNDRED FM (6"). Cf. *Hundred Mill* ib.

Wentworth

WENTWORTH

> *Winteuuorde* 1086 DB, InqEl, *-worða, -uurð* 1086 InqEl, *-word(a)* 1109–33, c. 1170 *ElyM*, 1291 Tax, *-w(o)rth(e), -y-* c. 1130 *ElyD et freq* to 1428 FA
>
> *Wynteworda* 1086 InqEl, *-wurth* 1252 *ElyCh*, *Wynthewurthe* 1252 Ch, *Wyntwourthe in the isle of Elye* 1580 AD vi, *Winworth* 1636 BedL
>
> *Wynterword, -wrd'* c. 1150 *LibEl*, *-wrth* 1285 *Ass*
>
> *Went(e)worth(e)* 1335 Sacr *et freq* to 1573 Ely, (*al. Wenford*) 1588 ib., *Wentford* t. Eliz ChancP, *-forth* 1583 Ct, *Wenworth* 1870 Witcham
>
> *Wyndeforde* 15th HMC vi, *Wyntforde* c. 1554 ECP, *Winford* c. 1600 (1724) *BadesladeA*, *Wingford* 1684 Moore

The new forms, *Wynterword* etc., though late, make it probable that Ekwall (DEPN) was right in associating this name with Wentworth (WRY), DB *Wintreuuorde, Wineworde*. Either '*Wintra*'s enclosure' or 'winter-enclosure,' *v.* worð. For *-ford* cf. Duxford *supra* 92.

NOTE. DUNHAM'S LANE. Cf. William *Dunham* (c. 1840 *TA*). GRANNY'S END RD is probably to be associated with the family of John de *Granden'* (1323 *ElyF*) which probably came from Great or Little Gransden (*supra* 161). Their holding is called *Grantisdens* t. Hy 8 *Rental*. MARROWAY RD is *Marroway* c. 1825 O.S. This runs along the parish boundary and derives from (ge)mǣre, 'boundary.'

GLOVER'S FM (6") is probably to be associated with the family of Robert *Glover* (c. 1840 *TA*).

OLD FEN DROVE. Cf. *Old Fen* c. 1840 *TA*. STAPLE LEYS (both 6"). *v.* Staple Leys Fm *supra* 234.

Wilburton

WILBURTON

> (*on*) *Wilburhtune* 970 (12th) BCS 1268, *Wilburton, -y-* 1251 *Ely-Couch et freq* to 1499 Ct
>
> *Wilbertone* 1086 DB *et freq* to 1553 Pat, *Wilbertuna, -tona, Wuil-bertona* 1086 InqEl, *Wilbretone* 1199 BM, *Wylbyrton* 1334 *Ely-Couch*, *Wilbirton* 1336 SR, *Wilbourton* 1375–7 Pat

'The farm of *Wilburh*,' a woman's name found also in Wilbraham *supra* 137. *v.* tūn.

NOTE. BALLAND LANE. Cf. *le ballonde* 1388 *Ct, Ballon Close* c. 1840 *TA*. 'Bean land,' *v.* land. CLARK'S LANE is so named c. 1825 (O.S.), and is probably to be associated with the family of Edward *Clarke* (c. 1840 *TA*).

TOWNS END FIELD is so named c. 1840 (*TA*) and was near the home of William and Ralph *Attetunesende* (1277 *Ely*). *v.* tūn.

MARTIN'S FM, MINGAY FM[1] and MITCHELL'S FM (all 6″) are probably to be associated with the families of William *Martin* (c. 1840 *TA*), John *Mingay* (1676 Bentham) and William *Michell* (1523 *SR*).

AUSTRALIA FM is near the parish boundary, *v. infra* 357. BERRISTEAD CLOSE (6″) is *Berestead Close* c. 1840 *TA*. Cf. *Hayfeilde al. the Buristeede* 1606 *Depositions* and *v.* burh (manorial), stede. BREACH CLOSES. Cf. *le Breche* 1394 *Ct, Breach Furlong* c. 1840 *TA* and *v.* bræc. DOCTOR'S LODGE. Cf. *Doctors Close* c. 1840 *TA*. DOG HOUSE FIELD, LITTLE FIELD (all 6″), LOW FEN, MILL FIELD and NEW DITCH FIELD (both 6″) are so named c. 1840 (*TA*). THE DOLES (6″) is *The Doles* 1604 *Atkyns, le Doules* 1626 *Ct, v.* dāl. MANOR HO (6″) and TWENTY PENCE FERRY are so named in 1829 (Wells). SKEG FEN (6″) is (*Wilburton*) *Skeggfen* 1604 *Atkyns, Kegffen* 1636 BedL. SKEG FEN DROVE is *Skeig Fen Drove* 1870 *Witcham.* Cf. Skegg's Lane *supra* 169. SPRINGWELL COTTAGE. Cf. *Springwell(e)* 1221 *ElyA*. WALKER'S GROVE (all 6″). Cf. *Walkers Close* c. 1840 *TA*.

Witcham

WITCHAM
  (*on*) *Wichamme* 970 (12th) BCS 1268, *Wicham, -y-* c. 1120 *LibEl et freq* to 1418 Pat, *Wychomfen* 1240 Rams, *Wytch(h)am* 1281 Ipm, 1314 Pat
  Wiccham, -y- c. 970 (12th) *LibEl et freq* to 1326 Cl, *Wiccheham* 1086 InqEl, *Wicceham* ib., 1170 LibEl, *Wic(c)heam* c. 1130–44 *ElyD*, 1254 Val
  Wiceham 1086 DB, *Wicheham* 1086 InqEl *et freq* to 1394 Cl, *Wichham, -y-* 1277 *Ely et freq* to 1422 FF, *Wycheham* 1285 *Ass*, 1418 *MinAcct*
  Wikham 1251 *ElyCouch*
  Whicham 1675 Ogilby

'Enclosure by or with wych elm(s),' *v.* wice, hamm.

[1] *Mingay Fm* 1821 Baker.

NOTE. BURY WAY is *Bureweye* 14th *ElyF*. It runs to Burnt Hill *infra*.
HIVE RD is *le Hetheweye* 1322 ib., *Hithewey* 1520 *CaiCh*, *Hiveway* 1693 *Ct*.
'Road to the landing-place,' *v.* hȳð. MARKET WAY is *Marketweie* 1215 *ElyCh*.
WARDY HILL RD is *Wardeyweye* 1311 *ElyCh*, *Wardyway* 1693 *Ct*, *v.* Wardy
Hill *supra* 230.

BURNT HILL is *Burnewrthehil* 1215–19 *ElyCh*, -*hel* c. 1225 *ElyM*,
Burghworth Hyll 1477 *Peterhouse*, *Burnhill* (*ffelde*) 16th *CaiCh*. There
is no old stream here and confusion of forms probably makes any
attempt at an etymology idle. OE *byrgen*, 'burial place,' found in
Burn Hill (PN Bk 165) is phonologically impossible here.

HYTHE FM[1] (6″) was probably the home of Agnes *atte hethe* (1306
ElyCh). *v.* hȳð.

WILBY HILL FM is *Wolby Hill* 1654 *BLAcct*, *Woolby Hills Farm* 1821
Baker, *Wolvey Grounds* 1870 *Witcham* and is probably to be associated
with the family of Roger de *Wylebeye* (13th *Elem*) and Adam de
Wileby (1337 *Ct*) which may have come from Wilby (Nf, Sf or Nth).

CLARE FM belonged to Clare College (c. 1840 *TA*). COWCROFT DROVE
(6″). Cf. *Cawcroft* 1637 BedL, 1650, 1653 *FenS*, 1654 *BLAcct*, *Cow
Croft* c. 1840 *TA*. GRAVEL FM and DROVE (6″). Cf. *Gravel Bridge
Ground* ib. THE SLADE is *le Slade* 1312 *ElyCh*, *v.* slæd. STUMP DROVE
(both 6″) is so named in 1870 (*Witcham*). SWARM HAUGH CLOSES is
Swarmhooveway 1693 *Ct*, *Swarm Hough Closes* c. 1825 O.S., *Swarm-
hoof Close* c. 1840 *TA*. The second element is probably holh. WITCHAM
HIVE is *Wicheham hive* 1690 Lea, *v.* hȳð. WITCHAM HYTHE is *Wicham-
hythe* 1251 *ElyCouch*, *v.* hȳð.

Witcham Gravel

WITCHAM GRAVEL is so named in 1829 (Wells). *v.* gravel.

Witchford

WITCHFORD

Wiceford(*e*) 1086 DB, *Wicceford* 1086 InqEl, 1170 LibEl
Wiccheforð, Wicheford(*a*), *Wicheforð* 1086 InqEl, *Wicheford*(*e*), -*y*-
  c. 1120 LibEl *et freq* to 1467 FF, (*infra Insulam de Ely*) 1298 *Ass*,
Wychefurth 1553 EA ix

[1] Cf. *Hethecroft* 1304 *ElyCh*.

Wicford, Wichforda 1086 InqEl, -(*e*)*ford*(*e*), -*y*- 1138 *ElyD et freq*
   to 1499 Ipm, (*cum Wynteworth*) 1336 *SR*, *Witchford* 1335 Sacr
Wieceforda, *Wichdford* 1086 InqEl

'Ford by the wych elm(s),' *v.* **wice**, **ford**.

NOTE. SEDGE WAY is *Segweye* c. 1250 *ElyM*.

WOLD (lost) is *Walde* 1170 LibEl, c. 1200 *ElyE*, (*le*) *Wold*(*e*) c. 1195,
13th *ElyE*, 1281 Cl, 1298 *Ass*, 1303 Sacr, *le Would* 1541 *MinAcct*,
le Woold t. Hy 8 *Rental*. *v.* **weald**. This name survived until the end
of the 18th century as the name of "some arable and pasture lands
near Witchford" (Bentham 75). It was the name for an extensive
tract covering approximately the whole of the high clay-lands of the
Isle of Ely proper, survivals of which are found in Woolden Lane in
Haddenham and Waller Fen in Sutton *supra* 232, 240. Other references are found in Wilburton, Witcham, Mepal, Downham and
Ely: *Weld'* 1221 *ElyA* (Ely), *le Longewold* 13th *ElyCh* (Ely), *Brodwold*
1386 *Wren* (Downham), *Brun*(*n*)*eswold* 13th *ElyM*, c. 1300 *ElyCh*,
Brounesweld 1312 *ElyCh* (Witcham), *Mepale weales* 1589 *SewersD*.
For *Brunneswold* cf. Leighton Bromswold (PN BedsHu 245–6) and
Newton Bromswold (PN Nth 193–4). The association of the name
Brūn with two such forest areas is noteworthy. For **weald** as the name
of another large area cf. Croydon Wilds *supra* 54 and Introd. xxvi.

ALDERFORTH. Cf. *Alderforde*(*fen*) 13th *ElyCh*, *Alderforthfen* 1514
Clare, *Alder Fourths* c. 1840 *TA*, *v.* **alor**, **ford**. COLDMOOR FM (6″) is
so named c. 1825 (O.S.). FROGS ABBEY is so named c. 1840 (*TA*),
v. infra 357.

XVII. HUNDRED OF NORTH WITCHFORD

Benwick

BENWICK [benik]

Beymwich 1221 *ElyA*, -*wyk* 14th *Cai*
Benewich 1244 Rams, -*wik*(*e*), -*wyk*(*e*) 1244 ib. *et freq* to 1331 ib.,
   Benwyk(*e*) 1256 Rams, 1399, 1549 *Ct*, *Bennewyke* 1489 ib.
Beynwyk(*e*), -*i*- 1251 *ElyCouch*, 1277 *Ely*, 1282 Pat, 1298 *Ass*,
   Beinwich 1277 *Ely*, -*wik*(*e*) ib., 1298 *MinAcct*, *Beynewyk* c. 1350
   Thorney

Bemwyk 1251 *ElyCouch*, 1256 Rams, *-wik* 1277 *Ely*
Ben(n)ick 1645 EA vi, 1763 Bowen

Probably 'bean-farm,' *v.* bēan, wīc. For *-ey-, -ei-* from *ēa*, cf. *s.n.*
Benfleet (PN Ess 142).

LILLY HOLT is *Lilly Ho(u)lt* 1620 *SewersD*, 1636 BedL, taking name
from *Lytleye* 1251 *ElyCouch*. This may have the same history as Lilly
Wood and Plantation (PN Ess 396, 420) and derive from lȳtel, 'little'
and (ge)hæg, 'enclosure,' but here the second element might also be
ēg, as it lies right in the fen.

TURF FEN is *Benwicke turfe Fen* 1606 *Depositions*. This was one of the
fens from which turves were cut for fuel. Cf. Frith Fen *supra* 179 and
also *Turfen* 12th *ElyCh* (Witchford), *Turffen de Maney* 1414 *Wren*,
le Turffenne 1566 *Ct* (Swaffham Prior).

IBBERSON'S DROVE and SMITH'S FM (both 6″) are probably to be
associated with the families of Isaac *Ibberson* (1820 BedL) and
Thomas *Smith* (1678 *FenS*).

BENWICK MERE is *Benwicke mare* 1606 *Depositions*. BRADNEY HO.
Cf. *Bradneymore* 1549 *Ct* and *v.* Bradney Fm *infra* 254. LITTLE
LONDON (6″), *v. infra* 357. PARSON WARE DROVE (6″). Cf. *Parsonage
Drove* 1821 Baker. PUDDOCK BRIDGE is *Puttocks Bridge* 1808 BedL.
Cf. *Puttockesdroveway* 1658 *BLAcct*. WHITE FEN (6″) is *Whites Fen*
1636 BedL.

Chatteris

CHATTERIS [tʃætris, tʃɑ·tris]

> *Cæateric* 974 (1334) BCS 1311, *Ceateric* 1077 (17th) ChronRams,
> 1253 BM, *Ceatrice* 1178 (1334) Rams, *Chatric'* 1199 CurR,
> 1200–5 Cur, 1251 Ch
> *Corateric* 974 (1334) Rams, c. 1350 (17th) ChronRams
> *Chateriz* 974 (1334) BCS 1310, 1086 ICC *et freq* to 1473 *Ct*, (*al.*
> *Cateriche*) 1325 Ipm, *Chateritz* 1207 Rams, 1345 Pat, 1347 FF,
> *Chatteriz* 1258 Cl, 1287 *Ct*, *Chateruz* 1279 RH
> *Chaterih* 1060 (1334) KCD 809, *Chateri(c)ht* 12th *LibEl*, 1108 ib.
> *Chatriz* 1086 ICC *et freq* to 1302 FA, *Chatrys* 1285 *Ass*, 1413 Pat,
> *Chat(t)res(se)* 1370 Ely, 1553 EA ix, 1594 RHistS (3) i, 269
> *Catareio, Cetereio, Cet'(e)io* 1086 ICC
> *Cietriz* 1086 DB, *Cetriz* ib., 1086 InqEl, *Cetricht* 1109 BM

Cætriz 1086 InqEl, *Catriz* ib., 1109–35 *ElyCh*, 12th Ord, 1200 Cur
Cateriz 1086 InqEl, 1130 P, 1177–89 BM, 12th *LibEl*, 1277 *Ely*,
    Catariz 1116 *LibEl*, *Catteris* 1529 BedL
Chetriz 1086 InqEl, *Cheterich* c. 1260 Gervase
Cateriht 1108, 1115 *LibEl*, *Catericlond* 1251 *ElyCouch*
Chateric(h)(e), *-y-* 12th HH *et freq* to 1353 Ipm
Chartriz 1200 Cur, *Chartiriz* 13th *St John's*, *Charteriz*, *-yz* 1441 Cl,
    Charterys 1443 Pat, *Chartresse* 1636 BedL
Chatteriz, *-yz* 1258 Cl, *Chateris*, *-y-* 1271 Ipm *et freq* to 1434 Pat,
    Chaterysse 1282 Ipm, *Chaterix* 1302 Sacr, *Chateres* 1499 Ipm,
    Chatteras 1539–40 *MinAcct*, *Chattres* 1579 Ely, *Chateries or*
    Cheaterich 1610 Camden

It has been suggested (IPN 23 and PN NRY 242) that this name is
of the same origin as Catterick which is there ultimately associated
with Welsh *cader*, OI *cathair*, 'hill fort.' In spite of certain resem-
blances, however, the earliest forms point to a different origin. The
first element, as suggested by Ekwall (DEPN), may be either a personal name *Ceatta* or British *cēt*, 'wood,' as in Chatham (Ess, K).
The second is probably the OE *rīc*, 'stream,' discussed *s.nn. Richeham*
(PN Ess 238–9) and Escrick (PN ERY 267–8). The rarity of forms
with *-tt-* suggests a preference for *cēto-rīc*, 'wood-stream.' Such
names as Langwood and Stocking *infra* 251 and field-names such as
Popilholt and *Southwode* probably mean that the district was once
well wooded. Forms with *z*, *itz* and *s* are due to AN influence which
has persisted (cf. IPN 102).

Note. Bridge St. Cf. *Brigge* 1473 *Ct*, the home of Stephen *atte Brigge*
(1399 *MinAcct*). Curtis's Row. Cf. William *Curtis* (1821 Lot). High St
is *le highestrete* 1539 *Trinity*. Mill End is *Myll ende* t. Hy 6 *MinAcct*.
Park St. Cf. (*le*) *Pearklane* 1552 ib.

Birch Fen (6″) is *Burchfen* 1621, 1657 CCC, *Birchffenn* 1738 ib. It
may perhaps be associated with *Holdebreche* 1240 Rams, *Olbriche* 1468
CCC, *Oldbryche* 1489 ib., *le Oldbridge*, *Byrcheseand* 1552 ib., *Old(e)-
bur(d)ge* 1621, 1636, 1712 ib., *Oldburgh* 1728 ib. 'The old piece of
newly-cultivated land,' *v.* eald, brǣc. For the change of *breche* to
birch cf. that of *brycg* to *burge*, *s.n.* Cambridge *supra* 36.

Holwoods Fm is *Hollod(e)* 1240 Rams *et freq* to 1510 *MinAcct*, *Holle-
wood* 1540 ib., (*Great*, *Litle*, *Abbots*) *Holwood* 1616–36 BedL, *The
Hollwoods* 1656 *Rental*. 'Watercourse in the hollow,' *v.* holh, (ge)lād.
Abbots from the Abbot of Ramsey.

HONEY HILL is *Huney(e)* 1229 Pat (p), 1378 *MinAcct*, 15th *Ely*, *Hunneye* 1240 Rams *et freq* to 1461 *MinAcct*, *Hunhe(ye)* 1254 *Ct*, *Honneye*, *-eie* c. 1266 *Chateriz*, 1324 *MinAcct*, *Hony Fen* 1636 BedL. According to the Liber Eliensis the funeral service of St Etheldreda was conducted by her priest *Huna* and the saint was buried "non in ecclesia...sed in eadem palude prope Ely, ad quandam modicam insulam, quae ejus nomine vocatur *Huneia*" (LibEl 59–60). This statement is unlikely in itself and in direct contradiction to the much earlier statement by Bede (Bk iv, c. 17) with regard to the burial of St Etheldreda. The story in the Liber Eliensis was probably invented as an explanation of the name *Huneia*. If that does stand for *Hunan-eg*, the *Hūna* was almost certainly not Etheldreda's priest. *v.* ēg.

HORSEWAY is *Hors(e)hythe*, *-i-* 1238 *ElyCouch et freq* to 1489 *Ct*, *Horsethe*, *Horse* 13th *Chateriz*, *Chartris Horseway* 1670 *FenL*. Either 'landing place for horses' or 'muddy landing place' from OE *horsc*, 'foul, muddy,' noted under Horkesley, Horsefrith and Horsepit's Fm (PN Ess 392, 278, 361). *v.* hȳð. For loss of *th* cf. Odsey *supra* 62.

HORSLODE FEN FM (6″)

> *Hornigslade* 1240 (1334) Rams, 13th *Chateriz*, *Horningslade*, *-y-* c. 1250 *Chateriz*, 1402 *CCC*, *Horneslade* 1430 *Ct*
> *Horyngslade(fen)*, *-ing-* c. 1275, 13th *Chateriz*, *Horynsslade* ib.
> *le Horslade* 1457 *CCC*, *Horseslade* 1471 *Rental*, *Horselodde* 1489 *CCC*, *-loud* 1539 *MinAcct*, *Horslods Fens* 1829 Wells

The farm is situated in the middle of the extensive Horseley Fen *infra* 251 which was also called *Horselode Fen*. The second element is probably OE (ge)lād, 'watercourse.' The first element may be either a personal name *Horning* from OE *hornung*, 'bastard' (cf. Horningsea *supra* 145), or it may be the significant word *horning*, 'bend,' suggested for *Horningstrate supra* 32.

NIGHTLAYER'S FEN with LONG and SHORT NIGHTLAYER'S DROVE (6″) is *Nightlayer (Drain)* 1750 Elstobb, 1891 *CCC*. We may possibly compare *Godyeuesleyr* 13th *WMP* (Babraham), (*le*, *ffirst*, *last*, *myddyl*) *ley(e)re* 1498, 1518 *Ct*, *Middiller'*, *lastlyer* 1521 ib., *lestlyre* 1537 ib. (Over), *Great Layers* 18.. *Map* (Soham). *layer* is presumably the common word *lair* (OE *leger*), but just in what sense it is used here is obscure.

OLD HALVES is *Oldhalf* c. 1300 *SewersD et freq* to 1616 BedL, *Oldhaw(e)*

1415–18 *MinAcct, Eldehalf* 1428 *Ct*, (*the*) *Old Haves* 1618 *SewersA, Old Halves* 1652 *FenS, the Old Hawes* 1678 ib., (*or Old Halfes*) 1682 ib., *Chartres old Haues* 1684 Moore. Here we probably have the nom. sg. of healh, 'nook, corner,' developing to ME *half*, plural *halves*. The exact meaning is difficult to determine, but there is a marked bend in the county boundary here.

RESTAGES (lost) is *le Restage* 1539 *MinAcct, Restages* 1652 *FenS*. Cf. *Redesteches*(*were*) 1240 Rams, *Redestyche*(*were*) 1254 *Ct*, 1471 *Rental, Restich corner* 1529 BedL. Perhaps 'a piece of land covered with reeds,' v. hrēod, stycce, wēr.

WARTH'S OLD HALVES (6″) is perhaps to be associated with (*marisco de*) *Ward*(*e*) t. Ed 3 *Ct*, 1378 *MinAcct* which probably derives from OE *waroð*, 'shore, low-lying land,' cf. PN D 82, 120, 223. *Warth's* may, however, be really possessive. Between 1754 and 1792 Thomas, John and William *Warth* held land near Normoor, Langwood Fen and Westmoor (BedL), but these places are some distance to the north. v. Old Halves *supra* 249.

WENNY FM and SEVERALS are *Wenney*(*e*) 1240 Rams *et freq* to 1510 *MinAcct, Wenheye* 1251 *ElyCouch, Wendy* c. 1555 *Cole* xxxvii, *Wenny Severals* c. 1825 O.S. Possibly from OE *wenn* and *ēg*, hence 'wen island.' Cf. Wanstead (PN Ess 109). For *Severals*, v. *infra* 354.

WILLEY FM is *Wyliethe*, -y- 1240 Rams, *Wilihethe, Wyliehithe*, -*hythe* 1251 *ElyCouch, Willyhythe*, -y- 1457–61 *MinAcct, W*(*h*)*ilhith* 1378–1418 *MinAcct, Wilheeth* 1401 *CCC, Willeye* 1552 *CCC, Welagh* 1772 Imb. 'Landing-place by the willows,' v. welig, hȳð. For loss of *th* cf. Odsey *supra* 62.

CARTER'S BRIDGE[1], CAWTHORNE'S FM (6″), CLARK'S FM and ROBINSON'S FM are probably to be associated with the families of William *Carter*, William *Cawthorn* (1812 Lot), John *Clerk* (1396 *CCC*) and Richard *Robynson* (t. Hy 6 *MinAcct*).

ACRE FEN is *le Acreffenne* 1682 *CCC*. BLOCK FEN (6″) is *le Blokfen* 1340 *Ct, Black Fen* c. 1554 ECP, *Block Fenn* 1618 *SewersA, Chartres Block Fen* 1636 BedL, v. *supra* 198. BURROW LANDS. Cf. *Boruesfeld* 1720 *CCC, Burrows* c. 1825 O.S. CAMPOLE DROVE (both 6″). Cf. *Camppolle* 1552 *CCC, Campole* 1750 Elstobb. COMMON FM. Cf. *le*

---

[1] *Garters* (sic) *Bridge or* 40 *foot Dreine* 1695 SN.

Comon 1647 *CCC*. CURF (FEN) is *Curf(f)e* 1552 *CCC*, 1637 BedL, 1651–86 *FenS*, *Cyrfe* 1621 *SewersD*, *Corfe* 17th *AdvL*, *Cuffe* 1668 BedL. Probably from OE *cyrf*, 'cutting.' DEAN HILL, MOUNT PLEASANT (*v. infra* 357) and TURF FEN are so named c. 1825 (O.S.). Cf. *la Dene* 1240 Rams. *v.* denu and Turf Fen *supra* 247. DELVE FM. Cf. *Delf(e)* 1240 Rams, (*le*) *Delf felde* t. Hy 6, 1510 *MinAcct*, *v.* (ge)delf. FERRY BURROWS is *the ferry borrowes* 1619 *SewersD*. FERRY BURROWS DROVE (6″) is *Ferryburrows Drove* c. 1825 O.S. FERRY DROVE (6″) is *the ferrey waie* 1621 *CCC*. Cf. *le fferye* 1471 *Rental*. FORTY FOOT FM (6″) takes name from *the* 40 *Feet* (drain) 1780 BedL. HOLWOOD HO (6″) is *Hollwood house* 1589 *SewersD*. Cf. Holwoods *supra* 248. HORSELEY FEN is *Horsley or Horselode Fen* 1750 *Elstobb*. *v.* Horslode Fen *supra* 249. HORSELEY FEN DROVE (6″) is so named in 1829 (Wells). HOW FEN is *Howfenn* 1680 *FenS*. LANGWOOD FM (6″) and FEN. Cf. *Langwodefen* 1251 *ElyCouch*. LANGWOOD HILL DROVE (6″) is *Langwood Hill Road* 1750 *Elstobb*. NORMOOR is *Normore* 1637 BedL. PICKLE FEN. Cf. *Pickerell's Fen* ib., *Pickeril Fen* 1750 *Elstobb*. SLADE FIELD is *Sladefelde* 13th *Chateriz*. 'Open land in the slade,' *v.* slæd. SLADE LODE BRIDGE (6″). Cf. *campo de Sladeford* 13th *Chateriz*, *Slade loade* 1668 *CCC* and Slade Field *supra*. STOCKING DROVE. Cf. *le Stokkyng(e)* c. 1250 *Chateriz*, *v.* stocking. TUCK'S GATE is so named in 1720 (*CCC*). WESTMOOR (all 6″) is *Westmore Mowfen* 1636 BedL, *v.* Mow Fen *supra* 227. WHITE HO FM is *Whitehouse* 1639 *CCC*.

Doddington

DODDINGTON

Dundingtune (sic) c. 975 *LibEl*, *Dudintone* 1086 InqEl, *Dudingtune*, -*y*- 1170 LibEl, -*ton(e)* 1199 EA vi *et freq* to 1559 *Rental*, *Dudinton(e)* 1170 LibEl, 1230 FF, *Duddyngton* 1534 *Rental*, 1539 *MinAcct*

Doddintona 1086 InqEl, *Dodinton* 1086 DB, *Dodinton(e)* 1086 InqEl, 1165–71 P, 1276 Pat, 1569 Ely, *Dodynton in Insula Eliense* 1345 *Walden*

Dodincgtune, *Dodingetone* 1086 InqEl, *Dodington(e)*, -*y*- 1256 Barnwell *et freq*, (*cum Merch*) 1285 *Ass*, (*al. Donyngton*) 1600 *Cole* xix

Dutintune 1086 InqEl, *Dutingtune* 12th *Libellus*, -*tone* 1277 *Ely*, *Dothyton* 1346 Pat

Dedyngton 1455 Pat

Donyngton 1510 LP, Dunnington 1536 Cole xxxvi, 1576 Saxton,
Donnington 1606 Depositions
Dynnington 1644 Hollar

'Dudda's farm,' v. ingtūn. For Dedyngton and Dynnington, v.
Introd. xxxv.

NOTE. EASTALL'S RD. Cf. Eststallmore 1620 SewersD, East Hall More 1636
BedL, Eastalls c. 1840 TA. TURF FEN LANE. Cf. Turf Fen ib. and supra 247.

BEEZLING FEN is le Bylling(es)fenne 1540 MinAcct, Bezeling(s) (a mow)
Fen 1829 Wells and is to be associated with Bilsingge 13th Chateriz,
Belsynges 14th ElyCouch, Byslinges 14th Wren, Bylsynggis 1453 Ct,
Byslynges 1492 ElyB, Besselinges lode 1605 Imb, Bilsinges 1617
SewersD. No satisfactory explanation of the name can be offered. It
is clearly an early name in ing or perhaps in ingas, but it is impossible
to suggest what the first element may be.

CONEYWOOD FEN is Cuniwode, -y- 1251 ElyCouch, 1277 Ely, Coniwode
1298 MinAcct, Cone(y)woodfen(e) 1620 SewersD, 1842 Walker. Perhaps 'royal wood,' cf. Conington supra 165 and wudu. In 1086
Doddington was part of the royal demesne.

COPALDER is Kekal(d)re 1244 Rams, 1277 Ely, Kechal(d)re 1256 Rams,
Kekaller 1286 ib., Cop(e)alder 1487 MinAcct, 1645 EA vii, Copoldree
1529 BedL, Copholder Bank 1830 ib. If this sequence is correct, this
alder was first distinguished by the addition of kek, possibly related
to kex, 'dry hollow stem,' and then confused with the common
copp(ede) alder or 'pollarded alder.'

RANSON MOOR is Ravenesho(fen) 1227 Ch, Ramyshomore 1345 Wren,
Ransmer' 1346 ElyF, Rameshammor', Raunshammor(e) 1389 ElyCouch,
Ransome moor(e) 1618 SewersA, 1637 BedL, Ransummore 1621
SewersD, Ransonmo(o)re 1636 BedL, 1690 Lea, Ranseymoore 1656
BLAcct, Ramson 1660 AdvProc. Probably 'marsh by raven's ridge or
spur' or by that of a man called Hrafn, v. hræfn, hōh. To the south-
east, towards the village, the land rises and this was probably the hōh.
South-west of Doddington, in a somewhat similar position, we have
How Moor infra 253. Some of the forms are probably due to con-
fusion with ramson, ransom, 'wild garlic.'

BARROT'S FM, CLARKE'S BARN, LAMBE'S PLANTATION (all 6″), LOOM'S
FM, SMITH'S HOWMOOR FM (6″) and THICKEN'S FM are probably to
be associated with the families of Henry Barrett (1529 Dugd), John

Clerk (1356 *Extent*), Richard *Lamb* (1678 *FenS*), Edward *Loomes* (1802 Lot), William *Smith* (1523 *SR, v.* also How Moor *infra*) and Bowen *Thickens* (1819 BedL).

Askham Field (6") is *Oskamfeld* 1472 *ElyB*, *Ascomb Field* c. 1825 O.S., *Aschim Field* c. 1840 *TA*. Cf. *Oxcamsyde* 1444 *Clare*. Beezling Drove (6") is *Beeslings Drove* 1717 *FenS. v.* Beezling Fen *supra* 252. Copalder Corner is *Cop Alder Corner* 1829 Wells. The Crease (6"). Cf. *Crease Drove* c. 1840 *TA* and Crease Bank *supra* 205. Dyke Moor is *Dickamoore* 1632 Hondius, *Dikeamore* 1636 BedL, *Dike Moor* 1637 ib. Eastmoor Fm (6") is *Eastmoor* 1668 BedL. Fields End Pond (6"). Cf. *Feldesende* 1444 *Clare, v.* feld. How Moor. Cf. *Hoo* 1221 *ElyA*, *Hoofen* 1251 *ElyCouch, v.* hōh. Park Field (6"). Cf. *Great, Little Park*(e) 1600 *Cole* xix, *Dunnington Parke* 1617 *SewersD*. Parson's Land Fm. Cf. *the Parson of Doddington's Water* 1529 BedL. St Bennett's Cross is (*stone called*) *St Benittes Crosse* 1606 *Depositions*. Tick Fen District Engine (all 6"). Cf. *Thickffenn* 1603 *Survey*. West Moor is *Westmor* 1221 *ElyA*.

March

March

> *Merc*(c) 1086 InqEl, *Merche, Mercha* 1086 DB, *Merch*(e) 1170
>> LibEl *et freq* to 1355 *Walden, Merch* 1819 Carter
> *Merk*(e) 1236 Ch, 1298 *Ass*
> *March*(e) 1286 *MinAcct et freq* to 1554 Pat, (*by Welle*) 1346 ib.
> *Mersh* 1576 Saxton, *Marsh* 17th *AdvL*

Probably, as suggested by Ekwall (DEPN), OE *mearc*, 'boundary,' with mutated *a* and palatal *c* from a locative form in *-i*. March was originally a hamlet of Doddington and was situated some two miles to the south of the modern town, near the old church of St Wendreda.

Note. Dartford Rd takes its name from *Der*(e)*forda, -e* c. 1120 *LibEl, HarlCh et freq* to 1316 *MinAcct, Dern*(e)*ford* 1286 ib., *Darteford* 1597 *Wisbech Map, Darford field* 1709 *FenS*. 'Wild animals' ford,' *v.* dēor. Cf. Darcey Lode *supra* 4.

Binnimoor Fen is (*Greate, Little*) *Benimore* 1621 *SewersD, Binnymore* 1636 BedL, *Binin Moore* c. 1650 *SewersA, Bynamoor* 1678 *FenS*. Binnimoor Drove (6") is *Bynnimore Drove* 1829 Wells. Forms are late, but this is probably 'within the marsh,' cf. *Binbrook supra* 44.

BRADNEY FM is *Bradenhee (piscariam)* 1221 *ElyA*, 1392 *Ely*, *Brad(e)ne* (*-cote*) 1298 *Ass*, (*-more*) 1345 *Wren*, *Great, Little Bradnymore* 1636 BedL. This, with Bradney Ho *supra* 247, is near an old course of the Nene, here called *brādan-ēa*, 'broad river.' Cf. *þurh an scyr wæter Bradan æ hatte* 12th ASC (E) *s.a.* 656, *Bradenee al. voc. Marchee* 1428 *Ct.* *v.* brād, ēa. It was later known as 'March river.' This is probably the same river as *Brod(h)ea* 1220–25 *Thorney*, *Brodhe* c. 1225 *ElyCh* in Whittlesey, near which lay *Brodeheyfen* 1394 *Ct*, and this form possibly underlies Broadall's District (PN BedsHu 214), near the old course of the Nene, which also flowed through Whittlesey. For this name no early forms have been noted, but we may compare the change from *Byhee* to *Byall* (*supra* 211). The lower course of the Nene in Elm is also probably referred to under this name in *Bradenhee* 1314 *Ct.* *v.* Nene *supra* 8–9.

BURROW MOOR (6″) is *Bir(e)were, -y-* c. 1175 *Thorney*, 1221 *ElyA*, 1298 *Ass, -mor* 1389 *ElyCouch*, *Burewere* 1221 *ElyA*, 1251 *ElyCouch*, *Burgwere* c. 1225 *ElyM*, *Buruwere* 1251 *ElyCouch*, 1277 *Ely*, *Borowe were* 1539 *Bodl*, *Borowmore* 1636 BedL, *Burrough Moor* 1637 ib., *Burrowe Moore* 1656 BedL. 'Fishing weir by the stronghold,' with mōr 'marsh' later substituted for wēr. There are remains of a square entrenchment near, *v.* AnctC 88, burh, wēr.

CHAINBRIDGE is *Chain Bridge* c. 1825 O.S. Cf. *the Chare* 1576 Saxton, 1607 Kip, (*the lake called*) *the Old Chair(e)* 1637 BedL, *the Chaine called March Chaine* 1680 *Wisb*, *March Chaine Bank* 1714 ib., *Old Chayre* 1747 Kitchin. *Chain* is apparently a late corruption of *Chare*, the name of an old stream here. Cf. Chain Fm *supra* 226.

CREEK. Cf. *Creake frythe* 1403 *SewersA*, *Creke hire* (sic) 1438 Imb, *Krick Weire* 1529 BedL, *Creeke* 1621 *SewersD*, *Cricke fen* 1651 *AdvProc*, *Creek* 1824 BedL. This name, with the neighbouring Creekgall Fen *infra* 270, is to be associated with that of a river in March called *Crekelode*, already decayed in 1550 (Imb) which "beginneth in the great Eae betwene Mershe and Well" and was six miles long (1529 *Dugd*). Leaving the old course of the Nene between March and Upwell, it flowed north through Creek and Creekgall Fen to Elm. The more distant Crouch Moor *supra* 227 similarly takes name from a second *Creake loode* (in Littleport) "wch hath been a gret sewar and speciall good drayne" (1563 *SewersD*). It is probably represented in part by the Old Crooked Dike, the county boundary, north of Crouch

Moor in Littleport (earlier *Crechemere supra* 227) which reaches the
Ouse at Brandon Creek (Nf). On the Little Ouse in Southery is Creek
Fm and in Feltwell (Nf) Creeks End Mill Drain, all possibly owing
their names ultimately to this *creek*. From Cold Harbour Fm in
Southery it is identified by Major Gordon Fowler as a "rapidly de-
creasing roddon" along the line of the Southery-Hilgay parish
boundary to Lows Fm and in the past has been mistaken for a Roman
road. Thus, despite the difficulties of tracing their exact courses, it
is clear there were formerly two, possibly three, streams called *Creek*
or *Creche* from which these places were named. Other forms are
(*caput del*) *Cricke* 1199 *ElyCouch*[1], *-lake* t. Hy 3 *WMP*[2], *le Krike*
c. 1250 *ElyM*[2], *Kirkelake* 1251 *ElyCouch*, *le Kirke* c. 1270 *Thorney*[2],
le Crike 1284 *Ct*[3], 1339 *Imb*[2], *le Kyrke* 1341 *ElyF*[2], *Cricklode* 1528
Imb[2,3], *Crekelode* ib.[4], *Creeke loode* 1563 *SewersD*[5], *Creakelode* (*al.*
Crane lode) 1574 *SewersC*, 1617 *SewersD*[6], 1618 *AddCh*[7], *Creeke* 1597
Wisbech Map[1], *Creeke loade* 1621 *SewersD*[8], *Crock Load* 1632
Hondius[9].

These names are to be connected with modern English *creek*,
generally regarded as Germanic, although its earlier history is unknown.
NED, *s.v. creek*, sb.[1], gives three types: (1) *crike* (c. 1250), corresponding to OFr *crique*, (2) *creke* (1512), earlier Du *krēke*, 'creek, bay,'
(3) *crick* (*kricke* 1582), only since the 16th century. Here we have
much earlier examples. They must have the same origin and are either
from an English cognate of OScand *kriki*, 'crack, nook, bend,' Sw dial.
krik, 'bend, nook,' *armkrik*, 'bend of the arm,' or are due to a confusion of this cognate and the Scandinavian word itself. OScand
kriki and an OE *cricc would give ME *kricke, crike, crich*(*e*). Lengthening and lowering of the *ĭ* in the open syllable in ME would give *crēke*
(modern *creek*) and *crēche*, thus accounting for all the forms. Further
evidence of a probable native origin is provided by Creeksea (Ess).
In PN Ess 212–13, the first element is doubtfully explained as *ciric*,
'hill' or 'barrow,' but the first sense is not altogether satisfactory, as the

[1] Wisbech.   [2] March.
[3] Elm.
[4] March to Southery (Nf), passing through Laddus Fens.
[5] Doddington.
[6] Decayed; "extends itself from the River of Ouse beneath Southrey Ferye into
Welney river."
[7] "fallyng from Wellny Water by the fower lodes endes unto ye Ryver of Owse
beneath Sothery ferry."
[8] "Extending from a place called Crechmere." Cf. Crouch Moor *supra* 226.
[9] Southery Ferry to Apes Hall in Littleport.

hill there is but slight, whilst no trace of a barrow has been discovered. Ekwall has since suggested (DEPN) that the first element is identical with *creek*, which not only suits the topography but also fits in with the forms for the Essex place, *Criccheseia* 1086 DB, *Crikesse* 1198, *Crickesheth'*, *Crekeseye* 1248, whilst *Crukesheth* 1288 points to a possible development as in Crouch Moor, where we may have to reckon also with analogical influence from ME *crouche*, 'cross.' The earliest recorded meanings of *creek* are (*a*) 'coastal inlet,' etc., (*b*) 'part of a river or river system,' the common American *crick*, 'brook, small stream,' occurring from 1674. Here, the original meaning was 'bend,' hence 'winding stream,' the fen by this, and the lake into (or from) which it flowed, *v.* (ge)lād, lacu. For the alternative *Crane lode* cf. Grandford *infra*.

Estover Fm is *Estiw(o)rth(e)* 1221 *ElyA*, 1277 *Ely*, 1300 Ch, 1308, 1331 Ipm, *Estworth* 1251 *ElyCouch*, 1298, 1307 *MinAcct*, 1331 *Bodl*, *Easterforth* c. 1630 *Map*, *Estwith* 1678 *FenS*, *Eastover* 1695 SN, *Easteuor* 1706 Moore, *Estopher Fm* 1852 Harding. This is not an easy name. On the Wisbech Map of 1597 it is *Eastry* as opposed to Westry *infra* 257. It may be that our earliest forms have lost an *r* through distant dissimilation in *Estriworth*, a compound of ēasterra, 'more easterly' and worð. Cf. Eastrea *infra* 259.

Grandford Ho with Grandford Drove (6″). Cf. *Granford* 1350 *Walden*, (*Crofts*) 1636 BedL, *Grainford* 1618 *SewersA*, 1637 BedL, *Cranford* (*Crofts*) 1636 ib. It has been suggested (CAPr vii, 119) that this is 'great ford' (OFr *grand*), so called as carrying the Great Fen Road, but such a compound does not seem very likely, although the Roman road did cross the Plantwater or old Ouse (Nene) at this point. The first element may be *cran*, 'crane, heron,' with common, confusion of initial *c* and *g*, but forms are too late for any certainty.

Norwood is *Northwode* 1251 *ElyCouch et freq* to 1369 Ct, *Norwood Green* 1637 BedL. There are also forms *Norwol*(*dam*) 1573 Imb, *Norwold* (*grene*) 1589 *Depositions*, *Norholde* (*Common*), *Norbolde* (*Dam*) 1597 *Wisbech Map*, *Northolde* (*Cawsey*) 1615 *AddCh*, *Norwald Greene* 1636 BedL. These are late and irregular and probably due to the influence of Northwold (Nf). Norwood Drove (6″) is *draua de Northwode* 1333 *Walden*. Norwoodside is *Northwood side* (*fen*) 1669 *ChancDec*.

RODHAM FM with RODHAM DROVE (6″). *Rodham* is a modern spelling of what the fenmen call a *roddon*, i.e. a meandering bank of laminated silt. Major Gordon Fowler suggests that it is allied to the word *roddin* or *rodden* which Wright (EDD) gives as denoting a narrow road, path, or sheep track, but this is very doubtful as that word is distinctively North Country.

WESTRY is *West(e)rey(e)* 1221 *ElyA et freq* to c. 1450 ECP, *Westerheye* 1221 *ElyA*, *Westry* 1597 *Wisbech Map*. Probably 'the western part of the island or marshland,' OE *westerra* and *ēg*.

EASTWOOD HO (6″) was the home of Adam de *Estwde* (1221 *ElyA*) and Nicholas de *Estwode* (1285 *Ass*).

CLIPSON'S FM, DAINTREE FM[1] (6″), DODD'S FM[2] (6″), KNIGHT'S END[3], LAMB'S FM, MOORE'S FM[4] (6″), SMITH'S BARN[5] (6″), STAFFURTH'S BRIDGE[6], WADE'S CHARITY FM[7] (6″) and WATT'S FM[8] (6″) are probably to be associated with the families of John *Clipson* (1771 BedL), Jordan de *Dauentre* (c. 1260 *ElyM*) which came from Daventry (Nth), Ralph *Dod* (1251 *ElyCouch*), Elizabeth *Knighte* (1688 *SewersA*), George *Lamb* (1801 Lot), Jonas *Moore* (1669 *ChancDec*), Thomas *Smith* (ib.), Abraham *Staffurth* (1818 BedL), Judey *Wade* (1669 *ChancDec*) and Joseph *Watts* (1821 Lot).

BADGENEY is *Bageney, -ie* 1523 *SR*, 1636 BedL, *Badgeny* 1669 *Chanc-Dec*. BEDLAM BRIDGE is so named in 1829 (Wells). BOTANY BAY is in a remote situation, *v. infra* 357. COLESEED HO is probably to be associated with *Colested Lake* 1669 *ChancDec*, a compound of ME *cole* and *stede*, 'place where cole-seed grows.' EARL'S FEN (6″) is *Earles Fenn* 1688 *SewersA*. FIFTIES FM. Cf. Manea Fifties *supra* 236. FLOOD'S FERRY (6″) is *Flood's Ferry* 1684 BedL, *Floydes Ferrey* 1687 *BLAcct*. GALL DROVE (6″) is *Gaule Drove* 1563 *SewersD*, *Gald drove* 1669 *ChancDec*, *v.* galle. GAULT BANK is so named in 1829 (Wells). HAKE'S DROVE (6″) is *Hacks Drove* c. 1825 O.S. HORSE MOOR FM is *Horsmore* 1636 BedL. HUNDRED FM. Cf. *the hundred acres horne* 1669 *ChancDec*. HYTHE HO. Cf. *Hethelod, -dol* 1221 *ElyA*, *v.* hȳð, (ge)lād, dāl. LINWOOD WOOD is *bosc. de Lindwod'* 1230 *FF*, *Linge Wood* c. 1630 *Map*, *Lynwood Corner* 1717 *FenS*.

---

[1] (*dwelling house called*) *Dawntree* 1636 BedL, *Dantrey* 1695 SN.
[2] *Doddys* 1438 Imb.   [3] *Knight(s) end (green)* 1669 *ChancDec*.
[4] *Moores drayne* 1656 *BLAcct*.   [5] Cf. *Smiths Croft* 1636 BedL.
[6] *Staffords Bridge* 1720 *BLAcct*.   [7] *Wades Charity* 1829 Wells.
[8] But cf. *Wattesat(t)ebarr(e)* 1320 *Elien*, 1341 *ElyCh, ElyF*.

'Lime-tree wood,' *v.* lind. MAIDEN STILE FM is *maiden stile* 1669 *ChancDec.* MIDDLE DROVE is so named in 1691 (*SewersA*). MILLHILL PIT. Cf. *Millhill Grene* c. 1630 *Map* and "messuage called *Estw(ode)* with a mill hill (*monte molendini*)" 1439 AD vi. OTTERHOLTS (all 6″) is *Otter Holts* 1637 BedL. PEASE HILL is *Peas(e)hill* 1597 *Wisbech Map*. PILLARD'S CORNER is *Pillers Corner* 1669 *ChancDec*. REED FEN is *Reades Fen* 1636 BedL, *Reed Fen* 1795 ib. REED FEN FM (6″) is *Reades fenn house* 1669 *ChancDec*. STOW FEN is *Stowefen* 1227 Ch, *v.* stōw. TOWN END. Cf. *Townesend Dike* 1636 BedL, *Towne end Greene* 1669 *ChancDec, v.* tūn. WEST FEN is *Westfen* 1251 *ElyCouch*. WEST FEN CLOSE is so named in 1579 (*Depositions*). WHITE MOOR is *Whitemore* 1325 *Walden*, *Whetmore* 1636 BedL. WHITEMOOR DROVE (6″) is *Whitemore Drove* 1669 *ChancDec*.

Whittlesey

WHITTLESEY

(*W*)*itlesig* c. 972 ASCh, *Witlesig* 973 (14th) BCS 1297, *Witleseie, Witt(e)leseia* 1086 InqEl, *Wit(e)les-, Wytles-, -eia, -eie, -eya, -ey(e), -e* c. 1120 *HarlCh et freq* to 1553 Pat, (*Andree, Sancte Marie*) 1256 Barnwell, (*Maries*) 1559 *Rental*

Withleseya c. 1020 (12th) LibEl, *-eie* 1086 InqEl, *With-, Wythleseia, -eya, -eie, -ey(e)* c. 1130 *ElyD et freq* to 1285 *Ass*

Witesie 1086 DB, *Witeseia* 1086 InqEl, *Wyteseye* 1291 Tax

Wytlesheye 1234 *ElyCouch*, *Wythlesheye* 1277 *Ely*

Whytesleye 1322 Pat, *Whitleseye* 1346 ib.

Wyddylsay 1518 Fenland vii, *Wic(k)lesey or Wittlesea* 1586 ChancP

'*Wit(t)el*'s island,' *v.* ēg. *Witil* occurs as the name of a moneyer. It is a diminutive of *Witta*. The same personal name is found again in the parish in *Witlesforde* 13th *Thorney*, in the neighbouring Whittlesey Mere, *Witlesmere* 963–84 BCS 1128 (PN BedsHu 191) and in Whittlesford *supra* 98. There were two churches here dedicated respectively to St Andrew and St Mary.

NOTE. BRIGGATE is *Brigstrete* 1459 *Rental*, *Brygate* 1603 *Survey*. Anglo-Scandinavian *gate* (*v.* gata) has replaced strǣt. EAST DELPH is *Estdelf* 1237 *Thorney*, *Delphlane* 1603 *Survey*. At the end of Delph Dike *infra* 264. GRACIOUS ST is so named in 1603 (*Survey*).

BASSENHALLY FM, FIELD (6″), MOOR (6″) and PITS (6″)

> *Bastenhale* 1246 *Thorney*, 1285–1390 *Ct*, 14th *ElyF*, (-*feld*) 1397
>   *Ct*, (-*weie*) 1446 *Thorney*, *Bastenalemoore* 1403 *SewersA*, -*halyee*
>   1446 *Ct*
> *Bastonhale* c. 1280 *ElyF*, *Bastone* 1393 *Ct*, *Bastonefelde* 1396 ib.
> *Bastingeshalewey* c. 1280 *ElyF*
> *Bas(s)nall Feild, Bassinally Feild* 1603 *Survey*, *Bassenhall Moore*
>   1637 BedL
> *Bassinghally* 1712 *Fenland* iv, (*Moor*) c. 1840 *TA*

This name, like Barston *supra* 135, earlier *Baston*, and Bastwick
and Woodbastwick (Nf) (cf. DEPN), probably contains OE *bæst* used
either of the lime-tree itself or of *bast*, the bark of the lime-tree. The
first element is either *basten*, hence 'nook grown over with lime-trees'
(*v.* healh) or more probably (cf. Barston *supra* 135) *baston*, 'nook by
lime-tree farm', *v.* tūn. The form *Bassinally* may be a reduction of
Bastenhalyee, i.e. ēa or stream by *Bastenhale* or of *Bastenhaleweie*,
i.e. road by *Bastenhale*. BASINGHALL FM (6″) is derived from such
a form as *Bastingeshale*. BASSNIMOOR FM derives from *Bastenalemoore*
1403 *SewersA*, *Bassenhall Moore* 1637 BedL.

BEGGARS BRIDGE FM is named from *Beggers Bridge* 1687 *BLAcct*.
Cf. *Beggers Drove End* ib. In 1668 (ib.) a wooden bridge was built
over Bevill's Leame near *Beggersdyke* (*Beggers Dike* 1637 BedL). The
names are presumably of nickname origin. It is curious that the same
term should have been applied to all three objects.

CANTER'S DOLES is *le Cantoureslande* 1285 *Ct*, *Canter Doles Common*
1573 DKR xxxviii. ME *cantour*, 'singer, precentor.' This was probably part of the endowment of the precentorship of Ely. *v.* dāl.

EASTREA is *Estereie* c. 1020 LibEl, *Estrey(e)* 1285 *Ct et freq* to 1459
Rental, *Estre* 1525 Ely, *Eastrea* 1561 BM, *Est tree* 1604 *Dugd*. EASTREA
FIELD (6″) is *Eastrea Field* 1668 *Fenland* i. 'The more easterly part
of the island (of Whittlesey),' OE *ēasterra* and ēg. Cf. Estover *supra*
256.

ELDERNELL is *Alrenhale* 1315 *Thorney*, *Aldernhale* c. 1350 ib., *Alder-
nall* 1436 *SewersC*, *Heldernale* 1454 *Fenland* v, *Ildernale* 1463 ib.,
Eldernale 1505 ib. ii, *Eldernall* 1563 ib. v, 1576 Saxton, *Eldernayle*
1569 CHuAS i, *Eldernhall* 1579 *Depositions*. 'Alder-tree nook.' The
first element is OE *ælren*, *elren*, adj. 'of alder,' from *alor*. *ælren* is also

used as a subst. (*allerne* c. 1250 NED) and may be so used here. *v.* healh.

FELDALE is *Feldhale* 13th *Thorney*, *Feldale* (*-snote*) 1398 *Ct*, *Fieldale* c. 1840 *TA*. 'Nook in the feld,' *v.* healh. For *-snote* cf. snote *infra* 344.

FLEGCROFT. Cf. (*le*) *flech*(*e*) 13th *Thorney*, 1328, 1423 *Ct*, *Flegcrofts* 1636 BedL, *Flagcroft* 1712 Fenland iv, *Flycroft* c. 1825 O.S. This name, with Flag Fen *infra* 264, is to be compared with East and West Flegg Hundred (Nf), DB *Eastflec*, *Flecwest*, 1175–95 P *Est-*, *West-fleg*(*ge*). These all contain the word *flegge* recorded in the Promptorium Parvulorum as the equivalent of *segge* and used apparently alike of the plant itself and of a district where it grows. As noted by Anderson (EHN i, 70) the word is to be identified with Danish *flæg*. It is related to the more common *flag*. For further examples from Cambridge-shire, *v. infra* 324.

FUNTHAMS with FUNTHAM'S DIKE and LANE (all 6") is *Funtune* 13th *Thorney*, *Funtum*(*e*)*welle* 1423, 1446 *Ct*, (*long, short*) *Fountains* (*well*) 1603 *Survey*, *Funtams* 1636 BedL. Possibly 'spring-farm,' *v.* funta, tūn.

GLASS MOOR is *Glosmor* 1397–9 *Ct*, *Glasse Moor* 1560 (1773) Fenland iv. Cf. *Northglostesende* 1277 *Ely*, *Gloskelake* 14th *Thorney*, *Glos*(*se*)-*lake* 1574 *SewersC*. The forms are too late and conflicting for any satisfactory suggestion as to the etymology of this name. *v.* lacu, mōr.

KING'S DELPH

   (*to*) *Cynges dælf* c. 1150 ASC (E) *s.a.* 963
   Kyngesdelf a. 1022 (1200) KCD 733, (*in*) *Kinges delfe* c. 1050
      (c. 1350) ib. 904, *Kingesdelf*, -*y*- c. 1223 *ElyCh et freq* to 1390 *Ct*,
      Kyngesdel 1477 ib.
   Cnoutes delfe Kynges 1052 (1334) Rams
   Kyndesdelf 1251 *ElyCouch*, *Kynkesdelf* 1277 *Ely*, *Gingesdelf* 1288
      Misc, *Kyndelf* 1349 Pat

This is now the name of a marsh in Whittlesey, but was originally that of an artificial water-course (probably Roman) reputed to have been made by King Canute. It is now known partly as Cnut's Dyke (*supra* 207) and partly as Oakley Dike (*supra* 208). *v.* also King's Dike *supra* 208 and (ge)delf.

LATTERSEY FIELD (6″) and HILL. Cf. *Latereshale* 1285 *Ct*, 1322 *Thorney*, (*campo*) 1398 *Rental*, *Latersale* 1328 *Ct*, *Latesaleffeld*, *Latersalde* 1446 ib., *Lottersey Feild* 1603 *Survey*, *Lattersal feild* 1636 BedL. The first element is probably a personal name derived from *lǣtere* in OE *blōd-lǣtere*, 'blood-letter,' *v.* healh.

LESH FEN (lost) is *le lesschfen* 1381 *Ct*. This name, like Sedge Fen *supra* 204, etc., contains the name of one of the valuable products of the fens. Cf. *leschiam voc. sedge* 1579 *Ct* (Swaffham Prior), *leshiam anglice voc. ffenne strawe* 1598 ib. In the first half of the 13th century, the men of Littleport were granted the right to cut *lesch* and rushes in Rack Fen. This was a valuable thatching material. Darby (*Medieval Fenland* 32, 34) suggests that it was probably used to cover all the species of the genus *Carex*, but as we find a distinction between Sedge Fen, Reed Fen and Rush Fen, it may have been used in a more restricted sense. This is the word which Ekwall finds in Lyscombe (Do) and Redlynch (So). Here all the early forms have *i*, from an OE **lisc*, 'reed,' but Ekwall points out that there seem to have been two bases, viz. *lisk-* and *lēsk-*. Cf. OHG *lisca*, 'filix, carex,' MHG *liesch*, Ger *Liesch* (n.), *Liesche* (fem.), 'Riedgras,' OLG *lesc*, 'scirpus,' MDu *lissche*, *lisch*, *lessche*, Du *lisch*, *lesch*, 'iris.' For Redlynch, a compound of *hrēod*, 'reed,' a meaning 'fen' is suggested for **lisc*, but in Cambridgeshire some kind of reed is clearly indicated. *v.* Studies[2] 109–10.

THE LIPNEAS (6″) is *Lipeneye* 1328 *Ct*, *Lypney* 1526 *AD*, *Lipney* 1560 Fenland iv, *Lypneas* c. 1840 *TA*. Forms are late, but this is probably 'Lippa's low-lying land.' Cf. *lippan dic* BCS 924. *v.* ēg.

MUST FM. Cf. *Roughmust* 1398 *Ct* and *Rough Musts* (10 closes) 1829 Wells, *Thakmust* 1402 *Ct*, *Blemust* 1430 *ElyCh* and *Blea Musts* (4 closes) 1829 Wells, *Musts* ib., and *Mustee* (herbag') 1402 *Ct*. All are clearly to be associated with *Must*, the old name for Muscat (*supra* 7), which must have been used both of a muddy stream and of a marsh. *Roughmust* is probably self-explanatory, *thak* for thatching came from *Thakmust*, *Blemust* was probably dark in appearance, cf. OE *blǣ-hǣwen* (BT), while *Mustee* is from *Mustea*. *v.* ēa.

NORTHEY is (*le*) *Northe*(*e*) 1280–1334 *Thorney*, 1398 *Ct*, 1457 *Rental*, *Northey* 1550 Pat, *Northea* 1636 BedL. Northey is by Cat's Water. The early forms point to ēa rather than ēg as the second element, Cat's Water al. Must may well have been called 'north river' here as distinct from the *Southmust*, *v. supra* 8. In its lower course it was known as Old Ea and South Ea. *v.* Old South Eau *supra* 10.

NORTH FEN is *Northeefen* 1386 *Ct*, *Northfen* 1390 ib. This adjoins Northey *supra* 261 and was apparently at first 'the fen by Northey,' later simply 'north fen.'

OLDEAMERE is *Oldemere* 1221 *ElyA*, 1302 *MinAcct*, *Holdemere* 1251 *ElyCouch*, 1316 *MinAcct*, *Oldeameere* 1712 Fenland iv, *Oldermere* c. 1825 O.S., 1842 *Walker*. 'Lake by the old river,' *v.* ēa. This is *Old Ee* 1356 *Extent*, *altam ripam voc. le Ee* 1389 *ElyCouch*, *the old Eawe* 1637 *BedL*, *Old Eau* 1706 Moore. See further *s.n.* Starnea Dyke *supra* 15.

SNOOTS (6″) is *The Snoots* 1712 Fenland iv, *v.* snote. In Whittlesey documents we have reference to numerous *snotes* including *Atlessnote*, *Ormmeressnote* 13th *Thorney*, *Fensnote*, *Scharpenhalesnot*, *Southale-snote* 1446 *Ct*, *Rotyngsnote* 1459 *Rental*, *Mednall Snout*, *Vicars Snout* 1603 *Survey*, presumably all of them points of dry land on the edge of the fens or of Whittlesey Mere. In *Thorney* we have reference also to *Barsnoht* and *Redisnoht*. This would seem to be the same word with a curious intrusive *h*. Cf. *infra* 344, 371.

STAMPFEN DROVE (6″). Cf. *Stamp cross* 1603 *Survey*, (low ground called) *the Stamp* 1650 *FenS*, *the Stamp Gravel* 1788 Fenland iv. This is one of the words used of "letts and impediments hindring the fall of the waters" in the fens, e.g. "gravels, dames...wares, *stamps*, slackes, cradgings" (1616 *BedL*). Cf. "*stampes* damys et alia ingenia in Ripa de Wysbech...per que aqua...artatur seu obstupatur" (1438 *Sewers*) and "ther is an hill or *stampe* growing or standing in the myddest of the River...that is a verie great anoyance and hindrance to the passage of the River" (1617 *Dugd* f. 34). Other references are "piscaria voc. *weares* uel *stampes*" (1588 *Ct*) in Newton in the Isle of Ely, *stampe* or *were* (1600 *AddCh*) in Elm and earliest of all, *Crouche-stampe* (1406 *ElyF*) in Lakenheath (Sf). NED (*s.v.* stamp sb.[2]) quotes a passage from Robert of Brunne (1338) where Sir John Beauchamp is drowned in "a water *stampe*." This must be the same word. The persistence of the form *stampe* from the 14th century onwards makes it impossible to accept the suggestion of the NED that it is an altered form of *stank*, 'pool.' More probably it is allied to ON *stampr*, 'large tub,' Ger *stampf*, 'mortar, swill-tub,' LGer *stampe*, 'drinking-glass.' Cf. *stamp* sb.[4] (NED) and Torp *s.v.* stamp.

STONALD FIELD (6″) is *Litlestanhale* c. 1246 *Thorney*, (*campo de*) *Stonhale* 13th ib., *Stonhalefeld* 1397 *Ct*, *Stonnall Feild* 1603 *Survey*,

Stonald (*Dole*) 1712 Fenland iv. 'Field by the gravel nook,' *v.* stān, healh.

TURNINGTREE BRIDGE (6″) is *Thurnyngtree, -ing-* 1403 *SewersA*, 1603 *Survey, Turnyngtre* 1446 *Ct, bridge nere Turningtree gravills* 1655 *BLAcct, Turntree Bridge* 1829 Wells. *Turning-tree* is found in the 16th century as a name for the gallows (NED), but here its history must be different. Cf. "stopps and letts al. *Turningtres* and *gravell wayes*" (1563 *SewersD*), also *le Turnyngtre apud calcetum de Stonteney* 1490 *Elien*. The *tree* or timber was evidently so called because it diverted or hindered the course of a stream.

WYPE DOLES is *Wepe* 1199 *ElyCouch*, (*le*) *Wype, -i-* c. 1250 *ElyM et freq* to 1597 *Wisbech Map, Vipe* 1458 Fenland iv, *the Tenants Doles in Wype* 1668 ib. i. This is probably from an OE *wīp, allied to the verb *wīpian*, 'wipe.' The ultimate history of that word is obscure, but Walde-Pokorny (i, 241) suggests that the original idea is of something which moves or swings (cf. the Latin cognates such as *vibrare*) and it may be that *wip* originally denoted a reed or something of that kind and then a clump of reeds, a reedy spot. Cf. Ekwall's association of Wispington (L) with ME *wisp*, earlier *wips, 'wisp of hay or straw,' used perhaps in the sense 'thicket' (DEPN).

ATKINSON'S BARN, BEALES'S DROVE[1], BIRD'S HUNDRED, CAMBER'S NEW DROVE, DEARLOVE'S COTTAGE, DRAKE'S FM, HUGHE'S FM, IVES DROVE[2], JONES'S DROVE, KATE'S FM[3], LINCOLN'S DOLES[4], RICHER'S DROVE, SHAW'S DIKE[5] (all 6″) and UNDERWOODS FM and GROUNDS[6] are probably to be associated with the families of Henry *Atkinson* (1650 *FenS*), Mychael *Beale* (1573 DKR xxxviii), John *Brid* (1276 *Pat*), *Byrd* (1396 *Ct*), Robert *Cambers* (c. 1840 *TA*), Richard *Dearlove* (ib.), Robert *Drake* (1390 *Ct*), Thomas *Hughes* (c. 1840 *TA*), James *Ives* (1600 Fenland iv), Isaac *Jones* (1650 *FenS*), Mr *Keate* (17th *AdvL*), Richard *Lincoln* (1335 *Thorney*), Thomas *Richer* (1381 *Ct*), Richard *Shawe* (1523 *SR*) and Lt.-Col. *Underwood* (1652 *AdvProc*).

ANGLE BRIDGE is so named in 1668 (*BLAcct*). ANGLE CORNER (6″) is *the Angle* 1668 Fenland i. BANK FM is so named c. 1825 (O.S.), from *Wyttlesey banke* 1618 *AddCh*. BLACK BUSH is *Black bushes* 1603

---

[1] *Belis* 1519 EA vii.
[2] *Ives's Drove* 1712 Fenland iv.
[3] *Mr. Kates Lands* ib.
[4] *Lincoln doles* c. 1350 *Thorney, v.* dāl.
[5] *Shawes dike* 1658 *BLAcct*.
[6] Cf. *Underwoods Eau* 1655 ib., (*Grounds*) 1829 Wells.

Survey. BLACKBUSH DROVE (6″) is so named in 1821 (Baker). BLACK
DIKE is *Blakedike* 1368 Imb. BRADLEY FEN is so named in 1603
(*Survey*). Cf. *Bratleweie* 13th *Thorney*, *Bradleyhowe* 1446 *Ct*. BUN-
TING'S DROVE (all 6″). Cf. *Buntinges Bower* 1574 *SewersC*. BURNT-
HOUSE FM is *the Burnt House* 1793 Fenland iv. CHAPELBRIDGE is so
named in 1829 (Wells). CHURCH FIELD (6″) is *Chirchefeud* 1328 *Ct*,
Kyrkefeld 1446 ib. COATES is *Cotes* c. 1280 *ElyF*, *Cootes*, *Coats* 1603
Survey. 'Cottages,' *v.* cot(e). COLD HARBOUR DROVE (6″) is *Cold
Arbour Drove* c. 1840 *TA*, *v. infra* 357. COMMON DROVE. Cf. *Common
long Drove* 1668 Fenland i. COUNTER DRAIN and COW WAY are so
named c. 1840 (*TA*). CROSS DRAIN is probably to be identified with
le Crossleme 1540 *MinAcct*, *v.* leam. CROSS DROVE is so named in 1712
(Fenland iv). DECOY FM (all 6″) is *Decoy House* c. 1825 O.S. DELPH
DIKE is *Delfdik* 1237 *Thorney*, 1248 *ElyCh*, -*dich* ib., *v.* (ge)delf, dīc.
DOG IN A DOUBLET BRIDGE (6″). Cf. "The floating *bridge* laid down
at the *Dog in Doublet*" (1787 Fenland ii), an inn. DUNCOMBE'S CORNER
is so named in 1810 (BedL). EARL'S LANDS FM (6″) is *Earl of Lincolns
Lands* 1712 Fenland iv. FIELD'S END BRIDGE is *Feilds end bridge* 1603
Survey. FLAG FEN (6″) is *Flegg Fenn* 1650 *FenS*, *Flagg Fenn* 1667 ib.
v. Flegcroft *supra* 260. GRANGE FM is *Grange* 1328 *Ct*. GRAVEL DIKE.
Cf. *Gravell*, *Long Gravel* 1603 *Survey* and *infra* 353. GULL FM is *Gull*
c. 1840 *TA*, *v.* gole. HALF ACRE DROVE. Cf. *the Common half Acre*
1668 Fenland i. HEMMERLEY GRAVEL (all 6″). Cf. *Hemberneye* 1393
Ct, *Hem(m)erly (way)* 1603 *Survey*, (*Gravel*) 1712 Fenland iv, *Heming-
ley Gravel* c. 1825 O.S., *v.* gravel. INHAM'S END is *Inhame Ende* 1603
Survey. Cf. *le Breyes Inham* 1390 *Ct* and *v.* innam. KINGSLAND is
the Kinges Landes 1650 *AdvProc*. This was presumably part of the
12,000 acres allotted to the Crown in 1634, *v.* Darby, *Draining of the
Fens* 40, 78. LAKE DROVE (6″). Cf. *Bradlakmor*, *Broodlakmor* 1398
Ct, *the Lake* 1603 *Survey*. *v.* brād, lacu, mōr. LONG DROVE is *Long
Drove way* 1668 Fenland i. LORD'S HOLT. Cf. *le lordesgres* 1398 *Ct*,
Lordes dyke end 1604 *Dugd*. MARRIOTT'S DROVE is *Mariot(t)esdrave*,
-*drove* 1387 Cl, 1438 Imb. NORTHEY FM is *Northey House* 1829 Wells.
NORTHEY GRAVEL is *Northee gravell* 1604 *Dugd*, *Northey Gravel* 1712
Fenland iv, *v.* gravel. There is a ford here. PLUMTREE FM (all 6″) is
Plummer's Fm 1797 ib. vi. PONDERSBRIDGE is *Ponds bridge* 1688
SewersA. POPELY'S GULL is *Popeleys Gull* 1821 Baker. PRIOR'S FEN
is *Priors Fenne* 1554 Pat. It belonged to the Prior of Ely. QUAKER'S
DROVE (6″) is so named in 1821 (Baker). REACH is *Reche* 1396 *Ct*,
Reach 1712 Fenland iv, (*Lots*) c. 1840 *TA*. *v.* Reach *supra* 136.

SLATEBARN DROVE (both 6″) is so named ib. SUET HILLS. Cf. *Suets Hill Drove* c. 1825 O.S. TEN ACRE DROVE (6″) is so named in 1842 (Walker). Cf. "Ten acres of ground and premises by the name of *Ten acres of fresh marsh*" 1682 Fenland i. TOWN FIFTY is *the Town Fifty* 1788 ib. iv. TURF DROVE (6″) is so named c. 1825 (O.S.). THE TURVES is so named in 1668 (Fenland i). THE WASH (6″) is so named in 1712 (ib. iv). *v.* The Wash *supra* 212. WEST FEN DROVE (6″) is so named c. 1825 (O.S.). Cf. *Westfen* 1314 *Ct.*

Wimblington

WIMBLINGTON

> *Wimblingetune* c. 975 (12th) *LibEl*, 12th *Libellus*
> *Wimblingtune* 12th *Libellus*, 1170 LibEl, *Wymb(e)lington*, *-yng-* 1251 *ElyCouch et freq* to 1617 Imb
> *Wimiligtune* 12th *Libellus*, *Wymelitone* 1221 *ElyA*
> *Wym(e)lington*, *-im-*, *-yng-* 1251 *ElyCouch et freq* to 1576 Saxton
> *Wimblitone* 1277 *Ely*, *Wymbleton*, *-i-* 1617 *SewersD*, 1638 ElyVis
> *Winelington* 1285 *Ass*
> *Wemblington*, *-yng-* 1298 *MinAcct*, *Wemyllyngton* 1541 ib.
> *Wylmyngton*, *Wil-*, *-ing-* 1337 *Chateriz et freq* to t. Hy 8 *Rental*
> *Wymyngton* 1386, 1388 Pat

'*Wimbel*'s farm,' *v.* ingtūn. The name is not on record, but it might be a pet-form of OE *Wynnbeald*. Cf. Wombleton (PN NRY 67). The place-name is not on early record and it is possible that *Wimblingtun* is actually a reduction of *Wynnbealdingtun*.

THE STITCHES (6″) with STITCHES FM is *Stetches* 1575 *SewersC*, 1829 Wells. 'Pieces of land.' Cf. *Stichebechefen* 1251 *ElyCouch* and *marisco de Rakestichst* 1302 *MinAcct* (Wimblington) and stycce.

STONEA [stouni] is *Staneie* 1170 LibEl, *Ston(e)heye* 1221 *ElyA et freq* to 1497 *ElyF*, *Stoney(e)*, *-a* 1251 *ElyCouch et freq* to 1760 EA xiii. 'Stony (i.e. gravelly) marshland,' *v.* stān, ēg.

LYON'S DROVE (6″) is probably to be associated with the family of William *Lyon* (1797 BedL).

APPLEBOROUGH WOOD (6″) is *Appleboro Wood* c. 1825 O.S.; *Applebury Wood* 1829 Wells. BLOCK FEN is *Blockffen* 1549 *Ct.* 'Black marsh.' Cf. Blockmoor Fen *supra* 198. BOOT'S BRIDGE is so named in 1829

(Wells). BOOT'S FM (6″) is *Boots* ib. BROWN'S HILL is *Browneshill* 1669 *ChancDec*. EASTWOOD END is *Estwoodend* 1565 Ely. Cf. *Estwode* 1251 *ElyCouch*. GRAY'S FM. Cf. *Graceffen* 1636 BedL, *Grays Fen* 1637 ib. John *Gray* had land here in 1826 (ib.). HARDING'S DRAIN (6″). We may possibly compare *Hartingesfene* 1620 *SewersD*, *Fen called Hartings* 1636 BedL. HONEYHILL FM (6″) is *Honey Hill* 1821 Baker. Cf. *supra* 166. HOOK. Cf. *Hochoue* 1277 Ely, *Wimblington Hooke* 1529 BedL, *v.* hōc, hōh. HOOK HO (6″) is *Hookehouse* 1621 *SewersD*. HORSE MOOR is *Horsmore* 1656 *AdvProc*. LATCHES FEN. Cf. *Lechewer* 1251 *ElyCouch*, *Leccwerefen* c. 1320 *Thorney*, *Latches Fen* 1821 Baker. *v.* lache, wēr. SEDGE FEN (6″) is *Seggefen* 1426 AD ii. Cf. Sedge Fen *supra* 204. STONEA GRANGE is *Stoney Graunge* 1600 *Cole* xix. Cf. Stonea *supra* 265. WIMBLINGTON COMMON is so named in 1680 (*FenS*).

XVIII. WISBECH HUNDRED

Wys(e)bech(e), *-i-* 1201 *ElyC*, 1251 *ElyCouch et freq* to 1438 Imb *Wisbiche* 1553 EA ix, *Wisbitche* 1617 *AddCh*

The courts leet for Wisbech Hundred (which here replace the tourn) were held at Wisbech at Pentecost in 1307, 1316, 1339 and 1465[1].

Elm

ELM [eləm]

Ælm c. 1150 ASC (E) *s.a.* 656
Elm c. 973 (c. 1253) *Peterb*, *Elm(e)* c. 1213 Fees *et passim*, (*cum Enemeth et Welle*) 1341 NI, (*iuxta Wysbech*) 1348 *Walden*, *villa Delm* 1284 *Ct*, *Delm* 1372 *SR*
Eolum 973 (15th) BCS 1297, *Elym* 1221 *ElyA*
Helm(a) c. 1155 *Thorney*, 1284 *Peterb*, *Helme* 1240–57 Pap, 1464 Pat, (church of) *Helm and Helmes* 1500 ib.

But for the forms *Eolum* and *Elym* this could be taken simply as 'at the elm.' For the form *Ælm* cf. ON *almr*, MLG *alm*. *Eolum* (dat. pl.) is however found as the name of one of the Germanic peoples

[1] *Ex inf*. Mr E. Miller.

visited by Widsith (*Widsith* 87) and if the coincidence of form is more
than a chance, we must believe that in addition to settlements of the
Wisse, Swæfe and *Seaxe* (*v. s.nn.* Ouse, Swaffham, Saxon Street
supra 13, 133, 127), there was a settlement of the tribe which Kemp
Malone (ESt lxvii, 321–4) has identified with the *Ilwan,* a tribe living
on the left bank of the river Vistula. No certain decision is possible.

NOTE. BRAMBLE LANE is *Brimble, -y- Lane* 1436 *SewersC,* 1543 *Ct, v.*
brēmel. GOSMOOR LANE is *le Gosmerlane* 1336 *Rental, Cosmore Lane* 1779
Wisb. Cf. *Gosemere* 1251 *ElyCouch.* 'Goose-mere,' *v.* mere. KIRKHAM LANE
is *Kyrkham lane* 1519 Ely and is to be associated with Walter de *Kyrkeham*
(1221 *ElyA*). Cf. *terram Roberti de Kyrkeham* c. 1300 *ElyM.*

BEAUFORD HO. Cf. *Beufeld* 1299 *Ct, Beauford* 13th *Ely, Beaudeforde*
1308 *ElyCouch, Bealford* 1316 *Cole* xxxvi, 1321 Ipm, *Beuford* 1331
Ipm, *Bodl, Bewford* 1456 FF, *Bewforth Hall* 1597 *Wisbech Map,*
Beawford Hall 1611 Imb. The first element may be OE *bēaw,* 'gadfly,'
hence feld and ford where these insects worried the cattle. Cf. Beaford
(PN D 86). The form *Bealford* is, however, difficult unless it is an
inverted spelling.

BEGDALE is *Be(c)k(e)dale(ffeld)* 1362 *SewersC,* (*bank*) 1377 Imb,
Beg(ge)dale 1380–1607 ib., 1597 *Wisbech Map, Begedalesfelde* 1380
Sewers. Adjoining this is Begdale Fm *infra* 297. In Swaffham Prior,
too, we have *Bekedale(feld)* 1319 *Extent,* 1322 *ElyCh,* 1330–54 *Ct,*
Begdalefylde 1493 Queens'. In neither parish is there anything which
can be called a *dale* and both names are perhaps manorial, deriving
from the same family, that of John de *Bekedale* 1314 *Ct* (Elm and
Wisbech), 1341 NI (Swaffham Prior) and Margaret de *Bekedale* 1327
SR (ib.).

COLDHAM is *Coldham* 1251 *ElyCouch et freq, Coldam* 1331 Rams, 1576
Saxton, *Cowldham* c. 1570 ChancP. 'Cold ham(m).'

CROWMERE is *Cromemare* 1597 *Wisbech Map, Cromere* (*Common*) 1821
Baker. Near by was *Crommedych* 1306 *Ct, Cromedich* 1380 *Sewers,*
Crome dike 1438 Imb. It would seem that the names must be related
but the relationship is obscure. The natural interpretation of *Crome-*
dich would be 'winding ditch,' *v.* crumb, dīc. Near by there is marked
on the Wisbech Map a *Currymare,* going back to *Curemere* 1251
ElyCouch, Coremere 1340 Imb, of obscure origin. We may perhaps
compare the West Country river-name Cory, Curry (RN 97–8).

FRIDAY BRIDGE is *Fridayesbrugg'* 1298 *Ass*, *Frydaybrigge* 1340 Imb. *fridai* is the name of a fishery of the monks of Ely in 1086 (InqEl), later *Frideiwere* (1251 *ElyCouch*). There was also a *Fryday lake* 1570 Imb in Elm. In Haddenham also we have *Frydaye weyr* 1549 *Ct*, *-ware* 1608 *AddCh*, and near Whittlesey we have *Fridaylake, -lone* 1244, 1286 Rams. These should probably be associated with fishing by the monks for Friday fare and not be associated with other Friday-names discussed in PN Sr 410-11.

GRAY'S MOOR is *Grasmere* 1251 *ElyCouch*, 1380 *Sewers*, *Grasemere* 1277 *Ely*, *Grasner* (sic) 1377 Imb, *Gresmere* 1336 (t. Eliz) *Rental*, 1411 *Ct*, *Gresemere* 1391 (1599) *Rental*, 1422 *Ct*, *Greysmore* 1549 ib., *Great Grasemoor, Gracemoor* 1810 *Wisb*. GRAY'S MOOR DROVE (6″) is *Gresmoredrove* 1449 *Ct*, *Grasemoor Drove* c. 1825 O.S. This name seems to be the same as Grasmere (We), *Ceresmere* 1203 Cur, *Gres(s)e-mere* 1246-54 Kendale, except that there the first element is OScand *gres*, here OE *gærs*, 'grass.' Ekwall suggests (DEPN) that in Grasmere the reference is to the grassy shores or to vegetation in the lake. That may be so here. For the modern form cf. Gracechurch (London), 1190 P *Gerscherche*. v. gærs, mere.

HALFPENNY FIELD is *Halpenyfeilde* 1336 (t. Eliz) *Rental*, *Halpenifield* 1377 Imb, *Halfpeny field* 1608 Imb. So called from the contribution levied for the repair of a neighbouring dyke. Cf. "for repair of the said New diche every acre of land from thence to Needham diche should pay a penny; and every acre from Needham diche unto Half-penny field...an halfpenny" (Imb 309).

LADDUS FENS

    (*of*) *ladwere* c. 975 ASCh, *Lodwer(e)* 1221 *ElyA et freq* to 1445 *Ct*, (*in Creklode*) 1528 Imb

    Lod(e)weres 1251 *ElyCouch*, 1431 *Ct*, *Fenne called Lodwas* 1553 EA ix, *Lodward* 1580 Imb, *Lodhouse* 1587 *Ct*, *Lodas Fenne* 1687 *BLAcct*

    Lot(h)ewere c. 1300 *Bodl*, 1334 Rams

    Lotquers t. Hy 3 *Ct*

    Ladwers 1580 Imb, *Ladus fenns* 1632 Hondius, *Ladwards or Ladus Fen* 1764 Ely

'Lode (i.e. *Crekelode supra* 254) weir(s') fen,' v. gelād. This is the name of an extensive fen stretching into Upwell where we also have LADDUS FM. The early references describe *Lodwere* as a *piscaria*.

LIVERMERE is *Liuer(e)mere, -y-* 1221 *ElyA et freq* to 1437 *Ct, Leuer(e)-mere* 1251 *ElyCouch et freq* to 1580 Imb, *Lethermere* 1381 *Ct,* 1438 Imb, *Lethmere* 1411 *Ct.* The name is probably identical with Liver-mere (Sf), *Leuuremer* c. 1050 (13th) KCD 907, *Liuermere* c. 1095 BuryDoc, *Liuermera* 1086 DB, *Lefremere* 1255 Cl, and possibly, as to the first element, with Liverpool (PN La 116–17) which has persistent *Liuer-* forms. Ekwall (DEPN) would associate the first element with the common word *liver* and apply it to the shape of the mere, but it is difficult to believe in two liver-shaped meres. Alternatively, he would connect Liverpool and Livermere with OE *lifrig,* 'coagulated, clotted,' ModEng (dial.) *livery* (of soil), 'heavy, tenacious,' ME *livered,* 'clotted,' applied once to the Red Sea. Neither of these words can give us the first element directly, but as they themselves must derive from the common word *liver* they suggest the possibility that *lifermere* might be used of a pool with thick, turbid water. From the semantic point of view the most natural association of Livermere would be with dial. *levers,* 'yellow flag,' going back to OE *leber, læfer,* ME *leure,* but if that is the etymology it would be difficult to explain the frequent and persistent *liure-* forms.

LONG BEACH FM is *Lang(e)bech(e)* 1221 *ElyA et freq* to 1570 Imb, *Landbech(e)* c. 1350 Rams, 1411 *Ct, -beach* 17th *AdvL.* 'Long brook,' *v.* lang and bece, 'brook, valley.' This has perhaps been confused with Landbeach *supra* 178.

NEEDHAM BANK and FIELD. Cf. *Nedham* 1221 *ElyA,* 1251 *ElyCouch,* 1277 *Ely,* (*campo*) 1390 *SewersC, -feld* 1445 *Ct, Needham Bank* 1590 *SewersC, Nedom(dyche)* 1390 *Ct, bank of Needham called Bishops Dike* 1649 BedL. This name occurs several times in East Anglia—Needham (Nf), Needham in Yaxley, Needham Market and Needham Street (Sf)—and also in High Needham (Db), all with similar forms (cf. DEPN). Ekwall has suggested that this name is analogous to Hungerton, meaning 'needy, poor homestead or village,' from OE *nīed,* 'distress, hardship' and also probably 'poverty.' *v.* hām.

WALDERSEA[1]

  Walderse 1248 *ElyCh et freq* to 1420 *Ct, Waldirsee* 1316 *MinAcct,*
     Waldersey 1368 Imb, *Waldersea* 1658 *BLAcct*
  Waltershe 1251 *ElyCouch, Walterse(e)* 1316 *MinAcct et freq* to 1480
     Ct, Waltersey(e) 1368 Imb *et freq* to 1597 *Wisbech Map*
  Waterse 1383, 1492 *Ct, Waterseye* 1438 Imb

  [1] Partly in Wisbech St Mary and St Peter.

The first element is probably the gen. sg. of the personal name *Wealdhere*, the variant forms in *Walter-* being due to the OFr *Walter* or to that tendency to unvoice *d* to *t* before *h* which Ekwall first noted in such names as Waltham from *Wealdham* (*Studia Neophilologica* i, 97 ff.). The second is probably ēg.

HILL HO (6″) was probably the home of Thomas *at Hille* (1449 *Ct*).

BOYCE'S BRIDGE[1], HAWSTEADS[2] (6″), STAG'S HOLT[3], TILNEY HIRNE[4] (6″) and WALES FIELD and BANK[5] (6″) are probably to be associated with the families of John *Boyce* (1482 Pat), Robert de *Haustede*, *Halstede* (1221 *ElyA*) which probably came from Halstead (Ess), John *Stegg* (1327 SR), Nicholas de *Tylney* (1221 *ElyA*) which came from Tilney (Nf), and Richard *Waleis* (1277 *Ely*). *v.* hyrne.

BAR DROVE is so named c. 1840 (*TA*). Cf. *Southbarre* 1464 *Ct*. BIRD'S BARN. Cf. *Brideslond* 1336 *Rental* and Bird's Hundred *supra* 263. CHAIN FM (all 6″) is *Chainbridge House* c. 1825 O.S. It is near Chainbridge *supra* 254. CREEKGALL FEN is *Creekefenne* 1597 *Wisbech Map*, *Cricke fen* 1651 *AdvProc*, *Creek Gall Fen* c. 1840 *TA*. *v.* Creek *supra* 254 and galle. GREEN DROVE is so named in 1723 (*Ct*). LONG DROVE (6″) is *Longysdrove* 1500 *Ct*, *Longsdroffe* 1533 *SewersC*, *Lunges droves end* 1619 Imb. MOLLS' DROVE and PEARTREE HILL FM are so named in 1829 (Wells). NEW FIELD (6″) is *Neufeld* 1491 Ely. OLD FIELD (6″) is (*in*) *veteri campo in villa de Elm* 1298 *AddCh*, *le Oldfeilde* 1336 (t. Eliz) *Rental*, *v.* eald, feld. REDMOOR BANK and FIELD. Cf. *Redmere* 1221 *ElyA*, *-felde* 1434 *Ct*, *Redmor(e)* 1306 ib., *-dyke* 1336 *Rental*, *Redmore bank* 1596 Imb, *Reed moore ffeilde* 1336 (t. Eliz) *Rental*. 'Reed-mere,' *v.* hrēod, mere. THE STITCH (6″). Cf. (a drove called) *the Stitch* 1713 *Deed*, *Richard's Stitch* 1806 *Wisb* and stycce. TOWN FIELD (6″) is *Townfeilde* 1336 *Rental*, *v.* tūn, feld. WALDERSEA HO is *Waldersey House* 1829 Wells. WALDERSEA MAIN DRAIN. Cf. *drayne of Walterseye* 1579 *Depositions*. WHITE HO FM is so named c. 1825 O.S.

---

[1] *Boyce Bridge* c. 1840 *TA*.
[2] *tenementum Hallested'* 1315 *Ct*, *Hausted* 1346 *ElyF*.
[3] *Steggesyerde* 1397 *Ct*, *-wood* 1533 *SewersC*.
[4] *Tylneyehyrne* 1199 *ElyCouch*.
[5] *terra Waleys* 1251 ib., *Walysfelde* 1324 *Ct*, *Walesdyke* 1336 *Rental*.

Leverington

LEVERINGTON

Leverington(e) c. 1130 *Ely et passim*, *-yngton(e)* 1234 *ElyC et freq*
to 1552 Pat
Leverinton', *-y-* c. 1210 *ElyCh et freq* to 1378 SR
Lieurington 1220 *ElyCh*, *Lyverington* 1246 *Wren*, 1506 *Ct*
Luringtune c. 1250 (1348) Ch, *Lewryngton* 1494 Ipm, 1541 *MinAcct*

'*Lēofhere's* tūn,' *v.* ingtūn.

NOTE. BLACK LANE is *le Blaclane* 1395 EA iv. BONA LANE is *Bony Lane*
1696, 1865 *Wisb*, *Bona Lane* 1876 ib. FENDIKE LANE. Cf. *le Oldefendichlane*
1340 *Ct*, *Leueryngton fendyk* 1448 ib. GREEN LANE is *Greenelane* 1620
SewersD. GULL LANE is *Golelane* 1446 *Ct*, *Goole lane* 1620 *SewersD* and
takes its name from *le Gole super le Fendyk* 1449 *Ct*, *v.* gole. HORSESHOE LANE
takes its name from *Horsho* 1251 *ElyCouch*, 1277 *Ely*, *the Horshooe by the old
river* 1340 Imb, *Horshooe* 1597 *Wisbech Map*, *the Horshew* 1690 Lea. This is
a bend in the Roman Bank shaped like a horse-shoe. There was another
Horssho c. 1270 *Thorney*, *Harschoe* (*hyrne*) 1597 *Wisbech Map* on the Old
South Eau in Thorney. Cf. also *the Horshooe ground* 1709 *FenS* (in Waterbeach). For a similar type of name cf. *Sadelbowe(cote)* 1244 Rams, 1251
ElyCouch on the Cambridgeshire-Huntingdonshire boundary in Whittlesey,
and Saddle Bow, a hamlet in a bend of the Ouse in Wiggenhall St Mary the
Virgin (Nf), *Sadelboge(gate)* 14th Lewes. It may be noted that these names
give us examples of *horseshoe* some 130 years before the earliest example in
NED. MAY'S LANE is *Meyeslane* 1438 *Sewers*. Cf. *domum Thom' le Mey*
c. 1254 *Thorney*. MILL LANE is so named in 1570 (Imb). It is earlier *le Kekys-
myllane* (1417 *Wisb*), so named from *Kekysmille* (1438 Imb) on the bank of
the Wisbech river. PAP'S LANE is *Pappyslane* 1461 *Ct*. *v.* Pap's Field *infra* 273.
PARK LANE is *Parkelane* 1620 *SewersD*. POPE'S LANE is *Popenhowlane* 1454
Will, *Popney Lane* 1505 *Deed*, *Popelane* 1570 Imb, *Popes Lane* 1634 *Wisb*.

BONE'S GOTE is *Bondesgote*, *-ys-* 1438 *Sewers*, Imb, *Bond's gote* 1570
ib., *Bonesgote* 1620 *SewersD*, *Bone's Gout* c. 1825 O.S. This is a compound of *bonde* (from ON *bóndi*), originally denoting a peasant proprietor (*v.* EPN), and ME gote, 'watercourse,' *v. infra* 327.

CAT FIELD (6″) is *Catefeld* c. 1250 *ElyM*, *Cattesfeld* c. 1260 *Thorney*,
Catfelde 1334 *Ct*. 'Open country haunted by the wild cat,' *v.* catt,
feld and cf. *Catefelde* 1446 *Ct* (Whittlesey).

CATTLE DIKE (6″) is *fossatum de Cattesfeld* c. 1260 *Thorney*, *Catffelde-
dyke* 1480 *Ct*, *Cattledike* 1570 Imb. 'The dike by Cat Field' (*supra*).
v. dīc.

DOWGATE BRIDGE (6″) is so named in 1821 (Baker). Cf. (*a gote called*) *Dogarde* 1368 Imb, (*gurgitem vocatam*) *Dieugard* 1438 *Sewers*. A pious or facetious French name for the gote from which the bridge took its name. 'God protect' those who came near it.

GOREFIELD is *Gorefeld* c. 1190 *ElyM*, *Gordefelde* 1520 *Ct*, *Gorefeild greene* 1620 *SewersD*. Probably 'fen feld' from OE gor, 'mud, marsh.' Cf. Havengore (PN Ess 185), earlier *Havenemersche*, PN Wa xlix, and Goredike Bank *supra* 206.

IVESDIKE FIELD (6″). Cf. *Eyisdich* 1331 *Ct*, *Evysdeke, Ewsdeke* 1543 ib., *Evisdike-, Eydikesbrigge, Evil dike brigg* (sic) 1570 Imb, *Isedike bridg* 1611 *SewersD*, *Ivesdike bridge* 1620 ib., *Eyes Dyke* 1768 *Wisb*, *Ivesdyke Field* 1806 ib. There has clearly been confusion in the later forms of this name. The first element is possibly the gen. sg. of ēg, 'marsh-land.' The forms with v are difficult of explanation, but may be due to association with the family of John *Ivy* and Thomas *Ive* (1454, 1600), which held land near the dike[1].

PLAIN FIELD (6″) is *Flaynefelde* 1335 *Wisb*, *Flannyffeild* 1436 *SewersC*, *Sleynffeld* (sic) 1524 Ely, *Flaynfelde* t. Hy 8 *Rental*, *Plainefeild* 1611 *SewersD*, *Flanefeilde* 1620 ib., *Flatmore al. Flain Field, Plain al. Flain-field* 1785 *Wisb*, *Flain Field* c. 1840 *TA*. This name would seem, by a curious chance, to be identical with Plainfield (Nb), earlier *Flaynefeld* (PN NbDu 157) and the first element would seem to be ON *fleinn*, 'pike, arrow.' The Leverington area, surrounded by lanes, does suggest an arrow-head in shape.

POCK FIELD (6″) is *Pokefeld(e)* c. 1190 *ElyM*, 1305 *Ct*, *Pock-, Pooke-feild(e)* 16th Fenland vii. 'Goblin feld,' *v.* pūca. Popple DROYE (6″) is *Pokeldrove* 1518 ib., *Pooke Field or Popple Drove* 1696 *Wisb*. 'Drove by Pock Field,' *v.* drāf. For the development cf. Cattle Dike *supra* 271.

SPITTLE FIELD (6″) is *Spetilfeld* 1411 *Ct*, *Spitlefeild* 16th Fenland vii. This was probably part of the endowment of the Hospital of St John the Baptist of Leverington (cf. L 228). *v.* feld.

TOWNHOUSES (6″) is a group of twenty-one houses, all brick, inhabited rent free by paupers. Six of them were erected by the terms of the will of Edward Cross in 1633 on land called *Midd Feather*[1]. Cf. *Mid-fether* 1586 *Ct* (Wisbech), *Middffetter* 1606 *Depositions* (Stretham), *Midfitters* 1653 EA xiii (Haddenham).

[1] *Ex inf.* Mr G. M. G. Woodgate.

WOLF LANE is *Wyrmfeld(lane)* 13th *ElyCh*, *Wormfeld* 1338 *Ct*, *Wyrfeld* 1369–75 ib., *Wurfelde* 1443 ib., *-lane* 1449 ib., *Wullfullane* 1498 ib., *Wolflayn felde* 1528 Fenland vii, *Wurfelayne* t. Ed 6 *Rental*, *Wolfflane* 1620 *SewersD*. Here in 1298 lived Richard de *Wirmefeld*, *Wermfeld* (*Ass*). 'Open country where snakes were numerous,' from OE *wyrm* and feld.

WRAT FIELD (6″) is *le Wrottefelde* 15th *Thorney*, *Wrotfeld* 1369, 1386 *Ct*, *Wratfeld* t. Hy 8 *Rental*, *Wrat*, *Wret Field* c. 1840 *TA*. 'Open land where crosswort grows,' from OE *wrætt* and feld. The forms in *wrot(te)* are surprising, but they have their parallel in the forms for Wratting and *Wratworth supra* 122, 80. Cf. *Wrottecroft* 1385 *Ct* in the same parish. Known also as *Cakers Hill Field* (1728 *Wisb*), it lies immediately north of Karrow *infra* 275.

FITTON HALL is *Fittonehall* 1366 *ElyCh* and was the home of Alanus de *Fittun* (c. 1213 Fees). Cf. *terram Alani de Fittune* c. 1254 *Thorney*. Here at an earlier date may have lived Ellich de *Fitton* (t. Hy 2 (1314) Ch). The first element is ON *fit*, 'meadow-land by a river,' cf. "sea banckes...for the defendinge of the landes, marshes, holms, *ffittyes*" (1617 *Depositions*). Hence 'tūn by the meadow-land.'

WOOL CROFT (6″) is *Wlcroft* 13th *ElyCh*, *Wollecroft* 1385 *Ct*, *Wul-crofte* 1455 ib., *Woolcroft* 16th Fenland vii. Here in 1221 and 1251 lived Richard de *Wlfuecroft*, *Wluescroft* (*ElyA*, *ElyCouch*). '*Wulf(a)*'s croft.'

BIRD'S DROVE[1], BRADLEY'S FM,[2] PAP'S FIELD[3] (all 6″) and RICHMOND FIELD[4] (6″) and HALL are probably to be associated with the families of Robert *Brid* (1308 *Ct*), Thomas *Bradley* (1611 *ParReg*), Roger *Pappe* (1357 Pat) and Geoffrey *Richemund* (1375 Ely).

ALLEN'S DROVE (6″) is *Aleynesdroue* 1398 *ElyCh*, *Alinne drove* 1570 Imb. BLACKLANE FIELD (6″) is *Blacklanefeld* 1395 EA iv, *Blak(el)enfeld* 1438 Imb. CHERRYTREE HILL is *Cherrye hill* 1586 *Ct*, *Cherry Tree Hill* 1810 *Wisb*. DECOY FM (6″) is so named in 1905 (*Wisb*). Cf. *the Coye* 1659 Fenland ii. *Coye*, denoting a decoy, is a loan word from Dutch. Cf. NED *s.v. Coy* sb.[1] FEN CROFT (6″) is *Fencroft* 1380 *Ct*.

---

[1] *Briddisdroue* 1411 *ElyCh*, *Birdisdroue* 1440 ib.
[2] *Bradleys Horse Pond* 1768 *Wisb*.
[3] *Pappesfeld* 16th Fenland vii, *Pups Field* c. 1840 *TA*.
[4] (*fossatum de*) *Richemund* c. 1260 *Thorney*, (*manor called*) *Rychemond* 1392 (1455) Pat, *Richmund field* 1570 Imb.

HAROLD'S BRIDGE. Cf. *Harold Dyke* 16th Fenland vii, *Harwell* or *Harrold, Harhald Common* 1756, 1790 *Deed, Harrold* c. 1840 *TA.* v. Harold Drove *infra* 278. HART FIELD (6″) is (*le*) *Harp(e)felde* 1436 *SewersC*, 1438 *Sewers, -field* 1570 Imb, 1786 *Wisb*, Hart-, *Hertfelde* t. Ed 6 *Rental.* The field is shaped like a harp. HASSOCKHILL DROVE is so named in 1905 (*Wisb*). Cf. *Hàssok* c. 1151 *Thorney* and *v.* hassuc. *v.* Addenda lx. HONEYHILL FM (both 6″). Cf. *supra* 166. LEVERINGTON COMMON is *Leverington Common or Turne Green* 1785 *Wisb*. LONG MEADOW FIELD (6″) is *Longemedwes* c. 1250 *ElyM, -medwe* 1333 *Ct*, *Langmiddow* 16th Fenland vii. MARGERY'S CROFT is *Margeryscroft* 1465 *Wren*. NEW FIELD is *Newefeld* c. 1190 *ElyM*. OUTNEWLANDS is *Out-Newlands* 1570 Imb. OX FIELD is *Oxfeld* 1376 *Ct*. PARK FIELD (all 6″) is *Le Parkefeld* 1369 *Ct*. RABBIT HILL is so named in 1782 (*Wisb*). REMER'S FIELD (6″) is *Raymerfelde* t. Hy 8 *Rental, Reym-* 1553 Pat, *Reymers* 1556 *Wisb, Remersfeilde* 16th Fenland vii. SEA FIELD is *Seefelde* 1467 *Ct*. 'Open land by the sea.' *v.* Sea Dike Bank *supra* 207. SHIRE FIELD is *Schyerfeld* t. Hy 8 *Rental, Sherefield* 1570 Imb. It probably owes its name to its position on the shire boundary. Cf. Lady Nunn's Old Eau, earlier Shire Drain *supra* 7, 15. Between it and the boundary is now Hart Field *supra*. SNAIL CROFT is *Snaylcrofte* 1385 *Ct*. 'Croft overrun by snails,' *v.* croft. WHITE ENGINE DRAIN (all 6″) is so named in 1696 (*Wisb*).

Newton

NEWTON

> (*to*) *niwantune* c. 972 ASCh, *Newenton, Nuenton* 1285 *Ass*
> *Neuton(e)* c. 1213 Fees *et freq* to 1457 Pat, (*iuxta Leuerington*) 1285
> *Ass*, (*in Mers(che)lond*) 1298 ib., (*by Wysbech*) 1354 Pat, *Newton(e)*
> 1291 Tax *et passim*, (*Colvyle*) t. Eliz *Cole* xxxvii

'The new farm,' *v.* nīwe, tūn. *Colvyle* from the family of John de *Colville* (1360 Ipm). *Merschelond* is the neighbouring Marshland (Nf).

NOTE. BREWER'S LANE is *Medwedraue* 1343 *Ct, Medowlane* 1438 *Sewers*, *Brewers or Meadow Lane* 1786 *Wisb*. FRANK'S LANE is *Frankslane* 1570 Imb and is probably to be associated with the family of John *Frankes* (1395 EA iv). Cf. *Frankisdrove* ib. GOODEN'S LANE is *Godings Lane* 1688 *Wisb, Gooden Lane* c. 1840 *TA*. GREENSTOCK LANE is *Green dyke or Greenstock Lane* 1786 *Wisb*. Cf. *le Grenedyk* 1395 EA iv, *Green Dike Stock* 1688 *Wisb*. HOGEN'S LANE is *Hoggens Lane* ib., *Huggins Lane* 1789 *Wisb*. MILL LANE is *le Millelane* 1395 EA iv.

BLACKDIKE BANK (6″). Cf. *le Blakediche* 1370 *Ct*, *Blakedyke* 1438 *Sewers*, *Averies trees or Black dike* 1570 Imb, *v.* dic. BLACKDIKE BRIDGE (6″) is on the Tydd St Giles's boundary and the bank apparently once continued through Tydd to the Shire Drain. In Tydd we have *Auereystrese, -trees* 1438 *Sewers*. This is probably to be associated with the family of Nicholas, son of John *Averey* (1305 FF).

GAUL FIELD (6″) is *Gavelfeld* 1395 EA iv, *Gallefelde* t. Ed 6 *Rental*, *Galls field* 1570 Imb, *Gawleffeilde* 1621 *SewersD*, *Gaulfield* 1688–1797 *Wisb*. OE *gafol*, 'tax, tribute' and feld. 'Land for which rent was paid' as opposed to the common fields. Cf. Galleywood (PN Ess 234), Galton (Do), *Gaveltone* DB, Gawlish and Galford (PN D 74, 187).

GULL FIELD (6″) is *Goolefyld* 1533 *SewersC*, *Gooldfield* 1611 EA xiii, *Goolefield* 1688 *Wisb*, *Gull Field* c. 1840 *TA*. Cf. *Fittongole* 1343 *Ct*, *Fytton goile* 1549 ib. 'Watercourse feld,' *v.* gole.

KARROW FIELD (6″) is *Kakerow, Cakerow* 1395 EA iv, *Karrow Field* c. 1840 *TA*. Near here lived Alexander de *Kakerowe* (1277 *Ely*). Cf. also Karrow Field *infra* 288, *Cakerow* t. Ed 1 *Rental* in Spalding (L), *Cak(e)row(e)(gate)* ib., 1321 Cl, *Carrowgate* 1699 Holbeach Landholders, in Holbeach (L), *Cacrowe* c. 1570 *Compotus* in Leverton (L)[1]. All these are examples of a name of derogatory type. The first element is the vb. *cack*, 'to void excrement.' The noun is not recorded before c. 1600, *v.* NED *s.v. cack* and *v.* also rāw.

BRADLEY'S BRIDGE and WHIRLER'S HILL (6″) (so named in 1688 *Wisb*) are probably to be associated with the families of Stephen *Bradley* (c. 1840 *TA*) and Reginald *Whirler* (1327 *SR*).

BLOCK'S DROVE is *Blokislane* 1395 EA iv, *Blocks Lane* 1570 Imb, *Drove* 1736 *Wisb*. CHAPEL DROVE (both 6″) is *Chappel Drove* 1705 *Wisb* and was so named from a chapel which stood by the sea here, cf. *Chappel of the See* t. Ed 6 *Rental*. CHURCH CROFT is *Kirkecroft, -y-* 1385 *Ct*, 1532 ib., *Church Crofts* 1688 *Wisb*. *v.* Introd. xxxv. CROSS DROVE (6″) is *Bychopdyke, Bychepisdych* 1395 EA iv, *Bishops Dike or Cross Drove* 1786 *Wisb*, *v.* dīc. The Bishop was the Bishop of Ely. EARL'S DOLES is *Erlisdoles* 1395 EA iv, *v.* dāl. FALL HIRN is *Fall Hurn Field* 1688

---

[1] For the Lincolnshire forms we are indebted to Dr L. W. H. Payling.

Wisb, v. **hyrne.** FENLAND FIELD is *Fenlond(e)* 1395 EA iv, *-feld* 1438
Sewers, v. **feld.** FENLAND GATE is *Fengate* 1395 EA iv, *Fenland Gate*
c. 1840 *TA*. 'Road to the fen,' *v.* **gata.** FITTON CROFT (all 6″) is
Fyttonecroftes 1438 *Sewers* and with FITTON END goes with the neighbouring Fitton Hall *supra* 273. GOATLANDS (6″) is *Dooles al. Goatelands*
1688 *Wisb.* It is near Four Gotes *infra* 285. *v.* **dāl.** HARD CROFT (6″)
is *le hardcroft* 1395 EA iv. LODGE FM. Cf. *ye Lodge Ground* 1705
Wisb. LONG FIELD (6″) is *le Longefeld* 1324 *Ct.* MAJOR DROVE (6″)
is so named in 1786 (*Wisb*). MARSH FM, on the seaward side of
the Roman Bank, is probably a modern name. Cf. *Newton Marsh*
1621 *AddCh.* MEADOW FIELD is *Medowfeld* 1395 EA iv. MIDDLE
DROVE is *Middeldraue* c. 1254 *Thorney, v.* **drāf.** MUD CROFT is
Mudcroft (*bridge*) 1436 *SewersA.* NEW CROFT is *le Newcroft* 1395
EA iv. NEW FIELD is *Newfelde* 1438 *Sewers.* NEWLANDS is *Newlond*
1376 *Ct, Newelondes* t. Ed 6 *Rental. New* perhaps because reclaimed
from the sea. It lies just behind the Roman Bank. NEWTON HALL is
so named in 1597 (*Wisbech Map*). OLD FIELD is *le Oldfeld* 1395 EA iv.
PARROCK FIELD is *le Parroche, Parrokes* t. Ed 6 *Rental, Parkefeld* 1395
EA iv. 'Small enclosure,' *v.* **pearroc.** ROWLES FIELD is *Rollysfeld* ib.,
Rolsesfelde 1438 *Sewers, Rowles Field* 1688 *Wisb.* SHORTLANDS is
Shortlond(es) 1395 EA iv. STERTS is *Stertis* ib., *Stertes* (*gate*) 1436
SewersC. v. **steort,** 'tail of land.' WEST FIELD (all 6″) is *Westfeld*
1395 EA iv. WILLOWHALL. Cf. *Wylugcroft* ib.

Outwell

OUTWELL

> *Udewuwelle, Udewelle, Wodewelle* c. 1130 (17th) ChronRams
> *Witewelle* 12th Lewes, *Vitwell versus Wisebech'* 1251 Ch, *Wythewelle*
>   1260 Rams
> *Well(e)* 1203 Cur, 1285 Pat, 1388 Cl, 1438 *Sewers, Welles* 1204 Cur
> *Vtwell(e)* 1221 *ElyA*, 13th *ElyG*, 1304 *Ct,* Utwell 1267 Pat,
>   *Vtwellys* 13th Lewes, *Vtwelles* c. 1282 ib.
> *Outwell(e)* 1324 *Ct et freq*
> *Owtewall* 1556 Pat

Outwell, partly in Norfolk (*Wella, Utwella* 1086 DB), once formed
a whole with Upwell *infra* 288. Some of the forms in *Welle(s)* given
there may refer to this place. The earliest forms of this name are
irreconcilable. One set would suggest OE **wudu,** alternating possibly

with OScand **viðr**, 'wood,' the others suggest OE *ūt(e)*, 'outer,' probably because lower down stream, farther out towards the sea than Upwell. Cf. *Wodebech* 1324 *Ct* (in Outwell).

COTTON'S COMMON (6") is probably to be associated with the family of Anthony *Cotton* (1536 *Cole* xxxvi).

SAYER'S FIELD HO (6"). Cf. *Saresherne, -hirne* 1380 *Sewers, Sayersfeld* 1438 ib., *Sayesfelde* 1553 *ElyCh*.

Parson Drove

PARSON DROVE

> *Person(e)sdroue* 1324 *Ct*, 1433 Cl, 1459 Fenland vi
> *Parsonsdrove* 1395 EA iv, (*al. Fenende*) 1397 *Wren, -droyve* t. Ed 6 Rental
> *Parson Drove* 1396 Ely *et passim, Parsonways End* 1582 *Wisb*
> *Persondrove* 1397 *Elien et freq* to 1553 Pat

OE **drāf**, 'drove,' *v. infra* 321. *Fenende* because the hamlet was in the fen near the boundary of Leverington. The first element is clearly the common word or name *persone* or *parson*. It has been suggested that the drove was the one along which the parson had to pass from Leverington to the chapel (Fenland i, 345). This may be so, but droves were commonly named from owners. Certainty is impossible, as the date of the foundation of the chapel is unknown.

NOTE. PULLEY'S LANE is *Polylane* 1438 *Sewers*. SILVER'S LANE is *Silverings Drove* 1864 *Wisb* and is to be associated with the family of Geoffrey *Silveroun* (1345 *Elien*). Cf. *Siluyrns* 1518–29 ECP, *the Silverings* 1864 *Wisb*.

BYTHORN [baitə·n] BANK (6") is *Byett Hyrne, Byte Hyrne* 1524 *Wisb*. 'Nook in the bend,' *v.* **byht**, 'bend of a stream' and **hyrne**. The bank runs along the Old South Eau and is near a sharp bend in the stream. The spelling pronunciation [baiθə·n] is also heard. *v.* Addenda lx.

CANNON FIELD (6") is *Kanunisfeld* 13th *St John's, Chanounesfelde* c. 1300 *St John'sH, Canonfield* 1570 Imb, *Channonfeild* 1611 *SewersD*, *v.* **feld**. It belonged to the canons of St John's Hospital, Cambridge.

CLOUGHS CROSS is *Clow(e)s crosse* 1438, 1528, 1570 Imb, *le Clouse* 1438 *Sewers, Clowsecrosse* 1469 Pat, *Clow(e)crosse* ib., 1594 Camden, *Clowes Crosse al. Shofftfenndike* 1579 *Deposition, Clows Cross* 1618 BedL, *Clough(s)crosse* 1636 ib. *v.* NED *s.v. clow* sb.[1] where it is shown that *clow* is a false singular from *clowes*, regarded as a plural but really a singular, going back to OE *clūse*, from Late Latin *clusa*, used in ME of a dam. Cf. *mulne cluse* c. 1225 Ancren Riwle, *clowys* c. 1440 Prompt Parv, *clowe* 1430 CathAngl. The form *clough* is probably an inverted spelling due to such parallels as *plough*, *plow*. It is commonly used of a sluice or floodgate and to the examples given in NED we may add "a *clow*...to prevent water passing from a pipe into Jeccon's gote" (1358 Imb 309), "one *clow* or one dam in the common sewer of Tyd" (1438 ib. 326). Near this clow stood a cross marking the boundary between Cambridgeshire and Lincolnshire. Cf. *le Clowes juxta Trokenhold ubi alia Crux lapidea figitur* (1597 *Wisbech Map*, where the cross is marked). Because of its position as a boundary the stream was also known as "*Clowse Crosse or Shiere Drane* which divideth the Isle of Elie from Hollande" (1596 Fenland v, 68).

HAROLD DROVE with HAROLD'S BANK (both 6″). Cf. *Goredyke al. Harroldedyke* 1588 *Ct*, *Shoffendike al. Harroldike* 1592 *Wisb*, *Harroldbank(e)* 1619 *SewersD*, 1782 *Wisb* and Harold's Bridge *supra* 274 which is on Elloe Bank. Harold Drove and Harold's Bank run east from this. Forms are late and it is clear there has been some transference of names. *Goredyke* is Goredike Bank in Newton *supra* 206 which runs at an angle from Elloe Bank near Harold's Bridge. *v.* also Shoffendike *infra* 286.

INHAM FIELD (NORTH and SOUTH) (6″) are *Inneme* 1239 *Ely*, *Suthinholm* 1298 *Ass*, *Northinnome* 1310 *Ct*, *the Sowthenham* 1366 *Wisb*, *Southinham* 1382 *Ct*, *Northinham* 1438 Imb, *Inhamfelde* 1393 *Ct*, *Southingham* 1438 Imb, *South Ennam Field* 1565 *Wisb*. 'Piece of land taken into cultivation,' *v.* innam.

THROCKENHOLT

> *þrokonholt* c. 1150 ASC (E) *s.a.* 656, *Throkenholt* 1229 *ElyCouch*, *Throkenold* 1439 Imb, *Throcknolt* 1548 *Ct*, *Thrognolt(e)* 1550–2 *Ct*, *Throcknall* 1619 Imb
>
> *Trokonholt* c. 1151–91 *Thorney*, *Trokenholt* 1218 *ElyCouch et freq* to 1438 Imb, *Trockenholt* c. 1240 (1348) Ch
>
> *Hoconhold* c. 1150 (1348) Ch
>
> *Trokeholt* c. 1151, c. 1350 *Thorney*, *Throkeholt* 1235 *ElyA*
>
> *Heremitorium quondam Endewicke dictum nunc vero Trokenholde nominat'* 1196 *Wisbech Map*, *Trokenhold(e)* 1251 *ElyCouch*, 1597 *Wisbech Map*, *-hout* 1293 Imb, *-haut* 1293 Pat

Trokkene c. 1191 *Thorney*, *Trokenhee* c. 1350 ib.

Thorkenholt 1234 *ElyC*, *Thorokinholt* 1301 *Ct*, *Torkenholt(e)* 1436 *SewersC*

Trokenhou 1291 *Cole* xliii, 1294 Imb

Trokonolum in loco Euerdewic c. 1320 *Thorney*, *Trokenholum in loco Endewico dicto* 1358 *Wisbech Map*, *Trokenhole* 1576 Saxton

Troknold 1570 Imb

The first element is an adj. *þroccen*, from OE *þrocc*, 'a piece of timber to which the ploughshare was fastened' (dial. *throck*), also used of the table of the moneychangers, fully discussed *s.n.* Throcking (PN Herts 187). The second element was originally holt, with later occasional substitution of ēa (with reference to the river) and holh. Hence probably, 'wood or hollow where throcks were obtained,' though the exact meaning of *þroc* is uncertain.

The earliest form for the lost alternative occurs in *aqua de Euerdwic* 13th *StNeot* for the Old South Eau *supra* 11. 'Dairy farm by the ford through the (South) Eau,' *v.* ēa, wīc. -*uerd*- preserves the old locative ending of ford.

BRIDGE DROVE[1], DIKE BANK and GATE END BRIDGE[2] (all 6″) were the homes of Henry *ate Brigge*, John Elyot *ate Diche* and John *ate Gatishend* (1327 SR). *v.* drāf. *gate* here is ME *gate* from ON *gata*, 'road,' used of the road formerly known as Parson Drove Green or *Gate*.

DIGLIN'S DROVE[3], FOUNTAIN'S DROVE[4], JOHNSON'S DROVE and MAY'S BRIDGE[5] (all 6″) are probably to be associated with the families of Thomas *Diglin* (1662 *Wisb*), John, son of Isack *Fountaine* (1668 Fenland ii), Thomas *Johnson* (1536 *Cole* xxxvi) and William *Mey* (1490 Ely).

ELBOW FIELD. *v.* Elbow Bank *supra* 206. FENHALL FIELD is *Fennehall* 1285 *Ass*, *Fenhalfeld* 1438 *Sewers*. OLD EAU FIELD is *Oldeafelde* t. Ed 6 *Rental*, *v.* Old South Eau *supra* 10. OVERDIKE BANK is *Ouerdyche* 1438 *Sewers*, *Ouerdyke* 1440 *ElyCh*. POPE FIELD is *Popisfeld* 1298 *Ass*, *Popifeild* 1533 *SewersC*, *Popishefeild* 1611 *SewersD*. WOAD MILLS and WOADMILL FM (all 6″). Cf. "There are Woad Mills on a farm at Parson Drove, known as the Woad Farm" (1892 Fenland ii).

---

[1] *le Briggedraue*, -*y*- 1385 *Ct*, 1399 *ElyCh*, -*droue* 1408 ib.
[2] *Gatysende* 1480 *Ct*. [3] *Diggles, Diglings Drove* 1864 *Wisb*.
[4] *Fountain Drove* 1905 ib. [5] *Meyesbrigge* 1438 *Sewers*.

Thorney

THORNEY

(i) *Ancarig (igland)* c. 1150 ASC (E) *s.a.* 656, *Ancraig (nunc...
Dornig)* 973 (14th) BCS 1297, *Ancraeie (nunc Thorneya)*
c. 1151 *Thorney*

(ii) *(into, æt, on, to) þornige* c. 960 (c. 1200) BCS 1131, c. 972
ASCh, c. 1000 Saints, c. 1100 ASC (C) *s.a.* 1049, *(on) þornege*
c. 1050 ASC (D) *s.a.* 1049, *Ðorneye* c. 1050 (c. 1350) KCD
904, *(of) þorneie* c. 1150 ASC (E) *s.a.* 1066, *Thorneia* 1086
InqEl, *Thorneiæ (propter condensitatem dumorum vocata)*
c. 1125 WMP, *Thornee* 1217 Pat, *Thorney(e)* 1227 Ch *et
passim*

Tornyg, Torny 1086 DB, *Torneia, -eie, -ey(e)* c. 1109, 1113
NthCh *et freq* to 1235 *Ely, Tornay* 1235 Cl
Thornheia c. 1250 MP

Originally this was 'hermit-island' from OE *ancor, ancra,* 'hermit,
recluse, anchorite.' Cf. Ankerwyke (PN Bk 245). Later 'island
covered with thorn bushes,' *v. þorn, ēg.* Cf. Thorney (PN Mx 165),
the name of the site of Westminster Abbey. *v.* Addenda lx.

NOTE. BUKE HORN RD is *Buke Horn Drove* 1829 Wells.

DOWSDALE PLANTATION (6″). Cf. *Dowysdale, Dowesdale* 1469 Pat,
Dovesdale 1529 BedL, *Douisdale* 1597 *Wisbech Map, Dows(e)dale* 1610
Speed and Dowsdale Arm *supra* 209. This is to be associated with
Dowsdale Bank in Croyland and Dowsdale in Whaplode (L), *Dousedale*
1331 *Spalding,* just over the Lincolnshire border. Possibly 'Dúsi's
valley,' *v.* dæl or, as the topography is not very distinctive, 'Dúsi's
share of land,' *v.* dǣl. *Dúsi* is an ODan personal name, found also in
Dowsby (L), *Dusebi* 1086 DB (*v.* DEPN).

GOLD DIKE (6″) is *Abbotesdik* 1228 *Thorney, Gooledyke* c. 1500 ib.,
Gold Dyke 1574 *SP, Goledyke* 1597 *Wisbech Map, Goldedike or Shepye
lake* 1579 *Depositions. v.* gole *infra* 327. *Gooledyke* is a late marginal
entry against *Abbotesdik,* so called because on the bounds of the Abbot
of Thorney. For *Shepye, v.* Old South Eau *supra* 10.

THE GORES and GORES FM (6″) is *le Gores vocat' le Fenne Gores* 1540
MinAcct, le Gores Fenne 1550 Pat, *Thorney Gores, Gores Fm* 1829
Wells. In the neighbourhood were *le Gorehirne* 1315 *Thorney, le
Oldegore* 1329 ib. In the last two names we probably have OE gāra,

'wedge-shaped piece of land,' cf. 'Parcels of Gores of Grass Lands,' 'the Bell Gore' in Whittlesey (1668 Fenland i). It may be that these are to be associated with the Gores, but it should be noted that there is another possibility. *gorce* from AFr *gortz*, pl. of *gort* from Lat *gurgitem*, 'whirlpool,' is used primarily of a whirlpool, but also of a 'stop in a river such as a wear' (*v.* NED *s.v.*). It may be that *le Gores* is for *le Gorce* and that we have reference to a weir or the like. *gores* itself was mistaken for a plural form and gave rise to a noun *gore* (NED *gore* sb.[4]) with the same meaning as *gorce*. Cf. quotation there given, 'weres, *gores*, etc.' (1523) and '*goors*, mills, piles' (1657).

KNARR FM is (*le*) *Cnor* t. Hy 2 (1314) Ch, c. 1151–1314 *Thorney*, (*le*) *Knarr(e)* 1199 *ElyCouch*, 1438 Imb, (*le*) *Knor* c. 1250 *ElyM*, c. 1270 *Thorney*, 1314 *Ct*, 1340 Imb. KNARR FEN is *Knarresfenne* 1541 *Min-Acct*, *Knarre Fenne* 1550 Pat. Cf. also Knarr Lake *infra* 293. It is difficult with the forms before us to know whether we have to do with ME *knarre*, 'rugged rock,' also 'knot in wood,' or the allied ME *knorre*, 'knot or excrescence on the side of a tree.' *knarre*, 'rugged rock,' is probably found in Knar and Knaresdale (Nb) (cf. DEPN and PN NbDu 129–30) and survives in dial. *gnarr* (*v.* EDD). The rock sense would clearly not fit here, but the name might denote a 'gnarled' tree. Similarly *knorre* might be used of a tree—some tree stump in the fenland. There has clearly been confusion between the words, and in the absence of any knowledge as to the exact site to which reference is made, the etymology must remain uncertain. Possibly the term is descriptive of 'rough, gnarled' ground, with reference to the stumps of projecting trees such as are found in parts of the fens.

PORTSAND FM (6″). Cf. *Porson drove* 1638 Imb, *Porsand* (*Banck*) 1654 Moore, 1690 Lea, *Postland* 1672 FenL, *Porsant al. Portland* 1697 SewersC, *Portson drove* 1772 Imb. The name clearly derives from Postland (L), on the other side of the Old South Eau, for which we have early forms (*island called*) *le Purceynt* 1415 Pat, (*water called*) *le Pursuaunt* 1555 ib., *Pursant* 1652 CWills, *Por*(*t*)*sand* 1680 Map, *Postland* 1775 PR[1]. This derives from AFr *purceynt*, adj. and sb., 'enclosure,' Lat *procinctus*, 'girt about, enclosed.' *v. purcinct* (NED).

SINGLESOLE FM

    Senglesholt 1204 Cur, 1251 *ElyCouch*, 1277 *Ely*, -*halt* 1227 Ch
    Singlesole 1574 SP, *Syngell Sole* 1589 SewersD, *Synglesole* 1597 *Wisbech Map*, *Single Sole Farme* 17th AdvL

    [1] Forms due to the kindness of Dr L. W. H. Payling.

This goes with Singlesole Fm on the opposite side of the Cat's Water in Eye (Nth). Probably, as suggested in PN Nth 235, '*Singull's* wood.' The personal name is probably a Scandinavian loan name from OGer *Singulph*. *v.* holt.

WRYDE CROFT is a large area of marsh, probably referred to in *Wrethefeld* 1318 *Ct*. Cf. (*le*) *Wride, -y-* c. 1250 *ElyM*, c. 1270 *Thorney et passim, -weare* 1617 *AddCh, Ryde* 1674 *BLAcct*. OLD WRYDE DRAIN (6″) is *drain called Old Wryde* 1753 BedL. *Wryde* 1597 *Wisbech Map* refers to OLD WRYDE FM (*Old Ryde* 1674 *BLAcct*). These, with WRYDE BRIDGE, WRYDELANDS FM and OLD WRYDE BANK HOLT (6″) all derive from a stream, *Wridelake* 1586 *Ct, Wrydestreame* 1597 *Wisbech Map, Wryde River* 1720 *BLAcct* which, flowing south of Thorney Abbey, wound round near Old Wryde Fm, passing near the site of East Wryde Fm. It was also known as *le Wride*, possibly a contraction of *wride-ēa*. Cf. the alternation between *Cricke* and *Crickelake, s.n.* Creek *supra* 254. This is from an OE **wride*, 'twist, turn,' from OE *wrīþan*, 'to twist,' hence 'the winding stream.' Cf. Wordwell (Sf), (*æt*) *Wridewellan* c. 1025 (11th) BCS 1018, *Wridewella* 1086 DB and Worlington (Sf), *Wirilintona* 1086 DB, *Wridelingeton* 1201 Cur. The first is an old name of the Lark, on which both are situated; the second means 'the tūn of the dwellers on the winding river' (Studies[2] 100).

ARCHER'S DROVE, GREEN DROVE, HARLEY'S DROVE, HARRIMAN'S DROVE, HUNT'S DROVE, SCOLDING DROVE (all 6″), TONEHAM FM and WARD'S CAUSEWAY (6″) are so named in 1825 (O.S.). BARLEES FEN and BAR PASTURES (both 6″) with BAR PASTURE FM. Cf. *apud Barram* 1315 *Thorney, Thorney barr* 1436 *SewersC, Barre* 1597 *Wisbech Map, the litle Barr pasture* 1604 *SewersC, Bar Pastures* 1829 Wells. The Pastures lie by Cat's Water and the bar probably has reference to some obstruction in that stream. BLUE BELL FM is *Blue Bell* ib. BOARDEN HO DROVE (6″) is so named in 1852 (Harding). Cf. *Boarden House* 1829 Wells. COBBLER'S FEN is *Coblers fenn* 1706 Moore. CROWTREE FM is *Crowetree* 1540 *MinAcct*. DAIRY FM (6″) is so named in 1836 (O.S.). ENGLISH DROVE (6″), FRENCH DROVE and STONE BRIDGE (6″) are so named in 1829 (Wells). There was a colony of French Protestant refugees in Thorney from 1653 to 1721, *v.* Darby, *Draining of the Fens*, 84–5. GRANGE FM is *grange of Thorney (formerly of Elye monastery)* 1553 Pat. KNARR CROSS FM is *Knarre, Knorre Crosse* 1579 *Depositions*. UPPER, MIDDLE and LOWER KNARR FEN (6″) are *Vpper*

Knarr Fenn 1706 Moore, *Great, Middle* and *Little Knar Fen* c. 1825
O.S. NEW and OLD KNARR FEN DROVE (6″). Cf. *Knar Fen Dr.* 1829
Wells, *v.* Knarr *supra* 281. MILL FEN (6″) is *Milleffenne* 1540–1
MinAcct. MORRIS FEN is *Marrys ffenne* 1540 ib., *Marys* 1550 Pat,
Morris Fen 1836 O.S. Cf. *Mariskote* 1438 Imb. OFr *mareis,* 'marsh.'
Cf. Morris Fm (PN Ess 229). NO MANS LAND (lost) is *Noman(n)es-
lond* 1191, c. 1350 *Thorney,* 1469 Pat, *No Mans Ld Hirne* 1829 Wells.
It was on the boundary of the lands of the monastery of Thorney,
v. hyrne and *infra* 357. NORTH FEN is so named in 1697 (*SewersC*).
RUFF FEN (6″) is *Ruffle Fen(n)* 1706 Moore, c. 1825 O.S., 1829 Wells.
ST VINCENT'S CROSS FM (6″) is *Vincet(t)crosse* 1604 *SewersC, St Vin-
cents Cross* 1821 Baker. THORNEY CAUSEWAY (6″) is *Thorney calsey
Way* 1808 L. *v. infra* 315. GREAT and LITTLE TOWERS FEN. Cf.
Torrer(re)sfenne 1540 *MinAcct,* 1550 Pat, *Great Towers fenn* 1690 Lea.
WILLOW HALL is so named in 1636 (BedL). *v.* Addenda lx.

Tydd St Giles

TYDD ST GILES

> *Tit* c. 1165 NthCh
> *Tid(d)(e)* 1170 LibEl *et freq* to 1559 *Rental, Thid* 1221 *ElyA*
> *Tyd(d)(e)* c. 1213 Fees *et passim,* (*Sancti Egidii*) 1250 *Ass,* (*Seynt
> Gilles*) 1504 *Wisb,* (*Seynt Gyell'*) t. Hy 8 *Rental*
> *Tedd Sente Gyls* 1570 (inscription on cover of church chalice)

This name and Tydd St Mary (L), *Tite, Tid* 1086 DB, *Tit* 1094
France, *Tid* 1168 P, must have the same origin, but there seems no
definite feature from which they might be named. They lie low on
opposite sides of the Old South Eau, surrounded by flat marshland.
Ekwall (DEPN) explains the names as OE *titt,* "a teat, here used in
the transferred sense of a slight hill...there is a slight rise near Tydd
St Mary" (cf. *tid,* 'small cock of hay,' Lincs. dial.), but a walk from
St Mary to St Giles leaves one with the impression of a dead level.
Alternatively, we may well have, as suggested by Zachrisson, an
i-mutated variant of *tod,* 'bushy mass (especially of ivy),' *v.* NED
s.v. tod sb.[2] NED associates that word with EFris (LGer dial.) *todde,*
'bundle, pack, small load (of hay, straw, turf, etc.)' and Sw dial. *todd,*
'a conglomerated mass (especially of wool).' Zachrisson notes the
further parallel of Ger *Tudden,* 'Höcker, Schwellung, Wullt' (Middendorff 137), ModIcel *toddi,* 'small wood.' "To judge from its

cognates, OE *tydd* means 'shrubs, low brushwood' or possibly 'hillock,' meanings often interchangeable in words of this type." Here the meaning may have been 'low brushwood' or 'shaggy tufts of grass, reeds, etc.,' later extended to a place where such grow. *v.* further StNP v, 3. *St Giles* from the dedication of the church.

NOTE. BEE'S LANE. Cf. *Beeslaneende* 1438 *Sewers, Beyslaneishend* 1505 *Ct, Little Broadgate or Beys Lane* 1806 *Wisb* (cf. High Broad Gate *infra* 287). It takes name from the family of William *le Be* (c. 1240 *ElyM*). BLACK LANE is *Blak(k)e(s)lane* 1438 *Sewers, Egate* or *Blacklane* 1788 *Wisb* and probably takes name from the family of William *Blac* (1221 *ElyA*). *v.* Eaugate Field *infra* 285. BOTTLE LANE is *Botellyslane* 1504 *Ct, Bottellane* 1570 Imb. Cf. *Botteleslane brigge* 1438 *Sewers, Bottlebrigge* 1570 Imb. *Bottel* is probably the common colloquial form of *Botolph*, St Botolph being the patron saint of wayfarers. Cf. Botolph Bridge (PN BedsHu 195, xli). CARVELEY'S LANE. Cf. Robert *Calverley* (1671 *Wisb*). CATS LANE is perhaps to be associated with the family of Peter and William *Cat* (1285 *Ass*). Cf. *Catts mere* 1632 Imb. *v.* Addenda lviii. CHURCH LANE is *Kirklane* 1438 *Sewers*. CHURCH LANE BRIDGE is *bridge in Kyrklane* 1570 Imb. *v.* Introd. xxxv. FEN LANE is so named ib. HALLCROFT LANE is *Hallcroftlane* 1438 *Sewers*. Cf. *Hallecroft* 1221 *ElyA*. KIRKGATE is *Kirkegate* 1376 *Ct, Kyrkgate* 1438 *Sewers*, 1579 *Ct, Churgate lane* 1497 ib., *Churchgate* 1577 ib. KIRKGATE BRIDGE is *the bridge at Churchgate* 1570 Imb. *v.* gata and Introd. xxxv. MOSS LANE is *Mosseslane* 1438 *Sewers, Mosslayne* 1579 *Ct*. Cf. Richard *Mosse* (1250 *Ass*). NEWGATE LANE is *Newgate* 1438 *Sewers*. *v.* gata. NORTH LANE is *Nortlane* c. 1350 *Thorney*. SANDY LANE is *Sondylane* 1438 *Sewers*. Cf. *Sonddilond* 1506 *Ct*. SWALLOW LANE is so named in 1667 (*Wisb*).

AUSTRALIA (6″) was built by John Morton (born c. 1840) who as a young man had made all arrangements to go out to Australia with a friend, who at the last moment refused to go. Morton saved up his money and built the house which he called Australia in memory of his disappointed ambition[1].

BLADDERWICK FIELD (6″) is *Blad(e)wicke* 1618 *AddCh, Bladderwicke Field* c. 1840 *TA*. We may compare *Blarewyke* 1316–51 *Spinney, Blathyrwyke, -er-* 1377, 1395 ib., *Bladerwyk* 1430 ib. (in Isleham) and Blatherwycke (PN Nth 156), where it is suggested that the first element may be OE *blæd(d)re*, ME *blather, blether*, 'bladder,' from some plant-name such as *bladder-wort, bladder-fern* or *bladder-campion*. In PN Wa xlvi, the suggestion of Mansion is cited, that a personal name *Bladra* is possible, but the threefold occurrence of the element compounded with wīc makes this unlikely.

[1] *Ex inf.* Mr G. M. G. Woodgate.

BLOWHEAD FIELD (6″) is (*campi*) *Bloheuede* 1438 *Sewers*, *Bolhedd* (sic) 1496 *Ct*, *Bloheade* 1579 ib., (*feilde*) 1618 *AddCh*. OE blā(w), 'cold, exposed,' and hēafod, 'head, headland.' Cf. Blofield (Nf), *Blafelda*, *Blawefelle* DB, *Blofeld* 1294 Bodl.

EAUDIKE FIELD (and BANK) is *Eedichfeld* 1331 *Ct*, *Edykfeld* 1382 ib., *Eadikefelde* 1578 ib., *Eaudike Field* 1790 *Wisb*, *Bank* 1821 ib. Cf. *Edich* 1277 *Ely*, *Bysschopesdyke* 1438 *Sewers*, *the Ee dike* (*or Bishops dike*) 1570 Imb. *v.* ēa and cf. *Edyk*' 1354 Works in Thurlby (L), and *les Edykes* 1365 ib. in Boston (L). The Bishops of Ely were responsible for the repair (cf. Imb 342).

EAUGATE FIELD. Cf. *Eagate* 1436 *SewersA*, (*way called*) *Eygate* 1531 *Wisb*, *Eaugate or Black Lane* 1788 ib. 'Road to or by the river,' *v.* ēa, gata and cf. Eaugate in Moulton (L), *Egate* 1331 *Spalding*.

EAULEET FIELD (6″) is *Elettfeild* 1436 *SewersA*, *Eletefelde* 1438 *Sewers*, *Elletfield* 1570 Imb, *Eauleet Field* c. 1840 *TA*. 'feld near the river confluence,' i.e. probably where Grange Dike and Lady Nunn's Old Eau meet at Grangehill Corner (cf. *infra*). *v.* ēa, (ge)lǣte.

FOUR GOTES is *the Four gotes* 1570 Imb, *Le Quatuor Goates* 1597 *Wisbech Map*, *Four Gouts* c. 1825 O.S. *v.* gote. This was the meeting-place of "*the four gotes* of Wisebeche, Leverington, Newton and Tyd S Giles" (1438 Imb), i.e. of Wisbech Drain, Leverington High Lode, Newton Lode and Tydd Drain.

FURLONG FIELD (6″) is *field called Spadeholme al. Furlong* 1605 *Wisb*. Cf. *Spadeholm*(*e*) (*feilde*) 1618 *AddCh*, 1667 *Wisb*. The first element here can hardly be the common *spade*. There is a rare ME *spay*, *spey*, MFlem *speye*, ModWFlem *speie*, *spei*, related to Flem and Du *spui*, 'a sluice,' recorded from 1415 to 1451 in NED. From this a verb might have been formed in the sense 'to provide with a sluice.' *Spayed-holm* would become *Spadeholm*, 'water-meadow with a sluice,' *v.* holmr. *v.* Addenda lx.

GRANGEHILL FM is *Graines Hill* c. 1600 (1724) *BadesladeA*, *Greyns Hill* 1650 *Wisb*, *Cranes Hill* 1655 ib. Cf. *Eegreine*, *le Egreindes*, *Tydde Eegreene*, *le Greendys* 1436 *SewersC*, *le Egryndes* 1438 *Sewers*, *Tydd Graynes* 1455 *Wisb*, *Edgreynes* (probably for (*at T*)*edgreynes*) 1469 Pat. This is clearly dial. *grain*, 'fork of a tree, fork of a river' (ON *greinn*), with reference to the fork made by the Shire Drain and Lady Nunn's Old Eau (*supra* 7, 15) with Grange Dike (L) at Grangehill Corner.

v. ēa and *grain* sb.[1], 2 in EDD. For intrusive *d* in *greindes* and other
forms cf. Jespersen i, 7, 61, Jordan § 202, Anm. For the combination
nds, pronounced [ndʒ], the spelling *nge* has been substituted.

HORN FIELD (6″) is *Horn(e)feld(e)* 1379 *Ct*, 1438 *Sewers*, *Hurnefield*
1570 Imb. Cf. *Horne lanes end* ib., *Hornelayne* 1578 *Ct*. OE *horn*,
'corner, bend' and **feld**. The field is in a corner of the parish. *Hurnefield* is from the related **hyrne**.

RYLAND FIELD (6″) is *Reyelondfelde* 1385 *Ct*, *Ryhlond* 1398 ib., *Rylond-
felde* 1438 *Sewers*. Cf. *Sothwer'relondfen* 1251 *ElyCouch*. This is
probably ME *atte reyland*, from *atter eyland*, 'at the low-lying land,'
v. æt, ēgland.

SHOFFENDIKE FIELD (6″) takes its name from (*le*) *S(c)hoffendyke* 1391
Wisb, 1438 *Sewers*, *New Fendike al. Shofendike al. Harhold* 1570 Imb,
Shooffe fenndike, Shofft fenndike 1579 *Depositions*. Cf. *Newfendyk* 1438
Sewers[1]. This is 'the fendike by the Shof' or 'the dike by Shof-fen.'
Shof is an alternative name for the Old South Eau *supra* 10. It is
Shof 1251 *ElyCouch*, c. 1270 *Thorney*, 1277 *Ely*, *cursus aque de Shoft*,
aqua dulcis de Scoft 1291 *Cole* xliii, xliv (the boundary between Cam-
bridgeshire and Lincolnshire near Throckenholt), *river of Schoft by
Trokenhaut* 1293 Pat, *the Shofe* 1340 Imb, *Schephe al. Schoffes* 1597
Wisbech Map. Cf. also *le Schof* 1349 *Walden*, *the Shoft* 1575 *Survey*
(both in Over), *sewer' de Scoftgraft* 1315 Cole xliii (in Donnington, L),
le Schust (sic) 1365 Works in Boston (L) and a dyke called *le Shuft*
1439 Pat in South Kyme (L). Cf. also *angustam aquam quæ vocatur
Thescuf* between Whittlesey Mere and King's Delph (664 BCS 22).
This word long persisted in the fens as a common noun. Cf. "every
small shuft of water [in Waterbeach, Stretham and Thetford] over-
flows and drounds our fens" (1677 Fen). This is probably one of the
river-names formed from original agent-nouns from strong verbs (cf.
RN xlviii). OE *scūfan*, originally a strong verb, 'to thrust, push,' was
used c. 1374 of winds or other natural forces meaning 'to drive,
propel, impel,' whilst from c. 888 it was used intransitively in the
sense 'to push one's way forward, to press on' (NED *s.v.* vb., 2 d, 6).
Hence 'the pusher' used of a river that made its way slowly and with
difficulty in this level district. For names of this type cf. Rendbrook
'the pusher' (RN 339).

[1] The present New Fen Dike between Sutton St James and Sutton St Edmund.

SUMMER LESURE FIELD [sʌme lesiu·ə] is *Sumerleswe* 1251 *ElyCouch*, *Somerlesowe* 1376 *Ct*, *Somerlesur* 1496 ib., *Somerleasure* 1577 ib., *Somerleasue (Feld)* 1579–81 ib., *Summer le Sieur Field* 1767 *Wisb*, *Summer Sewer Field* c. 1840 *TA*. 'Summer pasture,' *v.* lǣs and cf. Summer Lesure Field in Tydd St Mary (L), with similar early forms.

TREADING BANK, DRAIN and FIELD (6″) are *(le) Thre(e)dyng(e)* 1436 *SewersC*, 1497 *Ct*, *Tyd Thre(e)dinge (end)* 1436, 1437 *SewersC*, *Tyd Thredyng* 1438 *Sewers*, *Threding dike* 1438 Imb, *Tydd Treddyng* 1493 *Wisb*, *Tyd Thredding* 1570 Imb, *Treading (Bank)* 1786 *Wisb*, *(Field)* c. 1840 *TA*. Probably OE *þrǣding*, 'a threading, twisting,' from OE þrǣd, 'thread,' from the root of OE þrāwan, 'to twist,' an apt name for the bank which is probably old as it forms the boundary between Tydd and Newton. *v.* ing. For the type of name, cf. Trotton (PN Sx 44) where the first element is probably OE *trǣdding*, 'treading.'

COOPER'S FM, DODDIN'S FIELD[1] (6″), HANNATH HALL, HOLLINGWORTH HO (6″), KILHAM'S FM, OLDROYD'S FM, ROGERS'S DROVE[2] and SWAIN'S DROVE[3] (all 6″) are probably to be associated with the families of John *Cooper* (c. 1840 *TA*), William *Doding* (1221 *ElyA*), Joseph *Hannath* (1820 *Wisb*), John *Hollingworth* (1752 ib.), William *Kilham* (c. 1840 *TA*), Richard *Oldroyd* (ib.), Henry *Rogers* (1670 *Wisb*) and William *Swayne* (1600 ib.). CRANE COTTAGE and KENNY HO (both 6″) are to be associated with William *Crane* (1802 *Wisb*) and Mark *Kenny* (c. 1830–40 ib.).

THE ANGLE is so named c. 1840 (*TA*). It is an outlying corner of the parish. BROAD DROVE is so named in 1785 (*Wisb*). CROSS DROVE. Cf. *Crossgate* 1794 *Wisb*. *v.* gata. DUNTON BRIDGE is *Dunton Hall Bridge* 1753 BedL. It is named from Dunton Hall in Tydd St Mary (L) which, with Dunton Field, is *manor of Donton* 1572 *Sewers*, *Dunton Lande* 1625 *Terrier* and is to be associated with William de *Dunton* (1334 Pat). GREAT EAST FIELD is so named in 1865 (*Wisb*). FENGATE FIELD. Cf. *Fengate* 1496 *Ct*. *v.* gata. GARDIKE FIELD is *Gordikfeld* 1401 *Ct*, *Gardyk(e)(feld)* 1506, 1579 *Ct*. *v.* gāra. HIGH BROAD GATE. Cf. *(le) Brodgate* 1438 *Sewers*, *v.* gata. HIGH DIKE BANK. Cf. *Heyedyk* 1496 *Ct*, *High dyke* 1752 *Wisb*. HIGH SOUTH BANK is so named in

[1] *Dodyngesfelde* 1388 *Ct*, *Dodyngfeld* 1581 ib., *Doddingtonfeilde* 1618 *AddCh*, *Doddin Field* c. 1840 *TA*.
[2] *Rogers Drove* 1707 *Wisb*.
[3] *Shipboard or Swaine's Drove* 1788 ib. Cf. also *Shepesbourd, Skepp's board, Skepgatebrigg, Skeppers gate* 1570 Imb.

1806 ib. KARROW FIELD is *Carrowefelde* 1401 *Ct.* Cf. *Carrowe* 1379 ib. and Karrow Field in Newton *supra* 275. LONG BRICK FIELD is so named c. 1840 (*TA*). It is *field called Prickes* 1545 *Wisb*, *Long Bricks* 1668 ib., *Long Prick Field* 1865 ib. Possibly *prick* is here used of an ox-goad. NEW FIELD is *Neufeld* 1306 *Ct.* NORTH LANE FIELD is *Northlanefelde* 1438 *Sewers*. QUANEY FIELD is *Whaueneye* 1316 *Ct*, *Quaveneye* 1324 ib., *Qwaney*(*felde*) 1588 ib., *Quaney Field* 1785 *Wisb*. Identical with Quaveney Hill *supra* 220. SOUTH CROFTS is *Southcroft* 1504 *Ct.* HIGH and LOW SOUTH FIELDS are *Southfeld* 1334 *Ct*, *Low Sowthfeld* 1788 *Wisb*. TRITTON BRIDGE (all 6″) is *Treaton Bridge* 1687 *BLAcct*, *Tretham Bridge* 1821 Baker. It is named from Tritton Manor Fm in Tydd St Mary (L), *Treton Hall* 1535 VE, *manor of Trytton* 1625 *Terrier* and is to be associated with the family of Richard de *Treton* (1374 Pat). TYDD GOTES is *Tyd gote* 1414 *Ct*, *Tidd Goate* 1579 *Depositions*, *Tydd Goat* 1825 O.S. *v.* gote. TYDD GOTE BRIDGE (6″) is *Gotebrigge* 1438 *SewersC*. TYDD ST GILES MILL (6″) is named from the manorial windmill standing here in 1547 (*Wisb*).

Upwell

UPWELL

(*æt*) *Wellan* 963 (12th) BCS 1128

(*æt*) *wyllan* 970 BCS 1267, (*et*) *Willan* 970 (12th) LibEl, *Wyllan* 973 (14th) *Thorney*

Welles 974 (c. 1350) BCS 1310, 1077–1130 (12th) ChronRams *et freq* to 1368 Pat, *Wellis* 14th *Walden*

Welle 1086 InqEl *et freq* to 1549 Pat, (*immo Vpwelle*) 1285 *Ass*

Upwell(*e*) 1221 ElyA *et passim*, *Up*(*p*)*ewell*(*e*) 1269 Pat, 1287 FF, 1298 *Ass*, 1480 *Ct*

Opwell(*e*) 1301 *Ct*, 1376 *Elien*

Upwell, like Outwell *supra* 276, with which it once formed a whole (hence the plural forms), is on the Old Croft River (*supra* 9), *aqua de Welle* 1250 *Ass*, from which both Upwell and Outwell, with Welney (Nf), were named. It is partly in Norfolk. *Up* because farther upstream than Outwell. Cf. Waterbeach *supra* 184. Either Upwell or Outwell is referred to as *Waterwell* in 1342 (Cl).

BIRDBECK FIELD (6″). Cf. *Bud*(*e*)*beche* c. 1320 *Thorney*, (*campo*) 1403 *SewersA*, 1429, 1533 *SewersC*, 1442 Cl, (*Upwell*) 1620 *AddCh*, *Bod*(*e*)-

beche(feld) 1340 Imb, *Burbech Field* c. 1840 *TA*[1]. The first element is OE *budda*, 'dung-beetle' and the second *bece*, 'stream, valley' and the whole name is probably descriptive of a place where they breed. For the strange development to *bird* we may perhaps compare the form *sherne birds* for *sherne buds*, 'dung-beetles,' found in a 14th-century MS of Trevisa's translation of *Bartholomeus Anglicus* (*v.* PMLA l, 1042).

EUXIMOOR FM, FEN and DROVE with EXMOOR GRANGE are *Yekeswelle-moor* 1431 *Ct*, *Zekeswellmore* 1434 *Wren*, *Yekeswelmere* 1461 *Ct*, *Eux-moor* 1562 *Cole* iv, c. 1840 *TA*, *Ixwellmoor* 1605 Badeslade, *Eusimore* 1618 *SewersA et freq* to 1829 Wells, *Eximore* 1654 *Dugd*, 1723 Bade-slade, *Tuxmore Fen* 1654 *Dugd*. Probably 'marsh by cuckoo's spring or stream,' *v.* gēac, wielle, mōr. For the sound development cf. Exbourne and Exwell (PN D 140, 302).[2] *Tuxmore* is from *at Uxmore*.

MARMONT PRIORY FM is *Mirmand(e)* 1251 Cl, t. Hy 3 *Ct*, *Myr(e)-maund(e)* 1251 *ElyCouch*, 1277 *Ely*, *Mermaund* 1284 *Ct*, *la Myramande* 1285 *Ass*, *Mermonde* 1307 Imb, *Meremound* 1340 Imb, *Meremande* 1376 *Elien*, *Marmonde* 1539 *MinAcct*, *Marmount* t. Jas 1 *Rental*, *Orman's Fm* 1808 L, *Marmond Priory Farm* c. 1840 *TA*. A small priory was founded here c. 1200 (L 271), taking its name from Marmande (Lot et Garonne). Gröhler (ii, 247) derives the name from *Milmandra* (7th century), an early name for the river Trech on which it stands. Forms *Miramunt, Miremunt* (1254 Cl) for Marmande show that in France as in England there was an early tendency to confuse the second element of the name with Fr *mont, munt*.

OLD CHAIR DRAIN (*TA*) is "sewer called *the Chayre* in Upwell more" 1570 Imb, *The Chare* 1576 Saxton, *Well Chaire* 1669 *ChancDec*. This would seem to be yet another example of the word *chare* applied to a winding watercourse, *v.* Chear Fen *supra* 149.

SHREWSNESS GREEN

    Schrewehirst, -hyrst 1207 Rams, *Ct*, *Shrewshirst* 1597 *Wisbech Map*,
        Shreweshiste 1772 Imb
    S(ch)rewed(e)hirst c. 1250 *ElyM*, *-hyst* 1251 *ElyCouch*, 1277 *Ely*,
        Shrewid hist 1340 Imb

---

[1] *Burbech* (c. 1200 Rams), near the churches of Upwell and Outwell, probably refers to this place, but the form would seem to be a bad one.

[2] The relation of this name, if any, to places called *Hykleswere* c. 1170 *Thorney*, *Jechelwere* 1221 *ElyA*, *Yekelweres* 1277 *Ely*, *Echelueswere* c. 1235 *Chateriz*, in the neighbourhood, is obscure.

Shrewysnest (*point*) 1558, 1596 Imb, *Shrew(e)snest(e)* 1586 *Ct*, 1609
  AddCh, 1772 Imb, *Shrewnestpoynte* 1609 *AddCh*, *Shreusnest* 1655
  BLAcct
Susans Green 1830 Baker, 1835 O.S.

This is a difficult name. The second element was clearly **hyrst,**
'wood.' The first was probably OE *scrēawa,* found in OE in the sense
'shrew-mouse' and in ME in that 'a wicked, evil-disposed or malignant man, rascal, villain.' According to NED this is generally held
to be a figurative transference of meaning from the name of the animal
because of the superstitious belief in its malignant influence, but it is
also possible that these very superstitions gave the animal its name of
'the malignant being,' a sense which is found in other Germanic
dialects (*v.* NED *s.vv. shrew,* sb.[1], sb.[2] and cf. OHG *scrawa,* 'dwarf,
goblin,' MHG *schröuwel,* 'devil'). That we have this meaning here
seems to be confirmed by the forms *S(ch)rewed(e)hirst,* where the first
element must be the adj. ME *schrewede,* 'depraved, wicked, malignant.'
We have thus two alternative forms, *scrēawa-hyrst,* 'devil-wood' or
the like, and *scrēawede-hyrst,* 'devil-haunted' or 'malignant wood,'
and we may well have preserved in this name a reference to the general
belief in the existence of such beings in the fens. Other names in
which shrews are possibly associated with woodland or marshland are
the unidentified *scræwanleg* (BCS 723) in Devon and the Lathe of
Scray (PN K 241), *Shrewinghop* 1240 Ass, *Schreweshope* 1254 ib.
  At a later stage in the history of the name folk-etymology has been
at work. In place of *Shreweshist* and *Shrewid Hist,* pronounced
[ʃruˑzist], [ʃruˑdist], a form *Shrewsnest,* later *Shrewsness,* was developed as if for 'shrew-mouse nest.' Later there was further
corruption to *Susans. v.* Addenda lx.
  It may be added that there is a place *Shrewedich* c. 1270 *Thorney,*
1341 *ElyF* in the neighbourhood. Its relation to this name is obscure.

THURLAND'S DROVE (6″)

Trillinga c. 1155 *Thorney, -e* c. 1175 ib., *Trillingishord* 1284 *Peterb,*
  Tryllinge 13th *Chateriz*
Thrilling(e) 1175 *Thorney,* 1251 *ElyCouch, þrillinge* 1221 *ElyA*
  þrinlinge 1221 *ElyA*
Thyrlingewere 13th *ElyM, Thirling(e)* (*Halle*) 1551 *Pat,* 1589 BM,
  Thurlings 1706 Moore
Thurland' 1461 *Ct, Thurlands Drove* c. 1840 *TA*

This is described as a *piscaria*. Cf. also the 13th-century *Thyrlinge-were*. The drove is on the Upwell boundary, near Laddus Bank, but the exact site of *Trillinga* is unknown. We may well have here OE *þyrelung*, 'a piercing, a hole,' with reference to a gap or break in some fen-dike. Cf. Hole in the Wall Fm in Upwell (Nf). The early meta-thesis is, however, a little disturbing.

BACON'S FM[1], BURGESS'S FM (both 6″), COTTON'S CORNER, ORTON'S FM (6″), PIUS DROVE[2] (6″), RALINGHAM HALL[3] and WEST'S BRIDGE are probably to be associated with the families of William *Bacon* (1796 BedL), John *Burgess* (c. 1840 *TA*), Anthony *Cotton* (1529 BedL), Thomas *Orton* (1803 ib.), Hamo *Pius* (1347 *Walden*), Roger de *Ranillingham* (1275 RH), *Rauenigham* (1277 *Ely*), which probably came from Raveningham (Nf), and Thomas *West* (c. 1840 *TA*).

BLACK SLUICE BRIDGE. Cf. *Black Sluice* c. 1840 *TA*. CHRISTCHURCH was so named in 1862 when the church was built[4]. Earlier it was *Brimstone Hill* (1832 G). COLDHAM BANK (6″) is so named in 1637 (BedL). COLDHAM FIELD is *Coldehamfelde* 1397 *Ct*. These are near Coldham *supra* 267. LADDUS FM. *v.* Laddus Fens *supra* 268. LOW CORNER, POULTER'S DROVE and ROTTEN DROVE are so named c. 1840 (*TA*). MILL FM. Cf. *Millestede* 1341 *ElyF*, *v.* stede. PADGETT'S DROVE is *Padgets Drove* c. 1840 *TA*. TURF LOT DROVE (all 6″). Cf. *les Turfpyttes* 1445 *Ct* and The Lots *supra* 150. WELL FEN FM is *Welfen bi Gunildislake* 1221 *ElyA*, *Wellefen* 1386 *Ct*. *Gunildislake* is "the sluggish stream (*v.* lacu) belonging to a woman bearing the Anglo-Scandinavian name *Gunhild*."

Wisbech

WISBECH [wizbitʃ], [wisbidʒ]
  Wisbece 1086 DB, *Wisbecce* 1086 InqEl, *Wisbech(e)*, *-y-* 1284 Peterb *et passim*, *Wisbich(e)*, *-y-*, 1436 Pat *et freq* to 1594 Camden, *Wisbitch* 1588 Fenland i, *Wisbeeche* 1657 FF, *Wisbidge* 1664 BedL
  Wisebache 1086 InqEl, *Wysebach* 1470 ECP

---

[1] *Bacons* 1508 *Ct*.
[2] *Piisdrove* 1340 Imb, *Piys-*, *Pyisdrove* 1438 *Sewers*, *Pye's drove* 1570 Imb, *Little Pyes Drove al. Meye's Drove* 1714 *Cole*. Cf. *Meisdrove* 1438 Imb. If this identifica-tion is correct, the origin of the personal name *Pius* is obscure.
[3] *Rollingham* 1740 BedL.
[4] *Ex inf.* Rev. Seiriol A. J. Evans.

Wisebece c. 1150 ASC (*s.a.* 655), *Wisebec* 1173 P, 1199 Cur, *Wise-
      bec(c)h(e)*, *-y-* 1229 FF *et freq* to 1484 Pat
Wisebek 1217 Pat, *Wysebeck'* c. 1277 Misc
Wissebech(e), *-y-* 1291 Tax *et freq* to 1469 Pat
Weysebech 1342 Pat, *Wes(e)bech(e)* 1360 Ipm *et freq* to 1608 *FF*,
      Wosbyshe 1463 Pat, *Wesbiche* 1576 PC
Wyskebeche 1452 Pat, *Wyshebyche* 1511 EA vii
Wisbishe 1497 PCC, *Wysbitche* 1550 ib.

'The stream or valley of the *Wisse*,' either the Wissey or the Ouse,
or possibly both. *v.* bece and Ouse *supra* 11. For the *-be(c)k* forms
v. Hoback Fm *supra* 68.

Wisbech St Mary

NOTE. MOUSE LANE is *Mouth Lane* c. 1840 *TA*. Cf. *Mouthdrove* 1570
Imb. So called from *the Mouthe* (1597 *Wisbech Map*), constructed by Bishop
Moreton on Moreton's Leam to prevent flooding. WISBECH FEN RD. Cf.
Wysebechffen 1386 *Ct*.

ADVENTURERS' LAND is *Adventurers Land* c. 1840 *TA*. "the said Earl
(of Bedford) undertook so great a work upon the confidence he had
of the aid and assistance therein from divers other gentlemen, who by
his good example and encouragement would become *adventurers* with
him…proportion of land to be allotted…in recompense…shall be
divided into 20 whole shares, of which shares the said Earl of Bedford
doth agree to *adventure* for two whole shares…" (1631 BedL ii, 113).
Adventurers' because they *adventured* their capital as distinct from the
undertakers who *undertook* the actual draining. Cf. The Undertakers
supra 151.

BELLAMY'S BRIDGE is *Bel(l)ymyl(le)brigge*, *-mil-*, *-brygge* 1438 *Sewers*,
1476–1519 *Ct*, *Belamybrigge* 1401 ib. Cf. also *Belymeldyke* 1437 ib.,
Bellymelle 1515 ib., *Bellymylnebroke* 1549 ib. The first part of the
name is clearly descriptive of some feature of the mill which stood
by the bridge and stream here. With the forms that we have it is
impossible to say whether *bel(l)y* is to be associated with the common
word *bellow(s)* (OE *bælg*, *bel(i)g*) or with *belly* (ME *baly*, *bely*).

FOLLY FM (6″) is *Fallho* c. 1208 *Thorney*, *fallowe* 1310 *Ct*, (*Litle*) 1549
ib. This is probably a compound of *fealh*, 'fallow' and *hōh* in the
sense 'a cultivated rise or hill.' Cf. *Fawcliff* (PN Nth 15) and Fulham,
earlier *Falholm* ib. 227. Some little distance away, running north-east

from the opposite side of the South Eau Bank are FOLLY'S DRAIN and
DROVE (6″), for which we have forms *Faleys Drave* 1387 Cl, *Faulle
lane* 1570 Imb, *Fallayne* 1586, 1587 *Ct*. This looks like a weakening
of *Fallho*. The drove may have continued to near the farm before the
construction of Moreton's Leam and Guyhirn Gull, but, as often in
the Isle of Ely, the construction of drainage works makes certainty
impossible. *v.* **drāf** and **lanu.**

GUYHIRN

> *le Gyerne* 1275 *ElyF*, (*le*) *Gy(e)herne, -hyrne, -hirne* ib. *et freq* to
> 1513 *Ct*
> *Cuherne* 1278 *ElyM* (p)
> (*le*) *Gehirn'* 1438 *Sewers, Geyherne* ib., *-hirne* 1438 Imb
> *Guy(e)hyrne, -herne, -hirne, -hurne, -horne* 1438 Imb *et freq* to 1579
> *Depositions, -hearon* ib., *Gyhorn* 1819 Carter

This is a difficult name, perhaps a hybrid, a combination of OFr
guie, 'guide' (*v.* NED *s.vv. guy, guide*) and OE **hyrne**, 'angle, corner.'
Guyhirn must always have been a critical point in the drainage of this
part of the fens. The tide flowing up the Wisbech river came as far
as this. Ring's End (*infra* 296) is quite close. It was here that Bishop
Moreton erected his Tower House for the effective supervision of his
new drain, and long before the construction of Moreton's Leam, the
meeting here of the fresh waters and the tides probably led to the
construction of works for the safe guidance of their flow at this corner.

INLAY'S FM, with INLAY'S FIELD (6″), is (*le*) *Inlyk(e), -lik* 1251 *Ely-
Couch et freq* to 1586 Eg, *Inl(e)yfeild* 1536 *SewersC*, 1611 *SewersD*,
Inleys 1585 Eg, *Inlay's Field* c. 1840 *TA*. This is OE *in(n)līc*, adj.,
'inward, interior.' NED (*s.v. inly*) remarks that the word is unknown
during most of the ME period and appears to have been formed anew
from the corresponding adverb. The forms above help to fill the gap
between c. 900 and 1422. 'Inner field,' an apt description when
Rummer's Field was still a mere and New Field had not yet been
named. *v.* Addenda lxi.

KNARR LAKE is *Knorlake* 1772 Imb. Cf. *Knor* 1277 *Ely*, *le Knarredike*
1421–2 *Ct*, *Knarlake* 1570, 1605 Imb. *v.* Knarr Fm *supra* 281.

MURROW is *Morrowe* 1376, 1383 *Ely*, 1384 *Elien*, (*le*) *Murrow(e)* 1420–
1515 *Ct*, *Marrowe* t. Hy 8 *Rental*, *Murroughe* 1554 EA ix, *Wisbech*

Moorroe 1597 *Wisbech Map*. 'Row (of cottages) in the marsh,' *v.* mōr, rāw.

NYMANDOLE FIELD is *Ninemændale* 1221 *ElyA*, *Ninmandole* 1319 *Ct*, *Nyn-* 1369 ib., *Ni-*, *Nymandole* 1319–95 *Ct*, *-ffelde* 1447 ib., *Nymenes-dole* 1438 Imb, *Nyman(y)sdo(o)le* 1488–98 *Ct*, 1570 Imb. *v.* dāl. This is a *dole* shared by nine men or one which required nine men to plough or reap it. Cf. *Manimandole* 1309 *Ct* (Sutton).

RICHEY FIELD (6") is *Richey(e)*, *-y-* 1221 *ElyA et freq* to 1353 Sacr, *Recheye* 1338 ib., *Richeyfield* 1570 Imb. Probably 'low-lying land by the stream,' *v.* ēg and OE *rīc, found in Chatteris *supra* 247.

RUMMER'S FM with RUMMER'S FIELD (6") is *Rummere* c. 1226 *Thorney* (p), *Rughmere* 1285 Pat, *field called Rummere* 1336 ib., *Rummers (field)* 1570 Imb. 'Rough mere or swamp,' *v.* rūh, mere.

WILLOCK FIELD is *Wydelake* 1251 *ElyCouch*, 1277 *Ely*, 1291 *ElyF*, *Wylake* 1268 EA vi, *Willac* 13th *StNeot*, *Willake* 1277 *Ely* (p), 1570 Imb, *(feild)* 1536 *SewersC*, *Willelake* 1438 *Sewers*, *Willock* 1620 *SewersD*. It is named from *mare Wide vocatum juxta Welle…magnum et spatiosum lateribus aquarum et liberos exitus habens* c. 1300 GestH 390, *piscaria de Wyde* 1277 *Ely*. Hence, probably, 'the broad stream' (flowing from *Widemere*, 'the broad lake'). *v.* lacu.

BARRETT'S BRIDGE[1], BEVIS HALL,[2] CHEYNEY BRIDGE,[3] HALL'S FM[4] (6"), HIPTOFT FM and FIELD[5] (6"), MUNDFORD FIELD (6"),[6] PARNELL HO, TERRINGTON LAND FM[7] and THOLOMAS DROVE[8] are probably to be associated with the families of Thomas *Barrett* (1663 *Wisb*), Alan de *Beuveys* (1279 *ElyCh*) and *Beveys* (1327 SR), John *Cheyne* (1348 *Walden*), William *Halle* (1446 *Ct*), Gilbert de *Hyppetoft* (1285 *Ass*) which came from Hiptoft (L), Adam de *Mundeford* (c. 1213 Fees) which came from Mundford (Nf), Thomas and William *Parnell* (1818

---

[1] *Barrett* 1529 BedL, *Barrets brigge* 1570 Imb.
[2] *Beuvise Crosse* 1438 ib., *Bevys(e)(crosse)* 1438 *Sewers*, (*hall*) 1570 Imb.
[3] *Chenyesbrigge* 1536 *SewersC*.
[4] This may be local, from the family of John *del Halle* (1356 *Extent*).
[5] *Hiptoftes rent* 1474 Ipm, *Hiptoftefeilde* 1536 *SewersC*, *Hiptoft juxta Wisebech* t. Hy 8 *Cole* xxxvii.
[6] *feodo de Mundeford* 1285 *Ass*, *Mundesforthlond* 1325 *Ct*, *Mund(e)forthffelde* 1438 *Sewers*.
[7] *Tiryngton* 1358 FF.
[8] *Tolymer(e)sdrowe* 1275 *ElyCh*, *ElyF*, *-draue* 1370 *Ct*, *Tholymessedrove* 1438 *Sewers*.

BedL), John de *Tyrington* (1251 *ElyCouch*) which came from Terrington (Nf), and Walter *Tholymer* (1248 *ElyCh*).

BISHOP LANDS is *Bischopslands* 1460 Fenland iv, 1549 *Ct*. These were part of the possessions of the Bishop of Ely. BOARDEN HO TOLL and COLD HARBOUR CORNER are so named c. 1825 (O.S.). *v. infra* 357. BRIDGE HO (6″). Cf. *bridge of Wisbech* 1327 Pat. BUNKER'S HILL lies out in the fen, *v. infra* 357. CALVES FIELD (6″) is so named in 1570 (Imb). Cf. *Caluescroft* 1251 *ElyCouch*. CANT'S DROVE (6″) is *Cants Drove* 1821 Baker. GALL'S DROVE (6″) is *Galdrove* 1437 *SewersC*, *Gawyl drove* 1438 Imb, *Galleys drove* 1570 ib., *Galles Drove* 1587 *Ct*. Cf. Gaul Field *supra* 275. GULL BANK is *Gold banke* 1608 Imb. Cf. *Goldyke* 1437 *Ct*, *Goledyke* 1437 *SewersC*. *v*. gole. GUYHIRN FIELD (6″) is *Gehirnfeld* 1438 *Sewers*. *v*. feld. GUYHIRN GULL is *Guyhirne gole* 1570 Imb. *v*. gole. GUYHIRN WASH (6″) is *the Wash at Guyhurne* 1658 *BLAcct*. *v*. The Wash *supra* 212. INHAM HALL and FIELD (6″) are *le Innham* 1361 *Ct*, *Inhom* 1377 ib., *Inhamfeld* 1380 *Sewers*, *Inhams*, *Ynhams* 1586 *Eg*. 'Enclosure,' *v*. innam. KILN HO is *Kellus* 1251 *ElyCouch*, *Kelhus* 1277 *Ely*. Cf. *Kylhousdyk* 1252 *ElyF*, *Kylnehousdych* 1447 *Ct*. *v*. cyln. This example carries back the word *kiln-house* some 150 years. LONG DROVE (6″) is *longam drauam* 1221 *ElyA*, *le Longdroue* 1351 *Ct*. *v*. drāf. MURROW FIELD is so named c. 1840 (*TA*). NEW DROVE is so named in 1587 (*Ct*). NEW FIELD (all 6″) is *Newfelde* t. Hy 8 *Rental*. PLASH FM is named from *Murrow Plash* 1656 *BLAcct*. *v*. plæsc. SAYER'S FIELD (6″) is *Seyrfeld* 14th *ElyCh*, *Sayre field*, *Sayers field* 1438 Imb. WHITE ENGINE DRAIN (6″) is so named in 1785 (*Wisb*). WISBECH HIGH FEN is *Heyefen* c. 1250 *ElyM*, *the heighe fenne of Wisbeche* 1579 *Depositions*. hēah is here used in the sense 'chief, great.'

Wisbech St Peter

NOTE. GADD'S LANE is *Gadds Lane* 1808 *Wisb*. *v*. Addenda lxi. LORD'S LANE is *Bowmans drove al. Lordes lane* 1620 *SewersD*. NEW BRIDGE LANE is so named in 1611 ib. Cf. *Newbridgg drove* 1358 Imb. PANSWELL LANE. Cf. *Pan(ne)swell* 1542 *Ct*, t. Eliz *Cole* xxxvii. WEASENHAM'S LANE. Cf. *Wesingham, Wesynham brigge* 1438 Imb. The lane and bridge probably took name from a family coming from Weasenham (Nf).

BOLENESS FIELD is *Bolnehyrst field* 1438 Imb. Cf. *Bollenherst* 1310 *Ct*, *Bolnehyrst* 1334 ib., -*hirst* 1358 Imb, *Bolney hirst drayne* ib., *Bolnest* 1334 *Ct*, t. Hy 8 *Rental*, *Boleness* c. 1840 *TA*. Cf. Bolnhurst (PN

BedsHu 13). Both names should probably be interpreted as by Ekwall (DEPN) as from *bulena hyrst*, 'bulls' wooded hill.' For the development cf. Shrewsness *supra* 289.

NORTH BRINK FM and SOUTH BRINK (both 6″). Cf. *austral' ripa de Wysebeche* 1312 ElyF, *Hebrynkefeld* 1334 Ct, *Ebrynke* 1429 ib., *le Eye-brinke* 1586 ib., *Eabrinck(e)* 1615 AddCh. 'River bank,' v. ēa, brinke.

CRAB MARSH (6″) is *Crabbemershe* 1508 Ct. This is on the seaward side of Roman Bank (*supra* 206) and is so called from the growth here of *crab-grass* or glasswort (*salicornia herbacea*), a medicinal plant common in saltmarshes. Cf. *Crab Grasse* 1597, the only reference in NED before 1861. In 1617 one of the questions asked of deponents was whether "sampier, *crabbegrasse* or sea wormwodd growe upon any (*sic*) the marshes" in Leverington and Newton (*Depositions*).

FLATMOOR FIELD is *Flackemore* 1221 ElyA, 1310 Ct, *Flak(e)more* 1331 Ct, (*feilde*) 1436 SewersC, *Flat(t)mo(o)re* t. Hy 8 Rental, 1570 Imb. The first element is probably the word found in the phrases *fodit flackys* 1376 Ct and *flackes and semys super dictum fossatum* 1450 ib. in Wisbech. That would seem to be the word *flak* or *flack* used of a turf (EDD *s.v. flag*). Hence 'marsh where turves are cut,' v. mōr.

LICKING'S DROVE is *Ly(c)kyng(e)draue*, *-kk-*, *-ing-* 1312 ElyCh, ElyF, *-droue* 1392, 1449 Ct and is named from *Licking(g)e, Lykkyng(g)e* 1312 ElyCh, ElyF, 1383–1446 Ct, *Likkyng(e)* 1336, 1508 ib., *Leckyng* t. Hy 8 Rental. The name is probably to be associated with OE *liccian*, 'to lick'; cf. *licing den* 940 BCS 753 and v. KPN 249.

RING'S END is *Rings End* c. 1840 TA and is named from *banckes called the Rynge of Waldersey and Coldham* 1607 SewersD. The ring is described as the land "within a bank beginning at Keekes Mill (Hobb's Bank, on which is Ring's End Fm) and thence to Tower House and thence to Hobbs House (Hobb's Lots *infra* 297) and so to *Tilney Hurne* (*supra* 270) and thence by Maries dam and so by Elme Leame to Friday Bridge (*supra* 268) and thence by *Redmore Dyke* (*supra* 270) and Begdale (*supra* 267) and so by Gold Dyke to Keekes Mill again" (1607 Imb). It was a separate undertaking for the drainer (Fenland v, 161, 156). Hobbs House was near the end of Wisbech High Fen Dyke, on the boundary between Wisbech and Whittlesey, where we have *Ryngemer* 1314 Ct. This is possibly to be identified with *Ringemere* c. 1151, 1191, 1314 Thorney, on the bounds of Thorney and Wisbech. This may, however, have been identical with *Ryndge-mare* 1597 *Wisbech Map*, near Throckenholt. 'Round lake,' *v.* hring, mere. Cf. Ringmer (PN Sx 355). Between Wisbech and Thorney, too, was *Ringgebrigge* 1237 *Thorney*, 1248 *ElyCh*. There is a bridge across the Nene at Ring's End, near Guyhirne Station.

SIBALD'S HOLM (6″) is *Siboldesholm* 1221 *ElyA*, *Sybaldesholm(e)* 1251 *ElyCouch*, *Sybollysholme* 1508 *Ct*, *Sybilysholme* 1536 *SewersC*, *Syblesholme* c. 1840 *TA*. '*Sigebeald*'s holmr.'

WHEATMATH FIELD is *Wetemathis* 1302 *Ct*, *Le Qwetemathys* 1335 ib., *Whetmathis* t. Hy 8 *Rental*, *Wheatm(e)ats*, *-mates* 16th *Fenland* vii, *Whitemathes* 1570 *Imb*, *Whatmayes fild* 1583 *Eg*. OE hwǣte, 'wheat' and mǣð *infra* 338.

REDMOOR FIELD (6″) is *Redemore* 1543 *Ct*, *Redmore Field* c. 1840 *TA* and was probably the home of William de *Redmor* (1251 *ElyCouch*). 'Reed-marsh,' *v.* hrēod, mōr.

BEGDALE FM[1], COLVILLE HO, HARVEY FIELD[2] (6″), HOBB'S BANK and LOTS[3] (all 6″) and HOGG'S FM are probably to be associated with the families of John de *Bekedale* (1314 *Ct*), Robert *Colvile* (c. 1870)[4], Thomas *Heruy* (1436 *SewersC*), Henry *Hobbe* (1335 *Ct*) and George *Hogge* (c. 1840 *TA*).

BARTON FM is *la Berton* 1251 *ElyCouch*, *Wysebecheberton* 1316 *Min-Acct*, *Bartone Drove* 1409 *ElyCh*. *v.* beretūn. A manor of the Bishop of Ely. NORTH and SOUTH BRIDGE FIELD (6″) are *Briggefeld* 1369 *Ct*, *North*, *South Bridge Field* c. 1840 *TA*. BURCROFT FIELD is *Burcroft* ib. EAST FIELD is so named in 1358 (*Imb*). FENLAND FIELD is *Fenlond* 1331 *Ct*, *Fenland Field* c. 1840 *TA*. FOURSCORE FM (all 6″). Cf. *fourescore acres* 1251 *ElyCouch*, *fourscore* 1586 *Eg*. GUYHIRN CORNER is *Gyherne Corner* 1498 *Ct*. HARECROFT FIELD (6″) is (*campo de*) *Hare-croft* 1316 ib. HIRN FIELD is *le Hirnefelde* 1320 ib., *Hurnefelde* t. Hy 8 *Rental*, 1549 *Pat*, *Hornfild* 1564 *Eg*, *Harnfild* 1565 ib. *v.* hyrne, feld. LONGLAND FIELD (6″) is *Longland* 1358 *Imb*. NETTLE BANK is so named in 1842 (*Walker*). Cf. *Nettlecroft* 13th *ElyM*, *Nettyldykelane* 1438 *Imb*, 1498 *Ct*. NEW DROVE is so named in 1570 (*Imb*). OLD

---

[1] Cf. Begdale *supra* 267.
[2] *Hervysfelde* 1450 *Ct*, *Harvest felde* t. Hy 8 *Rental*, *Harvey Field* 1570 *Imb*. For the excrescent *t* cf. Hawkins's Harvest from one Ralph *Hervy* (PN Ess 428).
[3] Cf. *Hob's house* 1570 *Imb*, *Hobbs Lots* c. 1825 O.S. For *Lots* cf. The Lots *supra* 150.   [4] *Ex inf.* Mr G. M. G. Woodgate.

FIELD is *Holdefeld* 1320 *Ct*, *le Oldefelde* 1335 ib. *v.* **feld**. SANDYLAND
FIELD is *Sondilond* 1336 ib. SMALL MEADOW FIELD is *Smalemedwe*
1221 *ElyA*, *Smalemede* 1369 *Ct*. So named in contrast to *Gretemedwe*
1251 *ElyCouch*. SWILLINGHAM FIELD (all 6″) is *ten. Sweueling'* 1319
Ct, *Sweuehalyshyrne* 1401 ib., *Suollyngesherne* 1437 ib., *Swillingesherne*
1621 *AddCh*, *Swillingham* c. 1840 *TA*. *v.* **hyrne**. It was probably
held by someone coming from Swefling (Sf), DB *Sueflinga*. WHITE
HALL. Cf. *Whyttes*, *Whitis* 1518–29 ECP, *Whit(e)hall* t. Hy 8 *Cole*
xxxvii, 1607 DKR xxxviii.

THE ELEMENTS, APART FROM PERSONAL NAMES, FOUND IN CAMBRIDGESHIRE PLACE-NAMES

This list includes all elements used in uncompounded place-names or in the first or second part of compounded place-names so far as they are of toponymic, historical or general cultural interest. Under each element the examples are arranged in three categories, (*a*) uncompounded elements and those in which the first element is a significant word and not a personal name, (*b*) those in which the first element is a personal name, (*c*) those in which the character of the first element is uncertain. Where no statement is made it may be assumed that the examples belong to type (*a*). Elements which are not included in the *Chief Elements used in English Place-names* are distinguished by an (n) after them. The list is confined to names for which there is evidence before 1500.

āc Oaks. æcer *Linacre*. ǣl (n) Ely.
ælren (n) Eldernell. ǣmete *Ampthill*. æppeltūn Appleton.
æpse, æspe Apes Hall. æsc Ashley, Ashwell.
alor Aldreth, Alderforth, Copalder. *anger Anglesey, *Clayangles*.
bæst (n) Barston, Bassenhally. banke, ME Bank.
barre, ME (n) Barlees, Bar Pastures.
bēan Balland, Bancroft, Bannolds, Benwick. bēaw (n) Beauford.
bece Birdbeck, Hoback (2), Landbeach, Long Beach, Waterbeach, Wisbech.
*bele (n) Beald, Bield. beorc Bartlow.
beorg Barham, Bar(ra)way, Cambridge Hill. beorn Barnwell.
beretūn Barton (3). bern Moor Barns. bierce Barcham.
bī(g) Beesons, Byall, Sun Doles. bigging, ME Biggin (2).
binnan Bin Brook. blāc (n) Block Fen, Blockmoor (3).
blā(w) Blowhead. bóndi, ON Bone's Gote. *bor (n) Borley.
brǣc Breach (2), Birch. brame, ME Braham.
brēmel Bramble Lane.
brinke, ME Brink, *Eabrinck*, *Quaveneybrinck*.
brōc Brook (4), Brookend (2), Brook Field, Brookhampton, Bin Brook, Bourne, Callow and Hoffer Brook, (c) Vicar's Brook.
brunnr, ON Bourn.
brycg Cambridge, Friday Bridge, High Bridge (3) and some fifteen others.
budda (n) Birdbeck. bufan Burton.
burh Burrough, Burrow, Burwell, Alboro, Woodbury, (c) Vandlebury. (Manorial) Bury Crofts and Lane, Melbourne Bury, Westbury.
burna (a) Fulbourn, Melbourn, (b) Bassingbourn.
*byde (n) Bedwellhay. *bydel (n) Bedham.

byht (c) Bythorn, Baits Bite.

cake ME, (n) Karrow (2).   **calu** Cloderton (?).

cam, ME (n) Camel.   **camb** *Camgate* (with Cambridge Hill).

camp Camps.   **catt** Cat Fd, Catley.   **ceaf** (n) Cheveley.

cealc Chalk.

*cear (n) Chainbridge, Chain Fm, *Chare Lake*, Chear Fen and Lode, Old Chair Drain.

ceaster Chesterton, *Grantacaestir*.   **cēt** Chatteris, Chettisham (?).

cild Chilford, Childerley.   **cis** Chishall.

clæg *Clayangles*, Clayhithe, Claypit.   *clopp (n) Clopton.

clūse (n) Cloughs Cross.   **cnapa** (n) Knapwell.

*cnyll (n) Nill Well.   **cofa** Coveney (?).

*co(o), ME (n) Coe Fen.   **copp** Copley, Coploe.

coppede Cophall.   **cors** Crossfield.

cote Coates, Coton, (a) Caldecote, (c) Muscat, Pincote.

cran Cranmoor, Cranney, Grandford (?).   **crāwe** Croydon.

*crēowel Crow Hill.   *cricc (n) Creek, Creekgall, Crouch Moor.

croft (a) Croft, Bancroft, Burry Crofts, Church Croft, Cow-, Fen-croft, Fitton Croft, *Green-*, Hall-croft, Hard and Hare Croft, Horse Crofts, Mud, New and Newnham Croft, Ox-, Rye-croft, Snail Croft, South Crofts, (b) Margery's and Wool Croft.

cros Cross, Cloughs Cross.   **crouche** (b) Huckeridge.

cū Cowcroft, *Cowstreet*, Quy.   **cumb** Conger's Well.

*cwafen (n) Quaney, Quaveney.

cyning King's Delph, Dike and Path, Kingston.

dæl (b) Dowsdale (?), (c) Annesdale.

dǣl (n) Deal Grove, (b) Dowsdale (?).

dāl (a) Hill Row Doles, Nymandole, Sketchdoles, (b) Lincoln's Doles, (c) Earl's Doles.

(ge)delf Delve, Delph Bridge and Dike, Delphs, Delver End, East and King's Delph, Spaindelf, Swasedale.

denu Dean Hill, *Burden*, Croydon, Fox Hole Down (?), Heydon, *Ornel-dene*, *Shackledon*, *Spelverden*, Waterden, (b) Cumberton, Gransden.

dēor Darcey Lode, Dartford.

dīc Dike, Ditton (2), Blackdike (2), Cattle and Delph Dike, Eau-, Fen-dike, Fleam Dyke (Flendish), Gar-, Gore-dike, Gold Dike, Greenditch, Greenstock, High and King's Dike, High Ditch, *Marditch*, New and No Ditch, Overdike, Shoffendike, Whittlesey Dike, (c) Bran and Brent Ditch, Ivesdike.

dierne Dernford.   **dræg** Drayton (2).

drāf (n) (a) Bridge, Gall's, Licking's, Long (2), Middle, Norwood, Parson and Popple Drove, (b) Allen's, Bird's, Marriott's, Pius and Tholomas Drove.

dūn Down Field and Hall, Downham, Cloderton, Fox Hole Down (?), Hay Hill, Linden, Morden, Sun (Doles), Widden's Hill, Whaddon, Woolden, (c) Eversden.

*dung (n) Wilsmere Down.

ēa Rhee, *Eabrinck*, Eau-dike, -gate and -leet, Eau Fen, Bradney, Byall, Darcey, Deepney, Grangehill, Northey, North Fen, Old-eamere, *Shepeye*, South Eau, Starnea.

*ēan (n) Yen Hall. **ēastan** (n) Beesons.

ēasterra (n) Eastover (?), Eastrea.

ēg Eye, Ryecroft, Anglesey, Bar(ra)way, Blakeney, Cranney, Denny, Eastrea, Elmney, Fordey, *Gooley*, Henny, Lilly (?), Manea, Nornea, Quaney, Quaveney, Quy, Richey, Shippea, Smithey, Stonea, Thorney (2), Wardy, Wendy, Wenny, Westry, (b) Gamlingay, Honey, Horningsea, Lipneas, Shingay, Turbutsey, Waldersea, Whittlesey, (c) Coveney, Elney, Padney, Stuntney.

ēgland Ryland. **elm** Elm (?), (H)olmstead. **elmen** (n) Elmney.

ende Brook, Castle and Delver End, Eastern Brook, Fields, Gate, Gatley, Green, Lode, Mill (2), Moor, North, Offal and Town End, Townsend.

eofor Eversden (?). **eorðburh** Arbury.

espinei, OFr (n) Spinney.

fealh Folly.

feld Feldale, Askham, Birdbeck, Blacklane, Bridge, Brook, Cannon, Cat, Church and Coldham Fd, Cattle Dike, Crossfield, Down, Dunstal, East, Eaudike and Eauleet Fd, Ely Fields, Fenhall, Fenland, and Flatmoor Fd, Fordfield, Gardike and Gaul Fd, Gorefield, Guyhirn, Halfpenny and Hart Fd, Hayfield, Hill Row, Hirn, Horn, Inham, Karrow, Lindon End, Long, Meadow, New (6), North and North Lane Fd, Nosterfield, Nymandole Fd, Offal (2), Old (2) and Old Eau Fd, Ox-, Park-, Plain-field, Pock and Quaney Fd, Radfield, Rummer's, Ryland and Sea Fd, Slade-, South (2)-field, Stonald, Spittle and Swaffham Fd, Studfield, Westfield (3), Town and Wrat Fd, Wolf Lane (Field), (b) Doddin's, Harvey, Mundford, Rowles and Sayer's (2) Fd, Hasling-, Rose-field, Wales Fd, (c) Pope Fd.

fenn Fen (3), Fen-croft, -gate, -hall, -land, Birch, Block (2), Burnt, Burwell, Byall, Cawdle, Chear, Coe, East, Eau, Fodder (2), Frith (2), Fulbourn, Hall, Hay, High, Holt, Horslode, Joist, Langwood, *Lesh* and Low Fen, *Lugfen*, Middle (3), North (5), Ouse, Padnal, Sedge (4), Setchel, Smithey, Soham, South, Stow, Swaffham, Teversham, Waller, Well, West (5) and Wisbech Fen, (c) Beezling, Grunty and Rack Fen.

fit, ON (n) Fitton. **flak, ME** (n) Flatmoor.

flegge, ME (n) Flegcroft. **fleinn, ON** (n) Plain Field.

flīeming (n) Fleam Dike (Flendish). **fōdor** (n) Fodder Fen (2).

ford Fordey, Ford-field, -ham, Alderforth, *Alfordway*, Beau-, Brad-, Chil-, Dart-, Dern-, El-ford, Hoffer, Grand-, Lang-, Shel-ford, *Spelverden*, Staple-, Thet-, Witch-ford, (b) Armingford, Sipsey, Whittlesford.

fox Fox Hole Down, Foxlow, Foxton.

fugel Foulmire (?), Fowlmere, Fulbourn. **fūl** Foulmire (?).

funta Funthams (?).

fyrhðe Frith (2), Frith Fen (2), Thrift, (b) Chalice Fruit.

gærs Gray's Moor. **gafol** (n) Gaul Fd.

galle, ME (n) Gault. **gāt** Gatley.

gata, ON Gates End, Broad-, *Cam*-, Eau-, Fen-gate, Fenland Gate, Kirk-, New-gate.

*****gē** (n) Ely. **gēac** (n) Eux(i)moor. *****golde**, ME (n) *Gooley*.

gole, ME (n) Gold Dike, Gull (3). **gor** Gardike, Gorefield. **gōs** Gosmoor.

gote, ME (n) Bone's Gote, Four and Tydd Gotes.

græfe The Grove, Graveley. **grāf** Conger's Well.

grange, ME (n) Grange (4), Odsey Grange.

grein, ON Grangehill.

grēne, ME Green (7), Green End, Broad, Carlton, Thriplow, West and West Wratting Green.

grēot Girton. *****grunt** (n) Grunty. **gylden** *Gildene* Swaffham, Guilden Morden.

*****hæfer** (n) Harrimere.

(ge)hæg Hay (2), Bedwellhay, Empty, Impett's, Langley, Lilly (?), Starlock Hay, (b) Barsey, Willesey.

hæme Upend. **hǣð** Heath (8), Heath Barn, Horseheath.

haga Setchel. **halke**, ME (n) Hawk Mill.

hām (a) Down-, Ford-, Need-, So-, Stret-, (b) Babra-, Bals-, Bottis-, Chippen-, Cotten-, Hadden-, Hilders-, Isle-, Tevers-, Wilbra-ham, (c) Swaffham.

hamm Barham, Coldhams, Witcham.

ham(m) Barc-, Bra-, Chettis-, Cold- (2), Mettle-, Newn (3) -ham.

hāmtūn Brookhampton.

*****hasse** (n) Hasse. **hassuc** Hassockhill. **haugr**, ON Howhill.

hēafod Blowhead, Wellhead.

healh Hale, Old Halves, Anglesey, Bannolds, Bassenhally, Camel, Eldernell, Feldale, Fenhall, Fox Hole Drove (?), Marshal, North Hills, Stonald, Thorn and Yen Hall, (b) Brangehill, Clipsall, Hempsalls, Lattersey, Mepal, (c) Padnal.

heall Hall (8), Ashley and Church Hall, Cophall, Down Hall, Eye Hall, Fenhall, Fitton and Holmstead Hall, Hungry Hill, Merton, Mitchell and Nether Hall, Overhall, Streetly and Tunbridge Hall, Sylhall, Uphall.

hecg (n) Hinton Hedges, Manages. **henn** Henny.

heordewīc Hardwick. **hīd** Hyde.

hlāw (a) Bartlow, Copley, Coploe, Foxlow, Grinnel, Limlow, Mettle Hill, *Mutler Shot*, Portley, *Thurlow*, Wadloes, Wadloo, Waller, Wormwood Hill, (b) Cockle Hill, Thriplow, (c) Tadlow.

hlinc (a) Bedham, (b) Kirtling. **hōc** Hook.

hōh How, Howe, Folly, Northey, Staploe, Stonehorse, Westoe, (b) Armshold, Freckney, (c) Chilly, Ranson Moor.

holh Holt, Hoback (2), Holwoods, Shelfords, Whole Way, Winfold.

holmr Holme (2), Holmes (2), Long Holmes, Oxholme, Queen Holme, (b) Sibald's Holm.

holt (a) Apes Hall, Throckenholt, (b) Singlesole, (c) Ravens' Hall.

horh Orwellpit. **horn** Horn Fd. ***horning** (n) *Horningstrete*, Horslode.

hræfn Ranson Moor, Ravens' Hall.

hrēod Red Hill, Redmere, Redmoor (3), *Restages*.

hrȳðer Ruddery. **hunig** (n) Honey Hill.

hūs Kiln Ho, Mill Ho, Redhouse.

hwǣte Wadloes, Whaddon, Wheatmath.

hyll Hill (8), Hill Fd and Row, *Ampthill*, Bedham, Church, Croydon, Fox and Honey Hill, How-, Milk-hill, *Orneldene*, Red and Slough Hill, Stannel, *Thurlow* and White (2) Hill, (b) Edix Hill, Meggs Hill, Roswell, (c) Chronicle.

hyrne Horn Fd, Bythorn, Guyhirn, (b) Swillingham.

hyrst Boleness, Shrewsness.

hȳð Hive, Hythe (2), Aldreth, Clayhithe, Downham Hythe, Horseway, Willey, Witcham Hive and Hythe, (b) Swavesey.

impe, ME (n) Empty, Impett's.

ing (a) Braddons, Grunty, Harrimere, Licking's, Thurland's, Tillage, Wratting, (c) Chittering.

ing (connective) Top Moor, Weltmore (?).

inga Bassingbourn, Brangehill, Gamlingay, Haslingfield, Madingley, Shingay.

ingahām Badl-, Dull-, Will(2)-ingham.

ingatūn (b) Arring-, Litling-, Saws-ton, (c) Hinton.

ingtūn (b) Abing- (2), Dodding-, Hinx-, Ickle-, Imping-, Levering-, Oaking-, Trumping-, Wimbling-ton.

innam (n) Inham (2), Inhams (2), Inholms. **innlīc** (n) Inlay's Fm.

karlatún, ON Carlton. **kirkja**, ON Kirkgate.

klint, ODan *Clintway*. **knarre, knorre**, ME Knarr, Knarr Lake.

konungr, ON Coneywood, Conington.

lache, ME Latches Fen. **lacu** *Shepeylake*, Starlock, Willock.

(ge)lād Lode (2), Laddus, Lode End, Bottisham Lode, *Capload*, Chear and Cottenham Lode, *Dallode*, Darcey and Fenton Lode, Hallard's Fen, Holwoods, Midload, Reach Lode, Sealodes, Soham, Swaffham Bulbeck and Willingham Lode, (c) Horslode.

lǣs Leys, Staple Leys, Summer Leisure. **(ge)lǣte** Eauleet.

land Landbeach, Landwade, Balland, Bishop Lands, Brack-, Broad-, Fen- (2), Lay-, Long-land, Mead- (4), New-lands, *No Man's Land*, Outnewlands, Shortlands, Red-, Ry-, Sandy-, White-land, Wrangling, (b) Cole's Land.

lanu Bottle Lane, Church Lane (4), Mill Lane (3) and some twenty-five others.

lēah Ley, Leys, Ash-, Bor-, Brad-, Cheve-, Childer-ley, Dullingham Ley, Finch-, Grave-, Hay-ley, Silverley, Streetly, Swansley, Westley Waterless, Wetherley, (b) Brink-, Deris-, Eltis-, Mading-, Pap-ley, (c) Hatley.

līn *Linacre*, Lin-den, -ton.　lind Limlow (?), Linwood.

lotte, ME (n) The Lots.　lugge, ME (n) *Lugfen*.

lundr ON *Lunway*.

mǣd Meadow (2), Meadlands, Long (2), North and Small Meadow.

(ge)mǣne (n) Manages, Manea.

(ge)mǣre *Marditch*, Mareway, Stanton Mere Way, (b) Bluntishmere.

mǣð (n) Wheatmath.　mareys, ME (n) Morris Fen.

mearc March.

mere Mere (2), Cranmoor, Crouch Moor, Foulmire, Fowlmere, Gosmoor, Gray's Moor, Harri-, Liver-, Long-, Oldea-mere, Pickmore, Redmere, Redmoor (2), Rummer's, Soham Mere, Stanmoor, Stretham Mere.

mersc Marshal.　middel Mettleham (?), Milton.

mōr Moor (2), Moor Balk, Barns and End, Morden, Murrow, Ash-well Moor, Block(3)-, E(u)x(i)-, Flat-moor, Fordham and Glass Moor, Lode-, Middle(2)-moor, Pymore, Ranson Moor, Red-, West(3)-, White-moor, (b) Top Moor, Weltmore.

(ge)mōt Mettle Hill, *Mutler Shot*.

myln Bellamy's (Bridge) and other examples.

næss Ness.　nīed (n) Needham.　norðan (n) Norney.

ofer Over.　ord Orwell, Swasedale, (b) Kettlesworth.

oxa (n) Ox-croft, -field, -holme.

pæð King's and Small Path, (b) Bunting's Path.

park, ME Park (2), Parkfield, Abington and Wimpole Park.

pearroc Parrock Fd.　pēo, pīe Pymore.　pirige Perry (Way).

plaine, ME (n) The Plains.　pōl (b) Wimpole.

port Portley, Port Way (2), Littleport.　pūca Pock Fd, Popple Drove.

pytt Chalkpit, Claypit.

*quap (n) *Capload*.

rǣc Reach (2).　ramm Rampton.　rāw Karrow (2), Murrow.

*rīc (n) Richey, Chatteris.　rīð Meldreth, Ruddery, Shepreth.

rūh Rummer.　*rȳd (n) Reed (?).

sǣ Sea Dike, Sea Field.　*sǣg (n) Soham.

sǣte Grantchester.　sand Sounds, Sand St.

scēap Shepreth, Shippea.　*sceldu (n) Shell, Shelford.

sceolh (n) Shelfords.　scipen Shapens　scrēawa (n) Shrewsness.

*scydd Shudy Camps.　sēað (b) Odsey.

secg Sedge Fen (3) and Way, Setchel Fen.

seolfor (n) Silverley.　slæd The Slade, Slade Field.

slāh Slow Line.　slōh (n) Slough, Slough Hill.

snægel (n) Snailcroft, Snailwell.　spann (n) Spaindelf.

spell *Spelverden*.　spring Springwell.

stak, ME (n) The Stacks.

stān Staine, Stannel, Stanton, Starlock, Stonald, Stonea, Stow Bridge (?).

stapol Stapleford, Staple Leys, Staploe.

stede (H)olmstead, Market Place. **stēor** (n) Stourbridge.

steort Sterts. **stīepel** Steeple Morden.

stocking, ME Stocking (2), Stocking Toft.

stōw Stow, Stow Fen and Bridge (?), Long-Stowe, Northstow.

strǣt Streetly, Street Way, Stretham, *Allstreet*, Ashwell and Ermine Street, *Cowstreet*, *Euestrete*, *Eystrete*, *Granstrete*, Icknield Way, Wool Street (and several minor examples).

stunt (n) Stuntney (?). **stycce** Stitches, *Restages*.

stȳfic Stetchworth (?). **sumor** (n) Summer Leisure.

sūðan (n) Sun Doles. **swān** Swansley (?).

þēod Thetford. **þorn** Thorney (2), Thorn Hall.

*þrǣding (n) Treading. ***þroccen** (n) Throckenholt.

þȳrel Thurland's Drove.

topt, ON Toft. **trēow** (c) Garden Tree.

tūn Town End, Town Fd, Townsend, Barston, Bassenhally, Beesons, Bur-, Chester-, Clop-, Coning-, Dit (2)-, Dray (2)-, Fit-, Fox-ton, Funthams, Gir-, His-, Kings-, Kneigh-, Lin-, Mil-, New (2)-, Ramp-ton, Saxon, Long Stanton, Sutton, Utton's, Weston, (b) Barring-, Cax-, Comber-, Crox-, Harl-, Hars-, Haux-, Mal-, Wilbur-ton, (c) Hin-, Pepper-ton.

tūnsteall Dunstalls, Dunstal Fd. ***tydd** (n) Tydd.

ūt Outwell, Waterbeach.

vað, ON Landwade (?).

wǣd Landwade (?). **wæter** (n) Waterbeach, Waterless, Cat's Water.

waroð (n) Warth's Old Halves. **wēala** *Walworth* (3).

weald *Wold*, Waller, Woolden, Croydon and Hatley Wilds.

weard Wadloo, Wardy.

weg *Alfordwey*, Babraham Rd, Bourn, Ely and Icknield Way, Buckingway, Long Road, *Lunway*, Mareway, Port Way (2), Street Way, Whole Way and some eighteen others.

welig Willey. **wenn** (n) Wenny. **wēr** Laddus, Upware.

westerra (n) Westry. **weðer** Wetherley.

wīc Wicken, Ben-, Chis-, West-wick.

wice Witcham, Witchford. **wīchamm** Wickham. **wīd** Willock.

wielle Well, Ash-, Barn-well, Bedwellhay, Bur-well, Caudle, Cawdle, Chardle, Conger's Well, Cowdell, Crownall, Euximoor, Gatley End, Orwell(pit), Out-, Snail-, Spring-, Up-, Whit-well, (b) Crackwell, (c) Knapwell.

wiht (n) Utton's Drove, Widden's Hill. **wiluh** (n) Willow, Prickwillow.

wīngeard Vineyard. **winter** Wentworth (?).

*wīp (n) Wype Doles.

worþ (a) Estover, *Wal* (3)-, Went-, *Wrat*-worth, (b) Boxworth, Duxford, Els-, Knees-, Lol-, Pap-worth, Pampisford, (c) Burnt Hill, Stetchworth.

wrætt (n) Wrat Fd, Wratting, *Wratworth*.
wrang Wrangling.   **wride** (n) Wryde.
wudu Wood (3), Balsham, Borley and Bourn Wood, Coney-, East (2)-wood, Hardwick and Hildersham Wood, Langwood, Leys Wood, Lin-, Nor-, Over-wood, Short's Corner.

CELTIC NAMES

Chatteris, Chettisham (?), Crossfield and the river-names Granta, Kennett, Nene.

SCANDINAVIAN NAMES

Biggen, Biggin, Bourn, Brink, Carlton, Fitton, Grange(hill), How-(hill), Toft. Hybrids with a Scandinavian personal name as a first element: Caxton, Clipsall, Croxton, Dowsdale, Pampisford (?), Single-sole; with a Scandinavian significant word as a first element: Bone's Gote, *Clintway*, Coneywood, Conington, Flegcroft, *Lunway*, Plain Field. See further *s.vv.* **bekkr, gata, holmr.**

FRENCH NAMES

Belsars Field, Dowgate, Portsand, Spinney and the borrowed name Marmont. Guyhirn is a hybrid formation.

NOTES ON THE DISTRIBUTION OF THESE ELEMENTS

A few notes on the distribution of certain place-name elements may be given. The significance of the distribution depends to a considerable extent upon a comparison with the distribution in other counties, more especially in neighbouring and adjacent counties. The counties adjacent to Cambridgeshire are Beds, Hunts, Northants, Lincs, Norfolk, Suffolk, Essex, Herts. For the first three and the last two we have very full material at our disposal; for Lincs, Norfolk and Suffolk the material at present is not so full.

burh. There are several examples of **burh** used of some ancient encampment, but its manorial use in the ME form *bury* is rare, and in this respect it is marked off clearly from Essex and Herts.
cote is less frequent than in Northants, Hunts, Beds or Herts. It resembles Norfolk, Suffolk and Lincs in the rarity of this element. One is a DB manor.
croft is more frequent than in any other neighbouring county. All are names of unimportant places. Two-thirds of them are in the north of the Isle of Ely.

ēg is very common, as was to be expected in a county with so much well-watered land. Eight are DB manors.

ende is somewhat less common than in the adjoining counties.

feld is much more common than usual. The nearest parallel is Suffolk, but there it is found in names of more important places. One is the name of a DB manor. In such names as East, South and West Field we have reference to the open fields of the parish. The great majority of the examples are, however, to be found in the Isle of Ely in names of comparatively late formation. Here the sites of *field*-names frequently adjoin one another. The sense would seem to approximate to the modern sense 'enclosed area' rather than to the old 'open country.'

grēne is less frequent than in Essex and Herts, but more so than in Beds, Hunts or Northants. It often has reference to the parish green.

(ge)hæg is seldom found. It is much less frequent than in the comparatively well-wooded counties of Essex, Herts and Northants.

hām and hamm are as usual difficult to distinguish. Of the nineteen probable examples of hām all except three are DB manors and one out of the two examples of hamm is a DB manor. It resembles Norfolk and Suffolk and to some extent Essex in the frequent use of hām.

hāmtūn. There is one isolated example. So similarly in Norfolk.

healh is as usual common. The examples come from fenland parishes, particularly from the Isle of Ely.

heall is more common than usual. It is more frequent than in Herts, less so than in Essex. It is not so common in the Isle of Ely as in the rest of the county.

hīd. Only one example has been noted, in strong contrast to the neighbouring counties of Essex and Herts. There is a similar absence of *hīd*-names in Lincs, Norfolk and Suffolk.

hlāw is more common than in any adjoining county. The reference is sometimes to a hill, sometimes to a barrow. Ancient tumuli are still to be found in association with five of them. Of seventeen examples fifteen are found in the chalk belt in the south of the county. This element is very rare in Lincs, Norfolk and Suffolk.

hōh is known only in minor names, though these include one hundred-name. Its comparative rarity is probably due to the character of the landscape.

holt is rare, three of the four examples coming from the Isle of Ely.

hyll is fairly common and widespread, but is of course rare in the Isle of Ely.

ing is found in one name of a DB manor and in some half-dozen other minor names in fenland parishes, of which three are in the Isle of Ely. There is no example of an ingas-name.

ingahām is found in four names, three of which are DB manors. It is much less frequent than in Norfolk and Suffolk and about as frequent as in Essex.

ingatūn. There are four examples of this rare formation. Three are names of DB manors. ingatūn formations are similarly found in Norfolk, but not in Suffolk or Lincs.

ingtūn is more common than in Hertfordshire, Essex or Suffolk, and a good deal more so than in Norfolk. It is less common than in Hunts or Northants. The formations are, with one exception, from monothematic names. All but two of the examples are names of DB manors and, except for three in the northern half of the Isle of Ely, all lie in the valley of the Cam. In the west there are no examples in the hundreds of Papworth, Longstow and Wetherley or in the east in those of Flendish, Staine, Staploe, Chilford, Radfield and Cheveley.

land is more frequent than in any adjoining county except Essex. It is found only in names of unimportant places, two-thirds of which lie in the Isle of Ely.

lēah. Of the twenty-two examples ten are names of DB manors. Except for one example in the Isle of Ely these fall into two well-defined groups, one in the western clay-lands bordering on Hunts and Beds, the other in the south-eastern clay districts along the Suffolk boundary. It has roughly the same relative frequency as in Essex, Herts, Beds, Hunts and Suffolk. It is a good deal commoner than in Lincs and Norfolk.

mersc is strangely rare.

stede is found only once and there it is a carry-over from Essex.

stoc and **þorp** are noteworthy for their absence.

tūn. Of some thirty-four examples some twenty-seven are DB manors. Proportionately they are more common than in Essex or Herts or Lincs and occur with the same frequency as in Norfolk and Suffolk. Only one formation is from a dithematic name. They are fairly evenly distributed.

wīc is rare. Of the four examples two are names of DB manors.

worþ is fairly common, indeed more common than in any neighbouring county except perhaps Hertfordshire. Ten of the examples are names of DB manors.

PERSONAL NAMES COMPOUNDED IN CAMBRIDGESHIRE PLACE-NAMES

Names not found in independent use are marked with a single asterisk if they can be inferred from evidence other than that of the place-name in question. Such names may be regarded as hardly less certain than those which have no asterisk. Those for which no such evidence can be found are marked with a double asterisk.

A. OLD ENGLISH

Abba (Abington (2)), **Bæddel* (Badlingham), **Bælli* (Balsham), *Bār(a)* (Barrington), *Basa* (Bassingbourn), *Beaduburh* (f) (Babraham),

Beorn(a) (Brangehill), *Beornheard* (Barsey), **Blunt* (Bluntishmere), **Boduc* (Bottisham), *Brynca* (Brinkley), **Bucc* (Boxworth), *Cēnðegn* or *Cēnwine* (Kneesworth(?)), **Cippa* (Chippenham), *Cnapa* (Knapwell(?)), **Cofa* (Coveney (?)), *Cola* (Callow Brook), *Cotta* (Cottenham), *Crætta* or **Crǣta* (Crackwell(?)), *Cumbra* (Comberton, Cumberton), *Cyneðegn* or *Cynewine* (Kneesworth(?)), **Cyrtla* (Kirtling), *Dēor* (Derisley), **Ducc* (Duxford), *Dudda* (Doddington), **Dull(a)* (Dullingham), **Earn(a)* (Armingford, Arrington, Ermine St), **Earn(ing)* (Armshold), *Elli* (Elsworth), **Elti* (Eltisley), **Empa* (Impington (?)), *Eofor* (Eversden (?)), **Frǣcca* (Freckney), *Gamela* (Gamlingay), **Gīsla* (Isleham), **Granta* or *Grante* (Gransden), *Hǣda* (Haddenham), **Hǣsela* (Haslingfield), **Hǣtta* (Hatley (?)), *Heafoc* (Hauxton), **Hefin* (Hempsalls), *Hengest* (Hinxton), *Herel(a)* (Harleston, Harlton), **Hildrīc* (Hildersham), *Hoc(c)a* (Oakington), **Horning* (Horningsea, Horslode (?)), **Hræfn* (Ranson, Ravens' Hall), *Hūna* (Honey), *Icel* (Ickleton), *Lēofhere* (Leverington), **Lippa* (Lipneas), **Loll(a)*, *Lull(a)* (Lolworth), **Māda* (Madingley), **Mealca* (Malton), *Odda* (Odsey), **Pada* (Padnal (?)), **Pampe* (Pampisford (?)), *Pappa* (Papley, Papworth), *Pinn(a)* (Pincote (?)), **Salse* (Sawston), *Sc(ī)ēne* (Shingay), *Sibbe* (Sipsey), *Sigebeald* (Sibald's Holm), **Stunta* (Stuntney (?)), **Swǣf* (Swavesey), **Tāda* (Tadlow), **Tæppa* (Top Moor(?)), ***Teofer* (Teversham(?)), *Tīdbeorht* (Turbutsey), *Trump* (Trumpington), **Tryppa* (Thriplow), *Wǣndel* (Vandlebury (?)), *Wealdhere* (Waldersea), **Wifel* (Willesey, Willingham), *Wilburh* (f) (Wilbraham, Wilburton), *Willa* (Willingham), **Wimbel* or *Wynnbeald* (Wimblington), *Wina* (Wimpole), *Wit(t)el* (Whittlesey, Whittlesford), *Wulf(a)* (Wool Croft), *Wulfmǣr* (Wilsmere Down).

B. SCANDINAVIAN

Dúsi (Dowsdale), *Kakkr* (Caxton), *Klyppr* (Clipsall), *Krókr* (Croxton), *Singull* (Singlesole (?)).

FEUDAL AND MANORIAL NAMES

Feudal additions: Abington Pigotts, Hatley St George, Papworth Everard and St Agnes, Swaffham Bulbeck and Prior, Tadlow Tower, Weston Colville, Wilbraham Temple.

Feudal names added sporadically include (a) *Abington Comitis, Caumpes Comitis, Ditton Vallence, Harleston Typpetote, Histon Abbatis, Morden Peverel, Stowe Engayne, Swafham le Cunte, Swafham Monialium, Wendy Templariorum, Wikam Wolvis,* (b) *Stowe Wid, Kinges Wilburgham.*

Other Feudal names include The Caldrees, Jerusalem Wood, Sheene Fm, Tunbridge Hall.

Miscellaneous additions include (a) Great and Little Abington, Castle and Shudy Camps, Fen Ditton, Woodditton, Little Downham, Dry and Fen Drayton, *Waldraittone*, Great and Little Eversden,

Little Gransden, East and *Hungry* Hatley, Cherry Hinton, Guilden and Steeple Morden, Great and Little Shelford, Long Stowe, *Gildene Swafham*, Little Thetford, Great and Little Wilbraham, West Wratting, (*b*) *Abington in the Clay, Long Stanton Allhallows*, Long Stanton All Saints and St Michael, Tydd St Giles, Westley Waterless, Wisbech St Mary and St Peter.

FIELD AND MINOR NAMES

The arrangement is as follows: (*a*) field and minor names (excluding those which can be identified with modern field-names) which are mentioned in early documents, treating them under the heading of their most significant element; (*b*) common elements found in the field and minor names of Cambridgeshire, but recorded only in distinctively modern documents; (*c*) miscellaneous field-names not readily grouped under (*a*) and (*b*); (*d*) modern field-names arranged under hundreds and parishes in the same order as in the rest of the book, in so far as it has proved possible, with the early documents at our disposal, to attempt to interpret them, or indicate some fragment of their history. The basis for this study has been, wherever it exists, the Tithe Award, supplemented by the lists of modern field-names with the accompanying maps collected and recorded by the schools (*v.* Preface *supra* x). This treatment of field-names is necessarily somewhat uneven. Both sources are far from complete. Unfortunately, no lists of modern field-names have been received from the Isle of Ely, whilst from Cambridgeshire itself only 27 parishes supplied material. This naturally varied in value, often through no fault of the schools themselves. Some of it has been very useful. Tithe Awards, too, are not available for some 82 parishes, whilst in some of those surviving either no names at all are given or only those surviving on the ordinary map. The surviving field-names of Cambridgeshire, on the whole, lack distinction. Schools frequently record 'no name' for field after field. In Newton, for example, 22 out of 45 fields are now nameless. The names given are often obviously late, frequently recording merely the size, *Six, Thirteen, Fifteen* Acres, etc. In Eltisley, the first six fields are simply numbered, *First, Second Field*, etc., whilst we meet with such names as *Allotments, Engine Shed Field, Station Field, Tin Sheds Field*, and *Soldiers Field*, so called because devoted to allotments for ex-service men after the war of 1914–18. Thus it is frequently impossible to relate an abundance of medieval field-name material to those surviving, whilst, occasionally, where the modern names are more numerous and more interesting, early material is lacking.

(a) *Field and minor names arranged under the forms of their elements, mainly as recorded in EPN. For* (n), *v. supra* 299.

æcer is very common. We have fields of *Trey-* (1232), *Four-* (1298), *Sex-* (1319), *Seuen-* (1251), *Heyte-* (1302), *Nyne-* (1398), five of *Tenacres* (1251–1356), *le ffyften-* (1356), *Tuenti-* (1251), *Thrittyacres* (13th), *le Fourtiacr'* (1319), *le hundred acres* (1395) and *Two hundred-acres* (1336), the last two in the Isle of Ely, and a *Sengilaker'* (1480). Note also *Schort(e)heyte Acris* (1259), *-festeneacres* (1319). Various compounds of *half-acre* occur, including *Honyswet-* (1406), *Horse-* (1308), *Wrong-* (1247), *v.* wrang, *Godes-* (1348), *Petiteshalvaker* (t. Hy 3), the last probably from the personal name *Petit.* Descriptive of shape are compounds of *Brode-* (t. Ed 3), *Longe-* (1300), *Pyk-* (1313), *Piked-* (1260) (i.e. with *pikes* or corners), *Gored-* (1480) (from gāra), *Bowe-* (1313) (i.e. shaped like a bow); of size is *Garebroodeacre* (13th), *v.* gāra. We have reference to soil or colour in *Salt-* (13th), *Sond-* (1480), *Stoni-* (1309), *Blake-* (1328), *Red-* (1404), to crops in *Ben-* (1307), to vegetation in *Bremb-* (13th) 'brambles,' *Eldern-* (1523) from *ellern* 'elder,' *Karlok-* (1480) 'charlock.' *Chekker-* (1494) has reference to the general appearance, *Geldin-* (1295), *Gilden-* (1455) (from OE *gylden*) to appearance or fertility. Occasionally we have reference to animals as in *Hund-* (1313), *Ox-* (1319), *Swin-* (13th). Situation is indicated in compounds with *Stret-* (1221), *Pynfold-* (1452). Occasionally we have reference to ownership as in *Ailetes Aker* (1198), probably from OE *Aelfgeat*, *Adamesaker* (1285), *Mariotesaker* (1319), or to charitable uses as in *Lauediaker* (1280), *Belle Acre* (1432), *Chapelacre* (t. Ed 4), *Lampeaker* (1480). *le Nikeresaker* (1313) was frequented by nickers or water-demons (cf. PN Sx 562, PN Ess 598), *le Lodderesacre* (1319) by a beggar and carries the word *lodder* back some 100 years. See also *s.v.* hēafod.

æppeltūn, 'orchard,' has been noted occasionally. In three examples in Balsham it is compounded with the owner's name, *Palfreymanes-, Lyonnes-, Beaufizapelton* (1316).

ærn, 'house,' has been noted in *Newern* (1239).

ærs, ears (n), 'arse,' is found in one or two late names.

balke, ME (n), is fairly common and is used of the ridge separating two cultivated strips. This was sometimes used as a path as in three examples of *Weybalke* (1372–1480) and as a boundary as in *Mearebalke* (16th) from (ge)mǣre. Thrice we have reference to the beating of the parish bounds as in *le Prosessyonbalke* (1458). Note also *le comen balke* (1562) and *Endlessebalk* (1591). Other compounds are *Þornbalke* (13th), *le Brodebalks* (1312), *le longebalkes* (1480), and an occasional example with a personal name (e.g. *Lungechampnysbalk* 1323). Reference is made to the site as in *Halough-* (1480) from healh, *Byrybalke* (1395) from burh.

banke is found in *le Banke* (1455) and *Lynchebanke* (1483) (*v.* hlinc) in Ickleton. It is more common in the Isle of Ely where it is used of the banks protecting the low-lying lands against flooding: *Barrebanke* (1558), *Fishpoole banke* (1669), *Lirlyngbankes* (1395) on the lands of Matilda de *Lirlyng* (1302) from Larling (Nf). *Benchel* (1312) may contain **benc**, the OE cognate of the Anglo-Scand *banke*, discussed in PN W 423.

barre, ME (n), is used of a barrier to hold up the waters: *le Barre* (1279), *Barrewere* (1199), *Barrefeld* (1300), *Mareysbarre* (1368) from ME *mareis* 'marsh,' *Barrelode* (1498), *Doddington Barres* (1574). It survives in modern field-names such as *Barr Close, Bar Croft*.

bece. This element (cognate with ON **bekkr**) is found in the form *bece, bech, beche* in Landbeach and Waterbeach whilst *beche* is very common in the Isle of Ely. Three times only it is found in the form *bach(e)* in *Wisebache* 1086 InqEl, *Wysebach* 1470 ECP and *Bachecroft* 1438 Imb (in Wisbech). Among the examples of its use we may note *middelwere de batlebeche*, a fishery in Upwell (c. 1170 *Thorney*), *piscaria de Beche in marisco de Sutton* (c. 1295 *ElyM*), *ripa de Chisbeche* (t. Hy 3 *Cole* xli) in Upwell, probably a compound of *cis*, 'gravel,' and *water of Dreyebeec* (1328 Banco) in Sutton. All these names are consistent with an interpretation of *bece* as 'stream' or possibly 'valley.' The curious names *Vtmestebeche* (13th *StNeot*), *Vtewardebesche* (ib., c. 1320 *Thorney*), *Hinnewardbeche, Estbeche hinneward, Estbeche vtward* (ib.), all in Upwell, rather suggest a reference to land at varying distance from a stream or valley. Other examples are quite uncertain in their interpretation, such as *Herewardisbeche* (1334), *Wyllardisbeche* (1284) (where it is compounded with a personal name), *Horsbech* (1459), *Snitebeche* (1221) (from *snite*, 'snipe'). In Landbeach and Waterbeach we seem to have reference to the valley of the Cam, and in Wisbech to the valley or stream of the Wissey or Ouse. The interpretation in Birdbeck (*supra* 288, earlier *Budebeche*), which lies by the Nene, is specially difficult. In some names it interchanges with the corresponding Scandinavian loan-word, cf. *Estrebek* (14th), *Estrebec(h),Osterbec* (1387), *Lytlebek* (13th),*Litlebec(h)* (1387) inChippenham.

bedd has been noted in compounds with plant and tree names, *Wythibeddes* (1230), *Ahssebed* (1311), and *Lekesbedde* (1349).

bekkr, ON, 'stream, *beck*,' occurs in *la Bek* (1342) in Wicken, *le Becke* (1504) in Comberton and *Mildred becke* (1586) in Orwell. Cf. 'the little river or becke' (1553 WMP), *v.* also **bece** *supra*.

beorg, much less frequent than **hyll**, is found alone in the forms *Berewe* (1228), *Beru* (1274), *Berech* (1387) and *Borowes* (1389), and in the compounds *Wyteberewe* (13th), *Stanberue* (1278), *Hauekebereche* (13th), *Chircheborw* (1300). It is usually difficult to know whether these unidentified names have reference to a hill or to a barrow, but *Fowerberewe* (1279) in the bounds of Little Wilbraham and *Fowerbereghes* (1260), in Babraham, clearly have reference to groups of barrows.

bern is found occasionally. *Barnes* (1312), *Wilkinesbern* (1319), *Sextry barn* (15th) in Ely, so called because here were received the tithes which formed the endowment of the sacristy (NED *s.v. sextry*).

bigging, ME, is rare and late. *Biggyng* (1453), *Newbigging* (1457). It survives as *Biggin(s)*.

bōcland, 'land held by charter,' has been noted occasionally as in *Boclond* (14th), *Bokelond* (1326) and possibly *Buklond* (1513).

bois, ME (n), 'wood,' occurs in *le Southboys* (1339).

boþ, ODan, is found once in *Bury Boothes* (1561).

botm is occasionally found as in *le Botme* (1334), *le Botum* (1515), *Baryngden Botme* (1367), *le Gretebotom* (1456).

bræc, 'land newly taken into cultivation,' is fairly common as *Brache* (1235–1612), less frequent as *Breche* (12th–1494) and once as *Brayche* (1514). Compounds are rare: *Grethornbrech* (1236) and one each with **eald, sceort**, 'short,' **lang** (1461–4). It survives in *Breach* and *Britch*.

brædu (n), 'breadth, broad strip,' is fairly common, the first element being usually descriptive: *Litlebrade* (13th), *Litlebrede* (1251), *Broudbrede* (1491), *Middel-* (1240), *Hye-* (13th), *Blake-* (t. Ric 2), *Elde-* (1251) (*v.* **eald**), *Comoune-* (1323), *Hangendebrede, -brade* (1319), *Wrongebred* (1329) 'crooked' (*v.* **wrang**), *Stoni-* (1272), *Mers-* (1251), 'marsh,' *Garebrede* (1251) (*v.* **gāra** and cf. *Gorebrode s.v.* **brode**), *North-* (1414). It is compounded with tree and plant names in *Wile(we)-* (1251–77) 'willow,' *Thorn-* (13th), *Coppethornbrede* (1329). *Cherchebrede* (1472) was near or belonged to the church. The strip sometimes takes name from a neighbouring place, as in *Ganghullebrade* (1319), *Alvenehobrade* (14th), *Roudenebrede* (1319), etc., and, occasionally from an owner as in *Grimesbrede* (1251), *Wolfrichesbrade* (1319). *Pollardisbrede* (1329), *Heylokesbrade* from Robert *Heylok* (1387). Note also *le Stablebrede* (1319), *Tradebrede* (1319), probably from ME *trade*, 'way, path.' No examples of this element have been noted in the Isle of Ely. Later, it survives in *The Breeds*.

braken is very rare: *le Nethyrbrakne* (1359), *le Brakyn* (1429).

brēmel, 'bramble,' is used collectively in *Longe brimbil* (1301).

brinke, brenke, ME, is used occasionally of the edge of a steep place, especially of an edge of land bordering on water, as in *Brynke apud Reche* 1431 Ct, *Saltbryng, -bringge, -brinkke* (1349), *le Loderesbrynke* (1380) (from *loddere*, 'beggar'), *Lodesbrinck* (1415) (*v.* (ge)**lād**), *Wayourbrynke* (1447) (*v.* **weyour**).

brōc is common and, as in Sussex and Surrey, sometimes denotes a water-meadow, rather than a brook, e.g. 'herbagio in *the Brok*' (1362), *Fulebrok* (campus) (1251), *Reybroc* (1230), 'meadow by the low-lying land,' *v.* **æt, ēg**. Two compounds with **in**, *Inbroc* (1220), *Innebrok* (1319) should be compared with **inland**. The most frequent compounds are *Holebroke* (1231), *Smal-* (1373), *Wrang-* (1239) (*v*, **wrang**), *Ful-* (1219). We may note also *Narwebroc* (1219), *le Comen-*

broke (1525), *Tonebroke* (1361) 'village brook' (*v.* tūn), *Dambroc* (13th). We have reference to horses in *Horsbroc* (13th), and bulls in *Bolebrok* (1306), to birds in *Fynchybrook* (1487) and *Crowbroke* (1475), and to owners in *Toppes-* (1203), *Sigares-* (13th), *Ediuebroc* (1290) (from OE *Éadgiefu* (f)). *Hayl Broke* (1483–93), in Madingley, appears to be another example of the lost *Hail*, the original name of the Kym (PN BedsHu 7–8, RN 188–9), whilst *Idibrok* (1351), in Grantchester, may, perhaps, be compared with Ide (PN D 497).

brocc-hol is occasionally found as in *Brokhole, Brokholes* (1321), *Brokkeshole* (1521).

brode, ME (n), 'broad strip,' is found uncompounded and in the compounds *Gorebrode* (1202, 1300), probably a broad strip tapering to a gore or point (*v.* gāra), *Crowchebrode* (1494) and *Barlybrode* (14th). It survives in *The Broads*.

brycg. We may note: *Calvenebreg'* (1279) 'calves,' *Bedelisbrigge* (1314), *Prestisbregge* (1319), *Loderesbrugg* (1352) from ME *loddere*, 'beggar.' See also *s.v.* port.

burh is commonest in the manorial sense either finally as in *Clopton-bury* (1440), *Bonesbury* (1383) and *Bansibury* (1640) from Robert de *Bancies*, or more commonly, as a first element as in *Biricroft* (1251), *Beristrate* (1352), *Birysted* (1324), *Burieweye* (14th), *Beriyard* (1540). It survives occasionally as *Burry* and in *Burystead*. In Kneesworth we have reference to a *Maidebury* (1513), *Maydbury* (1686), *Mayden-bury* (1696) which would seem to relate to some unknown earthwork nicknamed 'Maiden-fort' as in Medbury (PN BedsHu 71–2) and Maidenburgh (PN Ess 371). burhsteall, 'site of a *burh*,' is found in *Burstallweye* (1250). burhtūn is found in *Burtoneweye* (1246).

burna is very rare: *Ringeburn'* (1231), *Emesburne* (t. Hy 3), *Mekes-brocburn* (1285).

OScand buskr, 'bush,' is found in *Briddesbuske* (1280), 'young birds' bush.'

butte, ME (n), occurs from 1342 in the plural, used of short strips, of uncertain length, ploughed in the angle where two furlongs meet at right angles. It is compounded with lang (1300), short (1626), grēne (1300) and myln (1322). *Hunibuttes* (1228) must have been sticky or muddy. Note also *Fiftenebuttes* (1432), *Ellenebuttes* (1432), probably 'eleven,' and compounds like *Schortemadebuttes* (1379) (i.e. short mead). Occasionally, we have a personal name *Aileuebuttes* (1250), from the OE woman's name *Æðelgiefu, Farmansbuttes* (1475).

byge (n), 'bend, curve.' *Walterisbig* (1151), *Nebroc atte Bege* (1200), *Leche-, Lachebey* (13th, 1387), in a stream (*v.* lache).

byht, 'bend,' is probably found in *Bytewere* (1277), *Bytrode* (1378), *Dreibet* (1251), from drǣge, *Gosebitt* (1422).

*bysc is rare and late. We may note *Medyl-* (1483), *Hawebus(s)h* (1548), from haga, *Sallowbush* (1623), from sealh 'willow,' *Vrchoun-nysbusch* (1515) 'hedgehog's bush' from ME *urchon*.

bytme (n), 'bottom,' is found twice in Ely: *le Bidme, Bithme, Suth-bedme* (13th).

cangle, ME (n), 'enclosure,' a variant of *chancel, has been noted twice on the Essex border (cf. PN Ess 434–5).

cattesbraȝen, ME (n), 'catsbrain,' has been noted three times, the earliest being *Cattisbrainis* (1319). In the course of the Survey this term has been found as a field or farm name in Bk, O, Wa, Beds, Hunts and Sr. It has been explained as the name for a coarse soil consisting of rough clay mixed with stones. Sir John Russell of Rothamsted has very kindly made enquiries on our behalf as to the use and meaning of this term. In addition to the counties just mentioned, it is still used in Shropshire and in Kent and there is an early reference to its use in Staffordshire, though the term seems no longer to be current there. This last reference is as follows: "But tho' there is little danger of *overmarling* such sorts of lands, yet of some others there may; and therefore in some places they always observe the *thickness* of their mold above the *Catbrain* (as they call it) i.e. a sort of barren *clay* and *stone* mixt; which if they find but *thin*, they *marle* that land proportionately less; but if *thick*, they also *marle* it accordingly; for to lay a good deal of *marle* upon *thin* land, will produce but a mean, if any cropp at all." This is the earliest reference so far found for the use of the term apart from its use in place-names. In Kent a correspondent of Sir John Russell noted that the term is used to describe a number of different geological and soil materials which all possess the common characteristic of exhibiting a fairly pronounced mottling in colour. It is also to be noted that in J. J. Graham's *Weardale, Past and Present* (1939), the author in his chapter on dialect says that *cats* = a mixture of clay with something else, e.g. 'cat's balls' were made of blue clay and crawcoal. He is speaking of the early 19th century. It may be that the reference to mottling as the characteristic feature of this particular type of soil gives a possible clue to the origin of the name. Most cats, especially of the wilder type, are striped or tabby and it may have been thought that an animal with striped or tabby fur must have brains corresponding.

causey, ME (n), 'paved way,' is occasionally found, sometimes in the form *calcey, calsey*.

checker, ME (n), denoting a field of chequered appearance, is occasionally found as in *Cheker* (1403), *Chekermedewe* (1406), *Chekerforlonge* (1491), *Chekker acre* (1494).

clæg is found in *le Clay* (13th), *Hangindeclay* (13th), *Dedeclai, Witteclay* (1250) 'white,' *Longeclay* (1319), *Redeclay* (1337) 'red.'

close, ME (n), is fairly common, but late. *le Clos* (1409), *Tyleclose* (1465), *Ynggoldesclosse* (1496). See also Camping Close *supra* 153.

clote, ME (n). *Welleclote* (1376), *Sewalesclote* (1380) in Upwell and Elm. Cf. *le Clote* (1375) in Elloe (L) near Croyland, *Aswykclote* (1415) in Croyland (L), *Pundaghclot* (1321) in Skeffling (Y). This is a fenland term, apparently something to do with draining and barring waters. Its history is obscure.

cnoll is rare, as in *Ramesknol* (1240), *Greneknol* (14th), *Pelrynescnol* (1309), i.e. 'pilgrim's.'

codd (n), 'bag, sack,' apparently used topographically of a hollow, is found several times in the compound *Watericoddes* (1202), *Watircod(d)es* (1325–64).

coninger, ME (n), is rare. We may note the forms *Conynger* (1287), *the Conynger* (1407), *Cunigera* (1388), *Conyger* (1549).

corner, ME (n), occurs occasionally, the earliest example being *Vernons corner* (1368).

cote is fairly common. We have two examples of *Newcot(e)* (13th, 1636), three of *S(c)hepecote* (1231–1473), four of *Swyne(s)cote* (1292–1376), two of *Lambecote* (1212, 13th) and one of *Muttoncote* (1443). *Waytecote* (1319) was a 'look-out cottage' (ME *waite*). Situation is denoted in *Estfenkote* (1251), *Mellecote* (1319) (from myln, 'mill'), *Seekote* (1466), 'by the sea,' in Wisbech, *Marekote* (1478), by Stretham Mere *supra* 239. *Maryshcote* (1570), in the marsh (ME *mareis*). Note also *Blakemonendaykote* (1294) and *Outlawes Cote* (1604). *Aldrehewenecote* (1298) is apparently for *ealra hīwena cote*, 'cottages belonging to the whole monastic community; it lay *juxta terram Prioresse de Stratforde*. We have occasional examples compounded with a personal name as in *Cobbecote*, *Wybbecote* (1319) from OE *Cobba* and *Wibba* and *Aldredecote* (1364) from OE *Ealdrēd*. In the Isle of Ely it is often used of fishermen's huts as in 'two *Fisharcotes* called *le Newkote* and *le Pykerelleskote*' (1473) in Wisbech, the latter belonging to the family of Thomas *Pekerell* (1430). It occasionally takes the form *court* in modern times.

croft, 'small enclosure,' is very common indeed. Descriptive of shape, position, etc. are *Bali-* (1240), probably from *bealg*, 'rounded,' *Crispe-* (1279), 'curly,' *Del-* (1319), in a valley (dell), *Hale-* (1290) from healh, *Hille-* (13th), *Hindre-* (1250) (an early example of *hinder*), *Hirne-* (1221), 'nook,' from hyrne, *Ho-* (13th) from hōh, *Lowe-* (1308), probably by a hill (hlāw), and numerous compounds of eald, brād, norð, sūð, ēast, west, lang, sceort, middel and lȳtel. The colour of the soil or its nature is indicated in *Grene-* (1250), *Rade-* (1319), 'red,' *Whight-* (1526), *Chalde-* (1526), 'cold,' from ceald, *Hore-* (1251) from horu, 'mud,' *Rou-* (1324), 'rough,' from rūh, *Ston(y)-* (1351–1432), *Mudde-* (1435), *Slo-* (1202) from slōh, 'slough.' Note also compounds with *Wode-* (1253), *Madwe-* (1251), *Gardeyn-* (1424) and *Watyrlesow-* (1395), i.e. 'water-meadow,' *v.* 1æs. *Sunderlondcroft* (13th) was remote or set apart for some special purpose, whilst *Sumerlondescroft* (13th) was used in summer. Reference is often made to some neighbouring building or feature: *Berne-* (1404), 'barn,' *Cote-* (1331), *Halle-* (1251), *Melne-* (1292), *Pol-* (1334), 'pool,' *Style-* (1336). We may note also two examples of *Thorpcroft* (1349, 1457), several of *Bery-*, *Biri-*,

Burycroft (1251–1497), attached to the manor-house (burh), and of *Cherche-*, *Churchcroft* (1283–1668), which may have been near the church or ecclesiastical property. Beneficial ownership is also indicated in *Bysshopes-* (1424), *Prestes-* (1314), *Deknes-* (1316), *Canons-* (1395), *Abbotis-* (1404), *Munkene-* (13th), *Nonnes-* (1400). Compounds with trade-names (used perhaps as surnames) are *le Barkers-* (1459), 'tanner's,' *Mangeres-* (1250), 'trader's,' *Potters-* (1283), *Smethes-* (1327), 'smith's,' *Tasilleres-* (1422), 'the user of a teazle in cloth-making,' and there are numerous compounds with personal names, including *Tedbrictes-* (1199), '*Thēodbeorht's*,' *Wlsis-* (1236) (OE *Wulf-sige*), *Wolveres-* (1290) (OE *Wulfhere*), *Alueue-* (1221) and *Wlueue-* (1280) from the OE women's names *Ælfgiefu* and *Wulfgiefu*, and various medieval surnames, *Fleminges-* (1274), *Katelines-* (1320), *Paynes-* (1251), *Qwyntynys-* (1380). *Carlecroft* (1308–23) in Foxton is a compound of ME **karl**, 'freeman.' Frequent reference is made to (*a*) crops, trees, etc. in *Bene-*, *Banecroft* (1251–1420), 'beans,' *Bere-* (13th), 'barley,' *Brembely-* (1501), *Gars-* (1233), *Gres-* (1285), *Gras-* (1319), 'grass,' from **gærs**, *Hasel-* (1235), *Henep-* (1251), 'hemp,' *Hey-* (1225), *Pery-* (1344), 'pear-tree,' *Pese-*, *Pise* (1200–1441), *Res(sch)e-* (1279–1319), 'rushes,' *Rey-*, *Rye-* (1412–16th), 'rye,' *þystli-* (1251), *Wate-*, *Qwate-* (1341), 'wheat,' *Wyle-* (1332), 'willow'; (*b*) animals and birds found there: *Bole-* (1435), *Bukkes-* (t. Hy 7), *Calues-* (1251), *Chalve-* (1286), *Calf-* (1342) from **cealf**, 'calf,' *Cow-* (1410), *Fesant-* (1450), *Fox-* (1460), *Frosche-* (1484) (OE *forsc*), 'frog,' *Gose-* (1280–1543), *Horse-* (1260), *Muse-* (1299), 'field-mice,' *Oxe-* (1251). *Wedrescroft* (t. Hy 2) may be from OE *Weðer* or the animal. We may also note *Cokkestolcroft* (1398), where the cucking-stool was set up, *Cokaynecroft* (1302), containing ME *cokaygne*, the imaginary abode of luxury and idleness (cf. Cockaynes, PN Ess 325). In modern field-names this survives as *Croft*, *Croat(es)*, *Craft*.

cros is fairly common, including *Charitie crosse* (1368), *Cherchecros* (1329), *le Hyecrosse* (1439), *Spittle crosse* (t. Ric 2), several examples of *Stoncrosse* (1376), *le Stumpidecrosse* (1501), *le Treencrosse* (1455) from OE *trīewen*, 'made of wood,' *Whyȝthcros* (1459), 'white,' and several containing a personal name as in *Balescros* (1260), *Paykescrosse* (1395). *Godlakescrosse* (1469) in Thorney probably marked the limit of the possessions of St Guthlac's monastery of Croyland.

crouche is about as common as cros. We may note *le Charitescrouch* (1298), *Howecruche* (1204), situated on a hōh, *le Cherchecrouche* (1352), *Ouerecrouche* (1359), 'upper,' *le Wytecrouch* (1363) and *Paryshcrouche* (1517). Sometimes we have reference to the village cross as in *Wycche-fordcruch* (1300), *Over Crutch* (1617) at Witchford and Over respectively. Sometimes they are associated with personal names as in *Brunilde Cruch* (1279), *Charlescrux* (1279), *Ionescruche* (1277).

crundel, used of quarries or chalkpits of irregular outline, noted hitherto only in D, Do, Ha, Sx, W and Wo, i.e. in the west and south-west, has been noted now appropriately enough in Balsham (*þrecrundles* 1251), Sawston (*Crundlesfeld* 13th) and Babraham (*Crundlisfeld* 1330) in distinctively chalk country.

cumb is found uncompounded in Barrington, Bottisham, Fulbourn, Ickleton and Melbourn (*le Cumbes* 13th, *le Combes* 1409, *Kumb* (1483) and compounded with **holh** in Melbourn (*Holcombespath* 1409), with **hyll** in Ickleton (*Combhyll* 1431) and with a personal name in Little Abington (*Famliscomb* 1359).

cyln. *Limekelne* (1200) carries that word back almost a hundred years.

dæl, 'valley,' that distinctively Anglian term, is undoubtedly found in Cambridgeshire, but it is very difficult to separate it from **dæl**, 'share, part,' which equally certainly occurs in this county side by side with the more usual **dāl**, 'dole' (*infra*). In most parts of England *dæl* would yield ME *del(e)* and be easy to distinguish, but in the East Midlands *æ* develops to *ā* and we clearly have examples of this change in Cambridgeshire (Introd. xxxiii). This makes it very difficult to know whether ME, ModEng *dale* in Cambridgeshire should be interpreted as 'valley' or 'share, part.' Field and minor names in *dale* are fairly common. In such names as *Depedale* (1293) in Fulbourn, *Forkedale* (1296) in Barton, *Twisedal* (1220) in Haslingfield (*v.* **twisla**), we are pretty certainly right in interpreting it as 'valley,' but when names in -*dale* are found in such parishes as Wisbech, Swaffham and Swavesey it is almost equally certain that we must have to do with the other word. Apart from this topographical test, compounds with personal names such as *Wivelesdale* (1360) in Haslingfield are entirely ambiguous. *Gilberdesdale* (1251) in Wisbech cannot be a 'dale,' and its true origin is suggested by the alternative form *Gilberdesdole* (1338). Similarly we have *Moruluesdale* (1205) and *Morolesdole* (1250) in Madingley. Occasionally too we have forms in *dele* such as *Faragesdele* (1274) in Steeple Morden (from William *Farage*), which must go back to **dæl**, and in general the exceeding frequency of compounds of *dale* with a personal name, often of late origin, fits better with the 'share' interpretation than the 'dale' one. Quite apart from their situation, the fields *Osemundesdale* (1251), *Doddingesdale* (1255), *Billeresdale* (1277), *Adgeresdale* (1251), *Modberdesdale* (1251) (from Peter *Moberd*), are more likely to be the 'shares' than the 'dales' of the men whose name they bore.

dāl, 'portion or share of land, especially of the common field,' is very common. Compounds are frequently descriptive of site, shape or colour, *Nort-*, *Sut-*, *Est-*, *Westdole* (1274), *Longe-* (1225), *Brod-* (1287), *Mochil-* (1389), *Olde-* (t. Ed 3), *Niew-* (13th), *Middel-* (1319), *Wrang-* (1317), *Wrong-* (1339), 'crooked' (*v.* **wrang**), *Thwert-* (13th), *Whart-* (1450) (ME *thwert*, 'cross'), *Sharp-* (1513), *Ouereste-* (1319), 'topmost,' *Mere-* (1277), 'boundary' (*v.* (ge)**mǣre**), *Goredole* (1298) (*v.* **gāra**), *Hyrne-* (1398) (*v.* **hyrne**), *Crocdole* (1251) (*v.* **krókr**), *For-*

(1200), *Forthdole* (1322) (*v.* forð, 'in front'), *Blak-* (1428), *Grene-* (1322), *Reddole* (1600). Size is indicated in *le Nyneakredoole* (1449). *Stakedole* (1319) was probably enclosed by stakes; *Pennydole* (1540), part of the Pennylands in Over, is named from its rent. *Stonidole* is common from 1212. The character of the site is often indicated: *Calugh-* (1418), 'bare' (*v.* calu), *Nakededole* (1484), *Smethdoole* (1484), 'smooth,' *Slyther-* (1480), 'slippery,' *Coldedool(l)* (1455), *Brende-* (1315), 'burnt,' *Hangendedole* (1319), on a slope. Reference is often to crops or plants grown or to animals or birds kept or found there: *Barli-* (1185), *Popi-* (1228), *Thorn-* (1250), *Ays-* (1247) (*v.* æsc), *Docki-* (13th), 'grown over with dock,' *Wrte-* (1285), 'vegetables' (*v.* wyrt), *Leuer-* (1376), 'wild iris' (*v.* læfer), *Whad-* (1274), 'wheat' (cf. Whaddon *supra* 68), *Ban-* (1397), 'bean,' *Thistel-* (1319), *Lynn-* (1401), from līn, 'flax,' *Brenbili-* (1283), *Bremly-* (1293), 'brambly,' *Breridole* (1398), 'briary,' *Walnotedoles* (t. Ric 2), *Flagge Doole* (16th), *Oxe-* (1300), *Schepe-* (1230), *Calue-* (1319), *Enede-* (1283), 'duck' (*v.* ened), *Gos-* (1362), *Crane-* (1371), *Snaylidole* (1332). Position is often indicated by reference to some neighbouring feature or building, including *Rydydooll* (1460) (*v.* riðig), *Sepewasse-* (1274) (*v.* scēap-wæsc), *Castel-* (1281), *Brigge-* (1280), *Melne-* (1319), *Doffusdole* (1358), 'dove-house.' *Stepeldole* (1591) may contain OE *stīepel*, 'steep place,' discussed *s.n.* Steeple (PN Ess 226–7). Note also *Teynterdole* (1542), 'field where cloth is stretched.' Compounds containing a personal name are frequent. Cf. *Normannes-* (1202), *Godgive-* (t. Hy 3) (OE *Gōdgiefu* (f)), *Coluillesdole* (1499). Note also *Maniman-dole* (1342) (cf. Nymandole *supra* 294), and two examples of *Cotmandole* (1489, 1540). These doles were also used as boundaries. Cf. *quandam metam siue dolam* (1406) in Landwade. In Barrington, we have frequent reference to 'one *fulledole*' (1250), a unit of area (note in MS, 'three fulledoles equal one acre'). In modern field-names this survives as *Dole(s)* and *Dowles* (cf. *ye Dowles* 1693).

dam, ME (n) is fairly common. *le Dam* (1319), *Blakedam* (1370), *Melnedam* (1279) (*v.* myln), *Mareysdam* (1368) (AFr *mareis*, 'marsh'), and a number of compounds containing a personal name, such as *Alviesdam* (1220) (OE *Ælfwīg*), *Hychecokesdam* (1398). Note *dam-mynges* (1307), 500 years earlier than NED.

(ge)delf is fairly common. Apart from *le Delfe* (1319) in Hasling-field, *Stonidelf* (1273) in Steeple Morden, *Stanydelffe* (15th) in Pam-pisford and *Standolff* (1513) in Kneesworth, where the meaning is probably 'quarry,' this element is confined to the fenland parishes where it is used in the sense 'artificial watercourse.' Cf. 'lada prioris voc. *Priurs Delf*' (1278) in Sutton. We may note *Smaldelf* (1320), *Neudelf* (1221), *Adthelwoldesdelf* (1251) (OE *Æðelweald*), *Baronesdelf* (1298).

dell is very rare. We may note *Gren-*, *Grindel* (1280–95) in Ashley, *Farndelle* (14th) in Arrington (*v.* fearn), *Dellcroft* (1319) in Meldreth and *Willemondesdelle* (1353) in Steeple Morden, 'valley of *Winemund* or *Wilmund*' (cf. Wymondley, PN Herts 148).

denu is fairly common. The first element is usually descriptive as in *Micheldene* (1280), *Litlen-* (1250), *Longe-* (1208), *Depe-* (1235), *Schalwe-* (1465), *Wrange-* (1373), 'crooked,' *Rue-* (1250) (*v.* rūh), *Hole-* (1250) (*v.* holh), *White-* (1397), *Stany-* (17th), *Risshe-* (1260), *Russh-* (1465) (*v.* rysc), *Brere-* (13th), 'briar,' *Hasyl-* (1392), *Hassokes-dene* (1240) (*v.* hassuc). Occasionally we have reference to birds or animals: *Hulverestresden* (1260), 'plover' (OE *hulfestre*), *Cattesdene* (1319), *Hartdene* (1290). Occasionally we have a compound with a personal name as in *Alwinesden* (1203), *Godmannes-* (1250), *Wiuerdes-* (1250) (OE *Wīgferð*). Occasionally this element occurs as *dane*: *Schytlowedane*, *Scotlowedane* in Steeple Morden (1340–66) (from *scite*, 'dung'), *v.* Introd. xxxiii–iv. It survives in modern names as *Dene* and *Dean* and occasionally as *Dane*.

dēop, 'deep,' is used substantively in the fens of a deep place in a stream and of a fishery: *le Depe* (1345), *Suttone Depe* (1278), *Blow deepe* (1605), perhaps from OE blā(w), 'dark, livid.'

dīc is very common, especially in the fenland parishes, where it is used both of a ditch and a dike. In early forms it is not always possible to decide to which it refers. Very common compounds are *Grenedich* (1250), *Maredich* (1285), *Meredych* (1410), 'boundary ditch' from (ge)mǣre, and compounds of lang, middel, smæl, wrang, blæc, hwīt, eald, myln, mǣd (*Made-* 1272, *Mede-* 1466, *Maddyche* 1513, *Maddage* 1727). Other descriptive elements are found in *Braddyche* (1489), *le Oueredich* (1357), *le Goardyke* (1336) (*v.* Goredike *supra* 206), *Casteldyke* (1477) by Wisbech Castle, *Twyslynge dytche* (1569), *Whislin Ditch* (1721), 'forking,' a derivative of twisla, 'fork,' *Dernadick* (1285), 'hidden' from dierne, *Fuldich* (t. Ed 4), 'foul,' *Cleydich* (1272), *Stondyche* (1447), *Holledych* (1344) from holh, 'hollow,' and several examples of 'rough ditches' such as *Rudich* (1205) from rūh. Reference is frequent to plants or trees growing in or near the ditch: *Thorndiche* (1340), *Leuirdych* (1290) from læfer, 'wild iris,' *Spirediche* (1466) from OE spīr, 'reeds' (cf. Spirewell, PN D 261), *Wylowedyke* (1469). The name often indicates the place bounded by the ditch: *Mordig* (1230), *le Pastourdich* (1312) from ME *pastour*, 'pasture,' *Dole-* (1483), *Drovediche* (1436) and *Croftdig* (1450). We may note also *(S)charneldich* (13th) in Ely, possibly from ME, OFr *charnel*, 'burial-place, cemetery,' and if so, carrying back this word over a hundred years, *Crisemaledych* (14th) from OE *cristelmæl*, 'cross,' and *Cukkyngstolldych* (1435). Very common in the Isle of Ely are new dikes and ditches (from 1294) and *Fendich, -dike* (from 1346). *Heydich* (1228) in Trumpington and *Heydych* (13th) in Foxton were probably boundaries of a woodland enclosure or *hay* (*v.* (ge)hæg). We have one 'thieves' ditch,' *Yeuesdych* (1387) and one *Grimmisdych* (1319), whether from the Anglo-Scandinavian personal name *Grim* or from the mythological *Grim* or *Woden* (cf. *Grims Ditch*, PN Herts 8, PN W 15, PN Mx 11), it is impossible to say. Other compounds with a personal name are common: *Bernuluesdiche* (1205), OE *Beornwulf*, *Wlwyisdick* (1282), OE *Wulfwig*, *Thokesdich* (1290), *Tokisdyke* (1315), ON *Tóki*, *Hilleryesdyke* (1336) from Gilbert *Hillary* (1358). Note also *Levedidich* (1325), 'lady's ditch.'

dræg is an element always difficult of interpretation (cf. Drayton *supra* 152, 166) and if we do not know the site of the place in the name of which this element is used, interpretation becomes even more difficult. In the fen-district the sense 'place up which something is dragged' is not possible; that of 'portage' is more likely, but the *Drey(e)-*, *Dray-* names in the Fenland district are too numerous for us to believe that they all derive from dræg, even in this sense. More probably they derive from the recorded OE *dræge*, 'drag-net, fish-net,' cf. 'uno *Dreye* per duas vices post le *Dreyefar*' (1336) where *far* is probably used of the 'passage' of a stream,' *v.* fær. Among these ambiguous compounds we may note *Draymere* (1251), *Dreyebeec* (1328) (probably for *Dreyebece*), *Dreydich* (1279) and *Dreywelle* (1312). *Dreyhirst* (1251) and *Dreyehyrst* (1277) were probably on slopes. We must remember also that *drey(e)*, *drei(e)* and even *dray(e)* may derive from drȳge, 'dry.'

drāf (n), ME *drove*, is commonly used in fenland parishes of a road along which cattle are driven. We may note *Litledraue* (t. Hy 3), *Smaldrove* (1358), 'narrow' (*v.* smæl), le *Vtdrove* (13th), le *Tundrove* (14th) (*v.* tūn), *Maresdrove* (1336) (AFr *mareis*, 'marsh'), *Twertdravam* (t. Hy 3) ('cross-drove,' ME *thwert*), the comon *Drove* (1565), *Kikking-drove* (1438), le *Droveweye* (1394). Compounds with a personal name are frequent, e.g. *drauam de Rosby* (14th) from Robert de *Roseby* (1221), *Meesdroue* (1358), *Mesedraue* (1413) from an ancestor of John *Mees* (1500). le *Wendlinge drove* (1336) was on the land of the abbot of Wendling. All these, with *Forthdrove* (1402) in Whittlesey, are in the Isle of Ely. Elsewhere we have only le *Droue* (1426) and *Newdrove* (1562) in Cottenham and another *Forthdrove* (t. Hy 3) in Papworth. *Droveway* is frequent in modern field-names.

drift, EModE (n), 'cattle-road,' is occasionally found: le *dryfte* (1563), described as a common pasture, *Tounmille Dryeft* (1457), the *horse dryfte* (1562), le *dryfte lane* (1563). Survives in *Drift Ground* and *Driftway*. The first reference for this usage in NED is 1686.

dufhous, ME (n), 'dove-cot,' is found occasionally: *Doffus*, le *Duf-hous* (1338), *Duffous* (1462), *Olde Duffehous* (1420), carrying back the history of this word nearly a hundred years.

dūn is fairly common. The first element is descriptive of (*a*) size, *Littledon* (1323), *Mechel-* (1360); (*b*) soil and appearance, *Cleidune* (13th), *Sandunne* (1260), *Ston(y)don* (1300), *Muse-*, *Mosdun* (1205–10) (*v.* mēos, 'moss'), *Fuldon* (1225), 'foul,' *Caloudun* (1250), 'bare' from calu, *Fawdon* (1593), 'variegated' from fāg; (*c*) birds and animals found or kept there, *Hauke-* (1329), *Falke-* (1447), 'falcon' from OE *fealca*, *Horsedon* (1279), *Retherdune* (t. Hy 3), 'cattle' from hrȳðer; (*d*) crops and plants growing there, *Hei-* (1217), 'hay,' *Rey-* (1250), 'rye' from ryge, *Ban-* (1251), 'bean' from bēan, *Whaten-*, *Quatendon* (13th), 'wheat' from OE *hwæten*, 'overgrown with wheat,' *Thorndone* (1313); and occasionally, an owner, as in *Sexferes-* (1292) from *Seaxfær* or *Seaxferð*.

dyncge (n), 'manure, manured land,' has been noted in *Deenge* (1219), *le Denge*, *Dunge* (13th), *Dynge-*, *Dengefurlonge* (14th).

ēa, 'river, stream,' is fairly common. *le Hee* (1251), *le Lyttle Hee* (1326), *Westhe* (1251), *North Ee* (1438), *Asteree* (1377), 'more easterly stream.' We have reference to its bed in *Chiselhe* (1279) from ceosol, 'gravel' and *Depee* (1378), 'deep,' to animals in *Hauer ee* (13th), 'he-goat' from hæfer, and *Quyee* (1453), 'cow' from cū, and to persons in *Algareshe* (13th) from OE *Ælfgār*, *Flemingeshee* (1314). It occurs occasionally as *Ree* (1405, 1526), cf. Rhee *supra* 14. There is sometimes confusion with ēg *infra*. Rare in the 14th century, it is common from the 15th century onwards: (*lacum voc.*) *Blakene*(*e*), *Blakeneye* (1311–16), (*chanel called*) *the Maid's Eye* (1605). It survives in the forms *ea*, *eau*. The latter form is a pseudo-French spelling from Fr *eau*. Its local pronunciation is, however, usually [i·]. Cf. RN 140.

ēg, 'island, low-lying marshy land,' is less common than one would expect: *Eye* (1313), *Neweye* (1399), *Bradeneye* (1258), *Lytleye* (1277), *Watereye* (1423). We have reference to animals in *Schepeye* (1310) and *Horseye* (1526). *Estanig* (t. Ric 1) is OE *be ēastan ēge*, 'east of the low-lying land,' *lada de Culanig* (1221), *Culdinglake* (1251–77), 'stream by *Cūla*'s island' (*v.* lacu), and *Presseye* (14th), 'priest's low-lying land.' This sometimes occurs as *Ray* (1361), *Rey* (1424) from misdivision of the dat. *at ther eye*. In *le Forty* (1342) we have OE *forð-ēg*, 'projecting peninsula,' discussed *s.n.* Forty (PN Wo 202–4, PN Ess 23).

ende is fairly common, both in the sense 'end' and 'district.' Most frequent are compounds with *North-*, *South-*, *Est-* and *West-* (1251–1549), tūn, generally in the genitive, as in *Tounisende* (1388), 'end of the farm or hamlet,' *Brokesende* (1287), *Papesande* (13th), *Fen hende* (1428), *fene yende* (1511), *Croftesende* (1230), *Dammeshende* (1251), *le Damme ende* (1455). We may also note *le littleend* (1328), *Lodesend* (1221), *Tondrauishende* (1358) (i.e. 'farm-drove'), *Dounende* (1378), *Greneende* (1415), *Moreend* (1489) and, with a personal name, *Paynesend* (1437).

fær, 'passage' (cf. PN Ess 61, *s.n.* Laver), has been noted in *Dreyefar*' (1336) (*v.* dræg) and *Trun*(*c*)*kefar*(*e*) (1343–9), from ME *trunke*, 'trunk of a tree,' probably used in a sense similar to that of the East Anglian *trunk-way*, "a water-course through an arch of masonry, turned over a ditch before a gate, probably so called from the trunks of trees used for the same purpose in ancient and simpler times" (NED *s.v. trunk*, v. 18).

falod, 'fold,' is not common, but it is more frequent than in Northants, whilst in Hunts, Herts and Essex examples are lacking. It is distributed throughout the county, except that only one example, and that a difficult one, comes from the Isle of Ely: *Derefold* (1246) from dēor, *Vrefolde* (1234), *Wyfold* (1285), *Vppefold* (1510), two examples of *Stodfold(e)* (1180, 1300) from stōd, 'stud, herd of horses,' two of *Stotfolde* (1300, 1441) from stott, 'horse, bullock,' and three of *Pinne-, Pynfolde* (1357–1489), 'pinfold.' The Isle of Ely example is *Tuyfolde* (1251), which looks more like an example of the adjective *twīfald*, 'two-fold.'

fealh, 'ploughed land,' has been noted in *Lytlefalowe* (1363) in Leverington.

feld is very common indeed. Particularly numerous are compounds of *North-* (1221), *Sud-* (1200), *Est-* (1221), *West-* (1199), *Middel-* (1221), *Alde-* (1220), *Elde-* (1274), *Olde-* (1324) (cf. Offal *supra* 78), and a parish-name, e.g. *Knesworthefeld* (1315), with reference to the common fields. So too, no doubt, with *Utfeld* (1251), *Infeld* (1340), *Netherfeld* (1232), *Ouerfeld* (1365) and *Tone-, Tunfeld* (13th, 1469). Compounds with a personal name are not frequent, but we may note *Brihtnothesfeld* (13th), *Podemansfeld* (1305). Beneficial ownership is indicated by *Monekesfeld* (1307), *Prestisfelt* (14th), *Spetylffelde* (1336), belonging to some hospital, and *le Duchefeld* (1476), *Doucher ffeilde* (1667) to the Duchy of Lancaster. We have several boundary fields, *Merefeld* (13th) from (ge)mǣre, one *Grenefeld* (1290) and many examples of *Wyte-* (t. Hy 3), *Whyte-* (1374), *Qwite-* (1324), 'white.' Common too are compounds with dūn from 1277 and *Stoni-* from 1326. The first element is often descriptive of shape and size, as *Brade-* (1285), *Longe-* (1483), *Michele-* (1243), *Mikelfeld* (1285), *Litleuelde* (1319), or situation, *Lowe-* (1312), *Hyghe-* (1510), *Derne-* (13th) from dierne, 'hidden.' This is also often indicated by reference to some neighbouring feature, natural or artificial, in compounds with beorg, brōc, brycg, crouche, denu, dīc, hǣð, hlāw, holh, holmr, hyll, mersc, mōr, myln, wudu. We may note also *Cherchefeld* (1339), *Berifelde* (1393) belonging to the manor-house (*v.* burh), and *Reefelde* (1504) by a stream (cf. Rhee *supra* 14). Sometimes it is the nature of the soil or character of the surface which is indicated, *Cley-* (1262), *Chalk-* (1313), *Peet-* (13th), *Smethe-* (1432), 'smooth,' *Clene-* (1342), 'free of weeds' from clǣne, *Wilde-* (1301), *Medowe-* (1287), *Falow-* (1480), *Somer-* (1277), 'one used in summer,' *Honie-* (1504), 'sticky,' and *Bren-* (1450), 'burnt' from brende. Occasionally we have reference to animals, but these are usually late, and, except for *Bolefeld* (1319) and *Stotfelde* (16th) from stott, 'horse or bullock,' not those of the farm: *Dere-* (1251–1392), 'wild-animal,' from dēor, *Hart-* (1290), *Catte-* (1447), 'wild-cat,' and *Fox-* (1615); or to birds, *Sparwe-* (1280), *Cok-* (1298), *Fineche-* (1432) and *Crowfelde* (1490). Reference to specific crops is not common and, except for *Grasfeld* (1250), is late.

Most common is *Pesefeld* (1347), 'pease,' then four examples of *Whete-* (1389), *Qwhete-* (1443), 'wheat,' and of *Barley-* (1428), three of *Stubbil-* (1426) and one of *Benefeld* (1315), 'bean.' We may also note *Stocfelde* (1250), *Truhfelde* (1300), 'trough' from **trog**, *Herberwhefeld* (1406) from *hereberg*, 'shelter,' *Dedcherlfeld* (1339). Cf. Street Way *supra* 30. *Berdefelde* (956 (12th)) in Stapleford would seem to be identical with Bardfield (PN Ess 504–5), but it is difficult to know just how to interpret it, especially as we do not know its site. Ekwall (*Studies*[2] 163–4) would associate it with a lost OE **(ge)byrd*, 'border, edge,' possibly 'by a stream.'

fenn is very common. In addition to the frequent Sedge, Turf, Mow and Cow Fen *supra* 204, 247, 227, 173, named from the products secured or the animals kept there, we have *Rushfenne* (1634), *Oxefen* (1328), *Hoggefenne* (1489) and *Bullockes Fenne* (1564), and also reference to birds in *Snyt(e)fen* (1350), 'snipe,' and *Purfenne* (1540) from OE *pūr*, 'bittern.' We may note also *Morefen* (1364), *Foulefen* (1343) from *fūl*, 'foul' or **fugol**, 'wild-fowl,' *Strodefen* (1227) from **strōd**, 'marshy land covered with brush-wood,' and *Hardefen* (1279), probably because less liable to flooding than others near. *Sokemannyfen* (1336) in Isleham contains ME *sokeman*, 'a free peasant owing suit of court.' Occasionally we find compounds with a personal name as in *Taberys-fen* (1390), *Sayesfen* (1453). Note *Fanfurlong* (1274) in Wendy, (14th) in Litlington, with ME *fan* for **fen**. *v*. Introd. xxxiii–iv.

fēorðung, 'fourth part,' is rare: *le Ferthingges* (1312), *Farthyng* (1514), *Oldeferþing* (13th). In *Ferthingfeld* (1302), *Ferþingplot* (1334) and four compounds of **hyll**, *Ferthinghil* (1319–1494) we may have reference to the rent or to the size.

flegge, ME (n), 'flag, marshy place overgrown with flags' (*v*. Flegcroft *supra* 260), is found in *Flegele* (1240), *Flegges* (1260), *Flegheye* (1356) and *Fleghangelles* (t. Eliz), probably a compound of **anger**.

flēot, 'creek, inlet,' is very rare: *Welmanysflete* (1438), *le Fluth* (1503).

ford is less frequent than one would expect. We have the usual common descriptive elements as *Lange-* (1251), *Alde-* (1246), *Stan-* (1253), etc., with an occasional personal name, *Wulmerford* (1389) from OE *Wulfmær*. *Wluefford* (1221) may be 'wolves' ford.' *Bereford* (1251) was probably one which would carry a good load of corn, OE *bere*, 'barley,' being used generically. Cf. Barford (PN BedsHu 50–2). *Lacheford* (1320) and *Letchfurth* (1553) are from **lache**, **leche**, 'slow, sluggish stream.' *Ruggeford* (1232) was probably frequented by woodcock (OE **hrucge*). *v*. Studies[2] 88 ff.

fox-hol is fairly common, often in the plural, from 1264 (*Foxholl*) and 1277 (*Foxholes*). The second element is sometimes confused with **hyll**, e.g. *Foxholes* (1267), *Foxhell* (1354), *Foxhyllys* (1492) in Melbourn, *Foxhole* (1228), *Foxhell* (1466), *Foxall* (1596) in Cottenham.

furh (n), 'furrow, ditch,' is not very common. We have several examples of *Watrefurches* (13th), *Waterfuruis* (1248), *Waterforo(w)es*

(1408, 1500), two of *Holefurghes* (1383), three of *Rennendeforw* (1300) and one of *Rennyngforgh* (1383), 'running.' *v.* Introd. xxxvii. We may also note *Sunderlongfurht* (13th).

furlang as the name of a division of the common field is very frequent, particularly in compounds with lang, sceort and middel. Note also *Tunforlong* (1251) (*v.* tūn), *Mane-* (1251), 'common' from (ge)mǣne, *Syxfurlong* (1302) and *Seueneforlong* (1319). Situation is indicated in *Ouere-* (1251), *Nether-* (1509), *Mare-*, *Mere-* (13th) on the boundary ((ge)mǣre), *Hangyng-* (1467) on a slope, *Crosse-* (1439), *Castel-* (14th), *Quarre-* (1402), *Drof-* (1431), 'drove,' *Dam-* (1389), and in compounds with brōc, brycg, dīc, feld, fenn, (*Fen-* 1260, *Fan-* 14th), grāf(a), pytt, stocc, wielle, wudu. For *Prefurlong* (1422) *v.* prey *infra* 341. The first element is sometimes descriptive, *Brad-* (1285), *Brochene-* (1251), *Suuort-* (13th) from OE *sweart*, 'black, dark,' *Brende-* (1397), 'burnt,' or has reference to the soil, *Sand-* (13th), *Cley-* (1432), *More-* (1342), *Malme-* (1432) from ME *malm*, 'light, loamy soil,' *Dynge-*, *Denge-* (14th) from dyncge, 'manure,' *Byttersalt-* (1503) and occasionally, to living things, *Snyte-* (1274), 'snipe,' *Snake-* (1292), *Sneyly-* (14th). The reference is at times to the crops grown, *Ruy-* (1248), 'rye' from ryge, *Wete-* (1513), 'wheat,' *Flex-* (1575), *Pese-* (1241), 'pease,' or to other plants, *Thorn-* (1319), *Russh-* (1473), *Rishe-* (1483), *Brer-* (13th), 'briar,' *Brembil-* (1480) and *Carlock-* (1591), 'charlock.' *Milkforlong* (1312) is uncertain. *Radelingesforlong* (1202) contains a compound of rēad and hlinc. It is very doubtful if compounds with a personal name are found.

fyrhþ(e), 'wood, wooded country,' is rare. Only three certain examples have been noted: *le Frithe* (1318) in West Wickham, *le Freth* (1319) in West Wratting and *the Frith* (1612) in Barrington. *Le Fryth* (1302) in Doddington is described as a fishery (*piscaria*), whilst in Wicken we have a 'marsh called *Jankynesfreth*' (1449). The element is common in the fens where it seems to have denoted fenland covered with brushwood (cf. Frith Fen *supra* 179). *Duditunefrith* (1221) in Doddington was six leagues across from Wimblington to Willey in Chatteris.

gærs, græs is rare. It has been noted in *Horsegers* (1225), *Radegres* (1221), 'red,' *Clauergers* (1232), 'clover,' *Dedegresslade* (1473) (*v.* slæd) and *Broadgrasse* (1600). Note also *le Landgres*, *-gerse* (1398).

gafeluc (n), probably a diminutive of OE *gafel*, *geafel*, 'fork' (the etymology is difficult, *v.* NED *s.v.* gavelock), is found in *Gauelockes* (1575) in Over and in *Gullocks* and *Little Gallocks* (1806) in Fulbourn. Its exact topographical application in these names is uncertain.

galle, ME (n), 'wet place,' occurs in *le Watergalle* (1312). It survives in the form gall, gaul, gald, gault.

gang (n), 'road, track' (cf. PN ERY 215, 323), has been noted in *Watergong* (1282), 'water passage,' in *Ganghulle* (1319), cf. Ganghill (PN Sr 151), and in *the pitanzers Botesgonge* (1570), i.e. 'boat-passage' from OE *bāt*. This was a technical term in Ely (cf. *one botesgonge* ib.), apparently meaning the right to sail a boat on a stream. Once we find a substitution of gata for gang, (*piscaria voc.*) *le Botesgate* (1539).

gannok, ME (n), is found in *Gannock* (1344), later *Cannokfeld, -lane* (1372) in Dullingham and in *Gannock Meadow* and *Gammock*. The interpretation of this element, found also in Ganwick Corner (PN Mx 77), Gannock in Sandon and Gannock in Reed (PN Herts 164, 161), is difficult. In the earlier volumes of the Survey (*loc. cit.*) the name was interpreted as being derived from OE *gamen-āc*, 'sports oak,' but Dr Angus McIntosh (RES xvi, 54 ff.) has shown that there is good ground for believing in the existence of a ME *gannok*, 'fortified place' or the like, an adaptation of the Medieval Latin form *Gannoc* of the name of the famous Welsh castle of Deganwy. If we could identify the sites of the Cambridgeshire place-names, we could be more definite. The form *Gammock* is late, and the only example which contains an *m*, suggestive of the old interpretation as *gamen-āc*.

gapp, ME (n), is very rare. *Kechemeyesgapp'* (1411).

gāra, 'triangular piece of land,' is fairly common. In the plural it occurs as *le Goris* from 1279 and *le Goren* from 1323. Compounds are either descriptive or possessive: *Tail-* (1260) from its shape, *Stony-* (1319), *Sneyl-* (1427), *Thorni-* (1202), *Wlfrunesgores* (1304), *Bacheleresgore* (1319), *Potterysgoryn* (1446). *Gyldyngore* (1298) and *Gyldengore* (1438) from OE *gylden*, 'golden-coloured.'

gardin, ME (n), is very rare. *Bretonesgardyn* (1360), *Shopgardeyn* (1478).

gata, ON 'road,' is common in the north of the Isle of Ely. Clear examples are *Northgate (communem viam)* (1343, 1529), *Mousgate* (1398), described as *drauam* (v. drāf), *Crossegate* (1438), a highway, and *viam voc. le Kirkgate* (1486) in Leverington, identical with *Kyrkstrete* (1393); *Mersgate* (1318) and *Mareysgate* (1368) probably mean 'road to the marsh' from OE *mersc* and ME *marais* respectively, *Seagate* (1579) in Tydd led to the sea, whilst two examples of *Hol(e)gate* (1228, 1337) probably correspond to the common *Hol(e)way supra* 24. Cf. also *Bradgate* (13th), *Nether gate* (1356), *Madwegate* (1303) and *Medowgatelane* (1587). *Vtgatefeld* (1249) was probably the field by the road leading out of the parish. *Chapelgate* (1391) and *Chirchegate* (1433) are ambiguous. They probably refer to the roads leading to the chapel and church respectively, but they may refer to gates, cf. *Chapelзate* (1396). It is very difficult to distinguish names containing ON gata from those containing OE geat, 'gate,' which in ME instead of the normal *yate* form usually shows a development to *gate* under the influence of the OE plural forms *gatu, gata, gatum*.

geat is certainly found in *Hachegate* (1366) from hæcc, *Neuhousзate* (1397), *Wellhousyate* (1449), *Hallegate* (1399) and probably in *Wodegate* (1251) and *Berygate* (1319) (v. burh). In West Wratting we find *Rugh(e)gate* (1234), *Denegate* (1250), *Crossegate* (1319) and *Ladigate*

(1443). Except, possibly, for the last, 'road' is here a better meaning than 'gate.' Note too the variation in the second element in *Bourstalleweye* and *Burtallegate* (1319) in the same parish. *le Botesgate* (1540) in Over is described as a fishery and can hardly be a 'gate.' Compounds of *gate* and a personal name are entirely ambiguous, such as *Aylbernesgate* (13th), *Geddyngsgate* (1400).

geard and **gierd** (n). It is usually very difficult to distinguish names containing **geard**, 'enclosure,' from those containing **gierd**, 'area of land varying in extent, usually 30 acres and commonly taken as a fourth of a hide,' for both are represented by *yerd(e)* in ME. It is clear that we have the latter in *Halfyerdecroft* (1303), *Halfʒerdelyngcroft* (1335) and *Yerdelonde* (1500). We probably have the former in *le Coleyerd* (1346), 'enclosure where cole or kale grows,' *Halleyerd* (1374), *Duffhousyerd* (1433) (*v.* dufhous), *le teynter yard* (1570) (cf. *supra* 319). Completely ambiguous are *le Neweyerdes* (1298), *la Contesseyerd* (1370), *le personeseyerd* (1391), *Melleriszerd* (1408) and (with personal names) *Geddyngesyerd* (1338), *Bettisyerd* (1395).

gole, ME (n), 'stream, channel, ditch, sluice,' is late but fairly common, as in *le Gole* (1395), *the gowlle* (1542), *Fittongole* (1343), *Barburisgole* (15th), *Semansgole* (1528). Cf. also *sluse or goole* (1423 *SewersC*), *atte Gole* (1308 *Ct*) (in Whaplode, L). It is probably identical with *gool*, still used in dialect (Y, L, Cu, Sx) in the senses 'whirlpool, ditch, wooden drainpipe' and related to *gull* used in Nth, Db, Herts, Mx, Sx of a breach or hole made by the force of a torrent, a natural watercourse, and in the Isle of Ely of a 'break in a bank,' cf. "mending the *gulls* in the bank" (1662 Fen), "*gulls* to be made before the snow goes away" (1670 *FenL*). Ekwall (DEPN *s.n.*) suggests that Goole (Y) which is *Gowle* in 1553 (PN SWY 148) may be identical with *gulla...in Merskland* in the Coucher Book of Selby (ii, 49). In PN La 53 he is probably right in associating these words with Swedish *göl*, 'pond,' MHG *gülle*, 'pool,' MLG *gole*, 'marsh,' EFrisian *göle*, *göl*, 'hole, pool,' MDu *gulle*, 'palus, vorago, gurges.' They survive in modern names in the forms *gool*, *gull*. In Somerset and Devon *goole* appears as *goyle*, *goil*. Cf. Naplease Goyle (PN D 599).

gote, ME (n), 'water channel,' also used of a sluice, is fairly common in the north of the Isle of Ely. Cf. PN NRY 327. *le Stathegote* (1320) had a staithe or landing-place, *Kirkegote* (1320) was near the church. Note also *Neugote* (1399) and a few compounds with personal or place-names, *Vykorisgote* (1368), *Loundesgote* (1376), *Helgays gote* (1570) (i.e. Hilgay (Nf)). Other examples from Lincolnshire are *attegote* (1316 Fleet) in Fleet, *le Newegote*, *le Thurgote*, *le Crossegote* in Surfleet, *le Stangote* in Gosberton, *Wygtoftgote* in Wigtoft, *Wystardegote* in Sutterton (1361 Works), *Gotehouselands* (1393 Cl) in Winthorpe and *le gote voc.* (*le*) *Walegote* (1396 Works) in Alford.

grāf(a), 'grove, copse,' is not common and is late: *Callesgrove* (1251), *Templegrove* (1330), *Frithgrove* (1361), *Welugrove* (1446) (i.e 'willow'), *Cherchegrove* (1501), *Asshegrove* (1544). This element is difficult to distinguish from **græfe** with the same meaning, which itself is liable to confusion with **græf**, 'pit,' 'trench.' **grāf** and **græfe** have certainly been confused in The Grove *supra* 241. From **græfe** we certainly have *Conygreaves* (1320), 'rabbit wood,' whilst *Depegrave* (1235), *le Graves* (1540) and *Slogravis* (1517), 'slough-pits,' are almost certainly from **græf**. Doubtful are *Lamberdesgrave* (1270) and *Chyldes-grave* (1395).

*****graft**, ME (n), 'a ditch, moat,' cf. OE *grafan*, 'to dig.' This has been noted in *Southgraft(e)(feld)* 1438 *Sewers*, 1444–1587 *Ct* (Tydd). Cf. Graft Drain in Pinchbeck (L), *Old graft* 1587 *Sewers*, *fenne gate grafte* t. Ed 1 *Rental*, Reedy Graft Drain (L), *Redygraft* 1465 *AD* vi, 1488 *Ct*, (*sewera de*) *Scategraft* 1295 *Cole* xliii in Gosberton (L), and *Greddikgraft* n.d. ib. (L). The word *graft* is recorded in NED *s.n.* *graft* sb.[2] as adapted from MDu *graft* and the examples given all have reference to foreign ditches and moats. It would seem from the examples given above that the word had at an earlier date also arisen independently in English.

grēne, ME is fairly common from 1250 (*Lagrene*). We may note *Kyngesgrene* (1298), *le Comungrene* (1323), *Wodehusgrene* (1311), *Gosegrene* (t. Hy 6) and a number of compounds with a personal name such as *Huntesgrene* (1250).

grund occurs twice compounded with **stān** (*Stangrunde* 1250) (cf. Stanground, PN BedsHu 199), once with **stǣnig, stānig** (*Stonigrund* 1290), in *Hardegrund* (1274) and in two examples of *Saffrongrounde* (1570, 1612). Note also *Hempen Grounde* (1539), *Fodderyng Grounde* (1550). *Ground* is very common in modern field-names, *Saffron, Clover, Whinney* (i.e. 'gorse'), *Lordship, Play Ground*, etc.

hæcc, 'gate,' is very rare and late. *le Hacche* (1424), *Cattishache* (1503).

(ge)hæg, 'enclosure,' is fairly common. *Barnhey* (1205) was by a barn, *Frithhey* (1253) a woodland enclosure, from **fyrhðe**, *Scephey* (1221) one for sheep, and *Foxhey* (1251) frequented by foxes. *Templehay* (1250) in Grantchester belonged to the Knights Templar and *Abbotteshegh* (1391) in Dry Drayton to the Abbot of Crowland.

hǣð, 'heath,' is rare: *le Heth* (14th), *Frithheth* (1279), *Heldeheth* (1279) from **eald**, 'old.' ME *hethe* is a common form of **hȳð**, 'hithe,' but these examples are from Steeple Morden, Ashley, Linton and Woodditton, where there can be no question of a landing-place.

haga, 'enclosure,' is very rare. *Berchawe* (1387), probably from **beorc**, 'birch-tree.' It survives in *Lock Hawe*.

halke, ME (n) is fairly frequent and denotes a nook or corner. It is perhaps a diminutive of OE **healh**. Cf. *le Halc, Halk* (1228), *le Halke* (1315, 1397), *Bruneshalk* (13th), *Madehalk* (1281) (from **mǣd**), *le Weyehalke* (1349), and cf. also Hawkwood (PN Ess 20).

hām and **hamm** are always difficult to distinguish. Examples are not common. *le Hamme* and *Ham* (1235, 1292) are derived from *hamm*, but compounds like *Totesham* (1271) and *Hambroke* (1369) are entirely ambiguous.

hāmsteall, 'farm-house and adjacent buildings,' is rare: *le Hamstell* (1458), *Suoneshamstal* (1251) that of the *swān* or peasant, *le hyhamstal* (1310), 'high,' and *Pulhameshamstall* (1385). It survives as *homestall*.

hassuc, 'coarse grass,' is rare. *Hassok* (c. 1150), *le Hassokis* (1343), *Blakehassokes* (1251).

haugr, ON 'barrow, hill,' is difficult to distinguish from hōh, 'hill, spur.' We probably have this Scandinavian word in *Tweynowes* (1526) in Meldreth, *Tremhowe* (13th), *Fremhoue*, *Thremhou* (14th) in Chippenham, groups of two and three barrows respectively, in *Nynehoues* (1319) in Newton, possibly the nine barrows on Thriplow Heath (Fox 329), *Konewesho* (1308), *Conegeshou* (1316) in Duxford, from ON *konungr*, 'king,' and *Hosmundeshou* (13th) in Bourn, from ON *Āsmundr*.

hēafod, 'head,' is used of the top of a strip of land. It is very common in the plural, rarely in the form *hauedes*, usually as *haveden*, with sporadic *heveden*, later as *hafden*, *hefden*, *hadon* or *hayden* and *haven*. It is compounded with descriptive elements in *Lang-* (1388), *Middel-* (1387), *Hey-* (1250). Note also *Highhaveden* (1278), *Gyldenhaveden* (1448), *Michelhadon* (1479). It has reference to the soil or position in *Brachehauedes* (1203) from **bræc**, *Wateryhavedenes* (1300), *Stonehaven* (1610), *Holleheueden* (1319) from **holh**, 'hollow,' *Madeheueden* (1338), *Meade heven* (1531), 'meadow,' *Dounehafdes* (1404), *Broke-* (1287), *Mores-* (1349), *Buttishaveden* (1439), *Gallowes-*, *Melneshaveden* (1349), *Wikhavedyn* (1331), *Stapelesheueden* (1200), or has reference to a neighbouring place or the parish, *Hardhulle-*, *Shelfordhaveden* (13th). We have reference to crops, plants, animals, birds, etc. in *Corn-* (1349), *Reed-* (1349), *Elder-* (1467), *Stot-* (1294), *Schepes-* (1315) and *Larke-haveden* (1475), and to the owner or cultivator in *Wlfsis-* (1337), from OE *Wulfsige*, *Wolmerehauedyn* (1395) from OE *Wulfmǣr*, *Babbinges-* (13th), *Bassetteshaveden* (t. Ed 1). Note also *Theueshaueden* (1432), *Lytlbushehaven* (1589). Only two examples come from the Isle of Ely, both in Sutton. This element survives in *Ditch Haden*, *Mill Hadin* and *Sweeting Tree Haden*. In *Herberdhouedlond* (13th) in Chatteris, we have the corresponding ON hǫfuð, as also perhaps in *Brokhoden* (1445) in Thriplow. In the singular we probably have this technical sense in *Stabelesaued* (1250), *Gyldonhed* (1510), *Smewynisheued* (1316) and *Halfhedd acre* (1569). It denotes 'head, commencing point' or 'source' in *Apewellesheved* (1304), *Blakwelleheued* (1319), *Wellehed* (1379), *Rigge-* (1211), *Wode-* (1244), *Fennesheued* (1338).

hēafod-land (n), a fuller name for such head-strips, is frequent, e.g. *Hauedland*, *Heuedlond* (13th), *Hedland* (1409), *Hadelonde* (t. Hy 7). Most compounds contain a personal name, *Leflinghauetlond* (1198), *Snarries-* (1210), *Ailfledeshauedlond* (13th) from the OE woman's name *Æðelflǣd*, *Oseualdes-* (1251), *Aschwiesheuedland* (13th) from OE

Æscwīg, Mobbs headland (1627). Note also *yᵉ lordschephadelond* (1496), and compounds with *Cley-* (13th), *Larke-* (1309), *Culuer-* (14th) from culfre, 'pigeon, dove,' *Crouch-* (1376). *Quarellyshavedlond* (15th) was by a quarry (ME *quarelle*).

healh is fairly common. It is noteworthy that, as in Northants, we have some forms derived from the nominative: *Littlehalgh* (1419), *Halugh* (1319), *Halw* (1319), *Halu* (1341), *Halowe* (1395), *Westhalf* (1225), *le Hafe* (1294). Cf. Old Halves *supra* 249. The more usual dative form is found in *Northale* (1202), *Sidehal'* (1221) from sīd, 'broad,' *Marishale* (1225) from ME *mareis*, 'marsh,' *Cattishale* (1344), *Renghale* (1387), 'circular' from hring, *Shephale* (t. Hy 7), 'sheep,' and in two with personal names, *Admarshale* (1225) from OE *Ēadmǣr* and *Dagenhale* (1279) from OE *Dæcca*. The plural is found in *Peshales* (1230), *Litlehales* (1349) and *Burwellehales* (1397).

heall is fairly common, usually compounded with *Up-*, *Nether-*, *Over-* or *New-*, and also with the name of the owner, *Beauchampishalle* (1388). We may note *le Seghalle* (1292) and *Coppydhalle* (1440), *Copt Hall* (1614), 'peaked,' found frequently elsewhere.

hēap, 'heap,' has been noted in *Sithepes* (13th) from OE *scite*, 'dung,' and *le Cleyhepe* (1476).

hearpe (n), 'harp,' used of a harp-shaped field, has been noted in *le harpe* (1395). In 1405, in Upwell, it is used of a fishery. It survives in *The Harp, Harp Close*.

hecg, 'hedge,' is found occasionally as *Hegge* (1287), *Longhege* (1523), *Shortehegge* (1473). It is usually compounded with a personal name denoting the owner, *Lefricheshegg* (1200) from OE *Lēofric*, *Wlstonhegge* (1280) from OE *Wulfstān*, *Pekkeresheg(ge)* (13th). *Wardhege* (1236) was a 'protection' hedge, from OE *weard*. *Irchuneshegge* (1207) was one where hedgehogs were numerous (ME *urchon*).

hiche, ME (n). *Litil Hiche* (1404) is probably an early example of *hitch*, 'enclosure of hurdles in which sheep were penned,' cf. PN Wa 335.

hīd, 'hide of land,' is very rare. *Hyde* (1249, 1251), two examples with a personal name, *Rumpes-, Dodes-* (1236); and *Wereslehide* (1234) in Gamlingay on the borders of Waresley (Hu).

hlaða, ON 'barn,' is found in *Westlathe* (1368) and *Castellathe* (1386) in Wisbech and in *Appellathe* (1320) in Upwell.

hlāw is fairly common both in the sense of 'hill' and 'barrow.' *Anlowe* (15th) may be either a solitary hill or a single barrow, but *Toulow* (13th), three examples of *þre(me)lowe* (13th), *Trimelowe* (14th) and *Thrymlowe* (1500), *Fourlowen* (14th) and *Fiflawe* (1279) have, no doubt, reference to groups of barrows. *Lychlowe* (13th) (OE *līc*, 'body') was, presumably, a barrow in Foxton, cf. Litchborough (PN Nth 25–6), whilst *Wenlowe* (1251) in Balsham, no doubt, was like a 'wen' on the ground, cf. Wanborough (PN W 283–4). *Harlowe* (1483) in Barton is 'army-hill,' cf. Harlow (PN Ess 36); *Cristemannelowe*

with *Cristenerydunelowe* (13th) in Steeple Morden is 'christians' hill.'
The sense 'hill' is also probably found in *Chalclouue* (13th), *Stonloue*
(1310), *Stanlowe* (1332), *Rogelowe* (1229), *Rue-* (13th), *Roulowe* (1319),
'rough' (*v.* rūh), *Schytlowe* (1274) (OE *scite*, 'dung'), *Boldynglowe*
(1287) (ME *bolling*, 'pollarded tree,' cf. Bolding Hatch, PN Ess 264),
Hawekelowe (1439), *Dunekeslawe* (1241) (ME *dunoke*, 'hedge-sparrow,'
carrying back this word some 230 years), *Cattelow* (1483), *Sepelowe*
(1210), 'sheep,' *Herdlowe* (1395). We may note also *Attewesternelowe*
(1267), *Bestynglowe* (14th), perhaps OE *be ēastan hlāwe* (cf. Beesons
supra 239), *Crop(pe)lowe* (1302, 1312), either OE *cropp*, 'sprout,
bunch' or ON *kroppr*, 'hump' (cf. Cropwell, earlier *Crophill*, PN Nt
234–5). *Brokenelowe* (1250) was perhaps a ravaged barrow. Occasionally the first element is a personal name as in *Wrabelowe* (13th)
from **Wrab(b)a* (cf. Wrabness, PN Ess 358), *Adyeleuelowe* (1276)
from OE *Æðelgiefu* (f).

hlinc is occasionally found as in *Lynches* (1311), *Lynch* (1374),
Shortlynges (1401). It survives as *Link*, *Links* and *Linches*.

hlӯp(e), 'leap, leaping place,' is found in March, Sutton and
Chatteris in the special sense *Fyshynglepys* (1441), as in *Horeldescroft-*,
Newe-, *Nordonelepes* (1240), *Vtlep* (1277).

hōc, 'hook,' used of a place at a sharp bend of a stream or of a
projecting spit of land, is rare: *le Hoke* (1287), *Brodhok* (1250), *Smale-
hokes* (1290), 'narrow' from smæl, *Blak-*, *Balkehook* (1404).

hōh, 'hill, spur,' is fairly common, but is difficult to distinguish
from haugr. It is found independently in *Howe* (1250), *Ho* and *Hoo*
(1280) and compounded with lang, middel, neoðera, ufera, micel,
grēne. The first element sometimes has reference (*a*) to the site or
soil, *Stan-* (1285), *Calu-* (1319), 'bare,' *Slape-*, *Slepe-* (1439–77) from
slæp, 'slippery place,' *Brec-* (1251) from bræc, *Hyrst-* (1221) from
hyrst, *Stokyng-* (1251) from stocking, *Water-* (13th), *Fen-* (14th),
Byneþenlosho (1251) from hlōse, 'pig-stye,' (*b*) to animals, *Shepe-*
(1364), *Stottebukes-* (1236), *Swynes-* (1250), *Hart-* (1285), *Cattes-*
(1285), (*c*) to birds, *Brid-* (14th), *Hauekes-* (1202), *Putokes-* (1251),
'kite,' *Arn-* (1323) from earn, 'eagle,' (*d*) to trees, plants, *Elren-* (1221),
i.e. ellern, 'elder,' *Farn-* (1320), *Asche-* (1315), or to crops, *Pesehowe*
(1367), and (*e*) to occupier or owner, *le Cotsetleshoue* (1309) from OE
cotsetla, 'cottager,' *Dudenho* (1199). Note *Athelingesho* (1260) from
OE æðeling, 'prince,' *Tunhoue* (1250) from tūn, *Seyntmaryhoue* (1407)
in Ely, which was probably part of the endowment of St Mary's
Church, and *Landmarehowe* (1340) from OE *landgemǣre*, 'boundary,'
which had developed to *Lylmerhowe* by 1517. *Bekenhowe* (1449) was
probably used for purposes of signalling. More than half the examples
come from the Isle of Ely and parishes with much fenland, so that
hōh must have often been used of a very low spur of land.

holh, 'hollow,' is found in *Hole* (1228), *Presteshol* (1250), *Langhole*
(1316), *Skyppynghole* (1483), *Beggershole* (1662), *Joan Sadds hole*

(1669) and, in the plural, *Blacholes* (1297), *Catesholes* (1324), *Snakes-holes* (1319). The nominative is found as *le Holwe* (1279), *the Holough* (1544). This survives in Swarm Haugh *supra* 245, earlier *-hoof, -hoove,* and in modern field-names as *Hove* and *Hoof.* Cf. *Cranehooffe* (1638), *Longhoofe* (1694) and Greenhalgh (PN La 154, 164), DB *Greneholf.* Cf. also healh *supra* 330.

holmr, 'marsh meadow,' is fairly common throughout the county, alone (*Holm* 1332 on), occasionally in the characteristic Danish form *Hulm(o)* (1279), and in various compounds. Descriptive are *Michel-* (1388), *Litleholm* (1319), *Brod-* (1395), *Vuer-* (13th), 'upper,' *Neu-* (1277), *Wrong-* (1316), 'crooked' (*v.* wrang), *Lang-* (1330), *Qwyte-* (1411), 'white.' We have reference to birds and animals in *Gosholm* (1232), *Coltholmes* (1499), *Cuholm* (1279), *Calf-* (13th), *Hare-* (1422) and to vegetation and crops in *Ruisse-* (1251), *Rissh-* (1342) (*v.* rysc), *Whete-* (1402), *Ry-* (1395). The owner or occupier's name is sometimes given, as in *Euermundesholm* (1251), *Stywardes-* (1319), *Martins-* (1389), *le Prystesholme* (14th). *Crysten'holme* (1544) belonged to Denny Abbey and *Seynt Marie Holme* (1287) was part of some ecclesiastical endowment. Occasionally there has been confusion between *-hom* or *-ham* and *-holm* as in *Calfholm* (13th), *Calfham* (14th); *Lang(e)holm(e)* (1319), *Langehom* (1319), *Langham* (1480). *Hogsholm* (1725) in Linton is *Hoggesham* (1470).

holt, 'wood,' is fairly common, but apart from four examples in Brinkley (*Litleholt* 1261), Trumpington (*Drye Holte, Duffield Holte* 1629) and Linton (*Museholte* 1279), described as a *viridarium,* where it probably has its usual meaning, all our examples come either from the Isle of Ely or parishes with much marsh, and here it is probably used, as in the common *osier-holt* (*v.* EDD and NED), of a bed or a plantation of small trees, as in *Ash Holte* (1558), *Alderholt* (1478) and *Osyerholte* (1539). It was probably extended to other marshy ground covered with plants as, e.g., in two examples of *Popilholt* (1347, 1409), probably from ME *popylle,* 'lollium' (Wright, *Voc.* i, 234), perhaps used of red darnel or ryegrass (NED *s.v. popple* sb.²), and *Hassokholte* (1454) from hassuc, 'coarse grass.' Several late examples are found with a personal name, *Spygotesholt* (1452) from John *Pygot* (1434), *Ploughwrytesholt* (1553), described as *ortum* or *pomarium,* whilst *Seynt Jonys Holt* (1464) and *Jesus Holte* (1577) were in ecclesiastical ownership.

horn has been noted in *le Horn* (1301).

hūs. We may note *Kelnehus* (1279), carrying back that word some 130 years, *Cheshous* (1319), *Schepehous* (1319), bridging the gulf between the OE references (c. 1000) and the earliest reference (1410) in NED and *Fysshous* (1420).

hyll is very common. Descriptive attributes are *Wyte-* (1247), *Blac-* (1432), *Grene-* (13th), *Red-* (1298), *Ded-* (1195), *Gore-* (1230), 'muddy' from gor, *Kallew-* (1260), 'bare' from calu, *Faw-* (1522), 'variegated' from fāg, *Rowe-* (1279), 'rough' from rūh, *Hongyr-* (1297) with poor soil, *Hangyng-* (1432), 'sloping,' *Copped-* (1379), 'peaked,' *Cnop-* (1376) possibly from ME *knopp(e)*, 'knob.' We have reference to soil in *Ston-* (1211), *Clai-* (13th), *Chalc-* (1300), *Sand-* (1340); to what grows there in *Pesehel* (c. 1250), *Bane-* (1302), 'beans,' *Gras-* (13th), *Brinbel-* (1250), 'brambles,' *Charlic-* (1300), 'charlock,' *Fern-* (1306), *Dock-* (1347), *Sno(w)re-* (1502–10), 'brushwood,' cf. Snower Hill (PN Sr 284); to animals, *Hauer-* (1228) from OE *hæfer*, 'he-goat,' *Co-* (1340), 'cow,' *Riþris-* (13th), 'cattle' from hrȳðer, *Tag-* (1527), 'teg, sheep,' *Houndes-* (1319), *Fox-* (1206); to birds, *Sug-* (t. Hy 3) from OE *sucge*, 'hedge-sparrow,' *Arn-* (1321), 'eagle' from OE *earn*, *Crow-* (1362), *Puttokes-* (1432), 'kite.' *Waytehil* (1290) was a look-out hill, *Chestre hil* (1395) in Knapwell probably takes its name from the moated mounds found there (cf. Fox 194), whilst *Gospel Hill* (1626) in Steeple Morden must have been on the parish boundary where the gospel was read during the beating of the parish bounds. We may note also *Galwhelle* (1336), *Wyndmullehill* (1372), *le Marcathil* (1429), *Aldermannehyl* (13th) and *Presteshil* (1250). Compounds with a personal name are usually late. Exceptions are *Dudewenehel* (1185) and *Wrenthelle* (12th), which seems to contain the OE **Wrenta* postulated by Ekwall (DEPN) for Wrentham (Sf) and Wrentnall (Sa). Note also *Stepemanneshil* (1312) in Eversden which may contain a personal name deriving from OE *stēap*, 'of high courage, noble' (cf. NED *s.v.* steep sb.[2], A.1.b).

hylte (n), 'wooded-place' (*v.* PN Sx xlv, PN D 400, *s.n.* Emlett), is found in *Fulhilt* (1226) from fūl, 'foul, dirty,' and *Huuerehilte* (1280), 'upper.'

hyrne, 'corner,' is fairly common, usually compounded with a personal name or another place-name: *Edwoldesheyrne* (13th), *Greggys-hirne* (1332), *Wodegateherne* (13th). Otherwise the first element is descriptive of its nature or position, *Sideherne* (1402), 'wide' from sīd, *Hayherne* (1337) from (ge)hæg. *Schipehirne* (13th), *Shephern* (1471) fed sheep. *Galweherne* (1377) was the corner where the gallows was situated.

hyrst, 'hillock, copse,' is not common. We may note *Bradherst* (1251), *Stonihyrst* (1251), *Thornhurst* (1398). *Bradherst* developed to *Brodest* (1495), cf. *supra* 289–90.

hȳð, 'landing-place,' is found as *Hethe* (1287), *Hythe* (1300), *Hive* (1670), cf. Witcham Hive *supra* 245, *Nowhethe* (1405), i.e. 'new.' *Lechehithe* (13th) was on a *leche* or stream, *Raueneshethe* (1316) was probably owned by one *Hræfn*, *Crowchehithe* (1575) was near a cross. It survives as *hithe* or *hive*.

ing. A noteworthy feature of minor names is the number of compounds of ing, particularly in the Isle of Ely. They are especially frequent in Upwell and some, at least, are stream-names. Occasionally they appear in a plural form, but can scarcely be regarded as **ingas-**

compounds. The names are usually very difficult of interpretation, partly no doubt because of their age, but partly also because we have not sufficient forms and are not able to locate the objects or sites to which they have reference. It is in this way impossible to hazard any satisfactory guess at the interpretation of such names as *Chisting* (t. John), *Sywinge* (13th), *Waddeng*, *Wadding* (1200–21), *Pudeleswaing* (t. Hy 3), *Burnigwere*, *Burringwere*, *Burningeswere* and *Camering*, *Kamerding*, *Kameredig* (1086), later *Kambirdenche* (1428), names of fisheries in InqEl, *Weuinge*, *Wewinge* (t. John), *Merveling* (t. Ric 1), *Deneking*, *Dineking* (1200, 1221). *Bollinges* (1251) may possibly be identical with Bowling (PN SWY 80), DB *Bollinc*, and be a derivative of *bolla*, 'bowl,' used of a hollow (cf. DEPN), but there is no certainty. *le Sthithing* (1308) may possibly be from OE *stiþe*, 'lamb's cress, nettle,' a name of the same type as Wratting *supra* 121.

inland (n), 'land round the home estate,' the lord's demesne, is fairly common from 1220. It later becomes *Indlonde* (1426) and *Illonde* (1432). It is compounded with heall, *Halleinlond* (1376), *Hallehyllond* (1402), *Halylond* (1408), *Halleillonde* (1436), and once with the name of the lord of the manor, *Botelersinlond* (1390).

innam (n), 'piece of land taken into cultivation,' is recorded in NED from the Danelaw and Northern England and is taken to be derived from a compound of ON *nám*, 'a taking.' In PN Sx 29, PN Sr 362, PN Ess 583, it is shown that there must have been a corresponding OE *innam*, developing late to *innam*, *innom*, *ennam* and (by confusion in the unstressed syllable) *inham*, *inholm*. It is fairly common in Cambridgeshire, as in *le Innome* (13th), *le Inham* (1364).

krókr, ON, 'bend, corner, nook,' has been noted in *le Croke* (1287), *Krocwere* (1277), *Crocdole* (1251).

lache, leche, 'slow, sluggish stream,' is occasionally found as in *Lechehithe* (13th), *Lacheford* (1320), *Lachepol* (1334), *Lache-*, *Leche-mere* (14th).

lacu, 'slow, sluggish stream,' is fairly common, particularly in the Isle of Ely. We have three compounds with stream, *Stremlake* (1251), references to birds in *Gose-* (13th), and *Bryddes-* (1419), to animals in *Swynes-* (1287), *Tagges-* (1404), 'sheep,' and *Fro(ss)che-* (1250), 'frogs,' and to the reeds and willows growing there in *Red-* (1313) and *Wythe-* (1399). Other attributes are usually descriptive: *Alde-* (1284), 'old,' a reminder that streams here were wont to decay, *Blake-* (1256), *Grene-* (1473), *Brod-* (1294), *Wronge-* (1306), 'crooked' (*v.* wrang), *Turne-* (1377) from OE **trun*, **turn*, 'circular,' here probably 'winding' (cf. Turncole, PN Ess lxi), *Hol-* (1250) from holh, 'hollow,' *Derne-* (1251), 'hidden' from dierne, *Muse-* (1240) from mēos, 'moss.' Personal names are not uncommon as in *Gunnildes-* (1251) from the ON woman's name *Gunnhildr* (*Gunnel Lake* 1714). Some of these names are formed by the addition of *lacu* to a stream-name ending in ing (*supra* 333). *Lippincge-* (1250, 13th), *Lyppinglake* (1251, 1277) may be such a derivative, cf. *Lipping* (1276 RH), a river in Lei (RN 256); *Seg(g)inc-, -inglak(e)* (1221–77) is perhaps a derivative of secg, 'stream flowing through a sedge-growing district'; *Peling-* (1327), *Pilling-* (1435) may derive from OE *pyll-ing*, from OE *pyll*, 'pool, pill, small creek,' cf. Pilling (PN La 140, 165), Pilling (RN 326); whilst *Settinglake* (1437–8) is perhaps from OE *sætung*, 'plot, snare,' used of a place where fish were trapped, cf. Settings Dike (PN ERY 10), *Sittingdyke* (1325). Note also *Processioners lake* (1575), no doubt on the parish boundary and *Whoredome Lake* (1637), probably one into which offenders were plunged.

(ge)lād, 'watercourse,' often artificial, is common, particularly in the Isle of Ely, as in *Oldlode* (1316), *Newlod* (1356). *Geynlode* (1251) is perhaps from OE *gegn*, 'direct or straight,' cf. Gainford (PN NbDu 90–1). Attributes are usually descriptive: *Est-* (1240), *North-* (1319), *Longe-* (1287), *Brode-* (t. Ed 3), *Smale-* (1374), 'narrow,' *Michele-* (13th), 'great,' *Dernelode* (1277), 'hidden' from dierne, *Heuedlade* (1251), 'head or chief' from hēafod, *Brodest-* (1378), *Twisle-* (1445) from twisla, 'fork.' Note also *Marketlode* (1287). *Laclade, -lode* (1086 InqEl) is a compound of lacu as is *Pokelodelake* (1397), one haunted by goblins (pūca), *Barrelode* (1498), one with some artificial obstruction for draining purposes. Compounds with a personal name indicate the owner, or sometimes the constructor, *Busshopplode* (1480), *Edyuelode* (1251) from a woman named *Ēadgiefu*, *Puttokislode* (1329) from Stephen *Puttok* (1304). Note *Maydenelode* (1277) and *Maidlode* (1528).

lǣs, 'pasture' (dat. lǣswe) is fairly common. It is found in *Lese* (1298), *Leswe* (1250), *Smythesleswe* (1236), *Croules* (1260), *Oxlese* (1359), *Coweles* (1393), *Cowlaswe* (1375). The nominative singular survives in the form *lease, leaze*, and through confusion with *ley* from leah sometimes appears as *leys*. The dative singular here as elsewhere develops to EModE *leause, lazure, lazer, lasure, lazar, lesure, leasure, leisure* (cf. Lazier Fen and Summer Lesure Field *supra* 238, 287). Occasionally such forms are found even in late ME as *Somerlesur* (1496), *unum Watyrlesur* (1451).

(ge)lǣt (n), 'watercourse, channel,' has been noted in *Whithlete* (1319), possibly a compound of 'withy,' and *le Oldletes* (1395), *Old Leeds* (1786).

land is the most common field-name element. It commonly has reference (especially in the plural) to the cultivated strips of the common fields. It is very often compounded with lang (1217), less frequently with wrang, 'twisted' (1221), *Blake-* (1225), *Short-* (1240), *Brade-* (1220), wōh, 'crooked' (*Woulond* 1230). Particularly frequent are references to crops and vegetation, especially beans, *Benlond* (1219), *Banelond* (1225), *Balland* (1575), which survives as *Bandland, Balland, Balance, Bean Lands* and possibly *Balaams*, less often to wheat and pease, *Wat(t)elond* (1219, 1277), *Peselond* (1251), hemp, *Henep-* (12th), brambles, *Brimli-* (1285), flax, *Flex-* (1250), *Lyn-*

(1319), and occasionally to other plants, *Farni-* (1270), *Fearm-* (1212), 'ferns,' *Thorni-* (13th), *Wad-* (13th), 'woad' and *Bere-* (1255), 'barley.' References to animals and birds are much less frequent: *Cu-* (1251), 'cow,' *Schepe-* (1312), 'sheep,' *Gose-* (1316), *Rok-* (1357). Soil or site are described in *Fule-* (1236), 'dirty,' *Wateri-* (1195), *Sur-* (1300), 'sour,' *Wylde-* (1377), *Cley-* (14th), *Sond-* (1255), *Stoni-* (1206), *Ley-* (1232) (frequent), *Lay-* (1250), 'fallow' from lǣge, *Madwe-* (1297), 'meadow,' *Moor-* (1397), *Hylly-* (1387), *Stokkede-* (1313), *Tongede-* (1319), *Brande-* (1274), *Brende-* (1328), 'burnt' from brende, *Gore-* (1336), 'triangular' from gāra, *Sunder-* (1318), 'outlying' from *sundor*, 'apart.' *le Deulond* (1360) is apparently 'dewland,' whilst *Marklond* (1521) was on the boundary (*v.* mearc). Technical uses are found in *Heuedlond* (13th), *v. supra* 329, *Yerdelonde* (1500) *v.* gierd, and inland *supra* 327, 334. Owners or occupiers are named fairly often, *Fransemanes-* (1274), 'Frenchman's,' *Pigates-* (1319), *Schepmannes-* (1405), *Akermanes-* (1221) from OE *æcerman*, 'husbandman, ploughman.' Lack of ownership is indicated in *Nomansland* (1405) and disputed ownership in *Flitene-* (1225), *Flitlonddene* (1260) from OE *(ge)fliten*, 'disputed' and *(ge)flit*, 'dispute.' *Meanland* (1549) was held in common, *v.* (ge)mǣne. Several examples of *Penylond* (1540–1609) have reference to rent. Cf. "copyholds (in Over) called *Penny Lands* formerly of the demesne, let (t. Hy 7) by copy of court roll to such as would give most rent and farm to hold them" (1575 *Survey*). Beneficiary ownership is implied in *le Ducherilonde* (1497), part of the Duchy of Lancaster estate, *le Treasorye landes* (1539), *the Poor mans Land* (1613) and ecclesiastical ownership in *Hinlandes* (1240) '*de dominio Abbatis*,' *Henlondes* (1341) from hīgna (gen. pl.), 'monastic community,' *Mounkes-* (1336), *Nonys-* (1372), *Pitensaryes lande* (1576), 'endowment of the pittancer of a monastery,' *Cherche-* (1316), *Chapele-* (1251), *Persons* (1549), *Seyntmary-* (14th), *Lady-* (1448), *Sextry-* (1570), 'endowment of the sacristy,' *Torche-* (1501), *Belle Rope-* (1504), and four examples of *La(u)mpelond(e)* (1250, 1580), for the maintaining of church lamps. *Clampland* in Tydd (1650) probably has reference to a stack of turf or peat (*v.* NED *s.v. clamp,* sb.³). Curious is *Fysselondes* (1250) in Ashley, which may have been manured with fish. *Temesedelond* (1200) in Harston and *le Temeselond* (1319) in Newton must contain *tem(e)sed*, past participle of OE *tem(e)sian*, 'to sift or bolt (flour, etc.) with a *temse*,' i.e. a sieve, common in the phrase *temse(d) bread*. Cf. also *Tamesedweye* (14th) in Stretham. Perhaps the reference is to the nature of the soil, fine and powdery, like sifted meal, and when wet resembling temse bread in the making. land is also found as a first element, compounded particularly with mǣd, *Landmade* (13th), *Londmedwe* (1339) and also in *Landgres, -gerse* (1398, 1459), *le londdich* (1381), *Londe Lake* (1331). Its meaning is not entirely clear, but perhaps it refers to something particularly belonging to the *land* or estate.

landgemǣre (n), 'boundary,' has been noted in *Landymere* (1334), *Landymerfurlang* (15th).

lane, lanu, 'lane,' is common, often with the name of owner or user as in *Aluiuelane* (1319) from OE *Ælfgiefu* (f), *Barkereslane* (1280), *Hunteslane* (1287), *Mellereslane* (1400), *Peddereslane* (1480), *Ferroureslane* (1309, William *le Ferrour*), *Waryneslane* (1293), *Wangfordeslane* (1319). The place to which it leads is indicated in compounds with *Chapel-* (1287), *Cherche-* (1362), *Bury-* (1473), *Fullyngmyll-* (1426), *Market-* (1432), *le Punfold* (1402), *Vineyard-* (1339), *Wode-* (1334), also in *Gyleslane* (1314), leading to St Giles Church. *Baldokeslane* (1280), *Fordhamlane* (1448) led to Baldock and Fordham respectively. Often the first element is descriptive, *Narwe-* (1335), *Smal-* (1345), *Sorte-* (c. 1280), i.e. 'short,' *Derne* (1370) (*v.* dierne, 'hidden'), *Derke-* (1425), *Blynde-* (1575), *Croked-* (1580). *le Flexlane* (1357), *Fenellane* (1526), *Saffronelane* (1556), *Fyshlane* (1583) were presumably lanes where these things were sold or along which they were taken. *Lovelane* (1431) and *Gropecuntlane* (1472) repeat well-known names found elsewhere. *Ferthynglane* (1418) and *Wynferthynglane* (1418) are obscure.

launde, ME, 'open space in woodland, glade,' is occasionally found in its ModE form *lawn*.

lēactūn, 'kitchen garden,' is found occasionally: *Leytone* (1279), *Leyghton* (1415), *Smidlaicthon* (13th), 'smooth,' *Recheleytones* (1347), near Reach *supra* 136, *Monekeslautone* (1387), *Pykerrelysleytone* (1427). It shows the double development to *leyton* and *laughton*.

lēah, 'wood, clearing,' is fairly common, but it is not always easy to distinguish names containing this element from those containing OE lǣg(e), used of fallow or unploughed land, or lǣs (*supra* 335). *Bradele* (1250), *Litley* (1423), *Rowleye* (1395), *Stonle* (1280) are pretty certainly descriptive compounds of lēah; *Derelegh* (1397), *Calverley* (1606), *Foglee* (1362) and *Pokle* (1570) are compounds of lēah with dēor, 'animal,' calf, fog (pasture) and 'pook' or goblin, and *Obbeleie* (1185) a compound with a personal name. It survives as *lay, ley, lea, lie.* Sequences such as *Hathleyes, -lese* (1501) and *Westelese* (1553), *Westleys* (1614) show that through confusion of suffixes, lǣs may develop to *leys*. Quite uncertain is the interpretation of the element in such weak plurals as *le Brodelayen* (1278, 1324), *Biggislayen* (1294), *Chircheleyne* (1470).

longe, ME (n), is fairly frequently used of a long strip as in *le Long* (1474). *Estlonge* (1217), *Estlonges* (13th), *le Northlonge* (1300) must have had reference to the direction in which the strip ran. Difference in length is indicated in *le Longelongeys, le Shortlongeys* (1449), *longelonge* (1513). *Flexlong* (t. Hy 3) grew flax, *Redlong* (1493) reeds, or perhaps was red in colour; *Wrongelong* (1322) was crooked (*v.* **wrang**). *Short* seems to have been used similarly of a short strip as in *the Shorttes* (16th).

lundr, ON, 'grove, wood,' is found twice in Little Gransden, *Langelund, Litlelund* (*boscus*) (1251) and once in Sawston, *le Lounde* (1328).

mǣd is very common indeed, but not so common in the Isle of Ely as elsewhere. It occurs both as *made* and *mede*, but only two examples of *made* have been noted in the Isle. Besides the usual descriptive compounds with **lang, sceort, brād, smæl, lȳtel** and **micel**, we have *Under-* (1316), *Bow-* (1480), 'curved' from *boga*, 'bow,' *Smethe-* (1298), 'smooth,' *Rowe-* (1406), 'rough,' *Hilli-* (13th), *Calo-* (1564), 'bare' from **calu**, *Sur-* (t. Hy 3), 'sour,' *Dygyd-* (1455), black, red and dark meadows. Oxen were the animals most frequently pastured there, *Oxe-* (from 1228), next cows, *Cu-* (from 1260) and then calves, *Caluere-* (1313) and horses, *Horse-* (1435). *Haye-* (1349), *Flax-* (1279) and *Russhe-* (1480) represent the most common products, whilst hawks and ducks are the only birds referred to, *Hauek-* (13th), *Ende-* (1312) (from *ened*, 'duck'). Position is often noted, *Fen-* (1251), *E-* (1251) from **ēa**, 'stream,' *Hel-* (1205), 'hill,' *Bede-* (1324) from *byde*, 'hollow,' *Frith-* (1251) from **fyrhþe**, 'woodland,' *Groue-* (1354), *Duffhous-* (1354), *Bery-* (1522), 'manor-house,' *Burgh-* (1285), *Tun-* (13th), *Castel-* (1460), *Los-* (1418), 'pig-stye' from **hlōse**. *Hwol-*, *Hwelmade* (1279) was circular from **hwēol**, *Formadwe* (1250) and *Fortmad* (1326) were in front of other land (from **fore** and **forð**), *Chekkermedwe* (1406) was variegated in appearance, *Dolmedue* (1225) was divided into shares (v. **dāl**), *Man(ne)medwe* (1251, 1322) was perhaps held in common (v. **(ge)mǣne**). Tenure is indicated in two examples of *Bonde(s)made* (1273, 1326) from ON *bóndi*, 'peasant proprietor,' and beneficial or other ownership by *Kinges-* (13th), *Bischopes-* (1279), *Lady-* (1300), *Cherche-* (1251), *Cuntrymanys-* (1391), *Chapell-* (1548) and also by a few personal name compounds, *Wlfmannes-* (13th), *Algarsmede* (1399), and lack of such in *Nomannesmad* (1315). Note also *Lammas meadowes* (1655), v. **lammas** *infra* 353.

(ge)mǣne, 'common,' is found in *Menwere* (13th), *Mannemedwe* (1251), *Meanland* (1549) and *Manedich* (1501).

(ge)mǣre, 'boundary,' occurs both as *mare* and *mere* and is thus difficult to distinguish from **mere**. *Greenmere* (1361) 'which divides the fields of Cherry Hinton and Barnwell,' *Grantedenemare* (1239), *Draitunemere* (1250), *le Knottedemare* (1307), *Marefurlong* (14th).

mǣð (n), 'mowing, place where corn was reaped.' Cf. *le Mathes* (1221), *Tomennes-, Thremannes-, Fouremannes-, Quinquemannes-, Sexmanmath* (14th), *Manymathlode* (1472) in Sutton.

malm, ME (n), 'light, loamy soil,' first noted in PN Herts 258 from t. Ed 6, occurs in *le Malme* (13th, 1312, 1401), *Whytmalm* (1338), *Malmeforlong* (1432) and *le Malmeweye* (1516).

*mealo (n), 'stones, gravel,' first discussed *s.n.* Wythemail (PN Nth 129–30), is found in *Gretmale* (1418) and *Malewecroft, Maluuecroft* (13th).

mearc, 'boundary,' is rare: *Lamarke* (1251), *Markemar'* (in the boundaries of Foulmere) (1279), *Markfurlong* (1447).

mere, 'pool, mere,' is common, but cannot always be distinguished from (ge)mǣre, especially as this also occurs as *mare*. Cf. Harrimere and Stretham Mere *supra* 199, 239. *Grindelmere* (t. Hy 3), *-mare* (1350) near Throckenholt, *Rissemare* (1246) in Whittlesey (*v.* rysc), *Typpesmere* (13th), *-mare* (15th), *Hornynggemare* (15th) in Isleham and *Potynggsmare* (1397) in Soham were all probably *meres*. *Smythismare*, *-mere* (14th) in Chippenham may have been a pool or a boundary. So too with *Pennesmare* (13th) in Meldreth and *Cwekeresmare* (1319) in Newton. *Gretemare* (1230), *Estmar'* (1365), *Longemar'* (1379) are doubtful. Certain examples of *mere* are five of *Gosemere* (1212–1315), three of *Frithmere* (1203–1316), *Lache-*, *Lechemere*, *-mare* (14th) from lache, 'stream,' *Hassocmere* (1328) from hassuc, 'clump of rushes,' *Dokemer* (1432), *Holmere* (14th) from holh, 'hollow,' *Gretemere* (1298), described as a fishery, *Wetheymere* (1397), *Mellemere* (t. Hy 7). *Scaldemere* (1250), *Skalde-* (t. Hy 7) is probably 'shallow mere' with Scandinavianising of OE sceald. *Pichenemere* (1280, 13th), 'pitch-black mere,' is from OE *picen*, 'pitchy, of pitch,' cf. *on þære picenan ēa* (BT). Note also *Portmere* (13th) from port, 'town,' *Thernyngmere* (1432) from OE *þyrning*, 'place where thorn-bushes grow,' *Cymere* (1241) from cȳ, 'kine.' *Braunchesmere* (1450) in Elm is named from the family of William *Braunch* who held land near here in 1436.

mersc, 'marsh,' is much less common than fenn. In the Isle of Ely it is limited to a salt-water marsh (and early forms are rare) whilst fenn is used of fresh-water marsh. *Mers(s)* (1250, t. Ed 1), *Stanmers* (1301), *Eldermarsh* (1303), *Orwellmersh* (1352), *Galughmersh* (1431), *Starkemersh* (1327), 'bullock or heifer marsh' from OE stirc, styric, *Tichemersshe* (1483) from ticcen, 'kid.'

middel is found several times in March, used apparently of a fishery, as in *Gredy middil*, *Hogges middle*, *Jellis middil*, *Sheting middil*, *Ung medil* 1528 Imb 329–30.

mōr is fairly common from 1250. We may note *Pichennemore* (1250), 'pitch-black,' from OE *picen*, *Sourmore* (1391), 'sour.'

morgen-giefu (n), 'morning-gift,' i.e. the gift given the morning after marriage by the husband to the wife, has been noted once in *le Morezewe* (1403), *Moryevecroft* (1471). Cf. Moor Fm (PN Ess 276) and Mooray (PN W 186).

mos, 'moss, peat-bog,' has been noted in *Mirillmosse* (1278).

myln, as usual, is common. We may note an early example of *Horsemelne* (1285), a compound first noted in NED in 1530, *Portmelne* (13th) (*v.* port), *Tounemelne* (1336) (*v.* tūn), *Galoumill* (1316), a water-mill called *the Easemill* (t. Hy 8) and a burnt mill, *Brendemylle* (1494). *Pokemilne* (1260) was haunted by goblins (pūca).

orceard is occasionally found as in *Elue orcherd* (1251), *le Orchert* (1303), *Orchardstede* (1199), *litilorcharde* (1436). The first element in the first example is quite uncertain.

ord, 'spit of land projecting into the fen or between two streams', is found occasionally near Ely as in *Blacwinesord, Padenhaleord* (1251).

pæð, 'path,' is fairly common. Compounds are usually (*a*) descriptive, *Smalepat* (1341), 'narrow' from smæl, *Slytherpathe* (1480), *Mydylpat* (14th), *Derne-* (1487), 'difficult to find' (*v.* dierne), *Thwerte-* (1324) from ME *thwert*, 'cross,' (*b*) indicating the place to which it leads, *Bregepath* (1235), *Chirchepaþ* (1327), *Wynt Mulne Path* (1347), *Gotemorpath* (1296), *Foxtonepath* (c. 1250), *Exnyngpath* (1329), (*c*) naming its users or owners, *Gatepath* (1246) from gāt, 'goat,' *Stodpaþ* (1270) from stōd, 'stud, herd of horses,' *Hors-* (1345), *Munkespad* (13th), 'monks,' *Clerkespath* (1451), *le Shepherdes-* (1360), three examples of *Theuespath* (1240–1660), *Boyespat* (t. Hy 3), perhaps 'boys' path,' *Thurstones-* (1250) from a personal name.

pasture, ME (n), is occasionally found as in *Bolokkyspasture* (1468) or the modern *Night Pasture*.

pearroc, 'small enclosure, field,' is occasionally found and appears in modern names as *parrock* or *park*.

pece, ME (n), is fairly common with (*a*) a descriptive epithet, *Geldene-* (1319), 'golden' from gylden, *Tayllyd-* (1431), *Harpepe(e)ce* (1622), *Mose-* (1334), *Mus(e)-* (1357) from mēos, 'moss,' *Bole-* (1512), 'bull,' (*b*) an occasional indication of owner or user as in *le Pynders pece* (1564), *Glovers peice* (1676), (*c*) a neighbouring place-name, *Foxholepece* (t. Ric 2), *Hertwelhylpece* (1450). *Piece* is very common in modern field-names such as *New Taken, No Mans, Gent's, Poors, Church, Bank, Scizzors, Paled Piece*.

pightel, 'small field, enclosure,' is rather more common than the nasalised form pingel. Apart from *le pytil* (1366), *the pightells* (1495), it has been noted only in compounds with personal names such as *Rundelespitell* (1250), *Lemanespichtel* (13th), *Haywardespistel* (1315), *Mellerespygehel* (1356). It survives as *Pightle, Pickle* and *Pykle* [paikl].

pinfold, EModE (n), 'enclosure,' has been noted only four times, the earliest being *Pynfolde* (1340).

pingel, ME (n), 'small enclosure,' occurs from 1408 (*le Pyngel*), *the Rushy pingle* (17th) and with an owner's name in *Gerenteryspyngyl* (1428). It survives as *Pingle* in the Isle of Ely.

pīpe (n), 'pipe, channel of a small stream,' is used occasionally near Wisbech of some landowner's drain as in *Rotespipe* (1358) from Walter *Rote* (1251), *Massynghams pipe* (1438), *Coldhampipemead* (1455).

place, ME (n), 'place, site,' is not uncommon, as in *le Marcatplase* (1330), *le Gildeplace* (1361), *Thunder Place* (1370), two examples of *Wastplace* (1371), *Berneplace* (1380), *Bowerplace* (1485), *Petyplace* (1539) and, with the owner's name, *Gambonesplace* (1367), *Magotisplace* (1372), *Prattesplace* (1376), *Grandfathers Place* (1511).

plæsc, 'shallow pool,' is surprisingly rare. Note *The Plashe* (1578). It survives as *plash* and occasionally as *splash*. Cf. Introd. xxxvi.

plegstōw, 'play-place,' is very rare. It has been twice noted in *Pleystowe* (1251, 13th).

plott, ME (n), has been noted in *Ferþingplot* (1334), twice in *Greneplot* (1235) and in *Shortplottes* (1388), *Brodeplott* (1431), *Rush plott* (1650).

pōl, 'pool, deep place in a river,' is fairly common and is several times described as a fishery. Note *Blakepol* (1251), *Lechepol* (1334), probably so named from water-leeches, *Ryngemerepoles* (1315), *Fennepole* (1465), *Horpool* (1529), 'muddy' from horh, *Cleypole* (1540). *Hachepol* (1389) was a fishery with a grating (hæcce), *Gosepol* (1251) was frequented by geese, whilst *Bukkepol* (1329) and *Horspole* (1467) were drinking-places for animals. Ownership is indicated in *Akermannespoles* (1221) and *Persespol* (1240).

ponde, ME (n), is not very common. We may note *le pond* (t. Ed 1), *Eliasponde* (1225), later *Elypond* (1480), *Nethir-* (1359), *Whit-* (1388), *Swan-* (1413), *Prestis-* (1425), *Fysheris-* (1443).

port, 'town,' is found in *Portfeld* (1279) in Cambridge, *Portmelne* (13th) and, no doubt, in *Purte(s)brege, -brigge* (1240–94), *Port(e)brigge, -bregge* (1272–1480), *Pourtebrygg, -bregg* (1320–1480) in Cambridge and *P(o)urt(e)brige, -bregge* (1250–14th) in Grantchester where we find the *Purte-* forms noted in PN Ess 587, lxi, 130 *s.n.* Purfleet.

prey, ME (n), 'meadow,' first noted *s.n.* Pray Heath (PN Sr 158–9), has been noted once in *Prefurlong* (1422).

pundfald (n), 'pound,' is found in *Pundefoldedole* (1280), *-lane* (1402).

*pynd (n), 'enclosure' (cf. Pen Hill (PN Sx 200) and PN Sr 364), has been noted in *le piend* (1354), *le Peend* (1400), *le pende* (1501), *le Nespeend* (1404), *the Newpinde* (1414).

pytt is fairly common, especially with reference to the material found there, particularly chalk and clay, *Chalcpettes* (1212), *Claipittes* (1200) carrying back the word over 200 years, less commonly to sand, loam and gravel, *Sondpyttes* (13th), *Lamputtes* (1228), *Chiselpettes* (1251), *Cheselpyttes* (1482) (v. ceosol, 'gravel'), occasionally to charcoal and lime, *Colpyt* (1322), *Lympet* (1313), *-pittes* (1424). Further we have *Turefpettes* (13th), *Stanpettes* (1251), *Marlepytte* (1439) and *Gravelpettys* (1496). We may also note *Shelwepettes* (1354), 'shallow,' *Bottomlespytt* (1467), *Watrypittes* (1395), *Thwartpittes* (1467) (ME thwert, 'cross'), *Fullerespet, -put* (14th). It is associated with animals in *Hoggepet* (1270), *Horsepit* (1250), *Wolpet* (1309), 'wolf-pit' or 'wulf-trap.' *Thefpeut* (1319) was one haunted by thieves; *Schokepet* (1431), *prispit* (1250), *Thurspit* (13th) were haunted by goblins and giants respectively (v. scucca, þyrs). *Wudecokespet* (1279) and *Crowspytt* (1467) were haunts of woodcock and crows, whilst *le Redeputtes* (1300) were full of reeds. Occasionally the first element is a personal name as in *Osewoldespit* (1228), *Kentynggesput* (1399).

quarre(r), ME (n), 'quarry,' occurs occasionally as *Quarree* (1364), *Quarrer*' (1372).

quike, ME, 'couch-grass,' survives in *The Quick*, *Quick Ground* and *Long Quick*. It is a variant of *Quitch* or *Couch* Grass, found in NCy and in Nf and Sf.

*ræc (n) is probably used in the sense 'a stretch of river' in *Brodreche* (1438) in Wisbech and *Ewerereche* (1435) in Haddenham, 'reach by the river-fishing-weir.' In *Stretreche* (1221) in Doddington it seems to be used of a stretch of road, a sense first recorded in NED in 1536. *v.* also Reach *supra* 136.

rāw, 'row,' is found in the sense 'row of cottages' in *le Newrowe* (1362), *Sevencoterowe* (1364), the common *Ratounrowe* (1401), *Ratterowe* (1436), *Wratt Row* (1701), 'rat-row' from ME *ratoun*, 'rat,' used contemptuously of miserable hovels, contrasted with *Meryrowe* (1518), 'pleasant row' from myrig, *Seekoterowe* (1466), *Dicherowe* (1487), and of a row of trees in *les Willerowes* (1398).

*ried, ***ryd** (n), 'clearing' (PN Ess 588) is rare; we may note *Red* (1228), *Wyterede* (14th), *Shortrede* (1475).

rīpig, 'streamlet,' is found occasionally as in *Rydye* (1320), *Redye* (1332), *Algarridi* (1260), belonging to *Ælfgār*, *Dalrydi* (13th) (*v.* dæl), *litelho ridi* (13th), *Chelwelrydy* (1347), 'cold spring streamlet' (*v.* ceald, wielle) and *Pouteredy* (1510) where eel-pouts were found.

rod, 'clearing,' is not common. We may note *le Rode* (1334), *Yrchunesrode* (1205) where hedgehogs (ME *irchon*) were found, *Linrode* (t. John), 'flax' from līn, *Longrode* (1343). *v.* also rōd *infra*.

rōd (n), 'rood,' measure of area, is found in *le Roudes* (1351) and *Catte Rude* (*tres rudes terre arabilis*) (1460). It is probably found also in the following, though the forms cannot be certainly distinguished from rod: *le Nyeroden* (1319), 'new,' (rood called) *Cursyd rode* (1432), *Weyrode selion* (1262) by a road, *le Cuttederode* (1480), *Lamperode* (1312), probably a rood rather than a clearing, devoted to the provision of a light in the church, *Baldewynesrode* (13th) in Ely, and *Bytrode* (1378) in a bend (byht) in Sutton where clearings are not impossible but unlikely. We have also numerical compounds, *Fyverod* (1319), *Sixrodes* (1441), *Severoden* (14th), *Tenroden* (1300), *Fourtyrode* and *le Sextirode* (1378), the last three being in Sutton.

roð (n), 'clearing' (PN Nth 119, PN Ess 503, 588), has been noted in *le Rothe* (1336) and *Rothelane* (1405) in Woodditton.

ryden (n), 'cleared land,' so common in Essex (PN Ess 588), has been noted only twice, *le Redenefeld* (1313) in Castle Camps and *Redenwey* (1355) in Bartlow, both on the Essex border.

ryding, 'clearing,' has been noted in the forms *Redinge*, *Redyng* (1313–1513). It survives as *Riding* and *Readings*.

rysc, 'rush,' in the plural form is occasionally used collectively of a place overgrown with rushes as in *le Reysshen* (13th), *le Reschen* (1313), *Longerussh*' (1349), *Dukrusschyn* (1300), *Candelrushes* (1402),

Candelroschyn (1446), the common rush used for making rush lights, carrying back this compound some 40 years.

sceaga, 'small wood, copse,' is very rare; we may note *le Schage* (13th).

scēap-steall (n) has been noted in *Scepestal* (13th).

sceard, 'notch, gap,' has been noted twice used independently, *le Sherde* (1393, 1526) and in *Brodesherd* (1251). *v.* also Wormwood Hill *supra* 89.

scēat, 'nook, corner,' is fairly common, but usually late. We may note *le Sotys* (1290), *Wrenthellesote* (13th), *Netherexsotes* (t. Hy 3), probably from 'ox,' *Middelschote* (1319), *Wyndemellschotte* (1468), *Rowe-* ('rough'), *Ouer-*, *Groveshott* (1483), *Brokeshott* (1593). It survives as *shot*. *Helneshet* (1280) and *Fyfshetes* (1251) are from the related scīete.

scipen, 'cattle-shed,' is late and rare; we may note *Shypen* (1419), *Shepen* (1498).

sealh, 'willow,' is found in *le Salowes* (1347), *Salle* (1346). It survives as *sallow*.

set(e)coppe, ME (n), 'seat-hill,' first noted in PN Ess 589–90, is found in *Setecoppe* (1314).

sīc, 'small stream in marshy ground,' is found occasionally as in *Sich* (1202), *Sik* (1230), *Syke* (1316), *Hollesyke* (1315) from holh, 'hollow,' *Redesyke* (1397) probably from hrēod, 'reed.'

sid(e)ling, ME (n), is used of a strip of land lying by some other portion or by a stream as in *Sidlinge* (1250), *le Sid(e)lynge* (1300, 1374, 1623), *Sydlynggys* (1394). Cf. PN Wa 343, PN W 454.

slæd, 'shallow valley,' as in Nth and Hu is common from 1220, as in *Depslade* (1493). In Northants it also means 'strip of greensward through a wood, a green road' (PN Nth 269) and this may be its meaning in *Heygrauesclade* (1260). In Essex it is also used of a boggy spot and of a stream (*v.* PN Ess 7, 11 *s.nn.* Fulfen Slade, The Slade), meanings found also here, especially in the Isle of Ely. Cf. *Le Slade vocat. Breredondich* (1381), *the old wereslade* (1300) by a fishing-weir, *Segesslade* (t. Hy 2), 'sedge,' *Merslade* (13th), *Marsh Slade* (1589), *Littelwelleslade* (1230) and ten examples of *Waterslade* (1251). Cf. also 'all *slades* and low places in the same drove and ways be amended' (1339). We have descriptive elements in *Brode-* (1307), *Mechele-* (1398), *Hokede-* (1305), *Dedegrasslade* (1453), references to situation in *Mid-* (1377), *Herne-* (13th) from hyrne, 'nook,' to pigs in *Swynes-slade* (1287) and to pigeons or doves in *Culuerslade* (1418) from culfre. Occasionally we have reference to persons, *Chapmanslad'* (1250), *Grimesslad* (1251), *Malkineslade* (13th). *Chircheslad* (1250) may have been near the church or in ecclesiastical possession. *v.* Addenda lxi.

slæp, 'slippery place,' has been noted in *Slape-*, *Slepehowe* (1439, 1477) (*v.* hōh) and *Redeslapp* (1617).

slōh (n), 'slough.' We may note *le Slo* (t. Ed 1), *Redeslogh* (1299),

Crouissclo (1240) frequented by crows, *Fulslow* (1280), *Voulslo* (1340), 'foul' from *fūl*, and *Edrichescloue* (1259) from OE *Ēadric*.

smēthe, ME, 'smooth place,' has been noted in *Smethe* (1250), *the Smeeth* (1636).

snād, 'a piece of land cut off,' has been noted in *le Snode* (13th), *Aluuredessnode* (1217) from OE *Aelfred*.

snote, ME (n), is common in minor names in the fenlands. We have *Alwredessnote* (c. 1225 *ElyM*), *parvam snotam* (14th *ElyF*) (Witcham), *Birssnota* (1251 *ElyCouch*) (Doddington), *Snota* ib., *le Sharpesnote* (1383 *Peterhouse*) (Haddenham), *Westsnote, le Snote* (13th *ElyCh*), *the Snowte* (1584 *Ct*) (Ely), *Snotas* 13th *ElyM* (Sutton), *le Snote* (1446 *Ct*) (Wilburton), *le Snote* (1309 *ElyCh*) (Wentworth), *Mychelsnote, le Smalesnote* (c. 1320 CAPr iv) (Littleport), *the Snout* (1669 *ChancDec*) (Wimblington). See also *s.n.* Snoots *supra* 262. In spite of two 13th-century forms in *snoht* (*s.n.* Snoots *loc. cit.*) we should probably derive this from ME *snute*, 'snout,' used with reference to some projection of drier land into the fen. NED records the sense 'a projecting point of land' from 1536. The persistent *snote* rather than *snute* is probably only a spelling form, *u* represented by *o* after *n* in the same way that it is commonly represented by *o* before *n*. The ultimate phonological development in Snout is from *snute*, in Snoots it may be from *snote*.

sol, 'muddy or miry pool,' has been noted in *a holm atte Sole* (1371), *le Sole* (1399), *Horsesolle* (1251). It survives in *Soles Ground*.

stæþ, 'landing-place,' has been noted in *le Stathe* (1473), *Stathstede* (1251), *le Stathegote* (1320), *Elvyestathes* (1395).

stān is found occasionally as in *campo voc. Atteston* (13th), *le Stoon* (1349), *le Brodeston* (1296), *Athelstanestan* (1218), *Millestonis* (1373).

standard, ME (n), is found twice, (*le*) *Standard* (13th, 1300), probably in the sense 'a tree or shoot from a stump left standing when a tree is copped or cut down.' Cf. PN Nt 277, 282.

stapol, 'staple, pillar,' is found in *Chippenham Stapell'* (13th), *le Stapylles* (1483), *Stapelweye* (1251).

steall, 'site, place, cattle-stall,' is found in *Newstale* (1235), *Bibele-stal* (1251), *Midstalewey* (1277).

steddle, ME (n) (cf. PN Sx 79, 341, PN Sr 365), perhaps 'a building of timber standing on legs or *steddles* to raise it out of the mud' is compounded with lang, *Langstedeles* (1364), *Lannstedel* (1377), *Lankstedel* (1379), and with myln, *Mellestedil* (1400).

stede, 'place, position, site,' is common. It is compounded (*a*) with a descriptive element, *Mukkilstede* (1342) from micel, 'great,' *Ringstede* (1231), 'circular,' *le Newestede* (1398), or with one referring (*b*) to the character of the land, *Mareystede* (1300) from ME *marais*, 'marsh,' *Orchardstede* (1199), (*c*) to its crops, *Wheatestede, Barlystede* (1605). As in Hunts (PN BedsHu 296), it often refers to the actual site of some buildings, what in Scotland would be called a *steading*,

le Biristed (1324) from **burh**, 'manor-house' (surviving as *Berrystead*).
Bothested (1561) from **bōþ**, 'booth, temporary shelter,' *Cotstede* (1240),
Kyrkested (1251), *Loftstede* (1219), *Mellested* (1220), *Mercatstede*
(1285), i.e. 'market,' *Stathstede* (1251) from **stæð**, 'landing-place,'
Tunstede (1487) and *Wicstede* (1250). We have also several examples
compounded with a personal name, *Wlfysstede* (1300) from OE *Wulf-
wīg*, *Dunnyngistede* (1341) from Hervey *Dunning* (t. Hy 3), *Sauserstede*
(1334) from Ralph *le Sauser*, *Kyngestede* (1364), *Stiwardestede* (1300)
and *Barkerestede* (1357). We have also *Plaistede* (1432), *Halkstede*
(1250) from **halke** and *Langefordestede* (1314), descriptive of its position, *Wormstede* (1472) where snakes (OE *wyrm*) were numerous.
Luuestede (13th) is enigmatic. We have also three examples of (*bi*)
Gangestide (1052–65), *Gangestede* (1053) in King's Delph in Whittlesey, *Gangsted* (1311) in Graveley and *Gongested lake* (1339) in
Upwell. This compound occurs also in PN BedsHu 296 and seems
to be identical with Ganstead (PN ERY 48–9), an OScand compound,
gagnstaðr, 'meeting-place, place of opposition,' referring to the 'site
of a fight,' with later substitution of the cognate OE **stede** for ON
staðr. It is noteworthy that all are situated in districts subject to
Scandinavian influence.

steort, 'tail of land,' has been noted once.

stīg, 'path,' is very rare. We may note *Swinesti* (1231).

stigel, 'stile,' has been noted in *Churchestille* (1525), *Pickard's stile*
(1570) and *Blackstile* (1617).

stŏc, 'place,' perhaps 'cattle-farm, dairy-farm' (*v. Studies*[2] 35–43),
is found independently as *Stoche* (1235) in Duxford and *Stoke* (1251)
in Long Stanton, compounded with **cealf**, 'calf,' in *Chaulstoch* (1316),
Calstok (1385) in Fulbourn, with a personal name in *Hudestoke* (1251)
in Ely and *Aleynesstoke* (1409) in Little Wilbraham.

stocc, 'stock, log, tree-stump,' is found in the plural in *Hye-*,
Lyttyll-, *Ouerstokken(e)* and compounded with **weg** in *Stok(ke)wey(e)*
(1455), all in Ickleton, and possibly in *Ravenesstocfeld* (1395) in West
Wickham (cf. *Studies*[2] 31).

stocking, 'group of stumps,' has been noted seven times, in
Sto(c)kyng from 1236 to 1542.

stōw, 'place,' does not occur, as so often elsewhere, compounded
with a saint's name. We have one compound with **wīc**, *Hyrauuicstouue*
(1170) and later examples in a more general sense, *Falowstowe* (1483),
Cowstowe (1570), *Westow* (1669). It is frequent in the Isle of Ely as
in *les Stowes in le Fendykfelde* (1401), sometimes with the owner's
name, *the stow of Geffrey Sutton* (1438), *Riche's stow* (1570), *Mr Parsons
Stowe* (1621). It seems to be used in a similar way to **stede**, but had
clearly also some special sense, particularly in the compound *stowcroft*
(cf. *infra* 346) and *stow-way*, still used in Wisbech of a passage from
one field to another formed by heaping earth above a pipe placed to
continue the flow of water along the dike separating the two fields.

It may be this which is sometimes described as a *porta*: *uno stowe iuxta le houtgate* (1347), *portas vocat' stowes* (1586), *unum cartestowe* (1396), *Adger(is)stou(u)kroft* (1320–33). One example (*Stowcrofte* 1593) has been noted outside the Isle, in Orwell. We have also one compound with dāl (*Stowdole* 1496) and two with stede (*Stowstede* 1541–86).

strǣt is common and is clearly not limited to names of Roman roads. It is compounded with very much the same elements as weg and occurs both as -*strate* and -*strete*. We may note descriptive compounds such as *Brodestrete* (1250), *Smalestrete* (c. 1250), *le Heystrete* (c. 1290), i.e. 'high' or 'chief,' *Litelstrete* (1387), *Michelstrete* (13th), *le Newestrete* (c. 1275), *Grenestrate* (1205), *le Horestrate* (1420) from horh, 'muddy,' *le Ouerstrete* (1285), *Netherstrete* (1300), *Wrongstrete* (1493), i.e. 'crooked'; compounds indicating the place to which it led such as *Beristrate* (1352) leading to the manor-house, *le Fordestrete* (13th), *Wellstrete* (1318); compounds with the user's name such as *Acremannestrete* (c. 1250) and *Willekinsstrate* (1303), and miscellaneous compounds such as *Likestrete* (c. 1260) from līc, 'body, corpse,' *Katstrete* (1205), *le Fullyngstrete* (13th) where 'fulling' was carried on, and *streete called lytyll London* (1573).

strengr, ON (n), 'watercourse,' has been noted in *Strenges* (1393) in Soham, *Sheldesstreng* (1277) in Ely (*v.* Shell *supra* 200), *Ewere-string* (1320) in Littleport 'by the fishing-weir in the river' (*v.* ēa, wēr).

strōd, 'marshy land overgrown with brushwood,' has been noted in *Strode* (1221).

stubb, 'stump of a tree,' is used independently in *le Stubbe* (14th) and is compounded with ellern, 'elder' in *Elrenestubbhowe* (1195), *Ellernestub* (1235), *Eldrenestub* (1250), with ǣcen, 'oaken' in *Echenstub* (13th) and with wiðig, 'willow' in *Withiestubbe* (1481).

stubbing, ME (n), 'place of stumps,' is occasionally found as in *le Stubbyng* (1243), *Ouerstobbing* (1299), *Heystubbinge* (1280).

stulpe, ME (n), 'a short post fixed in the earth as a boundary-mark' (cf. PN Ess 99, *s.n.* Stoop Bridge, another example of which is probably *le Stulbruge* (13th)), is found in *les Stulpys* (14th) and *Stulpysweye* (1451).

stycce (n) is in fairly frequent use to denote a piece of land. Cf. *Tenstichoue* 1221 *ElyA* (*v.* hōh) (Doddington), *una terra voc. a Styche* (1488 *CaiCh*) (Haddenham), *le Seuenestycche* (c. 1300) (Fen Drayton), *Middelstech* (13th *Elem*) (Ely), *i steche bitowne*, i.e. by the farm (1496 *Rental*) (Fulbourn), and *Restages supra* 250.

sumpe, ME (n), 'marsh, swamp' (PN Ess 187), has been noted in *the Sumps* (1636), *the Sumpts* (1678).

swæð, primarily 'the track left by a moving body,' develops in ME *swath* the sense 'mark left by the scythe of the mower, measure of grass land' as in *vnam swatham prati* (13th *ElyM*) (Ely), *tres swathes prati falcabilis in campo de Sutton* (1320 *ElyCh*), *4 longe swathes prati in ... Longswathesmedow each of which swathis contain in breadth 10 feet*

(1526 *WMP*) (Meldreth), *five Swathes* (1621) and (*le*) *Haywarde-swa(y)the* (1501, 1637).

swice (n), 'trap, snare,' has been noted in *Swike* (14th). *v.* NED *.v. swike* sb.² and cf. Sweech (PN K 518).

taile, ME, 'tail,' descriptive of a narrow strip of land, is found in *Snakestaylles* (1309), *le Longetaylles* (1403) and *Whiptayle* (1510).

þorn is found independently from 1296, several times in the compound *Smalethorne(s)* (1220). *Auethorn* (1321), later *Audorne* (1405), is probably an error of transcription for *Anethorn, Andorne*, 'single thorn' from ān(a).

þorp occurs in (*le*) *Thorp* (1296–9) in Portfield in Cambridge and in *Thorpcroft* (1349) which must have been adjacent.

topt, ON, 'piece of ground, messuage, homestead,' is fairly common as in *Toft* (1151), *Toftes* (1290), *Longtoftes* (1463), *Houndysthofte* (1483), *Toft(e)made* (1397), *-furlonge* (1460).

trade, trede, ME (n), has been noted in *Trede* (1250), *le Trade* (1319), *Tredfurlong* (1251, 1277), *Tradebrede* (1319). There is a ME *trede* recorded in 1440 in the sense 'track' and from 1225 in the plural *treden* in that of 'footprints.' Side by side with this we have ME *trad(e)*, MLG, OHG *trata*, 'way, path,' first noted in 1375. NED suggests (*s.v. trade* sb.) that this was apparently introduced into English in the 14th century from Hanseatic MLG, perhaps originally in nautical language in the sense 'course or track' of a ship. The above forms, with the variation in the vowel between *a* and *e*, suggest that the word existed earlier and point to an original OE **træd*.

trenche, ME (n), in *le Trenche, the Brodetrenche, le Longetrenche* (1546) must be used in the sense 'ditch' and not in that of a 'forest-track' as in PN Nth 270, PN Ess 591, PN W 448, though this may well be the meaning in *Trenchweye* (1312) in Eversden.

trēo(w), 'tree,' is compounded with a personal name in *Wullokesthre* (13th). We may note also *Midfentre* (c. 1151), later *Madgestree al. midd fenn tree al. halfe waye tree* (1579) in Thorney, *le Halfemile tree* (1540) in Thorney, *mile and half tree* (1604) in Whittlesey.

trōg, 'trough, hollow,' is probably to be found in *A(l)stonestrow(es)* (1354–85), *le Trouwe* (1294), *le Troȝth* (1417), *Trough* (1480), *le ferthere trough* (1494), all in Fulbourn, but we cannot be quite certain that some of these are not from trēo(w). It survives in *Trimtrough*.

tūn. Lost farms or hamlets have been noted in *Midelton* (1228) in Chesterton, *Neuton* (1229) in Gamlingay, *Middeltone* (1319) in West Wratting, *Sigereston* (1250) in Stetchworth (from OE *Sigehere*), *Beston* (1279) in Great Wilbraham (cf. Beesons *supra* 239), *Clauertone* (1280) in Chesterton ('clover-farm' from clæfre), *Bramston* (14th) in Litlington, *Plumpton* (1414) in Waterbeach and *Prestiston* (1432) in Barnwell. It is common in such compounds as *Tonewalle* (*communem puteum*) (1338) (*v.* wielle), *Tunforlong* (1251), *Tunfeld* (13th), *Tunmad'* (13th), *Tounmelne* (1336), *Tonebroke* (1361), *Tundrove* (14th), *le Towne*

Holtes (1424), *Ely Towne Ware* (1608), denoting something common to the hamlet or village. Cf. also *(H)eyeweyeabuuent(o)un, -aboue-* (1300–12) in Witcham. It survives frequently in modern field-names such as *Townsend Close* and *Field, Towns Hole Corner, Town Close, Dole, Land, Mead(ow), Spring* and *Wash, Town End Hove* and *Tween Towns*.

tūnman (n), 'villager,' has been noted in *Tonmanlond, Tunmanbroc* (1272), *Tunmannisaker* (1480), all in Cambridge, *Tunman(n)e(s)feld* (13th, 1300), *Tunmenhoue* (1309), from hōh.

tūnsteall, 'farm-site,' has been noted twice in *Tunstal(l)* (1207, 1360). It survives as *Dunstall* and *Dunstill*.

twisla, 'fork,' is found in *le Twiseles* (1294), *le Tweselles* (1483). It is compounded with weg, 'road,' in *Weitwiseles* (1236), *Weyetwesel* (1344). *Middeltuysel* (1251) was a fishery.

valley, ME (n), is late as in *le Valey* (1451).

vangr, ON, 'field,' is less frequent than in Hunts or Northants. It occurs five times in Barnwell, *Pese-, Stony-, Hulk-, Longhaueden-* and *Brytheswong* (1432) and once each in Whittlesey, *Long Wong* (13th), Boxworth, *Bradewonge* (1260) and Swaffham Prior, *Dencheburgwong* (1319).

viniterie, ME (n), presumably a small vineyard, has been noted in the names of two crofts, *le Vyntre* (1404), *the Vyntery* (1494).

vrá, ON, 'nook, corner,' is found once in *le Wro* (t. Ric 2) in Bottisham.

wayte, ME (n), 'look-out,' occurs in *le Wayte* (1278) and probably in *Weighthyll, -shott* (1589).

weald occurs as *le Welde* (1387) in Duxford. It is used in a series of names in the neighbourhood of Croydon and of *Wold* (supra 54, 246). One would naturally think that this indicated the presence of old forest-land, but it should be noted that we have reference in the case of Croydon Wilds to the grant of *pratum* or meadow land in this neighbourhood, a puzzling case if this is really forest land.

weg is very common. In addition to the names noted *supra* 18–33 we have compounds descriptive of (a) situation, *Este-* (1210), *Myddel-* (1285), *le Ouer-* (13th), *le Nether-* (1400), *Thuert-* (1231), 'athwart or cross,' *Ouertwertweye* (1397), (b) size or character, *Little-* (1356), *Mickle-* (1250), *Mochel-* (1346), *Twiseled-* (1387), 'forked' (v. twisla), *le Wrong-* (1451), 'crooked' (v. wrang), *Calow-* (1464), 'bare' (v. calu), *Endeles-* (c. 1195), *Rowe-* (1378), 'rough,' *Dichede-* (1236) with a ditch or dyke, *Stylewey (viam pedestrem)* (1483), *Gorewey* (1302), 'muddy' from gor, *W(h)yte-* (13th, 1319), 'white,' *Flod-* (1452) liable to floods, *Thyrsty-* (1504), *le Gutter Wey* (1531). *Heywey* (14th) may be 'highway' or 'hay-way.' Compounds with *Chalk-* (t. Ed 1), *Ston-* (1235), *Send-* (1348) and *Sand-* (1455) may be descriptive of the soil or of what is carried along the road. *le Barliwey* (t. Ed 1) and compounds with *Segh-* (1348) and *Rusch-* (1376) are probably of the latter type. The beasts that travel along them are indicated in *Retheres-* (1250) from OE *hrȳðer,* 'cattle,' *Hund(es)-* (1278–85), *Hors-* (1349), *Shep-* (1441), *Nete-* (1491) from OE *nēat,* 'cattle,' *Bullokes-* (1563), *Cow-* (1596); their human users in compounds with *Monke-* (1234), *Nunnes-* (1253), *Prestes-* (1308), *le Mongeris-* (1317), 'merchant's,' *le Persones-* (1342). *le Verdeweye* (1375) was used by an army (OE *fierd-weg*) and *Ferdmanewey* (13th) by the *fierd-men, Processionwey* (1564) by those who were beating the parish bounds. *Forthwey* (t. Ric 2) perhaps went straight to its object; *le Wyndweye* (1387) is ambiguous, it may be a 'winding' or a 'windy' road. We have indication of the marking, bounding or construction of the road in compounds with *Cruch-* (1250), i.e. 'cross,' *Stapel-* (1251), *Pile-* (1312) from OE *pīl,* 'stock, stake,' *Herdlys-* (1445), i.e. 'hurdles,' and *Stulpis-* (*supra* 346); of its destination or situation in compounds with *Welle-* (1195), *Cherch-* (1250), *Medue-* (1250), *Peseland-* (1250), *Milne-* (1251), *le Dofhous-* (1287), *Burstal-* (13th), *Burie-* (14th), i.e. 'manor-house,' *Merket-* (1300), *Watlond-* (1325), i.e. 'wheatland,' *Dam-* (1369), *Hil-* (1387), *Qwarre-* (1401), *Ford-* (1433), *Castel-* (1457), *Moore-* (1480), *Cote-* (1513). Frequently a particular town is indicated as in *Lundeneweye* (1230), *Seffordeweye* (1210), i.e. Shelford, *Cantebrigweye* (1319), *Wyue-lingweye* (1349), leading to Willingham, and *Minster Way* (1623) to Ely. Occasionally we have reference to a particular person as in *Blakeswey* (1240), *Aldricheswey* (1318), *Thurgaresweye* (1349), *Ruggeles-weye* (1203) (associated with Alured *Ruggel*). *Grymesweye* (1316) is ambiguous. It may have reference to a man bearing the Anglo-Danish name *Grim* or to Woden as in the numerous examples of Grims Ditch. Picturesque is *Skiwardweye* (1319).

welig, **wylig,** 'willow,' is common, occasionally with a personal name as in *Drakeswelews* (1473), *Fysheres willowes* (1584). We may note *Cristemanneswylewes* (1230) and *Daysterrewilug(h)* (1336–7) in Whittle-sey, but the association with 'Christian man' and 'daystar' is obscure, *Goswelugh* (1446), *Ravenswilgh* (1603).

wende, ME (n), 'turning, turn, bend' (cf. PN Ess 542 *s.n.* Wendens and Wendy *supra* 67) is used of a winding stream in *Brokwende* (1250). Cf. also *le Wende* (t. Ric 2), *Middelwende* (1300), *Bradewende* (1309), probably used of a road.

wēr, 'fishing-weir,' is very common, particularly in the Isle of Ely. We have reference to situation in *Northwere* (1086 InqEl), *Suth-* (1277), *Estweyr* (1549), *Middelwestwere* (13th), *Vttrewere* (1086 InqEl), *Uttreste-* (1170), *Middel-* (1170), *Midleste-* (1221), *Ouer-* (1221), i.e. 'upper,' *Vt-* (1221), *Bacweres* (1221), *Pol-* (1169), *Barre-* (1199) (*v.* barre), *Mare-* (1221) either on the boundary (*v.* (ge)mǣre) or more likely, in the mere, *Strem-* (t. Hy 3), *Lache-* (t. Hy 3) (*v.* lache), *Byte-* (1277) in a bend (*v.* byht), *Brug-* (1225), *E-* (1221) on the river (*v.* ēa), *Grante-* (1221) on the Granta at Ely, *Stret-* (1221), *Bed-* (1251) prob-ably from *byde,* 'hollow,' *Kroc-* (1277) in a corner (*v.* krókr), *Heth-*

(1330) by a hithe, *Stok-* (1315) (*v.* stocc), *Stonildewere* (14th), probably by a gravel slope (*v.* stān, hielde). *Boiwere*, *Buiwere*, *Biwere* (1086 InqEl) in Ely, *Bi-*, *Bywere* (1221–77) in Upwell, (1344–80) in Sutton, are probably from byge, 'bend of a stream.' We have a number of 'new' weirs, *Neo-*, *Newewere* (1086 InqEl), several examples of *Dep(e)-were* (1170–1450), and other descriptive attributes in *Little-* (1221), *Lange-* (1221), *Wrong-* (1378), 'twisted' from wrang, *Naked-* (1251), *Mery-* (1277), 'pleasant,' *Bytere-* (1251), *Grop-* (1086 InqEl), where fish had to be 'groped' for, *Hali-* (1294), 'holy,' *Men-* (13th), 'common' (*v.* (ge)mæne), *Nepe-* (1086 InqEl) from OE nēp, 'scanty, very low,' *Hake-* (1221) from OE haca, 'hook,' 'bend,' *Haked-* (1277) probably 'hooked, curved.' We have reference to frogs in *Paddok(es)-were* (1469), to swans in *Swanwere* (1306) and to sedge in *Segwere* (1169). *Sponware* (1284) seems to contain OE spōn, 'shaving, chip,' but in what sense is not clear. Beneficial ownership is indicated in *Bissopiswere* (t. Hy 3), *Cherchewere* (1170), *Chapelwere* (1366) and *Munkeswere* (1473), and there are many compounds with a personal name, *Dunni(n)g(es)were*, *Chelmes-*, *Vttrechelmes-* (1086 InqEl), i.e. *Cēolhelm*'s outer weir, *Alwoldinge-*, *Wlgares-*, *Benning-* (1221), *Archdeacons Ware* (1608). Note also *Letelknaueswere* (1341) from OE cnafa, 'boy, servant,' and *Cristemellware* (1531), *Christmereweyre* (1558) from OE cristelmǣl, 'cross.' *Spichwar* (t. Hy 3) contains the element *spic* discussed *s.nn.* Poles Pitch (PN Sx 190) and Fastbridge (PN Sr 222–3), denoting marsh land or a small stream. Cf. Wallenberg (KPN 39–40). The Westphalian *spik* and the Dutch *spike* were used of a 'fish-weir.' This may have been called simply *spic* to which was added *wer* when the meaning of this rare word was forgotten.

weyour, ME (n), 'horse-pond,' first noted in PN Ess 594, has been found four times as *Wayer'* (1326), *Wayour* (1343–96) and in the compound *Wayourbrynke* (1447).

wīc is less common than in Essex or Herts. It is well scattered throughout the county and is not always used in the sense 'dairy-farm.' No references to animals have been noted. Once we have reference to beans, *Benewyk* (1436), twice to sedge, *Seg(e)wyk(e)* (1285, 1498) and once to a kiln, *Kilnesvic* (1208). Twice it occurs uncompounded, *Wyche* (1392, 1467), once compounded with eald, 'old,' *Eldwic* (13th), and occasionally with the owner's name, *Tidbrihtwic* (1151) from OE Tīdbeorht, *Boydyneswyke* (1321), *Pollardeswyke* (1456); *Monekwyke* (1324) belonged to the monks of Thetford (Nf). Note also *Wycstede* (13th).

wielle, 'spring' or 'stream,' usually the former, is very common indeed. It is most frequently compounded with ceald, 'cold,' *Calde-* (1220), *Kald-* (1250), *Chalde-* (1300), *Chold-* (1219), *Chade-* (1204). Frequent too are compounds with *Litle-* (1250), *Blac-* (1230) and *W(h)yte-* (1280). Other descriptive elements are *Eld-* (1373), 'old' from eald, *Mikkil-* (1376), *Suete-*, *Swot-* (1250), 'sweet,' *Salte-* (1241),

Pisse- (1228), *Derne*- (14th), 'difficult to find' from **dierne**, *Spreng*- (1319), 'spring,' *Ful*- (1342), 'dirty,' *Stan*- (1282), *Crom*- (1353) from **crumb**, 'crooked,' *Hole*- (1293) from **holh**, 'hollow,' *Gysle*-, *Gosel*- (1387) from OE **gysel*, 'gushing' (cf. DEPN *s.n.* Gisburn WRY), *Rottewelle* (1483) in Cambridge and *Rutwell hill dean* (1643) in Bourn, also *Rutthall Dean* (1610), *Ruttedeane* (1668), 'snoring spring' from OE *hrūtan*, 'to snore,' and several examples of *Stoc(k)*- (1250–1512). These springs were frequented by horses, *Hors*- (1319), bulls, *Bole*- (1305–73), lambs, *Lambe*- (1340), pigs, *Swynes*- (1372), harts, *Hert*- (t. Ric 2), wild-cats, *Cat*- (1553), foxes, *Fox*- (1315), frogs, *Paddok*- (1395), kites, *Puttokes*- (1275), crows, *Crowes*- (13th), ravens, *Rauenes*- (1349) and bees, *Be*-, *Bu*- (13th). Trees and vegetation growing near were *Wyle*- (1303), 'willows,' *Ash*- (1604), cress, *Carse*- (1195), *Kerse*- (13th), *Cras*- (1251), *Cres*- (1309), rushes, *Risse*- (1250), *Resse*- (13th), reeds, *Bone*- (1415) from OE *būne* and barley and beans, *Bere*- (14th), *Bene*- (1470). *Wodewalle* (1353) was in a wood; *Sevewelles*, *Sewelles* (1250) and *Sywelle* (1395) were groups of seven springs, cf. Sewell, PN W 94, 107–8, whilst *Fourewell* (1389) refers to a less usual group of four. Compounds with a personal name are frequent: *Serlinges*- (1150), *Darnodes*- (1198), *Alemunde*- (1235), *Osemunde*- (1250), *Ha- kounis*- (1300), *Grimis*- (14th), *Normannes*-, *Anneis*- (13th). Note also *Athelingewelle* (1228) (OE *æðeling*, 'prince'), *Prestes*- (1185), *Maide*- (13th), *Mongeres*- (1312), 'trader's,' *Seynt Nycolas Welle* (1429) and *Kune*-. This element sometimes occurs in the Anglian form -*walle* as in *Witewalle* (1287), *Dernewalle* (14th).

wiht (n). There is abundant evidence for an element *wyght*, etc. deriving from OE *wiht*, especially in Fenland documents. It is used of a small enclosure, e.g. in Sutton, *unum wyghte* (containing half an acre) 1344 *Ct*, *unum whyghte* 1391 ib., *unum whitam* 1424 *ElyCh*. We read of *terras, wyhtas, piscarias et redditus* and that *una wyhta prout fossatis includitur* (1327 *ElyCh*). A grant of a messuage and *una wyczha* is made in Barway (1329 *StJohn's*) and of a messuage and a small *weyhta* (1336 ib.) and of *unum clausum vocat' a weight* (1462 *Pembroke*) in Soham. We may note also *le Wehttecroft* (1278 ib.), *le Hallewyght* (1370 *Ct*), *Shyllyngeswyghte* (1391 ib.), *Dereleghweyghts* (1397 ib.), *Spencer's* and *Monkes Weight* 18.. *Map* (all in Soham), *le Wyght de Alders* (1475 *Ct*) in Sutton, *Gilsons wyte* (1617 *SewersD*) in Mepal, *Guntons Wight* (1674 *BLAcct*) in Haddenham. Its ultimate history is obscure. It would seem that the word is the same as the *wiht* which gave rise to Great Whyte (PN BedsHu 216, xli). There and in White- hill (O), earlier *Wihthull*, the word seems to denote a 'bend' and to be associated with *wīcan*, 'to move.' Possibly from denoting land in a bend the name may have come to mean land surrounded by winding ditches. In the *wiht-tūn* which lies behind Utton (*supra* 173), it must still have something of its original sense, for the name can hardly have the sense 'enclosure-enclosure.' The actual site of Utton is unknown.

wīngeard (n) appears as *Wynyard* (1240), *Wyneʒerd* (1315), -*yerd* (1339) and as *Vineyerd* (1339) and *Vynyardes* (1529).

wiðegn (n), 'willow,' is found in *Schortewithins* (1344) side by side with *Longewydyes* (1384) from wiðig.

worþ, 'enclosure,' is found occasionally as in *æt Mawyrþe* (c. 975), *Hillingworth* (1331), *Stani-, Stanyw(o)rthe* (1302–90) (v. stān), *Ban(e)-worth(e)* (1332–1510) from bēan, 'bean.'

wrang, 'crooked, twisted,' in addition to its frequent adjectival use in *Wrongdole, Wrangdich*, etc. is also used independently as a noun for a crooked, twisted piece of land as in *Wrong(e)* (1260), (*la*) *Longe-wrong(e)* (1260, 1300), *Atelongwronge* (1255), *Byrswrong* (1251), *Sal-mans wronge* (1579).

wudu, 'wood,' is fairly common. We may note *Fildenewd* (t. Hy 2) which seems, paradoxically enough, to denote 'wood in the open country' (v. feld and cf. Fieldon Bridge, PN Wa 15), *Kywod* (t. Ric 1) from cȳ, 'kine,' *Hachwode* (1251) (v. hæcce), *Hangendewud* (1235), *Heywode* (1270) (v. (ge)hæg), *Sunderwde* (1279) from *sundor*, 'apart,' *Kyngeswode* (1230), *Menechenewode* (1251), 'nuns,' from OE *myncen*, *Presteswode* (1319) and an occasional personal name, as in *Good-redeswode* (1449) from William *Godred* (1403).

(b) *Some of the more common elements in field and minor names either not found or of rare occurrence in early records.*

bedlam survives as Bedlam in field-names and in Bedlam Fm in Haddenham, Fm and Hill in Manea, Fm, Bridge and Drain in March, for which we have no early forms. This must be the ME *bedlem*, the colloquial form for the Hospital of St Mary of Bethlehem in London which became a hospital for lunatics. Later, this became a common name for a madhouse and also for houses for discharged, but often only half-cured patients of Bethlehem Hospital. Some of these places may have been small private asylums, but as a rule we probably have here a derogatory nickname for places where only madmen would attempt to farm.

beggar is found in derogatory names such as *Beggars Bush* (1655) and *Beggers Welle* (1392) and *Beggersfeild* (1659).

cinquefoil in association with *field* and *close* is fairly common in the forms *Cinque Foil, Cinque Foin* and *Sainfoin*. The earliest examples are *Cinquefoil Close* (1797) and *the Cinquefoyne* (1809).

clamp, 'pile, stack,' is found in *Brick Clamp Close*. It also appears as *Brick Clump* and *The Clump*.

cow pasture(s) is fairly common. We also find *Brook* and *Horse Pasture*. First noted in *the Cowpasture, Cow Pasture Wood* (1614).

dolver is to-day a common term in the fens for 'a freehold piece of fenland' usually of about eight acres, cf. (from a 'particulars of sale' of 1859) "a Dolver of Fenland containing 8a 0r 36p more or less," "a half-dolver...containing 3a 2r 7p, more or less." According to EDD it means 'reclaimed fenland' and is used in Suffolk of 'a piece of land, bog or peat ground where peat is cut' or dug. The word must be associated with OE *delfan*, 'to dig.' In modern field-names it survives as *The Dolver(s)*, *Great*, *Little*, *Ladies*, *Horse* and *Tansey Dolfer*. Early examples are rare; we may note *the ix dolvers* (1599) in Whittlesey, *Delfer* (1660) in Cottenham.

folly[1] as used in place-names is fully discussed in PN Wa 382–5, PN W 451–2, and it is there shown that it commonly has reference to some example of human extravagance or folly, but occasionally is used of a small plantation, a usage which it is difficult to explain, unless it is due to early and false etymologising which associated the word folly (Fr *folie*) with *feuillée*, 'leafy place.' It has been noted in *Folly*, *Folly Close* and *Diepups Folly*. In Cheveley we have three examples, *Castle Folly* near the ruins of the castle where we might expect a reference to human folly, except that this probably corresponds to the modern Castle Plantation, and *Hay Stack* and *Red Gate Folly*, and all are probably small plantations. *The Folly* in Dry Drayton is a spinney. Earlier examples are *le Folys* (1391), *Little Swafham follis* (1719) described as a ditch (in Bottisham) and the curious *Foly loye* in Soham.

gravel is used of some artificial block in a fenland stream, cf. "there is a *gravell* maintayned by the Commoners of Cottenham into or nere the middest of the River at a place called 20 pence" (1617 *Dugd*), "Ouze...made shallow by *gravell* and fords (which they call hards)" (1618 BedL).

home is fairly common in *Home Close*, *Croft*, *Field*, *Meadow*, *Orchard*, *Pasture* and *Pightle*. It denotes land adjacent to the farm or homestead.

honey is used of sticky or muddy soil. *v.* Honey Hill *supra* 166.

lairstall is interpreted in NED as 'grave within a church.' This will hardly fit its use in field-names; there it probably denotes 'site of an animal's lair.'

lammas is found in *Lammas Close*, *Fen*, *Mead*, *Meadow* and *Pightle*, so called from the custom whereby certain lands became common pasturage from Lammas-tide (1st August) until the following spring. The earliest example noted is *two lammas leyes* (1666).

leam is used occasionally of a drain or watercourse in the fen district. Its history is obscure.

lot is common as in *The Lotts*, *Half Lot*, *Long Lot*, *Drove Lot*, *Pit Lot*, *Reach Lots*, *Frith Head Lot* and *Lots Close* and has reference to the allotment of reclaimed land in the fens by drawing lots. Cf. The Lots *supra* 150.

---

[1] Cook's Folly in Walthamstow (Ess), where this element was not recorded, was a large house (now demolished) with a pillared front like that of a Greek temple. The builder is said to have been ruined. In the Colchester district *folly* is used of a footpath.

lucerne, used of fields where *lucerne-grass* grows, is found in *Lucerne Field* and *Piece*.

paradise is a complimentary nickname, cf. *Paradise Close* (1666).

pen, 'enclosure,' survives in *The Pen, Little, Cooks, Hen* and *Cuckoo Pen*. Cf. *Oxpenne* (1546). *v.* penn. *Pen Hill* is more likely to be a hill marked by a *pen* than to be a hybrid of Celtic *penn*, 'hill,' and English *hill*.

rainbow is found occasionally as *Rainbow Field*. Earlier examples are *Reynbowe ffurlonde* (1316), *Rainbow* (*shot*) (1757). They may possibly be so named from a rainbow once seen stretching over them. More probably they were so called because they were ploughed 'rainbow,' i.e. with the plough following the curve of the field boundary (cf. PN Ess 600).

roundabout(s) occurs occasionally for a field surrounded by a wood or for a field surrounding a clump of trees.

runnel, 'small stream,' is found in *Long* and *Short Runnels* (1774) and *Rynnels* (1595).

ryegrass, one of several species of *lolium* extensively used as forage or fodder grass, is found both alone and compounded with *Field* and *Piece*.

severals refers to land in private ownership, especially enclosed land as opposed to common land.

shoals, *v. supra* 175.

shoulder of mutton and leg of mutton are both found with reference to the shape of the field.

skirt(s) is used in the fenland parishes of land on the edge or skirt of the fen, cf. *the skirtes* (*and borders*) *of Gruntie fenne and Rushe fenne* (1595 *Depositions*) and PN Ess 597. It survives in *Skirts, Skirt Ground* and *Skirt Land*.

slipe is common. It denotes a long, narrow strip and occurs also as *Slipes, The Slip* and in *Long* and *River Slipe*.

spong, 'narrow piece of land,' is found occasionally as *Spong* and *Sponge*. Cf. "a certain *spong* of pasture" (1604 *Atkyns*), *Free Spong*(*e*)*s* (*Close*) (1675 *WMP*) and PN Nth 277. ME *spong*, 'a long, narrow field.'

(c) *Miscellaneous field-names*.

Names referring to the discovery of dead bodies are not uncommon. Though these may, at times, refer to scenes of medieval tragedy, they more probably point to the discovery of some skeleton or even to the site of some ancient cemetery (cf. Street Way and *Deadman's Way supra* 30, 22). In Ickleton we have *le Dedeman* and *Dedmanhyll* (1455), another *Dedeman* is found in Foxton (1327), *Dedemannesdale* in Cambridge (1299), *Deadmans Bushes* (17th) in Burrough Green and *Dedesman lane* (1543) in Wisbech, whilst in Boxworth we have *Ded-*

cherlweye (1300) and in Guilden Morden, where an early Iron Age and Romano-British cemetery has recently been excavated (CAPr xxvii, xxxvi) we have *Dedcharle* (1525). In four instances the skeleton was that of a woman (OE *cwēn, wīf*), (*le*) *Dedequene* (1260) in Papworth and (1349) in Haslingfield, where we also find *le Dedwyf* (1400), a name recurring in *atte Dedewif* (1506) in Harlton.

Of the references to social classes in minor names, the most frequent is to OE *æcerman*, 'husbandman, ploughman,' in such names as *Akermanesland* (1221), *Akermanestret* (13th) and *Akermannespoles* (1221). The churl or free peasant (ceorl) gave name to *Cherlesfeld* (1221), whilst the corresponding Scandinavian peasant proprietor (ON **bóndi**) is represented by *Bondemadwe* (1259) and *le Bondesmade* (1326) and the peasant freeman (ON **karl**) as opposed to the *jarl* by *Carlecroft* (1308). Others are *Suoneshamstel* (1251) from OE **swān**, 'peasant,' *Sokemannyfen* (1336) from ME *sokman*, 'free peasant owing suit of court,' *Cotsetleshoue* (1309) from *cotsetla*, 'cottager.' Note also *Schepmanneslowe* (1405), carrying back the word *sheepman* nearly 200 years, and *letelknaueswere* (1341). Tenure is referred to in *Fullondgouelerthe* (1324) from *gavelerth*, 'the duty of ploughing so much ground for the lord,' and *Molland* (1461), 'emancipated copyhold held by payment of a quit-rent' (*v.* PN Ess 126–7, *s.n.* Mollands).

Noteworthy is the frequency of field-names formed with a prefixed prepositional phrase, a type particularly noticeable in Devonshire (*v.* PN D xxxvii). In addition to examples in major names (Introd. xxxvii n.) we may note

(i) *Atelongewronge* (1255), *Attewesternelowe* (1267), (*campo voc.*) *Atteston* (13th), *Atehithe* (13th), *Atecrofteshendes* (1301), *atte Dedewif* (1506).

(ii) *Byneþenlosho* (1251), *Bynethebradeweye* (1279), *Binethewodewey* (1294), *Beneþeyelowe* (1300), *Benethewey* (1317), *Bynethebrok* (1349), *Bynethewarennerescroft* (1380).

(iii) *Understanworþe* (1302), *Underbanhul* (1320), *Underlichelake heved* (1331), *Undernethedounehulle* (1383).

(iv) *Bituenestrete* (1251), *Betwenetosmaleweys* (1328).

(v) (field called) *Byondeton* (1316), *be ȝounde the toun* (1395), *beȝondtownefeld* (1431), *Balesdoun Beȝoundetoun* (1382), *Byhoundebrok'* (1308).

(vi) *Withoutenacres* (1301).

(vii) (*apud*) *Besuthen* (1339), *Bestynglowe* (14th) from *be ēastan hlāwe*, 'east of the hill.'

(viii) *Abovenyemadwe* (14th), (furlong called) *Above Metlecroft* (1315), *Abouetowres* (1422).

(ix) (land called) *Betwixtetheweys* (1522).

An interesting feature is the use of the superlative adjective in compounds, occasionally alone, as in the Ely fishing-weirs called *Vuerest* and *Niderest*, *Nithereast* (1086 InqEl), and in *Brodestlode* (1378), *Midlestewere* (1221), *Uttrestewere* (1170), *Vtmestebeche* (13th), *Ouerestedole* (1319).

No name has been noted referring to heathen worship, but we have reference to goblins in *Pokemilne* (1260), *Pokelodelake* (1397), *Pokle* (1570) and *Schokepet* (1431), and to giants in *þrispit* (1250), *Thurspit* (13th). *v.* pūca, scucca, þyrs.

In manorial names, the use of the French definite article before the surname, first noted in PN Ess xxxii, 297, is not uncommon. *le Kentes* (13th) alternating with *le Kentesgoren* (1260), the land of Walter de *Kent*, *le Drakes* (1325), *le Maners* (1360), later *Maneresfee* (1403), *le Rowys* (1455), *le Aleyns* (1472). We also find this used of ecclesiastical ownership in *le Carmes* (t. Ed 1) from the Carmelites of Cambridge and *le Munchenys* (1460) from the nuns of Stratford.

Among isolated names of interest are *plot called Littlebaldok* (1322) in Orwell which seems to be named from Baldock (PN Herts 120–1); *S(c)hakepoke* (1298–1438), the name of fisheries in Ely and Sutton perhaps so unproductive that the fisherman had to shake his 'poke' to find his catch; *Goldhoard al. Goldwellfurlong* (1590) was the site of some long-lost treasure trove; *le Ma(u)mpasse* (1570–87), one of the few French names, was a difficult passage; the boundary between Wisbech and Elm is referred to in *Devyse* (1438), from OFr *devise*, 'boundary,' a parallel to Devizes (PN W 242–3); *viam de la garite* and *Garitefeld* (1290) must have taken name from some watch-tower (OFr *garite*); *Frauncmauntel* (1315) perhaps had reference to some movable pent-house or an enclosure for fattening animals (ME *frank*, OFr *franc*); *Charlestyng* (1381) probably contains ME *thing*, 'possession' (cf. PN Nth 270); *le Shyouele* (1345), *le Shovell* (1522) and *le Spade* (1407) probably took name from their shape, whilst *Wanelsbreast* (1355), *Shortboulster* (1627), *Bunchedole* and *Philippesbunch* (1432) employ common terms in a topographical sense (ME *bunch*, 'protuberance, hump'). We have reference to places of punishment in *le Galwys* (1392), *le Pyllarye* (1453), *Cuxstoole meadow* (1577). *Draxes Entre* (1354) carries back the meaning 'passage between two houses' some fifty years. Very curious are a field called *Nean church* (1728) in Chatteris, *the Muses in Rotten Rowe* (1566) in Waterbeach, and *one acre at Pytteman* (1477) in Haslingfield. We have a *Christmas Bush* (1626) in Steeple Morden and a *Tybourne Greene* (1669) in March. *Alstonescastel* (1204) in Sawston may contain OE *cæstel*, 'a heap of stones,' cf. Studies² 136 *s.n.* Castley (WRY). *Pylekok* (1251, 1277) in Upwell is identical with the old name of Thornham Magna (Sf), *Pelecoc* 1230–40, *Pilecoc* 1255, which Ekwall derives from ON *pill*, Swed *pil*, 'willow' and OE *cocc*, 'heap' in the sense 'clump, cluster of trees,' hence 'willow-copse' (Studies² 83), an explanation eminently suitable in this district.

The modern field-names *The Sixes*, *Five Close* and *Friers Nine* are paralleled earlier by *le Syxtene* (1319), *apud Eyteandtwenty* (1432) and *le Sixes* (1600); to what the numerals refer is not clear.

For many we have no early forms at all. This is specially true of names of the nickname type which are common.

Sometimes they are complimentary as in *Apple Pasty Acre*, *Bright Jimmy*, *Butter Field and Mead*, *Butter Milk Field*, *Fillcups*, *Mount Pleasant*, *Saucy Close*, *Surprise Grove*, *Sweet Lips*, *Sweet Place*, *Sweet Plots* and *Venus Croft*.

More often they are uncomplimentary as in *Bugs Close*, *Buggs Hill*, *Burnt Ground*, *Cold Rain*, *Cuckolds Haven*, *Frogs Abbey* and *Frog's Hall* (used of marshy ground), *Hungry Hill*, *Jonah's Field*, *Knaves Acre*, *Lord Helpus*, *Louse Gap*, *Lousey Leys*, *Pickpocket*, *Rats Close*, *Sour Lay*, *Great* and *Little Shavings*, *Stark Naked Close*, *Starve Goose* (several). *Little London* is used of two cottages "now tenantless, out of repair, and not likely to be inhabited again" (F. A. Walker, *Dry Drayton* 31). *Coldharbour* is a nickname of reproach for an exposed place and has no special archaeological significance (cf. PN Sr 406–10).

Such nicknames are usually very late, but a few earlier examples are found: *Blakemonendaykote* (1294), *Milkfurlong* (1312), *le Watery* (1395), *Honeysweet acre* (1406), *le Plenty* (1445), *Nanlefte* (1279), a balke called *drawbacke* (16th), *Sharpshankes* (1510), *Spornewolf* (1332), a sand called *the Thief* (1605). *Derebouth* (1240) in Chatteris, *Derbought lane* (1521) in Wisbech and *Little Deerebought* (1685) in Wicken carry back the history of *dear-bought* some 150 years.

Very small fields are ironically named *Hundred Acres* and *Thousand Acres*. Remote fields are named from distant countries and places such as *America*, *Bunkers Hill*, *China Close*, *Dunkirk*, *Flanders Ground*, *Gibraltar Close*, *Isle of Elba*, *Jamaica*, *Jerusalem*, *New England*, *New Zealand*, *Scotland* and *Yorkshire*.

Shape is indicated in *The Cocked Hat*, *Elbow Pond*, *Gridiron*, *Harp Close*, *Horse Shoe Plantation*, *Hunch Back*, *Pancake*, *Peacock Tail*, *Saddle Shot*, *Scizzors Piece* and *Trundle Meadow*.

Lands used for charitable purposes bear such names as *Abbey Close*, *Chantry Close*, *Chapel Close*, *Church Close* and *Pit*, *College Close*, *Pest House Close* (cf. PN Ess 596), *Poors Piece* and *Garden*, *Priory Close* and *Templars*. Land in doubtful ownership is denoted by *No Mans Piece*, *No Mans Land*.

Entirely enigmatic are *Blind Feet Shot*, *Fighting Hedges*, *Hen and Chickens*, *Hung Tucks*, *Thummim*.

(*d*) *Field-names of which the history can for the most part be traced, arranged under hundreds and parishes.*

I. Armingford Hundred

ABINGTON PIGOTTS (*TA*). Paradise (Grove) (cf. *supra* 354). Spotmear (*Spotmere* c. 1236 *Wymond*, *-furlong* 1274 Cl. *v.* mere). Wendy Moor (*Wendimor* 1202 *FF*, *v.* mor and Wendy *supra* 67).

CROYDON CUM CLOPTON (*TA*). West Rea (cf. *Ree Place* t. Hy 8 CAPr xxxiii. Near here lived Humfrey *atte Ree* of Clopton (1272 *Ass*). *v.* Rhee *supra* 14).

EAST HATLEY (*TA*). For Black Leys, Ley Close, Long Ley, *v.* lǣs, lēah.

LITLINGTON (*TA*). Abbots Close (cf. *le habotts hedlond* 14th *Wymond*, so named from the Abbot of Wymondley (Herts)). Punts Close (cf. The Punts *supra* 152). South End Close (*le Sowthhende* 14th *Wymond*).

MELBOURN (*TA*). Mill Close (cf. *le Mellefeld* 1385 *Peterhouse*, *Milnefelde* 1401 Cl). Portway Close (*v.* Portway *supra* 28). Carden Hill Road (on pre-enclosure map; *Calewedonefeld, Caluedenefeld* 1319 *Extent, Calwedonehel* 1335 *Peterhouse*, *Calfdenfeld* 1439 ib., *Caudun(e)-feldhyll* 1492 *St John's, Cawden hill* 1584 *Ct, Carlton Hill* 1829 Wells. 'Bare hill,' *v.* calu, dūn, with some confusion with a first element cealf and a second denu).

MELDRETH[1]. Boy Bridge (*Boy bridge ditch* 1707 Meldreth. Cf. Boy Bridge *supra* 52). Gilton Arch (cf. *Gilton Ford* 1675 *WMP, Gilten Bridge* 1697 Meldreth, *Guilton Bridge* 1707 ib., *ground* 1726 ib. Possibly 'guildsmen's ford and bridge.' Cf. Ealing Bridge (PN Ess 37), but the phonology is difficult. The guild of Meldreth had property here in 1547). Manton (*Manton* (*Bank*) 1708 Meldreth). Meldreth Holme Bridge (so called in 1699 ib. Cf. *Little holm* c. 1300 *Christ's, Holmes Bryge* 1526 *WMP, v.* holmr). Peat More (*Pykemore* 1526 *WMP*, 1606 *Ct, Pikemore* 1578 ib., *Peekemore* 1594 ib., *Peek More* 1699 Meldreth, *v.* mōr. Perhaps so called from its pointed shape).

GUILDEN MORDEN (*EnclA* 1800). Chipping Furlong (*v.* cīeping, 'market'). For Gotswick Leys and Stocking Croft *v.* lǣs, stocking.

STEEPLE MORDEN (*TA*). Ashwell Way (*v.* Ashwell Street *supra* 19). Bennetts Bank (cf. *Bennet balk* 1626 *Eg* and *v.* balke). Clunch Pit (*Clunchpit hill* 1675 *Eg*). Ditch Fd (cf. *le Dik* 13th *Wymond*). Fox Holes (*Fox(h)ole* 13th *CaiCh, Foxhulforlong* 1407 *St John's, v.* fox-hol). Hawks (*Hawkeshegges* 1466 ib.). Holywell Close and Hollywells

---

[1] For much of this information we are indebted to the late Dr W. M. Palmer.

(*Hol(e)well(e)* 1274 Cl, 1296 *Ct*, *Hollowell* 1626 *Eg*. 'Hollow spring,' *v.* holh, wielle). Horse Doles (*Horsedoles* ib., *v.* dāl). Hundred Acres ((*le*) *Hundaker* 13th *Wymond*. The actual area is 1 rood, 3 perches, cf. *supra* 357). Lark Hill (*Lauerechell* c. 1212 *Wymond*, *Larkhill* 1592 *Bodl*, *v.* lāwerce). Mill Close (cf. *Melleholme* 1384 *StJohn's*). Odsey Hill (*v.* Odsey *supra* 62). Offals Wood (*le Eldefeld* c. 1272 *Wymond*, *Oldfeldebalke* 1466 *StJohn's*, *v.* eald, feld and Offal End *supra* 78). Reeve Shot (cf. *le Reueaker* 13th *Wymond*, *-acres* 1377 *StJohn's*. Field associated with the reeve). Tween Towns (is midway between Guilden and Steeple Morden, *v.* tūn and Between Ditches *supra* 241). Westbrook Hill (cf. *Westbroc* c. 1212 *Wymond*). For Cinque Foil Fd, Ley Fd, Calves Pightle, Slipes, Town Land, *v.* cinquefoil, lēah, pightel, tūn. For Small Gains *v. supra* 357.

The School adds Crow Hill (*Crouzhulledoune* 1380 *StJohn's*, *Croughhull* 1402 *Ct*, *Crowhull* 1473 *StJohn's*. The first element here may be OE *crōh*, 'saffron.' Cf. *Saffron ground furlong* 1675 *Eg* (in this parish), or it may be OE *crōg*, *crōh*, 'vessel, pitcher, crock.' This is, perhaps, more likely, as the hill is only just south-east of a Roman cemetery where, among other things, vases have been discovered). The Diggings (the site of former coprolite diggings). The Duckuss (the site of 'Duckett's Mansion'). Gallows Hill (*Gallowhill* 1592 *Bodl*, where the gallows stood).

TADLOW (*TA*). Aldcocks (perhaps to be identified with *Oldewyke* 1429 *Ct*. 'Old dairy farm,' *v.* eald, wīc). Cf. All Docks and Aldicks (PN Ess 640, 648). For Cinque Foin Close, Black, Dry and Long Leys, Church, Home and Wood Pightle, Sallow Hill, *v.* cinquefoil, lǣs, pightel, sealh.

WENDY (*TA*). Gammons Grove (*Gambons* 1465 FF. So called from the family of William *Gamboun* 1394 Cl). For Great and Home Pightle, *v.* pightel.

WHADDON (*TA*). Church Close (cf. *Chircheholme* 1513 *Christ's*, *v.* holmr). Courts Hill (cf. *le Cotes* 1398 ib. and *v.* cote). Dovehouse Close (cf. *Dovehouseyarde* 1554 Pat). Hargoods (*Hargat(e)(dich)* 1336 *Christ's*, *Hardgatedyche* 1513 ib.). Holmes (*in Hulmo, in Nova Holm'* 1224 FF, *Holm* 1377 WMP, *v.* holmr). Long Meadow (*le Langemade* t. Ed 1 *Christ's*). Meldreth Holme (*Melredholme* 1513 ib., *v.* Meldreth *supra* 60 and holmr). The Moor (*le mor* 1309 ib., *v.* mōr). White Lands (*qwhytlond* 1398 *Christ's*). For Cinque Foin Fd, Pightle, River Slipe, *v.* cinquefoil, pightel, slipe. For Ridgeway Fd, *v. supra* 29.

II. Wetherley Hundred

ARRINGTON (*TA*). West Fd (cf. *Estfeld* 14th *CartMisc*). Hither and Further Wile and Wiles Pightle are, perhaps, to be associated with

Croydon Wilds *supra* 54. For Dean Fd, Long Leys and Pightle, *v.* denu, lǽs, pightel.

BARRINGTON (School). Church Hill (so named 1613 *HardwickeA*). Frexlands (*Flexlond* c. 1250 *Trinity*, where flax grows). Long Burrow (*Longeburwe* ib. Cf. *le Shorteburgh* 1425 *StCatharine's*. 'Barrow' or 'hill,' *v.* beorg). Middle Dean (cf. *Langedene, Prestesden* c. 1240 *Trinity, Storkesdene* c. 1279 *StCatharine's, Wrancdene, Wrankedene* c. 1250 *Trinity, Wrangeden* c. 1280 ib. (*v.* **wrang**)), *le Quarryedeane* 1571 *StCatharine's, v.* denu).

BARTON (*TA*). Church Close (cf. *Churchelandes* 1510 *StCatharine's*). Dicks Meadow (*Dykkes medowe* 1515 AD v). Priors Close (cf. *the pryours wey* 1524 ib. Merton Priory held the advowson). Round Close (cf. *le Rowndeplot* 1457 *StJohn's*). Stocks Close (cf. *Stocfurlang* 1203 FF. *v.* stocc).

COMBERTON (*TA*). Bean Hill (cf. *Benelonde(wey)* 1504 *Queens'*). Brocks Close (cf. *Brokkeshole* ib., *v.* brocchol). Harborough (*Harbourghfeld* 1518 *StJohn's, the Harbour Field* 1706 *Terr. v.* herebeorg, 'army-quarters,' with reference possibly to the unexplored mound at Comberton on the line of a supposed Roman road, *v.* Fox. 198). Hundred Acres (actually 1 rood, 36 perches, cf. *supra* 357). Mereway (*v. Mereways supra* 27). Toftshill (1706 *Terr.* Cf. *Toft hyll* 1504 *Queens'* and Toft *supra* 164). For The Doles, Gore, Kenting's and Robs Leys, *v.* dāl, gāra, lǽs.

COTON (School). The Brook (*le Brooke* 1436 *Clare*). Brook Close (cf. *Brokfurglong* (sic) 1235 *FF*). Clint Fd and Clint Hill (*Clintfeud* 1235 *FF, Clynt* 1395 *StJohn's, v. Clintway supra* 21). The Marsh (cf. *Marshffurlong* 1510 *StCatharine's*).

ORWELL (*EnclA* 1836). Downhill (*Downehill* 1600 *Depositions*). For Oxleys, Pickle Pasture, *v.* lǽs, pightel.

SHEPRETH (*TA*). Archer Meadow (cf. *Archesford* 13th *Chateriz* and *Archefoertheweye* 1392 *Ct* in Barrington). Carvers Meadow (cf. *Cal(d)berwe* c. 1280 *Chateriz,* 1328 *Trinity, Calwverfeld* 1458 *Peterhouse.* 'Cold hill or barrow,' *v.* beorg). Five Fools Mead (*le Fyfhowes* 13th *Chateriz.* 'Five barrows,' *v.* haugr). How Moor (cf. *Litlehowe* ib., *v.* haugr or hōh). Oslocks Meadow (adjacent to Horselick's Field *infra* 361).

WIMPOLE (*TA*). Broad Meadow (*Broadmead* 1320 *Add*). Brook Close (cf. *the brooke* 1494 *Hardwicke*). Dovehouse Close (cf. *the douffouspitill* 1316 *Add*). Moor Close (cf. *Mordole* 1231 *FF, Wynepolmore* c. 1250 *StJohn'sH*). Pond Fd (cf. *Pondes* 1501 *Add*). Priest Path (*le Prystis Path* 1429 *Peterhouse*). Burndole (*TA*) is now known as Burnt Dole (School). Ship Walk preserves the local pronunciation of *sheep*. Wimpole Hill is locally *Oddidod*, i.e. *hoddydod*, 'snail' (School).

III. Thriplow Hundred

FOWLMERE (*TA*). Holms (*le Holme* 1447 *Rental, v.* holmr). New Close (id. 1588 AD vi). Hangman's Mound is said to be where sheep stealers were hanged. Long Close (id. c. 1840 *TA*). Rayners (*Rayners Close* ib.). For Severalls *v.* severals.

FOXTON (School). Chardle Spring (*Cheldewellefelde* 1247 *Chateriz*, *Caldewell(e)* c. 1280 ib., *Chaldewelle* 1308 ib., *Chawdwell* 1520 ib. 'Cold spring,' *v.* cald, wielle and cf. Chardle Ditch *supra* 57). Draymer's Fd (*Dreymere(hil)* 13th *Chateriz*, 1308 *Trinity*, (*Smale-*) *dryemere* 1316–23 ib. 'Drag-net mere,' *v.* dræge, mere). Footpath to Fowlmere (*Fulmerepat* 1308 *Trinity*). Ham Fd (*Ham(feld)* 1308–28 ib. *v.* ham(m), probably hamm as it adjoins a brook). Hooper's Fd (*Hopper Field* c. 1840 *TA*). Horselick's Fd (*Oseloke* 1328 *Trinity*, *Ostlick Meadow* c. 1840 *TA*. 'Muddy enclosure,' *v.* wāse, 'mud' and loc(a). Cf. Oslocks Meadow *supra* 360).

NEWTON (School). Great and Little Brook Fd (*Brokfeld* 1319 *Extent*. Cf. *le Brokdole* ib. and *v.* brōc, dāl). Clunch Pit Fd (*Clunch Pit* c. 1840 *TA*). Collins Field (cf. *Collin Bush* ib.). White Fd (*le Wyt(h)efeld* 1319 *Extent*, *Whitefelde* 1418 *Ct*) (*TA*). Foxton Brook (id. 1567 AD vi). Great Mead (cf. (*le*) *Mechele-*, *Michelemede* 1319 *Extent*). Lease Meadow (*Lessesmade* ib.). Long Lands (*Longelond* c. 1250 *ElyM*). Lugslow (*Loggeslowe* 1319 *Extent*, *Lugeslow* 1564 *WMP*. Cf. *Lugges-londe* 1418 *Ct*). Mereway Shot (*v.* Mereways *supra* 27). Rowditch Shot (cf. *Roughdich* 1418 *Ct*). Thorn Shot (cf. *le Thorn, le Thorndole* 1319 *Extent*). Tibs Ham (*v.* ham(m)). White Hedges (*Whithedge* 1564 *WMP*). For Gore Shot *v.* gāra, scēat.

LITTLE SHELFORD. Cow Holm 1802 *EnclA, v.* holmr.

STAPLEFORD (School). Church Fd (*le Cherechefeld* 13th *ElyCh*). Mingle Lane (*le m(e)yndlandes* 1469, 1504 *Pembroke, Mingelandes* 1654 ib. From ME *meinde*, 'mingled,' perhaps used of lands which were intercommunal). Mutler Shot (*v.* Thriplow Hundred *supra* 82).

THRIPLOW (*TA*). Bushes Close (*le Bussh* 1445 AD vi). Church Close (cf. *Cherchefeld* 1314 ib. v). Pitters Alley (cf. *le Puthoo* 1445 ib. vi, *le Putthowe* 1576 *Ct*. 'Pit-hill,' *v.* pytt, hōh). Squirrels Close (*Squyreles* 1391 AD vi from the family of John *Squirel* (1360 ib.)). Townsend Close (*Townysendes* 1457 *St John's, Townesendelande* 1484 ib., *v.* tūn). For Bury Wells, *v.* burh (manorial).

IV. Whittlesford Hundred

Duxford (*TA*). Biggins (*Byggen* 1589 *Ct*, *v.* bigging). Blackland
(*le Blakelonde* 1296 *CaiCh*). Daber Noons (named from the family of
Roger *de Abernuin'* 1200 ChR). Little Holme (*le Holm* 1302 *CaiCh*,
v. holmr). Middle Fd (*Middelfeld* c. 1250 ib., *v.* feld). Moor Close
and Fd (cf. *le More* 1308 ib., *v.* mōr). Turf Pits (*le Turpyttes* 1589 *Ct*).

Sawston[1]. America is in a remote situation, cf. *supra* 357. Bitterum
Fd (*Bit(t)erholm* c. 1235 *ElyCh*, *ElyM*, *Bitherholm* c. 1260 *St John'sH*,
Bytter Holme Meddowe 1580 *Survey*, *v.* holmr. The first element is
probably OE *biter*, 'bitter,' here perhaps a variant of the more com-
mon *sour*, used of waterlogged lands as in Sour Grounds (*Sower
Grounds* 1763 *Huddleston*) in Sawston. Cf. *Bittermede* 1251 Ch (Long
Stanton)). Butlers (*Botelers* 14th *Huddleston*). Camping Close (id.
1703 ib., *v. supra* 153). Church Fds (cf. *Cherchefeld* 1401 ib.). The
Cross (id. 1687 ib.). Dovehouse Meadow (*Doffhousmede* 1391 ib.).
Harboroughs [ɑ·bərəz] (*Arburys*, *Awberys*, *Alberys* 15th–17th ib.).
Kettleley's Walk (an old rope-walk named after a rope-maker). Ladies'
Wash (tradition has it that this pool was used by the squires' ladies
as a bathing-pool). Monks Orchard (*Munkesortyarde* 14th *Huddleston*,
Moncks Orchyarde 1591 ib., probably with reference to the monks
of the Abbey of Gresteyn). Owbanks (*Hobacks* 1763 ib. Cf. Hoback
supra 68). Pampisford Hay [pɑ·nzə] (id. 1703 ib. Cf. *le Hay* 1328
Queens', *v.* (ge)hæg). Partridge Hill (*Parthrych holle* 1401 *Huddleston*,
Pertriche hill 16th Queens', *Pattarigge hill* 1612 ib.). Sawston's Orchard
(id. 16th *Huddleston*, named from the family of William *Sawston* (1554
ib.)). Stakon's Fd al. Stakenses (*Stakens*, *Stakeings* 17th, 1763 ib.
This is a ten-acre field. In the Court rolls there were various *stakings*
belonging to different people and also to the town itself. Cf. *Stacon
Lane* (PN Mx 29) and Stakenford (PN Wo 150)). Also called Tom
Tits). Town Close (id. 1613 *Huddleston*). West Moor (cf. *Weste-
mormade* 1396 ib., *v.* mōr). Whitefield (*Wytefeld* 1461 ib. Very chalky
soil).

Whittlesford (School). Barfield (cf. *Barrebrooke* 1449 *Pembroke* and
v. barre). Bridgemoor (*le Breggemoore* ib., *v.* mōr). The Splash (*The
Plashe* 1578 *Huddleston*, *v.* plæsc).

V. Chilford Hundred

Great Abington. On a map of 1716 we have Hungry Hill (*supra* 357)
and Sunken Church Fd. The latter would seem to take its name from
the *Sunkin-Church* mentioned by Morant, *History of Essex* (ii, 556),
"By the roadside which leads from *Chesterford* to *Gogmagog-hills*…

[1] In this parish we are much indebted to the School and to Mr T. F. Teversham.

are some ruins of a Building, by the neighbourhood called *Sunkin-Church*." Cf. *Sunkenechyrche* (t. Hy 3) in Brixworth (PN Nth 274).

BABRAHAM (School). Steeple Hill (cf. *le Stapele* 1199 FF, *le Stapelacre* 1420 *Clare*, v. stapol. So named from some post or pillar). Sunderlands Belt and Corner (*Surderland* (sic) 1141–7 Colch, *le Sunderlond de Baburgham* 1390 *ElyF*, *Sunderland* 1802 *EnclA*. v. sundorland, 'separate land.' Belt and Corner are some distance apart, both on the parish boundary, the latter at the junction of the parishes of Babraham, Sawston and Pampisford. The last reference is from Sawston. This was probably a detached part of the Stapleford possessions of Ely).

BARTLOW (*TA*). The Breeds (cf. *Chirchebrede* 1409 Pat, v. brædu).

CASTLE CAMPS (*TA*). Goodwood Fd (*God(e)wude* c. 1275 *AddCh*). Great and Little Impy (cf. Empty Common *supra* 40). Stone Fd (*le Stonfeld* 1313 *AddCh*). Tangley Common (*Tangeleye* 1346 *Cole* ii. Cf. Tangley (PN Sr 256–7). The interpretation of *tang* is difficult. It may derive from a lost OE *tang(e)*, 'tongue or *tang* of land').

SHUDY CAMPS (*TA*). Calves Ley (cf. *Caluescroft* c. 1300 *ElyM*). Church Fd (*Cherchefeld* 1219 *FF*). Elbrows (sic) (cf. *Eldebery* 1303 *Waltham*, v. eald, burh). Lindcrofts (*Lincroft* 13th *Waltham*, v. līn, 'flax' and croft). Pollywells (*Polheiwell* c. 1275 *AddCh*. v. pōl, (ge)hæg, wielle). Readings (*le Redinge* 1313 *AddCh*, v. ryding). Sheep Close (cf. *Schepesland* 13th *Waltham*). Stockings (*Stokinge* ib., v. stocking). Stone Fd (*Stanfeld* ib., *Stonfeld* 1338 Seld ix). For Lousey, Ox and Stoney Leys, Back and Moat Pightle, Severals, v. læs, pightel, severals.

HORSEHEATH (*TA*). Dovehouse Fd (cf. *Duffhouse Crofte* 1536 *Jesus*). Moor Meadow (cf. *Morland* 1207 FF, v. mōr). For Berry Field, Chalk and High Leys, Calves Pightle, v. burh (manorial), læs, pightel.

LINTON (*TA*). Ballydon Hill ((*Over*)*balydon*(*felde*) 1487, 1515 *Pembroke*, *Balyngdon* 1522 ib., *Balyndon* 1531 *WMP*. Probably 'rounded hill,' from OE *bealg* and dūn. Cf. Balham (PN Sr 33–4) and Bardon Hill (PN Wa 241)). Bush Pasture (cf. *Buntyngysbusch* 1474 *Pembroke*, *Katsbush* 1531 *WMP*). Clay Pit (*Cleypettes* 1474 *Pembroke*). Holly Bush (*Holybusshe* 1523 ib.). Pepperidge Furlong (cf. *Pepper close* 1609 *Deed*). Pinnings Ditch (*Pininchesdich* 1279 RH. Cf. *Pynacre* 1531 *WMP*). Great Warren (possibly to be associated with *Warendene* 1279 RH). For Linches, Catley Leys, Westrop Meadow, v. hlinc, læs, þorp.

WEST WICKHAM (*EnclA* 1812). Doddle Fd (*Doddewellefeld* 1322 *Queens'*. 'Dodda's spring,' v. wielle, feld). Readings Fd (*Redings* 1650 ib., v. ryding).

VI. Radfield Hundred

BALSHAM (School). Ashley Fd (*Ayssele* 1251 *ElyCouch*, *Ashley* 1801 *EnclA*, *v*. æsc, lēah). Big and Little Bavis (*the Bavies* ib.). Hay Hill (*le Hay* 1251 *ElyCouch*, *v*. (ge)hæg). New England (id. 1801 *EnclA*, is in a remote part of the parish). Portfield (*v*. Icknield Way *supra* 27). For Honey Hill, *v*. *supra* 166. For Long Slipe, *v*. slipe. On *EnclA* (1801) we have Wash Dale, *v*. dæl.

BURROUGH GREEN (*TA*). Chalk Pit Fd (*Chalkepitfyld* 16th *Pembroke*). Grove Fd (*Grovefyld* ib.). Sheldricks (*Sheldrakes* 1804 Borough). Stonehurst Wood (*Stonhous* 1315 *Clare*, *Stonehurst* 1663 Borough. Cf. Scaldhurst (PN Ess 180), earlier *Caldhous*). Duxey Hill Fd (*Duxly Hill* 1584 Borough, *Duxleys* 1674 ib., *Dukesley Hill, Fd* c. 1840 *TA*). The Leys (cf. *Near, Far Ley* ib.). Ploughed Atkyns (cf. *Adkins* 1674 Borough).

CARLTON CUM WILLINGHAM (*EnclA* 1799). Apsie Fd (cf. *Aspond-ffelde* 14th *Lewes*). Barnfield (cf. *Bernemedewe* ib.). For Night Pasture, Outfield, *v*. pasture, feld.

STETCHWORTH (School). Brook Bottom ((*le*) *Brok* c. 1250 *ElyM*). Brook Bottom (Ditch Side) (*Brokedichdene* ib.). Plum Tree Leys (*Plumterlee* c. 1270 ib., *v*. lēah).

WESTLEY WATERLESS (*TA*). The Moor (*la More* t. Ed 3 *Cole* xviii, *v*. mōr). For Leasow Plantation, Long and Short Plash, Slipe, *v*. læs, plæsc, slipe.

VII. Cheveley Hundred

ASHLEY CUM SILVERLEY (School). The Breach (*le Brache* c. 1290 *Hosp*, *Breche* 13th ib., *v*. bræc). Burrough Fd (*Burufelde* 13th *Hosp*, *Burgfelde* c. 1300 ib., *v*. burh). Canada Allotments are in very bleak, open country. Church Fd (*le Cherchefelde* c. 1250 *Hosp* is the site of Ashley Old Church). The Downs (*le Dune* c. 1287 ib., *v*. dūn). Hawk Fd (*Halc-, Halke-, Haukfelde* c. 1280 ib. Cf. *le Halke, Siluerlehalke, Sortehalke* c. 1280 ib. *v*. halke). Heath Fd (*Hatfelde* c. 1280 *Hosp*, *Hethfelde* c. 1287 ib., *v*. hǣð, feld). High Fd (*le Heyfelde* c. 1250 ib.). Great Lees (*la Leye* c. 1250 ib., *v*. lēah). Park Nook Fd (cf. *le Parkes-yate* c. 1290 ib.). St John's Ley, Pasture and Wood are relics of the possessions here of the Hospital of St John of Jerusalem. Spaithwaine (*Sparu(e)-, Sparwethorne, Spaurethorne* c. 1280–1317 ib. 'Sparrow thorn bush'). Wickhams (*Wic-, Wikham* c. 1280–1300 ib., *v*. wīc, ham(m)).

CHEVELEY (*TA*). Broadway (*v. Broadways supra* 20). Middle Fd (*Middelfelde* c. 1240 *Hosp, v.* feld). Saxon Pasture (cf. Saxon Street *supra* 127). West Fd (*Westfelde* c. 1240 *Hosp*). For The Leys, *v.* læs.

KIRTLING (School). Bury Land (*v.* burh (manorial)). Queen Fd and Meadow are near the Queen's Head Inn. For Thrift Meadow and West Croats *v.* fyrhðe, croft.

WOODDITTON (School). (Little) Empty Fd (*Imp(h)eyfeld* 1338, 1501 *Ct.* 'Field by the enclosure of saplings,' cf. Empty Common *supra* 40). Fisher's Meadow (cf. *Fishisgate* 1336 *Ct, Fysshyscroft* 1411 ib.).

VIII. Staine Hundred

STOW CUM QUY (*TA*). Byron Meadow is probably to be associated with *Bryans* 1419 Cl, *Briansclose* 1586 *CCC*, so called from *Brian* de Stapilton (1419 Cl). Dove House Close (*Duffhowse Close* 1553 Pat). Lotts (cf. The Lots *supra* 150). New Meadow (*Novum Pratum* 1279 RH).

LITTLE WILBRAHAM. St Catherine's Fd formerly belonged to St Catharine's College.

IX. Flendish Hundred

FULBOURN (*EnclA* 1806). King's Croft (cf. *Kynggeslond* 1496 *Rental*). Oxmeadow ((*le*) *Oxemede* 1435 *MinAcct, -medow* 1509 *Ct*). Woodbridge Fd (*Wdebrige* c. 1225 *AD, Wodebriggefeld* 1322 *Peterhouse*). For Long Sponge, *v.* spong.

X. Chesterton Hundred

CHESTERTON (*TA*). Butts Close (*But Close* 1552 Pat, *v.* butte). Camping Close (*v. supra* 153). Dovehouse Close (*Douehouseyarde* 1499 *MinAcct*). Paradise (*close called Paradise* 1555 Pat, *v.* paradise). Rumbland (*Rumelonde* 1228 Merton, *Romelond* 1277 *Bodl.* 'Empty, unoccupied land,' *v.* rūm and cf. Rome Land (PN Ess 30). West Fd (*le Westfelde* c. 1480 *CTerr*). For Homestall, Holt, Newnhams Holt, *v.* hāmsteall, holt.

CHILDERLEY (*TA*). Honey Hill (cf. *supra* 166). For Bean Lands *v.* land.

COTTENHAM (*TA*). For Dovehouse Close and Holme Meadow, *v.* dufhous, holmr.

HISTON (1746 *Terr*). Bellrope Leys was doubtless an endowment for supplying the church bell-ropes, *v.* læs and cf. PN Nth 281. The

Breach Way (cf. *le Shortebrath* (sic) c. 1450 ElyA, *v.* brǣc). Brook-field (cf. *le Broke* ib.). For Ye Beck Close, Great and Little Barrow Fd, Bishop Craft, Bandeland, *v.* bekkr, beorg, croft, land.

XI. Longstow Hundred

BOURN (*TA*). Home Meadow (*Holm meadow* 1704 *AddCh*, *v.* holmr). For Scotland Fm and Starve Goose Close *v. supra* 357. For Goswell Leys *v.* lǣs.

CALDECOTE (*TA*). For Layton Green Close, the Ley and Long Ley, Calves and Home Pightle, *v.* lēactūn, lēah, pightel. For Broadway Furlong cf. *Broadways supra* 20. Linwoods Close is probably for *Lindwood Close*, i.e. 'lime-tree close,' *v.* lind.

CROXTON (School). For Mill Dole, Debden, The Dane, High Hayden, Two Leys, Broad Moor, Riding, *v.* dāl, dēop, denu, hēafod, lǣs, mōr, ryding. For Leg of Mutton Wood and New Zealand, *v. supra* 357.

ELTISLEY (*TA*). Croes Nest Furlong is near Crow's Nest Fm *supra* 171. Ditch Haden Furlong (cf. *le Dychfurlong* 1387 *Pembroke*, *Withie-hafden* 1344 ib., *Smalhadon* 1500 ib. *v.* wiðig, hēafod). Downham Dean (cf. *le Dene* 1399 *Pembroke*, *Dungelonddene* 1404 ib., *Dowlonddene* 1500 ib., *v.* denu. The first element is doubtful. Cf. Wilsmere Down *supra* 71). Kings Fd (*Kengesfeld* 1380 *Pembroke*). Port Way Furlong (*v.* Port Way *supra* 28). Willow Way (cf. *Longewilous* 1500 *Pembroke*). Winsborough Hill would seem to be a corruption of *Wynnesmerehille* 1408 ib. For Hay Close, The Pightle, *v.* (ge)hæg, pightel. The School adds Duffers Close (i.e. *Dovehouse*). Hillings (*Hillands TA*). York-shire (in a remote situation).

GAMLINGAY (*TA*). Brook End (cf. *le brok* 1229 *StNeot*, *le Brokfurlang* 1239 ib.). Sinks Common (*v.* Gamlingay Cinques *supra* 161). Mag-gotts House (cf. *Magodespit* 1251 *ElyCouch*, *Magotespyt* 1277 *Ely*, probably from a personal name). Stockings Close (*le Stocking* 1246 *StNeot*, *v.* stocking). For Broad Lays, Pightel, *v.* lǣs, pightel. For Cold Harbour and Folly Close *v. supra* 357, 353.

LITTLE GRANSDEN (*EnclA* 1813). Stocking Fd (*Stokinge* 1251 *Ely-Couch*, 1277 *Ely*, *v.* stocking). For The Leys, *v.* lǣs.

HARDWICK (*TA*). For Stocking Close *v.* stocking.

HATLEY ST GEORGE (*TA*). For Drift Way *v.* weg. For Honeyhill Close *v.* Honey Hill *supra* 166.

TOFT (*TA*). Brook Close (*Broc* 13th *StJohn's*). Rottendell (cf. *Red(d)eden* c. 1250 *StJohn'sH*, 13th *StJohn's*, probably 'cleared valley'). Staines Fd (cf. Staine Hundred *supra* 129). For Dovehouse Dole, Foxholes, Lousey Leys, Waterslade, *v.* dāl, dufhous, foxhol, lǣs, slæd and *supra* 357.

XII. Papworth Hundred

BOXWORTH (*TA*). Cats Hole Close (cf. *Catteshoweshaveden* c. 1285 *StCatharine's*, *Catsoweye* 1464 AD iv, *Catsowhill* 1510 *StCatharine's*, *Catteswell close* 1577 AD v. 'Wild-cat's hill and spring,' *v.* hōh, wielle and hēafod). For Swath's Meadow *v.* swæð.

FEN DRAYTON (*TA*). The Hales ((*le*) *Hale* c. 1250 *StJohn'sH*, 1422 *StJohn's*, *Esthales* 13th ib., *v.* healh). Mill Fd (*le Milnefeld* 1342 *StJohn's*). Perchen and Lete Meadow (cf. *Pyrchyndiche* 1379 *StJohn's*, *Lied* 13th ib., *le Longelede* c. 1300 *StJohn'sH*. The latter is OE lǣd, an *i*-mutated form of lād, 'watercourse,' *lead*, 'an artificial watercourse,' first recorded from 1541 except for *ledam* (13th), *s.n.* Leads Ho (PN ERY 43)).

OVER (School). Bury Close (cf. (*le*) *Buryholme* 1489 *Ct*, *Burye yard* 1540 *MinAcct*, *v.* burh (manorial). Bodies have been dug up in the grounds of Hereward Ho, near the church, and tradition has it that this was the site of Hereward's camp. The early forms give no support to this story). Doles Fd (cf. *Burydole* 1489 *Ct*, *Barkersdole*, *Ilgerysdole* 1540 *MinAcct* and *v.* dāl). Mill Fd (*le Milnefeld* 1333 *StCatharine's*). Punyards is the local pronunciation of *Pond-yards*. Snudd Fd (1826 *CCC*) is *le Snod* 1349 *Walden*, *v.* snād, 'piece of land cut off.' Soldiers' Land is a name dating from 1918; allotments here were granted to ex-service men.

PAPWORTH ST AGNES (*TA*). Sprawsdens (*Sproweuesdene* c. 1260 *StJohn'sH*, *Sprouysden* ib., 13th *StJohn's*, *Sprowesdene* ib. '*Sprow*'s dene,' *v.* denu. *Sprow* is found in the Liber Eliensis as the name of a man in the 10th century). Scotland is claimed by no farmer and is waste (School). Gostails (c. 1840 *TA*) is now corrupted to Gostrilles (School). For Homestall, Church Leys, *v.* hāmsteall, lǣs.

SWAVESEY (*TA*). Hobbledods perhaps derives from a corruption of *hodmandods*, *hoddydod*, 'a snail or its shell.' Lords Close (cf. *Lordesdole* 1287 *Rental*, *v.* dāl).

WILLINGHAM (*TA*). Broadway Punt and Punt Wash (cf. Punt, Broadways and Wash *supra* 152, 20, 212). Fardell Close (*Fardole* 1575 *Rental*, *v.* dāl). Snout Fen (*Snotefen* 1251 *ElyCouch*, *Snootfenne* 1621 *SewersD*, *v.* snote). West Fd (*Westfeld* 1221 *ElyA*, *v.* feld). West Meadow (*Westmede* ib.). Whittens Close (*Wyttons close* 1575 *Rental*. *v.* Utton's Drove *supra* 173). Wrangland Shoals, Wrangling Shoals (*Wrangland* ib., cf. Wrangling Corner *supra* 181). For Berry Croft,

Gore Close, Lock Hawe, Small Holt, Hurst Fm, Pightle, *v.* burh (manorial), gāra, haga, holt, hyrst, pightel.

XIII. Northstow Hundred

GIRTON (*TA*). For Camping Close and Starve Goose Close *v. supra* 153, 357. For Pightle *v.* pightel.

MADINGLEY (*TA*). For The Knowl *v.* cnoll.

RAMPTON (*TA*). Balsars Fd (*v.* Belsars Field *supra* 174). Hempsall ((*The*) *Hempsal*(*l*) 1605 Imb, 1754 Venn. It adjoins Hempsalls *supra* 174). For Lockspit *v.* Lockspit Hall *supra* 150. From Venn (1754) we have Britch Fd, Lambcoat Fd, Huntington Gore, How Furlong, Lane Leys, Mear and Moor Furlong, *v.* brǣc, cot(e), gāra, hōh, lǣs, (ge)mǣre, mōr. For Portway Furlong *v.* Portways *supra* 28.

LONG STANTON (*TA*). Stanwell Fd (*Stanwell'* 1228 *FF*, (*-feilde*) 1617 *EgCh*). For America Close cf. *supra* 357.

XIV. Staploe Hundred

BURWELL (*TA*). Burnt Fen (*Le Brundefen* 1294 *Ct*, *Brendffenne* 1460 *Pembroke*, *v.* brende). North Fd (*le Northfeld* 1232 *FF*). South Fd (*le Southfeld* 1307 *Ct*, *v.* feld). Reach Ground (*v.* Reach *supra* 136 and ground). For White Shot *v.* scēat.

CHIPPENHAM (School). The Croft (cf. *viam vocat' atte Croftesende* c. 1305 *Hosp*). The Half Acre is [hævəkə].

ISLEHAM (*TA*). Beck Close (*le Bekke, Bekkecroft* 15th *Pembroke, v.* bekkr). Dunstall Fd (*Dunstal* 14th *Pembroke, v.* tūnsteall). Herrings Meer (*Heringemere* 1247 *FF, Heringesmere* 13th *ElyM, Heryngesmere* 1344 Ipm, 'mere of *Hēring*,' a personal name found in ASC). South Fd (*Sut*(*h*)*feld* 13th *ElyCh, v.* feld). For Brink Fen Ground, Skirt Ground, *v.* brinke, skirt(s).

SOHAM (*TA*). Mardale (*Mardellpath* 1503 *Pembroke*). Cf. Marble Hill (PN Mx 30). For Camping Close *v. supra* 153. For Osier and Sprights Holt, Willow and Wood Pightle, *v.* holt, pightel. Bonnets Close (the profit from this was originally used to provide bonnets for the poor of Isleham (School). Gooseberry Arcade (once given over to the growing of gooseberry bushes) (ib.).

The Isle of Ely

XV. Ely Hundred

ELY (*TA*). Butlers Close (*Clogges Ware al. Butlers Ware* 1608 *AddCh.* Cf. *Cloggeswere* 1251 *ElyCouch*, *v.* wēr). Cow Fen (*Coufen* t. Hy 3 *WMP*). The Dairies (cf. *Dyerhaihoue* 13th *ElyM*, *ElyE*, *Dededirhay* 1404 *Ct*, *Derehey* 1564 ib., *v.* (ge)hæg, hōh. The first element is uncertain). Dead Hills Fd (*Dedhil* c. 1195 *ElyE*). Dedden Fd (*Depedene* 13th *ElyM*, 1300 *ElyCh*, *Debdenfelde* 1494 *Ct*, *v.* denu). Docking Ground (cf. *Docckenefurlong* 13th *Elem*, i.e. overgrown with dock). Fernywell (cf. (*le*) *Fernihou*(*e*) 13th *ElyCh*). Finnual Close (cf. *Finewell*(*e*)*wey*(*e*) 13th *ElyM*, *Elem*, *Fynniwelleweye* 1300 *ElyCh*, *Fynnell*(*feld*) 1528 CAPr xxxvi. Probably 'woodpecker spring or stream,' *v.* fīna, wielle). Grizzle Hill (*Greslove* 1221 *ElyA*, *Graslowe*, *Grasseloue* 1277 *Ely*, *Gresseleyhyll* 1528 CAPr xxxvi. 'Grass hill,' *v.* gærs, hlāw). Hangmans Hill (*Hangemanshyll* 1584 *Ct*). Knowles Ground (*Knol* 13th *Elem*, *v.* cnoll). Priest Meadow (*Prestesmedwe* 13th *ElyCh*). Sallow Hill (*Seuelowes* 1251 *ElyCouch*, 1277 *Ely*, the (*ye*) *Sellowes* 1611 *AddCh*, 1618 *Sewers*. Apparently 'seven hills' or 'barrows,' *v.* hlāw). Shepherds Piece (cf. *Sephierdeshoue* 13th *ElyCh*). Snout Close (cf. snote *supra* 344). Turf Fen (cf. *supra* 247). Wash Land (cf. The Wash *supra* 212). For The Spong *v.* spong.

LITTLE DOWNHAM (*TA*). Long Balance is probably for *Ballands*, i.e. 'beanlands,' *v.* land. Dole Fd (cf. *Dolemedwe* 13th *ElyCh*, *v.* dāl). Hawkley ((H)*aukele* 1309 *ElyCh*, 1387 *Wren*. 'Hawk clearing or wood,' *v.* heafoc, lēah). The Holmes (*Holm* 1251 *ElyCouch*, *le Holmes* 1415 ib., *v.* holmr). Long Lots (cf. The Lots *supra* 150). For Hoe Furlong, Stony Hoof, the Holts, Broad Hurst, Hurst Fd, the Lay, *v.* hōh, holh, holt, hyrst, lēah.

LITTLEPORT (*TA*). East Fd (*Estfeld* 1221 *ElyA*). Knoll Ground (cf. *Nole Bridge* 1829 Wells, *v.* cnoll). For Hoof Close *v.* holh.

XVI. South Witchford Hundred

COVENEY (*TA*). Park Pightle and Wood (cf. *the Parke* 1676 *Pembroke* and *v.* pightel).

HADDENHAM (*TA*). Bottle Croft (*Bottelcroft* 1380 *Peterhouse*). Broad Water Close (*Bradewater* 1383 ib.). Calley Croft (*Callicroft* 1636 BedL). The Doles (*le Dolys* 1428 *Peterhouse*, *v.* dāl). Grays Hoof Plantation (cf. *Grayes* t. Jas 1 *Cole* xxxvii and *v.* holh). Heater Croft (cf. *Leys in the Hether Croft* 1701 *HardwickeA*). Towns End Close (so named 1697 *Cole* ix, *v.* tūn). For The Brinks *v.* brinke.

MANEA (*TA*). Derey Lode (*Deree* 1378 *Ct*. 'Wild animal stream,' *v.* dēor, ēa and cf. Darcey Lode *supra* 4). Freemans Lots (cf. The Lots *supra* 150).

MEPAL (*TA*). Gall Fen (cf. Gall Fen *supra* 235). Widen Close (*Widden* 1654 *BLAcct*, *Widdin Parts* 1870 *Witcham.* *v.* Widden's Hill *supra* 240).

SUTTON (*TA*). Cox's Nest (*Cocks Nests* 1637 BedL). Dovehouse Way (cf. *le Dofhousweye* 1287 *ElyCh*, carrying back this word over 100 years). Half Lot and Long Lot (*v.* healh and The Lots *supra* 150). Holbrook (cf. *Holebrocweye* 1292 *ElyCh*, *v.* holh, broc). Holt Lot (cf. *le Holt* 1379 *Ct*, *v.* holt and The Lots *supra* 150). Lockspit (cf. *Hyde's Lockspits* 1786 BedL and Lockspit Hall *supra* 150). Pudding Holme (*Puddyngholm* 1438 *Ct*, *v.* holmr. *pudding* is probably used of sticky soil). For Madams and Turf Dole, Water Gull, Pingle, *v.* dāl, gole, pingel.

LITTLE THETFORD (*TA*). Camping Close (*v. supra* 153). Stonebridge Fd (so named 1676 EA xiii).

WENTWORTH (*TA*). Camping Close (*v. supra* 153).

WILBURTON (*TA*). Flexon Fd (cf. *Flaxlondweye* 13th *ElyM*).

WITCHAM (*TA*). Gritham Close (cf. *Grethom*(*broc*, -*weye*) c. 1300–2 *ElyCh*, *Gretham*(*furlong*) 13th, 1302–4 ib., *Grittom way* 1693 ib. 'Gravel enclosure,' *v.* grēot, hamm). Lockspit (*v.* Lockspit Hall *supra* 150). Medlands (*v.* Witcham Meadlands *supra* 237). Widden Close (*v.* Widden's Hill *supra* 240). For North Doles, Hale Fen, The Pingle and Penny Pingle, *v.* dāl, healh, pingel.

WITCHFORD (*TA*). Beale Close (*Bile Closse* 1528 CAPr xxxvi, *Beelle closes* 1571 *Ct*, *v.* Beald Fm *supra* 223). Wheat Ground (cf. *Watelond* c. 1250 *ElyM* and *v.* hwǣte, land). For Church Holt, Matthews Pingle, *v.* holt, pingel.

XVII. North Witchford Hundred

DODDINGTON (*TA*). Great and Little Alleys (*Allehoue* 1221 *ElyA*, *Lordes Alleyez* 1492 *ElyB*, *v.* hōh). For Town Dole, Fen Ground, Garden Holt, Beagles Leys, *v.* dāl, ground, holt, lǣs.

WHITTLESEY RURAL (*TA*). Berrystead Close ((*the*) *Berysted* (*Close*) 1636 BedL. 'Site of the manor-house,' *v.* burh, stede). Long and Short Doles (*les Dooles* 1398 *Ct*, *v.* dāl). Five Swarths (*v.* swæð). The Gores (cf. *Aldegore* c. 1223 *ElyCh*, *Eldegore* 1248 ib., *Olde-gore* 1394 *Ct*, *the Bell Gore* 1668 Fenland (to the Bellman of Whittlesey). *v.* eald, gāra. Grass Close (cf. *le Grescroft* 1398 *Ct* and 'parcels of Gores of Grass Lands,' *the Constables Grass* (to the constables for keeping each of them a common Bull and Boar for the use of the Inhabitants), *the Bulls, Boars, the Bellman's* and *Herds Grass* (to the several neatherds) 1668 Fenland i, *v.* gærs). Grithill Balk (*Grethal(e)* 13th *Thorney,* 1393 *Ct, Grethill Snout* 1603 *Survey.* 'Gravel-nook,' *v.* grēot, healh and Snoots *supra* 262). Musket Hill (*v.* Muscat *supra* 7). Pingle Lots (cf. *the Pingle* 1668 Fenland i, *Northerell Lotts* 1603 *Survey, Fenlotts* 1636 BedL, *v. supra* 340 and The Lots *supra* 150). The Setts (cf. *vj settis in Kyngesdel* 1477 *Ct, Pryors Setts, Settes lotts* 1603 *Survey*). Swingland Snoots (*Swyngland Snout* 1603 *Survey.* Cf. Snoots *supra* 262). For Town End and Wheelpit Hove, *v.* tūn, holh.

XVIII. Wisbech Hundred

ELM (*TA*). Bishops Bank (cf. *Biscopeswere* c. 1130 ChronRams, (bank called) *Bysshopesdych* 1380 *Sewers.* The Bishop of Ely had land here).

LEVERINGTON (*TA*). Church Croft (cf. *Kyrkefelde* 1462 *Ct, the Kyrke-londe* 1519 Fenland vii).

NEWTON (*TA*). Smeeth (*le Smeth, le Smith* 1395 EA iv. 'Smooth place,' *v.* smēðe).

UPWELL (*TA*). Broken Wash (cf. *Broken(e)* 1203 *Ass et freq* to 1449 *Ct, Brokenes* 1251 ElyCouch, *Brokendyke* 1390 *Ct, the Broken dyke alias Oldfield dyke* c. 1530. The original name seems to have been *brocen-ēa,* 'broken river,' and the dyke to have been named from it. *v.* Wash *supra* 212. Church Fd (*Kirkefelde* 1489 *Ct*). Pigs Drove (cf. *Piggeshirne* 1320 *Ct, -feld* 1369 ib., *-drove* 1430 ib., from the family of John *Pigge* (1320 *Ct*). Pull Yards (*le Poleyerd, Pooleyard* 1539 *Min-Acct, v.* pōl, geard).

WISBECH ST PETER (*TA*). Stowcrofts (*Stowcroft* 1314 *Ct, v.* stōw, croft). Tillery Fd (*le Tyllerie* 1351 *Ct, the Tylere* 1376 Imb, *le Til-(l)erye* 1411, 1422 *Ct, le Tylerye* 1469 *Sewers, Tyleryfeld* 1508 *Ct.* 'Place where tiles are made.' This word is first recorded in NED in 1846).

APPENDIX

The three following parishes were transferred to Cambridgeshire from Essex in 1895 for civil purposes. They were originally treated in *The Place-names of Essex* (pp. 520–1, 529–30 and 644).

Great and Little Chishall

CHISHALL (GREAT and LITTLE) [tʃisəl]

Cishella(m), -ā, Cishelle 1086 DB
Cheshill', -hull' 1199 Cur, *Overecheshelle* 1251 FF, *Cheshulle* 1263 ib., *Chessalebusshes, -bury* 1456 *MinAcct*
Chishull(e) 1212 RBE, 1234 FF, 1303 FA, 1327–33 Londin, *-hill* 1222 FF, 1248 *Ass*, 1269 FF, 1428 FA, *-hell* 1238 *SR*, 1239 FF, *Magna Chiselhelle* 1248 *Ass*, *Graunt Chisull* p. 1420 FA
Chyshull (Little) 1269, *-hill* 1270 FF, 1428 FA, *Chishall* 1363 IpmR
Chishyld 1274 RH
Over, Nether Chessell 1548 Pat, *Chessell Mag. or Chishall, Chessell* 1594 N, *Over, Nether Chissell* 1607 EA ix

'Gravel-hill,' *v.* cis, hyll. Identical with Chishill (K). The 1248 *Chiselhelle* is probably an error, but may contain the recorded *chisel*, *v.* ceosol. *Over* is Great, *Nether* is Little Chishall.

Great Chishall

BOVERIES (lost) is *Bu(u)eries* 1199 *FF*, *(vill)* 1254 *Ass*, 1387 *Walden*, *(in) Bovariis* 1200–70 FF, *Boveryes (town)* 1262 ib., *(ex parte aquilonari de Hichenild)* 1387 *Walden*, *Bouuerie* 1298 FF, *Boverias* 1387 *Walden*. Cf. *Boverie* (PN Nth 274) and Beufre Fm (Ha), *la Boverie* 1300 *Rental*. It is of the same type as Vetchery (PN Sx 350) and Vachery (PN Sr 232) and is derived from OFr *boverie*, 'place where oxen are kept.' It was on the north side of Icknield Way.

SHAPENS is *Shupenes* 1272 *Ass*, *S(c)hep(e)n(eys)* ib., 1280–94 FF, 1332 *SR*, 1338–55 Cl, *Shypenes* 1290 FF, *Shipyns* 1362 FF, *Chepyns* 1503 *Will*. 'Cattle-sheds,' *v.* scipen.

BARNARD'S WOOD (6″). Cf. *Barnys, Barnes Gate* 1542 *Ct*. CHISHALL DOWN is *Chisille-, Chis(h)elledune* 1387 *Walden*. *v.* dūn. WALDEN LANE (6″) is *Waldon' lane* 1542 *Ct* and leads to Saffron Walden.

Little Chishall

CUMBERTON BOTTOM. Cf. *Comberdeneveld* 1387 *Walden* and *Cumberden* c. 1470 *Ct* in the neighbouring Barley (Herts). Perhaps '*Cumbra*'s valley.' Cf. Comberton *supra* 73.

Heydon

HEYDON

Haindena 1086 DB
Haidenam 1086 DB, *-den* 1222 FF, *haidene* 1086 InqEl, *-denn* 1194 Abbr, *Haydon* 1238 *SR*, *-den* 1345 Cl
Heidenñ 1199 CurR, *Heiden(e)*, *-y-* 1202 FF *et freq* to 1339 Cl, *-don(e)* 1246–54 FF, 1274 RH, (*Great*) 1290 FF, 1308 Abbr, *-denne* 1318 *Ass* (p)
Eydene 1285 Ipm

No certainty is possible with regard to this name. Heydon lies at the head of a well-marked valley, and it is clear that unless we lay stress on the three *denn*-forms the second element is **denu**, 'valley,' rather than **denn**, 'swine-pasture.' The first may be the common word **heg**, hence 'hay valley,' or it may be (ge)**hæg**, hence 'valley or swine-pasture marked by an enclosure.' Professor Chadwick notes that Bran or Heydon Ditch (*supra* 33), called also GREEN DITCH (6″), forms part of the western boundary of Heydon, and suggests the possibility that the *hey* is here used of the boundary dyke. Such an extension of the use of OE (ge)**hæg**, 'boundary hedge,' would perhaps have its parallel in *Hayditch*, one of the alternative names for Gryme's Dyke (PN Ess 374), itself the outer ditch of *Wildenhay* (cf. EAS xviii, 1–6).

HEYDON BURY is *Hayden-bury* t. Eliz ChancP. *v.* **burh** (manorial). THE PICOTS (6″) was in the possession of the *Picot* family from the time of Henry I to that of Edward II (M ii, 600).

FIELD NAMES: Brand Ditch Fd (*Brundishfield* 1610 *Cole* v. *v.* Bran Ditch *supra* 33). Lang Mead Fd (*Langemade* 1208 FF).

INDEX

OF SOME WORDS OF WHICH THE HISTORY IS ILLUSTRATED IN THIS VOLUME

INDEX

OF PLACE-NAMES IN CAMBRIDGESHIRE

The primary reference to a place is marked by the use of Clarendon type. Street-names are for the most part included in the Index.

With the exception of certain names of special interest, names which at once suggest the parish in which they are to be found, e.g. Whittlesford Bridge and Mill (in Whittlesford), are not included in the Index.

In grouping names together no distinction has been made between (a) names written in one or two words, e.g. High Fen Fm and Highfen Fm have been grouped together, (b) between s and 's, e.g. Earl's Fen and Earls Hook have been grouped together. Where grouping has made the inclusion difficult, the definite article before a name has been omitted. Parish- and river-names have been given separately.

No attempt has been made to index the field-names.

INDEX

OF PLACE-NAMES IN COUNTIES OTHER THAN CAMBRIDGESHIRE

[*References to place-names in Beds, Bk, D, ERY, Ess, Herts, Hu, Mx, NRY, Nt, Nth, Sr, Sx, W, Wa and Wo are not included, as these have been fully dealt with in the volumes already issued upon the names of those counties.*]

CAMBRIDGE: PRINTED BY W. LEWIS, M.A., AT THE UNIVERSITY PRESS